Errin O'Connor

D0861658

SharePoint® 2013 Field Guide

Advice from the Consulting Trenches

UNLEASHED

SAMS | 800 East 96th Street, Indianapolis, Indiana 46240 USA

SharePoint® 2013 Field Guide: Advice from the Consulting Trenches

Copyright © 2014 by Pearson Education, Inc.

All rights reserved. No part of this book shall be reproduced, stored in a retrieval system, or transmitted by any means, electronic, mechanical, photocopying, recording, or otherwise, without written permission from the publisher. No patent liability is assumed with respect to the use of the information contained herein. Although every precaution has been taken in the preparation of this book, the publisher and author assume no responsibility for errors or omissions. Nor is any liability assumed for damages resulting from the use of the information contained herein.

ISBN-13: 978-0-789-75119-5
ISBN-10: 0-789-75119-4

Library of Congress Control Number: 2014932531

Printed in the United States of America

First Printing September 2014

Trademarks

All terms mentioned in this book that are known to be trademarks or service marks have been appropriately capitalized. Sams Publishing cannot attest to the accuracy of this information. Use of a term in this book should not be regarded as affecting the validity of any trademark or service mark.

Warning and Disclaimer

Every effort has been made to make this book as complete and as accurate as possible, but no warranty or fitness is implied. The information provided is on an "as is" basis. The author and the publisher shall have neither liability nor responsibility to any person or entity with respect to any loss or damages arising from the information contained in this book.

Bulk Sales

Sams Publishing offers excellent discounts on this book when ordered in quantity for bulk purchases or special sales. For more information, please contact

U.S. Corporate and Government Sales
1-800-382-3419
corpsales@pearsontechgroup.com

For sales outside of the U.S., please contact

International Sales

international@pearsoned.com

Editor-in-Chief
Greg Wiegand

Executive Editor
Loretta Yates

Development Editor
Mark Renfrow

Managing Editor
Kristy Hart

Project Editor
Elaine Wiley

Copy Editor
Cheri Clark

Indexer
Tim Wright

Proofreader
Sarah Kearns

Editorial Assistant
Cindy Teeters

Cover Designer
Mark Shirar

Senior Compositor
Gloria Schurick

Contents at a Glance

Contents

About the Authors:
The EPC Group Team of Experts

Errin O'Connor is the founder and CEO of EPC Group and has completed more than 900 SharePoint and "Microsoft stack-related" implementations, including efforts relating to business intelligence (BI), custom application development, hybrid cloud strategy, Microsoft Azure, Office 365, SQL Server 2012/2014, Amazon Web Services (AWS), and Microsoft Project Server. This is Errin's third Microsoft SharePoint book; he is also the author of *Microsoft SharePoint Foundation 2010 Inside Out* and *Windows SharePoint Services 3.0 Inside Out*, both by Microsoft Press. Errin continues to work closely with EPC Group's clients to develop and implement scalable SharePoint 2013, Office 365, and SharePoint Online initiatives, as well as BI, ECM/RM, and hybrid cloud strategies with identity management, security, and compliance in mind. Errin can be contacted directly via email at errino@epcgroup.net.

Miranda Salley is the Vice President of EPC Group and she manages the full range of EPC Group's technology consulting and solutions offerings. Miranda also oversees EPC Group's operations and marketing teams and tailors EPC Group's go-to-market strategies. She works with the full range of Microsoft technologies, including EPC Group's hybrid cloud advisory practice, to ensure that the organization continues to stay on the leading edge of consulting. Miranda has over 14 years of experience in information technology, marketing, sales, and communications management. For the past 10 years, Miranda has served as a volunteer technology teacher, and a life skills and career mentor, as well as a leading board member for various Boys & Girls clubs and not-for-profits, allowing her to further her passion for technology and community responsibility. Miranda can be contacted directly via email at contact@epcgroup.net.

Timothy Calunod has been an active and involved SharePoint enthusiast since SharePoint's first release. He has worked with every version of SharePoint in terms of design, implementation, architecture, administration, maintenance, troubleshooting, and solution creation to meet the unique needs of SharePoint deployments in various organizations and industries. Timothy has worked on hundreds of initiatives and is able to adapt to the technology requirements of EPC Group's clients, whether it be for a business intelligence initiative, for a hybrid and federated SharePoint 2013 and Office 365 initiative, or to develop a governance and architecture strategy for a SharePoint implementation to support more than 250,000 users.

Joseph Jorden is a leading industry expert in designing and implementing various complex technical solutions for clients both large and small. Joe's primary field of expertise is in custom software development for EPC Group's clients, focusing on SharePoint 2013 as well as all areas of custom .NET application development including application architecture, custom workflow development, SharePoint development and administration, SQL Server development and administration, database design, and security. Joe is also the author of numerous technical books on SQL Server, SQL Reporting Services, and business intelligence.

Andrew Christen has over 11 years of experience in developing, designing, coding, and testing applications using C#, ASP.NET, SharePoint 2013, SharePoint 2010, SharePoint 2007 development, C++, BizTalk, and multiple other scripting languages. Andrew's industry-leading architecture skills that he provides to EPC Group's clients expand beyond SharePoint development into seamless integration of other line-of-business (LOB) systems, C#/ASP.NET financial and inventory systems, custom .NET applications, and responsive web design, as well as architecting and designing web services using SOAP and XML. Andrew has extensive experience in SQL Server 2012 business intelligence, as well as migration initiatives from non-SharePoint systems into new SharePoint 2013 environments.

Daniel Galant has focused on educating clients on the latest SharePoint 2013 technologies, as well as architecting the overall design and implementation of Microsoft solutions for EPC Group clients both large and small. Daniel's experience includes SharePoint system design, implementation, branding, and administration, as well as information architecture design and analysis. Over the past 15-plus years, Daniel's expertise has also included Active Directory migration and consolidation, Exchange architecture deployment and administration, and network architecture and security. Daniel's background in training helps him to convey difficult and often misunderstood technical topics in an easily relatable manner, and he has twice been awarded Microsoft MVP status.

If you are interested in contacting EPC Group.net for a possible project engagement, feel free to reach out to us via email at contact@epcgroup.net or email Errin O'Connor directly at errino@epcgroup.net.

Dedication

*To Miranda, the smartest and most kind person I have ever met,
and to the unbelievable patience you provided me during this
year-and-a-half undertaking.*

—Errin O'Connor

Acknowledgments

This book has been one of the most challenging efforts of my life; there are so many sacrifices that go into it, and the individuals who support you through it cannot be thanked enough in a handful of words.

This book would not have been possible without Miranda Salley's support and unbelievable patience, as she not only supported me in the writing and editing of the book but also ensured that the EPC Group organization and our clients' needs were always met. I cannot ever thank her enough for ensuring that all aspects of the EPC Group, in terms of both our staff and our amazing clients, were always put first while I spent the past year and a half writing this book.

I would also like to thank the Pearson organization for their support in allowing me to rewrite almost the entire book when Microsoft released their 2012 R2 technology updates. This included the changes in Office 365 API Tools, SkyDrive's rebranding to OneDrive, and the Microsoft Azure (Windows Azure) rebranding efforts. My goal was to publish a book that would be relevant in covering all the latest technologies and that would not be outdated after only six months, and Pearson allowed me to achieve that goal.

We Want to Hear from You!

As the reader of this book, *you* are our most important critic and commentator. We value your opinion and want to know what we're doing right, what we could do better, what areas you'd like to see us publish in, and any other words of wisdom you're willing to pass our way.

We welcome your comments. You can email or write to let us know what you did or didn't like about this book—as well as what we can do to make our books better.

Please note that we cannot help you with technical problems related to the topic of this book.

When you write, please be sure to include this book's title and author as well as your name and email address. We will carefully review your comments and share them with the author and editors who worked on the book.

Email: consumer@samspublishing.com

Mail: Sams Publishing
             ATTN: Reader Feedback
             800 East 96th Street
             Indianapolis, IN 46240 USA

Reader Services

Visit our website and register this book at www.informit.com/title/9780789751195 for convenient access to any updates, downloads, or errata that might be available for this book.

Introduction

The main goal of this book is to provide a central resource that shares lessons learned, best practices, and an unfiltered version of real methodologies covering what really works and what pitfalls you should avoid. Within the next 18 chapters, I have put together a compilation of what I have learned from working with clients "in the trenches" on consulting initiatives of all shapes and sizes, from small to mid-size organizations, as well as enterprise and global organizations.

Although every SharePoint 2013, Office 365, and/or SharePoint Online initiative does have very specific and granular underlying business and technical requirements, there is an approach you can take to ensure that your implementation is a success. With the ever-changing IT landscape around the private (that is, on-premises), public (that is, cloud), and hybrid (that is, resources both on-premises and in the cloud) cloud, this book dives into implementing this new technology with a "hybrid mindset" to ensure that your organization's IT roadmap will align with your SharePoint 2013, Office 365, and/or SharePoint Online roadmap with scalability and security in mind.

There must be a strong focus on implementing your initiative with "future compatibility" in mind as relates to the information architecture (IA) as well as the underlying system architecture, but doing so with governance and identity management in mind. This includes the initial planning all the way through the implementation, configuration, custom development, go-live, and post-support to ensure that your organization focuses on end-user adoption and implementing this technology right the very first time.

I have covered SharePoint 2013 on-premises as well as implementations in the cloud in Office 365 and utilizing SharePoint Online but also how best to plan for and become familiar with Microsoft Azure, Amazon Web Services (AWS), Office 365 API Tools, SharePoint 2013's new app model, OAuth, OData, business intelligence (BI), Power BI, and tools such as Windows Intune and System Center.

This is the third SharePoint book that I have written, and I felt that my first two SharePoint books, on SharePoint 2007 and SharePoint 2010, did not allow me to have the "unfiltered" feel that I have attempted to convey within this new publication. In 15 years of owning a SharePoint- and Microsoft-focused consulting firm, I have always worked with clients to try to limit the licensing they have had to purchase. I have no stake in whether a standard or enterprise license of a Microsoft product is purchased and try and walk through some of the "marketing fluff" that comes with new releases.

The "cloud" is here but that can still mean you have a private "on-premises" cloud. Your organization may also want to focus on moving some resources into the "public cloud" or just go "all in" and move nearly everything into a public cloud. Regardless of the underlying infrastructure, there are key considerations for compliance and regulatory elements, as well your organization's future IT roadmap and the service level agreements (SLAs) you must provide to your users no matter what platform you may be focused on or considering.

There is a massive amount of hype around the cloud and what Microsoft's plans are for SharePoint in the future. Microsoft is starting to work on the next on-premises version, so as much as Microsoft would like you to move all of your data into Office 365, SharePoint Online, Microsoft Azure (Windows Azure), or other underlying offerings, I have developed this book to ensure that your organization's requirements are taken into consideration and the "marketing fluff" can be avoided.

There are some great new resources with the new Office 365 API Tools, along with new features and functionality within Visual Studio 2013 as well as Windows Server 2012 R2, SQL Server 2012/2014, and the openness that the new SharePoint 2013 App model allows for connecting to external data sources, that are also covered in great detail.

I also have focused on trying to get you to think about metadata (content types) and how best you can implement a core set of metadata so that you can more easily find content with the new SharePoint 2013 supercharged search engine, which now includes FAST Search in one single "SharePoint 2013 Search" offering.

Whether you are upgrading or migrating from a previous version of SharePoint, or are new to SharePoint, this book covers all aspects of every type of SharePoint implementation I have experienced since I started beta testing "Tahoe" (SharePoint 2001) back in late 2000. With the new offerings of SharePoint 2013, Office 365, and SharePoint Online, this publication will provide you the "from the consulting trenches" perspective in this fifth version of SharePoint, to cover all the moving pieces that encompass a successful initiative that will stand the test of time.

Who Should Read This Book?

This book has been written as a resource for anyone who will be involved in a SharePoint 2013, Office 365, and/or SharePoint Online initiative. The book covers topics from both sides of the coin, from extremely advanced topics for SharePoint architects, developers, and administrators, to power users, end users, and IT executives who may want to understand what the full life cycle of a successful initiative will entail.

This book covers topics for individuals of any "competency level" from those implementing a new SharePoint 2013 ECM/RM initiative or for readers who want to know how to implement a power-user strategy or even a successful training initiative. This book also covers the aspects of project management for those who may be managing these efforts and the communication and teamwork from various stakeholders that is required. There are granular areas that also cover compliance and regulatory issues for records managers or those who may work in the legal department for data such as PHI, PII, and HIPAA, as well as data stored in data centers in the EU and related global datacenter considerations.

This book also covers SharePoint 2013, Office 365, and SharePoint Online development strategies for developers interested in both learning and performing custom development; it also provides insight into the new "hybrid development mind-set" that is key to being a successful developer within these technologies.

Software Requirements

This book targets SharePoint 2013, Office 365, and SharePoint Online, as well as Microsoft Azure (Windows Azure), Windows Server, SQL Server, and Visual Studio. There are references to links to download trial versions of each of these technologies, as well as links to sign up for trials for any cloud-based services such as Office 365, Microsoft Azure, AWS, and even Visual Studio Online.

Code Examples

Source code for examples in this book can be downloaded from www.samspublishing.com.

CHAPTER 1

Introduction to SharePoint 2013 (On-Premises, Office 365 Cloud, and Hybrid)

When one is approaching a SharePoint 2013 initiative, there is a defined strategy with related implementation methodologies that will ensure its success. I started working with Microsoft SharePoint in late 1999 when it was originally code-named Tahoe. Since then, I have personally worked with all five versions (2001, 2003, 2007, 2010, and now 2013) on architecting and deploying SharePoint in hundreds of organizations of all shapes and sizes all over the globe. SharePoint is Microsoft's flagship product and one of the fastest-selling software solutions in history that is deployed to meet a wide variety of organizational business and functional requirements.

It's important to note that this product can sometimes be referred to as either SharePoint 2013 or Office 365's SharePoint Online. During the writing of this book, Microsoft has used both references in different whitepapers and press releases, as well as the term SharePoint Online, but I am going to cover an implementation from all sides, including Microsoft Azure and all the latest Windows Server 2012 R2 releases, as well as Visual Studio 2013 and SQL Server 2012 R2 and SQL Server 2014.

This book has been developed to provide "from the trenches" proven strategies for multiple audiences, from the IT solution architects tasked with implementing this game-changing solution to the CIOs and business leaders whose jobs may be on the line for the success of its implementation. It is also meant to be a reference for end users and power users, as well as developers, support personnel, and even enterprise content managers and records managers.

This publication addresses the SharePoint 2013 platform from all sides in a three-dimensional way to ensure that your SharePoint implementation is done right the first time with scalability, performance, high availability, and end-user buy-in in mind. Development best practices, governance strategies, power-user cultural adoption, and migration strategies are also discussed in great detail. SharePoint 2013's business intelligence (BI), enterprise content management (ECM)/records management (RM), and all available capabilities that are included in this release are addressed from initial requirements gathering all the way through deployment and post-implementation support.

This book is for individuals who are wanting real guidance, strategy, and a no-nonsense methodology for approaching their SharePoint 2013, Office 365, or combination in a hybrid cloud scenario where there are services that are hosted both onsite and within the cloud.

This is not a publication that takes a Microsoft TechNet-type approach and repeats the same "point and click" information that is obtainable via an online search, because there is a massive treasure-trove of online references via Microsoft TechNet and MSDN, as well as from the thousands of bloggers who have published articles on various topics.

I have written two previous books on SharePoint 2007 as well as SharePoint 2010, and the "click here and then click there" approach that I have followed in these past publications is not the way the following 18 chapters are structured. This is meant to answer best practices, roadmap strategies, and methodologies that my team at EPC Group and I have used for over a decade and continue to use every day.

The approach to almost any SharePoint 2013/Office 365 SharePoint Online initiative should start off by developing a 24- to 36-month roadmap, which is a key factor in ensuring your overall organization's long-term SharePoint success. This SharePoint 2013 roadmap should be developed to document not only the initial SharePoint business and functional requirements but also the other technologies associated with SharePoint. It should provide placeholders for any current unknowns or elements currently being discussed, such as your organization's bring-your-own-device (BYOD) strategy or long-term information management strategy's enforcement by a retention schedule.

A SharePoint roadmap should cover everything from the server and storage design of the system architecture to the metadata, taxonomy, security, and navigational hierarchy of SharePoint's information architecture. The strategies and best practices regarding SharePoint roadmap development and the related governance strategies are covered in detail throughout this book.

Key SharePoint 2013 Methodologies and Best Practices

As mentioned previously, key methodologies, strategies, and lessons learned that stemmed directly from initiatives executed within organizations of all verticals since the induction of SharePoint in 2001 will be followed, such as these:

▶ Defining an "anchor application/killer app" or key set of SharePoint 2013 features that will continue to draw users to SharePoint for many years to come

▶ Global and large enterprise implementation-specific considerations

▶ Upgrading from one or even multiple versions of an existing SharePoint deployment to SharePoint 2013

▶ Understanding the Cloud (Private, Public, Hybrid, SaaS, PaaS, IaaS, and so on)

▶ Integrating SharePoint with external data sources (Oracle, custom SQL databases, HR systems, ERP systems, Documentum, and so on)

▶ Best practices around developing internal power users and ensuring SharePoint's continued growth and progression within your organization

▶ Social strategies that will ensure proper and governed enterprise buy-in

▶ Multilingual implementations and architecting a SharePoint solution for 100 or even 1,000,000 (one million) users

▶ Performance considerations across multiple data centers or locations

▶ Disaster recovery, business continuity, data replication, and archiving

▶ SharePoint content publishing best practices and implementing the "one version of the truth" concept

▶ Mobility, BYOD, and external security considerations

▶ SharePoint governance best practices and how to develop a SharePoint steering committee

▶ Implementing true records management (ECM/RM) with SharePoint 2013, including working with your organization's retentions schedule and strategies around disposition, eDiscovery, and compliance

▶ Metadata and core content type discovery exercises

▶ Long-term support of SharePoint 2013, as well as strategies around Microsoft SQL Server 2012/SQL Server 2014 and Windows Server 2012

▶ Understanding Microsoft Azure as well as other offerings such as Amazon Web Services (AWS)

▶ Developing custom web parts, workflows, apps, and solutions

▶ Content database sizing, SQL Server best practices, and shredded storage

▶ Identity management and authentication

> **NOTE**
>
> This is just a short subset of the methodologies this book provides to you with "advice from the consulting trenches" to ensure that your SharePoint 2013 is implemented right, the first time.

This book was written for you to avoid having to purchase two or three separate SharePoint books on specific topics that do not cover the entire range of the true best practices. This is meant to be a central best practices "advice from the consulting trenches" reference on planning, deployment, configuration, development, runtime strategies, and support. Every aspect of a SharePoint 2013/Office 365 deployment is addressed from a perspective of someone who has been there, in the trenches, sitting across from clients who have a variety of goals.

This powerful platform can easily meet specific business and functional goals around implementing an organizational intranet, collaboration platform, enterprise content management, or records management solution. Other organizations may be interested in implementing a professional (social) networking or business intelligence platform, as well as rolling out workflows to streamline business processes while ensuring extranet and mobile compatibility. All the elements mentioned previously must be accomplished while staying in line with compliance and governance standards, as well as mobility and your organization's overall IT roadmap.

Time-Tested SharePoint Deployment Strategies from the Trenches

There is a method to the madness and a way to implement SharePoint 2013 right the first time. It is key to think in terms of beginning the overall initiative by gathering the key stakeholders from multiple departments where you and the project team members can start to whiteboard the overall solution and SharePoint roadmap with its long-term success in mind.

This "bottom-up SharePoint 2013 implementation approach" will open up the proper mind-set for a successful implementation and ensure that roadmap development is initiated to take into consideration future phases and other possible initiatives.

If a SharePoint project fails or falls short of expectations, it is typically due to the hard questions not being asked or addressed due to time and budgetary constraints or the project team not having been "in the trenches" seeing the various types of "SharePoint curveballs" that can be thrown their way.

For example, I was recently involved in an enterprisewide SharePoint Server 2013 initiative with approximately 11,000 users and data centers in three countries. In the very first discovery meeting with the IT director, he asked, "How is your firm's approach different from other consulting firms and why and how does your methodology differ to make sure this project is going to be a success? This is an extremely high-profile project with just about zero room for error."

The answer to that question is based on the strategy of avoiding the typical "top-down SharePoint implementation approach." When referring to the "top-down" implementation approach, I am referencing the "build it and they will come" mentality in which SharePoint sites are implemented across the organization and allowed to proliferate without proper governance, security strategies, and the identity of a core set of content types that manage the actual types of content (documents and so on) that SharePoint will be storing. Allowing users to have too many permissions, like allowing a user to create subsites within their departmental or project site and then be given full permission control of that new subsite, can cause major content sprawl and nongoverned growth. Eliminating risks by applying proper governance will reduce the instances in which content (documents, records, and so on) may not be protected in a manner to meet specific compliance standards or in which three or four sites are created that are very similar in nature and end up going unused long-term.

The "bottom-up SharePoint 2013 implementation approach" is based around identifying, from the very beginning, the types of content that will be stored, the matching metadata or core content types for that content, and the types of users and possible scenarios that the organization may experience not only in phase 1 but also in phase 2 or phase 3. When referring to looking at a SharePoint 2013 initiative from all sides in a three-dimensional way, I am referring to the project team members, both technical and nontechnical, understanding at a high level how content is stored, secured, and accessed by users authenticated not only within their organization's network but also by approved users who may be utilizing their laptop or tablet device waiting to catch a flight and sitting in an airport connected via a public Wi-Fi. The mobile, BYOD mentality is here and the strategy and policies must be addressed in your SharePoint roadmap not only for current staff but also for those future clients or partners you may want to access via a "SharePoint supplier portal" or for staff to access business intelligence data.

If the more difficult SharePoint roadmap strategies are left unanswered and rather are left to be answered at a later phase, this can end up costing the organization more time, budget, and risk because certain areas may need to be rearchitected or redesigned to meet future organizational needs.

When SharePoint is architected without future phases in mind, you also risk the possibility of losing buy-in and support from the user base which can stifle the momentum and long-term adoption of the SharePoint platform.

WARNING

GET YOUR SHAREPOINT ROADMAP IN PLACE ASAP!

I can't stress enough how important it is to address mobility, scalability, compliance, and governance as soon as possible in your initiative. SharePoint will more than likely grow in content and user requests at a much faster pace than planned. It is critical to have your SharePoint 2013 support model and defined processes in place for managing end-user requests in the early stages of your SharePoint initiative.

Initial Roadmap Questions

Thinking in terms of SharePoint as a Service (SPaaS) or SharePoint as a Platform (SPaaP) that will grow in size and importance over time will help instill the strategy of SharePoint offering "services" to your organization and will open up the hybrid SharePoint implementation mind-set. For example, some initial questions for any SharePoint 2013 implementation may start with these questions:

1. What technologies are the organization currently using?

    a. Are you already utilizing a previous version of Microsoft SharePoint? (Is SharePoint already installed, etc.?)

    b. If SharePoint is not currently utilized, what other technologies or line-of-business (LOB) systems are you trying to move away from in going to SharePoint 2013?

2. What is the organization's stance on the cloud, and will you possibly be implementing only SharePoint Online without Office 365's other technologies such as Lync or both SharePoint Server 2013 on-premises and Office 365?

3. What are the initial goals you are trying to accomplish by implementing SharePoint 2013, and what are some other functionalities or offerings that SharePoint 2013 brings to the table that you see possibly being utilized in the future?

TIP

This question is key because 90% of all SharePoint implementations end up being morphing into a hybrid environment to meet multiple organizational needs.

---

4. Is a main goal of SharePoint 2013 to be

    ▶ An intranet and/or collaboration platform for the organization?

    ▶ An enterprise content management/records management platform?

    ▶ A collaboration service for departments or team members to work together on to increase productivity?

    ▶ A business intelligence or reporting service to offer features like dashboards, KPIs, and score cards?

▶ A workflow service or business process automation platform to help take existing paper-based processes and turn them into online forms with specific workflows?

▶ An extranet that will allow your company to work more collaboratively with external partners, customers, or other approved audiences?

▶ An Internet-facing SharePoint service to replace your company's current website?

▶ A social and/or professional networking platform?

▶ A central platform to house or host your organization's existing applications or custom applications?

▶ A mobile or "edge device" type of service to answer the BYOD questions?

▶ A replacement of an existing system such as Documentum, LiveLink, eRoom, SAP, FileNet, DocuWare, or eDocs?

▶ A Learning Management System(LMS) or training platform to reduce travel costs of staff or to provide a central location to increase or streamline organizational training needs?

▶ A platform to allow you to migrate your existing network file-share content to increase security, as well as putting structure around currently unstructured content?

5. What does your organization's current Active Directory (AD) infrastructure look like and how is it managed?

▶ Are there AD groups around specific departments or are there also other custom AD and SharePoint security groups that were created to meet cross-functional projects or user security requirements?

6. What is your current hardware situation and/or strategy?

▶ What is your current virtualization strategy?

▶ What type of storage are you utilizing and do you have any metrics around content growth?

▶ Do you have more than one data center or possibly globally dispersed data centers or DR sites?

▶ Are you currently utilizing or planning to utilize cloud-based or SharePoint Online/Office 365 solutions?

7. What is the organization's current mobile or BYOD strategy?

8. What has worked well in the past to train your organization's staff?

9. Are there content owners or staff members who have been identified as possible SharePoint power users?

10. Is the organization looking at the Microsoft Azure platform or other possible external hosting options like Amazon Web Services (AWS)?

TIP

These are just a few initial questions, but they help set the stage around developing a SharePoint 2013 roadmap and implementation strategy that is forward thinking and addresses possible future needs.

In your organization's initial SharePoint 2013 envisioning and requirements gathering sessions, the goal should be to get as many stakeholders from different departments and/ or divisions within the organization as involved as possible in the project so that they understand its overall proposed life cycle and what may be expected of them.

Inevitably, there will be differing opinions from project team members on things such as the overall site structure, taxonomy, hierarchy, and even security model around permissions strategies. The SharePoint 2013 project will likely be one of the most high-profile efforts taking place in the organization, and with that there is also the realization that many of the questions that need to answered or tasks that need to be accomplished will be assigned to staff with existing work already scheduled on other efforts and meetings already scheduled on their calendar. This is an area where setting the initial tone of what is expected from the project team by its key stakeholders or project sponsor is very important. A SharePoint 2013 effort requires many elements to be done in parallel, and if certain questions are not being answered or team members are left in limbo about the direction on a specific project task or milestone, it can cause major delays and team member frustrations.

There is also an intangible element around the creation of a SharePoint 2013 cultural adoption and change management strategy as part of the overall project effort that will drastically increase user buy-in on both the initial and the long-term usage of SharePoint. Power users, sometimes referred to as super users, tend to not be included in initial SharePoint 2013 design sessions, which is a mistake.

Identifying staff members who are excited about technology and are willing to be a SharePoint power user will provide a return on investment (ROI) in three or four major areas. The development of a power-user strategy is discussed in granular detail in Chapter 9, "Governance Strategies for SharePoint 2013, Office 365, and SharePoint Online."

Power users should be given initial training and SharePoint 2013 introductory materials very early on in a SharePoint initiative. These users may not have extensive IT backgrounds but they will be your "first line of defense" for championing SharePoint, as well as assisting users in their departments or specified areas, by providing answers to initial questions and getting the overall organization comfortable with using this game-changing platform. A best practices power user strategy not only will reduce the number of SharePoint support calls or Help Desk tickets by up to 50% but also will provide invaluable feedback as well as ideas about "quick wins" that IT may not have even considered.

From the very beginning of a SharePoint 2013 initiative, a large number of SharePoint-specific technical terms will be used and a wide array of team members from different departments will attend specific meetings, so setting up a SharePoint 2013 introductory training site is extremely valuable. Having a video library available for project members to access with short one- to five-minute topic-driven SharePoint 2013 videos as well as a "common set of SharePoint 2013 terms" will ensure that every project member is on the same page.

SharePoint training sites, and related materials are typically designed and delivered near the end of a SharePoint project before going live into production, but a scaled-down version of these with some core technical overview videos and documents, as described previously, should be made available as soon as possible in your initiative.

Your project meetings and discussions with team members will be much more productive with a reference or specific example of what you are describing in terms of SharePoint 2013 rather than speaking in terms of an abstract technology. This is something that is guaranteed to kick-start your project and get some real momentum going very early on in your initiative.

Presenting SharePoint 2013

Microsoft SharePoint 2013 or Office 365, as you will need to be prepared to hear it referenced in different IT or business circles, has a number of new key features and functionality improvements over SharePoint 2010 or SharePoint 2007. I have found that a large number of organizations still have business-critical and highly customized SharePoint 2007 platforms in use, and the methodologies described within this book cover how you should approach these different scenarios.

Many organizations that are experienced with previous versions of SharePoint will find SharePoint 2013's features to be easily adaptable, and those that have not yet implemented SharePoint will also find that a best practices governance model and clear roadmap will make this powerful technology very manageable. Regardless of the technology that is currently implemented, SharePoint 2013 will provide very tangible return on investment and increased productivity to your organization.

TIP

If your organization does not currently have a SharePoint governance model in place, this book will help you to develop an industry-leading "from the trenches" governance model, including operational governance, in a later chapter.

Overview of SharePoint 2013 Key Features

When you are reviewing all the powerful features available in SharePoint 2013, it is key to analyze them in terms of the available service offerings this platform contains. More important, when reviewing and analyzing these features, be sure to keep your organization's business requirements in mind so that you take an agnostic implementation approach, which is key to implementing a hybrid SharePoint platform. You are implementing SharePoint 2013, but don't just think in terms of SharePoint but focus on your business needs and the overall big picture.

This will help you align SharePoint 2013's key features with your overall short-term as well as long-term goals with, of course, your SharePoint roadmap in mind.

When you are looking at all the features and functionality of SharePoint 2013, it can initially be a little overwhelming or even give you a sense of "where do I even begin." This can be simplified by thinking in terms of all the different features, apps, and functionalities in SharePoint 2013 as different service offerings. For example, in a previous section several examples of SharePoint service offerings were provided, such as a SharePoint "intranet" service or a SharePoint "enterprise content management" or "business intelligence and reporting" service. This helps break down SharePoint 2013's massive number of features into manageable offerings and will also assist in developing a governance strategy around these different "services."

SharePoint 2013's On-Premises and Office 365

SharePoint 2013 can be deployed in an on-premises model, a SharePoint Online/Office 365 model, or even a combination into a hybrid infrastructure model. I have also seen several organizations implement a hybrid infrastructure model in which SharePoint Server 2013 on-premises was deployed for their intranet and enterprise content management needs (records management and compliance), with Office 365 being offered to the organizations' partners and/or external users such as clients and even Microsoft Azure or AWS being used for other storage or application purposes.

It is key to identify the type of content that will be stored in SharePoint as well as any compliance or regulatory-related considerations because the platform must be suitable for highly sensitive areas of the business. Will SharePoint's content contain any trade secrets, personal files, or healthcare records? There has been a push in recent years around compliance with sensitive information such as personally identifiable information (PII), which is regulated by various laws and compliance bodies.

Personally identifiable information generally includes the following:

▶ Full name (if not common)

▶ National identification number

▶ IP address (in some cases)

▶ Vehicle registration plate number

▶ Driver's license number

- Face, fingerprints, or handwriting

- Credit card numbers

- Digital identity

- Date of birth

- Birthplace

- Genetic information

There are also data considerations regarding protected health information (PHI) that falls under the U.S. Health Insurance Portability and Accountability Act (HIPAA). PHI is linked based on the following 18 identifiers, which you should consider with special care:

1. Names

2. Dates (other than year) directly related to an individual

3. Phone numbers

4. Fax numbers

5. Email addresses

6. Social Security numbers

7. Medical record numbers

8. Health insurance beneficiary numbers

9. Account numbers

10. Certificate/license numbers

11. Vehicle identifiers and serial numbers, including license plate numbers

12. Device identifiers and serial numbers

13. Web uniform resource locators (URLs)

14. Internet Protocol (IP) address numbers

15. Biometric identifiers, including finger, retinal, and voice prints

16. Full-face photographic images and any comparable images

17. Any other unique identifying numbers, characteristics, or codes except the unique code assigned by the investigator to code the data

18. All geographical identifiers smaller than a state, except for the initial three digits of a ZIP Code, according to the current publicly available data from the Bureau of the Census

I have seen enterprise organizations that have specific types of data that have regulatory or legal-related information lean toward the use of the on-premises approach rather than the SharePoint Online model, but this is still evolving as hosting and cloud offerings take shape and address some of these data and privacy concerns.

The other major consideration relates to the amount of environmental control your organization requires for the deployment of any custom solutions you may need to fully control and govern.

The SharePoint Online/Office 365 off-premises hosted model can be extremely convenient for organizations that do not want to host their SharePoint 2013 environment and have no issues with following the custom deployment or storage guidelines set by the hosting provider. This model works very well for organizations that want to quickly have access to SharePoint 2013 without having to carry the expense of the maintenance and overall overhead of a dedicated environment.

This is a key decision point as well in your overall SharePoint 2013 roadmap. Always thinking in terms of future phases and possible requirements regarding items such as Active Directory Federation Services or Azure Active Directory for any business intelligence or reporting you may have planned for future phases will save time and future budget. Ensuring that there is sufficient control over the environment for any requirements you may have regarding customization, like workflows that cross into other LOB systems and these similar types of "one-offs" or variables, will ensure that you select an environment model that will meet your organization's needs for years to come.

SharePoint Server 2013 Technology Updates

The following 18 chapters cover many of the intricacies of this new release, such as Microsoft's new Workflow Manager, which provides the capability to host workflows in a high-scale, high-density, and multitenant environment for SharePoint Server 2013 (see Figure 1.1).

This new workflow engine is not supported by any SharePoint Foundation 2013 releases, and Office 365's workflow capabilities are also different from those of the on-premises version. This new workflow framework, Workflow Manager, is not installed by default and must be installed as a prerequisite to installing SharePoint Server 2013. If Workflow Manager is not installed, SharePoint Server 2013 will still revert to being compatible with only the workflows that work with SharePoint 2010 until Workflow Manager is installed.

The architecture of your SharePoint Server 2013 platform should take into consideration the number of workflows that your organization uses or plans to use. If your organization is a heavy user of workflows, you should consider installing Workflow Manager on a separate farm. For enterprise or global organizations, Workflow Manager should almost always be implemented on its own server or server farm to ensure performance and scalability.

SharePoint 2013 Workflow Platform

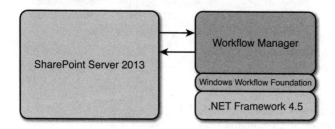

FIGURE 1.1   An overview of SharePoint Server 2013's new workflow platform.

Table 1.1 covers the main differences between the features available in SharePoint Server 2013 and those in SharePoint Foundation 2010.

TABLE 1.1   SharePoint Server 2013 Versus SharePoint Foundation 2010

SharePoint 2013 Feature	SharePoint Foundation 2010	SharePoint Server 2013
Records Management and Compliance		X
Provides records management and compliance features in SharePoint Server 2013 provide improved ways to help you protect your business. The records archive and the in-place record retention from earlier versions of SharePoint Server are still supported. SharePoint Server 2013 adds retention policies that are applied at the level of a site.		
Social Computing		X
Enables social computing features in SharePoint Server 2013 offer an improved administration and user experience, in addition to new functionality for enterprise users to share and collaborate with others in their organization. The introduction of Community Sites offers a forum experience to categorize discussions around subject areas, and connect users who have knowledge or seek knowledge about subject areas. Improvements to My Sites offer a more intuitive workflow for users to develop their personal profiles, store content, and keep up-to-date with activities of interest.		
Business Intelligence		X
BI in SharePoint 2013 provides comprehensive BI tools that integrate across Microsoft Office applications and other Microsoft technologies. These BI tools are Excel 2013, Excel Services in SharePoint 2013, PerformancePoint Services in SharePoint Server 2013, Visio Services in SharePoint, SharePoint 2013, and Microsoft SQL Server.		

SharePoint 2013 Feature	SharePoint Foundation 2010	SharePoint Server 2013
User Authentication and Authorization	X	X
User authentication in SharePoint 2013 is the process that verifies the identity of a user who requests access to a SharePoint web application. User authorization in SharePoint 2013 is the process that determines the users who can perform defined operations on a specified resource within a SharePoint web application. SharePoint 2013 supports user authentication based on the following methods:		
Windows claims		
Security Assertion Markup Language (SAML)-based claims		
Forms-based authentication claims		
eDiscovery		X
Enables eDiscovery functionality in SharePoint Server 2013 provides improved ways to help you protect your business.		
Web Content Management		X
Provides new and improved features for web content management that simplify how you design publishing sites and enhance the authoring and publishing processes of your organization. SharePoint Server 2013 also has new features that use the power of search to surface dynamic web content on publishing sites.		
Workflow		X
SharePoint Server 2013 brings a major advancement to workflow: enterprise features such as fully declarative authoring, REST and Service Bus messaging, elastic scalability, and managed service reliability. SharePoint Server 2013 can use a new workflow service built on the Windows Workflow Foundation components of the .NET Framework 4.5. This new service is called Workflow Manager and it is designed to play a central role in the enterprise.		
Note: SharePoint Foundation 2013 is compatible only with workflows that work on SharePoint 2010.		
Search	X	X
Empowers users to quickly locateimportant sites and documents by remembering what they have previously searched and clicked. The results of previously searched and clicked items are displayed as query suggestions at the top of the results page.		
Note: Advanced search as well as tailored customized search is available only in SharePoint Server.		

SharePoint 2013 Feature	SharePoint Foundation 2010	SharePoint Server 2013
Access Services		X
This allows creation of new Access service applications using the Access 2013 Preview client. You can view, edit, and interact with the Access Services database in a browser.		
Access Services 2010		X
Access Services 2010 allows continued maintenance of SharePoint 2010 Access Service applications by using Access 2010 clients and Access 2013 Preview clients. It doesn't allow users to create new applications.		
App Management Service	X	X
This feature allows you to install apps from an internal app catalog or the public SharePoint App Store.		
Excel Services		X
Enables users to view and interact with Excel files in a browser.		
Machine Translation Service		X
Enables the feature that performs automated machine translation.		
Managed Metadata Service		X
Access managed taxonomy hierarchies, keywords, and social tagging infrastructure as well as Content Type publishing across site collections.		
PerformancePoint		X
Access the information you need when you need it with interactive dashboards and score cards. Easily analyze root causes and make effective decisions by using new features like the Decomposition Tree, visualizations, and improved filtering.		
PowerPoint Conversion		X
Allows you to convert PowerPoint presentations into various formats.		
Secure Store Service		X
Provides single sign-on authentication to access multiple applications or services.		
State Service		X
Provides temporary storage of user session data for SharePoint Server components.		

SharePoint 2013 Feature	SharePoint Foundation 2010	SharePoint Server 2013
Usage and Health Data Collection	X	X
Collects farmwide usage and health data and provides the capability to view various usage and health reports.		
User Profile		X
Adds support for My Sites, Profiles pages, Social Tagging, and other social computing features.		
Visio Graphics Service		X
Allows you to view and publish Microsoft Visio diagrams in a Web browser.		
Word Automation Services		X
Performs automated bulk document conversions.		
Work Management		X
Provides task aggregation across work management systems, including Microsoft SharePoint products, Microsoft Exchange Server, and Microsoft Project Server.		
Microsoft SharePoint Foundation Subscription Settings Service	X	X
Tracks subscription IDs and settings for services that are deployed in partitioned mode. Windows PowerShell only.		

Feature Comparison of SharePoint On-Premises Versus Office 365/SharePoint Online

SharePoint on-premises and Office 365/SharePoint Online have different feature offerings. Table 1.2 covers the main differences between these offerings.

> **NOTE**
>
> Office 365/SharePoint Online has several different offerings including those for small-business and enterprise. EPC Group uses both SharePoint Server 2013 on-premises and Office 365 Enterprise (E3) because we have a hybrid configuration to support our clients. Table 1.2 is meant to represent a sample of the Office 365/SharePoint Online offerings as they have been frequently updated over the past six months, and I want to ensure that you review the latest and greatest offerings at Microsoft.com before selecting any licensing options.

TABLE 1.2   SharePoint Server 2013 Versus SharePoint Foundation 2010

		SharePoint Server On-Premises		Office 365/SharePoint Online	
		Standard	**Enterprise**	**Plan 1**	**Plan 2**
		Licensing Options	Licensing Options	Monthly Fee	Monthly Fee
Apps	**App Catalog and Marketplace**	X	X	X	X
Collaboration	Team Sites	X	X	X	X
	Work Management	X	X	X	X
	Social	X	X	X	X
	External Sharing			X	X
Search	Basic Search	X	X	X	X
	Standard Search	X	X	X	X
	Enterprise Search		X		X
Content Management	Content Management	X	X	X	X
	Records Management	X	X	X	X
	eDiscovery, ACM, Compliance		X		X
Business Intelligence	Excel Services, PowerPivot, PowerView		X		X
	Score Cards and Dashboards		X		
Business Solutions	Access Services		X	X	X
	Visio Services		X		X
	Form-Based Application				
	SharePoint 2013 Workflow		X	X	X
	Business Connectivity Services	X	X		X

X = Capability Included

SharePoint Server 2013's Capabilities

In the subsections that follow, SharePoint Server 2013's capabilities as well as new offerings are covered. The remainder of this book focuses on the capabilities of SharePoint Server 2013.

Enterprise Content Management, Records Management, and Compliance

SharePoint Server 2013's enterprise content management, records management, and compliance features are vast and range from being able to implement a records retention schedule around millions of documents to manage the entire life cycle of your organization's content, to providing your eDiscovery capabilities that are seamless and can be tailored to your specific needs.

The first two questions that I typically ask a client when architecting a SharePoint Server 2013 document management (ECM/RM) solution are "What is considered a record within your organization?" and "Does your organization have a defined retention schedule?"

It is key to scope out exactly what you are wanting to accomplish when approaching a SharePoint 2013 document management initiative because SharePoint's out-of-the-box document libraries provide capabilities for storing content, but SharePoint's information management design can be configured to follow specific retention or compliance policies as well as a multitude of other specific needs your organization may require. Table 1.3 shows an example of how the type of record correlates to an organization's record category, which is an example of how you can begin to look at the content within a specific department or a division.

TABLE 1.3   Example of How a Type of Record Correlates to a Record Category

Type of Record	Record Category	Description
Benefit plans, insurance plans, pension plans	Employee Benefit Descriptions	Descriptions of all employee benefit plans
Payroll time sheets, supplementary payroll information	Payroll Records	Summaries of hours worked, overtime, and salary paid
Vendor invoices	Invoices	Records of goods or services purchased from vendors
Product surveys, questionnaires, training manuals, training videos	Training Materials	Provides internal or external training
Shipping forms, shipping reports	Shipping Records	Documents the shipment of materials
Press releases, newspaper articles	Press Releases	Public relations information about products and services
Emergency contact sheets, medical plan enrollment forms, résumés, benefits status reports	Personnel Records	Records of individuals' employment histories and related personnel actions

Understanding what your organizational requirements are in terms of document management will allow you to put in place a core set of metadata/content types that are also flexible enough in nature to ensure that users can easily store as well as retrieve content. Identifying the type of content that will be stored will enable you to create governed site templates in SharePoint that contain core metadata/content types within document libraries and lists you can utilize whenever a new site is created to ensure governed site proliferation.

There are also elements to SharePoint 2013 document management that are advanced in nature that allow for retention-based document life cycle management as well as disposition of content based on rules and workflows. This life cycle includes document creation, review, approval, and ultimately disposition. Identifying these core content attributes as soon as reasonably possible will pay huge dividends over having to go back and apply the information management policies in a future phase after thousands of documents have already been stored. Figure 1.2 is a high-level example of the life cycle of a record and how retention rules can be applied to ultimately delete and "destroy" an organization's record to reduce legal exposure and improve records management.

The entire approach and best practices records management methodologies, from initial content analysis to content type planning and the development and implementation of proven information architecture for SharePoint 2013, are described in Chapters 2, "Proven Implementation Strategies for SharePoint 2013 and Office 365 | SharePoint Online," and 5, "Implementing a Best Practices SharePoint 2013/Office 365 Information Architecture." Proven strategies of all aspects of a SharePoint records management or ECM implementation, such as content expiration, multistage retention policies, and implementation of eDiscovery and compliance, are a very granular focus in these later chapters of this book.

SharePoint Server 2013 has some exciting new features related to performing bulk metadata updates as well as providing metadata-driven navigation that are extensively covered in these later chapters. These features increase SharePoint's information management capabilities as well as usability and buy-in from end users, making not only storing content but also retrieving content much easier.

Search Capabilities in SharePoint 2013

There are some very exciting and noticeable search updates and new features in SharePoint 2013 search capabilities. Microsoft has basically taken the two different offerings they had available in SharePoint 2010 around SharePoint Server 2010 Search and the FAST Search Server 2010 and combined them with a set of new and improved features that make finding your content very easy.

Users can now rest the pointer over a search result to preview content in the hover panel, which allows them to distinguish results much faster. SharePoint 2013 has search results lists which show users the links that are most often selected after a specific search, and it will also help return to content that you have already searched by remembering the links, sites, and documents you have searched and clicked in the past.

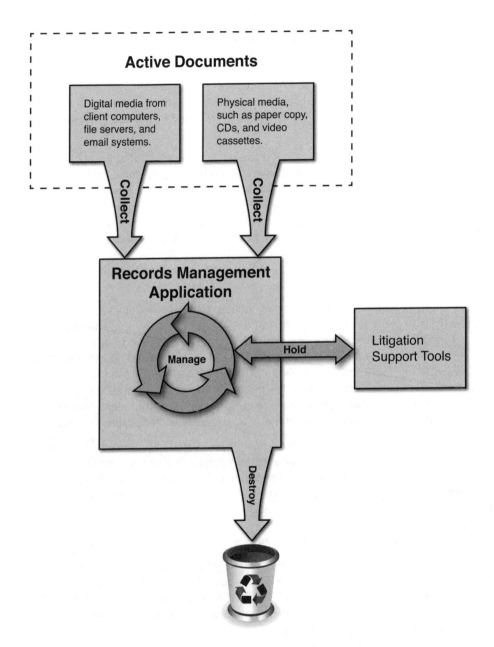

FIGURE 1.2   An example of a document's overall life cycle.

There are added improvements in areas such as people searches with integration to Lync, as well as other social search improvements such as newsfeed results that show the number of replies, as well as likes of specific content.

There is also the capability to offer customized behavior of search results for specific audiences or sites without having to implement a custom search solution as you would have in previous releases of SharePoint.

I have spoken with a number of clients recently with SharePoint 2010, as well as SharePoint 2007 currently installed, who have said their users are not using SharePoint's search because it's just not giving them the results they are expecting. This issue should be resolved with SharePoint 2013 with the analytical-based search engine that gives search results similar to a popular site like Amazon.com in that SharePoint helps guide you to suggested content based on your criteria.

SharePoint 2013's search features, as well as the strategies regarding the planning and configuration of search, are discussed in greater detail in Chapter 14, "Search Web Content Management, Branding, and Navigational Strategies," and are covered not only from a standard content retrieval perspective but also from an eDiscovery perspective.

You will find that in SharePoint 2013 there are many moving parts that relate to each other and that is the importance of ensuring that a proven strategy is followed as some configurations elements must be planned and implemented which are prerequisites of other critical features. This approach will provide for not only the expected feature results but also the long-term scalability and performance required to meet your organization's service level agreements (SLAs). Figure 1.3 shows the overall high-level architecture of SharePoint 2013's Search.

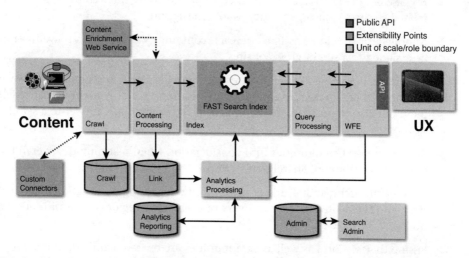

FIGURE 1.3   SharePoint 2013's search architecture.

Social Features and Capabilities in SharePoint 2013

The social computing features in SharePoint 2013 have been redesigned to focus more on how users have experienced social media in other areas (LinkedIn, Facebook, and so on) while maintaining and actually increasing security. I prefer the terms "professional networking" or "professional computing" regarding these social features because governance and compliance are key to these capabilities' long-term success. Having been involved in more than a hundred "My Site" and professional networking projects in SharePoint, I can say that there has been mixed acceptance and usage of this capability in a large number of organizations in previous versions of SharePoint, and there are several key strategies that need to be followed.

SharePoint 2013 has built on and improved the My Site capabilities and has also added Community Sites, which provides a new layer to social (professional) computing in SharePoint. Communities encourage the collaboration of organizational communities or topic-driven communities that build on a knowledge management or "Communities of Practice" type of approach while also continuing to maintain a user's dedicated My Site.

Microblogging has been introduced to enable users to participate in conversations or discussions with a Twitter-like tag (starting with the # symbol) and a "Like" feature, as well as improved capabilities to quickly follow people and specific documents or sites.

I have experienced much more acceptance and buy-in from "SharePoint business owners" around these capabilities in SharePoint 2013 deployments. I have also seen several key strategies increase this acceptance by suggesting the following:

▶ My Site templates should be governed to provide only the web parts, apps, and related features your organization wants to support.

▶ A moderator should be assigned to each community much like a power user would be assigned to a site or group of sites.

▶ The moderator should be empowered and provided incentives much like power users to maintain permissions or monitor conversations not only for governance enforcement but also to possibly rewrite or provide a combination answer to a set of discussion posts.

▶ Be sure to take Communities into consideration when planning the overall hierarchy and taxonomy of SharePoint.

▶ Plan for the architectural side of communities regarding the creation of site collections and the related disaster recovery or even archiving of communities that may no longer be utilized.

▶ Ensure that My Sites as well as Communities are reviewed and fall under your information management governance strategies. Also ensure that the capability to store content is there and a sensitive document or record has the capability to be securely stored.

SharePoint 2013's social computing features and related best practices methodologies, from architecture and design to governance, compliance, and long-term user adoption strategies, are covered in greater detail in Chapter 16, "Social Networking and My Site Strategies."

Yammer

Microsoft's reported $1 billion purchase of Yammer also provides a huge curveball to those organizations that are exploring the new social capabilities of SharePoint 2013. In my personal opinion, if you do not yet have an investment in a third-party social networking solution such as Yammer, you should hold off until SharePoint 2013 is implemented and you have your users using the new My Site capabilities.

Office 365's licensing has been updated recently to include Yammer in SharePoint 2013's newsfeeds, and you now have an option of integrating Yammer into SharePoint's newsfeeds. I think providing too much social capabilities right from the beginning and not focusing on your organization's specific roadmap, unless you are implementing SharePoint 2013/Office 365 specifically for a social networking initiative, should wait until a later phase 2, because this can be a project in itself and overwhelm your user base.

Web Content Management in SharePoint 2013

SharePoint 2013's Web Content Management includes improved capabilities in the publishing of content by site owners, power users, and site designers. One major complaint regarding SharePoint 2010's and 2007's WCM capabilities related to the pains content owners experienced when updating their site content, which ultimately leads to sites not being updated as often and being much less relevant to users and the overall organization. SharePoint 2013 now allows users with content publishing capabilities to copy content from applications like Microsoft Word and paste it directly into a Rich Text Editor Web Part, a Content Editor Web Part, or an HTML field control and have it automatically process the content and provide correct HTML markup displays of that content in the styles provided by the organization or site owner.

This is a very important milestone in SharePoint's web content management capabilities to provide for a "smart" content conversion type feature that will increase updates and also enhance governance around the styles of the content users will experience.

One of the other new web content management (WCM) features introduced in SharePoint 2013 directly meets a business requirement I have heard about time and time again when clients mention the lack of video capabilities in SharePoint. In SharePoint 2013, there are many new features for videos and digital asset management, as well as how videos play on pages. There is also a new "video" content type that will increase search and filtering capabilities of video content and provide a faster upload experience in saving content.

A thumbnail preview is automatically created when a video is uploaded to an asset library, and content authors can choose a frame from the video and use that as the thumbnail preview image, much as you would when uploading a video to YouTube.

Also in SharePoint Server 2013, content authors can insert an iFrame element into an HTML field on a page that enables authors to embed dynamic content from other sites (videos, maps, links, and so on). There is the capability to govern this iFrame feature as well, which I have seen to be one of the initial governance-related questions when discussing content on SharePoint 2013 intranet projects, as well as on other sites like those for corporate communications and marketing departments. There is the capability to specify trusted external domains for which URLs can be accepted from, and site collection administrators can add to this list of "trusted external content providers" as required under the HTML Field Security setting on the Site Settings page.

There are also improvements related to the storage and WCM features of images. SharePoint 2013 now supports image renditions that let content contributors display differently sized versions of an image on different sites and pages.

For large enterprise and global organizations there has been a focus on improving the variations feature for multilingual sites, as well as site redirecting capabilities to route specific users to the appropriate variation of the site based on the language setting of the user's browser. This resolves one of the business requirements that I have experienced in the past for global clients who had team members traveling abroad. Some of these clients had experienced issues with the content of SharePoint due to language packs and had to go to additional trouble and workarounds to view the content in the language they required.

SharePoint 2013's WCM architecture planning and implementation are covered in greater detail in Chapter 14. This is another example of how important it is to have a roadmap and strategy in place or to develop one that will take into consideration all of these variables.

For example, you can now provide friendly URLs by using managed navigation and category pages that will build the URL for the site based on the term set specified. If we take a quick step back to think through this process, the underlying architecture of SharePoint 2013 that is designed should take into consideration metadata as well as taxonomy and navigational business and functional needs to take advantage of some of these powerful new features. This book covers these strategies "from the consulting trenches" based on experience from a variety of past successful SharePoint 2013 implementations having designed global deployments with consideration of specific laws and governing regulations in specific countries.

When you are planning global SharePoint deployments, it is key to consider some of these "SharePoint curveballs" to ensure that your architecture will meet the various requirements that might be thrown your way and to ensure that you have a strategy and the ability to adapt without having to rearchitect or redesign areas of SharePoint 2013.

Scalability best practices relate not only to the system side of SharePoint regarding servers, network performance, and high-availability performance but also to the scalability of the actual information architecture of SharePoint regarding its navigation, metadata, security model, and variety of other areas that fall under "operational" governance, which is covered in great detail in Chapter 9.

Understanding Mobility in SharePoint 2013

Mobility and the capability to provide a secure and governed BYOD strategy to your SharePoint 2013 users is quickly becoming one of the most high-profile milestones for SharePoint project sponsors and project managers across the globe. This strategy must not only take into consideration the management of the mobile devices but also delve down to the granular level of the mobile application experience provided for the devices your organization supports.

Thankfully, SharePoint 2013's new features and capabilities support these requirements. This also comes down to the planning and execution of a best practices strategy for sites, site content, the type of mobile device, and the experience you want to provide to these users while maintaining organizational information management policies and intellectual property (IP) security at all times.

I have been deeply involved with SharePoint 2013 and enterprise mobility strategy initiatives at several Fortune 500 organizations, as well as government and healthcare-related institutions, and have navigated through the potholes. I cover these best practices and strategies in detail in Chapter 14. This book covers the mobility and BYOD strategies and configuration recommendations from both sides of the coin. The user experience (UI) of SharePoint and the content for which you want to make mobility accessible must also align with the devices, the security policies, the governance strategies (what if a mobile device is lost, and so forth), and your organization's custom development best practices.

It is not enough to just worry about which browser your organization's SharePoint users may use; you also need to consider which device, OS, resolution, and permission strategies should be specified. This is actually one of the most exciting topics and milestones to work on and achieve within a SharePoint 2013 initiative. In many cases, this has been the 800-pound gorilla (that is, your organization's BYOD strategy) that IT and possibly legal have been debating, and it now must be addressed and at the very least planned for within your organization's SharePoint roadmap. There are also added features available within SharePoint 2013, such as new mobile browsing experiences that are smartphone/mobile browser specific, as well as geographical and business intelligence capabilities.

This book also covers the mobile development best practices in areas such as the jQuery Mobile framework, as well as responsive design strategies, to ensure accessibility on mobile devices' touch, channels, tiles, fonts, and performance capabilities.

Business Intelligence in SharePoint 2013

Business Intelligence is one of the most discussed topics regarding SharePoint 2013. I think it has to do with not only SharePoint's new BI capabilities but also the life cycle of where SharePoint is now on its fifth release and SQL Server 2012's new big data and BI features which SharePoint 2013 integrates.

SharePoint 2013 provides new capabilities for a more seamless integration with Excel 2013, Excel Services in SharePoint 2013, PerformancePoint in SharePoint 2013, Visio Services in SharePoint, native SharePoint data, and Microsoft SQL Server 2012 and 2008.

There is a new "In-Memory BI Engine" (IMBI) that works in conjunction with Excel for nearly instant analysis of millions of rows of data. There is also a new Power View add-in for Excel that provides interaction with modeled data with visualizations, smart querying, and even animations.

PerformancePoint's integration with SharePoint provides for interactive key performance indicators (KPIs), dashboards, reports, and quick filtering of data to provide analytics and data with BYOD and scalability in mind.

In a number of SharePoint BI initiatives I have been involved with, a major factor in success was planning and the available data "streams" and methods for which that data was provided. In almost any BI initiative, you will have questions regarding the requirements of the designed analytical report, KPI, or dashboard in terms of real-time versus nightly or even on a specific time schedule. There are also factors regarding your organization's infrastructure and some possible limitation in some scenarios with SharePoint Online/Office365 and Power BI data accessibility, but these questions are addressed and strategies are explained later in this book, in Chapter 8, "Business Intelligence Overview for SharePoint 2013 and Office 365."

Identity Management in SharePoint 2013

Claims-based authentication enhancements and the use of extending the Open Authorization 2.0 (OAuth 2.0) web authorization protocol provide SharePoint 2013 with the capability to seamlessly authenticate not only with Exchange Server 2013 and Lync Server 2013, but also to the apps in the SharePoint Store and App Catalog. Claims-based authentication is now the default for new web applications in SharePoint 2013 when they are created within SharePoint's Central Administration.

SharePoint 2013 also supports Windows claims, SAML-based claims, and Forms-based authentication claims. Windows Classic model authentication has been deprecated in SharePoint 2013, but the enhancements in the claims infrastructure allow for easy migration from classic model to Windows-based claims mode with the new `Convert-SPWebApplication` Windows PowerShell cmdlet.

Overview of the SharePoint 2013 Upgrade Process

The methodologies and "from the trenches" best practices provided by this book are extensive around all areas of the upgrade process from previous versions of SharePoint (2007/2010) to SharePoint 2013, as well as the migration from non-SharePoint LOB systems such as Documentum, LiveLink, and eRoom.

The upgrade and migration technical strategy will vary based on your existing SharePoint 2007, SharePoint 2010 environment, or other LOB system, but there are core questions that need to be asked of both IT and the business to implement a best practices strategy.

I was recently involved in an upgrade and migration initiative for a client that had a highly customized SharePoint 2007 (MOSS) farm with a large number of team sites that were used for collaboration as well as a Documentum environment they had been utilizing as their organization's ECM platform. The main goals of the effort were to migrate away from two different systems with two different licensing models and support processes to one centralized SharePoint as a Service (hybrid platform) for SharePoint 2013 to be the organization's central ECM and collaboration solution.

The book covers in detail the different strategies, both non-SharePoint LOB system migration initiative and upgrade best practices for existing SharePoint environments to SharePoint 2013, that will ensure the initiative's success.

One of the major upgrade path changes Microsoft has put in place with SharePoint 2013 that you should be aware of is that 2013 does not support in-place upgrade for an existing environment. You must utilize the database-attach upgrade method to upgrade your databases to the new SharePoint 2013 environment.

There is also a change in the upgrade process designed to provide additional flexibility to SharePoint farm administrators and site administrators. The upgrade process has changed from previous upgrade methods in past versions to separate upgrades of the software and databases from upgrade of the sites. This boils down to upgrading the data and sites after the content and services databases have been copied over to the new SharePoint 2013 farm. The upgrade and migration to SharePoint 2013 are covered in great detail throughout this book "from the trenches," providing examples of proven strategies that have been used in a large number of successful SharePoint 2013 efforts.

Branding in SharePoint 2013

The overall branding approach in SharePoint 2013 has drastically changed from previous versions. Visual Studio or SharePoint Designer is no longer required to brand your SharePoint environment; rather, HTML, CSS, or JavaScript can be utilized. SharePoint 2013's Design Manager, a new interface and central hub for managing aspects of branding your SharePoint 2013 site, is available at the top-level site of a SharePoint site collection. Design Manager is a part of the Publishing Portal site collection template in SharePoint 2013. It is key to plan for the appropriate templates when provisioning sites in SharePoint 2013 so that you can take advantage of certain capabilities.

With the new branding capabilities in SharePoint 2013 via utilizing Design Manager, it is possible to utilize HTML editors or even programs like Adobe Dreamweaver or Microsoft Expression Web to brand your SharePoint environment.

SharePoint Server 2013 supports device-specific targets, as shown in Figure 1.4. It does so by creating channels that allow a specific publishing site to be rendered in multiple ways using different designs targeted to specific devices you want to support in your overall SharePoint governance model and SLAs with your user base.

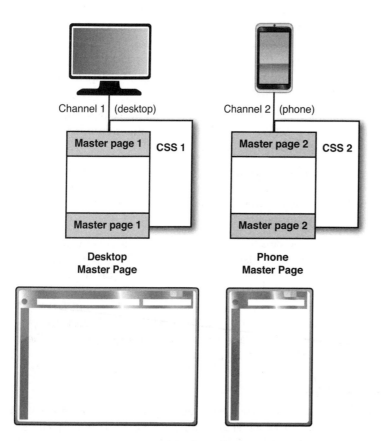

FIGURE 1.4   SharePoint 2013's branding capabilities across different browsers and devices.

The planning for your organization's branding or "look and feel" must also take into consideration SharePoint 2013's new capabilities for mobility as well as WCM to ensure that specific devices such as smartphones or tablets that you may want to provide a seamless user experience with are compatible with the branding you have implemented.

SharePoint 2013 utilizes templates to define and render SharePoint pages, and the structure of these pages contains multiple elements. There is a new "Change the Look" feature, as shown in Figure 1.5. The first element, master pages, defines the shared framing elements (that is, the chrome) for all pages in your site. The second element, page layouts, defines the layout for a specific class of pages. Lastly, pages are then created from a page layout by authors who add content to page fields.

Branding best practices, as well as proven strategies for gathering and translating business design requirements into functional and proven branding solutions for your organization's SharePoint deployment, are covered in great detail in Chapter 14.

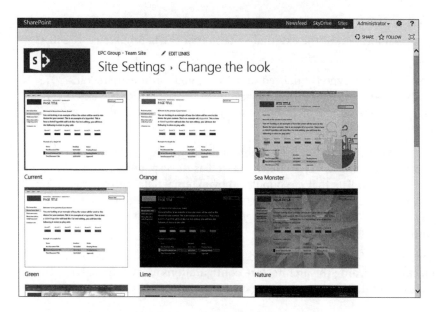

FIGURE 1.5   SharePoint 2013's "Change the Look" feature.

Custom development best practices are covered in Chapter 13, "Development Strategies and Custom Applications in SharePoint 2013, Office 365, and SharePoint Online," around creating custom apps, workflows as well as the related strategies around application life-cycle development.

Business Connectivity Services Overview in SharePoint 2013

SharePoint Server 2013 includes the Business Connectivity Services (BCS), which allows for secure connections to data sources that exist outside of SharePoint. The BCS in SharePoint 2013 does not have any changes in terms of creating the service application topology, but there are several enhancements and new capabilities that are delivered in this new release, such as these:

▶ The support of Open Data (OData) Business Data Connectivity (BDC) connection

▶ Performance enhancements in relation to connections to external lists

▶ The capability to support SharePoint apps and Office apps

▶ The capability to receive events from external systems with new event listeners

There is a Business Data Connectivity metadata store, which is a database within SQL Server 2012/2014 or SQL Server 2008, where the BCS stores the definition of external content and all the relevant connection information such as its location and the data type.

The way the BCS data works from a high-level perspective is that the definition of the specific external data source or content you are connecting to is referred to as the External

Content Type. When you take the External Content Type along with the details and definition of the actual location of the external system, that is what makes up the BDC model.

When an Enterprise Content Type is finalized or defined, you can use SharePoint 2013 via a browser or SharePoint Designer 2013 to manipulate the data from the external data source by utilizing an external list which is very similar to SharePoint lists that are available right out of the box in SharePoint.

Another feature that you will quickly notice when utilizing the BCS in SharePoint 2013 is the performance improvements in external lists, as well as the capability to actually export data that you are viewing in lists that are populated by external data into Microsoft Excel. If you have a workbook in Excel linked to an external BCS list, you also can refresh the data in that Excel workbook, which is very powerful, giving yet another way to perform BI and data analysis in real time in SharePoint 2013.

The Business Connectivity Services are discussed in very granular detail in later chapters, and best practices regarding the architecture configurations, data connectivity, and processes, as well as custom development in regard to the BCS, are also covered.

Summary

The goal of this chapter and of future chapters is to provide methods and best practices strategies that I have seen work well in organizations across the globe that were developed over 13-plus years of SharePoint consulting.

There have been lessons learned, mistakes made, sleepless nights, and battles fought over the hundreds of SharePoint implementations that my organization's EPC Group and I have worked on, but the main goal of this book is to provide you with a time-tested approach and the tools you need in order to succeed.

The following chapters build on this foundational chapter to address specific requirements and matching strategies to implement SharePoint 2013/Office 365 right the very first time.

CHAPTER 2

Proven Implementation Strategies for SharePoint 2013 and Office 365 | SharePoint Online

This chapter provides a best practices approach on how to plan, manage, and implement a SharePoint 2013/Office 365 | SharePoint Online initiative. Every SharePoint effort is different in terms of having its own set of IT and business challenges, possible pitfalls, and overall goals, but there are core methodologies and strategies that your organization can follow to ensure its success. A tailored strategy can be built for your initiative by ensuring that the specific underlying project tasks, milestones, and granular questions that need to be answered are factored into your project plan and integration roadmap.

The goal is to provide you with these "from the trenches" methodologies that have been developed from several hundred SharePoint implementations and provide this "knowledge transfer" to you on what really works and what doesn't.

Where to Begin

SharePoint 2013 may be the core technology and platform your organization is implementing, but don't just focus on the technology side of this initiative. By establishing a phased success criteria and working with the business and key stakeholders to define the project objectives, establishing an overall project plan and timeline, you will ensure that the initial pieces are in place. Someone should be identified as the person who owns the overall control and execution of the project. Multiple stakeholders and team members will be involved with the execution of the actual tasks, but by first identifying the objectives and implementation plan, you will put a stake in the ground that the team can work toward.

There are some key implementation questions from the project management and planning perspective that should be initially answered, such as these:

- What is the organization trying to accomplish with this initiative (SharePoint 2010 to SharePoint 2013 intranet, enterprise content management platform, technology/ platform replacement initiative, and so on)?
- Are there any timelines or dates that need to be met?
- Are there any existing SharePoint 2013 development/test or Office 365 environments already set up that the project team should be aware of?
- What is the overall budget for the initiative?
    - Infrastructure/licensing
    - External consulting resources/internal budget costs for IT
    - Travel, separate training budget identified or procured, and so on
- Who are the key stakeholders, business owners, and project sponsor(s)?
- Is there a specific department, pilot group, or audience for any initial milestones or possibly phase 1 goals, or does this apply to the entire organization?
- What is the availability of the team members who have the knowledge and answers for the questions that will need to be answered?
- Are there any legal policies, retention schedules, or compliance that must be followed in regard to the content or records, in-scope?
- Are there other systems that exist within the organization that will need to be utilized, and, if so, who are the owners (e.g., business and technical)?
- Are there any branding standards that must be followed?

TIP

Different technologies are available to track the overall effort, but SharePoint itself should be utilized whenever possible to manage the project documents and milestones to ensure that the team is "practicing what they are preaching." This is not always possible, but when this is an option, I would recommend using SharePoint for project collaboration if a secure environment is available.

Establishing a roles and responsibilities document, as well as creating a defined Communications Management Plan, will ensure that the project team understands what is expected of them in terms of all project communications.

SharePoint Communications Management Plan Example

This example is of a Communications Management Plan for the SharePoint initiative being conducted. This communications mechanism will be provided to the project team and will identify the schedule, contents, purpose, and person responsible for each communication. The Communications Management Plan provides direction for several key areas covered in the following subsections.

Scope

The Communications Management Plan encompasses communications managed by EPC Group's project management. This plan applies to all project team members and staff, both internal and external, involved in the project. Project management expects strict conformance to this documented communication process in the management and communication of internal and external team information.

Objectives

The objective of the Communications Management Plan is to clearly define the standards and processes of communication used to facilitate successful completion of the project. Through the communication management process, the EPC Group project team and client project team will have a transparent and identified method for sharing key communications and important project documents. This plan ensures that project sponsors and stakeholders are provided with timely information regarding the project's progress and status.

Stakeholders

Table 2.1 shows the initial baseline information that should be captured and communicated to all project team members and stakeholders.

TABLE 2.1   Capturing and Communicating Project Team Information

EPC Group

EPC Group				
Last Name	First Name	Role	Phone	Email

Customer

Client				
Last Name	First Name	Role	Phone	Email

Communication Path

The diagram shown in Figure 2.1 shows the communication path for this project.

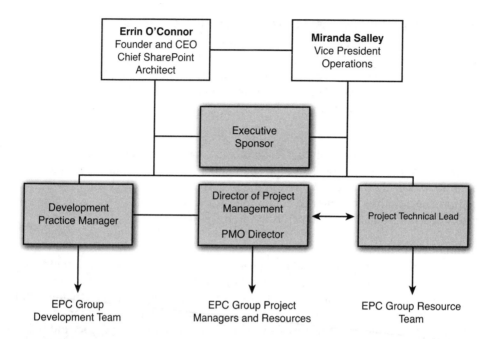

FIGURE 2.1   An example of a high-level initial communication diagram for a SharePoint initiative.

Communication Best Practices

The general rules for communication for this project will apply as listed here:

- ▶ Formal communications shall be documented in writing.

- ▶ The subject line for all project-related emails should include the project name or an abbreviation for the project followed by a short description of the email.

- ▶ The Project Manager should be copied in all communications, even if no direct action is required.

Communication Matrix

Table 2.2 shows an example of the types of communications that will exist within your initiative.

TABLE 2.2   Communication Matrix Example

Communication Type	Responsible Party	Audience
Status Updates	EPC Group/Client Project Managers	EPC Group/Client Project Managers, Operations Team
Change Request(s) Meetings	EPC Group/Client Project Managers	IT Managers, Development Managers, Network Engineers, Project Sponsors

Table 2.3 defines the purpose and frequency of each type of communication meeting.

TABLE 2.3   Communication Frequency Matrix

Item	Description	Frequency
EPC Group Internal Status Meetings	Discuss progress, issues, and/or risks to the project with the major project resources and stakeholders.	Weekly
EPC Group/Client Status Meeting	Discuss progress, issues, and/or risks to the project with the major project resources and stakeholders, customer(s), sponsor(s).	Weekly
Change Requests Meetings	Documented request to modify scope. These meetings are scheduled to discuss the operational need or requirement, impact, and schedule if approved.	As needed
EPC Group Development Meeting	Internal call with the development group to get the status on development progress, identify issues and/or risks to delivery dates, get clarification on specs (if needed), and confirm that deliverables are completed according to the specs.	As needed

Communication Schedule

Table 2.4 shows an outline of a communications schedule.

TABLE 2.4   Communication Schedule Example

Communication Item	Audience	Responsible Person	Frequency	Day	Time

Table 2.5 shows an example of a contact list template that can be used by managers in the event that an issue needs to be escalated.

TABLE 2.5   Communication Escalation List Example

Role/Title	Name	Phone	Email

Modifications to the Communications Management Plan occur when events that require forms of communication not previously listed occur. The communication type, description, frequency, and so on can be updated as needed.

SharePoint Public Relations and Communications Strategy

The overall SharePoint roadmap's communication messages are critical to SharePoint's success in terms of not only the content of the communication but also its timing. Sending out planned communications that will help you ensure SharePoint's "care and feeding" should be continuous throughout its life cycle and even into the future in SharePoint's next release, years down the road.

It is key to always try to connect the business and IT leadership messages, as shown in Figure 2.2, into one cohesive "core end-user" message.

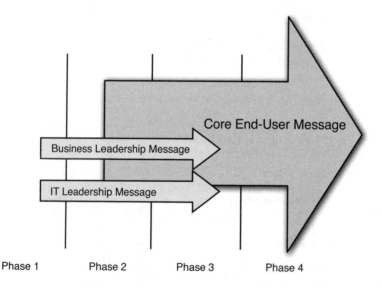

FIGURE 2.2   It is key to connect the business and IT leadership core messages to the SharePoint project team as well as the end-user community.

SharePoint Public Relations Objectives by Phase (Example)

As a SharePoint 2013 public relations campaign is planned and executed, it is key to have specific messages that you want to communicate to the user community, as shown in Figure 2.3, within each project phase. This will help the organization understand that SharePoint is a long-term platform meant to meet the organization's business and functional requirements.

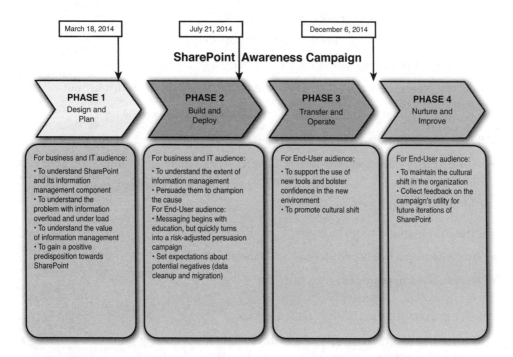

FIGURE 2.3   Aligning your SharePoint PR and communication campaign messages with key success criteria within each project phase will help you meet your overall goals and measure their success.

Providing a public relations (PR) campaign and very specific goals to achieve will allow you to measure specific SharePoint metrics throughout the different phases to gauge success as well as possible areas of improvement or even retraining.

TIP

All of these messages within the different phases are meant to be high-level core messages, but I would strongly recommend that the organization's SharePoint Governance strategy be tied in and communicated at every opportunity. SharePoint Governance plays a part in nearly every item I have identified here within this PR and communications strategy.

In Phase 1, it is important for the business and IT audience to:

▶ Understand SharePoint and its information management component

▶ Understand the need to identify and/or develop your mobile and BYOD strategy and related message

▶ Understand the problem with information overload and under load

▶ Provide a clear "Social Communication" message

▶ Understand the value of Information Management

▶ Gain a positive predisposition toward SharePoint

▶ Identify power users and know you will need to champion them throughout SharePoint's life cycle

And it is important for the end-user audience to:

▶ Feel that they have been provided with accessible training and information about the new tool, and to be given a message to help them embrace SharePoint within the organization

In Phase 2, it is important for the business and IT to:

▶ Understand the extent of Information Management

▶ Be persuaded to champion the cause

And it is important for the end-user audience to:

▶ Understand that messaging begins with education, but quickly turns into a risk-adjusted persuasion campaign

▶ Set expectations about potential negatives (data cleanup and migration)

In Phase 3, it is important for the end users to:

▶ Support the use of new tools and bolster confidence in the new environment

▶ Promote cultural shift

In Phase 4, it is important for the end-users to:

▶ Maintain the cultural shift in the organization

▶ Collect feedback on the campaign's utility for future iterations of SharePoint

Key Objectives of a SharePoint Awareness Campaign

The SharePoint Awareness campaign for business and IT users is only part of the overall PR campaign that spans the entire project's life cycle.

Awareness and understanding lay the foundation for the persuasion that must take place for SharePoint to be adopted quickly and consistently, which helps the various audiences reach their goals more efficiently.

For the enterprise, it means realizing protection from Information Management risks sooner and leveraging financial gain from the resulting productivity.

SharePoint Awareness Campaign Communication Channels

There are multiple ways to present a SharePoint awareness campaign to the various types of users, from end users to power users and from site collection owners to corporate communications. An example is shown in Figure 2.4 of providing one "core message" in seven different ways.

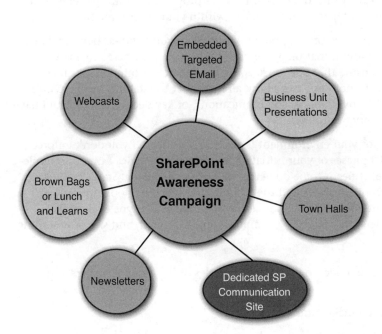

FIGURE 2.4   Your SharePoint PR and awareness campaign can be communicated in seven different core ways.

SharePoint's components should be defined, configured, and planned for in both the near term and the long term to set your SharePoint 2013 initiative apart from other organizations and provide for tangible ROI and an immediate cultural shift into improved collaboration, information management, and staff productivity.

High-Level Overview of a SharePoint 2013/Office 365 Deployment

In Chapter 1, "Introduction to SharePoint 2013 (On-Premises, Office 365 Cloud, and Hybrid)," the importance of a SharePoint roadmap was discussed, and along with that roadmap it is equally important to develop and implement a governance strategy. SharePoint Governance should not just be a 40-page Microsoft Word document that you refer team members to or have them sign off on. Instead, it should be "operational governance," which is the configuration of SharePoint 2013 in such a way that the right templates are created and utilized for site creation and within these templates your organization's information management policies are automatically contained. The branding strategies you develop should also automatically be configured into the available sites or "look and feel" options so that they can be followed right out of the gate.

The sites and communities that are created should also contain the security (AD Groups/SharePoint security groups) within them when they are provisioned from the templates and contents of the different SharePoint "galleries" within your environment.

Almost every moving piece, task, or component within SharePoint should have a related governance policy. I have found that mapping your project's requirements to a governance strategy will help ensure that you are keeping governance in mind at all times. It will also save you time to not have to go back after the fact to establish a governance strategy and even rehash conversations, communications, or key decisions that could have been captured from the very beginning.

SharePoint Governance for your environment is absolutely critical. If you don't enforce Governance in the initial phases of your initiative, it's going to be twice as hard to implement down the road, but it needs to be done regardless of your current state. To look at governance from both the business and the technical perspectives, look not only at SharePoint's branding and look and feel, but also at site quotas, file type exclusions, appropriate content policies, My Site and Community management, and site provisioning.

This will help you to:

▶ Develop a governance model that includes the roles of the content owners and teams

▶ Develop an organizational communication plan

▶ Create portal/site standards, including development and security standards

▶ Set the organization's operational and content management processes

▶ Identify end-user support processes and tools

▶ Plan monitoring and compliance policies and procedures

▶ Manage user requests (new sites and custom development)

▶ Develop SharePoint branding and look-and-feel standards

At a high level, SharePoint Governance consists of two major areas:

▶ Infrastructure Governance (see Figure 2.5)

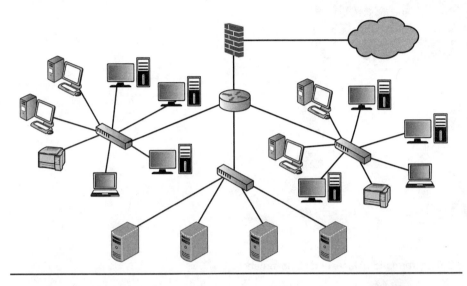

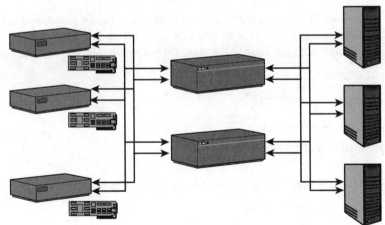

FIGURE 2.5   Infrastructure Governance.

▶ Information Management Governance (see Figure 2.6)

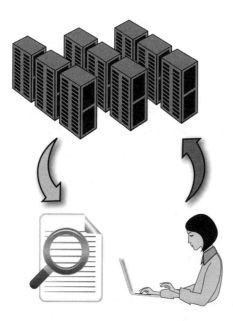

FIGURE 2.6   Information Management Governance.

From these two major areas, I prefer to break it down further and create four major topic areas so that the requirements are gathered to properly architect and design tailored, organizationally specific SharePoint Governance Policies. These are the four major topic areas:

▶ Environment and Security Governance

▶ Custom Development Governance

▶ Content-Related Governance

▶ Administrative and Training Governance

These four major topic areas contain a large number of granular subtopics:

▶ Environment and Security Governance

  ▶ SharePoint Disaster Recovery Governance

  ▶ Defining SharePoint SLAs

  ▶ Defining SharePoint Maintenance

  ▶ SharePoint Security Governance

  ▶ Site Provisioning Governance

  ▶ Search-Related Governance

  ▶ Continued...

- ▶ Custom Development Governance
    - ▶ Development of Organizational SharePoint Development Standards
    - ▶ Development of Deployment and Code Promotion Requirements
    - ▶ SharePoint Branding Governance
    - ▶ Apps, Third-Party Solution, and Custom Solution Purchasing Policies
    - ▶ SharePoint Designer 2013 Policies and Procedures
    - ▶ Workflow or Business Process Automation Governance
- ▶ Content-Related Governance
    - ▶ Enterprise Content Management–Related Policies
    - ▶ Content Type/Managed Metadata Policies
    - ▶ Retention and Site Storage Policies (quotas, file upload limits, and so on)
    - ▶ My Site/Social/Communities Policies/Yammer Strategies
    - ▶ Power User and Content Updating Guidelines
    - ▶ Executive and Legal Content Policies
    - ▶ Document Libraries and List Customization Policies
    - ▶ Continued...
- ▶ Administrative and Training Governance
    - ▶ SharePoint Training Guidelines
    - ▶ SharePoint Communication Plan Guidelines
    - ▶ SharePoint Steering Committee, Governance Committee Policies
    - ▶ Organization's SharePoint Support Model (Tier 1, Tier 2, Tier 3, and so on)
    - ▶ Business Intelligence, KPI, Executive Dashboard, and SharePoint Reporting Guidelines
    - ▶ Continued...

The overall performance and user requirements metrics need to be captured for the infrastructure components in areas such as these:

- ▶ What is the user base or requirements related to concurrent users?
- ▶ What is the expected load?
- ▶ Is the organization's architecture virtual, physical, and so forth?
- ▶ Are we implementing SharePoint 2013 on-premises only?
- ▶ What is the growth or adoption rate expected over the next 36 months?

▶ Are there any performance metrics?

▶ What SharePoint Services need to be offered?

▶ Are there geographical areas that need to be put into consideration?

▶ What are or will be our AD, SharePoint, and SQL Server locations?

▶ Are there identified service level agreements (SLAs) or peak hours?

▶ What are our monitoring and maintenance strategies?

▶ What is our network speed or do we have any third-party solutions such as Riverbed or F5?

▶ Are there any encryption requirements?

▶ Are we dealing with any blade distribution?

▶ Is there any custom code that needs to be considered?

▶ Will we have development and staging environments?

▶ What are the current software development policies or standards?

▶ Will we have any external SharePoint apps?

▶ Are there any logistical concerns or delays we need to be aware of regarding acquiring hardware?

▶ Have we built into our schedule the time needed for performance and reliability testing as well as DR?

Identifying the Core Tasks and Milestones of Your Initiative

There are a wide variety of tasks that must be accomplished throughout the life cycle of a SharePoint 2013 initiative, and every deployment's project plan or work breakdown structure (WBS) will be unique to the effort. By breaking down the overall project into smaller project components and work elements, you will be able to understand the total amount of work involved for each phase or subset of tasks to meet a given milestone. You will also be able to capture the actual cost of the effort and track the budget as you progress and also identify any areas where additional costs may be incurred that were not originally planned.

I have been involved in scoping many SharePoint 2013 initiatives for clients from the initial presentation of SharePoint to the business to working with IT to develop a statement of work regarding what it will take to accomplish the effort. Because my organization also works with a large number of organizations in a "Trusted SharePoint Advisor" role, I take an agnostic approach to this to assist organizations in understanding what the effort will realistically take in terms of budget, effort, and cultural adoption. There is a political side to any major IT initiative because staff members and even executives have a lot at stake, not only for their jobs but in terms of how the project is executed, delivered, and accepted by the overall organization.

You can put into place a risk mitigation strategy for your SharePoint initiative. However, the political or internal "company politics" are something that each organization will need to judge internally, and sometimes certain areas will need to be approached with a little more tactical care than you might expect. One strategy that has been effective in lowering the amount of "company politics" that can sometimes slow down or get in the way of certain areas of your SharePoint initiative is to try to include as many key stakeholders or specific business owners in the initial strategy and project kickoff meetings as possible so that they feel they are involved and their opinions are being taken into consideration.

The following tables are baseline examples of the components of a SharePoint project plan or WBS to help you build a tailored schedule of your own.

SharePoint Server 2013/Office 365 Project Plan Template

The table that follows is broken up into seven sections, shown as Tables 2.6 through 2.12. Each shows examples of milestones you should build on in your SharePoint 2013/Office 365 initiative's project plan.

TABLE 2.6   SharePoint 2013/Office 365's SharePoint Online Project Plan Template Example—Part 1

Task #	Project Tasks Description
1	**Project Start**
2	Initiate Planning Efforts
3	Establish Objectives and High-Level Requirements
4	Define Scope
5	Define Project Solution and Project Delivery Processes
6	Estimate Size
7	Review Direction
8	**Project Planning Activities Begin**
9	Create Work Breakdown Structure
10	Perform Resource Planning
11	Create Project Schedule
12	Prepare Budget
13	Conduct Schedule Review
14	**Begin Supporting Plan Definition Activities**
15	Create Communication and Controlling Procedures
16	**Project Initiation and Planning Wrap-Up Activities**
17	Compile and Inspect Project Definition Document
18	Review and Approve Project Definition Document

Task #	Project Tasks Description
19	**Initiate Project Execution**
20	Prepare for Kickoff
21	Create Project Site in SharePoint and Project Schedule in Project Server
22	Conduct Project Review and Kickoff
23	**Begin Requirements Gathering Activities**
24	Conduct Initial Requirements Gathering Sessions/Determine Audiences
25	**Begin Content Sessions**
26	Conduct Session 1
27	Conduct Session 2
28	**Begin Requirements Gathering Sessions**
29	Conduct Department or Audience Session 1
30	Conduct Department or Audience Session 2
31	**Equipment Sessions**
32	Equipment Requirement Session 1
33	Equipment Requirement Session 2
34	**People Sessions—Team Member Discussions**
35	Conduct People/Group Requirement Session 1, Etc.
36	**Begin Backend Application/Additional Data Sources Discussions**
37	Conduct Backend Application Investigation
38	**Begin Steering Committee Sessions**
39	Conduct Steering Committee Member Interviews
40	Develop Requirements Document
41	Conduct Requirements Document Review and Apply Updates
42	**Obtain Requirements Document Client Sign Off**
43	Conduct Phase End Assessment

TABLE 2.7   SharePoint 2013/Office 365's SharePoint Online Project Plan Template Example—Part 2

Task #	Project Tasks Description
44	**Initiate Onsite Reviews**
45	Conduct First Onsite Review Planning Session
46	Conduct Second Onsite Review Planning Session
47	**Begin Development Environment Configuration and Deployment**
48	Hardware and Software Procured
49	Provide Team Support in Development Configuration

Task #	Project Tasks Description
50	**Governance Document Development Begins**
51	Governance Overview Meeting
52	**Discover Working Sessions**
53	Define Overall Services
54	Define Software
55	Define Policies
56	**Design Working Sessions**
57	Build Organizational Diagrams
58	Build Proposed Model
59	Define Information Management
60	Define Organizational Structure
61	**Governance Document Draft**
62	Construct Services Documentation
63	Construct Equipment for Environment Documentation
64	Construct Software Documentation
65	Construct Information Management Documentation
66	Construct Organization Documentation
67	Construct Policies Documentation
68	Review Draft Governance Documentation with Client
69	**Governance Document Final**
70	Construct Services Documentation
71	Construct Equipment for Environment Documentation
72	Construct Software Documentation
73	Construct Information Management Documentation
74	Construct Organization Documentation
75	Construct Policies Documentation
76	Review Draft Governance Documentation with Client
77	Obtain Governance Document Client Sign Off
78	**Roadmap Development Activities**
79	Develop Roadmap Document
80	Review Roadmap Document
81	Obtain Roadmap Document Client Sign Off

TABLE 2.8   SharePoint 2013/Office 365's SharePoint Online Project Plan Template Example—Part 3

Task #	Project Tasks Description
82	**Design Efforts Begin**
83	Design Process Overview Meeting
84	**Server Configuration Related Activities**
85	Identify Document Management Approach
86	Identify Existing Content Sources—Content Audit or Inventory
87	Determine Content Migration Methodology
88	Review Server Software Requirements
89	Plan Recycle Bin Use and Site Recovery
90	Determine Site Provisioning Model and User Experience
91	Identify Number and Usage Patterns of Users for Server/Hardware
92	Identify Number and Usage Patterns of Document Management Users
93	Identify Number and Anticipated Usage Patterns of Search Users
94	**Planning Capacity Activities**
95	Determine Normal Load from Roles and Usage Patterns
96	Determine Number of Documents Stored and Document Store Size
97	Estimate Index Size
98	Determine Needs for Growth
99	Determine Peak Load Factor
100	Evaluate Caching, Load Balancing, and Other Scaling Techniques
101	Determine Future Scale-Out Approach
102	Whiteboard System Architecture
103	Update Design Document
104	**Security Related Efforts Begin**
105	Security Review and Lockdown (Device Governance) Discussions
106	Determine Authentication Provider—Identity Management Requirements
107	Review Security Requirements
108	Review AD Groups (Also Existing SP Security Groups)
109	Review Security Design
110	Review Infrastructure Components
111	Identify and Document Threats
112	Document Security Model
113	Update Design Document
114	**Performance-Related Activities**
115	Determine Requests per Second
116	Measure Caching Performance and Optimizations

Task #	Project Tasks Description
117	Review Connectivity and Bandwidth Requirements
118	Review Current Network
119	Establish Minimum Performance Levels
120	Performance Testing of Network
121	Review Network Performance
122	Diagram Future Network Topology
123	Update Design Document

TABLE 2.9   SharePoint 2013/Office 365's SharePoint Online Project Plan Template Example—Part 4

Task #	Project Tasks Description
124	**Failover and Disaster Recovery**
125	Establish Failover and Disaster Recovery Requirements
126	Create Failover and Disaster Recovery Plan
127	Determine Need for Third-Party Tools
128	Plan Recycle Bin Use and Site Recovery Plans
129	Document Failover and Disaster Recovery Plan
130	Test Failover and Disaster Recovery Plan
131	Update Design Document
132	**Localization-Related Activities**
133	Determine Language Used for Server Farm
134	Determine Need for Variations
135	Install Needed Language Packs
136	Review Search Settings for Locale
137	Update Design Document
138	**Maintenance Activities**
139	Plan Backup and Restore
140	Plan Other Routine Maintenance
141	Determine Quotas to Manage Site Collection Storage Sizes
142	Configure Zones, Alternate Access Mappings, Etc.
143	Determine Disposition Schedules and Notifications
144	Update Design Document
145	Create Detailed Wireframes for Site and Page Structure
146	Identify Additional Content and Design Requirements
147	Identify Custom Development Requirements
148	Establish and Maintain User Experience Best Practice Guidelines

Task #	Project Tasks Description
149	Maintain Brand Consistency and Design Standards for Templates
150	Update Design Document
151	Review Design Document
152	Obtain Design Document Client Sign Off
153	**Design Phase End Review**
154	Conduct Design Phase End Assessment
155	Design Phase End Review Complete
156	**Company Training Strategy**
157	Create Training Strategy
158	**Migration Strategy and Recommendations**
159	**Begin Integration Plan Development**
160	Determine BCS/External Data Source Requirements
161	Determine Need for Excel Services
162	Determine Need for InfoPath Forms Server
163	Determine Search Requirements
164	Determine Need for Antivirus
165	Determine SharePoint 2010/2007 Existing Content Metrics for Migration
166	Exchange 2013 Integration/Incoming Email Planning
167	Identify Other Systems for Integration
168	Determine Integration Strategy
169	Develop Plan for Integration
170	Migration Strategy and Recommendations Complete

TABLE 2.10   SharePoint 2013/Office 365's SharePoint Online Project Plan Template Example—Part 5

Task #	Project Tasks Description
171	**Initiate Client Training Activities**
172	Create SharePoint 2013 Tailored Training Guide
173	Obtain SharePoint 2013 Training Guide Client Sign Off
174	Phase End Review Phase 1
175	**Initiate Data Analysis**
176	Finalize Project Documentation
177	Conduct Project Analysis
178	**Begin Closure and Archival Activities**
179	Closeout Project Plan

Task #	Project Tasks Description
180	Conduct Project Closure Meeting
181	Finalize Phase 1 Phase End Reporting
182	Archive Artifacts
183	Execute Phase 2 Planning
184	**Project Management Activities**
185	Attend Team Work Session
186	Attend Weekly Status Meetings
187	Monitor and Control Project
188	**Phase 2 Begins**
189	**Begin Branding Discussions with Marketing/Corp. Communications**
190	Obtain Branding Standards/Discuss Mockups/Wireframe Development
191	Local View Style Sheet
192	Local Browser Style Sheet
193	**Deploy IA and Taxonomy**
194	Build Navigation
195	Configure Page Variations
196	**Provisioning Tool**
197	Install Site Provisioning Tool
198	**Development and Content for Sites/Pages**
199	Locations Page
200	Policies and Forms Pages
201	Application Page
202	Advance Search
203	Search Result Page
204	Global Directory Page
205	Team Sites
206	Communities Sites
207	Department Landing Page
208	Local Landing Page
209	News Page
210	Survey Page
212	Site Map/Glossary
213	Finalize Pages with Custom Components

2

TABLE 2.11   SharePoint 2013/Office 365's SharePoint Online Project Plan Template
Example—Part 6

Task #	Project Tasks Description
214	**App Parts / Web Parts (Custom) Development Begins**
215	Create Custom Weather App Part \ Web Part
216	Create Custom Stock Web Part
217	Create Time Converter Web Part
218	Create Custom Streaming Video Web Part
219	Create Search Result Web Part
220	Location Fly-Outs—Custom Navigation Configuration
221	Rotation Web Part—Global Announcements
222	Global Directory Search
223	Custom Online Help and Governance Sign-Off Forms
224	Implement RSS Features
225	**Configuration of Out-of-the-Box Web Parts on Home Landing Page**
226	Configure Local Content Web Parts
227	Configure Subscribe Link
228	Configure Feedback Icon
229	**Global Search Configuration Based on Requirements**
230	Managed Metadata Property
231	Configure Global Search Scopes
232	Configure People Search Scopes
233	Configure Crawl Components
234	Federated Search—Rollup or Replicate to EU Farm
235	**Workflows Development and Configuration Activities**
236	Ensure Workflow Manager Configuration
237	Content Approval Workflow Deployment
238	Expiration Workflow Deployment
239	Disposition Workflow Deployment
240	Deployment Workflow
241	Site Inactivity Workflow
242	**Global Directory/Profile Services Configuration**
243	Employee Directory
244	Location Tree
245	**Third-Party Tools Procurement/Installation**
246	Installation and Configuration of Management Tool
247	Development Complete
248	**Deployment to QA**

Task #	Project Tasks Description
249	Validation Hardware Has Been Obtained
250	**QA Server Build (Network Related, Windows Server 2012, SQL Server 2012/2014, etc.)**
251	QA Install SharePoint Server 2013
252	QA Install and Configure Third-Party Tools
253	QA Migrate Configuration
254	Migrate Code to QA Environment
255	QA Migrate IA and Taxonomy
256	QA Documentation
257	**System Testing QA Begins**
258	QA Conduct Unit Testing
259	QA Conduct Performance Tuning

TABLE 2.12 SharePoint 2013/Office 365's SharePoint Online Project Plan Template Example—Part 7

Task #	Project Tasks Description
260	**Validation and Testing Processes**
261	Create and Approve Test Plan
262	**Functional Testing**
263	Create Functional Test Scripts
264	**Execute Test Scripts**
265	Conduct Break Fixes
266	Rreview and Approve Testing Results
267	**UAT Testing Processes Begin**
268	Create User Test Scripts
269	Validate Users Have Been Trained for Testing
270	**Production	Execute User Test Scripts**
271	Conduct Break Fixes
272	PROD Review and Approve User Testing Results
273	Deployment to Production
274	**Build Production(Network Related, Windows Server 2012, SQL Server 2012/2014, etc.)**
275	PROD Install SharePoint Server 2013
276	PROD Install and Configure Third-Party Tools
277	Production Migrate Configuration
278	Migrate Code to Production
279	Production|Migrate IA and Taxonomy

Task #	Project Tasks Description
280	**System Testing of Production**
281	Production Conduct Unit Testing
282	Production Conduct Performance Tuning
283	**Update Browser Default Homepage**
284	Contingency Plan—Rollback
285	**Deployment to Production Complete—System Ready**

The granular technical strategies and configuration options for the items contained in this sample high-level project plan are detailed in the following chapters.

Identifying Common Terms and Features of SharePoint 2013

There are several common terms and features in SharePoint that you and your project team will need to understand in both a technical and a business perspective. These common areas within SharePoint 2013 exist on all versions and environments whether on-premises SharePoint Server, on-premises SharePoint Foundation, or an Office 365 | SharePoint Online implementation.

Sites and Site Collections

SharePoint sites store and share the information using web parts, apps, lists, and libraries that are the core components within SharePoint. SharePoint sites present the content stored within lists and libraries for a given team, organization, or project. SharePoint sites come in various templates, with each template containing a unique set of lists, libraries, and pages. After the business and functional requirements are defined, the appropriate template can then be selected to meet those needs. During the requirements gathering and governance strategy development of your initiative, you can create templates that contain lists and libraries with the information management policies and approved branding elements which will ensure that SharePoint grows in a managed and strategic manner.

Site collections are a group of sites that form a hierarchy with a single top-level site with a collection of subsites. There can be additional subsites created within these sites but they all will roll up to their top-level site collection.

The overall approach to developing a best practices SharePoint information architecture and taxonomy, as shown in Figure 2.7, is discussed in greater detail in Chapter 5, "Implementing a Best Practices SharePoint 2013/Office 365 Information Architecture," Chapter 6, "Using Out-of-the-Box Web Parts in SharePoint 2013/Office 365," and Chapter 7, "Implementing a SharePoint 2013 System Architecture with Future Hybrid Scalability in Mind."

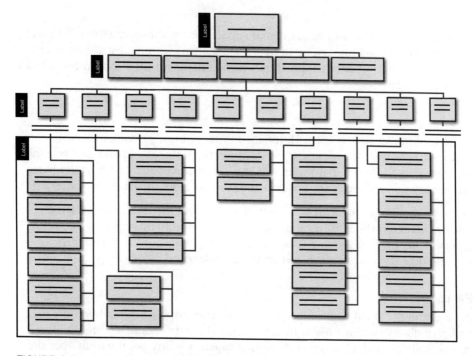

FIGURE 2.7   An example of a high-level overview of SharePoint's information architecture and taxonomy for your planning.

The Ribbon

The ribbon is a feature of SharePoint similar to the ribbon that exists within Microsoft Office. The ribbon, as shown in Figure 2.8, enables you to manage SharePoint via small icons within the site rather than text, to give you visual indicators of the setting that you are looking to configure. The ribbon adjusts the options available to you as you select various objects and make selections on a page.

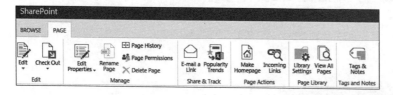

FIGURE 2.8   The Ribbon enables you to perform SharePoint management and design tasks with visual indicators.

Lists

The list feature is one of the most fundamental applications within SharePoint 2013 and is used as a storage location for a group of items. These items within a list are really any object that you are tracking information about, such as items within a contact list, a tasks list, or even a calendar.

Libraries

Libraries are very similar to lists but with the main intent of storing content. Document libraries, for example, are the libraries where documents are stored and also give you the options to configure the additional features of SharePoint Server 2013, such as site-based retention, information management policies, and content types (managed metadata).

Libraries can be thought of in terms of repositories that store the records and related content where users can then utilize SharePoint's search and filtering options to quickly find the documents they are looking to access. Libraries have reportlike capabilities to filter, sort, and organize documents based on the metadata and content types applied.

Web Parts

Web parts are basically small applications or modules that display information on a page or from a list or library. When a list or library is created in SharePoint, a corresponding web part is actually created, giving you the option to use it at any point within your site.

Web-part functionality, as shown in Figure 2.9, varies from adding text or images to displaying business intelligence or reports from data sources stored both inside and outside of SharePoint. SharePoint 2013 comes with a variety of web parts right out-of-the-box, and you also have the option to develop custom web parts to meet your organization's specific business or functional needs.

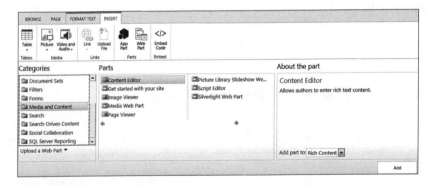

FIGURE 2.9   Web-part's allow you to display your organization's relevant data within a site.

As SharePoint has grown in popularity throughout the years, there have also arisen many third-party providers of custom web parts. With SharePoint 2013, you also have the

SharePoint Marketplace available, which adds additional options you may want to review to meet specific needs.

Content Types

A content type within SharePoint defines the attributes of a list or library item as well as a document or folder. You are able to configure a content type to specify the following:

- ▶ Metadata to associate with items of its type

- ▶ Workflows that can be started from items of its type

- ▶ Information management policies

- ▶ Properties to associate with items of its type

- ▶ Document templates (for document content types)

- ▶ Custom features to meet your organization's needs

When you associate a content type with a list or library, you are specifying that the list or library can contain items of that content type. You can also associate workflows, policies (template shown in Figure 2.10), properties, and templates directly with a list or library.

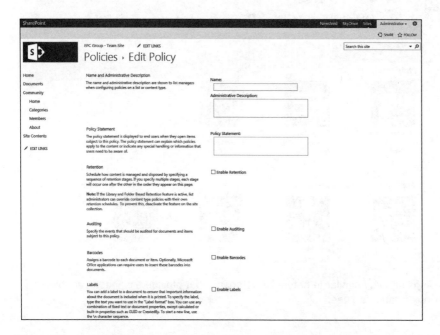

FIGURE 2.10   SharePoint 2013 allows for the creation of policies to configure and enforce information management.

With SharePoint Server 2013, you can also create a custom content type inside a content type hub that is defined in a managed metadata service (MMS) instance. When a managed metadata service is created in a content type hub, the content type will be available to other site collections that are part of web applications associated with that managed metadata service instance.

> **TIP**
>
> SharePoint Foundation 2013 does not contain the MMS and the content type hub.

Apps

SharePoint 2013 introduced a new feature called apps, as shown in Figure 2.11, which are self-contained pieces of functionality that extend the capabilities of a SharePoint site. Apps can be executed outside of SharePoint Server, in the client machine, or in the Cloud and are an extension of SharePoint's capabilities.

FIGURE 2.11 Apps are very similar in nature to web parts that provide expanded capabilities throughout your organization's sites.

It is key to think of apps in terms of apps for smartphones and similar devices, and at some level web parts in SharePoint can also have this similarity in terms of "mini-apps" or modules, as shown in Figure 2.12.

FIGURE 2.12   Apps are a common features within tablets, smartphones, as well as in the Windows App Store and iTunes App Store.

The apps capabilities follow SharePoint 2013's branding and overall user interface (UI) and can be appear full-screen (immersive) or through an IFrame.

Understanding the Audiences for Apps

The following are examples of audiences and user bases for apps, as well as some of the advantages or selling points that the new apps feature is marketing to the SharePoint community:

- ▶ Information workers
    - ▶ Familiar app concepts and components
    - ▶ Find apps in SharePoint Store or app catalog
    - ▶ Self-service provision, upgrade, and delete
- ▶ Developers
    - ▶ Leverage existing knowledge and expertise
    - ▶ Manage application life cycle independently of platform
    - ▶ Revenue potential of SharePoint Store

▶ IT Managers

   ▶ Govern the visibility and availability of applications

   ▶ Manage service independently of applications

   ▶ Customizations pose virtually no risk to service

TIP

Examples of apps for SharePoint can be found, as shown in Figure 2.13, at the following link: http://office.microsoft.com/en-us/store/apps-for-sharepoint-FX102804987.aspx

---

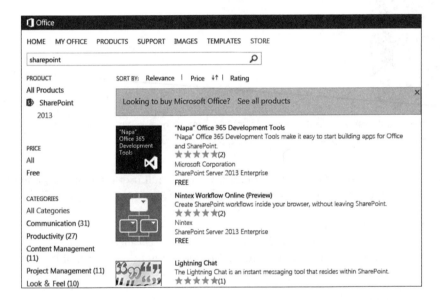

FIGURE 2.13   Microsoft's Office Store provides Apps for SharePoint as well as other Microsoft integrated products.

Getting Acquainted with SharePoint Server 2013/ Office 365's Architecture and Understanding Its Components

With all the available features and related components of SharePoint Sever 2013, it is key to ensure that the core architecture is implemented with high-availability in mind while you quantify your environment's actual availability goals and metrics. Most SharePoint environments become one of the most high-profile and critical environments in the organization and "too big to fail." By following best practices strategies, you will lessen the risk of downtime as well as reduce any downtime that may be caused in unavoidable or disaster recovery (DR) scenarios.

SharePoint is not typically utilized as an e-commerce platform, so a direct correlation between lost revenue as a result of reduced service and complete loss of service is not the metric that is usually calculated. SharePoint service level agreements (SLAs) and a service loss typically have differing consequences but can be equally damaging to the organization. A loss of confidence by the user base or your customers can be equally costly and diminish the respect of IT and the corporate brand.

A successful SharePoint architecture design should meet the specific needs of the business and must provide an optimal balance between business requirements, IT service level agreements, infrastructure costs, and IT support capabilities.

TIP

An SLA is typically an agreement between IT and the business or user representatives.

An SLA identifies the required services as well as the IT support that the business can reasonably expect. A large number of organizations tend to have an initial but not fully mature SharePoint SLA in place. Most SharePoint SLAs are lacking clear, specific, and precise expectations.

SharePoint 2013 Server Farm Overview

There are three main layers of a SharePoint Infrastructure: the Web layer, the Service Applications layer, and the Data layer, as shown in Figure 2.14. Within these three layers are the web servers, service applications servers, and database servers. With SharePoint Server 2013's new workflow framework utilizing Workflow Manager, as shown in Figure 2.15, there are added capabilities to host workflows in a high-scale, high-density, and multitenant environment. Therefore, the workflow load anticipated should be planned for because it may require a dedicated server or servers/environment depending on your organization's requirements.

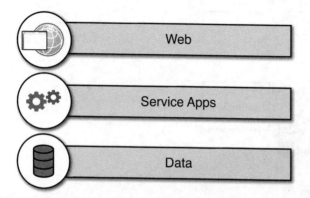

FIGURE 2.14   The three main layers of a SharePoint 2013's infrastructure.

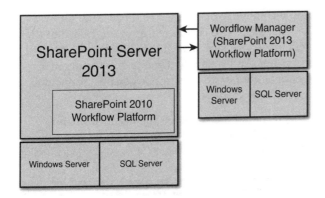

FIGURE 2.15   SharePoint Server's new workflow framework utilizing Workflow Manager.

With the service application layer existing on a separate server or farm, this allows for the isolation of service apps like the User Profile Sync and the capability to patch or resolve any tasks in isolation from the overall farm. An example of a SharePoint farm and the corresponding features it is designated to support is shown in Figure 2.16.

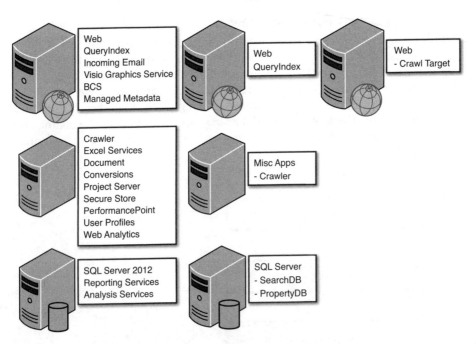

FIGURE 2.16   A high-level overview of a SharePoint 2013 farm and the areas the servers are designated to support.

Five Layers of SharePoint Security

Within SharePoint Server 2013, there are five layers of SharePoint security that you should consider:

1. Infrastructure Security and Best Practices

   a. Physical Security

   b. Best Practice Service Account Setup

   c. Kerberos Authentication

2. Data Security

   a. Role-Based Access Control (RBAC)

   b. Transparent Data Encryption (TDE) of SQL Databases

3. Transport Security

   a. Secure Sockets Layer (SSL) from Server to Client

   b. IPSec from Server to Server

4. Edge Security

   a. Inbound Internet Security (Forefront UAG/TMG)

5. Rights Management/Identity Management

Data Management Architecture and Remote BLOB Storage (RBS)

SharePoint Server 2013 provides the capability to manage data with much more flexibility over previous versions. There can be pros and cons to added features and functionality because they can add another layer of complexity and maintenance to your support and governance model.

Shredded Storage and the RBS "In the Trenches"

The shredded storage capabilities along with RBS can reduce the I/O between the web server and SQL Server for Microsoft Office document formats. This really reiterates the "bottom-up" implementation strategy for developing a SharePoint roadmap, as well as identifying the actual content that will be stored (Office documents, CAD drawings, large content, videos or media content, and so on) in SharePoint as soon as possible.

Although shredded storage can reduce storage of Office document versions and achieves a type of "de-duplication" process, non-office formats may not benefit from this technology. SharePoint 2013's real-time RBS receives each shred as a separate BLOB versus how SharePoint 2010 processed an entire file as one BLOB. There are scopes tailored to your organization that should be considered based on the type as well as the amount of data that is in-scope for your SharePoint 2013 initiative, both in initial phases and in the future. These differences are shown in Figure 2.17.

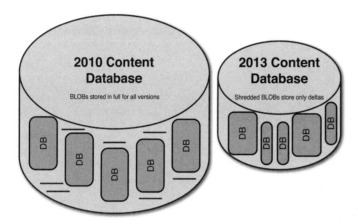

FIGURE 2.17   The new capabilities in SharePoint 2013's content database and shredded BLOBs.

Understanding the Core Databases in SharePoint 2013

The ability to understand the overall high-level architecture and information flow of SharePoint from early on in the initiative is an opportunity that is missed in many SharePoint implementations. There will be very technical team members involved in your initiative who speak the same "technology" language as you do, as well as project managers, content owners, and representatives from departments like marketing or corporate communication who may not have a technical background but deeply understand the business.

Instead of waiting until later in your initiative when training materials are typically developed or training sessions are delivered, you should start from the very beginning of the effort to explain this information flow and these core concepts of the overall planned architecture.

Most everyone on the project team may understand that SharePoint utilizes SQL Server to store its content, but spending a little extra time to explain how SharePoint data and its configurations are processed is very important.

Three foundational databases are created upon SharePoint 2013's installation, which are the Configuration, Central Administration Content, and Content database. The following three subsections provide high-level overviews of these three databases and the related content and information they store regarding your overall platform.

Configuration Database

The SharePoint 2013 configuration database contains data about the following key areas:

▶ SharePoint databases

▶ Web applications

▶ Site templates

- Internet Information Services (IIS) websites

- Web applications

- Trusted solutions

- Web part packages

Central Administration Content Database

The Central Administration content database in SharePoint 2013 is considered to be a configuration database. This database stores all configuration data for the Central Administration site collection.

If and when additional features and components are installed, such as SQL Server 2012 PowerPivot for SharePoint 2013, the Central Administration content database also stores the Excel worksheets and PowerPivot data files used in the PowerPivot Management Dashboard.

Content Databases

Content databases store all content for a SharePoint 2013 site collection, which includes site documents or files in document libraries, list data, web part properties, and audit logs. All the files that are stored for a specific site collection are located in one content database on only one server. In SharePoint 2013, a content database can be associated with more than one site collection.

SharePoint 2013's Additional Databases

There are several additional databases created by SharePoint 2013 that should be taken into consideration by the technical teams that will own and support SQL Server. These are covered in greater detail in the following chapters.

These additional databases are extremely granular in detail, but having the project team focus on and understand the three main databases (that is, Configuration, Central Administration Content, and Content databases) will ensure that the high-level information flow of SharePoint's content and configurations is understood. This information will provide for more educated and informed conversations by the project team from the very beginning of the initiative.

Summary

This chapter is meant to assist you in building on a strategy to approach, plan, and execute a SharePoint 2013/Office 365 initiative. Every organization will have granular components that are specific to its business and functional requirements, but there are proven underlying strategies that will assist in ensuring your project's success.

The following chapters in this book explain the capabilities of specific components and services in SharePoint 2013/Office 365 from a real-world perspective and a "from the trenches" perspective.

CHAPTER 3

Governed Utilization of the Features and Functionality in SharePoint 2013/Office 365

With Microsoft having referenced SharePoint 2013 as, SharePoint Server 2013, Office 365 (Enterprise), and SharePoint Online in many news articles, recent conferences and publications, the term SharePoint 2013 is used in this book to refer to SharePoint Server 2013 and Office 365 | SharePoint Online for this and all following chapters, but the integrated solutions such as Microsoft Lync, Microsoft Exchange, and Microsoft Dynamics CRM are specifically referenced as they may be specific to an existing on-premises environment you currently have implemented or features of an Office 365 plan for which your organization may have procured.

At EPC Group, we have SharePoint Server 2013 on-premises as well as Office 365 Enterprise, the E3 plan, along with SharePoint 2013 instances in the Microsoft Azure platform and in Amazon Web Services (AWS) because we believe that the future of SharePoint is going to be that of a very hybrid nature. Both Microsoft Azure and AWS have trial offerings that you can also test and integrate at any time to begin to gain experience in the hybrid cloud.

I believe that SharePoint's on-premises version will not be phased out for at least six to seven more years, and Microsoft has recently announced they have already begun working on the next on-premises release. This is my personal opinion, but I think with what has been released by Microsoft's rather vague references regarding "the cloud versus on-premises" and their ratcheting back of "cloud first" in press releases, they very much initially overstated how many firms would be "all in" in moving to the cloud in SharePoint 2013's release. The public, private, and hybrid cloud offerings and technology are covered in much more granular detail in Chapter 5, "Implementing a Best Practices SharePoint 2013/Office 365 Information Architecture."

The out-of-the-box SharePoint 2013 features that can quickly be deployed to your organization's user base are vast, but the key to a successful SharePoint 2013 implementation is rolling out SharePoint in a governed and methodical manner.

One of the key areas to keep in mind that will ensure long-term SharePoint success and save the organization's information technology (IT) budget over time is thinking of SharePoint's user base from a device-centric approach and considering the related audiences and roles associated with them.

There will be various departments, user types, and specific content they will want to access. What type of device will these users use to access SharePoint?

There will obviously be internal users with secured authentication accounts using company-issued laptops, tablets, and mobile devices, as shown in Figure 3.1, but what is the expected user experience you are going to provide to these users? Your organization's "bring your own device" (BYOD) policy may be in its infancy or even well-defined, but mapping out this strategy from the beginning is very important. Will your organization support a wide array of devices as SharePoint matures and new technology is developed?

FIGURE 3.1   An example of the wide array of devices from which users may access SharePoint.

It is important to have a common user experience throughout your user base, and it can vary based on the device and the related browser. This needs to be governed and support based on your organization's policies, but you should always think in terms of being device as well as browser agnostic whenever possible; you should also follow a Responsive Web Design (RWD) user interface (UI) design for your SharePoint sites, communities, and branding elements, as well as all custom development. The Responsive Web Design methodology (e.g., Responsive Design) is important because it assists in providing your users an optimal viewing experience with common reading and navigation that will allow for functions such as panning, scrolling, and resizing across devices.

When planning your user base and the related features and functionality you will provide, it is also important to map out not only the devices, such as those in Figure 3.1, but also the locations of the users, as illustrated in Figure 3.2. If you're a large or global organization or one that has users in multiple locations, in various countries, or possibly spread throughout the globe, you will need to keep the user experience and RWD in mind from a "device channel" perspective.

FIGURE 3.2   An example of a possible user base across the country or even across the globe.

Understanding Device Channels in SharePoint 2013 (BYOD)

Regardless of the type of implementation your organization is trying to accomplish in phase 1, it is key to understand the underlying capabilities of SharePoint 2013 to ensure that your initial plans take full advantage of SharePoint's out-of-the-box capabilities. SharePoint 2013 contains a device channel feature that is part of the SharePoint 2013 publishing infrastructure that will enable your organization to render site content, its images, and even the underlying content type while maintaining the same URL (uniform resource locator) across a selection of different devices.

On a recent project, EPC Group's architecture team was tasked with implementing SharePoint 2013 with a specific and aggressive go-live date. This phase 1 deadline was for internal users with Active Directory accounts and was not targeted toward external or "mobile" users of the organization. It was key to walk through the Responsive Design considerations with the stakeholders of possible future phases and future mobility needs because there was a custom branding and UI design that their marketing department was having us implement in phase 1.

The design was very appealing and looked great, but it was important to help both IT and the business understand that the "look and feel" that would be implemented should follow Responsive Design but also take into consideration the "device channels" or ways the users within their company would access SharePoint long-term so that this branding would be compatible in future phases.

There is a difference in the "desktop version" of the SharePoint site compared to a "mobile rendering" of a SharePoint site. Your overall design must support a variety of devices that your organization may currently support as well as take into consideration possible devices that may be allowed in the future.

TIP

When a user from a mobile device (smartphone, tablet, and so on) opens a SharePoint 2013 site, the device's browser submits something technically referred to as an HTTP GET request that includes a "user agent string." This string contains information about the device, enabling that specific browser to then be redirected to a governed and specific master page view for that device (Windows Phone, iPad, Android, iPhone, and so on). Thinking in terms of not only initial users in phase 1 but also future phases in which mobile devices will be utilized will save a great deal of future time and effort.

In most SharePoint 2013 implementations, the initial strategy will target internal users; however, the mobile or BYOD strategy will quickly follow so it's key to think in these longer terms regarding design. It's also important to get an initial inventory and/or develop a "governed device list" for your organization to know exactly how users will be accessing SharePoint content.

Most devices allow for users to go to an app store to purchase or download additional browsers, so implementing your "supported" list is key to being able to let users know whether their device's entire configuration is supported by the organization's SharePoint 2013 deployment.

Table 3.1 shows an example of how you can start a device inventory of what will be allowed in the initial phase as well as what might be allowed in future phases.

TABLE 3.1   Device and Related Browser Inventory

Device Type	Audience for Device	Known Browser Type	Is This Supported in SharePoint 2013?
iPhone	Executives, power users	Safari	Yes
Windows Phone	Some users in marketing, external user group "a"	Internet Explorer	Yes
Android	External user group "b", some IT team members, etc.	Chrome	Yes

SharePoint 2013/Office 365: Preparing for Governance

SharePoint 2013's out-of-the-box core end-user features, such as lists and libraries as well as apps, web parts, and the sites and site collections they exist on, will be the most used areas of SharePoint, but using them and deploying them with governance in mind is key to your success. The policies of how these components operate (are governed) guide your SharePoint user community and its related components. SharePoint 2013 offers end-user capabilities such as these:

▶ **Collaboration Tools:** SharePoint sites facilitate team participation in discussions, shared document collaboration, blogging, building communities, and professional networking.

▶ **Content Management:** The document collaboration features allow for easy checking in and checking out of documents, document version control and recovery of previous versions, enforcement of retention schedules, information management policies, eDiscovery, destruction or information management workflows, and document-level security.

▶ **Business Intelligence:** This enables people to connect to, find, and act on information locked away in line-of-business systems by using a framework to integrate them securely into SharePoint search results, configurable and actionable dashboards, KPIs, reports, apps, mash-up interfaces, and web parts.

▶ **Search:** A feature and overall capability that provides users with the ability to find information that is security trimmed and stored in almost any structured or unstructured repository as well as "people information." SharePoint 2013's search includes the previous SharePoint Server 2010 Search capabilities as well as FAST search into once seamless "SharePoint 2013" offering.

In keeping the SharePoint as a Service (SPaaS)/SharePoint as a Platform (SPaaP) strategy in mind, which will grow in size and importance over time and will open up the hybrid SharePoint implementation mind-set, the strategies in the following sections should be strongly taken into consideration and molded around your organization.

Preparing for SharePoint Site and Site Collection Governance

To paint a picture of how to prepare for SharePoint Site and Site Collection governance, I will walk through a few examples that apply to most organizations. SharePoint sites are usually created for collaboration or content management within the organizational structure or, alternatively, for a particular line of business (LOB) or department.

For example, as determined by the Site Owners, users from other locations may have access to content inside of these sites as well. Types of communication and collaboration in SharePoint include, but are not limited to, the following:

▶ Project sites

▶ Division department sites

▶ Professional networking (communities/My Sites)

▶ Team sites

▶ Content management/records management sites

Local sites may be created under the local SharePoint "root sites" or within the specific line of business or department. Functional area sites may reside below the local SharePoint "root sites." The sites may be further split out below the functional area by business units. The sites may also be further split out with approval of the Site Collection Owner below the functional area.

Site collections can facilitate collaboration within groups, within organizations, and between teams. For example, when a request is granted for a site collection, a governed model should ensure that the requestor chooses or is assigned the user to be the Site Collection Owner and the Site Collection Administrator with the approval of the Farm Administrators.

For example, a SharePoint Farm Administrator can assume the role of the Site Collection Administrator. Also, a Site Collection Administrator may be responsible for, but not limited to the following:

▶ Site Collection security

▶ Site Collection features

▶ Site Collection audits and usage logs

▶ Site creation

▶ List, library, and content type creation outside the scope of default items governed by the Farm Administrators

Site Collections should maintain data storage, quotas, size limitations, and threshold settings in the manner specified by the organization's SharePoint governance policy.

Preparing Your Organization's SharePoint 2013/Office 365 Organizational Support Governance

SharePoint 2013's governance is developed, monitored, and ultimately enforced by specific roles that can be referred to as the SharePoint "People Organization." A best practices example of how your organization can implement this People Organization is detailed next.

SharePoint Service Operations Teams

The SharePoint Services Operations (SSO) teams consist of the following "roles" or "groups" of support members.

SharePoint Services Team (SST)

The SharePoint Services Team oversees staff providing SharePoint system administration and multi-level support. The SharePoint Services Team drives the process of aligning the SharePoint Service with evolving business requirements and strategic direction.

The SharePoint Services Team consists of the SharePoint Services Team Manager, SharePoint System Architects, SharePoint Farm Administrators, and Site Collection Administrators. The SharePoint Services Team directs all aspects of the SharePoint Services to ensure an effective and stable service offering in relation to SharePoint.

Farm Administrators

The SharePoint Services Team Farm Administrators manage the operation of the production, QA, and development environments for SharePoint. The SharePoint Services Team controls the SharePoint application and helps execute approved change requests.

The Farm Administrators within the SharePoint Services Team may have the authority of full central administration rights, full SharePoint services rights, and provision security for the site collections, and they assign permissions to the Site Collection Administrator.

The Farm Administrators are essential members of the SharePoint Services Team, and they should frequently collaborate with other Farm Administrators and Site Collection Administrators to resolve problems, to assist with issues, and for knowledge transfer and continuous training. The Farm Administrators may have the same access to all SharePoint environment instances.

Site Collection Administrators

Site Collection Administrators manage the SharePoint site collections and are part of the SharePoint Services Team with the specific goal of promoting new collaboration tools and other SharePoint applications within their location for the sites they manage to help improve efficiency and increase productivity.

Site Collection Administrators do not, in most cases, have access to the operating system. The Site Collection Administrator is an integral member of the SharePoint Services Team.

The Site Collection Administrator will also be

▶ Comfortable working with new SharePoint applications

▶ Able to quickly learn the capabilities of SharePoint tools

▶ Able to demonstrate strong functional knowledge of the tools to others

Possible additional tasks could be delegated such as the following:

▶ Creating subsites within existing sites

▶ Managing security of the SharePoint site with approved Active Directory Groups

▶ Creating new workflows and managing site content

System Administrators

The System Administrators manage the operating systems of all SharePoint Environments (Production, QA, and DEV) and do not always have central administration rights, and they usually do not have administrative access within SharePoint. The System Administrators follow the procedures for maintenance, backup, recovery, and overall change management set forth by the SharePoint Services Team for the organization.

The System Administrators provide monitoring of the system through

▶ Usage analysis and tuning

▶ Automatic monitoring and event notifications

The System Administrators perform maintenance on the servers and provide support for hardware and software updates. They provide documentation on the installation and configuration of the system in its environment. Your organization SharePoint platform install and configuration must be documented well enough so that it can be reinstalled and reconfigured to the last known good operating standards.

Database Administrators

The Database Administrators are responsible for installation, configuration, backup, recovery, and monitoring of the SQL Server 2012 databases required by SharePoint. Database Administrators typically do not have central administration rights and have no special administrative access within SharePoint.

The Database Administrators are typically not a member of the SharePoint Services Team but work with the SharePoint Services Team in case of issues such as business continuity exercises, disaster recovery, and content database issues.

SharePoint Roles

The following sections detail granular SharePoint roles as well as the related granular best practices considerations regarding each role.

High-Level Operational Roles

Permissions and responsibilities of the operations roles are persistent throughout SharePoint. Resources may serve multiple roles within the operations roles. The roles and responsibilities defined in Table 3.2 are specific to SharePoint 2013 products and technologies and third-party tools used for operations and maintenance of the SharePoint service.

Table 3.2 shows the roles along with the related responsibilities, tasks, and any additional permission-related information.

TABLE 3.2   Roles and Related Responsibilities/Permissions

Role	Responsibilities and Tasks	Responsibility Assignment	Permissions
SharePoint Services Owner (SSO)	–Responsible for the effective provisioning and ongoing management of the centralized SharePoint platform –Leads SharePoint Steering Committee –Leads SharePoint Services Team –SharePoint Steering Committee	SharePoint Services Team/TBD	TBD
SharePoint Service Manager	–Assists in the SharePoint Steering Committee –Assists in leading the SharePoint Services Team –Ensures that tactical initiatives align to strategic intentions –Reports to Steering Committee on the level of activity	SharePoint Services Team/TBD	TBD

Role	Responsibilities and Tasks	Responsibility Assignment	Permissions
SharePoint System Architects	–Active Directory –Profile Synchronization –Patch/Release Management (validation and testing) –Responsible for SharePoint farm infrastructure design, installation, guidelines, and best practices –System Administrator's day-to-day support	SharePoint Services Team/TBD	–Full Control given at the web application policy level for every web application in all farm locations –Admin Control, full control to all central administration and SharePoint services in all farm locations
Network Engineers	–Firewalls –WAN optimization –Remote access management –External access management –Load balancing	TBD	–Will not have access to SharePoint or site configuration settings and will not be able to make any changes to the application
SharePoint Records Manager Administrator	–Responsible for new or modified records retention schedule categories –Performs legal research to determine applicable federal, state, local record-keeping laws, citations, or requirements –Works with the SP Administrator to ensure that content types are accurate –Consults with Site Owners as needed before site decommissioning	Records Management/TBD	–Will not have access to SharePoint or site configuration settings and will not be able to make any changes to the application

Granular Operational Roles

Resources may serve multiple roles within operations because it is typical in an enterprise implementation for SharePoint Architects and Administrators to perform multiple roles.

Permissions and responsibilities in the operational roles will exist within the central SharePoint Services Team, whereas development roles may exist independently throughout an organization if it is regionally or globally dispersed. The roles and responsibilities defined in Table 3.3 are specific to SharePoint products and technologies and third-party tools used for operations and maintenance of SharePoint.

Table 3.3 shows the roles along with the related responsibilities, tasks, and any additional permission-related information.

TABLE 3.3   Roles and Related Responsibilities/Permissions

Role	Responsibilities and Tasks	Team	Permissions
Farm Administrators	–Responsible for SharePoint farm's configuration, SharePoint services, policies, procedures, and governance/best practice enforcement –Day-to-day support for Site Collection Administrator –Serves as SharePoint champion for all locations	TBD	–May or may not have system administrative or SQL administration rights –Full Control: Full control given at the web application policy level for every web application in all farm locations. –Admin Control: Full control to all central administration and SharePoint services in all farm locations
SharePoint System Administrator Also referred to as: SharePoint Solution Architect	–Responsible for day-to-day maintenance of the SharePoint Platform	TBD	–Will not have access to SharePoint or site configuration settings and will not be able to make any changes to the application
SQL Database Administrator	–SQL Server database backup and recovery, SQL configuration, SQL upgrades and monitoring –Responsible for databases, site collection, and site backups	TBD	–Will not have access to SharePoint or site configuration settings and will not be able to make any changes to the application –SQL Administrative rights
Network Engineer	–Firewalls –External crawl content monitoring –Antivirus –Possible mobility management activities –Possible BYOD enforcement activities	TBD	–Will not have access to SharePoint or site configuration settings and will not be able to make any changes to the application

3

Role	Responsibilities and Tasks	Team	Permissions
SharePoint Solution Development Architect	–Responsible for following best practices development standards as defined by the SharePoint Solutions Review Board –Responsible for developing custom solutions such as apps, web parts, master pages, workflows, custom events, and custom organizationally specific records management features	TBD	–Full Control: to the development environment

End-User Roles

These roles are managed by the SharePoint Services Team with limited rights given to specific SharePoint 2013 skilled individuals.

Users may, in some cases, belong to more than one role and have additional permissions. Users may also be removed from lower-level roles because higher-level roles/permissions may encompass the permissions of the lower-level role.

Table 3.4 shows the roles along with the related responsibilities, tasks, and any additional permission-related information.

TABLE 3.4   Roles and Related Responsibilities/Permissions

Roles	Responsibilities and Tasks	Training	Permissions
Site Collection Administrator	–Manage features and solutions for site collection –SharePoint site provisioning for site collection	Instructor led with good understanding of site administration, security, content creation, feature deployment	Access defined at the SharePoint application level; no access at the system level
Site Collection Owner	–Site Collection Owner –Content creation –Manage content –Subsite management	Instructor led with good understanding of site administration, security, content creation, and records retention schedules	Access defined at the SharePoint application level; no access at the system level

Roles	Responsibilities and Tasks	Training	Permissions
Site Owner	–Site Owner –Content creation –Manage content *Note:* Annual/monthly auditing will be determined at the beginning of Phase 2 based on SLAs and the organization's Policy.	Instructor led with good understanding of site administration, security, content creation, and records retention schedules	Access defined at the SharePoint application level; no access at the system level.
Member	–Content creation (documents, lists) –Contribute to collaboration sites (blog, wiki) –Initiate workflows	Computer-based training video (CBT) with good understanding of document libraries and lists and records retention	Access defined at the SharePoint application level; no access at the system level
Approver	–Approve content (documents, lists) –Initiate workflows	CBT with good understanding of content approval and workflows and records retention	Access defined at the SharePoint application level; no access at the system level
Visitor	View content	N/A	N/A

Implementing a Best Practices Information Architecture from the Very Beginning

One of the great things about SharePoint is that it is very easy for users to store content, create content, and navigate. This can also become a challenge because from an IT and records management (RM) or information management perspective, it is important to get in front of this "challenge" as soon as possible so that a organizationally specific IM policy can be put in place before there are thousands or even hundreds of thousands of documents, records, and related content.

There is no magic answer to address this issue within all organizations because it differs among companies, their users, and the type of business or vertical the company is in, as well as the culture of the organization. There are, for example, some construction or manufacturing companies that have embraced new technology and others that have waited to see how some of the new offerings in information technology will take hold and flourish or possibly stall.

There are healthcare institutions that have focused on collaboration and document management and others that have been focused on other areas such as Electronic Medical Records (EMR) projects or other patient-specific productivity initiatives.

Some government institutions have embraced and taken records management and the institution's retention schedule head-on, and others have waited to see what regulatory or related laws may pass before implementing this technology.

My main point here is that regardless of your current state, it's time to address the roadmap and focus on implementing SharePoint 2013 within your organization to meet the specific short- as well as long-term goals of the organization.

Understanding Your Organization's User Base

Understanding your organization's user base, as well as the types of documents, content, and records they currently utilize or may want to utilize, will put you in a more educated position to implement a solid SharePoint platform.

Identifying Your SharePoint User Audience

There will obviously be several different user audience types within your implementation, but what is the best way to go about understanding how they may use SharePoint on a day-to-day basis, as well as determining the types of content and content volume they may access and create?

You can determine this by performing interviews with the specific groups, teams, or departments either via conference calls and Lync/WebEx-type virtual meetings or in person, depending on how dispersed the team members are and their availability. Another way to approach this is by sending out questionnaires to the team or the specific set of department stakeholders with core questions such as these:

- ▶ What are the standard functions that your department/team/business unit conducts in a given day or a given week (that is, what does a "day in the life" of your users look like)?

- ▶ What types of documents does your "area" create or have stored (that is, Word, Excel, PowerPoint, PDF, or are there any large files like CAD drawings, diagrams, media/video files, and so on)?

- ▶ Are there specific users who own or create specific records or documents for your given "area" (that is, are there any "records managers" identified that you should be aware of)?

- ▶ Are there any document retention schedules that exist within the organization that your "area" (department, business unit, team, and so forth) must follow or should be following in the near future?

- ▶ Are there any current workflows or business automation processes that you should be aware of?

- ▶ How are the documents within the given "area" stored currently (is there a network share, existing document management system, and so on)?

- ▶ Is there a current SharePoint system or other technology implemented where frequently used documents or even published content is stored? If so, please provide additional information.

▶ Would it be possible to get a "count" or possible estimate of the amount of content that currently exists (for example, 25GB and 125,000 documents)?

▶ Are there any common templates that are used to create common or frequently used documents for your "area"?

▶ Are there any scanning or OCR (optical character recognition) requirements within your "area"?

▶ Are there any existing systems that "tie in" or integrate with your existing documents or processes that you should be aware of?

TIP

This exercise needs to be completed for every area or department, team, business unit, or community because this will assist in your development not only of the SharePoint roadmap but also for your information architecture, navigational strategy, and governance strategy.

Laying Out a Plan for Document Libraries

As mentioned in the previous chapters, document libraries are collections of files in SharePoint 2013 that users share with other users within a given SharePoint site. Now that you understand the types of users as well as the documents they use, store, and work with, you will need to implement an information architecture that consists of the proper governed document libraries to meet these needs.

Some document libraries are used specifically for that area or department or such, and you may consider those "private" documents libraries that are accessible only by the team members or users of that given group.

Other document libraries are cross-functional and are accessed and used by many different users or groups within the organization. These document libraries may store "public" or frequently used content or may even be a document library that is created for a specific project the organization is conducting that many different users and groups need to access and contribute to.

TIP

When you start to understand the types of users and the content they are using and now are digging into the types of document libraries that need to be created to meet both the business and the functional needs, you need to start thinking about the security (e.g., Active Directory Groups or SharePoint Security Groups) that will need to be created and managed to properly protect and govern this content.

Introduction to SharePoint 2013 and the Hybrid Cloud Mind-Set

Questions about the evolution and maturity of the hosted and hybrid cloud, as well as some of the data, privacy, and security concerns that exist around it, are questions that you will need to be able to answer with facts and a clear understanding when asked by key project stakeholders and users, as well as by your organization's legal and compliance stakeholders.

As mentioned, SharePoint's 2013 "on-premises" environment, versus "hosted, off-premises," or "hybrid" environment, contains different offerings and capabilities as well as security, regulatory, and privacy implications. SharePoint 2013 stakeholders can sometimes find themselves at a fork in the road or between two possible paths, as illustrated in Figure 3.3, when selecting the type of environment or offering that will best service the organization in regard to cost, maintenance, and intellectual property security.

FIGURE 3.3   The SharePoint on-premises versus Office 365/hosted architecture decision.

There are also security- and regulatory-related questions that must be answered and addressed regarding storing personally identifiable information (PII), protected health information (PHI), HIPPA, and FDA (Title 21 CFR) Part 11. For global organizations, there are other regulatory concerns such as those of data centers in the European Union (EU) and Safe Harbor regulations that the U.S. and the EU have agreed to via the United States Department of Commerce and the seven principles of data protection and security.

> **TIP**
>
> A few new abbreviations are used throughout the Microsoft community regarding the cloud. Two of the more frequently used new acronyms are CAM (Cloud App Model) and SPO (Office 365).

There are also considerations related to the ability of your organization to develop custom solutions (workflows, apps, custom events, and so on) and promote these customizations to the cloud rather than into your on-premises environment, which you have full control over.

I have had hundreds of conversations with CIOs, CTOs, and key business stakeholders at organizations throughout the globe about this topic, and there are key considerations that must be vetted and understood when choosing a path for the organization even if a hybrid approach (that is, both on-premises and Office 365) is selected.

I was having this environmental conversation with a well-known oil and gas company's CIO I was working with who had extensive intellectual property (IP) for which the organization had invested millions of dollars on researching and collecting. His statement to me during this conversation was, "There is no way I am going to risk our IP by hosting this information in a cloud for which I cannot guarantee I have full control."

Another conversation that comes to mind is with the Enterprise Application's Director, for which SharePoint was managed, of a Fortune 500 military contracting and aerospace company. He said, "We have a ton of business intelligence needs that require us to access multiple internal systems, and there is just no safe way to deploy this custom code to the cloud and then "hook" into our SAP and other systems from SharePoint due to permissions and federation issues we have discovered." He made an interesting point during this conversation: "Do I want to have to get other IT hosting providers to have to review and approve my custom code prior to implementing it into their cloud after we develop it? This could cause additional delays I am just not comfortable with...."

In contrast, I had a conversation with the IT leader of a Fortune 500 manufacturing company who said they found Office 365 to be an excellent solution for servicing partners and clients who need quick collaboration sites set up that were also housed outside their company's DMZ (a term commonly referred to as outside the company's internal network database and perimeter), and the on-premises solution was not meeting their current needs.

I am not pushing you toward one environment or another but playing a bit of devil's advocate regarding some of the concerns and elements you need to keep in mind when going "all in" on one type of environment or another.

> **TIP**
>
> When selecting the type of environment your organization goes with in the on-premises versus cloud discussion, it is always important to ask the hard questions about the capability to migrate specific or defined content back into the on-premises environment from

the cloud should your organization ever have that requirement. This may occur in an eDiscovery process or some other auditing or BI type of effort, but it is key to be prepared and ensure that your provider can adequately meet this requirement.

Key Features of Office 365

Office 365 (O365) is an attractive offering to some organizations whose IT model as well as related content security governance will properly be met with the requirements of O365. Office 365 has an updated user interface and much improved administration controls with an improving cloud-app development model.

Office 365 has several key features:

▶ **OneDrive**

OneDrive is a core element of Office 365. It offers users organizational control to allow them to do the following:

  ▶ Sync and share documents.

  ▶ Collaborate on document security with individuals both inside and outside of their organization.

  ▶ Access content and information anywhere and from a multitude of devices.

  ▶ Control content life cycle and versioning.

  ▶ Manage access permissions.

  ▶ Access OneDrive with native mobile client apps for Windows 8 and iOS.

▶ **User Interface Updates (UI)**

The Office 365 user interface has been redesigned to allow for usability improvements in navigation to include features such as these:

  ▶ *Drag and drop:* This enables users to upload content to sites by dragging items from their computer into a SharePoint document library.

  ▶ *On-hover:* This is a new "callout" feature that works with any document within a SharePoint document library, as well as from a search results, that enables viewing, sharing, and following or "jumping" right to specific content.

  ▶ *Touch:* This feature allows for large "touch targets" for easy navigation on mobile devices and should be part of your mobile device management and BYOD considerations for your organization's governance strategy.

▶ **Yammer (in Office 365's Offerings)**

Yammer is a key element of Microsoft's social networking (that is, professional networking) strategy, and it is designed to bring additional collaboration, file sharing, and knowledge exchange within your company.

Depending on the release cycle you are currently in, it may be optional or may be included with the Office 365 investment. Key features of Yammer include these:

▶ Enables enterprises to become social quickly

▶ Offers easy access to groups and feeds

▶ Provides easy access across different devices and browsers

▶ Offers easy-to-use administration tools

▶ **Office 365 Guest Links**

Office 365 allows users to share everything, including sites, folders, and individual documents, using the Guest Link feature, which enables users to invite guests from inside and outside the enterprise firewall to share and collaborate on specific documents. These permissions can be added and revoked like any other permission element in Office 365.

▶ **Public Website Feature**

The public website feature in Office 365 comes with a large number of customization options for sites and individual pages. There are added publishing capabilities, web parts, and built-in Search Engine Optimization (SEO) property options and advanced design options.

You are also able to disable this feature and have it remain invisible until needed per the governance policies that are developed to control the SharePoint platform. The public website feature also enables users to utilize the Design Manager to completely redesign the sites from scratch.

TIP

Any customization and branding work done in the public website feature must follow the organization's governance strategy as well as any corporate logos or style elements.

▶ **e-Discovery**

Office 365 Enterprise comes with an e-Discovery management site, via integrated Exchange Online, that enables organizations to add sources and create queries to discover content across SharePoint sites and SharePoint document libraries, mailboxes, and discussions, while keeping them in place in Office 365, Exchange Online, and Lync Online.

▶ **Site Mailbox Feature**

The Site Mailbox feature combines Office 365's document management capabilities with Exchange Online's email solution. Teams can organize project-related content and email into a single view while keeping documents in their proper location. With the Site Mailbox feature, site mailboxes can be accessed through Outlook 2013, as well as Office 365.

▶ **Enterprise Search**

Office 365 search has been greatly improved in the relevancy of search results, enabling users to find the content they are searching for with the appropriate results. SharePoint Server 2013 and Office 365 have the same search engine and capabilities, with the added FAST features that were optional in SharePoint 2010 included natively. This enables users to control the search experience and also provides powerful metadata-driven results and filtering options.

▶ **Office 365 PowerShell Capabilities**

Office 365 enables administrators to use Windows PowerShell to manage their subscriptions as well as scripting tasks associated with provisioning new sites, site collections, and performing upgrade activities. SharePoint 2013 has a web-based companion tool called the Windows PowerShell Command Builder Tool for "power users or super users" with relatively moderate IT skills.

▶ **Office 365 API Tools**

The new Office 365 API Tools continues to extend the platform and will open up more possibilities around the hybrid cloud by adding not only the ability to access SharePoint 2013 on-premises, but also extending the platform in Microsoft Office 2013 by adding the ability for both sites and native applications to consume Office 365 data.

Yammer Considerations

Microsoft acquired Yammer in June of 2012, and understandably it takes time to finalize a technology roadmap within a technology of this magnitude. Office 365 users have been provided with an option to replace Office 365's activity-stream component with Yammer's, which is the first step and integration point between Yammer and SharePoint.

Microsoft has also offered the capability to embed a Yammer group feed into a SharePoint site. This is available through the "Yammer application" available in the SharePoint App Store, which will work with both on-premises and Office 365.

Microsoft has also provide organizations with the option to replace the newsfeed in SharePoint 2013/Office 365/SharePoint Online with Yammer.

OneDrive for Business (Previously SkyDrive Pro) Considerations

OneDrive for Business, previously SkyDrive Pro, has made several recent updates, such as providing SharePoint users who have Personal Site Use Rights with access to Microsoft's cloud-based OneDrive to store data and providing that same access via OneDrive from their smartphone or mobile device (see Figure 3.4).

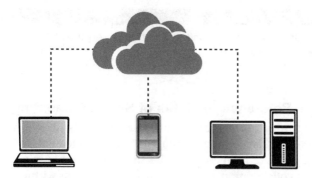

FIGURE 3.4   Showing a diagram of the workflow of OneDrive for business.

Social Computing in SharePoint 2013

Social computing, or what I like to refer to as professional networking to assist in sometimes overcoming some internal political hurdles, is one of the most powerful and sometimes underused features of SharePoint. Those who have worked with SharePoint 2010 or 2007 in the past will be familiar on some level with SharePoint My Sites capabilities, depending on whether the organization opted to implement them. In SharePoint 2013, however, the professional networking capabilities of SharePoint include not only radically improved My Site features but also a new Community Site template, which adds a new layer to this social computing powerhouse platform.

A Community Site is a new SharePoint 2013 site template that provides a forum type of experience within the SharePoint platform. This of course will add to your governance planning, but the way it has been architected into the SharePoint 2013 fabric, it adds a great deal of value and cements SharePoint 2013 as the social computing tool for enterprise organizations.

If your organization has worked with knowledge management (KM) initiatives in the past, it is helpful to think in terms of these communities to help categorize and spawn discussions among different groups or team members across the organization. This feature does not replace My Sites at all but rather is an added layer to help promote open communication and collaborative exchange by enabling users to share things like best practices and lessons learned, as well as to share and promote their personal expertise.

I have had the opportunity to work with organizations in the past on their knowledge management initiatives in SharePoint. I wish this feature had been included in past releases of SharePoint but it's here now and KM directors should take notice.

The Community Portal, which is a collection of the individual Community Sites on differing and specific topics, provides discussion lists and web parts directed specifically at the knowledge management and "community" experience.

TIP

The SharePoint 2013 community features are available only in SharePoint Server 2013 and are not made available in SharePoint Foundation 2013.

Understanding the Community Reference in Terms of Social Computing

It can become a bit confusing when referring to the "community" features of SharePoint 2013 because the term itself is also used to refer to other common SharePoint elements. It's important to keep the specific use of the term in context. The SharePoint Community Sites are for the enhancement of social collaboration and knowledge management within the organization.

You may also hear users or stakeholders refer to "communities" in terms of the IT community or SharePoint's "Power User" community which are, in fact, communities but more granularly they are just specific user groups or sets of individuals.

I think this is important so that you are able to set the tone with the SharePoint stakeholders and user base when describing the different SharePoint terms so that there is no confusion or overlap of terms.

Features and Practices of SharePoint Communities in Terms of Social Computing

This new Community Site feature in SharePoint 2013 enables users to further organize discussions as well as categorize feedback and knowledge and apply "metadata" or content types such as "lessons learned" and "best practices." It also enables users to get feedback from other team members within the organization who may have come across the same issue that a current Community is discussing and offer invaluable feedback to the Community users to solve a specific problem in a much faster manner.

Just as a SharePoint site or set of SharePoint sites should have a "power user" or "super user" assist in owning issues and championing the specific sites, communities need moderators to manage the community by enforcing the organization governance as well as reviewing and addressing posts for appropriate content.

There is also a new feature that allows each community to contain information about its member and content reputation that will help them earn "status" or the "gifted badges" type of recognition from the Community moderators when they do things such as posting discussions, promoting or liking content, or providing feedback by using the "marked as a best answer" feature in SharePoint 2013 communities.

A new SharePoint community can be created either at the site collection level or at the site level. The decision of where to create the sites, at which level, can be influenced by which features you would like to provide (that is, activate and so on) within a specific community or a greater set of community sites.

Understanding the Community Portal Template Versus the Community Site Template

SharePoint 2013's Community Portal template is actually an enterprise site template with a web part page and has the inherent capability to provide search-driven results, that is, audience-driven results. This template provides additional web parts such as the "Popular Communities" web part to display communities that are flourishing and are very active, which is ultimately determined by the number of replies to posts as well as the number of members within the community.

The Community Portal page can be accessed from the Sites link on a user's My Site.

> **TIP**
>
> It is important to note that you can have only one Community Portal per SharePoint Server 2013 farm.

The Community Site template contains the same base list, libraries, and features of a standard SharePoint Team Site template.

It is important to add the SharePoint Community features to your overall SharePoint Roadmap as well as governance model because this provides an additional layer of sites as well as a possible hierarchical element to your existing navigation and overall SharePoint topology.

Many of the terms used within SharePoint communities are common to other areas of SharePoint Sites; however, the following terms are new and you should understand and champion them when implementing communities into your SharePoint 2013 platform:

▶ **Moderator**

The moderator is a community member who has permission and access to tools to manage, or moderate, the community settings and members. The moderator should be deeply involved and tasked with reviewing and addressing posts that are flagged as inappropriate, as well as sometimes combining sets of "discussions" or threads to better organize them for consumption by the user base.

The moderator should also set rules per the organization's governance model for discussions and the quality of content that exists within the community, as well as champion the community to ensure that it's being used and does not become "stale" and irrelevant.

▶ **Reputation**

Each and every member of a SharePoint Community Site earns a reputation within the community based on specific activities and feedback from other members. This can occur when the member's posts are liked or an answer to a discussion is rated as a best answer provided. The new reputation functionality is maintained at the site level and is specific only to that individual Community Site.

A member may be more knowledgeable in a specific area or Community and thus may have a stronger reputation in a different community due to his or her skill set and vast knowledge base on a specific topic or interest.

▶ **Gifted badges**

The Community moderator can provide or assign a community member with a gifted badge to designate the user as a special contributor of the community. These gifted badges help community users understand who are the possible experts in a given community and provide them with insight on who may be able to give them the best and most informed information.

▶ **Best reply**

Within a SharePoint Community discussion, multiple replies will be given on a specific topic or question, but one reply can be designated as the best reply. The best reply designation can be given by either the user who originally posted the topic or question or the moderators of the community. When a user starts to build up a number of best reply tags, the user will start to build a reputation within the community.

My Sites in SharePoint Server 2013

A My Site is a personal site for a given user that allows them to display information such as their profile and relevant skillsets, as well as information regarding sites they are interested in and a newsfeed of recent activities. This also provides the users with access to their OneDrive, as well as their blog, aggregated list of tasks, and other personal information.

A user's My Site consists of two site collections, the SharePoint 2013 farm's My Site host site collection and the user's individual site collection.

> **TIP**
>
> When a My Site host site collection is created and users then create their individual site collections, this data is maintained in one or more content databases that are associated with the web application that you specify to host My Sites. It is possible to add content databases to this web application if multiple databases are required for storage due to size and other considerations are necessary. Also, the My Site host site collection and the related configuration that enables and creates individual My Sites site collections must be enabled before users can create My Sites.

Ensuring Best Practices My Site Architectural Configuration

SharePoint Server 2013's My Sites, as shown in Figure 3.5, do have core architectural and configuration requirements or prerequisites that must be put in place to ensure that all My

Site functionality is made available and that they function in a best practices and high-performing secured manner.

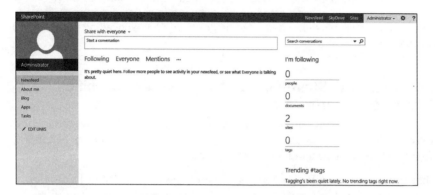

FIGURE 3.5   A newly created SharePoint Server 2013 My Sites.

SharePoint Server 2013's managed metadata service application enables web applications to store and access keywords from a managed metadata term database. These features are required for My Sites users to specify keywords as their areas of expertise in the Ask Me About section, as well as to utilize the new hashtag feature in Posts and Newsfeeds, and for social tagging by using the "Tags and Notes" feature within My Site.

The managed metadata service application must be configured as the default keyword term store for the web application.

I would also recommend for any SharePoint 2013 implementation that the SharePoint Server Search service application be enabled, but in terms of My Sites it is absolutely a requirement. This enables users to search from within their My Sites for people in the organization based on names or areas of expertise, which I believe is one of the most popular features of My Sites. This also enables users' search results to access the hashtags in microblog posts.

Expertise Search/People Search

The expertise search capabilities within SharePoint Server 2013 My Sites is another very popular features that should be enabled within your organization because it provides tangible return on investment (ROI). The People search and expertise tagging will help your organization's users to locate other team members who have identified themselves as having significant experience with a particular subject area or topic.

The My Site features in SharePoint enable users to add terms to their profile that describe areas in which they have experience and thus populate the searches of users using the expertise search.

> **TIP**
>
> If your organization's deployment is global in nature, it is key to take specific regulations of certain geographical locations as well as specific countries' laws into consideration because there are limitations in specific areas of the globe where certain information in My Site profiles cannot legally be shown and must be governed and removed or "trimmed" for you to be in compliance.

What Are Communities in SharePoint 2013 in Terms of Specific Audiences, Users, or Departments?

When SharePoint is implemented within an organization, there are business requirements that must be accomplished, as well as the information technology goals and key benefits that are embraced by IT to deploy SharePoint and support it for the long term.

From the very beginning, communities or "sets of certain types of users" start to develop, and those related users within those communities have their own sets of goals, processes they want to improve on, and collaboration or increased knowledge sharing in the governed and secure manner that SharePoint offers.

This is true for a SharePoint implementation of any kind, whether it be an enterprise content management (ECM) initiative or a new intranet or an increased "social" or "professional networking" related strategy the culture is striving to embrace.

Three core types of communities exist within any SharePoint 2013 implementation. There are, of course, many subcommunities and types of users that flow out of these main community types, but these are the three that can be identified at the very top level:

▶ The "Knowledge" community and related users, whose goal is collaboration, knowledge sharing, social/professional networking, and retaining this knowledge for the long term.

   A goal of this community is to prevent knowledge loss when staff members leave the organization and to provide their best practices, lessons learned, and intellectual property knowledge when new staff come into the company.

▶ The "Power User"/"Super User" community, which provides the "care and feeding" as well as support to ensure that the Knowledge community continues to thrive. This group is made up of team members or users who work with the Knowledge community as well as the business leaders who set these goals and the IT and Operational community that "keeps the lights on" and ensures security, performance, governance, compliance, and business continuity.

▶ The "Operational" community, which supports both the Knowledge community and the Power User/Super User community. This community is made up of the technical staff with roles such as the SharePoint administrators, Site Collection Owners, Site Owners, infrastructure, networking, and security.

   The Operational community is also getting ever-growing requests to support the Knowledge community, which is knocking at the door regarding mobility, smartphones, tablets, and the bigger BYOD questions.

The Knowledge Community

One thing I have stressed with my team members at EPC Group, the SharePoint and Microsoft consultancy I founded about 15+ years ago, is to take the word "SharePoint" out of many conversations and focus on the business and functional goals at hand. Microsoft SharePoint is the technology you are using to accomplish these goals, but think in terms of how the technology can meet the needs of the communities.

There is a bit of a new blurry line when talking about SharePoint communities today, with SharePoint 2013 having a new level or hierarchy of Community Sites (templates) that support specific communities. However, I think it's key to think in terms of knowledge management and Networks of Excellence (NoE) that initially created many of the best practices and strategies that drive SharePoint communities today.

So, taking a step back and using the NoE concept in the knowledge management world, the following are roles, responsibilities, and best practices that should be taken into consideration.

Executive Community Sponsor

▶ Approves and supports the business case and vision for knowledge sharing at the functional, business unit, operational, and/or executive levels

▶ Signs off on the business case, vision, and resources for knowledge sharing

▶ Remains involved through executive briefings and communications with the organizational community sponsors

Community Sponsor

▶ Sets goals and related performance criteria for the community

▶ Fosters widespread interest and enthusiasm for knowledge sharing and community participation

▶ Directs and presents the strategic input of the community to executives

Community Leader

▶ Directs the activities and sets the priorities of the community

▶ Manages the usage and appropriation of community resources

▶ Ensures the quality and timeliness of community activities/deliverables

▶ Develops a team concept within the community dedicated to learning and innovation

▶ Participates in and leads all aspects of community planning, design, development, and deployment

▶ Oversees the processes, content, technology (portal administration), and people resources to increase the effective sharing of best practices and lessons learned across business units

▶ Works closely with knowledge-sharing leaders and staff to incorporate training and standards

▶ Measures community maturity and effectiveness with accountability

▶ Communicates knowledge-sharing success stories and lessons learned

▶ Gives recognition to the community, and enables award or recognition of submissions

▶ Guides research and benchmarking projects (where applicable)

▶ Encourages qualitative and quantitative benchmarking to identify new areas of improvement opportunity

▶ Appoints, coaches, and supports the community coordinators

Community Coordinator

▶ Ensures effective content management by collecting and managing the right information that supports the community

▶ Ensures that SharePoint's content is updated and relevant to the user's needs

▶ Monitors collaborative spaces (sites) to extract new knowledge and to identify issues that require responses

▶ Builds awareness of and access to the right people and right information that supports employees' daily workflows (day-to-day tasks)

▶ Maintains processes for knowledge acquisition, storage, maintenance, and dissemination

▶ Facilitates community interaction and outreach to increase the number and contributions of active members

▶ Links community members with subject matter experts to answer questions or provide solutions

▶ Collects and packages knowledge-sharing success stories and lessons learned and champions these to other communities to keep a sense of competition within various communities to strive for excellence

Community Core Team Member

▶ Actively participates in and steers network activities under the guidance of the community Sponsor

▶ Builds regional sponsorship for and engages regional members in knowledge-sharing activities

▶ Formulates and executes plans to deploy community deliverables at the regional levels

▶ Provides a link between the strategies of the community and the strategies of the regional business units

▶ Develops relevant measures of success for the community

▶ Engages local community coordinators and subject matter experts (SMEs) in knowledge-sharing activities

In identifying these different roles, there is a best practices framework to be followed to ensure SharePoint Community effectiveness, as shown in Figure 3.6, along with 10 critical success factors.

FIGURE 3.6   EPC Group's SharePoint Community effectiveness framework.

In identifying this framework, there is a best practices SharePoint Community operating model, as shown in Figure 3.7, that should be followed to ensure SharePoint compliance as well as continued care and feeding of the community.

There is always the question of "the users and participants have a day job and tasks they must manage, so how can this be worked into the SharePoint network and overall participation?" Figure 3.8 details an approach to this question.

Within any network, critical or very time-sensitive issues or areas of possible improvement will come to the attention of community leaders and the roles identified previously.

Figure 3.9 details a workflow or process showing an example of how these community items can be dealt with head-on; it also puts a timeframe out there for resolution of issues so that they are not prolonged and the community itself does not become irrelevant because users have stopped providing or sharing knowledge due to an unresolved issue.

EPC Group's Community Operating Model

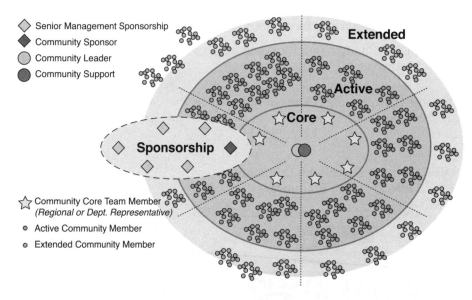

FIGURE 3.7   EPC Group's Community operating model.

Expanding the Intersection Between "Day Jobs" and Community Activities

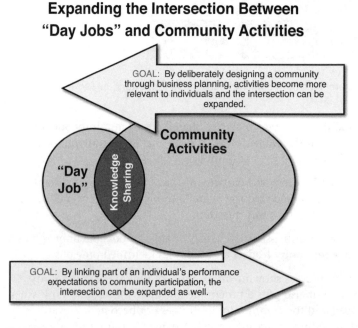

FIGURE 3.8   A graphic showing the intersection between a user's "day jobs" and the user's community activities.

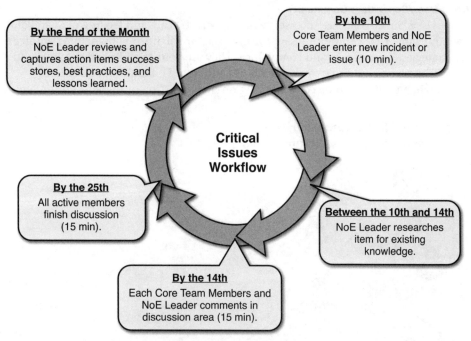

Critical Issues Workflow

By the End of the Month
NoE Leader reviews and captures action items success stores, best practices, and lessons learned.

By the 10th
Core Team Members and NoE Leader enter new incident or issue (10 min).

By the 25th
All active members finish discussion (15 min).

Between the 10th and 14th
NoE Leader researches item for existing knowledge.

By the 14th
Each Core Team Members and NoE Leader comments in discussion area (15 min).

FIGURE 3.9   A workflow example showing how community items can be addressed head on but how a timeframe can be assigned for issue resolution.

Lastly, you want to ensure that you have defined metrics, as shown in Figure 3.10, and have an understanding of the maturity model, as well as how relevant each community's knowledge is, to ensure that it is being updated and used, and that ROI is being gained from the network. Figure 3.10 compares the knowledge gained from communities to the time spent to provide a starting point for your organization.

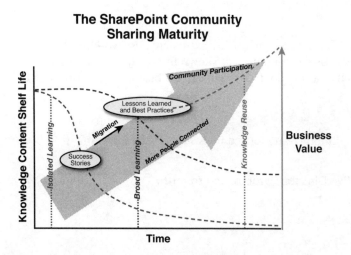

The SharePoint Community Sharing Maturity

FIGURE 3.10   EPC Group's SharePoint Community sharing maturity metric diagram.

The Power User/Super User Community

The Power Users/Super Users are the users who support the care and feeding of SharePoint, as shown in Figure 3.11, communities and really "keep the lights on" by helping enforce security strategies, governance, and compliance. They are your "first line of defense" and will limit IT involvement in extremely common issues that IT should not have to be pulled into when they should be concentrating on more pressing or higher-priority items.

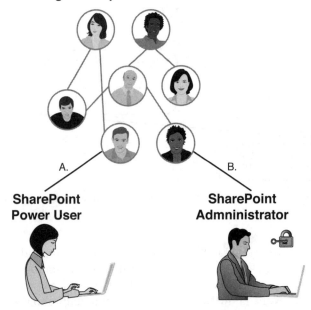

Who Should First Engage with the Knowledge and Operational Communities

A.   B.

SharePoint Power User   **SharePoint Admninistrator**

FIGURE 3.11   Power Users or SharePoint Administrators: Who should be your organization's first line of defense?

Because IT and the Operational community are usually extremely busy working on keeping the lights on, the Power User community, as shown in Figure 3.12, should be your first line of defense as well as a friendly face to engage the business and work with IT to resolve community issues.

The Operational Community

The SharePoint Operational community and related roles support the following in SharePoint 2013:

▶ People (permissions, Active Directory, groups, and so forth)

  ▶ Roles and teams

  ▶ Sponsorship

▶ Process and policies (enforcement)

    ▶ Security

    ▶ Content management (policy enforcement from a technical level)

    ▶ Hardware and services

    ▶ Procedures (from an automated or technical level)

▶ Communication and training (from a technical level)

    ▶ Communication plan

    ▶ Training plan

    ▶ Support plan

Who Should First Engage with the Knowledge and Operational Communities

SharePoint Power User

- There are frequent situations where a Power User could handle non-administrative tasks in their site/department/region.

- Users, new to SharePoint, account for a large number of the SharePoint-related Help Desk tickets.

- How could a Power User help those users (initial training, mentoring, etc.)?

FIGURE 3.12   Power Users should be your organization's first line of defense to handle common and easily answered questions from your SharePoint 2013 user base.

Summary

This chapter covered the core strategies for implementing some of the most high-profile features of SharePoint 2013, such as sites, site collections, and the social computing (that is, communities and My Sites) while ensuring that the implementation is done in a governed, best practices manner.

This chapter also covered the initial considerations for your organization regarding implementing a best practices information architecture. This was covered in a manner that will ensure that you are considering the types of users as well as the types of devices and the users' locations that will be accessing the SharePoint platform.

The next chapter goes into detail on how SharePoint 2013 integrates with Microsoft Office 2013.

CHAPTER 4

Understanding SharePoint 2013 and Microsoft Office Integration with Office 365 Now in the Picture

In the preceding chapter, Office 365 was briefly discussed in terms of "on-premises" versus the "cloud," but with SharePoint 2013's release, there are a great many other elements to be taken into consideration.

In any of the previous releases of SharePoint, I would have primarily focused on areas such as the integration points with applications like Microsoft Outlook and its capability to seamlessly display SharePoint calendars, or like Microsoft Word and the capability to edit documents stored in SharePoint document libraries directly within Word. These features are still available with SharePoint 2013's release, but when you are architecting and implementing a SharePoint implementation for your organization, there are many more factors regarding SharePoint 2013 and Office 2013 to take into consideration.

There are several popular "buzzwords" related to SharePoint 2013's new capabilities, and one of the main talking points you may hear is that Microsoft is releasing SharePoint 2013 with "cloud first" in mind. This can be a little confusing or worrisome to those who may not have their organization's overall cloud roadmap defined. In reality, "cloud" can actually represent an externally hosted cloud, an internally hosted on-premises cloud, or, probably more commonly accepted, a hybrid cloud where a mix of both on-premises and hosted architecture is utilized.

Microsoft has essentially released SharePoint 2013 and provided the same framework that powers the SharePoint capabilities in Office 365. This chapter explains the overall approach, touches on some much needed considerations, and clarifies the "art of the possible" with these major new moving architectural considerations.

SharePoint 2013 and Office 365: An Overview

While working on the development of this book, I have also been engaged with my consulting firm EPC Group and my staff on several initiatives for which the SharePoint 2013 and Office 365 conversation really required additional understanding and clarification from the different stakeholders within different organizations.

The project stakeholders within IT may have a total understanding of the Office 365 offering but the organization's legal and compliance stakeholders may still be unclear or hesitant because of the similar naming of products and their past understanding of SharePoint. There are terms that can be very "down in the technical weeds," such as Reverse Proxy and SSO or MSOL Tools, that can quickly sidetrack the conversation.

This also requires reexamining your SharePoint governance model because there are key functional pieces in 2013 that now have their own layer or uncoupled type of behavior that must be signed off on and understood by all stakeholders.

The on-premises and/or cloud or off-premises architecture is typically clear, but the term "hybrid" is referred to when one of the following five "non-SharePoint elements" is configured to support a hybrid SharePoint 2013 deployment:

- Reverse proxy and certificate authentication
- Identity provider (ADFS, etc.)
- MSOL tools
- SSO with O365 (single sign-on)
- Dirsync (Azure Active Directory)

Overview of Office 365 Plans

Office 365's underlying licensing model represents an array of plans and capabilities. The Office 365 business offerings, as shown in Figure 4.1, are centered on small business, midsize business, and the enterprise.

Most businesses will require a plan that includes the capability to enable Active Directory integration (with Active Directory Federation Services [ADFS] and Directory Sync) and single sign-on (SSO) with local Active Directory credentials to seamlessly access Office 365 in the cloud.

FIGURE 4.1   Reviewing the plans available for Office 365 on Microsoft.com.

As shown in Figure 4.2, the enterprise plan, also referred to as the "E" plan, allows for hybrid configurations of Exchange, Lync, and SharePoint, but it's important to review your specific requirements and discuss them with a licensing and Office 365 plan expert who is knowledgeable about the latest plans, capabilities, and prices, and the future of each plan. Microsoft continues to add capabilities to its Office 365 plans, and I can't stress enough how important it is to stay up-to-date on the available options before moving forward with any Office 365 plan.

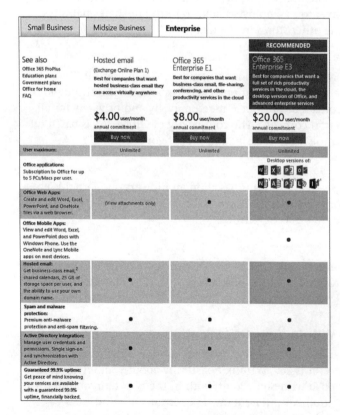

FIGURE 4.2   A look at Office 365 plan examples for the enterprise.

When looking at the Office 365 plans for the enterprise, you will see many options for integration with Exchange and other technologies that your organization very well may not even be considering moving or integrating with the cloud, so discussing your organization's SharePoint and overall IT roadmap and having a clearer understanding of it will allow you to review these plans with a much more educated perspective about what you may or may not want to consider.

Key Cloud Terms

You will hear many different technical references within an Office 365 architectural or business planning conversation, so it is key to understand the core terms as detailed in the sections that follow.

Tennant

A tenant is required for the setup of an Office 365 account with Microsoft or the Office 365 provider. A tenant is the domain login (.yourcompany.com) that you use to log in. Office 365 shares a global name space. Consequently, company "A" in the United States may already have registered and be utilizing Office 365, and company "B" in the United Kingdom, possibly an affiliate company, would not be able to use that same tenant name.

When you hear the multitenant system, think of this in terms of a single store in a mall that is unique and has its own inventory, employees, and so forth but shares hallways, stairs, elevators, and such with the other stores in the mall.

DNS Records

The Domain Name System, or DNS, translates domain names to the numerical IP addresses needed for the purpose of accessing computer services and devices throughout the globe. There are multiple records that must be entered publicly and privately for all the services in Office 365 to function correctly. The complexity of Office 365 is based on the configuration that is required to ensure security and proper governance.

ADFS and ADFS Proxy Servers

The Active Directory Federation Services (ADFS) is based on an industry-supported Web services architecture. Organizations' internal ADFS servers and external ADFS proxy servers will be essential for single sign-on to be accomplished.

Directory Synchronization Server

The Directory Synchronization Server is key to a proper single sign-on architecture because this will synchronize the entire Active Directory, or a subset of it, to your organization's tenant account in Office 365.

Implementing Office 365 Within Your Organization

Several key strategies are involved in a best practices implementation of Office 365 and the overall SharePoint 2013 service. It is key to think holistically about your environment and what you're trying to accomplish with SharePoint, both in the near term and in the long term. Within an implementation, keep the following questions in mind:

▶ What are the core strategic initiatives that your organization has planned within the next 24 months in terms of your SharePoint roadmap, and how will Office 365 benefit these efforts?

▶ What will the overall balance of on-premises versus hosted within your organization be, and have the key stakeholders in your organization, including legal and compliance, been included in the development of this strategy?

▶ How will this data be protected at an information management level, and how will the security or control differ between on-premises and cloud-based?

▶ What is your organization seeing in terms of proliferation within its users' overall mobile device usage, and what is your opinion of the best way to develop a stated BYOD strategy for the organization that would gain initial buy-in?

▶ Are there any set requirements related to the integration of other line of business (LOB) systems, and will the environment affect the access to this other data source? (Think of it in terms of future business intelligence [BI] initiatives.)

Key Components of a Hybrid Office 365 Initiative

Office 365 may be the core technology and platform an organization is implementing, but do not focus solely on the technology side of this initiative because many of the key success components are business-related processes that need to be thoroughly analyzed. By establishing a phased success criteria, just like that of an on-premises deployment, working with the business and key IT stakeholders to define the project objectives, establishing an overall project plan and timeline, you will ensure that the initial pieces are in place. There should be a project manager or specific group identified who will own the overall control and execution of the project.

Multiple stakeholders and team members will be involved with the execution of the actual tasks, but by first identifying the objectives and implementation plan, you will put a stake in the ground that the team can work toward.

Office 365 and Lync

Microsoft Office 365 is closely bundled with Lync 2013, which has been a big marketing win for Microsoft in getting potential clients to explore the offerings. Figure 4.3 details a hybrid Office 365 and Lync topology, which has a number of more granular components that your organization should investigate to fully understand its capabilities and organizational impact.

TIP

I would recommend downloading several of the Microsoft Lync whitepapers available on TechNet to get a better understanding of not only the Lync technology but also possible prerequisites your organization may need to consider. These can be found at the following URL: http://technet.microsoft.com/en-US/lync/

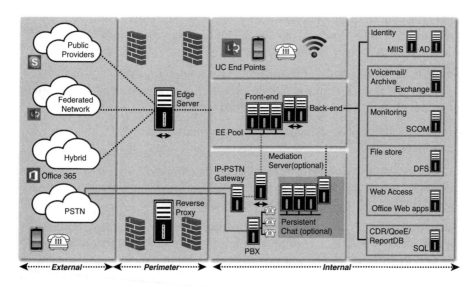

FIGURE 4.3   Overview of a hybrid Office 365 and Lync topology.

There are additional considerations related to on-premises versus cloud or online when you are analyzing your organization's Lync roadmap, as shown in Figure 4.4. This can also be researched at the TechNet URL listed in the Tip.

Feature	On-Premises			Online		
	Standard	Enterprise (Std Req'd)	Plus (Std Req'd)	Plan 1	Plan 2	Plan 3
Rich Presence, IM (1:1 and multiparty), Office interoperability	●			●	●	●
Public Cloud IM/P federation (Windows Live, AOL, Yahoo!*)	●			WL Only	WL Only	WL Only
Skype federation for Presence/IM/voice	●			●	●	●
Persistent Group Chat	●					
Lync to Lync calling (voice and HD video, 1:1)	●			●	●	●
Skill Search (requires SharePoint)	●					
Content Collaboration (desktop sharing, application, etc.)		●			●	●
Multiparty (3+) audio/video/content collaboration (scheduled and ad hoc)		●			●	●
Meeting Controls (Organizer, Lobby Experience, Join From)		●			●	●
Enhanced in-meeting note taking		●			●	●
Interoperability with 3rd party video systems		●				
Lync audio conferencing		●	●			
Interoperability with 3rd party audio conferencing providers		●			●	●
Lync Multi-view Video		●			●	●
Lync to Phone (PSTN)			●			
Lync PBX Replacement Functionality (Malicious Call Trace, E911, call park)			●			
Automated call distribution (unassigned number, attendant console, queuing)			●			
Lync Mobile Clients	●	●	●	●	●	●
Lync Web App			●		●	●
● : Existing ● : New						

FIGURE 4.4   The features of Lync, as well as the offerings for both on-premises and online or in the cloud.

Office 365's Security Considerations and Components

In reviewing Office 365's capabilities, a key factor in all your decisions must be the security integration elements of Office 365. Figure 4.5 details three separate Office 365 identity integration scenarios. I find that it is always important to have the on-premises options available to compare with cloud offerings because this helps bring clarity to many questions.

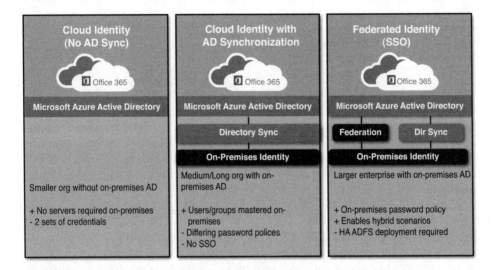

FIGURE 4.5   Identity integration scenarios and Office 365.

Being able to "whiteboard" the possible integration options your organization may be considering is key to a best practices Office 365 architecture. The hybrid, on-premises and cloud combination, as shown in Figure 4.6, will be a more common architecture over the next five years as the cloud offerings mature and organizations identify what benefits the cloud may offer them, as well as what risks the cloud may bring that need to be avoided.

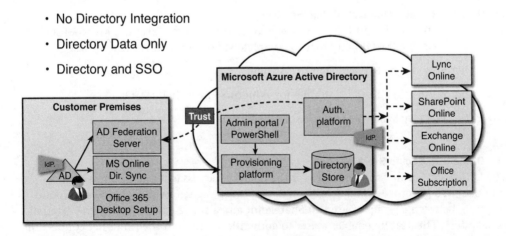

FIGURE 4.6   Examples of a combined hybrid, on-premises, and cloud architecture.

> **TIP**
>
> You may notice the reference to Microsoft Azure in several of the figures in this chapter. Microsoft Azure is Microsoft's application platform for the public cloud that enables organizations to build a web application that runs and stores its data in Microsoft data centers. More information on Microsoft Azure can be found at the following URL: http://azure.microsoft.com/en-us/

Office 365 Reverse Proxy and Authentication

There are several very technical terms that may be used during meetings with stakeholders by both the business and IT, and one of those is "reverse proxy." When using hybrid features for Office 365, the system sends requests from sites in the cloud to your organization's on-premises farm. To accomplish this, your organization needs to establish a reverse proxy for these calls to be channeled through to secure the process so that those requests can be authenticated before they are forwarded to SharePoint.

Identity Provider Overview—Office 365

Another term that you may hear referenced in an Office 365 conversation is "identity provider." To have a single sign-on experience, your organization needs to have a federated identity provider like Active Directory Federation Service. This requires the following:

▶ Two or more load-balanced ADFS servers

▶ An SSL certificate for the ADFS site

▶ A proxy device, like the ADFS proxy server

▶ A UPN of a registered domain (that is, ".local" or similar suffixes will not work) for all users

MS Online Overview (Microsoft Online Services)

Your organization will most likely require your users to access tools from Microsoft Online Services, MS Online (MSOL), in order to complete various functions such as these:

▶ Microsoft Online Services Sign-In Assistant

▶ Microsoft Online Services Module for Windows PowerShell (MSOL PS)

▶ The Directory Synchronization tool (dirsync)

The Office 365 Secure Store

The Office 365 Secure Store provides for the ability to access external business application data in a governed and defensible manner. It is designed to allow for a background mapping between a group of users in SharePoint and a single user known to the external data system. This feature enables a user to authenticate through their Internet connection at any given location into SharePoint. The Secure Store Service uses mapped credentials known to the external business application to render any necessary external data on the site for the authenticated user.

An Office 365 deployment can quickly derail if users are getting prompted time and time again for their credentials, so the secure store is critical to this process. It allows users to access the required data without prompting them to enter usernames and passwords specific to the external application, thus limiting the need for multiple passwords and the core element of the SharePoint as a Platform or SharePoint as a Service strategy.

Planning for Apps in SharePoint and Office 2013

When you're planning your organization's strategy around Microsoft Office 2013, Office 365, and SharePoint 2013, there is an additional list of considerations that apps have brought into the overall scheme of things.

There will be some organizations that have not yet moved to Office 2013 and are still on the Office 2010 platform. This is not a showstopper at all. A good rule of thumb is that you will not lose any integration points you are already used to having with Office 2010, but you will gain all the new technology and features when your organization upgrades to Office 2013. SharePoint 2013, though, does give you a nice business case and a compelling reason to push for an Office 2013 upgrade, apps being one of them.

With SharePoint 2013 and the Office 2013 combination, you have a "roaming CAL (client access license)" concept or the "wherever you go, Office 2013 roams with you" thought process. This is true for both on-premises and cloud or hybrid deployments and also plays into your organization's BYOD strategy.

One major element to Office 2013 is that it brings the Web to Office client applications and the capability for your organization to add web-based features to the Office applications by using apps for Office.

SharePoint 2013's App Catalog

Just like the app stores you have used on your smartphones and mobile devices or via Apple's iTunes, Office 2013 provides an Office App Store, as shown in Figure 4.7, for Microsoft Office solutions. It enables your organization to buy solutions as well as build up your "internal app store," which is technically named the App Catalog.

Your organization's SharePoint 2013 App Catalog, as shown as an option on the Apps page in Figure 4.8 and located within SharePoint's Central Administration, provides a central location for available "solutions" for your organization. To some, this is similar to the SharePoint Center of Excellence shared applications repository or thought process of building a SharePoint solution that can be utilized by or shared with the overall company.

If a department like Human Resources or Marketing is getting a major return on investment out of an app or solution that is available in your organization's App Catalog, why shouldn't the other departments in your organization also be utilizing these tools that will further collaboration and productivity?

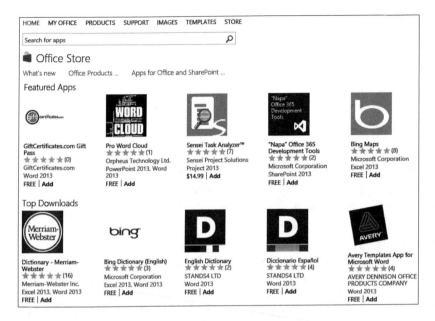

FIGURE 4.7   A sample of the apps listed in the Microsoft Office 2013 App Store.

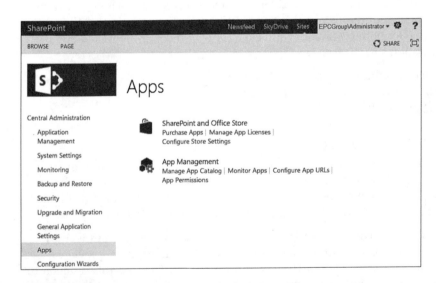

FIGURE 4.8   SharePoint Server 2013's Apps page showing links to the Catalog in Central Administration.

You are able to also create organizationally (departmental, business unit, project, and so on) specific apps for your company as you build up your corporate App Catalog and convert existing web parts into apps, so there really can be one centralized "app" way of thinking in terms of SharePoint 2013 solutions to your user base.

WARNING

Only One App Catalog for "Apps for Office" per Web Application

There is a limitation of one app catalog for Apps for Office per SharePoint 2013 web application. Only users with permissions to access and perform tasks within SharePoint Central Administration will be able to set up an app catalog.

TIP

To set up the app catalog for a web application, perform the following:

1. Browse to the Central Administration Site (Start > Programs > Microsoft SharePoint 2013 Products > SharePoint 2013 Central Administration).

2. In the left task pane, click the Apps link.

   At the bottom of the page, click the Manage App Catalog link under the App Management group.

   Note: Make sure you have the right web application selected in the Web Application Selector.

3. Specify the primary site collection administrator and the list of Readers and click OK.

This should create the Marketplace Host site collection that will host the app catalog document library. Click the App Catalog link to browse to the app catalog document library.

Office 365 Compliance

Within most Office 365 initiatives, there seems to be a lack of understanding of its compliance and regulatory capabilities. Microsoft has gone to some lengths to provide customers with a very strong starting point around Office 365's auditing and compliance capabilities, and as the platform continues to mature, there are a number of additional compliance milestones within Office 365's technology roadmap. A hybrid Office 365 architecture, an example of which is shown in Figure 4.9, is new to many in the IT field and rightly has many concerned about its security and compliance standards to protect their company's data and sensitive communications.

Auditing and Compliance Capabilities

Office 365 provides detailed auditing and related policies related to the logging of events down to the actual editing, viewing, and deleting of SharePoint's content within lists and libraries, as well as within its email capabilities of Exchange.

Auditing can be enabled as part of your organization's information management policies, and these audit logs and audit trails are available to administrators to view, summarize, and export to provide requesters within specific information. This data not only is available for investigation and compliance-related activities but also can be used to understand how your organization is using Office 365 and the overall return on investment (ROI) it may be providing to your company.

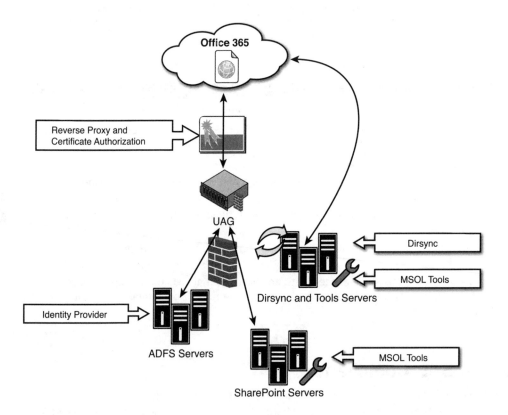

FIGURE 4.9   An example of an Office 365 hybrid architecture.

ISO 27001, FISMA, HIPPA BAA, EU Model

Office 365 was architected around and/or has obtained the following compliance standards and related industry policies and certifications:

▶ **ISO 27001:** Office 365 service was built based on ISO 27001 standards and was the first major business productivity public cloud service to have implemented the rigorous set of global standards covering physical, logical, process, and management controls.

▶ **FISMA:** Office 365 has been granted FISMA Moderate Authority to Operate by multiple federal agencies. Operating under FISMA requires transparency and frequent security reporting to our U.S. Federal customers.

TIP

The Federal Information Security Management Act of 2002 is a United States federal law enacted in 2002 as Title III of the E-Government Act of 2002. The act recognized the importance of information security to the economic and national security interests of the United States. The FISMA act requires each federal agency to document and implement an agencywide program to provide information security for the information and information systems that support the operations of the agency. This includes those provided or managed by another agency or contractor or another source.

▶ **HIPPA BAA:** Office 365 became the first major business productivity public cloud service provider to offer a HIPAA BAA to all customers.

TIP

HIPPA is a U.S. law that applies to healthcare entities that governs the use, disclosure, and safeguarding of protected health information (PHI), and imposes requirements on covered entities to sign business associate agreements with their vendors that have access to PHI.

▶ **EU Model Clauses:** Office 365 became the first major business productivity public cloud service provider to sign the standard contractual clauses created by the European Union (known as the "EU Model Clauses") with all customers.

TIP

The EU Model Clauses address the international transfer of data. Office 365 is possibly the only cloud service that has received broad validation from European data protection authorities (DPAs) regarding its approach to the EU Model Clauses, including from Bavaria, Denmark, France, Ireland, Luxembourg, Malta, and Spain.

TIP

Office 365 has obtained independent verification, including ISO 27001 and SSAE16 SOC 1 (Type II) audits, and is able to transfer data outside of the European Union through the U.S.–EU Safe Harbor Framework and the EU Model Clauses.

How Safe Is My Organization's Office 365 Data?

A major area of concern about Office 365 is the lack of understanding about how and where the data itself is stored and what proactive measures are being taken to ensure that your data is safe. As part of my research for this publication and my ongoing consulting efforts at EPC Group in relation to Microsoft SharePoint 2013 and Office 365, I was able to take a tour of an Office 365 data center/facility and hear firsthand from Microsoft some of the steps they are taking to help customers feel at ease about their data.

With any data that is outside your organization's direct control (that is, outside of your on-premises network), there are justifiable concerns. One of the main detractors a lot of large organizations or organizations with sensitive or proprietary data are wary of the hosted cloud model. The sections that follow detail what Microsoft is doing in terms of protecting data within Office 365, as well as the precautions they are taking to address these security concerns.

The Physical Hardware of Office 365

The actual Office 365 data itself is stored in the Microsoft network of data centers led by Microsoft's Global Foundation Services. These data centers are located around the world in strategic locations to take into consideration business continuity, disaster recovery, and government stability throughout the globe. Microsoft has architected and literally built these data centers from the ground up to protect services and data from not only natural disaster but physical intrusion or physical attack and unauthorized access as well. Per Microsoft's statement, "Data center access is restricted 24 hours per day by job function so that only essential personnel have access to customer applications and services." There are multiple failover controls and security processes.

There are required security processes including badges and smart cards, biometric scanners, on-premises armed security officers, and 24-7 continuous video surveillance, including various two-factor authentication methods. There are also motion sensors and security breach alarms, as well as seismically braced racks where required, and automated fire prevention and extinguishing systems in case of natural or man-made disasters.

Network Security in Office 365 at Microsoft

The overall networks that run the underlying Office 365 infrastructure are segmented to provide physical separation of critical backend servers and storage devices. These are set apart from any public-facing interfaces, and the implementation of edge router security provides the ability to detect intrusions and signs of vulnerability. All the client or external connections to Office 365 use SSL for securing Outlook, Outlook Web App, Exchange ActiveSync, POP3, and IMAP as stated by Microsoft in a recent press release. All customer connections are encrypted using industry-standard transport layer security (TLS)/Secure Sockets Layer (SSL), which uses a secure client-to-server connection to help provide data confidentiality and integrity between the desktop and the data center. The TLS between Office 365 and external servers for both inbound and outbound email is also enabled by default.

Antivirus and Anti-Spam

Microsoft has publicized that Office 365 utilizes a multi-engine anti-malware that protects against 100% of known viruses and that is continuously updated. The solution also provides for anti-spam protection, capturing 98%-plus of all inbound spam, while the underlying engine uses advanced fingerprinting technologies that identify and stop new spam and phishing vectors in real time.

Can Others See Your Data?

A major concern most customers have is whether others can see their data. Office 365 is architected as a multitenant service but that also means that customers do share hardware resources. Office 365 is designed to host multiple tenants securely through data isolation as each tenant is segregated through Active Directory, which isolates customers using security boundaries or silos. This is architected in a manner to help ensure that different companies that share hardware resources—that is, co-tenants—will not have their data accessed or compromised by another tenant that is not associated with that organization. Microsoft does provide the option for organizations to procure dedicated hardware for an Office 365 deployment if required, but that is a path that in some cases seems counterintuitive to the main reason Office 365 exists.

What Type of Encryption Is Deployed?

Microsoft stores Office 365 customer data in two different states. Data is stored at rest on storage media and in transit from the data center over a network to a customer device. All email and related content are encrypted on disk using BitLocker 256-bit AES Encryption. This protection architecture covers all disks on mailbox servers and includes mailbox database files, mailbox transaction log files, search content index files, transport database files, transport transaction log files, and page file OS system disk tracing/message tracking logs.

> **TIP**
>
> BitLocker 256-bit AES Encryption is a combination of full disk encryption designed to protect data for entire disk volumes. It uses the AES encryption algorithm. The Advanced Encryption Standard (AES) is a specification for the encryption of electronic data established by the U.S. National Institute of Standards and Technology (NIST). AES is widely used by the U.S. government as well as governments throughout the globe.

The BitLocker 256-bit AES encryption policies are also applied to all email contents including these types:

- ► Mailbox database files
- ► Mailbox transaction log files
- ► Search content index files
- ► Transport database files
- ► Transport transaction log files
- ► Page file OS system disk tracing/message tracking logs

Is Microsoft Being Proactive?

Microsoft uses a methodology for the protection of Office 365 referred to as "Prevent Breach." This is a defensive strategy aimed at predicting and preventing a security breach before it happens, but the defensive strategy connotation realistically contains offensive measures, including port scanning and remediation, perimeter vulnerability scanning, OS patching to the latest updated security software, network-level DDOS (Distributed Denial of Service) detection and prevention, and multifactor authentication for service access.

The processes Microsoft's staff uses also involves continuous auditing of all operator and administrator access, as well as a review of subsets of actions. Access is granted for specific tasks on an as-needed basis to troubleshoot issues of the service should they arise. An interesting element I found is that the staff's email is actually segmented during work on specific issues for an added layer of protection in regard to communications with other staff members during troubleshooting and so forth.

As in most data centers and highly sensitive environments, the staff members must pass background checks, and should an employee leave the organization, all of that employee's accounts are deleted and his or her access is audited and scrutinized to prevent any lagging accounts from existing within the environment. The following is a list of prevention breach items that Microsoft has established regarding the proactive nature of Office 365 security:

▶ Port scanning and remediation

▶ Perimeter vulnerability scanning

▶ OS patching

▶ Network-level DDOS detection and prevention

▶ Auditing of all operator access and actions

  ▶ Zero standing permissions in the service

  ▶ Just-in-time elevations

  ▶ Automatic rejection of non-background-check employees to high-privilege access

▶ Automatic account deletion

  ▶ When employee leaves

  ▶ When employee changes groups

  ▶ When there is lack of use

▶ Isolation between mail environment and production access environment for all employees

▶ Automated tooling for routine activities

Summary

This chapter covered many of the common questions and concerns regarding Office 365 and its high-level architecture. This information is meant to assist organizations in getting a better understanding of the on-premises versus cloud architecture, as well as some of the factors that should be taken into consideration when a best practices SharePoint 2013 roadmap is being implemented.

The next chapter goes into detail regarding SharePoint 2013's information architecture and the considerations for deploying sites, navigational hierarchies, and related taxonomies. The later chapters in this book also go into greater detail regarding compliance, Microsoft Azure, and the hybrid cloud, because this will be key to current and future roadmap planning around SharePoint and its long-term success.

4

CHAPTER 5

Implementing a Best Practices SharePoint 2013/ Office 365 Information Architecture

One of the most costly mistakes an organization can make during a SharePoint 2013 implementation is not putting enough effort into the overall planning and design of SharePoint's information architecture (IA). Equally important are the requirements of SharePoint's underlying system architecture that must provide the user base with optimal performance and future scalability considerations, as well as provide for the protection of sensitive data and intellectual property.

A lack of guidance exists within the SharePoint community and there are communication disconnects on how to best approach these efforts. They are critical because they are the foundational layers for which SharePoint's navigational topology and underlying metadata (content types and so on) tie directly into web applications and content databases. With SharePoint 2013's evolving hybrid deployment nature and some recent highly publicized news events, data spillage and security vulnerabilities are also frequently a part of this design conversation.

There are more moving pieces than ever before, and you need to ensure that you have a strategy that will allow for updating the information architecture design as well as the capability for the system architecture design to scale.

This chapter provides insight into how best to develop a proven IA design, and later, in Chapter 7, "Implementing a SharePoint 2013 System Architecture with Future Hybrid Scalability in Mind," we will discuss how to implement a best practices underlying SharePoint 2013 system architecture design.

The information architecture ties into the overall topology of SharePoint's infrastructure, from the underlying system architecture to the actual flow of content, its ownership, and the capabilities of SharePoint 2013.

Organizations must focus on both the near-term and the longer-term roadmap of SharePoint 2013/Office 365, as well as the actual capabilities that exist within SharePoint to handle these requirements, to ensure that the IA aligns with the infrastructure and platform's capabilities, as shown in Figure 5.1.

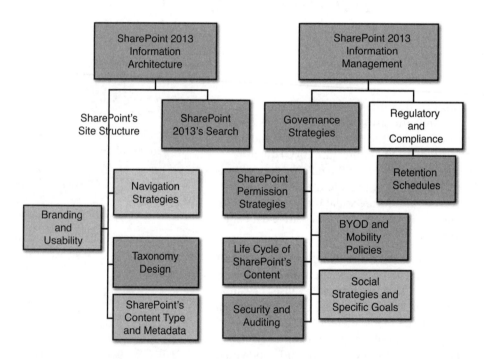

FIGURE 5.1   SharePoint 2013's information architecture components overview.

An issue that occurs on almost every SharePoint 2013 initiative relates to what the right path and tactical approach should be to inventory the existing information, content, and intellectual property. There is also a question about how that corresponds to a "workable" overall IA design while ensuring that the underlying system architecture can support the content (content database size, number of site collections, and so on) and usability as well as desired devices (browser, BYOD, and the like) required by the users. Other similar challenges organizations face stem from a combination of having a fairly good understanding of where most of the information and content is stored but not completely understanding either who the exact owners of the content are or who within the organization may need to access it.

If you already have a previous version of SharePoint implemented, these issues will still arise for you as much as for those who are implementing a new SharePoint 2013 platform for the first time. I have seen organizations that have a previous version of SharePoint implemented actually have more issues in this area because of the massive content sprawl that may have taken place due to not having governance or a previous best practices information architecture in place.

Planning SharePoint 2013's Taxonomy, Navigational Hierarchy, and Overall Topology

It is important to keep in mind that there is no single path or magic bullet to developing a best practices IA, but rather core guiding principles will ensure that your overall design is implemented in a structured manner that will accomplish your current business needs as well as have the ability to meet future growth and organizational changes. This chapter covers the broad 360-degree spectrum, as shown in Figure 5.2, of SharePoint's capabilities, underlying technical architecture, topology, and information architecture principles.

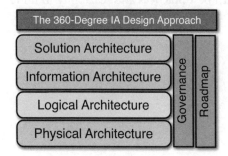

FIGURE 5.2   SharePoint's underlying technical architecture, topology, and information architecture.

The overall (IA) design will vary based on the type of organization for which it is being implemented, as well as its size and corporate structure. Some organizations also have additional regulatory or compliance considerations that will factor into your more granular IA requirements.

A scalable SharePoint 2013 IA design should provide for the intake of future requirements within the organization's overall current SharePoint roadmap. Most all organizations have a set number of milestones and business requirements defined for the initial phase 1 implementation effort. This may be upgrading an existing SharePoint 2007 or 2010 version of SharePoint to the new 2013 platform or implementing a new SharePoint 2013 business intelligence solution or an intranet for the organization to improve collaboration and increase knowledge sharing between co-workers.

Previous chapters have discussed how critical it is for an organization to have a best practices SharePoint roadmap defined. SharePoint 2013's IA design is at the very core of being able to accomplish this roadmap and new milestones that may exist in future phases such as a new ECM/RM initiative or business intelligence (BI) effort.

These future phases may require that additional metadata or content types be added to meet specific granular requirements. Implementing new features and functionality will more than likely mean new and more active users and the additional content that accompanies them. The flexibility of your IA design should also provide consideration for any known growth that you are aware SharePoint will need to handle.

The IA has a number of underlying technical components that tie directly into SharePoint's physical architecture. There are also a number of business considerations that must be accounted for, such as any major goals or drivers for expanding technology, offering a more robust and centralized enterprise search, or providing secure mobile access to the enterprise. Understanding SharePoint 2013's capabilities during this IA design will also provide insight into any future customizations that may need to be planned for within the overall budget and corresponding timeline.

By utilizing a three-prong information architecture approach along with combining SharePoint 2013 specific methodologies and proven technical considerations, your organization can rest assured the IA is being designed with best practices and scalability in mind. These are the three major areas of consideration for SharePoint 2013's information architecture, as shown in Figure 5.3:

► The "Context" information architecture

► The "Users" information architecture

► The "Content" information architecture

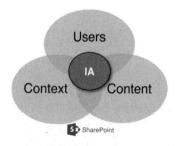

FIGURE 5.3   Approaching SharePoint 2013's information architecture in terms of Context, Users, and Content.

SharePoint 2013's initial business and functional requirements, as well as the organization's overall long-term SharePoint roadmap, will play a major role in the Context area of the IA design, as shown in Figure 5.4.

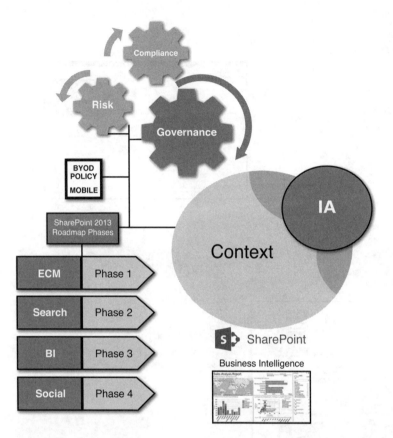

FIGURE 5.4   SharePoint 2013 Context area considerations for your information architecture approach and design.

I would also recommend identifying any cultural influences or related technology initiatives while keeping compliance, risk, and governance in mind that should be taken into consideration within the Context area. The out-of-the-box (OOTB) capabilities SharePoint provides for in search, eDiscovery, and enterprise content management (ECM)/records management (RM), as well as communities, social, and professional networking, must also be analyzed. The architecture required to scale to meet the contextual needs of the organization should also be discussed during the initial information architecture planning discussions to ensure that any updates to the organization's information architectural roadmap are identified and communicated to the proper stakeholders.

The second area of consideration within SharePoint's IA design, Content, centers on the documents that exist within the organization, as well as the existing structure or underlying system for which they are stored. These Content IA considerations, as shown in Figure 5.5, should provide insight into the types of data that exist within the organization as well as its overall volume.

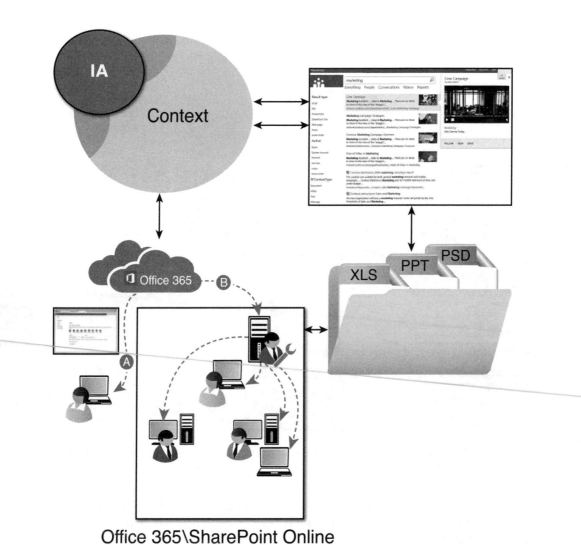

Office 365\SharePoint Online

FIGURE 5.5   SharePoint 2013 Content area considerations for your information architecture approach and design.

The Users area of the IA, as shown in Figure 5.6, provides insight into the day-to-day utilization of SharePoint's users and the core content they access within their department or business unit. This entails the identification of specific audiences along with the content and data they own and collaborate on that enables them to successfully perform their job duties.

It is important to have a good understanding of who the core contacts are within any given department or business unit that will be a part of SharePoint 2013's content editing and contribution.

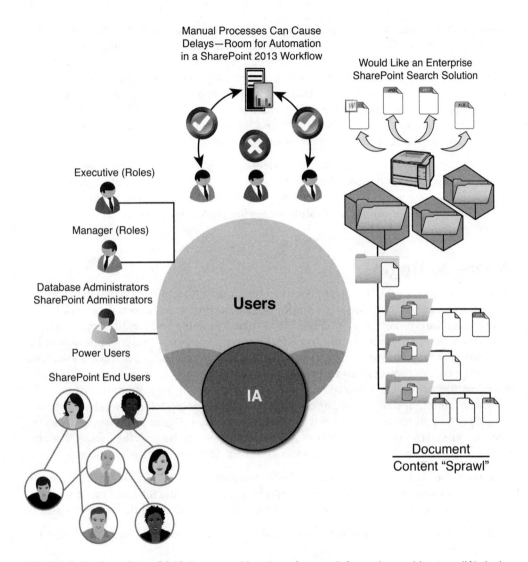

FIGURE 5.6   SharePoint 2013 User considerations for your information architecture (IA) design.

EPC Group has seen a noticeable increase in "enterprise search experience" initiatives driven by the new features available out-of-the-box within SharePoint 2013's Search. Organizations increasingly want to have a central "one version of the truth" platform that also has a governed and approved branding design to enable users to "query the entire enterprise" and receive extremely accurate search results for not only SharePoint data but also other line-of-business (LOB) systems such as Documentum, LiveLink, eRoom, and SAP.

Another area in which we have seen a huge spike in client interest is the SharePoint Server 2013 BI initiatives or Office 365 Power BI efforts. Organizations are focusing on not just one major functionality or "service" of SharePoint 2013 within a given project phase but in some cases many parallel efforts to accomplish multiple business requirements. This major shift in the expectations from SharePoint's previous versions and the consideration of having parallel initiatives being implemented, for example, around both a SharePoint enterprise search effort and a SharePoint BI and reporting initiative requires a new approach to the overall information architecture design.

SharePoint 2013 literally has become the "one-stop shop" for many organizations that require a robust and centralized platform that has the capability to securely access all of the organization's content and provide policies and rules that govern it, while also providing tools to analyze its contents, all while increasing productivity and collaboration with its team members.

Where to Begin

As mentioned previously, the three-prong information architecture approach provides placeholders for the requirements that must be documented but also sets expectations for the SharePoint project team to design an IA that is scalable and has the organization's long-term SharePoint roadmap in mind. The Context, Users, and Content approach to the information architecture design, as mentioned previously, is meant to instill a 360-degree view of the overall project goals and future business needs, as well as the other "moving pieces" within the organization that are not typically taken into consideration. It is extremely important to think of not only what content is going to be created and where it is going to be stored but also how it is going to be viewed. Figure 5.7 shows an overview of SharePoint 2013's content from both an authoring perspective and the perspective of how users access it and some of the devices and their properties they may utilize.

Based on the availability of the stakeholders or team members within the organization for which you may need to facilitate meetings and gather specific information, it is a best practices approach to first start with a more broad set of questions in these initial sessions.

What currently exists? The following questions can assist you with finding your initial IA baseline:

▶ What content management, content storage systems, or technologies currently exist within the organization?

▶ Do you need to take into consideration any previous versions of SharePoint?

▶ Does your organization have a complex or even massive file-share environment in place?

▶ Is there an existing intranet with documents or static content that will need to be analyzed and considered? If so, who owns or updates this content?

▶ What does your organization consider to be a record?

▶ Is there a retention policy or schedule in place from your legal or compliance department?

▶ Are there environmental considerations such as both a "private cloud" (that is, on-premises) and a "public cloud" (that is, hosted Office 365) that may have separate IA requirements or hybrid architecture considerations?

▶ Are there any globally specific regulations such as those in the European Union (EU)? If so, some social features and components as well as their specific fields may need to be excluded within the SharePoint Governance model and vetted by the legal and compliance stakeholders.

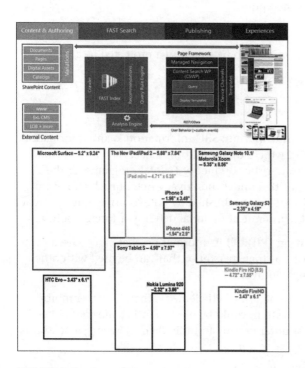

FIGURE 5.7   An overview of how users may access content and details regarding the user experiences and limitations on some popular devices that must be planned for in the design.

Some of these questions can be political land mines that you may need to carefully step around while also ensuring that the right audiences or stakeholders are included and briefed on the SharePoint effort so that they have a communication channel into at least part of the decision-making process. Do not bring a blank piece of paper to the meeting and just ask them, "What do you need and how do you want it?"

You must be prepared in every SharePoint information-gathering session with questions, topics, and agenda items that are relevant to the audience you are interviewing. You must have a solid idea of your baseline requirements, as well as how those baseline requirements play into the phase or even multiple parallel phases you are addressing, while always keeping the long-term roadmap in mind.

There are also specific regulatory considerations, laws, and industry-specific questions that must be considered because if they are ignored the organization may be open to litigation or penalties. The following questions should be asked and considered regarding any data being stored within SharePoint:

▶ What is sensitive information?

▶ How should you protect it?

  ▶ Does your organization use encryption?

  ▶ How is sensitive-information-classified?

  ▶ Does this sensitive information need to be stored in a protected location?

▶ What compliance is required under privacy regulations?

Different types of information include

▶ **Sensitive but unclassified (SBU) information:** SBU information is any information, the loss, misuse, or modification of which, or unauthorized access of which, could adversely affect the national interest or the conduct of Federal programs, or the privacy to which individuals are entitled under the Privacy Act, but which has not been specifically authorized under criteria established by an executive order or an act of Congress to be kept secret in the interest of national defense or foreign policy.

▶ **Personally identifiable information (PII):** PII is information that can be used to uniquely identify, contact, or locate a single person or that can be used with other sources to uniquely identify a single individual.

▶ **Sensitive PII:** Sensitive PII is a combination of PII elements that, if lost, compromised, or disclosed without authorization, could be used to inflict substantial harm, embarrassment, inconvenience, or unfairness to an individual. Here are some examples of sensitive PII:

  ▶ A social security number by itself

  ▶ An individual's first name or first initial and last name in combination with any one or more of the following types of information, including, but not limited to

    Social Security number

    Passport number

    Credit card number

    Home telephone number

    Personal cellphone number

Clearances

Bank numbers

Date and place of birth

Mother's maiden name

Financial records and the like

Note that this information may be in the form of paper, electronic, or any other media format.

▶ **Protected health information (PHI):** PHI is any information about health status, provision of healthcare, or payment for healthcare that can be linked to a specific individual. Under the U.S. Health Insurance Portability and Accountability Act (HIPAA), PHI that is linked based on the following list of 18 identifiers that must be treated with special care:

Names

Dates (other than year) directly related to an individual

Phone numbers

Fax numbers

Email addresses

Social Security numbers

Medical record numbers

Health insurance beneficiary numbers

Account numbers

Certificate/license numbers

Vehicle identifiers and serial numbers, including license plate numbers

Device identifiers and serial numbers

Web uniform resource locators (URLs)

Internet Protocol (IP) address numbers

Biometric identifiers, including finger, retinal, and voice prints

Full-face photographic images and any comparable images

Any other unique identifying number, characteristic, or code except the unique code assigned by the investigator to code the data

Who are the individuals who will be able to provide you with insight into what content exists and who may own or access this content? As the requirements-gathering sessions progress, you may find that there are multiple versions of documents stored in several locations, but ensure that you are working toward an IA design that will provide a "one version of the truth" principle to eliminate duplicate content that can lead to inaccurate reporting and metrics.

You may experience team members that are "content hoarders" in some departments, divisions, or business units that will push back on your requests and may not provide you exactly what you are wanting in initial sessions. These types of issues must be identified, addressed, and resolved. These individuals must be approached by either a manager or a stakeholder who can provide them with an enforceable directive to ensure their participation and assistance with the content identification and clarifications specific to their area of the IA design.

> **NOTE**
>
> It is very important to keep in mind that your analysis effort regarding the design of SharePoint 2013's IA is one of the more difficult and tedious processes within the overall implementation. The identification and content analysis effort you are performing is more than likely a task that has been put off by the organization for many years. If it was easy, anyone could do it—but it is not, and you must remain focused and consistent in your effort because consistency is key!

There may be questions regarding content and how it's used that may not be able to be answered until a future phase or until some other external business decision is made, which may cause you and the project team concern. There is no way to control these issues that are out of your hands and it may affect the IA.

In these cases, you need to follow the most scalable model that will allow the IA to meet current requirements, as well as those on the future roadmap that you have been able to identify.

After you have identified the key users and stakeholders that have the in-depth knowledge of the content in a given area or department, you should also consider that user or stakeholder to be a future SharePoint Power User or Content Owner because this will ease the transition over to the new platform.

It will be very beneficial for you to document the users' input carefully and under no circumstances put the content and/or documents that are required for this user or set of users to do their job in a "migration" holding pattern or somehow affect the permission and access to the content.

> **NOTE**
>
> All business- or mission-critical content must be identified, and these types of users, the ones who really understand the content in their department or given area, can help you ensure that this content is approached with extreme care and consideration.

The question of "what is a record" in your organization is typically defined by managers, and those organizations that are larger in nature may have a records manager or compliance officer who can help you make huge strides toward your goals. These managers or officers can help you understand what the organization's key underlying records are. In many organizations, the retention schedule or related "company enterprise content management initiative" may not yet have all of these spelled out in a manner that you can immediately use, but this is where you can start to see how the IA will scale and can identify some timelines around when this information can be provided or when it may be available.

How Should Your Information Architecture and Related Taxonomy Be Structured?

The information architecture design and related analysis you perform will be the driving factor in areas such as site structure and the services and functionality provided by SharePoint 2013.

Whether your organization's SharePoint 2013 implementation should be departmentally structured and closely follow the company's organizational chart or should have a functional hierarchy based on the major functionalities of business units and their related divisions should be determined after you fully understand the options SharePoint 2013 provides to you and your team.

The following sections detail the granular features and functionally within SharePoint 2013 that will enable you to configure this powerful platform to meet your organization-specific needs.

The technical side of the design of SharePoint's IA can be confusing to nontechnical project team members or content owners, so it's important to keep your audience in mind when discussing certain components and technical terms. If you walk into a meeting with content owners or a records manager without SharePoint technical knowledge, you will lose their attention and interest very quickly if you jump right into a conversation about site collections and web applications. It is your job to take the "business speak" and turn it into "technical speak" in defining your requirements.

This "technical business analyst" type of approach will make your discussions with the business much more productive and will require some preparation before the actual meeting(s). Have a defined plan and approach with questions specific and meaningful to that particular stakeholder, department, or set of users ready before engaging with them.

Understanding SharePoint 2013's Logical Architecture

To drill down into the overall logical architecture of SharePoint 2013, the underlying technical components and features that factor into the design of SharePoint 2013's IA are as listed here:

▶ Service applications

▶ Application pools

▶ Web applications

▶ Zone(s)

- ▶ Site collections
- ▶ Sites
- ▶ Lists and libraries

SharePoint 2013 allows for individual services to be configured and controlled at an extremely granular level. These "service applications" allow for key features and the resources they provide to be shared across a SharePoint farm and throughout sites. The following is a list of the service applications in SharePoint 2013:

- ▶ Access Services Web Service Application
- ▶ App Management Service Application
- ▶ Business Data Connectivity Service Application
- ▶ Search Service Application
- ▶ Excel Services Application
- ▶ Managed Metadata Service
- ▶ PerformancePoint Service Application
- ▶ PowerPoint Conversion Service Application
- ▶ Secure Store Service Application
- ▶ Machine Translation Service
- ▶ Usage and Health Data Collection Service Application
- ▶ User Profile Service Application
- ▶ State Service
- ▶ Visio Graphics Service Application
- ▶ Security Token Service Application
- ▶ Application Discovery and Load Balancer Service Application

Figure 5.8 provides an overview of SharePoint 2013's service applications, as well as how they flow into the overall information architecture.

SharePoint 2013's Application Pool and Web Application capabilities, as shown in Figure 5.9, have a different configuration model than those in previous versions of SharePoint. In most cases, there should be one web application and one related zone. You also can utilize host-named site collections that have much improved scaling capabilities with reduced resource consumption.

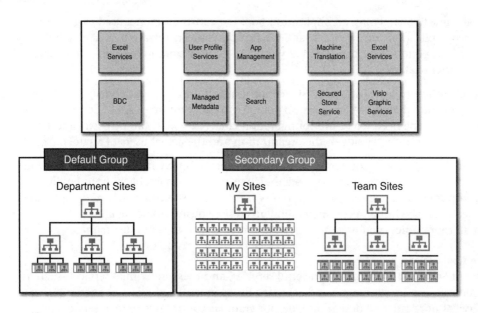

FIGURE 5.8   A detailed overview of SharePoint 2013's information architecture flow and structure.

Application Pool

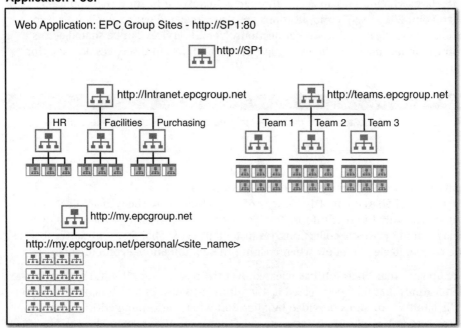

FIGURE 5.9   SharePoint 2013's Web Applications showing an example of a best practices configuration.

If you are new to SharePoint, an application pool is a construct model used to gather or group web applications in a logical manner based on your organization-specific requirements such as performance needs and any security- or configuration-specific elements such as authentication.

Taking advantage of the host-named site collections option is recommended; that is the same architecture that Office 365 uses, so planning for any future possible hybrid architecture will reduce the need for future configuration changes, which can be costly and time-consuming on both the IT side of the organization and the actual users of SharePoint.

There are always specific requirements that an organization may have that can cause you to go with a different configuration model, such as the need to enable apps in environments with multiple zones or the need to mix host-named site collections and path-based site collections. The initial recommendation given previously should be followed in almost all cases, unless you have specific requirements such as those just named.

Service Applications
SharePoint Server 2013 has many powerful services, and these individual services, such as Excel Services, can be configured and activated independently. SharePoint Server 2013's new services infrastructure design provides for granular control over which services are deployed and how services are shared.

These are technically referred to as service applications, which are really powerful resources that SharePoint allows you to share across sites throughout a SharePoint 2013/Office 365 farm which users can access through a SharePoint hosting web application. SharePoint 2013's service applications are also associated with SharePoint's web applications via service application connections. Not all services can be shared across a SharePoint farm but many of the most high-profile and powerful services do have this capability.

> **NOTE**
>
> These 16 service applications are discussed in greater detail in later chapters of this book.

Web Applications and Performing IA Administrative Tasks
At the very core of SharePoint 2013/Office 365's capabilities are the web applications, which are technically Internet Information Services (IIS) websites. This topic gets over-complicated, along with site collections, on just about every SharePoint initiative, because there are core strategies to follow when creating these foundational components.

With the updates that Microsoft has released over the past six months and with new or upgraded features that may be released in the future, it is always recommended that you follow the latest instructions provided by Microsoft when performing critical functions such as creating web applications, new site collections, or other related IA tasks.

This is not a cause of concern or a statement that Microsoft is constantly changing frequent or fundamental architecture and administration tasks that you may perform on a weekly or monthly basis. Rather, this is a practice that will ensure that you will always know that you have reviewed the published Microsoft steps so that you will have that added peace of mind.

TIP

It is key to ensure that you have the appropriate permission level when performing administrative tasks such as creating web applications or new site collection, but the documentation of these actions is equally important.

Your organization should follow your existing change control or documentation process whenever these types of administrative tasks are performed. If you do not currently have a change control process identified or created within your organization, the following chapters will provide guidance regarding SharePoint 2013/Office 365 governance and the types of policies and procedures your organization must have in place to ensure SharePoint's long-term success.

To create a web application in SharePoint 2013, follow the steps found at the link that follows to ensure that you are following the process that matches the latest feature releases from Microsoft regarding SharePoint 2013 in conjunction with the on-premises, Office 365, or hybrid architecture you currently have in place: http://technet.microsoft.com/en-us/library/cc261875.aspx

5

TIP

This type of direction (that is, providing you with the official Microsoft link), along with providing the "in the trenches" related strategies you should follow, will be used throughout this book. It would be incorrect to assume that the type of SharePoint 2013/Office 365 environment an organization provides to their user base and the directions you should follow can be stated once with the thought that they will not be modified as future releases/updates are provided; rather, the directions should be clarified in detail using this method to ensure that you have the latest and greatest information available.

A user may be creating an administration task via their browser on their individual desktop or device and not fully understand the specific SharePoint 2013/Office 365 environment they are working with because it may have been updated by IT; but to them, the URLs are still the same and they assume that the environment must be as well. Microsoft has stated they will provide specific updates or guidance via these official Microsoft links to ensure users have the specific set of tasks and options available to them that align with the environment for which they have deployed and include any possible variables for additional consideration.

This is a best practices step that your organization should always follow regardless of how comfortable performing a repetitive task may be. The release cycle for new updates is much faster than ever before, and Microsoft has hinted at following more of Apple's model in requiring the latest and greatest updates.

A good example of this is found with Microsoft's recent update to administrators of Office 365 environments. Internet Explorer 8 will soon no longer be supported and an update to Internet Explorer 9 will be required, as detailed in the following link: http://office.microsoft.com/en-us/support/supported-browsers-in-office-2013-and-office-365-HA102789344.aspx

Updating to Internet Explorer 9 may seem like a small and trivial task to some users, but with large organizations or those environments that allow external users to access specific content, these types of updates must not only be taken into consideration but also communicated to the user base, both internal and external.

Zones

Zones in SharePoint 2013 are representations of differing logical paths that are able to gain access to the same sites in a web application. Many different zones can be included within a web application. As mentioned previously, in most cases there should be one web application and one related zone, and you can also utilize host-named site collections that have much improved scaling capabilities with reduced resource consumption.

For more information on zones in SharePoint 2013/Office 365, refer to the following link: http://technet.microsoft.com/en-us/library/cc262350.aspx

SharePoint 2013's security is one of a "claims-based authentication" first strategy, and this provides for many variables for not only user authentication but also specific app authentication and the new server-to-server authentication model. This is covered in greater detail in future chapters to also include best practices administration practices.

Site Collections

SharePoint site collection capabilities have been updated in SharePoint 2013/Office 365 and are the most common and important component in creating a best practices information architecture.

Site collections not only are a major configuration component that contain a group of SharePoint sites within them but also have a direct correlation to a person or number of persons who will end up supporting these specific sets of sites.

You will commonly hear the term "site collection owner." This person has ownership and permissions to perform actions for all the users within this grouping or set number of sites that the collection falls under.

It is also key to understand the requirements of the site/sites within the site collection because when the site collection is created, it comes with a set of native features and functionalities that need to be specifically considered before its creation.

The web applications discussed previously are the actual hosts for a SharePoint site collection. Web applications have the capability to host a large number of site collections, so the underlying requirements of the users and related content are key to architecting the correct number of site collections, as well as how they should be managed both near-term and longer-term.

Some SharePoint 2013/Office 365 initiatives may require only a limited number of site collections to be created, whereas others may have more granular requirements that call for a very defined set of site collections. This also brings the underlying system architecture of SharePoint 2013/Office 365 into play here, because some site collections may be required to be created only in the organization's SharePoint 2013 on-premises environment due to the nature of content (PII, PHI, HIPAA, and so on), whereas others may be able to be created in the cloud for sites that do not contain data with regulatory requirements or implications.

The underlying system best practices configurations as well as approach are discussed in Chapter 7, as well as in later chapters covering SharePoint administration and governance.

To create a new site collection in SharePoint 2013, follow the steps found at the link that follows to ensure that you are following the process that matches the latest feature releases from Microsoft regarding SharePoint 2013 in conjunction with the on-premises, Office 365, or hybrid architecture you currently have in place: http://technet.microsoft.com/en-us/library/cc263094.aspx

Architecting for Success Regarding URLs in SharePoint 2013/Office 365

The URLs (links) of site collections and the underlying sites created that are used to access SharePoint 2013/Office 365 sites are extremely simple to create from an administrator's standpoint. However, the architecture and planning of these links is key because the organization's current and future requirements should always be accounted for as users frequently bookmark and embed links in documents. Figure 5.10 details an example of an organization's SharePoint URLs for different types of sites as well as users.

USER BASE OF THE ORGANIZATION—PARTNERS and EMPLOYEES INCLUDING REMOTE and SEARCH

**Partner Companies
(Business-to-Business)**
https://partnerweb.epcgroup.net

Individual Partners
https://partnerweb.epcgroup.net

Internet and Remote Employees
https://intranet.epcgroup.net
https://teams.epcgroup.net
https://my.epcgroup.net
https://partnerweb.epcgroup.net

Search Crawl Account
https://intranet.epcgroup.net
https://teams.epcgroup.net
https://my.epcgroup.net
https://partnerweb.epcgroup.net

FIGURE 5.10   URLs created for SharePoint 2013/Office 365 sites as well as the types of users for which they are being accessed.

Sites

SharePoint 2013/Office 365 sites, which I am sure is obvious by now, are what users access to view SharePoint's content as well as access all of its features and capabilities. Sites are covered in great detail in almost every chapter of this book in one way or another, but the most important concept to understanding and keep in mind at all times regarding how best to architect SharePoint 2013/Office 365's sites is to do so in a device- and browser-agnostic manner.

Users will always want to access SharePoint's search capabilities and the out-of-the-box features, such as storing or accessing their content in document libraries. As the technology advancements in mobility continue and as the hybrid cloud architectural considerations grow, the worst thing an organization can do is paint itself into a corner where SharePoint's sites were developed in a manner that didn't consider future requirements and the long-term SharePoint roadmap.

The following sections go into detail regarding the lists and libraries which you can create and configure in SharePoint's sites, and Chapter 6, "Using Out-of-the-Box Web Parts in SharePoint 2013/Office 365," covers the web parts and additional functionality that come OOTB with SharePoint 2013's latest release.

Lists and Libraries

Lists and libraries are covered in detail in the following section.

Translating Your Business and Functional Requirements into SharePoint 2013/Office 365 Lists and Libraries

Successfully translating your organization's business and functional requirements into a best practices information architecture design will include the creation of SharePoint lists and libraries.

Lists and libraries are the central features in SharePoint 2013 for storing content, records, list items, and records. This section covers how to create lists and libraries based on your organization's functional requirements.

In SharePoint 2013, there is a new app model, and technically lists and libraries and their referring web parts can now all be referred to as "apps."

Microsoft had tapped into the new app world that we live in today. From a user's perspective, there is really no difference between a web part and an app, but from a developer's or an IT perspective, there definitely is. The development of custom SharePoint solutions and apps is covered later in this book. Microsoft has also rebranded "Office Web Apps" to "Office Online" to help resolve some of this confusion.

Just as you can go out to the app store for your iPhone or Windows Phone or really almost any mobile device, you can also go to Microsoft.com and the SharePoint App Store, per the following link: http://office.microsoft.com/en-us/store/apps-for-sharepoint-FX102804987.aspx

Later in this book, I also cover the process you can follow to get a custom app you have developed into the SharePoint App Store.

I want to make sure that everyone is on the same page regarding the SharePoint App versus SharePoint web part topic before moving on so. That way, you will understand what I am referring to when I discuss web parts as well as lists and libraries. In some project, IT, or business conversations you may have in the future, all of these may be referred to as simply a "SharePoint app," so it's important to understand this thought process.

Creating Lists from a Built-in Template

When determining the types of lists your organization will create and provide to various SharePoint audiences, you should initially review the out-of-the-box templates that come native within SharePoint 2013. Microsoft has provided various list templates solving many common business and functional requirements, such as a tasks list, calendars, a contacts list, and an issue tracking list template.

To create a list from one of the built-in list templates, click on the Settings or the "gear" icon in the upper-right corner of the page and select Add an App. The Your Apps page then opens with various app templates to select from, similar to what's shown in Figure 5.11.

FIGURE 5.11   SharePoint 2013 comes with a variety of App templates to instantly meet specific business and functional requirements.

> **TIP**
>
> By creating list and library templates that follow your organization's governance strategy, you will be able to enforce governance as soon as a new list or library is created.

Going forward, you can browse and review the built-in templates available within SharePoint 2013, including other types of apps such as libraries, discussions, and surveys.

TIP

If this option does not exist, you may not have permission to create a list.

You may want to create a Contacts list, for example, to store contact information for your company's marketing department. First, you select the Contacts app and give it a name, as shown in Figure 5.12. After you click Create you are brought to the site contents page where your new list shows up. In our case, we can see that the Marketing Contacts list is listed and it has the "new!" keyword beside it.

FIGURE 5.12   Providing a specific name for a new Contacts list that is being created for the marketing department.

Figure 5.13 shows the new Contacts list and some basic columns that can be automatically created and instantly used out-of-the-box. When creating a list in this manner, keep in mind that not all the columns are created out-of-the-box and will be displayed by default.

FIGURE 5.13   The new Marketing departments Contact list that was created from the Contacts template.

If you were to look at the list settings or click on New Item, you would see that additional columns are available, such as Job Title, Fax Number, and Mobile Number. In the following sections, the steps you can take to modify this list to meet your specific requirements are discussed.

Figure 5.13 shows that with just a few simple clicks, a new list was created, enabling users to start storing and sharing contact information within this list.

Creating Custom Lists

There will be times when you are utilizing an OOTB SharePoint 2013 template that you will realize that the options available will not meet your needs. When you need a custom list and require it immediately, the added features in SharePoint 2013 enable you to create a custom list with a blank canvas and to add content types or fields to your custom list.

In this sample scenario, a custom list will be created that will store uniform sizes needed for the players on a Little League baseball team that your organization is sponsoring as part of an internal community program or charity initiative.

In the following scenario, the process of the development and rollout of custom lists and custom columns will be reviewed. This process is started by going to the Add an App page and then selecting Custom List (see Figure 5.14).

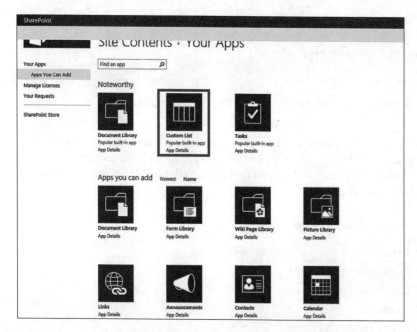

FIGURE 5.14   Selecting Custom List within the Add an App page.

For this new custom list, name it "Little League Uniforms," and click OK.

To ensure that the process of adding custom columns has been successfully executed, you must review specific list requirements. Select the List tab on the SharePoint ribbon menu, and then select List Settings to review and confirm your specific list requirements. SharePoint 2013 contains a large number of custom and configurable settings that can be modified under the List Setting option.

In this scenario, the focus will solely be on adding fields to the list, allowing the option to record specific uniform sizes needed for the Little League baseball team the company has sponsored. In the following section, list settings, as shown in Figure 5.15, will be reviewed, focusing on proper utilization and best practices.

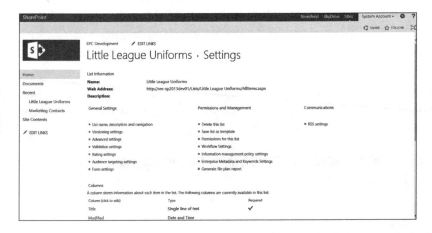

FIGURE 5.15   The settings for a list available within the List Settings page.

When you scroll down the List Settings page, the Columns section for lists as well as the default columns and fields that are included OOTB with a custom list are shown. To begin creating new columns for this custom list, you first need to define which types of fields are required, as shown in Table 5.1.

TABLE 5.1   Fields Required in the Custom List

Column Name	Data Type	Is Required?
Player Name	Single Line of Text	Y
Shirt Size	Choice Field	Y
Pant Size	Choice Field	Y
Hat Size	Choice Field	Y
Shoe Size	Number	N

In this scenario, the Title column can be created by default in a custom list with the same list data type that should be utilized for Player Name, as shown in Table 5.1.

The Title being utilized for the Player Name field is vital and can easily be renamed to meet specific needs. Figures 5.16 and 5.17 show that by clicking the Title column in the List Settings page, you will be able to edit it to meet your specific requirements.

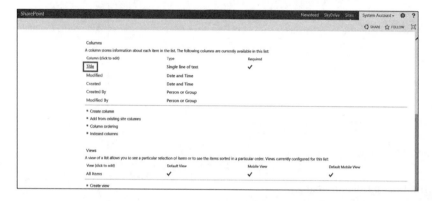

FIGURE 5.16   Clicking on the Title column within the List Settings page enables you to edit the settings of the column to meet your needs.

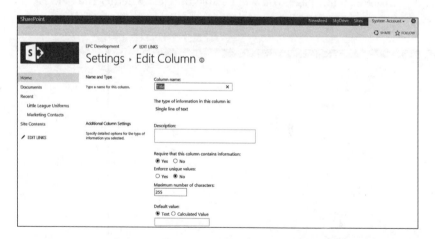

FIGURE 5.17   Within the Edit Column page, you are able to edit the column data to meet the requirements of your custom list.

Under the Column Name option, update the name of the column to "Player Name" and click OK to save the updates. To add the remaining columns required for this custom list, you will need to create them. To create a new column, click the Create Column link in the List Settings page and specify the column name required. As an example, let's look at the Shirt Size column. Figure 5.18 shows the Create Column page where you can create this new column.

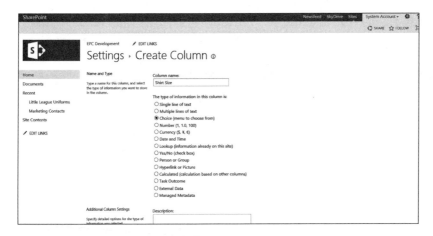

FIGURE 5.18   The Create Column page.

You begin by providing the Name and Type of the column, and in this case it should be called "Shirt Size." For the data type of the new column, Shirt Size, you should select the Choice type. In the Create Column page, you will be able to select whether the field is required, and you can also provide the list of choices for the field (see Figure 5.19).

FIGURE 5.19   Additional options available when you are creating a new list.

The same process can be repeated for the remaining columns needed for your custom list. After all the columns have been added, you can view the new list, shown in Figures 5.20 and 5.21. These figures show both the default list view and the create item view of the new list. Creating a custom list can be very useful and a quick way to provide a custom solution to meet your organization's needs and move it away from, for example, manual processes like an Excel spreadsheet that is updated and emailed to a group of people to collect feedback or information.

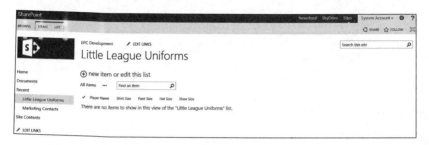

FIGURE 5.20   The default view for this new custom list.

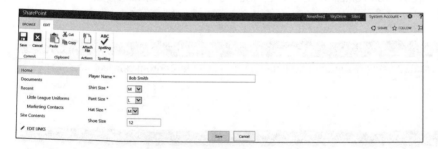

FIGURE 5.21   Showing the available options for the custom list after the new item option was selected.

The next section reviews the options available for creating list templates.

Creating a List Template

In this section, we will look at creating list templates to decrease the amount of time it takes to create multiple SharePoint lists with the same footprint. We will utilize the example from the preceding section in which a custom list was created to track uniform sizes for a Little League team that was being sponsored by an organization.

To create a list template, click on the List Settings page for the list you would like to create a template of, and click on the Save List as Template option under Permissions & Management. You then need to provide a filename for the new template, as shown in Figure 5.22, which will ensure that it's easily identifiable. SharePoint also provides the option Include Content, which enables the list content be included and saved within the list template. As an example, call this template "Uniform Sizes," click OK, and then confirm it by clicking OK again.

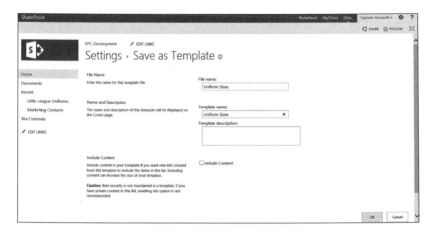

FIGURE 5.22   The Save as Template page when you are creating a list template.

TIP

If a list was created using a custom list definition, the Include Content box will be grayed out.

WARNING

Be Aware of Any Sensitive Data or Permissions When Creating a Template!

When you are creating a list template from an existing list, it is key to review the data in the list being saved as a template. If you have sensitive data in the existing list, I would not recommend saving the existing content. There are also considerations regarding permissions because any item permissions that have been applied to the existing list will also not be saved in the new template.

If you now look at the Add an App page, you will see the Uniform Sizes list template available to create a new list, similar to how the Contacts list template was utilized in a scenario earlier in this chapter (see Figure 5.23). List templates can save time for users and can be a very useful option for any site collection.

Creating a Document Library

As previously discussed, Document libraries are truly a set of files that can be shared with other users in SharePoint. A large number of features and policies can be applied to the Document library, but when thinking through your organization's taxonomy and site structure, you can consider them as an individual silo containing files to be shared and securely accessed.

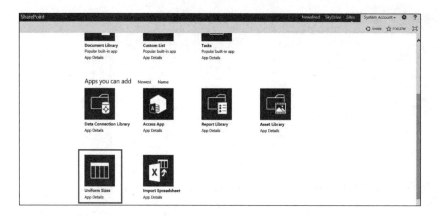

FIGURE 5.23   The Add an App page showing the new list template.

Most of the available document management features in SharePoint 2013 are delivered using document libraries. It is important to plan out your document management needs and determine the best way to set up your document libraries.

As with the lists previously created, developing a document library can be done from the Add an App page in the settings or gear menu. SharePoint treats document libraries very similar to lists, but allows documents to be stored in them.

To create a new document library, click on the Add an App page, select the Document Library template, and give the library a name, as shown in Figure 5.24. After saving the document library, you can open it to view the default view, as shown in Figure 5.25.

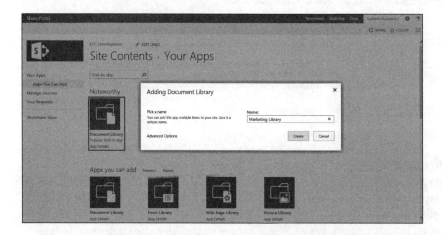

FIGURE 5.24   Providing a name for a new document library that is being created.

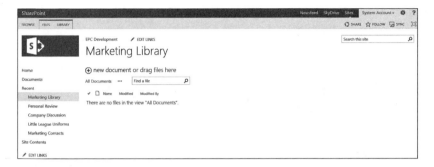

FIGURE 5.25   The default view of a new document library that was created from the Document Library template.

Now that we have created a new document library, you now have the option to add columns, create views, or even edit it in datasheet view just as with lists. Now let's take a look at adding a document to the library. As you can see in Figure 5.26, when you are adding a document to the library, it first asks you to select the document you want to upload. If there were other fields that were in need of being populated, SharePoint would then ask for those values. In this case, there were no other fields and the document has just been added to the library.

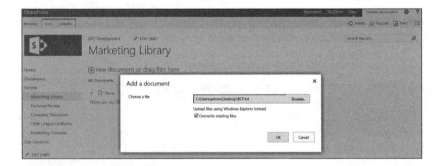

FIGURE 5.26   Upload dialog for new document.

Defining Site Columns

Until now, we have been creating lists and/or library columns that are contained only in the list or library in which they are created. Another option available is to create a site column definition that can be reused throughout all the subsites and that can be added to lists or libraries. In this section, we will look at how to define a site column, and later in this chapter we will take a closer look at how to work with them in a list or library. To define a new site column, you need to go to Site Settings, under the Settings/Gear menu, and then under the Web Designer Galleries section, as shown in Figure 5.27, you will then find the Site Columns option.

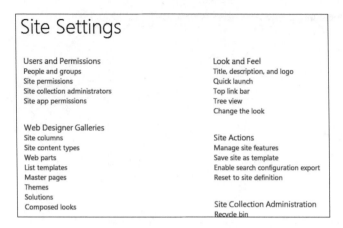

FIGURE 5.27   The Site Columns menu option under Site Settings.

In most cases, it is recommend to create site columns at the top-level site so that they are available to all subsites in your site collection. This may not always be the case, depending on the requirements of your environment or information management policies. To add a new site column, click the Create link at the top of the Site Columns page, as shown in Figure 5.28.

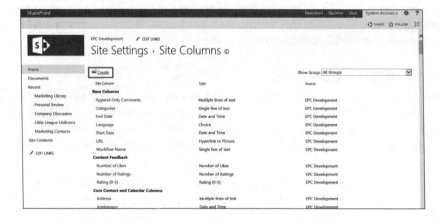

FIGURE 5.28   The Create option to create a new site column in a document library.

As you can see in Figure 5.29, there are more data types available for site columns than for list or library columns. These extra data types are normally reserved for publishing sites. When creating a site column, you must also select a group for the column, which helps categorize it for when it may need to be utilized later.

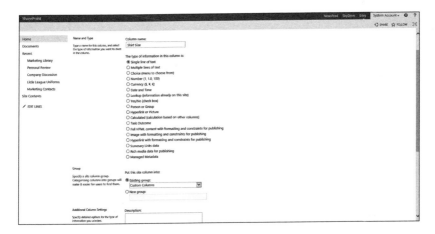

FIGURE 5.29   The Add Site Column page for creating a new column.

Modifying Lists and Libraries

Now that we have reviewed the process for creating lists and libraries, it is the ideal time to review how these can be modified after they have been created. Most organizations need to make updates or changes to their lists and libraries as the business and organizational requirements change and SharePoint evolves. Whether the need is to add a column, change the name, or even delete a list, this section provides insight into the settings available for lists and libraries that enable them to be modified.

Modifying List and Library Settings

Now you are able to review the types of settings that can be changed in lists and libraries. The goal is to provide an overview of which types of settings can be changed within a list or library. After reviewing changes in lists and libraries, we will unveil a variety of settings for lists and libraries that are available from a best practices and "in the trenches" approach.

When adding columns to a custom list, you first need to go to the List or Library tab on the ribbon menu and select either List Settings or Library Settings. In Figure 5.30, the settings available for a list are shown.

We will now take a deeper look at the General Settings for lists and libraries.

Updating General Settings

When you are viewing General Settings available for a list or library, the following options are available:

▶ List Name, Description, and Navigation

▶ Versioning Settings

- ► Advanced Settings

- ► Validation Settings

- ► Rating Settings

- ► Audience Targeting Settings

- ► Form Settings

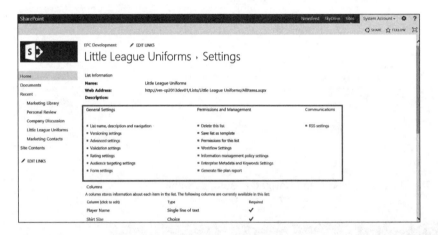

FIGURE 5.30   The settings available for a SharePoint 2013 list that are available out-of-the-box.

We will start by looking at the List Name, Description, and Navigation settings. In Figure 5.31, you can see that these settings are fairly straightforward. You can update the name of the list, give the list a description, and specify whether the list is shown on the Quick Launch menu.

In these settings, you can specify whether content approval is required, as well as which items must remain in draft state until they are approved. As shown in Figure 5.32, you can specify item/document versioning settings, such as the number of versions to retain for recovery and whether to update version numbers for every edit. Finally, you are able to set draft item security, which limits the users who can see items still in the draft stage, which can be very useful for document libraries.

Under General Settings, the Advanced Settings option, as shown in Figure 5.33, provides users the ability to enable/disable multiples features for a list or library, including content types, attachments, folders, and search options. These settings enable the user to set item-level permissions based on the access they have been granted. This setting can limit users to only view/edit the items that they created or prevent any edit permissions at all. General Settings and Validation Settings are vital pieces of these functionalities, which are covered going forward in greater detail.

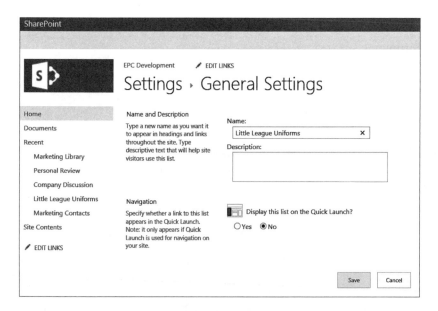

FIGURE 5.31   The Title, Description, and Navigation settings within a list.

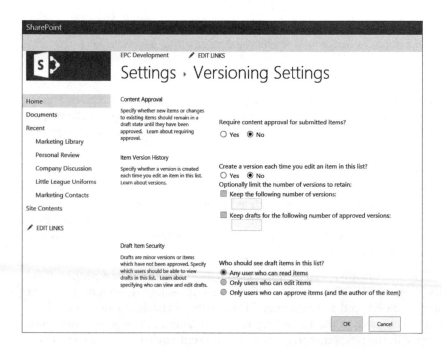

FIGURE 5.32   The Versioning Settings available within a SharePoint 2013 list.

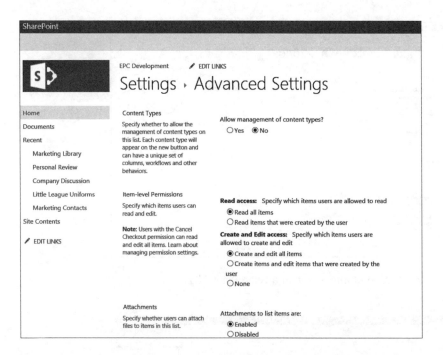

FIGURE 5.33   The Advanced Settings option for a SharePoint 2013 list.

Validation Settings, as shown in Figure 5.34, are a convenient tool when you are creating a solution using a SharePoint list or library. Validation enables you to specify rules based on the data contained in the list fields to validate the list item. For example, let's take a look at the custom list we created earlier in this chapter to store the uniform sizes for our Little League baseball team. We can create a rule that says, "Shoe Size must be less than 15," from a formula such as this: (= [Shoe Size] < 15). The formulas work very similar to Microsoft Excel formulas and include many of the same functions available in Excel.

SharePoint 2013 also provide Rating Settings, as shown in Figure 5.35, which enable you to specify whether your list can be rated by users, as well as the type of rating system that will be used. You may allow users either to just "Like" your list or to actually rate your list on a scale.

Audience targeting enables users to specify their target audience for a list item. When you are enabling audience targeting and creating a column in your list or library, end users now can be specifically associated with the users or group that the list item is targeting. This information can then be used by web parts, such as the Content Query Web Part, to filter results based on the user's context.

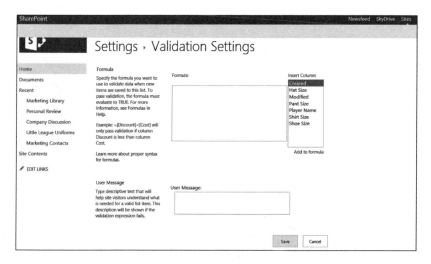

FIGURE 5.34   The Validation Settings within a SharePoint 2013 list.

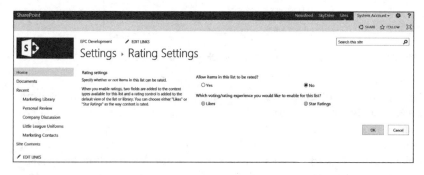

FIGURE 5.35   The Rating Settings within a SharePoint 2013 list.

Deleting a List or Library

When a list or library is no longer being used, there must be parameters in place to audit and explore the value of these sites. Deleting unused lists and libraries makes for a clutter-free SharePoint environment. Deleting a list or library is an easy task that can be accomplished in the List/Library settings page, which can be accessed from the ribbon menu. Select Delete This List, as shown in Figure 5.36, or Delete This Document Library, and confirm the action by clicking OK.

It is crucial to consider the impact of deleting the list from your site. You will want to make sure that the list or library is not being used by any custom solutions or web parts in your environment. You also want to make sure that deleting the list will not cause issues with any lookup columns. Always remember, however, that when a list or library is deleted, you can still recover it from the Recycle Bin.

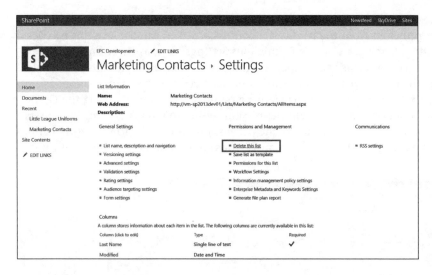

FIGURE 5.36   The Delete This List link within a SharePoint 2013 list.

Changing Permissions for a List or Library

By default, list and library permissions are inherited from their parent site. We will now cover granting unique permissions that are not inherited from the parent site. One thing to remember when creating unique permissions for a list or library is that after you stop inheriting from the parent site, all permissions added to the parent need to also be added to the list as needed. If you select the Permissions for This List link on the List Settings page shown earlier, you should now see the page as shown in Figure 5.37.

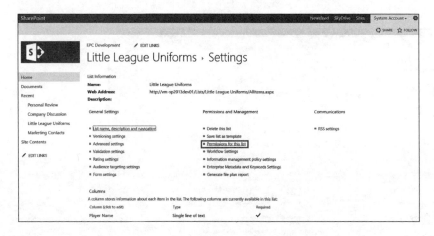

FIGURE 5.37   The Permissions for This List link within a SharePoint 2013 list.

The first step to creating unique permissions for a list or library is to ensure that it is not inheriting its permissions from the parent site permissions. You can achieve this by clicking Stop Inheriting Permissions on the Permissions Settings page, as shown in Figure 5.38. A prompt to confirm this action appears, and you should click OK. This then leads you to granting the desired permissions using the Grant Permissions menu option, as shown in Figure 5.39. Now you can start granting permissions manually using the Grant Permissions menu option. You can grant permissions either to groups or directly to users. If at any time you want to remove the unique permissions and revert to inheriting permissions, you can simply select the Delete Unique Permissions menu option and confirm it.

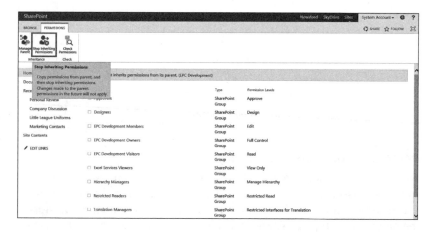

FIGURE 5.38   The Permissions page and the Stop Inheriting Permissions option within a SharePoint 2013 list.

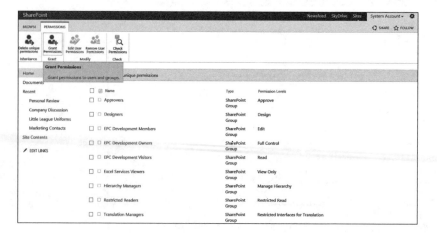

FIGURE 5.39   The Grant Permissions menu option within a SharePoint 2013 list.

Out-of-the-Box Workflow Settings

By default, no workflows are created in SharePoint. OOTB you are provided two work-flow options that can be attached to a SharePoint list. These are the disposition approval workflow and the three-state workflow. To add these to your list, you need to go to the Workflow Settings page and select Add a Workflow, as shown in Figures 5.40 and 5.41.

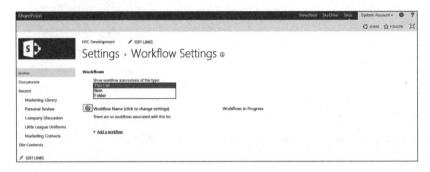

FIGURE 5.40   The out-of-the-box workflow settings within a SharePoint 2013 list.

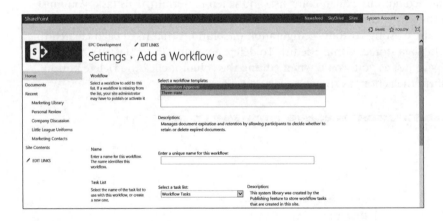

FIGURE 5.41   The Add a Workflow screen within a SharePoint 2013 list.

This Settings page also enables you to manage and remove workflows from a list after they are attached.

RSS Setting on Lists or Libraries

To change the RSS settings on a SharePoint list, you need to go to the Modify RSS Settings page, as shown in Figure 5.42, for the List Settings menu. From here you can change settings such as the Title, Description, and Icon for the RSS feed. Fields that are available in the RSS feeds and the display for those can be changed as well.

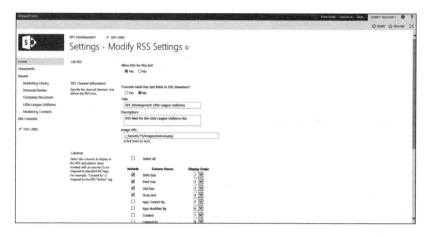

FIGURE 5.42   The Modify RSS Settings page within a SharePoint 2013 list.

Changing and Deleting List Columns

You can edit any column in a SharePoint list, and when performing this task, you must consider how the corresponding list data type will affect the current items in the list. This can also affect any existing custom configuration or solutions that have been created that are based on the data stored within the list. To delete a column in a list, you go to the Edit Column page just as you would when editing the column, click the Delete button, and then confirm the action, as shown in Figure 5.43.

FIGURE 5.43   The delete list column prompt on the Modify RSS Setting page within a SharePoint 2013 list.

Reordering List Columns

SharePoint allows for reordering of the columns in your list from the columns added to your list, enabling necessary organization. When you select the Column Ordering link, as shown in Figure 5.44, the Change Column Ordering page, shown in Figure 5.45, loads. This page enables you to change the ordering of the list columns. This changes the order in which data is entered into the list for new items, as well as when existing list items are updated. After the columns are modified and in the desired order, click OK to save the changes.

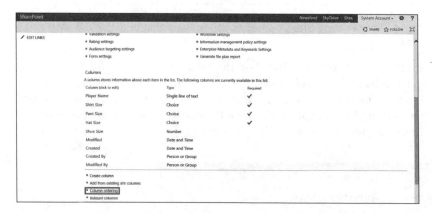

FIGURE 5.44   The Column Ordering option within a SharePoint 2013 list.

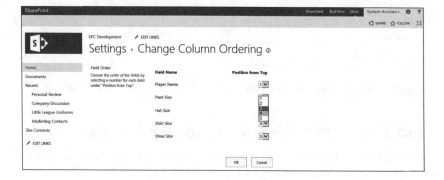

FIGURE 5.45   The Change Column Ordering page within a SharePoint 2013 list.

Working with Site Columns in a List or Library

SharePoint 2013 lets you define site columns that can be used in lists and libraries throughout your site and all subsites. In this section, we will look at how you can add a site column to a list in SharePoint 2013. To begin, select the Add from Existing Site Columns link in the List Settings page shown in Figure 5.46.

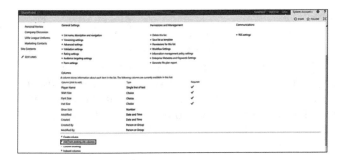

FIGURE 5.46   The Add from Existing Site Columns option within a SharePoint 2013 list.

You can search for existing site columns based on the group they belong to and add them directly to a SharePoint list. Figure 5.47 shows the Add Columns from Site Columns page, where you can add new site columns to a list. After the site columns that you want to add are identified, you can simply click OK to add them to your list, and they immediately are available to be utilized as new data fields.

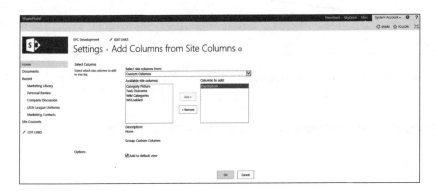

FIGURE 5.47   The Add Columns from Site Columns page within a SharePoint 2013 list.

Creating and Modifying List and Library Views

List and library views enable users to filter and modify the data that is in a list or library to better meet their business needs. SharePoint 2013 makes it easy to create or modify views in your SharePoint lists. In this section, we will look at how to create a new view and even how to modify existing views.

Creating List and Library Views

Creating a list or library view is easily accomplished in SharePoint 2013. Although you can still create a full view using the same process that was used in SharePoint 2010, SharePoint 2013 provides a new way to create a view directly from the list. By filtering and sorting the list, SharePoint 2013 will enable you to save these preferences as a view for later use, as shown in Figure 5.48.

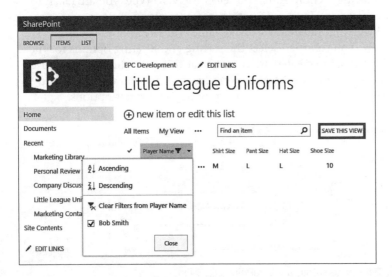

FIGURE 5.48   The Save This View option within a SharePoint 2013 list.

This option makes it very easy for any user to create a simple view based on other views currently available in your lists. The other option is the more well-known way of creating a new view. To create a new view from scratch, select the Create View menu option on the list ribbon menu, as shown in Figure 5.49. You can now select the type of view that will meet your specific requirements. These are the available options:

▶ Standard View

▶ Calendar View

▶ Datasheet View

▶ Gantt View

▶ Custom View in SharePoint Designer

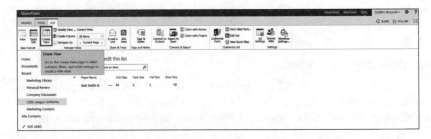

FIGURE 5.49   The Create View menu option within a SharePoint 2013 list.

The most common view used in SharePoint 2013 is the standard view. Figure 5.50 shows the View Type page, which has the options just described. The standard view serves as a reference point in the following section. After you select the view type, you are taken to the Create View page, as shown in Figure 5.51, which provides many options to create your desired view. Start by giving the view a specific name and selecting the columns you want to display in the view. You can then select the sorting and filtering options for the new view. Many new views that are created are complete at this time and are ready to be utilized, but there are also many additional options available for you to continue to specific granular areas, such as the new view's style, grouping, and totals options.

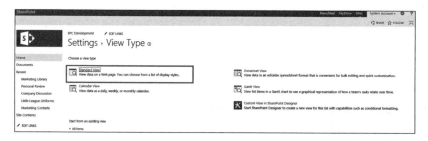

FIGURE 5.50   The View Type page within a SharePoint 2013 list.

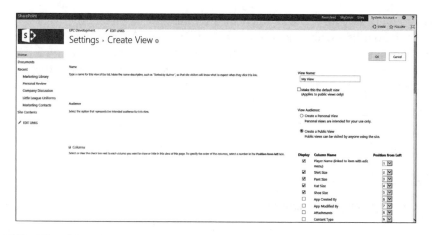

FIGURE 5.51   The Create View page within a SharePoint 2013 list.

Modifying and Deleting List Views

After a list view is created, you can edit it by selecting the Modify View menu option from the list ribbon menu, as shown in Figure 5.52. Modifying a view is similar to creating a brand-new view. When modifying a list or library view, you can add columns, change the view name, and even change the other options that are available to you when creating a new view, as shown in Figure 5.53.

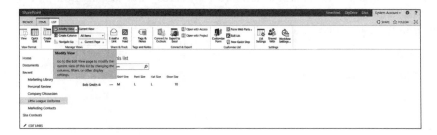

FIGURE 5.52   The Modify View option within a SharePoint 2013 list.

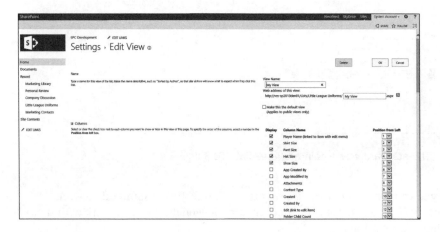

FIGURE 5.53   The Edit View page within a SharePoint 2013 list.

From the Edit View screen, you can both modify the view and delete it, which is very similar to modifying a list column. To delete a list or library view, go to the Edit View screen and click Delete. You must confirm the delete action by clicking OK on the subsequent prompt.

Working with List Content

Now that both lists and libraries have been created, it is time to review how you can work with the data that they store. In this section, we will be looking at how you can work with list content in the standard and datasheet view, and we will also look at how you can access the RSS feed associated with your list or library.

Working with List Content in Standard View

In SharePoint 2013, the standard view is the view that will most commonly be used and is displayed by default. Working with data in a standard view is easy and for the most part self-explanatory. The standard view for a SharePoint list, as shown in Figure 5.54, enables you to perform common tasks such as these:

▶ Create a new item

▶ View/edit a current item

▶ Start a workflow on an item

▶ Tag an item

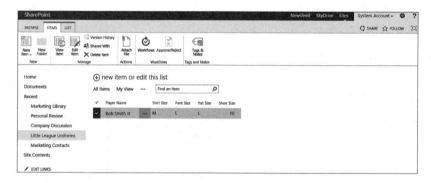

FIGURE 5.54   The standard view within a SharePoint 2013 list.

Additionally, you can create a new item using the link directly on standard view. As shown in Figure 5.55, you can see how the standard view enables you to work with data by using the item context menu.

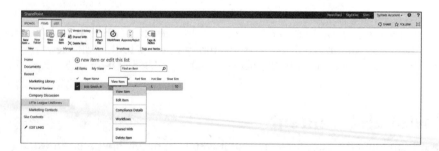

FIGURE 5.55   The item context menu within a SharePoint 2013 list.

Working with Lists and Libraries in Datasheet View

In SharePoint 2013, you can access the datasheet view through the Quick Edit ribbon menu option under the List or Library tab, as shown in Figure 5.56. The datasheet view enables you to quickly add items to a list and works more like an Excel spreadsheet than a web-based user interface. The datasheet view also enables the user to quickly add a column, as shown in Figure 5.57.

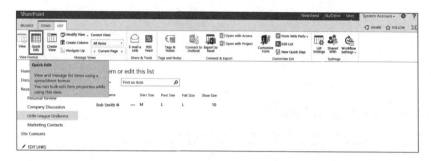

FIGURE 5.56   The Quick Edit menu option within a SharePoint 2013 list.

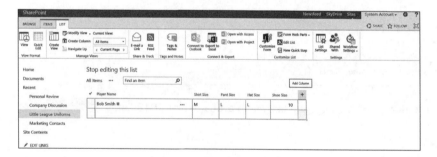

FIGURE 5.57   The datasheet view and Add Column option within a SharePoint 2013 list.

Just as with the normal list views, you can create custom datasheet views for your lists. This is extremely useful when you need to quickly enter data without having to worry about fields that are not required or not needed. Datasheet views can also be used to edit data items currently in the list, which can come in handy when you need to do mass-edit tasks on multiple list items.

Viewing RSS Feed

To view the RSS feed, select the List tab on the SharePoint ribbon menu and click the RSS Feed ribbon menu option, as shown in Figures 5.58 and 5.59. As you can see in Figure 5.58, you can subscribe to the RSS feed directly.

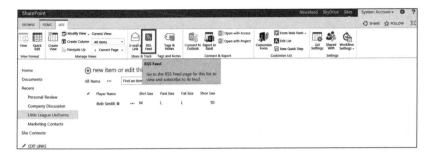

FIGURE 5.58   The RSS Feed menu option within a SharePoint 2013 list.

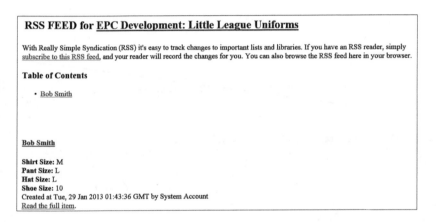

FIGURE 5.59   The RSS Feed for a custom list within a SharePoint 2013 list.

Creating Discussions and Surveys

Being able to create conversations around specific topics to gain feedback from your organization allows you to better interact and take action on the knowledge of others within your organization. SharePoint 2013 provides the ability to create discussion boards as well as surveys for users to provide this candid feedback as well as to share the knowledge they have to solve specific problems or gain additional critical insights.

Creating a New Discussion Board

Creating a new discussion board is as easy as creating a new list from a built-in template. Go to the Add an App page, select the Discussion Board template, and provide the new discussion board with a name, as shown in Figure 5.60. When you navigate to the new discussion board, you will see the default view, as shown in Figure 5.61.

FIGURE 5.60   The Discussion Board template in the Add an App page.

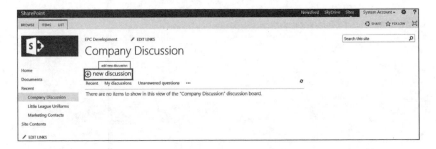

FIGURE 5.61   The default view of a Discussion Board.

Now that a new discussion board has been created, a new discussion can be created. To create a new discussion, click the New Discussion link, as shown in Figure 5.61. Next, provide a subject and body for the discussion and click OK. Creating a new discussion also provides a field to specify whether you are posing a question to the discussion board's audience, as shown in Figure 5.62.

After the discussion is created, we can now take a look how the discussion will look to users, as shown in Figure 5.63, who will be viewing and replying to it. Users will need to have the appropriate permissions to access the list in order to reply to a discussion, and you also can set permissions on specific discussions to limit the users or groups or users who may respond.

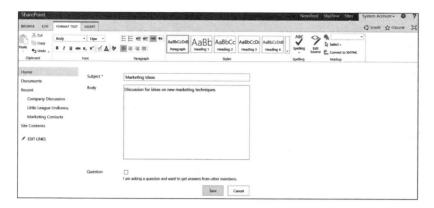

FIGURE 5.62   Showing the creation of a new discussion within a discussion board.

FIGURE 5.63   A new Marketing Ideas discussion topic created within a discussion board.

Creating a New Survey

Surveys are very useful within any organization and are a solution that is not used nearly enough. Surveys can be used to gauge acceptance of a company policy or even provide a vehicle for self-evaluations for team member reviews. SharePoint 2013 has a built-in template to enable users to easily create a survey in a matter of minutes. To start, go to the Add an App page, select the Survey template, and provide a specific name, as shown in Figure 5.64. Now that we have our new survey, we can start adding questions. To start adding questions, select the Add Questions menu option under the survey settings menu.

In the New Question screen, you can enter a question, select the response type, and even provide response options. On this page, you can also select whether a question is required and whether the response must be unique among all previous surveys. Unlike with a normal list, when you add questions to a survey, it allows you to add multiple questions one after the other and, when you are done, just click Finish. After you have added all of your questions, users can now take the survey. Figure 5.65 shows a simple survey that was created as an example for this exercise.

FIGURE 5.64   The Survey template in the Add an App page.

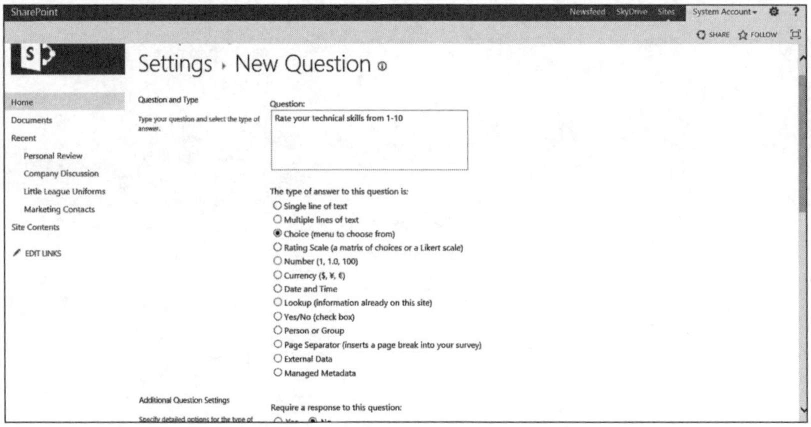

FIGURE 5.65   The New Question page in a SharePoint 2013 list.

The previous sections discussed how to design and create new SharePoint 2013 lists and libraries, as well as modify them to meet your organization's specific business and functional requirements. Lists and libraries are the most used features in SharePoint, and mastering the techniques of how to configure and provision lists to meet your organization's governance policies will ensure that information is stored in a secured manner and is easily retrievable by users to meet their specific needs.

Summary

This chapter covered core strategies for implementing a SharePoint 2013/Office 365 information architecture and underlying strategies and methods by which the data is displayed to users through lists, libraries, and app features.

Chapter 6 goes into granular detail on how best you and your organization can utilize the out-of-the-box web parts (apps) in SharePoint 2013/Office 365, and Chapter 7 digs into best practices system architectural methodologies.

SharePoint 2013/Office 365 is actually very easy to use after it is properly configured, and there are massive capabilities that come right OOTB with this technology. Getting users to understand how easy it is to use without becoming overwhelmed or discouraged is your job, and the faster you can make this happen the better.

CHAPTER 6

Using Out-of-the-Box Web Parts in SharePoint 2013/Office 365

What is a web part? If asked, many of us may be hard-pressed to answer that question because we know what our web parts (apps) do, but we may not know what they are.

You can think of a web part as a small application that runs on a web page. It can be used to display and manipulate data from just about any available source. All web parts have some features in common: a title bar, a configuration menu, toolbars, and so on. Web parts can also be customized. End users can set properties on each individual web part to change the way they display data.

With Office 365/SharePoint Online, there are some additional options that may be available with the specific licensing model that your organization has selected. The following sections cover the core web parts of SharePoint 2013 to ensure that you are able to get the most out of these powerful features.

Here in Chapter 6, we are going to peruse the web parts that come with SharePoint 2013 Office 365's SharePoint Online out-of-the-box (OOTB) by category. Let's start off by discussing the blog-related web parts that come with SharePoint.

Blog Web Parts

The web parts listed in the Blog category of OOTB web parts are all meant for use on a site created with the Blog template.

As shown in Figure 6.1, the Blog Archives web part is a simple tool for displaying older blog posts organized by month.

FIGURE 6.1   The Blog Archives web part as seen in a blog site.

When you click on one of the months in the list, you are taken to a page that displays all the posts for that month, as shown in Figure 6.2.

FIGURE 6.2   The Blog Archives web part takes you to a blog archive page for the selected month.

As depicted in Figure 6.3, you would use the Blog Notifications web part to configure how notifications are sent to you for a specific blog or to access the blog as an RSS feed.

FIGURE 6.3   Use the Blog Notifications web part to configure how notifications are sent or to access an RSS feed for the blog.

The Blog Tools web part, as shown in Figure 6.4, provides links to manage various aspects of the blog site. Using this tool, you can link to pages that will do the following:

▶ Create a blog post

▶ Manage posts

▶ Manage comments

▶ Manage categories

▶ Launch a blogging app (if one is installed)

You can also use this tool to change the post layout. This does not link you to another page; it just changes the layout right then and there.

FIGURE 6.4   Use the Blog Tools web part to link to various configuration pages for your blog site.

Business Data Web Parts

All the web parts in the Business Data category work with external data through one of SharePoint's external service providers, such as the Business Data Connectivity service.

The Business Data Actions web part shows you all the actions that are available for a given external content type. To display the list of actions, you have to configure the web part to look at a specific external content type and then choose the actions you want to display. The tool pane for configuring the web part is shown in Figure 6.5.

The Business Data Connectivity Filter web part enables you to filter the data displayed in other web parts based on the value obtained from an external content type. The configuration screen is displayed in Figure 6.6.

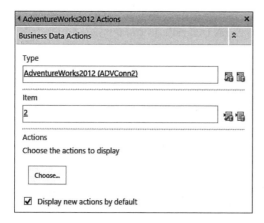

FIGURE 6.5   The Business Data Actions web part displays actions for external content types.

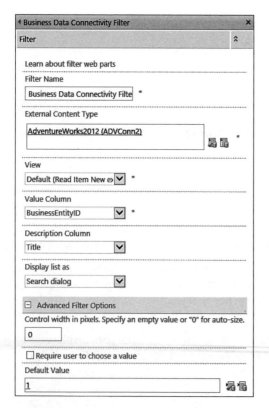

FIGURE 6.6   You can filter the data from other web parts using the Business Data Connectivity Filter web part.

You can use the Business Data Item web part to display a single data item from an external content type. This web part is typically used in conjunction with the Business Data Item Builder web part on a profile page to display a single data item. You will need to configure some settings, such as the external content type, from the tool pane, as shown in Figure 6.7.

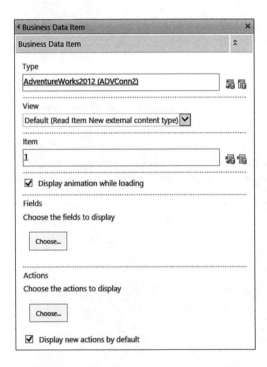

FIGURE 6.7   The Business Data Item web part can be used to display a single item from an external content type.

The Business Data Item Builder web part is a special web part that is only used in conjunction with other web parts, like the Business Data Item web part. Its sole purpose is to retrieve an item ID from the query string parameters in the URL and pass that ID to the connected web part. It has no configuration settings to change and it is displayed on the web page only in edit mode, so end users never see it.

The Business Data List web part is fairly simple in execution. It displays a list of all the items returned by the read list action of an external content type. All you need to do, as shown in Figure 6.8, is configure the external content type and the view from which to display data.

FIGURE 6.8   The Business Data List web part displays a list of all data returned from a given external content type.

Use the Business Data Related List web part when you need to display related items using an association as defined in the BDC model. You can see the configuration options for this web part in Figure 6.9.

FIGURE 6.9   The Business Data Related List web part is used to pull related items using a predefined association.

The Excel Web Access web part enables you to work with an Excel spreadsheet as a web page. All you need to do is upload the spreadsheet to a document library and point the web part to the spreadsheet, as depicted in Figure 6.10.

Both the Indicator Details and the Status List web parts are for backward compatibility with SharePoint 2010 status lists. In SharePoint 2013, we can use KPIs and other BI tools to achieve this level of functionality.

The Visio Web Access web part enables you to interact with Visio diagrams on a web page. You just need to configure the web part to point to an existing Visio drawing. The configuration panel is shown in Figure 6.11.

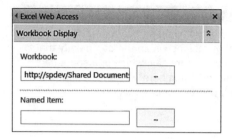

FIGURE 6.10   Use the Excel Web Access web part to interact with a spreadsheet right on the web page.

FIGURE 6.11   Use the Visio Web Access web part to interact with a Visio drawing right on the web page.

Community Web Parts

As a whole, communities are a new concept in SharePoint 2013/Office 365's SharePoint Online. Think of a community site as a discussion board's older brother. You can have several discussions in the site organized by category. When people join the community, they become members and they can contribute to discussions. The more a member contributes, the higher level the member will earn and the more badges he will earn. Community discussions are also moderated by preselected users. The moderators make sure that the discussions stay safe for work.

Organizations that have opted to integrate Yammer into their SharePoint 2013/Office 365's SharePoint Online platform may have additional options, web parts, and related features available to them. Yammer's features and functionality will be covered in greater detail in Chapter 16, "Social Networking and My Site Strategies."

NOTE

SharePoint 2013/Office 365's SharePoint Online Community sites have a default security group that is named "Members," as well as a list that resides within the community that shows a list of the users who have decided to join this community, which is also named "Members." This list within the site is separate from the "Members" security group, within the community's security settings and has no correlation to the other list, but rather just the same naming convention.

There are six web parts that are designed to work specifically on a site that has community functionality turned on (like a site created using the Community Site template).

The About This Community web part is a fairly simplistic web part that is used to display the community description and the date the community was established. You can see this web part in Figure 6.12.

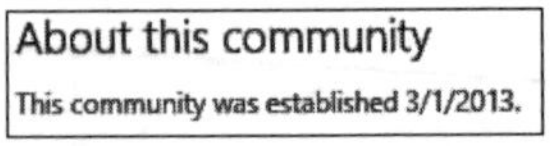

About this community

This community was established 3/1/2013.

FIGURE 6.12   The About This Community web part displays metadata about the community.

The Join web part enables users who are not yet members of a community to request access as a community member. This is not security access, mind you; this access just allows the user to join in discussions, earn badges, and the like. This web part is visible only to users who are not members of the community yet.

The My Membership web part displays all the information you could ever want to know about your standing in the community in question. This web part displays your name, when you joined, badges you've earned, and your reputation score based on your participation in the group. Figure 6.13 shows this web part filled in for a new user.

FIGURE 6.13   The My Membership web part displays all the information you could hope to know about your standing in the community.

The "Community" Tools web part (depicted in Figure 6.14) provides links to manage various aspects of the community site. Using this tool, you can link to pages that will do the following:

▶ Manage discussions

▶ Create categories

▶ Create badges

▶ Assign badges to members

▶ Manage reputation settings

▶ Manage community settings

Community tools

Manage discussions
Create categories
Create badges
Assign badges to members
Reputation settings
Community settings

FIGURE 6.14   The Tools web part gives you quick access to the necessary configuration settings for your community.

The What's Happening web part gives the user a brief overview of activities on the site. It lists the number of current members, discussions, and replies, and it shows who the top contributors are. Figure 6.15 displays the What's Happening web part for a community site.

What's happening

2
members

2
discussions

0
replies

Top contributors

Administrator
▪▪▪▪▪

Joe
⚡ First Timer

FIGURE 6.15   What's Happening gives a brief rundown of the activity on the community site.

Content Rollup Web Parts

Web parts in the Content Rollup category are used to display content from the current site and other sites in various ways. How that data is displayed depends on the web part being used.

To start off, both the Categories and the Sites in Category web parts were deprecated in SharePoint 2010; they are still around in SharePoint 2013 to help those users who still need to migrate from SharePoint 2007.

The Content Query web part enables you to display data from any list on the current site. You can filter and sort the data from any list to display the data the way you want it displayed. The web part has two main sections to configure in the tool pane, the Query and Presentation sections.

There are several pieces of information in the Query section, as shown in Figure 6.16, that you can configure to obtain specific granular data. You can configure which list (or lists) to get data from, what type of data you are looking for, and even what content type to display. You also can filter the data being returned in this section.

FIGURE 6.16   You can configure the Content Query web part to display data from any list on the site using the options in the Query section of the tool pane.

As shown in Figure 6.17, you can configure the web part to filter and sort data the same way you would configure a standard list view.

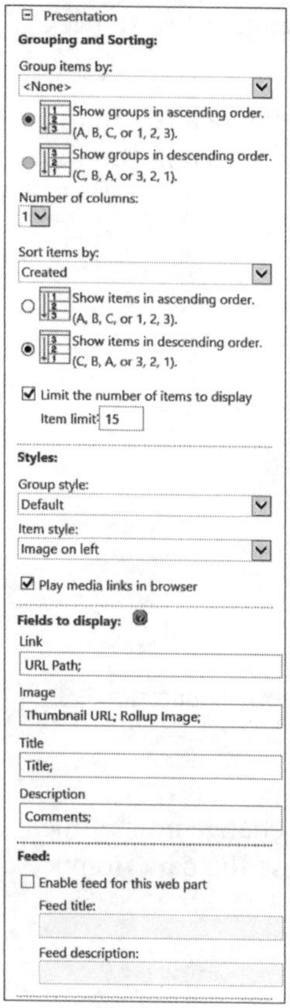

FIGURE 6.17   You can also apply custom filtering and sorting in the Presentation section of the Content Query web part.

If you want to tweak the display even further, you can modify the XSLT files that SharePoint uses to format the data displayed in the web part. Just open SharePoint Designer 2013, expand All Files, open the Style Library, and go into the XSL Style Sheets folder, where you will see several style sheets that work with various web parts.

The ContentQueryMain, Header, and ItemStyle style sheets work in conjunction with the Content Query web part to display data. You can modify these three style sheets to make advanced configurations to the way the web part displays data.

The Content Search web part is brand-new in SharePoint 2013. This web part issues a query to the SharePoint Search service and returns any content that matches the query. This means that your web part always displays the newest content available. You can use the web part right out-of-the-box, but who wants to do that? There is a lot to configure to make the web part behave exactly the way you want.

If you look at the tool pane, you will see four subsections in the Properties sections: Search Criteria, Display Templates, Property Mappings, and Settings. We're going to work backward here and start with Settings.

If you look at the Settings subsection, as shown in Figure 6.18, you will see a few settings that you can change to affect the way results are displayed on the page, such as the starting index of the results to display.

FIGURE 6.18   You can configure a small number of settings to change how results are displayed in the Content Search web part.

In the Property Mappings subsection, shown in Figure 6.19, you can change how properties are mapped in the results. For example, if you want the URL to use the data from a custom URL field, you can set the mapping in this section.

FIGURE 6.19   You can change some of the default property mappings in the results set in the Content Search web part.

Looking to the Display Templates subsection, shown in Figure 6.20, you can change the way the web part behaves overall by selecting a new control template and item template. By changing these, you can have the web part behave like a list, a paged list, or a slide show with various formats.

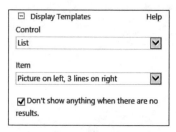

FIGURE 6.20   By changing the settings in the Display Templates subsection, you can change the way the Content Search web part displays data.

Now, on to the fun part of the Content Search web part, the Search Criteria setting. Just looking at the section itself, as shown in Figure 6.21, you probably wouldn't think it looks like much. There is a setting enabling you to limit the number of items displayed and a button. Just wait until you click the button, though.

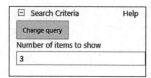

FIGURE 6.21   The Search Criteria subsection doesn't look like much, but wait until you click the button.

Clicking the Change Query button in the Search Criteria subsection brings up a whole separate app (for lack of a better term) in a lightbox that affords you very granular control over the query that the web part issues.

The first page of the Build Your Query app has two modes. The Quick mode gives you basic control over which query to execute. You can select a built-in query from the drop-down list and it lets you restrict the query by app or by tag. The Advanced mode, as shown in Figure 6.22, gives you a great deal more control over the query. Using Advanced mode, you can set keyword and property filters, and even enter the query text directly by hand.

The Refiners page lets you configure what is returned in the result set by changing the properties of the query. If you are familiar with SQL at all, you can think of this page as a WHERE clause. If you were to select Wiki Page from the list of refinements, only wiki pages would be displayed in the results. You can see the Refiners page in Figure 6.23.

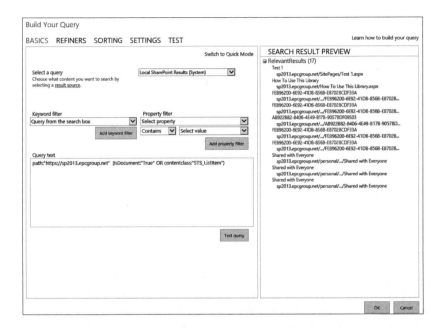

FIGURE 6.22   Using Advanced Mode to build your Search Criteria.

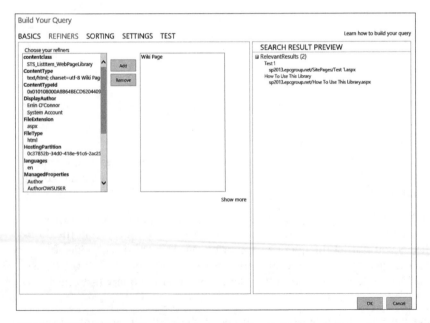

FIGURE 6.23   Think of the Refiners page of the Build Your Query app as a WHERE clause.

The Sorting page of the Build Your Query app shows up only if you set your query to Advanced mode instead of Quick mode. This page, shown in Figure 6.24, enables you to configure how the results are sorted.

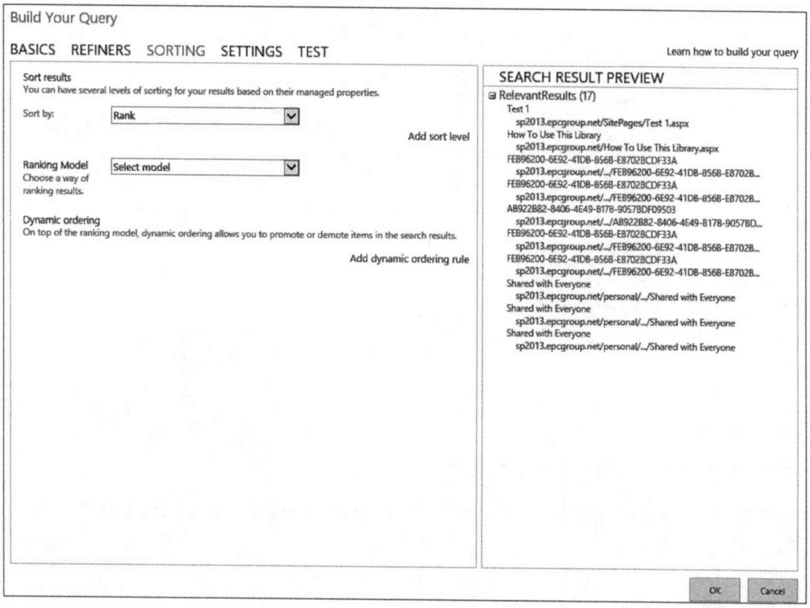

FIGURE 6.24   The Sorting page of the Build Your Query app is an advanced feature that lets you configure various sorting options.

The Settings page, shown in Figure 6.25, enables you to change some basic settings such as whether to use query rules or URL rewriting. The Test page, shown in Figure 6.26, lets you test your query before applying it.

The Project Summary web part is the next web part in this section. This web part displays tasks from an associated list as a timeline with a convenient countdown timer for the next task that is due. To get the timeline to display, you have to specifically add the tasks to the timeline in the task list; without that the web part will simply show a list of upcoming tasks for the logged-in user.

If you just want to see the timeline without the rest of the summary information, you can add the Timeline web part to your page. You can see the Project Summary web part in Figure 6.27.

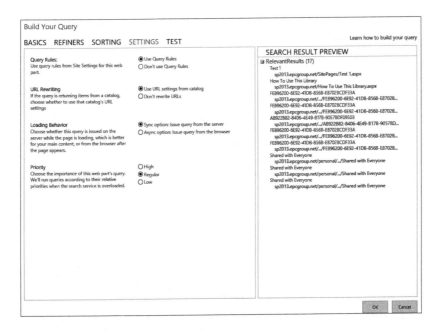

FIGURE 6.25   The Settings page of the Build Your Query app is used to set some basic query configuration options.

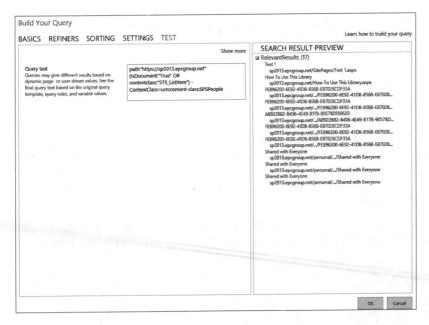

FIGURE 6.26   The Test page of the Build Your Query app lets you test your query before you apply it.

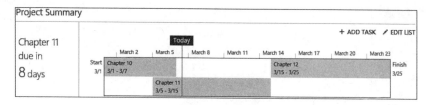

FIGURE 6.27 The Project Summary web part gives a quick overview of tasks from an associated task list.

Next, we move on to the Relevant Documents web part. This document displays a list of documents that the current user has checked out, modified, or created. The web part can be configured to display or not display documents in any of these three states, as shown in Figure 6.28.

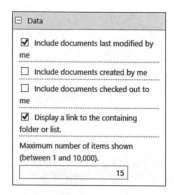

FIGURE 6.28 The Relevant Documents web part shows documents that the user has touched in some way.

As the name implies, the RSS Viewer web part displays an RSS feed on the page. Using the tool pane, shown in Figure 6.29, you can configure the RSS feed URL, the refresh time, and a limit on the number of items to display. If you would like to change the way the data from the feed is displayed, you can edit the XSLT used to transform the data by bringing up the XSL editor.

The Site Aggregator web part is nothing new and it has not changed in SharePoint 2013. The data displayed depends on the URL entered. If you configure this web part with the URL of a SharePoint site, it displays documents from that site. If you configure it with the URL of a non-SharePoint site, it displays the entire site. Think of this web part as a browser inside the page. You can see just how little there is to configure in Figure 6.30.

FIGURE 6.29   The RSS Viewer web part displays an RSS feed on the web page.

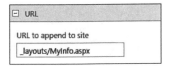

FIGURE 6.30   The Site Aggregator web part displays data from other websites, whether or not the site is a SharePoint site.

The Summary Links web part has also been around for several versions of SharePoint and hasn't really changed. This web part enables a user to add and group links on a web page. You can see the web part in Edit mode in Figure 6.31.

FIGURE 6.31   The Summary Links web part displays links organized into groups.

The Table of Contents web part displays the hierarchy of your site with links to the various sections. As you can see in Figure 6.32, there are quite a few settings you can change to modify how this web part finds and displays the hierarchy of the site.

FIGURE 6.32   You can configure the Table of Contents web part to display the hierarchy of your website any way you like.

The Term Properties web part does exactly what the name implies; it shows the specified property of a term in the managed metadata store. By default, this shows the name of the term associated with the page, but as you can see in Figure 6.33, you can configure the web part to show properties from any term in the store.

Web Services for Remote Portals (or WSRP) is a standard that states how a web service should supply fragments of HTML to callers. The WSRP Viewer web part is designed to display HTML retrieved from WSRP producers. You can see how it is configured in Figure 6.34.

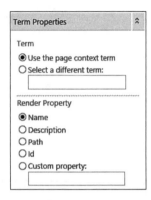

FIGURE 6.33   The Term Properties web part can be configured to show the properties of any term in the metadata store.

FIGURE 6.34   The WSRP Viewer web part can be configured to display HTML content from a trusted WSRP producer.

Last for this category: the XML Viewer web part. This web part takes in XML (either from a URL or entered directly) and transforms the XML using an XSLT style sheet. The resulting HTML is displayed on the page. You can see the configuration options in Figure 6.35.

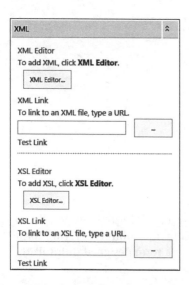

FIGURE 6.35   The XML Viewer web part transforms XML and displays the resulting HTML on the web page.

Document Sets Web Parts

When people are working on a project, they rarely create a single document and leave it at that. Projects in the real world are composed of multiple related items. A document set is a special content type that enables you to manage these multiple related items as a single entity.

There are two web parts in the Document Sets category that can be used in conjunction with a document set: Document Set Contents and Document Set Properties. The Document Set Contents web part shows you what is contained in the document set, and the Document Set Properties web part displays the properties of the document set. These two web parts are normally used together on a document set content page.

Document Sets will be covered in greater detail in Chapter 10, "Enterprise Content Management (ECM), Records Management (RM), and eDiscovery Best Practices."

Filters Web Parts

All the web parts in the Filters section are used to filter data in a connected web part elsewhere on the same page. The only exception here is the Apply Filters Button web part, which enables a user to manually enter and then apply a filter. The following filters are available:

▶ Choice Filter

▶ Current User Filter

▶ Date Filter

▶ Page Field Filter

▶ Query String (URL) Filter

▶ SharePoint List Filter

▶ SQL Server Analysis Services Filter

▶ Text Filter

Forms Web Parts

Both of the web parts in this category enable you to display a form for the user to fill out and submit. The HTML Form web part enables a user to fill in and submit an HTML form, and the InfoPath Form web part enables a user to work with a form designed in InfoPath.

Media and Content Web Parts

The web parts in the Media and Content category enable the user to work with media such as images and sound recordings, as well as other mundane content such as scripts and pages.

The first web part in this category is the Content Editor web part. This is a WYSIWIG ("what you see is what you get") HTML editor that enables users to enter whatever content they would like and format it in whatever way they please. Users can either edit the web part directly or, as shown in Figure 6.36, display HTML that is stored in a web page elsewhere on the site.

FIGURE 6.36   The Content Editor web part enables a user to add fully formatted HTML content to a page.

In SharePoint 2010, many administrators used this editor to sneak some JavaScript onto the page, but that is no longer necessary because there is a new web part designed for that purpose which is the Script Editor web part.

The Get Started with Your Site web part is one of the first things you see on a new website. There are several icons with links to various pages that will help a new user start building out her site. You can see the web part in Figure 6.37.

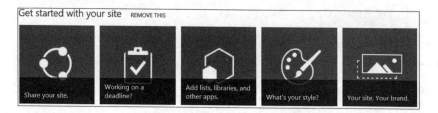

FIGURE 6.37   The Get Started with Your Site web part displays a series of icons with links to pages that are helpful to new users.

There are two Viewer web parts in this category: the Image Viewer web part and the Page Viewer web part. Each does just what its respective name implies. The Image Viewer web part displays an image on the page, and the Page Viewer web part displays another web page in an IFrame.

The Media web part also qualifies as a Viewer web part, but it is a bit more complex than the Image Viewer or Page Viewer web parts. This web part enables you to display a video or play an audio file on a web page. Not only that, but it gives the user the necessary controls to play, pause, fast forward, and so on. You can see the Media web part in Figure 6.38.

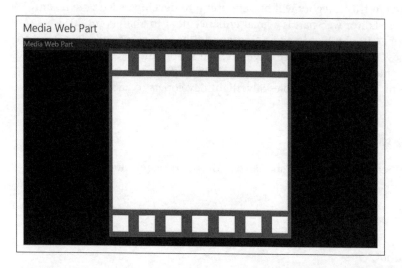

FIGURE 6.38   The Media web part enables you to display media, like a video, on a web page.

The next web part is the Picture Library Slideshow web part. As the name suggests, with this web part, you can display a series of images from a picture library as a slide show. You can see all the configuration options in Figure 6.39.

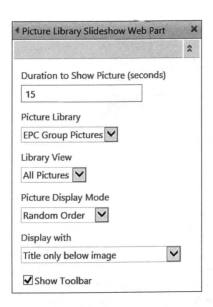

FIGURE 6.39   The Picture Library Slideshow web part displays a slideshow on your web page.

The last two web parts in this category will be very useful to developers who are reading this chapter. The Script Editor web part is a great enhancement in SharePoint 2013, because in SharePoint 2010 you had to add a Content Editor web part to add JavaScript to your SharePoint pages. This is not the case anymore; the Script Editor web part is designed for the sole purpose of adding script to your pages. The Silverlight web part is also still available in SharePoint 2013, which enables Silverlight developers to add your apps to a page.

Search Web Parts

The web parts in the Search category are specialized for use in Search sites. There are several in this category:

- ▶ Refinement
- ▶ Search Box
- ▶ Search Navigation
- ▶ Search Results
- ▶ Taxonomy Refinement Panel

Search-Driven Content Web Parts

The web parts in this category all serve a common purpose: They display data from the search index. You will have to have search up and running and have an index built to use them. There are several to work with:

▶ Catalog-Item Reuse

▶ Items Matching a Tag

▶ Pages

▶ Pictures

▶ Popular Items

▶ Recently Changed Items

▶ Recommended Items

▶ Videos

▶ Web Pages

▶ Wiki Pages

The Search-related web parts will be covered in greater detail in Chapter 14, "Search, Web Content Management, Branding, and Navigational Strategies."

Social Collaboration Web Parts

The Social Collaboration category contains web parts that help users get in touch with one another. They are primarily for use on a My Site. They are as shown here:

▶ Contact Details

▶ Note Board

▶ Organization Browser

▶ Site Feed

▶ Site Users

▶ Tag Cloud

▶ User Tasks

The Social Collaboration-related web parts will be covered in greater detail in Chapter 16.

Summary

In this chapter, we reviewed a high-level overview of all the web parts that come out of the box with SharePoint 2013/Office 365's SharePoint Online. We discussed each of the major categories and discussed many of the web parts contained therein. Many of these web parts are discussed throughout additional chapters in this book as specific business and functional scenarios are discussed and to ensure SharePoint sites are kept up-to-date and relevant.

In Chapter 7, "Implementing a SharePoint 2013 System Architecture with Future Hybrid Scalability in Mind," we will dig into SharePoint 2013's system architecture, and we will take a look at what your organization must take into consideration with your long-term roadmap and the ever-changing hybrid cloud and Microsoft Cloud OS strategy.

CHAPTER 7

Implementing a SharePoint 2013 System Architecture with Future Hybrid Scalability in Mind

Understanding On-Premises, Cloud, and Hybrid Environments in SharePoint 2013

The on-premises versus cloud environment debate about SharePoint started several years ago. That debate became much more heated when Jared Spataro, Director of SharePoint at Microsoft, announced during a conference that SharePoint 2013 was being developed using a "Cloud First" strategy and that Office 365 customers could expect to have access to the benefits of the new release sooner than on-premises deployments.

Microsoft has recently reiterated this stance at the Microsoft SharePoint Conference 2014, and my personal opinion is that this Cloud First announcement has Microsoft testing the waters to see how many organizations will opt to dive right into Office 365 while also leaving the door open so to not alienate SharePoint's long-term "bread and butter" on-premises deployment base, which has driven SharePoint to be the fastest-growing non-Windows product in Microsoft history. Around the same time, Microsoft began referencing on-premises SharePoint deployments as the "private cloud" and off-premises environments as the "public cloud" or a variance of an external-based "cloud." You could make the argument that the reference to SharePoint 2013 being developed using a Cloud First strategy could fit in either the private or the public cloud.

In this chapter, we will discuss deploying SharePoint 2013 on-premises in a private cloud, as well as the SharePoint Online/Office 365 public cloud, as well as the mixture of both public and private clouds into a "hybrid cloud" deployment scenario, as depicted in Figure 7.1.

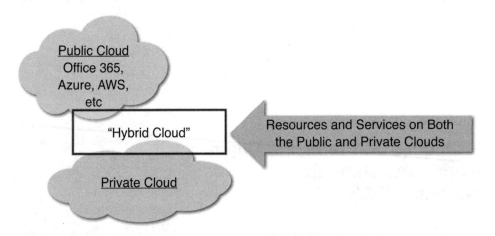

FIGURE 7.1   The hybrid cloud: A mixture of both on-premises and public cloud resources used by an organization.

What Is a SharePoint "Private Cloud"?

To first describe and baseline a private cloud deployment, the following items will typically be considered and implemented:

▶ Hosting SharePoint as infrastructure for a specific workload or combination of workloads such as these:

  ▶ Application platform for line-of-business (LOB) application

  ▶ Business intelligence implementations

  ▶ Collaboration, community, and/or project sites

  ▶ Internet/intranet publishing portal

  ▶ Personal sites

  ▶ Enterprise search

▶ SharePoint private clouds have the following features:

  ▶ Scalable, flexible architectures

  ▶ Ability to host many "customers" or tenants

  ▶ Repeatable, predictable automated deployment and provisioning

  ▶ Upgrade, failover, and patching resiliency

NOTE

Many of these items can also be achieved in a hybrid cloud environment, which is what most of the clients I have engaged with since SharePoint 2013's release are planning for in their SharePoint roadmap.

There are several factors that influence an organization's decision regarding which architecture (that is, on-premises private cloud, public cloud, or hybrid cloud) they are going to design and implement for their short-term and long-term SharePoint roadmap needs, such as these:

▶ The overall size of the organization and user base

▶ Security issues

▶ Legal and compliance issues

▶ Any project or deployment time constraints

▶ Complexity of customers' current environment

▶ Physical locations

▶ Current identity infrastructure

▶ Current IT infrastructure model and future IT roadmap

▶ Network bandwidth issues

▶ Software/hardware issues

▶ Any vendor service level agreement (SLA)

▶ High-availability/backup issues

▶ Internal resource issues and related training

▶ Support alignment

▶ Service reporting

▶ Standards adoption and management

▶ Development alignment

▶ Infrastructure alignment

▶ Development platform management

▶ Governance

▶ User issues

▶ Management and tools

▶ Development standards creation

▶ Information architecture and search

▶ Business requirements

▶ Infrastructure guidance

When you are taking complex environments into consideration, there are also items such as these:

▶ Multitenancy (Office 365 issues when a user goes outside of IT to create a new "environment")

▶ Multiple farms

▶ Security (FBA, SAML claims, extranets)

▶ Global clients with PHI, PII, Safe Harbor, intellectual property, EU pushback, or NSA concerns due to recent news

It is key to also look at your current operations and how well your organization will be able to adapt to change. There are existing maintenance windows that perform key backup and business continuity actions as well as LOB data connectivity updates and code promotion policies that must be considered, as shown in Figure 7.2.

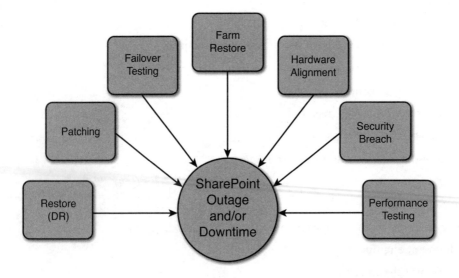

FIGURE 7.2   Identify your current "maintenance window" type of requirements and ensure that those are considered during your infrastructure planning and internal advisory discussions.

Storage Design

In Chapter 5, "Implementing a Best Practices SharePoint 2013/Office 365 Information Architecture," we discussed SharePoint site storage and underlying data considerations from the information architecture (IA) perspective. In this chapter, we are looking at storage in terms of the actual system architecture design perspective. The following initial items should start this conversation:

▶ How has storage been allocated for this effort or what may be available for this initiative?

▶ What are the actual costs of storage and/or purchasing or procuring in various-size allocations?

▶ Will you ever need to store more than 4TB? *Note:* In most cases, you should not have to surpass this limit in your phase 1 roadmap planning.

▶ How are content databases arranged in terms of the information architecture and site collection design?

The storage design and requirements will continue to be clearer to you and the team as some additional questions are asked and the technical architecture design process that's next described begins.

Technical Architecture Design Process

As you consider the questions asked in the previous sections, also consider the following list of technical architecture design process points. This is a proven check list of items that should be followed:

▶ Begin with one or more of the following:

  ▶ Business requirements of the organization

  ▶ Functional requirements of the organization

  ▶ User experience and devices from which SharePoint 2013/Office 365 will be accessed

  ▶ Logical design

  ▶ Boundaries of SharePoint 2013/Office 365

  ▶ Information architecture design

  ▶ Technical architecture

▶ Define, iterate, and revise

▶ Outcome

  ▶ Server counts

  ▶ Database design

  ▶ Server roles

▶ Storage requirements

▶ Sites/Portal/etc. design

Figure 7.3 illustrates a decision-tree process that should be followed during this exercise.

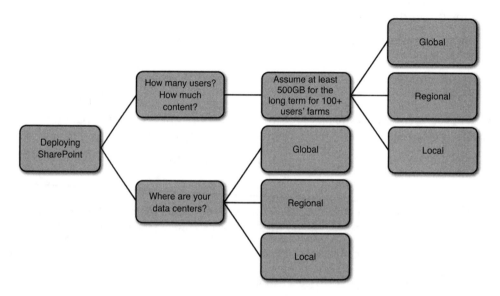

FIGURE 7.3   The technical architecture design decision process.

Ensure That Your Design Starts with What You Currently Know

Ensure that this process first takes into consideration the items that have already been uncovered and are known to the project team. These items also take into consideration any roadblocks or lessons learned that you may have gained from previous IT initiatives within your organization. The following is a list of items you should consider that you may already have a good deal of insight into:

▶ Constraints

   ▶ Cost

   ▶ Data center utilization goals

   ▶ Evolving business needs

▶ Risks

   ▶ "Undersizing"

   ▶ "Oversizing"

   ▶ Unknown limits and workload patterns

   ▶ Legal and compliance requirements

Reviewing Other Cloud Successes and the History Behind Recent Cloud Pushes and Mandates

The methodologies in this chapter regarding the private versus public cloud and the overall hybrid approach considerations have been developed based on approximately 50-plus SharePoint 2013 hybrid projects as well as seeing firsthand how cloud computing technology has evolved over the past five to six years. Several years ago, EPC Group was engaged with NASA in their enterprise SharePoint efforts, and I had the opportunity to work closely with then NASA CIO Chris Kemp, who led an extremely successful effort on the NASA Ames "Nebula Cloud Computing Pilot," which he spearheaded. The goal of the Nebula Cloud Computing Pilot project was to leverage the web as a platform and take the lead in open, transparent, and participatory space exploration and government. Kemp's Cloud efforts at NASA were simply a resounding success.

I worked with Mr. Kemp and NASA for several months and received some great insights into his vision of the cloud and the success that NASA was experiencing.

These conversations took place between the completely separate SharePoint efforts that the EPC Group team and I were spearheading at NASA in planning the future governance and architectural strategy for SharePoint for NASA. Seeing one of the world's largest cloud efforts at that time while working on a specific separate SharePoint initiative was an eye-opener for me as to how different underlying architectural platforms and systems can live in parallel to meet different functions and requirements.

During the SharePoint effort at NASA, I traveled with Mr. Kemp, whose background also included beingone of the founders of the popular Classmates.com, to many of NASA's major centers and facilities on several road trips or "mini-SharePoint roadshows" to help the organization understand how important governance is and the underlying architecture that should be considered.

The insights I gained have been extremely valuable over the past few years as the cloud has grown in being able to provide some very real-world examples of what should be planned for and considered for both the near and long term.

A short time after working with NASA's CIO Chris Kemp and seeing NASA's cloud effort firsthand, I was able to meet with Vivek Kundra, the first-ever CIO of the United States who was a presidential appointee by President Barack Obama. Mr. Kemp had actually been working with Mr. Kundra at NASA's Ames Research Center when Kundra launched Apps.gov, which enables federal agencies to subscribe to cloud IT services.

Mr. Kundra saw the potential in leveraging cloud services as an alternative to physical hardware in an effort to reduce costs and the overall federal government's infrastructure management. During his tenure as the CIO of the United States, Kundra published the "25 Point Implementation Plan to Reform Federal Information Technology Management," which included the original Cloud First push for the government to achieve IT efficiently. As part of this plan, Cloud First required each government agency to identify three cloud initiatives.

I think that it is important to take some external factors into consideration when reviewing certain technology pushes or major waves and especially those that come with a presidential mandate. At that time, in late 2010, the U.S. Government was recovering from the financial crisis and many of the lending and banking issues that came out of that in which cost cutting and reducing the bottom line were extremely critical. I am in no way saying that this decision about implementing an effort to cut costs and reduce the bottom line is not right or something that should not have been pursued.

As a business owner myself, I am always looking at the bottom line and ensuring that there are not areas where budget is being spent that are not providing any ROI or benefits to our clients and overall organizational mission and strategy. It would be irresponsible or wasteful for anyone to not look at the bottom line or to simply allow available budget and dollars to be spent where they are not needed. Rather, the dollars should be put to use to better an organization or effort in which they are involved.

The U.S. General Services Administration (GSA) has since closed Apps.gov and phased it out to a "storefront" that the GSA set up for government agencies to research and purchase cloud offerings and services. However, the GSA launched a new site on gsa.gov that provides government agencies help in complying with the cloud mandates and provides templates to IT owners around Inventory, Application Mapping, Migration Planning, and Migration execution strategies, as well as some other core elements that must be followed when cloud-based IT services are being procured within the Federal Government.

Recent SharePoint 2013 Cloud Initiatives

Since the SharePoint 2013 release, I have engaged, along with my with senior architecture colleagues at EPC Group, with organizations that are very interested in moving to the cloud, as well as those that currently feel they do not see their organization moving to the cloud for at least the next two or three years or until they feel it gets a little more mature. There are also organizations we have worked closely with that do not ever see moving to the cloud and that feel there is too much risk involved with their intellectual property and in handing off the keys to the underlying IT castle to an outside provider.

In conjunction with the feedback received from clients or potential clients in technical deep-dive meetings and roadmap development sessions from more than 30 organizations with at least 1,000 or more users, I launched a "Private, Public, and Hybrid" research initiative at EPC Group. This research initiative was launched to develop a mechanism and measurable framework to provide accurate and updated recommendations regarding the cloud and hybrid cloud computing to our clients as their "trusted advisor" without any influence from either service providers or mass-marketing campaigns that have flooded this technology space.

This internal research initiative was the largest ever conducted at EPC Group in our 15-year history. It included several visits to Microsoft, as well as other leading cloud provider data centers such as Amazon (AWS), to address a list of concerns that EPC Group had compiled both internally and from our clients. This effort allowed me to ask questions first-hand of the operations and management teams managing the vast amount of hardware, technology, and data that resided in these centers.

This research initiative led to some very lengthy whiteboarding sessions and technical deep dives into areas such as providers' service level agreements (SLAs) and standard operating procedures for specific scenarios. This was extremely insightful for me while at the same time a bit sobering as I saw how quickly new technologies in cloud computing are coming to market and being tested.

Based on this research initiative, I formally developed the "SharePoint 2013 P.P.H. (Private, Public, and Hybrid) Decision Framework" to assist organizations in planning their private, public, or hybrid cloud in an unbiased manner while also presenting related pros and cons as well as the types of risks associated. This strategy and thought process is followed in relation to cloud decision points in this chapter. One of the key areas you must focus on in reviewing cloud architecture options involves risk mitigation and gauging the impact and consequences of specific risks.

One of the major goals in developing this framework was to ask the tough "what if" questions and throw out specific scenarios on how a cloud provider's procedures cover them or mitigate and resolve the issues. For us to conduct this research and framework development initiative and dig into sometimes sensitive "standard operating procedures" or configurations, the providers we worked with understandably required us to consent to nondisclosure agreements to protect their intellectual property and any infrastructure configurations and nonpublished operating procedures.

Digging In and Covering SharePoint-Specific Topics

There are specific requirements and prerequisites as well as predictable and repeatable results that must be established before a consulting firm should ever throw out the term "best practice," and I believe that this has been accomplished in the new framework previously described that's meant to "demystify" the cloud.

A common misconception is that IT or external resources have a vested interest in advising an organization to implement SharePoint 2013 on-premises rather than investigating the additional options involved in a possible cloud-based or hybrid-based environment.

There is no getting around the fact that a successful SharePoint implementation is driven by key principles and best practices, and this applies regardless of where the actual deployment is applied. Over the past few years, I have found that there are, in many cases, more technical requirements requiring the senior or expert level (SME) external resources of an organization to properly implement a secured cloud environment housing the data of an enterprise SharePoint 2013 deployment.

It is critical that these very important decisions regarding SharePoint's architecture and your longer-term roadmap be made based on requirements and the corresponding capability of the specific on-premises, cloud, or hybrid offering to meet those requirements, because your organization's critical systems as well as the intellectual property at the very core of a company's existence are at stake.

I do think that some cloud providers are prematurely pushing or possibly overmarketing the jump into a cloud that is really not enterprise ready when many questions remain improperly addressed regarding legal, regulatory, data spillage, data breach, and a related list of concerns that are discussed later in the chapter. Also—and I should preface the following statement with complete and full disclosure that I am neither a Democrat nor Republican—I do believe that the Obama Administration was very premature in their edict for all U.S. Government agencies' projects to follow a Cloud First policy. There have been immense struggles that have been experienced because of the enterprise content management (ECM)/record management (RM) initiatives, as well as other canceled SharePoint and technology initiatives that were previously scheduled to move forward within an existing on-premises virtualized environment. In many cases, IT management was weary and unsure of the operational and governing policies or rules they had to follow in deploying possibly sensitive or secured content to a cloud outside their firewall and within their direct reach of control.

As with any new major architectural or computing innovation that comes to market, there is going to be a marketing "hype cycle" that will occur, and in reading the detailed estimates put out by major IT analysts, their firms, and IT publications across the globe, organizations were obviously providing initial feedback and communications in regard to their near-term and aggressive interest in the cloud. I believe there was also a much different "wildcard" factor involved in the initial aggressive analyst reports of companies pushing toward the cloud and then the prevailing and much lower number of actual cloud migrations that had been completed.

I believe that the wildcard that may have skewed the initial reports was driven in part by organizational leadership's requirements to cut costs and the many mentions of these Cloud First recommendations by major software companies and state and government agencies. The other factor, I think, that caused many companies to put a hold on their cloud migration plans was some of these regulatory, intellectual property, and security-related concerns that realized and warranted more research before the actual migration effort could be authorized.

During several SharePoint 2013 initiatives I have been involved in, the security and privacy laws of European countries (EU) as well as PHI, PII, and HIPAA, as shown in Figure 7.4, have been identified as a major milestone or "risk" item on many SharePoint 2013 project plans. There must be an in-depth analysis of your data security requirements to determine whether any departments, business units, or even sister companies need to take laws and mandates such as Safe Harbor, FISMA and HIPAA into consideration.

FIGURE 7.4   There are many different laws and international agreements covering data and related information security that your organization may need to take into consideration.

Figure 7.5 details the locations of many of Microsoft's data centers for additional insight into planning any globally dispersed SharePoint environments and related location-based procurement needs.

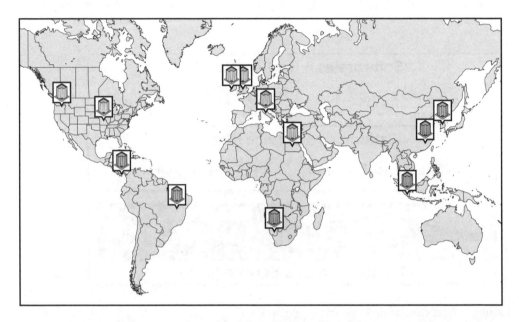

FIGURE 7.5   An overview of Microsoft's current global footprint supporting their cloud offerings.

Three Major Types of Cloud Services

It is important to understand the different options available for hosting, as well as the underlying options provided. There are currently three common offerings of the cloud:

▶ **SaaS**—*Software as a service* involves software such as Office 365. Software as a service has been a very popular on-demand software delivery mechanism typically delivered via web browser and other optional plug-ins.

▶ **PaaS**—*Platform as a service* encompasses all the development, service hosting, and service management environments needed to operate an application that uses on-demand compute and storage capacity and network bandwidth. These PaaS offerings also provide for the database and related services to be managed by the provider. Microsoft Azure and SQL Azure are great examples of a PaaS offering.

▶ **IaaS**—*Infrastructure as a service* provides raw computer and storage capacity with management tools available to be controlled by the client. Microsoft's System Center suite, which is run on the Hyper-V Cloud server environment within a Microsoft data center, is a perfect example of IaaS. Certain configurations of Microsoft Azure are also sometimes referred to as IaaS.

The SaaS model has been popular for many years and is typically straightforward or well understood. The PaaS and IaaS offerings have more recently started to compete with each other in some areas based on the options selected from the provider. Figure 7.6 details the three major offerings gives examples of some popular industry solutions within each offering.

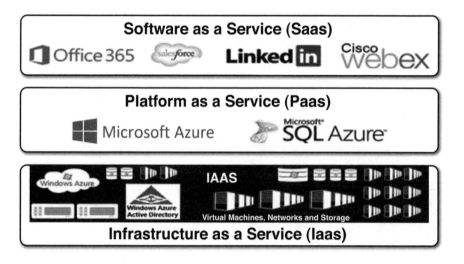

FIGURE 7.6   Examples of SaaS, PaaS, and IaaS.

There are eight key IaaS high-level principles:

▶ Perception of infinite capacity

▶ Perception of continuous availability

▶ Drive predictability

▶ Take a service provider's approach to delivering infrastructure

▶ Resiliency over redundancy mind-set

▶ Minimize human involvement

▶ Optimize resource usage

▶ Incentivize desired resource consumption behavior

Reviewing Microsoft Azure

Microsoft Azure's infrastructure as a service (IaaS) introduces new functionality that allows full control and management of virtual machines along with an extensive virtual networking offering and enables the use of almost any language, framework, or tool to build applications. Microsoft Azure features and services are exposed using open REST protocols, and the Microsoft Azure client libraries are available for the multiple programming languages that are released under an open-source license.

Microsoft Azure is stated to deliver a 99.95% monthly service level agreement and enables organizations to build and run highly available applications without focusing on the infrastructure. Microsoft Azure provides for automatic OS and related service patching, as well as built-in network load balancing and resiliency to hardware failure.

Microsoft Azure model follows the "pay only for the resources your application uses" model that is becoming popular for many cloud providers and is available in multiple data centers around the world. With Microsoft Azure's distributed caching and Content Delivery Network (CDN) services, you can reduce latency and deliver greater application performance anywhere in the world.

Microsoft Azure's flexible cloud platform enables you to host and scale out your application code within compute roles while storing the code in the relational SQL databases, NoSQL table stores, and unstructured blob stores. You also have the option to use Hadoop and business intelligence services to data-mine while also having additional messaging capabilities to enable scalable distributed applications as well as to deliver hybrid solutions, as shown in Figure 7.7, that run across a cloud and on-premises enterprise environment.

FIGURE 7.7   Microsoft's approach to Microsoft Azure hybrid cloud.

Windows Azure provides for scalability and has a fully automated self-service platform and advanced interface, as shown in Figure 7.8, that enables you to provision resources quickly and elastically grow or shrink your resource usage based on your organization's needs.

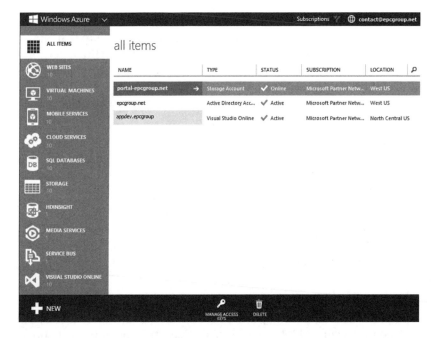

FIGURE 7.8   Microsoft Azure's Management Portal.

TIP

Hadoop, which derives from the Apache Hadoop project, is a software library framework that allows for the distributed processing of large data sets across clusters of computers using simple programming models.

Hadoop is designed to scale up from single servers to thousands of machines, each offering local computation and storage, which has been growing in popularity within cloud computing. Hadoop does not primarily rely on hardware to deliver high-availability, but rather the Hadoop library itself is designed to detect and handle failures at the application layer to deliver a highly available service on top of a cluster of computers.

TIP

Microsoft Azure Content Delivery Network (CDN) is designed to deliver high-bandwidth content by caching blobs and static content.

TIP

Microsoft offers various trials and "test-drive" options for you to begin testing Microsoft Azure and the various components. These can be accessed at the following link: http://azure.Microsoft.com/en-us/

I would recommend setting up a trial environment for yourself and any key technical project members for your SharePoint 2013 initiative so that you understand what is available to you in future phases in case Microsoft Azure's offerings could meet future business or technical requirements.

Reviewing Amazon Web Services

Amazon Web Services (AWS) provides infrastructure services that allow customers to run Microsoft Windows Server applications and provides preconfigured virtual machines (VMs). AWS and Microsoft Azure are very competitive and have a lot of similar offerings around the ability to stand up preconfigured VMs. AWS can host custom .NET applications as well as enterprise deployments of Microsoft Exchange Server, SQL Server, and SharePoint Server 2013.

AWS also provides Microsoft License Mobility through Software Assurance, which allows Microsoft customers to use their own Microsoft Server licensing on AWS without additional licensing fees.

> **NOTE**
>
> This BYOL (bring your own license) type of offering is also available in Microsoft Azure, but AWS was smart to also clear this type of offering on their platform to further the competition with Microsoft Azure.

> **TIP**
>
> Amazon Web Services also offers various trials and test-drive options for you to begin testing and understanding the available platforms that may best fit your organization. Additional information regarding AWS services and trial information can be found at the following link: http://aws.amazon.com/
>
> AWS, like Microsoft, offers an app store–like platform called Amazon Marketplace that can be found at the following link: https://aws.amazon.com/marketplace

What Are Your Organization's Compliance Policies?

Protection of your organization's intellectual property, as well as the ability to adhere to regulations and laws such as PHI, PII, FISMA, and HIPAA, must be a top requirement and an inherent capability of any architecture consideration for SharePoint 2013.

As a baseline, how do you currently protect sensitive and very important data that exists in your enterprise?

It is also important when developing compliance policies to actively look for ways to reduce any exposure risks that may exist.

Depending on the size of your organization, you may have designated resources for litigation, eDiscovery, and maintaining your current "compliance status." Small to mid-size businesses, though, will more than likely have resources that wear "many different hats," and SharePoint Server 2013 will provide you with many industry-leading capabilities to manage compliance. It is also important to ask questions of your organization such as these:

▶ How does your organization quickly find information?

▶ How does your organization ensure policy consistency?

▶ How does your organization scale the compliance solution to the enterprise?

▶ What is the current strategy on cost control and information management or compliance?

Instances of Data Breaches and Implementing Proactive Security Policies

Over the past few years, there have been some very high-profile instances of data breaches in environments of all types. The NSA IT administrator Edward Snowden, who accessed and shared classified NSA data, has been the most widely publicized case. There has been an added push to mitigate future data breaches and examine how these types of incidents actually occurred.

Do you, or does the assigned person within your organization, have reporting capabilities regarding user access and security levels? What about the ability to view "approved" security levels or have an available feature that sends out an alert if an unapproved security level is applied to an individual? Being more vigilant about securing your organization's data should be one of the leading drivers of your SharePoint and overall IT roadmap because many organizations have become complacent in this area.

In many cases, an organization's records "retention schedule" would provide you insights into what content is sensitive, proprietary, or regulated and how can it be identified. The issue here is that 30% to 40% of organizations throughout the globe do not have an "approved retention schedule" or are in the process of developing one. I have personally been involved in working with organizations' legal and compliance departments in the development of their retention schedule, and it is not an easy or sexy task to accomplish.

In many cases, it comes down to the content owner or even power users who understand what type of content exists within their "area" or "department." I have recently been involved in several SharePoint 2007 and SharePoint 2010 to SharePoint 2013 upgrades/ migrations in which governance was not previously enforced and content sprawl within document libraries in multiple, and in many cases very similar, sites exists.

Because of some of these more highly publicized cases of data breaches and extremely sensitive information being exposed, six of the world's top government security agencies, as detailed in Figure 7.9, have published their own recommendations regarding "Cloud Security Recommendations." These are designed to assist organizations by providing "lessons learned" around some of the growing threats that they have been addressing.

FIGURE 7.9   Overview of six of the world's top government security agencies that have developed cloud security-related recommendations.

Understanding the Implications of International Law and Your Organization's Data

For the past six or seven years, there has been a growing and very public backlash against laws in the U.S. and those laws that govern U.S.-based data centers, such as the Patriot Act. The U.S. is not alone; there are similar laws in numerous countries that have been much less publicized. When you are implementing a global SharePoint 2013 implementation in which data centers around the world are in scope, it is very important to understand how this may affect your deployment.

For many years, countries such as Germany and others in the EU have enacted very strict privacy laws that ban information from being published or readily available not only in public information and search platforms but in private and company-owned systems as well. SharePoint's My Site functionality is a good example here; EPC Group has had to develop and apply features to some of our clients in these areas that block some personal fields from "People Search," such as a person's manager, his home or cell numbers, and many variations of this.

Many large Fortune 1000 U.S. organizations have a stance around being English-only and have successfully been able to avoid some of these region-specific implications. However, this issue is heating up again and becoming an area of concern that should be discussed within your organization's IT departments as well as legal and compliance to ensure that you're following certain protocols and county-specific laws because there can be daily fines levied against companies as well as temporary "freezes" placed on data or system access.

Microsoft has been proactive regarding many regulatory issues, both in the United States and in the EU, in obtaining certifications and approvals in areas such as the EU Safe Harbor Certification, HIPAA, FERPA, SAS 70, and ISO 27001, to name a few. This will undoubtedly grow or continue to be updated, so it is very important that you or a designated individual within your organization monitor updates from Microsoft as well as other Cloud providers should you have global offices that may be affected and governed by specific laws.

7

I remember vividly when I received a phone call from IT and business stakeholders one evening from a client of EPC Group that had regional offices in a relatively small country in Africa. Because of recent laws there, as well as the regime change that had recently taken effect in that country, the government had seized the client's servers and temporarily shut down all Internet access and their ability to access their data.

This client is a household name in the oil and gas field throughout many areas of the world, but this country's government was not impressed and did not care about even the day-to-day drilling and oil production taking place. Production ground to a screeching halt. The total cost of this shutdown was estimated by this client on day two of this incident to be in the ballpark of $6 million per day, and they had to get this issue resolved one way or another.

In a nutshell, this country had recently passed a law stating that all data that is accessed by a computer system in their country in relation to oil well data had to actually reside or be stored within the country's borders. The incident started when a local government official performed an audit on this company in performing a set of random searches in SharePoint 2007 that returned results about some oil well specifications that were nearby but were stored in a SharePoint department/team site in London.

This issue, which was ultimately resolved within seven days, is obviously unique and bordering on the bizarre, but I remember it vividly because I do not think I slept for more than five hours that entire week. It is pretty clear that a "data loss" type of issue here, with a $6 million-a-day price tag and severe impact on the business, had to be resolved "yesterday." There have been a handful of other incidents like this that I have personally seen or been engaged by a client to assist in resolving, and this has led to some of my more cautious or sometimes doomsday-like questions at times during road mapping and architectural design sessions for some of EPC Group's global clients.

Within the overall architectural roadmap planning, you must have contingency plans regarding data protection, compliance, data loss, and data spillage for your organization's environments. When you engage in a deployment initiative to the cloud where sensitive data exists, you may not have the 24/7 access to immediately act on an issue, so investigating the cloud providers' SLAs and policies on these types of issues must be discussed, documented, and fully disclosed.

I have had some issues with cloud-provider representatives not knowing the answers to these questions, which in some cases is understandable due to the possible role they have at the provider, but any cloud provider you select should be able to quickly direct you to contacts that handle these issues as well as to very granular documentation regarding how these issues are dealt with and what you can expect from them.

It has been frustrating to view some of the SLAs and granular information provided by some providers who give sometimes vague responses, and EPC Group has stepped in based on our research and related hybrid cloud advisor strategies to help hold these providers accountable. Under no circumstances should you ever procure a cloud service and begin a public or hybrid cloud initiative where you do not have an exit strategy available and put yourself in a cloud vendor lock-in scenario. You must have the option available, should you want to move your data back on-premise or even to another provider, to perform a "reverse migration" or new migration to your desired provider.

These types of topics will continue to mature over time, and cloud providers will eventually all have representatives or technical teams up to speed on these granular issues. However, I am concerned about "data spillage" issues within cloud providers that can have extremely sensitive data be mistakenly made available to users or other even search engines and the nightly "content source crawl" results where this data must be identified, cleansed, and the issue solved right away.

I have a concern about companies that are not at all at fault but somehow their SharePoint or Office 365 search results, or even custom .NET application running on an IBM cloud, Azure or AWS platform, start returning results with content you have never seen before and you have no idea of its data source. There are cases where, due to this type of data spillage, your environment could be taken down temporarily by the provider or even a government agency who has been made aware of this sensitive data breach.

TIP

It is key to consider the possible differences in your organization's current disaster-recovery or business-continuity plan versus a cloud-based disaster recovery (DR) plan. The following is a high-level initial list of elements that must be taken into consideration in a cloud-based DR plan:

▶ Environment and Security Governance of the cloud provider

▶ SharePoint Disaster Recovery Governance regarding redundant copies

▶ Ensuring cloud-based Disaster Recovery has the ability to follow records retention deletion policies per the organization's approved retention schedule

▶ Availability to "intake" or copy cloud-based backups back "in-house" for eDiscovery or litigation matters to follow any court orders or to assist your organization's legal counsel

▶ Defining SharePoint SLAs

    1. Setup

        ▶   Installation

        ▶   Registration

    2. Configure

        ▶   Cloud Mapping

        ▶   Network Mapping

    3. Protect

        ▶   Enable Protection

        ▶   Recovery Plans

    4. Failover

        ▶   Planned Failover

        ▶   Unplanned Failover

    5. Monitor

        ▶   Jobs

        ▶   Resources

7

The environment you select to deploy your organization's SharePoint 2013 environment on in your 24- to 36-month SharePoint roadmap must take all of these issues into consideration because sometimes the pros outweigh the cons. Other times the cons, although mathematically slim in possibility, would so outweigh the pros that the risk of downtime would not even be something the organization would consider.

Should I Prepare for a Hybrid SharePoint Platform?

The previous sections discussed some of the differences between SharePoint 2013 on-premises (private cloud) and hosted (public cloud), as well as a hybrid SharePoint 2013 deployment, which allows for a middle ground for you to tailor based on specific requirements, concerns, security requirements, and custom development strategies. There is an inherent trade-off between complete control of your SharePoint environment and customization strategy and a managed service or SLA that you will adhere to for your environment.

As detailed in the preceding section, there are major considerations that must be vetted by both the business and technology sides of the company and the review of content or intellectual property and even governing laws at a state, province, or country level. There are also considerations related to business intelligence and the organization's requirements to connect to other line-of-business systems and how the cloud or hybrid cloud may affect or work with this other data and related permission strategies.

There are 9 key architectural areas to consider within a SharePoint 2013 deployment:

▶ Deployment architecture

▶ Network architecture

▶ Infrastructure and server architecture

▶ Permission architecture

▶ Cloud architecture

▶ Software architecture

▶ Business architecture

▶ Data architecture

▶ Information architecture

A hybrid SharePoint 2013 environment enables your organization to be flexible and provide for the capability to store sensitive and highly confidential content on-premise within your own data center while storing collaboration or non-sensitive data within a public cloud such as Office 365, Microsoft Azure, or AWS. The issues that have continued to compile in the news with the NSA's IT administrator Edward Snowden's leakage of classified data has undoubtedly hurt the reputation of the public cloud. The NSA's PRISM data mining program has also piled on concerns around organization's asking themselves, "How safe is the cloud?"

One of the largest impacts that EPC Group has seen around this issues has been with some clients or potential clients who have offices in the EU whose executive management or IT leaders have absolute refused to store data within cloud storage facilities based within the US. This is another key reason I believe that the hybrid cloud model will continue to take hold as it gives organization's options around where specific types of data are stored while still giving them secure "identify management" options to access it in a seamless manner.

SharePoint 2013/Office 365 hybrid deployments also provide organizations with robust options for business intelligence (BI) initiatives because the private side of the hybrid cloud will more than likely already exist on the company's network in their Active Directory (AD) forest, which will allow BI initiatives to securely access other line-of-business systems within the organization. Office 365's Power BI capabilities also allow cloud-based data the analytical and robust reporting required which can be seamlessly federated via Azure Active Directory, a REST-based service that provides identity management, to your on-premises data to allow you to architect and tailor the security model that will work best for your organization.

One major concern of organizations in past releases of SharePoint was how some "Test" or "Development" environments that were not properly implemented, that were not backed up or under the organization's disaster recovery strategy, or that duplicated the effort of the organization's central SharePoint deployment quickly became a "Production"-like environment.

In SharePoint 2010, 2007, or 2003 implementations there is concern about the risk that these types of environments (that is, Development environments that quickly became a SharePoint production environment with a great deal of content) can bring when they are not following the company's overall IT strategy, SharePoint roadmap, and governance policies and are causing additional effort, risk, and concern about document security.

At the very beginning of your organization's SharePoint 2013 initiative, a companywide SharePoint Governance and Communication strategy message must be established and communicated to all team members, both non-IT and IT, because an employee or team member who would like a place to store and access content without going through the proper channels can establish an unapproved SharePoint site by sending an email or placing a phone call to a very long list of hosting providers.

This user who may not know or understand the organization's SharePoint roadmap and/or governance strategy could unknowingly be putting the organization at great risk in a number of areas. This team member may not understand the implications of storing data in an environment that they know little or nothing about.

This is a key reason that preparing this strategy and a SharePoint hybrid-capable type of corporate communication message can be extremely valuable without ruling out possible hybrid needs of future projects, vendors, and so forth.

TIP

For SharePoint 2013 development, try to develop with an "Office 365 solution" mind-set regardless of whether your company has a completely on-premises SharePoint 2013 roadmap. You will be able to reuse this solution and ensure its compatibility for the future to keep your options open and to not have to open a completely new development project should you ever have a one-off that has this need.

SharePoint 2013's System Architecture

SharePoint implementations can be best approached by categorizing the underlying servers and hardware regardless of virtual versus physical, by categorizing the system architecture to cover these underlying components. The SharePoint system architecture roadmap components must be developed by the business and functional requirements of the information architecture, which contains the planning for sites, document libraries, and ultimately the content. SharePoint 2013's underlying system architecture must take into consideration the needs of the organization in terms of metrics such as these:

▶ Number of SharePoint users as well as any possible future estimates if expansion is on the horizon

▶ Amount of content to be stored by individual departments, business units, and users

▶ Size of that content and considerations for large files such as CAD drawings or media files such as large videos

▶ Performance requirements of these users, as well as their location

▶ Number of data centers and their locations

▶ Onsite deployment, cloud deployment, or hybrid (mixture of both onsite and cloud)

▶ Immediate requirements of the business (that is, company intranet), as well as longer-term requirements (that is, business intelligence and analytical SharePoint service) that may require security around federation or other access needs

▶ Disaster recovery strategies

▶ Network security, Active Directory, performance, acceleration needs, and so on

▶ Development environment and related Visual Studio/Team Foundation Server (TFS) strategy

SharePoint 2013 System and Server Architecture Overview

The following hardware and software related sections cover the SharePoint 2013's underlying system architecture recommendations. Microsoft has published their recommendations covering server resource minimums, but I will also run through sample recommendations for development, QA, and production deployments for a SharePoint 2013 on-premises environment for a baseline example. It is key to plan for the future so opting to plan for just the minimum requirements is not advised. Figure 7.10 reflects the minimum requirements for a SharePoint Server 2013 server deployment.

Physical Architecture Farm Model (Minimum)	RAM (Per Server)	CPU (Per Server)
Single Server	24 GB	4 Cores
Small Farm 1 Web Server + 1 App Server + SQL Server	16 GB Web/App Server(s) 16 GB SQL Server(s)	4-8 Cores
Medium Farm 2 Web Servers + 1-2 App Server(s) + SQL Server Farm	16 GB Web Server(s) 16 GB App Server(s) 32 GB SQL Server(s)	4-8 Cores
Large Farm 2-3 Web Servers + 2-3 App Servers + SQL Server Farm	16 GB Web Server(s) 16 GB App Server(s) 32 GB SQL Server(s)	4-8 Cores

FIGURE 7.10   The minimum server requirements as stated by Microsoft for a SharePoint 2013 deployment.

NOTE

In many areas, these minimums are referred to as the physical-architecture minimums, but these are also related to VM deployments. It is key to never plan for just the minimum recommendations because future scalability upgrades are much more time-consuming after your deployment is live and being utilized by your users.

Hardware/Software Recommendation Example for an On-Premises SharePoint 2013 Deployment

The following subsections outline an example for recommended hardware and software specifications for a three-environment SharePoint 2013 deployment, which are as listed here:

▶ Development

▶ QA

▶ Production

All environments in this example will be virtualized and will be allocated resources and configurations at the OS level of the virtual servers before the farm installation and configuration.

Development Environment Configuration

The SharePoint 2013 development environment in this example will consist of a single server with all roles, including database, configured for the environment. The purpose of this environment is for developing the custom applications and solutions that will be used in the production environment in a later section. The development server will be equipped with adequate RAM for performing testing and validation tasks.

Table 7.1 details the server requirements and setup for the development environment single-server installation.

TABLE 7.1   Server Requirements and Setup for the Development Environment Single-Server Installation

Server Type	Purpose	Requirements
SharePoint Server/Database Server (1 node)	Single-server installation with all roles; includes SQL server installation	Server: 1 node CPU: 1 core, 2.20GHz RAM: 24GB Disk: RAID on VM Storage: 150GB –80GB for OS –20GB for logs –50GB for database

QA Environment Configuration

The SharePoint Quality Assurance (QA) environment in this example will be identical to the production environment listed later in this example in terms of server allocations but not in relation to specific amounts of resources such as RAM or disk space. This environment will emulate the working environment of the production environment without the performance workloads expected and will have minimum resources allocated to each server. However, to properly validate applications and solutions, the appropriate number of servers as well as server types will be deployed.

Although application validation, benchmarking, use case testing, and training may occur in this environment, the performance of the environment does not have to reflect the full production workload because this would not include standard daily operation tasks and services.

Although Office Web Apps will be deployed for use in the production environment, it will not be included in the QA environment, although the Office Web Apps Farm can be used by hosts for any SharePoint farm.

The QA environment for this example, as shown in Table 7.2, will include the following topology and resource allocations.

TABLE 7.2   Server Requirements and Setup for the QA Environment Installation

Server Type	Purpose	Requirements
SharePoint Database Server (1 node)	Database storage content	Servers: 1 node CPU: 4 core, 2.67GHz min. RAM: 12GB Disk: RAID on VM Server Storage: 250GB –130GB for OS –20GB for logs –100GB for database
SharePoint Web Front Ends (2 nodes network load-balanced)	Main client communication point, content rendering layer, customized web-based functionality	Servers: 2 nodes network load-balanced (network device) CPU: 4 core, 2.67GHz min. RAM: 12GB Disk: 120GB –100GB for OS –20GB for logs
SharePoint Application: Business Intelligence Services (1 node)	Provides dedicated business intelligence services (BCS, Excel, PerformancePoint, Visio Graphics, PowerView)	Servers: 1 node CPU: 4 core, 2.67GHz RAM: 12GB Disk: 120GB –100GB for OS –20GB for logs
SharePoint Application: Central Administration, All Other Services (1 node)	Provides dedicated and separated functionality for administration and non-BI services (User Profiles, Search, Managed Metadata)	Servers: 1 node CPU: 4 core, 2.67GHz RAM: 12GB Disk: 120GB –100GB for OS –20GB for logs

Production Environment Configuration

The SharePoint production environment in this example will have an identical server allocation but an increased per-server resource allocation to support expected sustainable workloads for daily operations and services.

Although the SharePoint 2013 applications and solutions will be the primary focus and initial consumption source for all resources, the organization may eventually expand the usage of the production farm in both the number of expected users and additional services and features beyond custom applications or even business intelligence.

Because of the expected growth in usage and services, each server node will have a present and future resource allocation to indicate what will be recommended per server during that period. The present period is indefinite and may last for some time, although the recommendations reflect a period when concurrent usage and sustainable workloads reach their expected maximum capacity, as well as the additional services beyond areas such as BI that will be added to the farm.

Additionally, because of both the performance and the monitoring needs, each SharePoint server will have additional disk space volume allocations for separating the OS and paging files from the log files for SharePoint.

The production environment in this example, as shown in Table 7.3, will include the following topology and resource allocations.

TABLE 7.3   Server Requirements and Setup for the Production Environment Installation

Server Type	Purpose	Requirements
SharePoint Database Server (1 node)	Database storage content	Servers: 1 node
		CPU: 4 core for present, 2.67GHz min., 8 core for future
		RAM: 24GB for present, 48GB for future
		Disk: RAID on VM Server
		Storage: 750GB
		–150 for OS and paging
		–100 for SQL transaction logs
		–500 for SQL database files
SharePoint Web Front Ends (2 nodes network load-balanced)	Main client communication point, content rendering layer, customized web-based functionality	Servers: 2 nodes network load-balanced (network device)
		CPU: 4 core, 2.67GHz min.
		RAM: 12GB for present, 16GB for future
		Disk: 220GB
		–120 for OS and paging
		–100 for logs
SharePoint Application: Business Intelligence Services (1 node)	Provides dedicated Business Intelligence services (SQL Reporting Services, PowerView)	Servers: 1 node
		CPU: 4 core, 2.67GHz
		RAM: 12GB for present, 16GB for future
		Disk: 220GB
		–120 for OS and paging
		–100 for logs

Server Type	Purpose	Requirements
SharePoint Application: Central Administration, All Other Services (1 node)	Provides dedicated and separated functionality for administration and non-BI services (User Profiles, Search, Managed Metadata)	Servers: 1 node CPU: 4 core, 2.67GHz RAM: 12GB for present, 16GB for future Disk: 220GB –120 for OS and Paging –100 for logs

Office Web Apps Server

For this example, a single-server farm for Office Web Apps, recently rebranded to Office Online, will be included for Office Web Apps support. This server will be deployed in its own farm and can be used by any of the farms. Because of the resource-intensive processes for this server, the resource allocation will be similar to the application server in the production farm.

Note: Office Web Apps have been renamed to Office Online, but the current Office Web Apps Server, referenced here, is still the correct on-premise technical server name. The Office Web Apps Server will be renamed in the future to align with the new Office Online rebranding, but it is key to think of these technologies in a similar way to avoid confusion within IT, as well as with the business.

The Office Web Apps server, as shown in Table 7.4, will include the following resource allocations.

TABLE 7.4   Server Requirements and Setup for the Production Environment Installation

Server Type	Purpose	Requirements
Office Web Apps Server (4 node)	Office Web Apps view and editing server and farm	Servers: 4 node CPU: 1 core, 2.67GHz min. RAM: 16GB for present, 24GB for future Disk: RAID 1+0 Storage: 150GB –120 for OS and paging –30 for logs

Server Deployment Topology Examples

The following examples show various server deployment topologies, from limited deployment topologies to medium, as well as large and hybrid farm topologies.

The following topologies are listed:

▶ Limited deployments topology, as shown in Figure 7.11.

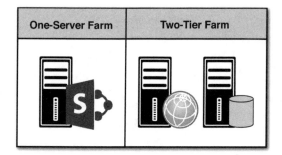

FIGURE 7.11   Limited deployments topology.

Limited deployments are typically used for product evaluation, development, and testing, or for environments that have limited numbers of users and don't require fault tolerance.

▶ Small/multipurpose (four-server farm) SharePoint 2013 topology, as shown in Figure 7.12.

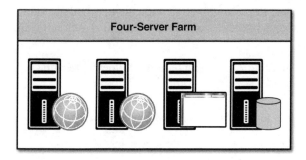

FIGURE 7.12   Multipurpose (four-server farm) SharePoint 2013 topology.

Small farm architectures serve a larger number of users and scale out based on how heavily services are used. Not all small farms are fault-tolerant. A dedicated application server is added for environments with moderate service usage.

▶ Medium farm SharePoint 2013 topology, as shown in Figure 7.13.

Medium farm architectures can be multipurpose or optimized for specific purposes. Medium-size farms are fully fault-tolerant. Some environments might require more web servers. Factor 10,000 users per web server as a starting point.

▶ Medium (six-server) farm plus Office Web Apps SharePoint 2013 topology, as shown in Figure 7.14.

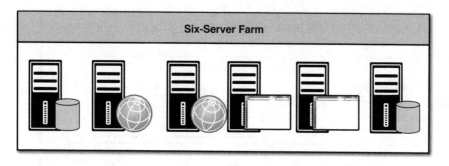

FIGURE 7.13   Medium farm SharePoint 2013 topology.

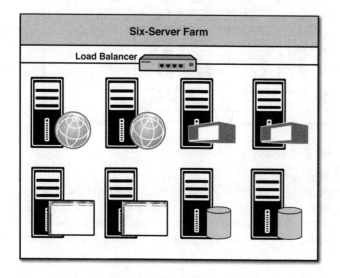

FIGURE 7.14   Medium (six-server) farm plus Office Web Apps SharePoint 2013 topology.

The medium fully fault-tolerant, virtual environment includes Office Web Apps Server VMs and includes a plan for scaling out databases. This also can be configured to call out all search application roles.

Office Web Apps Server VMs can share the same host as a SharePoint Web or application server. If more than one Office Web Apps Server VM is included in the architecture, a load balancer should be added or you should configure Application Request Routing in IIS.

▶ Large farm SharePoint 2013 topology, as shown in Figure 7.15.

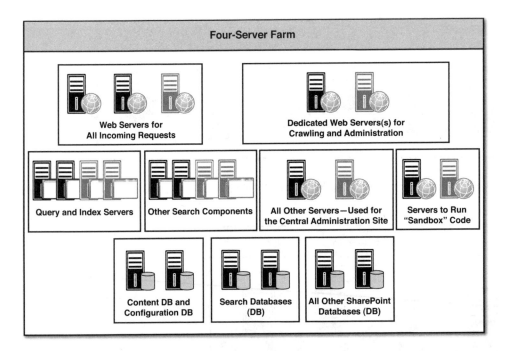

FIGURE 7.15   Large farm SharePoint 2013 topology.

This type of server typically supports 10,000 to 20,000 users. For 90,000 users, this architecture starts with six Web servers to serve user requests and leaves room for additional web servers, if needed. Two to three Web servers that are dedicated for search crawling is a good starting point, depending on rates of change and freshness requirements.

In regard to application servers, four servers are recommended to be dedicated for distributed cache, Central Administration, Access Services, App Management, Business Data Connectivity, Excel Services, Machine Translation Service, Managed Metadata, PerformancePoint, PowerPoint Conversion, Secure Store Service, State Service, Usage and Health Data Collection, User Profile, Visio Graphics Service, Word Automation Services, Work Management, and Workflow.

In regard to configuring the Search Server architecture, the correlation between items and volume of data will vary depending on the types of data that are crawled. It is important to understand the characteristics of the data within the environment. Above 40 million items, consider a dedicated search farm.

▶ Hybrid farm SharePoint 2013 topology, as shown in Figure 7.16.

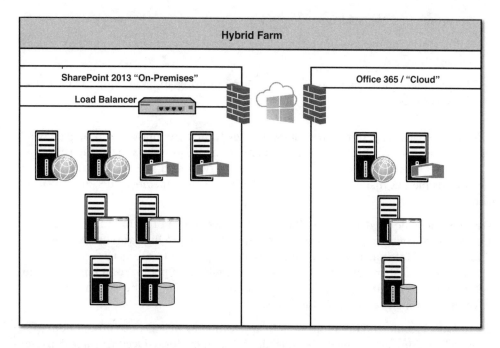

FIGURE 7.16   Hybrid farm SharePoint 2013 topology.

A hybrid environment that uses SharePoint Server 2013 and other cloud services such as Office 365's SharePoint Online, Microsoft Azure, or AWS enables solutions that integrate functionality between services and features such as Search, Microsoft Business Connectivity Services, and Duet Enterprise Online for Microsoft SharePoint and SAP in both environments.

There are options your organization should take into consideration when architecting SharePoint 2013's Search server architecture, such as the need for Internet-based users to search both environments, as well as which sets of SharePoint's users may require a hybrid search experience. The options that exist are "one-way outbound topology," "one-way inbound topology," and "two-way (bidirectional) topology."

Key Areas to Consider Regarding Scalability in Your SharePoint 2013 Architectural Roadmap

It is important to implement a highly available as well as scalable SharePoint 2013 platform and avoid some of the known pitfalls that degrade its performance, such as the following:

▶ Having all SharePoint services in the "default" service group

▶ Having JavaScript that has not been optimized or deployed in a best practices manner

▶ Procuring or having inadequate hardware

▶ Not paying enough time and attention to SQL Server's configuration and its optimization

▶ Not providing the proper tools to allow for monitoring and reviewing the underlying server logs

If you are experiencing performance issues, it is key to first attempt to perform exercises such as load testing in a similar or replicated environment, as well as reviewing the IIS logs, the server's performance, and latency for web, service, and SQL servers. There are some obvious metrics that are sometimes overlooked, such as memory, RPS, and the CPU's statistics.

There are some major updates or architectural considerations in relation to SharePoint 2013, such as discouraging dedicated service farms that end up increasing server count as well as overall maintenance requirements. It is also important to use as few application pools as possible in SharePoint 2013 because each application pool takes up memory and resources, and it is better to share these resources to avoid some of the caching errors that have come up in many enterprisewide farms.

There is also a recommendation for one web application as well as one corresponding zone as well as using host-named site collections that allow for reduced resource consumption and much better scalability. You are always able to have multiple host names in regard to secure site access (SSA).

SharePoint 2013's Search and Scalability Recommendations

SharePoint 2013's search, which now includes fast search, has very different metrics involved in the scalability of search. For example, for every 10 million items, there is a scaling recommendation to add an index partition. With 20 million items, the scaling recommendation is to add a new crawl database, and with 30 million items, it is recommended to go with a dedicated search farm. I have also seen some great results when providing a dedicated host for crawling on the crawling target server.

Your search will always function at a higher level when it is originally architected with best practices in mind with defined targets and proper logical and physical architecture.

SharePoint 2013's SQL Server 2012 Scalability Recommendations

There are a lot of similarities in recommendations from past versions of SharePoint. It is key to ensure that you always use SQL aliases whenever possible because this makes later migrations or database moves much easier and can save 100 or more hours of rework if those changes are ever needed.

There are several candidates for aliases, and if you begin with one SQL Server instance and three aliases, you will have the option to scale and later move any highly used databases into a dedicated SQL node.

SQL Server 2012 R2 comes with new AlwaysOn for redundancy capabilities, which is native in SQL Server 2014. This does require Windows Server Failover Clustering (WSFC).

Understanding SharePoint Server 2013 Search Architecture

One of the big-ticket areas Microsoft rolled into SharePoint 2013 is the integration of FAST Search as a native capability, as well as providing a new rich user interface through to a completely revamped back-end architecture.

Some of the previous SharePoint version search features still exist, such as full document and content searches, people and profile searches, and connecting Search to external systems with the BCS, but you will see a major search improvement with this new release.

Figure 7.17 shows SharePoint 2001, 2003, 2007, and 2010's previous search pages.

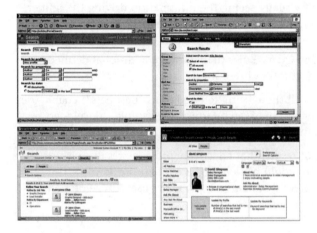

FIGURE 7.17   SharePoint 2001, 2003, 2007, and 2010's previous search pages.

EPC Group has taken a survey of the last 30 SharePoint 2013 deployments after the actual go-live and users being live within the new platform, and the following were the top "liked" or "much improved" features of search that users responded to in this survey:

▶ The full content preview for office documents with the search hover panel

▶ Improved search time to find the desired content that was actually being specifically searched for

▶ Capability to search for skills of other employees, which users found to not be useful in previous versions, causing them to eventually give up that type of search

▶ The new Search web parts

▶ The custom or tailored search results page, which made searching "more comfortable" and "not as clunky"

▶ Seeing what others have searched for and the capability to go back to previous searches where they were able to find what they were looking for after they had forgotten what they had previously searched for

The SharePoint 2013 Search interface includes elements such as search refiners that enable users to take a subset of Search results and "refine" them based on metadata associated with the content.

These are the updated or new refiners in SharePoint 2013:

▶ Entity extraction introduces the capability for entities such as people's names or company names to be extracted from the contents of documents and made available as a metadata selection in the refiners.

▶ Deep refiners ensure that the entire Search index is used to calculate the refiner information.

▶ Visual refiners provide a way of visually seeing the information driving the refiner, complete with an interactive slider to do the actual refining.

SharePoint 2013's Search also has new Query Rules that allow for additional defined areas such as promoted results and other features as listed here:

▶ Promoted results (you might recall these being referred to as "best bets") enable users to define a link to be shown for specific Search terms; for example, "developers" shows a link to the SP2013 training on MSDN.

▶ Result blocks are an inline set of results that effectively provide "results within results" based on the query. This could be rich media content previews for the current search, content from external systems, or any other useful type of a screen-shot or snapshot of content from the Search index.

The following is a list of the underlying core elements in SharePoint 2013's search:

▶ Content source

▶ Search schema

▶ Query rule

    ▶ Customization of returned results

    ▶ Captures intent, composed of

        Query condition

        Query action

        Publishing options

▶ Query transforms

    ▶ Web parts

    ▶ Query rule

    ▶ Result source

Figure 7.18 shows SharePoint 2013's capability to scope a search source.

FIGURE 7.18   SharePoint 2013's capability to scope a search source.

Figure 7.19 shows an example of a tailored display template in SharePoint 2013's Search.

FIGURE 7.19   An example of a tailored display template in SharePoint 2013's Search.

SharePoint 2013's New Auditing, Logging, and Monitoring Capabilities

SharePoint 2013 now comes with native event logs, as well as trace and usage logs. This has been a welcome set of new features by SharePoint administrators as well as companies that did not want to go out and invest in a third-party solutions but rather prefer to use 2013's native capabilities.

There are also some very powerful web analytics and health reports that enable you to much more closely monitor what users are experiencing in Search and ensure that they are getting the results they are searching for. There are also new administrative reports as well as a developer dashboard, and I have to mention that the new Timer Job Status reports that would have been so nice in previous versions when troubleshooting complex workflows are now available.

These new capabilities also include SQL Server monitoring, as well as the capability to review memory counters, disk counters, and performance counters. You can enable these features on specific sites or on specific site collections or even at the farm level. It is very helpful in providing you with tools to enforce your SharePoint governance strategy as well as permissions and possible scalability issues and red flags that you would be ready to react to and resolve.

SharePoint administration reporting can be separated into five categories:

▶ Permissions

   ▶ Troubleshooting why users cannot see the content they should

   ▶ Reporting for different types of compliance

   ▶ Auditing who has access to sensitive content

▶ Usage/Activity

   ▶ Finding which content is, or is not, being used

   ▶ Planning for future growth

   ▶ Understanding hardware requirements

▶ Storage

   ▶ Monitoring growth for performance reasons

   ▶ Understanding hardware requirements

   ▶ Reorganizing taxonomy based on storage needs

▶ Audit

   ▶ Showing who accessed what and when, to adhere to internal or external compliance requirements

▶ Performance

   ▶ Monitoring page load times to uncover problems

   ▶ Planning for increased usage

Figure 7.20 shows the out-of-the-box usage and activity reporting in SharePoint 2013.

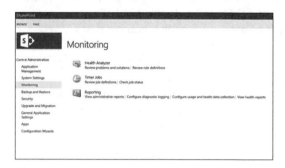

FIGURE 7.20   SharePoint Server 2013's out-of-the-box usage and activity reporting functionality.

SharePoint 2013 BYOD Best Practices

Remote workers and internal or onsite workers empowered with "bring your own device" (BYOD) policies can push the boundaries of IT and the typical IT-driven culture. A lot of IT organizations are playing catch-up in the areas of governance and their information management policies and have pushed back on BYOD due to the added complexity around security and compliance it brings and the way it ultimately forces specific polices to be approved. There is a trade-off between not allowing BYOD and the work required to actually implement a BYOD strategy and taking the risk of users finding shortcuts and utilizing other methods or access points to share files or obtain reports.

There are proven productivity increases that organizations with a BYOD policy have realized and ROI that comes with empowering users. The gains you see may in some cases be inevitably offset with some users taking advantage of the added capabilities, but those one-off cases should not stifle the overall organization's momentum toward technology innovations that can keep them ahead of their competitors.

The flip side of the coin regarding BYOD is that it can bring a 24/7 "working window" into the picture that some organizations may see as encroaching on the work/life balance but also what may define the actual workplace or given workday.

One of the major issues with BYOD has been with the security risks that can be increased, but in SharePoint 2013's case, there are solutions such as Microsoft's System Center's Windows Intune that can be put in place to assist in resolving some of these challenges. There must be a balance of privacy in conjunction with other obligations such as legal risks that may come with personal or PII/PHI data.

Enforcing a policy, where possible, that makes the user who is requesting to use his own device (BYOD) aware of any possible challenges, sign-offs, or privacy-related data policies is the best first step because there must be expectations from both sides (IT and the business) in introducing strategy such as those related to BYOD.

EPC Group's internal BYOD policy follows certain password requirements with a pin addition as well as some layer of file encryption. Our consultants may be onsite at any given client and require access to a document off of our SharePoint Server 2013 intranet or ECM platform that a client requests, and we must be able to immediately meet that request. The interesting part of developing and designing enterprisewide strategies around BYOD or even areas such as cloud or hybrid computing is that it does require us to test, perfect, and then implement these solutions ourselves at EPC Group, because the "eating your own dog food" rule almost always applies in these technology areas. In addition, we have implemented device locking as well as remote wiping if a device is lost or stolen, as well as secure backups and either certificate/encryption or virus protection.

Summary

This chapter covered core strategies for implementing a best practices system architecture. It also covered considerations regarding the on-premises private cloud and off-premise public cloud, as well as organizational considerations for the hybrid cloud.

This chapter also discussed scalability considerations, key questions, and metrics you must prepare for in the deployment and external access BYOD considerations.

CHAPTER 8

Business Intelligence Overview for SharePoint 2013 and Office 365

There has been a huge effort by Microsoft in SharePoint 2013's release, as well as in the underlying SQL Server 2012 R2 and SQL Server 2014 database technology, to provide organizations with a centralized location and "information worker"–friendly interface to deliver business intelligence (BI) related to mission-critical metrics to better understand your organization's data.

BI initiatives can be complex, and with the variables in where your data is stored, as well as the related security, availability, and performance considerations, careful planning must be completed. A lot of BI initiatives also have the underlying architecture of SharePoint and the line-of-business (LOB) data sources and corresponding reporting requirements being analyzed and designed in parallel, so keeping scalability in mind at all times is key.

This chapter covers SharePoint Server 2013's BI capabilities as well as the underlying Microsoft vision as SQL Server 2012 R2 and SQL Server 2014 is released and adapted by organizations and Microsoft Office 365's Power BI capabilities also begin to come into their own.

Business intelligence initiatives are meant to improve organizations by providing business insights to team members, which in turn will lead to better, faster, and more relevant decisions. With the new technology releases from Microsoft, BI can come in the form of a combination of SQL Server and the delivery intelligence through Microsoft Office, SharePoint Server 2013, and/or Office 365's SharePoint Online.

The following is an overview of Microsoft's BI stack, as shown in Figure 8.1, and related offerings:

▶ **Business Intelligence Center site:** A Business Intelligence Center is a SharePoint site that enables organizations to centrally store and manage data connections, reports, score cards, dashboards, and web part pages.

▶ **Excel 2013:** Use Excel 2013 to create a wide range of powerful reports, score cards, and dashboards. Microsoft Excel 2013 has several components that your BI effort may utilize, such as PowerPivot and Power View, and within SharePoint Server 2013, there is the related Excel Services feature, also discussed in the following text.

▶ **Excel Services:** This is a SharePoint service application that enables the loading, calculation, and browser-based rendering of Excel workbooks in SharePoint Server 2013. Excel Services is designed to be a scalable, robust, enterprise-class service that provides feature and calculation fidelity with Excel. *Note:* Microsoft recently updated their licensing requirements, and it is important for you to understand the features and related licensing your organization has available.

▶ **PowerPivot:** PowerPivot is an add-in for Excel to create powerful data models that can include calculated fields, reports, and score cards. PowerPivot's deep integration with Excel Services enables users to create relationships between data from different sources and to view complex data in a more refined, normalized form.

▶ **Power View:** Use Power View to create various interactive reports that include charts, tables, maps, bubble charts, and other views. Excel Services 2013 takes advantage of the new Microsoft data modeling and visualization engine that sits atop the SQL Server Reporting Services add-in to SharePoint.

▶ **PerformancePoint Services:** Use PerformancePoint Services to create and share centrally managed dashboards that include various up-to-date reports and score cards.

▶ **Visio Services:** Use Visio Services to publish visual diagrams to SharePoint sites. Visio Services is scalable and is an enterprise-class service that provides feature and rendering fidelity with Visio, as well as rich browsing and navigation capabilities that are supported in a zero-footprint Web client.

▶ **The SQL Server business intelligence stack:** SQL Server has five key underlying BI capabilities: OLTP (Online Transaction Processing), SQL Server Integration Service, Data Warehouse capabilities, Reporting Services (SSRS), and Analysis Services.

▶ **The cloud-related business intelligence stack:** Microsoft's cloud offerings include BI capabilities within SQL Azure, SQL Azure Reporting Service, OData capabilities, and Microsoft Office 365's Power BI.

Organizations look to BI solutions to improve decision making, cut costs, and identify new business opportunities. These efforts tend to also uncover metrics that were previously unknown and enable the organization to address them and develop a corrective path to increase the bottom line and provide real ROI to the organization.

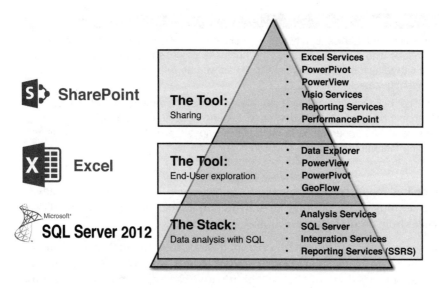

FIGURE 8.1   Microsoft's business intelligence stack.

Business Intelligence Considerations in SharePoint 2013

Business intelligence capabilities in SharePoint 2013 are vast and in many cases are achieved with a combination of SharePoint and Microsoft Office or SharePoint and SQL Server.

When you are approaching a BI initiative, there are several questions that should be addressed from the very beginning, such as the following:

▶ What is this BI initiative trying to accomplish and who is the audience it is being developed for?

▶ Where is the data located? Is the data all within SQL Server, or does this BI initiative need to pull in data from other external line-of-business systems such as Oracle or SAP?

▶ What are the expectations of the reporting? Are these reports going to be from yesterday's "data dump" or does the user require "real-time" up-to-the-minute type reporting?

▶ Is there a current reporting process in place that users are unhappy with, and is this initiative meant to replace that current process?

▶ What reports are the users wanting to see and what format are they supposed to be in?

8

TIP

A business intelligence initiative ideally has a "technical business analyst" involved. This should be someone who both understands the business process and reporting needs of the users and can relay those requirements to IT, as well as relaying any push-backs or limitations IT identifies back to the users.

This role is critical because formalizing the actual format of the reports and what their desired look should be can be one of the most challenging parts of this BI effort. Therefore, someone who understands both "business speak" and "technical speak" is critical to helping this effort become a success.

▶ Can the desired report(s) be provided in a sample format from what may already exist, or if nothing exists, can they be drawn up in a mock-up format so that IT can review them from an underlying technical perspective?

▶ How easily can IT "hook" into these external data sources? Are nightly data dump types of files/access available or does there need to be a new "view" created in the external data source's database that this BI initiative can access to pull this data into SharePoint Server 2013 via the right tool or path?

After these core questions are answered, you will have a much better idea of the path as well as the relevant technology you need to utilize within Microsoft's BI stack. The next step is configuring your baseline BI environment and getting familiar with the tools and related functionality so that you can make intelligent decisions as well as provide accurate feedback to stakeholders during the BI effort.

Following is an example of the steps required to implement your baseline business intelligence environment:

1. Configure Excel Services:

   ▶ Configure the Excel Services unattended service account.

   ▶ Configure a data access account.

   ▶ Publish a workbook with an external data source.

   ▶ Test the data refresh.

2. Configure Visio Services:

   ▶ Configure a managed account for Visio Services.

   ▶ Configure a Visio Services service application.

   ▶ Configure Visio Services Global Settings and Visio client for data access.

3. Configure PerformancePoint Services:

   ▶ Create an account for the application pool.

   ▶ Grant content database access to the managed account.

   ▶ Create a PerformancePoint Services service application.

4. Configure Secure Store:

   ▶ Configure a managed account.

   ▶ Configure a Secure Store service application.

   ▶ Generate an encryption key.

5. Configure the Excel Services unattended service account as follows:

   ▶ Configure a managed account for Excel Services.

   ▶ Register a managed account in SharePoint Server.

   ▶ Grant content database access to the managed account.

   ▶ Configure an Excel Services service application.

   ▶ Configure trusted locations.

   ▶ Configure Excel client data access.

   ▶ Create a SQL Server account(s).

6. Configure the required account within the source environment for which this BI initiative is "pulling" the data as well as corresponding SharePoint accounts as required per the business and technical requirements gathered.

7. Create an Active Directory group.

8. Create a Business Intelligence Center, as shown in Figure 8.2.

9. Set permissions on the Business Intelligence Center.

FIGURE 8.2   A Business Intelligence Center site in SharePoint 2013.

Self-Service Business Intelligence Architectural Overview

Microsoft has introduce a huge push toward "self-service business intelligence" (SSBI) and providing users with tools that enable them to run reports and perform BI actions as needed at any time without the need for IT's intervention.

> **NOTE**
>
> "Self-service business intelligence" can be a great thing when done in a governed manner, but it's key to first gain some "quick wins" and roll out a few reports to key business areas so that the impact of your BI initiative can be seen and recognized.

The goal of SSBI is to empower analysts so that they can design, customize, and maintain their own BI solutions, but it is important to note that SSBI is not meant to be a complete solution or a replacement for corporate BI initiatives and standardized reports offered by the organization.

SSBI can enable information workers to remain focused on delivering enterprise requirements and day-to-day reporting tasks and deliver and support a managed BI environment. This also provides a partnership and communication channel between IT and business analysts to encourage collaboration on new ideas on reporting capabilities from both the business and the IT sides of the organization.

Microsoft Excel Services, PowerPivot, and PowerView

Excel has more capabilities and relevance in BI within SharePoint than any other Microsoft Office program. The following sections detail the wide range of powerful capabilities for reports, score cards, and dashboards, as shown in Figure 8.3, which Excel and SharePoint 2013 can deliver to your organization.

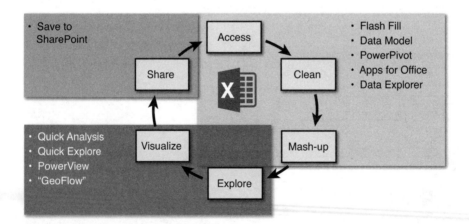

FIGURE 8.3   The wide range of BI and data analysis capabilities Excel technology offers through its integration with SharePoint 2013.

Excel Services

Excel Services, among many other things, enables manual business processes such as the emailing or sharing of spreadsheets that cause manual errors to stop and a centralized version of the truth to be established.

The following is an overview of Excel Services 2013:

▶ Excel Services 2013 is a SharePoint service application that enables the loading, calculation, and browser-based rendering of Excel workbooks (Enterprise Edition only).

▶ It is designed to be a scalable, robust, enterprise-class service that provides feature and calculation fidelity with Excel.

▶ Excel Services 2013 delivers rich analysis capabilities that are supported in a zero-footprint web client with a familiar interface.

▶ It enables live connections to data sources to be queried to deliver up-to-date data throughout analysis.

PowerPivot

PowerPivot is an add-in for Excel users that provides the capability to create powerful data models that can include calculated fields, reports, and score cards. PowerPivot sits among the three-dimensional business intelligence model that Microsoft's BI stack offers, as shown in Figure 8.4.

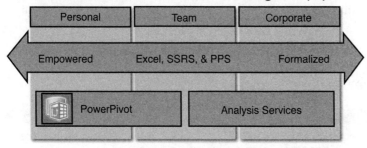

FIGURE 8.4   PowerPivot sits among the three-dimensional business intelligence model in Microsoft's BI stack.

The following is a summary of PowerPivot and SharePoint 2013:

▶ PowerPivot for SharePoint extends SharePoint 2013 and Excel Services to add server-side processing, collaboration, and document management support for the PowerPivot workbooks published to SharePoint.

▶ The PowerPivot Gallery, a special type of document library, is provided to browse published PowerPivot workbooks and to configure automatic data refresh.

▶ The PowerPivot Service deploys the embedded data model to an Analysis Service instance within the SharePoint farm, and Excel Services is used to query the deployed data model.

▶ Data connections can be defined to query the PowerPivot data model by using the document URL.

Excel Power View

Power View sheets can be added to a workbook to enable an interactive data exploration, visualization, and presentation experience, and they are also "presentation ready" at all times.

Power View reports can be based on an embedded PowerPivot data model or an external tabular data model that can be optimized to fully exploit the capabilities of the Power View experience.

Power View, in SharePoint Server 2013's release, offers much deeper integration with Excel Services. Using the xVelocity in-memory analytics engine, it uses in-memory compression and data filtering to ensure that large data sets are processed quickly, and it enables users to create relationships between data from different sources. In this way, users can view complex data in a more refined and normalized form even if the data exists in multiple data sources.

This data modeling and visualization engine sits on top of the SQL Server Reporting Services add-in to SharePoint and provides an easy way to deliver interactive data modeling and visualization tools to your users.

TIP

The xVelocity in-memory analytics engine is the next generation of the VertiPaq engine that was introduced in SQL Server 2008 R2, with PowerPivot for Excel 2010 and PowerPivot for SharePoint 2010. VertiPaq is an in-memory columnstore engine that achieves breakthrough performance for analytic queries by employing techniques such as columnar storage, state-of-the-art compression, in-memory caching, and highly parallel data scanning and aggregation algorithms. In SQL Server 2012, the xVelocity in-memory analytics engine has been enhanced to support both self-service BI (PowerPivot) and corporate BI (Analysis Services tabular mode) scenarios.

The xVelocity engine has two usage scenarios in the context of business intelligence:

▶ Information workers can use PowerPivot for Excel to integrate data from a number of sources, cleanse and model the data, enrich the data with business logic, analyze the data, and build reports and visualizations. Since PowerPivot uses the xVelocity engine under the covers, information workers are not limited by the restrictions of Excel. They can work with several million rows of data and still benefit from split-second response times.

▶ BI developers and IT professionals can use SQL Server Data Tools to create an Analysis Services Tabular project and build a BI Semantic Model. The model can contain data from a number of sources, business logic expressed in the form of DAX calculations, role-based security, and large data volumes that can be managed using partitions in the xVelocity engine. When the model is deployed to an Analysis Services server, information workers can use tools like Excel and Power View to interact with the model and achieve split-second response times from the xVelocity engine.

Microsoft PerformancePoint Overview in SharePoint 2013

PerformancePoint is one of the most used BI components within SharePoint 2013, and it is primarily used to create and share centrally managed dashboards. In many cases, PerformancePoint reports are designed in a manner to be updated at any time and modified to be viewed in various ways, such as reports or even KPIs and score cards.

PerformancePoint reports as well as the web part and related features available will enable you to filter data to provide a specific report or to drill down to find specific and more granular data and underlying metrics.

PerformancePoint 2013, and the related site and capabilities, comes with Dashboard Designer natively within the site's ribbon. This integration has been a welcome new feature to many users I have spoken with because they feel it's more user-friendly and easier to user.

PerformancePoint 2013 and SharePoint 2013 introduce some new user interface (UI) enhancements as well as new server-side enhancements. The user interface enhancements in PerformancePoint 2013 include the following:

▶ Theme support, which enables you to change the look and feel of core PerformancePoint functionality.

▶ iPad interface, which means, among other things, that iPad-using executives can access your PerformancePoint dashboards using this highly interactive form factor—including the ability to use touch intuitively and effectively.

The server-side enhancements in PerformancePoint 2013 include these:

▶ PerformancePoint now provides the capabilities to migrate dashboards that have been successfully created and tested in a development environment over to the production environment. PerformancePoint finally fits into first-class software development life cycle (SDLC) models with this functionality as in prior versions, dashboard creators had to re-create and publish their dashboards again from development to production once they were created, tested and approved.

You are now able to bundle a dashboard just like any other SharePoint artifact into a single file and hand that off to an administrator or a relevant team member for deployment.

▶ PerformancePoint has improved integration with SQL Server Analysis Services (SSAS) by supporting its concept of an "effective user." If your organization is leveraging SSAS effective-user functionality, SharePoint 2013 supports it natively with a simple configuration step.

▶ Business Connectivity Services can now connect diagrams directly to external data, opening a wealth of opportunities for user-driven data displays. Because SharePoint can provide and control access to key data, administrators can easily share data sources through the SharePoint interface.

▶ Functionality in the Dashboard Designer tool, as shown in Figure 8.5, has been improved, and it enables users to define data sources and regions on a page that hold such artifacts as filters, grids, charts, and graphs. With the push of a button, it creates web part pages and connected web parts that represent the dashboard.

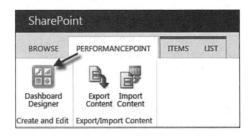

FIGURE 8.5   A SharePoint 2013 site with the Dashboard Designer shown in the ribbon.

Visio Services Overview in SharePoint 2013

Visio Services in 2013 comes with a list of new capabilities in this latest release. It is a SharePoint service application that enables the loading and browser-based rendering of Visio diagrams, as shown in Figure 8.6. These are the major features and capabilities of Visio Services in SharePoint 2013:

▶ It is designed to be a scalable, robust, enterprise-class service that provides feature and rendering fidelity with Visio.

▶ It delivers rich browsing and navigation capabilities that are supported in a zero-footprint Web client.

▶ Live connections to data sources are queried to deliver up-to-date data.

▶ It renders diagrams in the browser with high-quality PNGs for full fidelity.

▶ There is no dependence on Silverlight and native support for Visio file format.

▶ Diagram consumers do not need a Visio client and are available across devices using desktop browsers and mobile browsers.

▶ Users interact with content with pan, zoom, hyperlinks, and view shape data.

▶ BCS connectivity enables users to connect diagrams directly to external data via SharePoint BCS.

▶ Commenting is now available to allow for feedback from end users. With this new feature users can comment on a full diagram or even a single shape, which helps teams to collaborate on data more effectively.

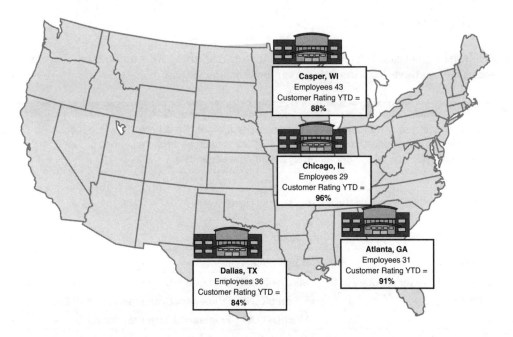

FIGURE 8.6 A Visio Services diagram stored within a SharePoint site.

Database Connections and External Data Sources

Although SharePoint is a very agile piece of software that is capable of holding just about any type of data you can throw at it, most organizations are going to store data in various disparate systems. This means that you will, at some point, have to connect SharePoint data with information stored in an external data source.

As an example, you may have inventory information stored in an Oracle database and sales information stored in a SQL Server database. Your salespeople will surely want to know if you have product available to sell, but with the information stored in two different systems, they would need to look at two different applications to find out whether you have product in stock. With SharePoint's capability to display data from external data sources, you can display information from both systems on a single page and make the salespeople's jobs much easier.

Of course, you are not limited to Oracle and SQL Server when creating external data sources. We will look at how to use each of the external data source connections available to you in SharePoint 2013, including these:

▶ Database

▶ SOAP Service

▶ REST Service

▶ XML file

▶ Linked data sources

Depending on the type of database that is being utilized, there are a number of different variables and methods for connecting to an external database.

TIP

You will notice that ODBC-compatible data sources are not listed here. This is because data views do not support connections to ODBC data sources and should not be used, even though you may see them as an available connection type.

Table 8.1 details the database types and connections.

TABLE 8.1   Database Types and Connections

Database Type	Connection Type
Microsoft SQL Server (2000–2012)	Microsoft .NET Framework Data Provider for SQL Server
OLE-DB Compatible	Microsoft .NET Framework Data Provider for OLE DB
Oracle	Microsoft .NET Framework Data Provider for Oracle

After you choose your data connection type, you will need to decide which authentication method you will use to connect to your database. You can either connect to the database by saving the username and password, or connect by using a custom connection string.

In this section, we are going to create a data source that connects to a SQL Server database using both authentication methods. Connecting to any other available data source follows the same pattern.

TIP

To complete this section, you will need to download the AdventureWorks database for your version of SQL Server. For SQL Server 2012, it can be downloaded from here: http://msftdbprodsamples.codeplex.com/releases/view/55330

Connect by Saving the Username and Password

Using this method, SharePoint will actually generate a connection string for you that stores the username and password in the data-source connection. It is important to note that SQL authentication saves the username and password as text in the data connection. This means that any user with permission to open the site in SharePoint Designer 2013 can view these credentials. You will see a security warning to that effect when you create a new connection using this method.

TIP

To use this method, you will need to ensure that SQL Server authentication is set to mixed mode because this method only allows you to use SQL logins.

To connect by saving the username and password, perform the following steps:

1. Open SharePoint Designer 2013 and select Data Sources in the navigation pane.

2. On the Data Sources tab of the ribbon, in the New group, click the Database Connection button.

3. On the Source tab of the Data Source Properties dialog box, click the Configure Database Connection button.

4. In the Configure Database Connection dialog box, in the Server Information section type the name of the server where your database resides in the Server Name text box.

5. In the Provider Name drop-down box, as shown in Figure 8.7, select Microsoft .NET Framework Data Provider for SQL Server.

6. Under Authentication, click Save This Username and Password in the Data Connection.

7. Type your username in the User Name box.

8. Type your password in the Password box.

9. Click Next.

FIGURE 8.7   The completed database connection configuration with username and password.

10. You are presented with a dialog box warning you that the username and password you entered will be stored as plain text in the data connection. Click OK to continue.

11. In the Database list, select AdventureWorks2012 (or whichever version of AdventureWorks you may be using). At this point, you have the following options:

a. Click the Select a Table or View radio button and then select the table or view you want to query from the list; then click Finish.

This option creates a default query that selects all records in the table or view. After you click Finish, you can modify the default query by clicking Fields, Filter, and Sort in the Data Source Properties dialog box.

b. Click the Specify Custom Select, Update, Insert, and Delete Commands Using SQL or Stored Procedures radio button, and then click Finish.

This option is available only if your administrator has turned on the Enable Update Query Support option in SharePoint Central Administration.

You can create custom SQL commands by using this option. When you click Finish, the Edit Custom SQL Commands dialog box opens. More on this later in this chapter.

For our purposes, click the Select a Table or View radio button, as shown in Figure 8.8; then select Address from the list of available tables and click Finish.

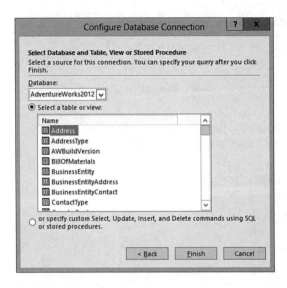

FIGURE 8.8   Selecting the desired database and related table or view for the Data Source.

12. In the Data Source Properties dialog box, as shown in Figure 8.9, click the General
tab and type TestDBConn as the name for the data source; then click OK.

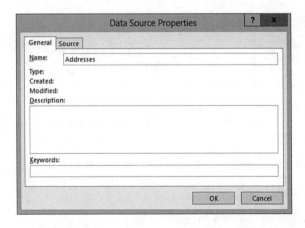

FIGURE 8.9   The completed Data Source Properties dialog box.

13. The new database connection now appears in the Data Sources list.

Connect by Using a Custom Connection String

A connection string is used to provide any information that a data provider might need to
connect to a data source, such as the username, password, or database name. To connect
by using a custom connection string, perform the following steps:

1. Open SharePoint Designer 2013 and select Data Sources in the navigation pane.

2. On the Data Sources tab of the ribbon, in the New group, click the Database Connection button.

3. On the Source tab of the Data Source Properties dialog box, click the Configure Database Connection button.

4. In the Configure Database Connection dialog box, as shown in Figure 8.10, check the Use Custom Connection String check box and click the Edit button.

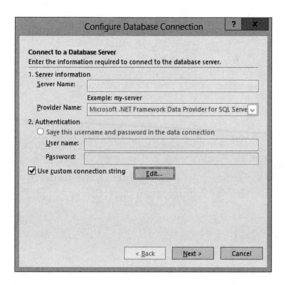

FIGURE 8.10   The Configure Database Connection dialog box.

5. In the Provider Name drop-down box, select Microsoft .NET Data Framework Provider for Microsoft SQL Server.

6. Enter your connection string in the Connection String box, as shown in Figure 8.11. It should look something like this: Data Source=*ServerName*;Initial Catalog=*Database*;User Id=*username*;Password=*password*.

7. Click the OK button to complete the connection string.

8. You are presented with a dialog box warning you that the username and password you entered will be stored as plain text in the data connection. Click OK to continue.

Edit Connection String

Select the provider name and then enter the text required to connect to the database.

Provider Name:

Microsoft .NET Framework Data Provider for SQL

Connection String:

Data Source=SPDev;Initial Catalog=AdventureWorks

OK   Cancel

FIGURE 8.11   The Edit Connection String dialog box.

9. In the Database list, select AdventureWorks2012 (or whichever version of AdventureWorks you may be using). At this point, you have the following options:

   a. Click the Select a Table or View radio button and then select the table or view you want to query from the list; then click Finish.

      This option creates a default query that selects all records in the table or view. After you click Finish, you can modify the default query by clicking Fields, Filter, and Sort in the Data Source Properties dialog box.

   b. Click the Specify Custom Select, Update, Insert, and Delete Commands Using SQL or Stored Procedures radio button, and then click Finish.

      This option is available only if your administrator has turned on the Enable Update Query Support option in SharePoint Central Administration.

      You can create custom SQL commands by using this option. When you click Finish, the Edit Custom SQL Commands dialog box opens. More on this later in this chapter.

   c. For our purposes, click the Select a Table or View radio button; then select Address from the list of available tables and click Finish.

10. In the Data Source Properties dialog box, click the General tab and type `TestDBConnCustom` as the name for the data source; then click OK.

11. The new database connection now appears in the Data Sources list.

Create Custom SQL Commands

When creating a new database connection, you have the option to create custom SQL commands for the standard CRUD (Create, Read, Update, Delete) commands. The option enables you to use a completely custom SQL command written on the fly, or you can select an existing stored procedure and add any needed parameters.

This is especially useful if your company, like many companies, allows access to the database only through stored procedures. To test this, perform the following steps:

1. Open SharePoint Designer 2013 and select Data Sources in the navigation pane.

2. Open the TestDBConn data source created earlier in the chapter.

3. On the Source tab, click the Configure Database Connection button.

4. Click Next, and then click OK on the subsequent warning.

5. Click the radio button to specify custom commands, as shown in Figure 8.12, and click Finish.

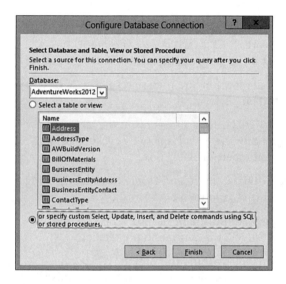

FIGURE 8.12   Selecting the custom-commands radio button.

6. On the Select tab, click the Stored Procedure radio button, as shown in Figure 8.13, and select the `uspGetEmployeeManagers` stored procedure.

7. This particular stored procedure requires a parameter, so click the Edit Command button to add the parameter.

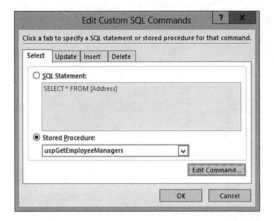

FIGURE 8.13   Selecting the `uspGetEmployeeManagers` stored procedure.v

8. You will notice that there are several methods for filling in the parameter as listed in the Parameter Source drop-down list:

- ▶ **None:** This enables you to hard-code the parameter value.

- ▶ **Cookie:** With this option, you can set the value using a cookie. You can also set a default value to use if the cookie is not present.

- ▶ **Control:** You can use this to retrieve the parameter value from an ASP.NET control on the page where the data source is used. This parameter is useful only in code.

- ▶ **Form:** This sets the parameter using a value in an HTML form field. You will need to know the ID of the parameter when setting it here.

- ▶ **Profile:** This is used to set the value of the parameter to a value stored in the user profile.

- ▶ **QueryString:** This option sets the value of the parameter based on a query string parameter set in the URL.

- ▶ **Session:** This sets the parameter to a value stored in the HTML session data.

- ▶ **RouteData:** This option sets the parameter based on a value stored in the route data taken from the URL. This is really useful only when you're using an MVC or single page application.

9. Leave the Parameter Source value as None, as shown in Figure 8.14, and enter 100 as the parameter value.

10. Click OK three times to get back to SharePoint Designer.

8

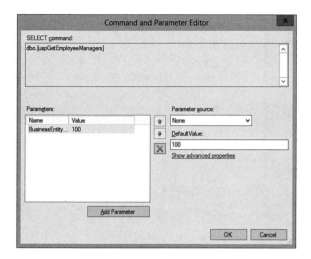

FIGURE 8.14   Setting the parameter for the stored procedure.

SOAP Service Connection Review

If you've been working with computer systems for any length of time, you likely know what a web service is: It is a piece of software that facilitates communication between computers over a network. There are two major classes of web services: SOAP and REST. We'll get more into REST later in this chapter.

SOAP web services exchange XML data over a network using the HTTP protocol, the same protocol used for transmitting web pages from a server to your browser. Each of these web services includes a Web Service Description Language (WSDL) file that describes the web service and its capabilities for remote applications.

To add a SOAP web service as a data source in SharePoint, you must know the URL for the WSDL file associated with the web service. These URLs usually end in .WSDL or ?WSDL.

SharePoint provides several web services that can be used for retrieving and manipulating data. We are now going to use the webs web service to create a SOAP service connection. To test this, perform the following steps:

1. Open SharePoint Designer 2013 and select Data Sources in the navigation pane.

2. On the Data Sources tab of the ribbon, in the New group, click the SOAP Service Connection button.

3. In the Data Source Properties dialog box, in the Service description location box on the Source tab, type this URL for the web service:

    http://*your_server*/_vti_bin/Webs.asmx?WSDL

    Be sure to replace *your_server* with the actual name of the server running SharePoint.

4. Click Connect Now.

Notice that after the connection has been established, the Connect Now button changes to a Disconnect button and the other options on the tab become available.

5. In the Select Which Data Command to Configure list, there are four available options, but you can use only the Select option. You cannot use the Insert, Update, or Delete options when creating a data view. For this example, make sure that the Select option is selected.

6. You may see several options available in the Port list, based on the web service you are connected to. For this example, just select WebsSoap.

7. The options displayed in the Operation list are defined by the web service you are connected to. For this example, select the GetWebCollection operation, as shown in Figure 8.15.

FIGURE 8.15   The completed SOAP Service connection dialog.

Based on the operation you select, you may need to provide parameter values. You can do that by selecting the parameter and clicking the Modify button. Our example doesn't use parameters, so you do not have to set any here.

8. On the General tab, enter TestSoapConn as the connection name and click OK.

REST Service Connection Review

In 2000, Roy Fielding, one of the primary authors of the HTTP specification, wrote a dissertation in which he coined the term Representational State Transfer, which we have shortened to REST. Unlike SOAP, REST is not a protocol. It is a description of how systems should be architected to interact over a network.

Although there are various things that make a web service RESTful, the main property that we are concerned with here is how RESTful services are accessed. When conforming to the REST architecture, all data elements are accessed through a standardized interface. In the case of a SharePoint REST data source, this interface is a URL in the _api space.

It is important to note that this data source can be used to connect to any server-side script that returns XML, like an RSS feed for example. We, however, are going to look at how to create a data source that connects to one of SharePoint's RESTful connections:

1. Open SharePoint Designer 2013 and select Data Sources in the navigation pane.

2. On the Data Sources tab of the ribbon, in the New group, click the REST Service Connection button.

3. Leave the HTTP method as GET and leave the command to configure as Select.

4. In the Select Connection Info section, as shown in Figure 8.16, enter the following URL (remember to use your actual server name):

   http://*your_server*/_api/web/Lists/GetByTitle('Pages')

FIGURE 8.16   The completed REST Service connection dialog.

5. On the General tab, enter TestRESTConn as the name and click OK.

Reviewing an XML File Connection

You may be wondering why you would want to use an XML data connection. One of the tools included with SQL Server is SQL Server Integration Services (SSIS), which enables you to import data, like XML files, into a database which you could then connect to using a database connection.

Wondering why you would want to use an XML data connection is a valid argument, but not all companies that have SQL Server use SSIS. First, they may not have the right SQL Server license. SSIS comes with Standard and Enterprise licenses, but it does not come with anything lower than Standard. SharePoint, however, will work on Express with Advanced Services, which means that SSIS is unavailable.

Second, SSIS is a fairly complex piece of software in itself, and many companies simply do not have the expertise in-house to build SSIS packages that will reliably import XML files into databases.

That being said, it is completely possible that, even though you have SQL Server installed, you may end up using an XML file as a data source in SharePoint. There are three ways to add an XML data source:

▶ Create the XML file in SharePoint Designer 2013 and save it in your website.

▶ Import an existing XML file.

▶ Connect to an existing XML file on your network.

It is important to remember that when you are using an XML file as a data source, it must be well-formed XML. Invalid markup may cause errors that can be difficult to track down. You can validate the XML file using the Verify well-formed XML functionality in SharePoint Designer, which you will see shortly. Additionally, the XML file must either contain and conform to a schema or it must contain data from which a schema can be inferred (which will happen automatically with well-formed XML).

We're going to create a new XML file first, and then we'll create an XML data source that connects to the file:

1. Open SharePoint Designer 2013 and select Data Sources in the navigation pane.

2. Click on the File menu and select Add Item.

3. In the Pages section, click More Pages.

4. Click XML and then click the Create button.

5. Enter `TestXML` as the filename and save it to the Site Pages library.

6. Click OK. This opens a new XML file with an XML DOCTYPE declaration.

7. Enter the following XML in the file:

```xml
      <?xml version="1.0" encoding="utf-8" ?>
<spouses>
    <spouse>
          <BusinessEntityID>100</BusinessEntityID>
          <FirstName>Lelu</FirstName>
          <LastName>Song</LastName>
    </spouse>
    <spouse>
          <BusinessEntityID>93</BusinessEntityID>
          <FirstName>Kawkaba</FirstName>
          <LastName>Ho</LastName>
    </spouse>
    <spouse>
          <BusinessEntityID>100</BusinessEntityID>
          <FirstName>Amy</FirstName>
          <LastName>Krebs</LastName>
    </spouse>
    <spouse>
          <BusinessEntityID>100</BusinessEntityID>
          <FirstName>Jane</FirstName>
          <LastName>Hamilton</LastName>
    </spouse>
</spouses>
```

8. Click on the Edit tab of the ribbon.

9. In the Code Formatting section, click the Verify well-formed XML button to check your XML for errors.

10. Click the Save button on the ribbon to save your XML file.

Now we'll create an XML data source that connects to the XML file we just created:

1. Open SharePoint Designer 2013 and select Data Sources in the navigation pane.

2. On the Data Source tab of the ribbon, in the New group, click the XML File Connection button.

3. Click the Browse button, as shown in Figure 8.17, and locate the TestXML file you just created in the Site Pages library and it will then appear as the source.

4. On the General tab, enter TestXMLConn in the File Name box and click OK.

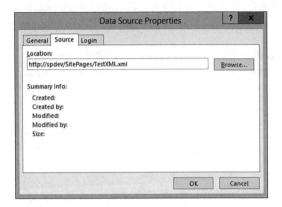

FIGURE 8.17   The TextXML file was via the browse button and is now correctly referenced as the source.

Reviewing Linked Data Sources

Data is almost never stored in a single table, or even a single database. Even the sample database we've been working with in this chapter (AdventureWorks2012) has a plethora of tables to hold many kinds of data. Bearing this in mind, SharePoint enables you to create a single data source that displays data from other linked data sources.

There are two ways to link data sources: merge and join. Merging a data source displays all the data from both data sources as rows of data. This means that if you join one data source with 100 records with a data source that has 50 records, your linked data source will display 150 records. To merge two data sources, they must have the same set of fields.

Joining data sources will display all the data from both data sources as columns. This means that you will not increase the number of records, but rather the number of columns displayed in a record. The two data sources must have one field in common to join successfully.

We are going to create a linked data source by creating two other data sources and joining them. One data source will connect to the Person table and the other will connect to the EmailAddresses table. We will link the two based on the common BusinessEntityID field.

Note: For this example, we will use data sources that are configured to use custom queries.

To create a linked data source using SharePoint Designer 2013, perform the following:

1. Open SharePoint Designer 2013 and select Data Sources in the navigation pane.

2. On the Data Sources tab of the ribbon, in the New group, click the Database Connection button.

3. On the Source tab of the Data Source Properties dialog box, click the Configure Database Connection button.

4. In the Configure Database Connection dialog box, in the Server Information section, type the name of the server where your database resides in the Server Name text box.

5. In the Provider Name drop-down box, select Microsoft .NET Framework Data Provider for SQL Server.

6. Under Authentication, click Save This Username and Password in the data connection.

7. Type your username in the User Name box.

8. Type your password in the Password box.

9. Click Next.

10. You are presented with a dialog box warning you that the username and password you entered will be stored as plain text in the data connection. Click OK to continue.

11. Click the radio button, for using custom commands, and then click Finish.

12. Click the Edit Command button.

13. In the command window, as shown in Figure 8.18, enter this command:

```
Select * from [Person].[Person]
```

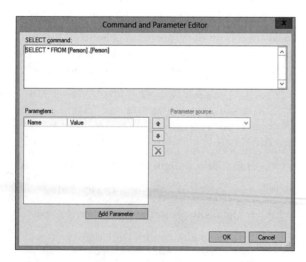

FIGURE 8.18   The completed custom query dialog.

TIP

We would ordinarily use fields in the select statement instead of the * (asterisk) identifier, which is shorthand in SQL for selecting all fields. We would also use a `where` clause to limit the number of rows returned, but at the time of writing, SharePoint Designer will crash if you try either of these best practices when creating a linked data source.

---

14. Click OK.

15. In the Data Source Properties dialog box, click the General tab and type `TestLinkConn1` as the name for the data source; then click OK.

16. On the Data Sources tab of the ribbon, in the New group, click the Database Connection button.

17. On the Source tab of the Data Source Properties dialog box, click the Configure Database Connection button.

18. In the Configure Database Connection dialog box, in the Server Information section, type the name of the server where your database resides in the Server Name text box.

19. In the Provider Name drop-down box, select Microsoft .NET Framework Data Provider for SQL Server.

20. Under Authentication, click Save This Username and Password in the Data Connection.

21. Type your username in the User Name box.

22. Type your password in the Password box.

23. Click Next.

24. You are presented with a dialog box warning you that the username and password you entered will be stored as plain text in the data connection. Click OK to continue.

25. Click the radio button for using custom commands and click Finish.

26. Click the Edit Command button.

27. In the command window, enter this command:

```
Select * from [Person].[EmailAddresses]
```

28. Click OK.

29. In the Data Source Properties dialog box, click the General tab and type `TestLinkConn2` as the name for the data source; then click OK.

Now that we have the two data sources to link, we can configure the linked data source:

1. On the Data Sources tab of the ribbon, in the New group, click the Linked Data Source button.

2. On the Source tab of the Data Source Properties dialog box, click the Configure Linked Source button.

3. In the Link Data Sources Wizard dialog box, as shown in Figure 8.19, expand Database Connections in the Available Data Sources pane.

FIGURE 8.19   The completed Link Data Sources data selection dialog.

4. Select TestLinkConn1 and click Add.

5. Select TestLinkConn2 and click Add.

6. Click Next.

7. On the next page, select the option to join the contents of the data sources, as shown in Figure 8.20.

8. On the next page, select BusinessEntityID, as shown in Figure 8.21, as the field to link for both data sources.

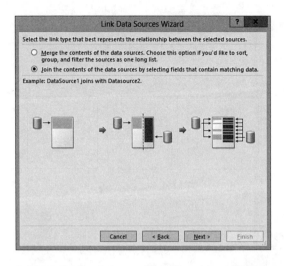

FIGURE 8.20   Select the option to join the data sources.

FIGURE 8.21   Select BusinessEntityID for both data sources.

9. On the last page, as shown in Figure 8.22, leave the default so that all available fields are selected and click Finish.

10. In the Data Source Properties dialog box, click the General tab and type TestLinkConn as the name for the data source; then click OK.

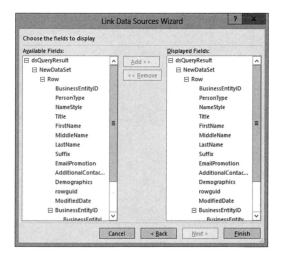

FIGURE 8.22   Select the default fields for the data source.

Testing a Data Source

Now that you have created a series of data sources, you probably want to know how they are used on a page. We will create a page that displays data using the linked data source created in the preceding section. The principles are the same for any data source you add to a page, though. To test this, perform the following steps:

1. Open SharePoint Designer 2013 and open the File tab.

2. In the Pages section, click the More Pages button.

3. On the subsequent page, select ASPX and click the Create button in the right pane.

4. In the Name text box, enter TestDS and then click OK.

5. You see a dialog asking whether you want to edit the page in advanced mode. Click Yes.

6. Place your cursor after the opening form tag and hit Enter to create a new, blank line.

7. On the Insert tab of the ribbon, in the Controls section, click the Data Sources drop-down list, as shown in Figure 8.23, and select TestLinkConn.

    If Data Sources is grayed out, click the refresh button in the quick links menu above the ribbon.

8. You should now see some new XML added to the page describing the data source, and the Data Source Details pane should be visible.

9. While holding down the Ctrl key, click the FirstName, LastName, and EmailAddress fields in the Data Source Details pane, as shown in Figure 8.24.

FIGURE 8.23   Select the TestLinkConn data source from the Data Sources drop-down list.

FIGURE 8.24   Select the right fields in the Data Source Details pane.

10. Click the Insert Selected Fields As drop-down and select Multiple Item View.

11. This adds the necessary XML and corresponding XSLT to the page for displaying the data from the data source.

12. Click the Save button in the quick links area above the ribbon.

13. On the Home tab of the ribbon, click the Preview in Browser button to view the web page.

Microsoft's Power BI for Office 365

Microsoft Office 365's Power BI contains a collection of features and services that enables organizations to visualize data and share these discoveries in a very similar manner as discussed in the earlier sections of this chapter.

Power BI provides organizations with a cloud-based self-service BI infrastructure and brings the Excel workbook sharing, discussed in earlier sections, together with online collaboration. There is a centralized Power BI Admin Center for managing your organization's Power BI infrastructure.

In the new hybrid cloud environment that is developing in most organizations throughout the globe, the Data Management Gateway is a feature that will connect on-premises data to the cloud.

Power BI works seamlessly with Excel to create content, data models, and visualizations while also providing the capability to share, collaborate, and extend those insights.

> **NOTE**
>
> It is important to review your licensing model to ensure that you have this capability available. For example, Excel is not part of Power BI for Office 365, but your organization's licensing model more than likely already provides you with Microsoft Excel.

Power BI's features and functionality are robust and are as listed here:

▶ Power Query enables users to easily discover and connect to data from public and corporate data sources.

▶ Power Pivot enables users to create a sophisticated data model directly in Excel.

▶ PowerView creates reports and analytical views with interactive data visualizations.

▶ Power Map provides for users to explore and navigate geospatial data on a 3D map experience in Excel.

▶ Power BI Sites, as shown in Figure 8.25, enable users to share, view, and interact with reports in these collaborative Power BI Sites.

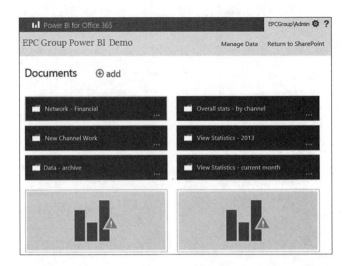

FIGURE 8.25   A Power BI Site for users to share, view, and interact with the available reports.

▶ Power BI Q&A is a feature that uses natural language queries to find, explore, and report over your data.

▶ Query and Data Management provides for users to share and manage queries and data sources, and view query usage analytics.

▶ Power BI app, available via the Power BI Windows Store, enables you to view reports on the go with your mobile device.

Summary

We have discussed Microsoft's BI stack and the features available, as well as the steps your organizations should take in implementing a successful BI initiative.

BI initiatives are on many organizations' radars to implement in 2014–2018 so that they finally can get true and centralized versions of the truth regarding their underlying business metrics.

The hybrid cloud is continuing to grow and is becoming a "norm" in more organizations, so it is key to understand where your data is stored as well as the security, compliance, and availability of that data to be consumed. If you have data that exists both on-premises and in the cloud, you want to ensure that your BI initiative and SharePoint roadmap take these variables into consideration.

In the next chapter, we will discuss SharePoint Governance and the many moving pieces it encompasses.

CHAPTER 9

Governance Strategies for SharePoint 2013, Office 365, and SharePoint Online

Governance Best Practices "from the Trenches" for SharePoint 2013 and Office 365's SharePoint Online

Governance is sometimes used as a catchall term to refer to nearly any and all functionality and how it should be managed with a SharePoint 2013 and/or Office 365 SharePoint Online initiative. The word "governance" is also one that is sometimes frowned upon in some organizations due to previous failed governance projects. If your organization's management has experienced previous failed efforts or has an overall distaste for the term "governance," you should consider using an alternative word or term to describe the development of your governance strategy and related policies.

Governance is a key component to ensure long-term success and is unique for every organization. It should define who will manage the environment or overall platform and define the related granular roles and responsibilities within an organization to establish rules for its appropriate usage. It should also outline how the business and technical users leverage the environment with a careful balance of required restrictions and enterprise compliance policies with well-defined procedures for growth and future change.

The strategies within this chapter have been developed by the team at EPC Group over the past 15 years to ensure that your organization's governance plan covers nearly all scenarios you may experience throughout the platform's life cycle. These strategies are outlined in the following four major pillars:

▶ People

   Roles and responsibilities

▶ Process

   How to accomplish common tasks as well as new business and technology requests

▶ Technology

   Leveraging features and tools to enforce policies

▶ Policy

   Collection of principles and clear definitions on how the platform is utilized

One of the keys to implementing a successful SharePoint governance strategy is to do so in a manner and mind-set that reflects "operational governance." One of the best ways I have heard this described was when a client's CIO once said to me that he felt their organization's SharePoint and Office 365 governance strategy would be an overall successful if it detailed not only how "the SharePoint ship was built but also how they should drive the SharePoint ship, maintain the SharePoint ship, and even how the SharePoint ship should be winterized."

Governance and its overall strategy should be controlled by a SharePoint/Office 365 Steering Committee that is responsible for ensuring best practices governance policies, as well as implementing and making available to users the features and functionality that will support the organization's mission.

Defining Your Organization's SharePoint Vision and Mission Statement

It is important that a clear message be communicated to your organization regarding the company's current and future SharePoint and/or Office 365 mission and overall vision that leadership has set for its various functions. The following is an example of an organization's SharePoint and/or Office 365 vision and overall mission statement:

"SharePoint provides a centralized environment where day-to-day activities and related documents and policies are organized in an intuitive manner with powerful search capabilities to all our team members. With this technology initiative, the organization has the latest industry-leading tools available for team members to quickly access the information and data required and then instantly collaborate on it. From any Internet-connected computer or device, team members will be able to realize greater efficiency in accessing important business systems, people information, company forms, news, benefits, calendars, and other relevant company information. This new centralized platform will provide tools for teams to collaborate and share documents, timelines, status reports, and other relevant communications, thus providing additional benefits to our customers and industry partners in a secure and efficient way."

The Scope of SharePoint 2013/Office 365's SharePoint Online Governance Strategy

To properly define the scope of your organization's governance strategy, you should begin by compartmentalizing the different technical, architectural, and functional areas, as shown in Figure 9.1, so that you can start to address each at a granular level. Starting at a high level, SharePoint governance consists of two major topical areas:

▶ Infrastructure Governance

▶ Information Management Governance

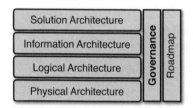

FIGURE 9.1   The various technical, architectural, and functional areas in scope for the SharePoint governance initiative.

You then break down these two major areas further to create four new main topic areas, which will enable you to begin the analysis and requirements gathering to properly architect and design tailored and organizationally specific SharePoint governance policies:

▶ Environment and Security Governance

▶ Custom Development Governance

▶ Content-Related Governance

▶ Administrative and Training Governance

These four major topic areas contain a large number of granular subtopics such as the following:

▶ **Environment and Security Governance**

    ▶ SharePoint Disaster Recovery Governance

    ▶ Defining SharePoint SLAs for System Architecture and the overall underlying architecture

    ▶ Defining SharePoint Maintenance

    ▶ SharePoint Security Governance

    ▶ Site Provisioning Governance

    ▶ Lync Server and OneDrive for Business Governance

▶ Defining compliance and regulatory governance

▶ Continued...

▶ **Custom Development Governance**

▶ Development of organizational SharePoint Development Standards

▶ Creation of Deployment and Code Promotion Standards

▶ SharePoint Branding Governance

▶ Visual Studio 2012/2013 and Team Foundation Server policies and procedures

▶ Continued...

▶ **Content-Related Governance**

▶ Enterprise Content Management–Related Policies

▶ Site Storage Policies (quotas, file upload limits, and so on)

▶ My Site and Social Computing Policies

▶ Power User and Content Updating Guidelines

▶ Executive and Legal Content Policies

▶ Apps, Libraries, and List Configuration and Customization Policies

▶ Continued...

▶ **Administrative and Training Governance**

▶ SharePoint Training Guidelines

▶ SharePoint Communication Plan Guidelines

▶ SharePoint Steering Committee Policies

▶ Enterprise SharePoint Support Model

▶ Executive Dashboard/SharePoint Reporting Guidelines

▶ Continued...

The scope of your organization's SharePoint governance strategy should be tailored to not only provide the information listed previously but also clearly define the following granular areas:

▶ Branding and "look and feel"

▶ Monitoring and compliance policies and procedures

▶ Management of user requests (new sites and custom development requests)

Key Objectives of the Governance Strategy Guide

Key objectives are defined outcomes implemented to meet business goals and provide a means to determine the overall effectiveness of the solution.

Your organization governance strategy is enacted to carry out the following:

- ▶ Create a consistent and standardized environment for collaboration

- ▶ Create a simple and convenient system for qualifying and storing content

- ▶ Provide a system for discovering content through simple navigational tools and effective search

- ▶ Ensure that the environment is managed and supported in a highly available manner

Guiding Principles for SharePoint Usage

Guiding principles shape how the overall solution will meet the key objectives defined by the organization. The following principles define the methodologies, rules, and descriptions used to manage the organization's SharePoint solution:

- ▶ Define groups for controlling polices and standards for SharePoint

- ▶ Define how the SharePoint application is delivered

- ▶ Define how sites are provisioned

- ▶ Ensure that the appropriate access levels are provided to users to ensure that compliance is strictly enforced

- ▶ Define resolutions for conflicts and required support

Roles and Responsibilities

A role in your organization's governance strategy assigns a set of responsibilities for the support of the SharePoint environment and includes areas such as daily maintenance and administration, design and branding, and change management. Each role is applicable to certain areas of functionality or specific business purposes. Some roles may cross or blend with other roles depending on the availability of resources.

A key factor in a governance role is to ensure that vital aspects of the SharePoint environment are managed, reviewed, adjusted, or removed to maintain an efficient and useful system. This governance strategy includes input and influence from several key groups, including business-focused members as well as SharePoint technical experts and key executive leadership, as detailed in Table 9.1. In the sections that follow, this is defined at a more granular level to form the organization's SharePoint governance.

TABLE 9.1   Roles and Responsibilities of Key Technical Experts That Will Help Ensure the Success of Governance

Role	Responsibilities and Tasks	Group	Permissions	Trustee
SharePoint Executive Board Manager	–Responsible for all SharePoint product and technology efforts –Leads SharePoint steering committee –Leads SharePoint executive board –Major SharePoint technology decision maker	SharePoint Executive Board	–N/A	Executive Board
SharePoint System Architect	–AD and Exchange integration	SharePoint Executive Board	–Admin Control has full control to all central administration and SharePoint services in all farm locations.	SharePoint Executive Board Manager
	–Profile synchronization		–Has system administrative and SQL admin-istration rights in development, QA, and production systems.	
	–Patch management (validation and testing), responsible for SharePoint farm infrastructure design, installation, guidelines, and best practices			
	–Governance model/best practices enforcement			
	–System Administrators day-to-day support			
	–Search administration			
	–Farm Administrators day-to-day support			
	–Third-party configuration			

Role	Responsibilities and Tasks	Group	Permissions	Trustee
SharePoint Application Architect	–SharePoint development team lead	SharePoint Executive Board	–Admin Control has full control to all central administration and SharePoint services in all farm locations.	SharePoint Executive Board Manager
	–Third-party configuration		–Has system administrative access and SQL administration rights in nonproduction systems.	
	–Line-of-business integration			
	–Governance model/best practices enforcement			
SharePoint Farm Administrator	–Manage operations of production, QA, and development environments for SharePoint	SharePoint Executive Board	–Full Control has access to all web applications.	SharePoint Executive Board Manager
	–Control the application at the operating system (OS) level and above		–Admin Control has full control to all central administration features and service applications.	
	–Cooperate with systems administrator to maintain SharePoint farm			
	–Help execute approved change requests			

Overview of Key Groups, Roles, and Users

Within your organization, the roles and responsibilities of the overall SharePoint and/or Office 365's SharePoint Online Service platform are split into these basic areas:

▶ Management groups

▶ Administrative/power user roles

▶ Developer roles

▶ User roles

Management Groups

The following subsections detail the different groups that have a stake in managing the SharePoint solution and its related services.

The overall management of SharePoint, Office 365, and SharePoint Online is controlled by the SharePoint Executive Board, which drives the process of aligning the SharePoint Service (that is, the overall technology platform) with evolving business needs and the overall company direction.

SharePoint Steering Committee

The SharePoint Steering Committee is composed of key stakeholders and oversees the strategic service direction and provides policy guidance.

The SharePoint Steering Committee should include a number of roles throughout the organization, including key members of senior management, business owners or key SharePoint stakeholders, and members of the SharePoint technical team, which I will refer to in the following sections as the "SharePoint Services team."

SharePoint stakeholders are defined as those in the business units that rely on the organization's SharePoint Services as a part of their business operation. The SharePoint Steering Committee should meet regularly to revisit structure, responsibilities and membership to ensure maximum effectiveness. The Steering Committee should also review potential scope changes for the organization's SharePoint-related initiatives and roadmap to address changes in business conditions and technology.

The role of the SharePoint Steering Committee will be to carry out these tasks:

▶ Align SharePoint, Office 365, and SharePoint Online initiatives with the overall business goals

▶ Set the strategic and functional guidance for the SharePoint Services team

▶ Continually assess SharePoint project viability

▶ Determine corporate standards and ensure they are communicated

▶ Approve all governance, standards, and policies

▶ Approve content publishing policies and assign departmental and functional ownership

▶ Approve SharePoint's branding, usability, and overall "look and feel"

▶ Approve changes to the official and published SharePoint Governance Strategy document available to the organization

▶ Review licensing purchases of Microsoft software as well as related software vendors who's product integrates with the organization's Microsoft solutions to ensure that there are no duplications of licensing

▶ Assess and approve the organization's BYOD policies and ensure that they are communicated

▶ Continually review compliance and regulatory laws that may affect the platform and its content

▶ Determine policies for OneDrive, Skype, Office Online, Microsoft Lync, and Exchange integration with SharePoint, Office 365, and SharePoint Online

▶ Perform audits on any of the organization's public cloud or hybrid cloud efforts to include a review of the cloud provider, SLAs, and updated pricing models, as well as any outages

▶ Ensure that the organization's SharePoint training strategies continue to fit the needs of the organization and that training does not become stagnant but is proactive in nature

The recommended structure of the SharePoint Steering Committee, as detailed in Table 9.2, calls for the committee to be chaired by the SharePoint Executive Board Manager. The committee should meet at least quarterly to review the following:

▶ Site structure

▶ Administrative responsibilities

▶ User adoption and metrics or criteria defined to measure success

TABLE 9.2   Structure of the SharePoint Steering Committee

Member	Purpose	Responsibilities
SharePoint Executive Board Manager	Has oversight of all discussions for change requests and implementations, and communicates with SharePoint Executive Board about requests and changes	−Present change requests −Oversee discussions regarding viability of requests −Present findings to Executive Board −Approve changes and project scope −Approve governance
SharePoint Operations Team	Provides technical insight and functional application for proposed changes and determines feasibility for implementing those changes	−Determine technical viability of change requests −Design and implement approved change requests −Assess current solution for continued viability
Business Unit Representative	Examines proposed changes and provides business guidance and value for proposed requests	−Determine business use case for change requests −Design use case scenarios −Determine business representative for solution −Determine and develop training requirements for solution

9

Based on this recommended structure, the next step is to determine the key stakeholders who should be involved in the SharePoint Steering committee. Typically, these are business leaders, IT managers, key technology stakeholders, legal representatives, and records management owners, as detailed in Table 9.3.

TABLE 9.3   Key Stakeholders Who Typically Make Up the Granular Roles of the SharePoint Steering Committee

Role	Responsibilities and Tasks
SharePoint Steering Committee Chair	The person responsible for chairing the SharePoint Steering Committee and owning sign-offs and casting the overall vote or decision should any impasse occur.
SharePoint Services Owner	The overall service owner of SharePoint who is responsible for all SharePoint product and technology efforts. Leads the SharePoint Steering Committee meetings and provides strategic guidance to the SharePoint Services team.
SharePoint Services Team Manager	The manager of the SharePoint Services team who is responsible for managing the day-to-day activities of the SharePoint Services team and delegating the incoming requests coming into the team from the different business units throughout the organization.
Records Management Representative	A key stakeholder for Records Management within the organization who ensures that the technology and business decisions being made regarding SharePoint's features for content and records management functionality continue to follow the records management standards within the organization.
Development Team(s) Representative	A key stakeholder or manager representing the SharePoint development teams to provide updates on development efforts such as custom SharePoint solutions, apps, workflows, business intelligence (BI) initiatives or other tailored organization solutions. This representative should also provide updates on capabilities of the team, code development and management practices, and the use of Microsoft Azure or other cloud-based VMs for development.
SharePoint Training Representative	A key stakeholder from training who will continue to monitor the ongoing activities of the SharePoint 2013 initiative while continuing to deliver training to the different audiences to meet the ongoing and possibly changing needs and requirements of the SharePoint user base within the organization.
Help Desk Representative	A key stakeholder from the organization's help desk, if applicable, who will monitor the activities of SharePoint and report to the committee on metrics regarding support calls and possible resolutions to reoccurring issues, and who will ensure that the help-desk team continues to be properly trained and proactive regarding the overall SharePoint Services provided to the organization.

SharePoint Governance Committee

The Governance Committee is the executor and manager of the governance plan in terms of form, execution, and modification, and provides oversight to the proper application and support of the governance plan itself.

The Governance Committee, as shown in Table 9.4, is made up of users from many different business units within the organization and includes identified SharePoint technical experts, business managers, daily users, legal counsel, and other applicable units.

TABLE 9.4   Example of an Organization's SharePoint Governance Committee

Member	Purpose	Expectation
Executive Sponsor	Management or other decision-making group that provides the support and drive for the collaboration of setting goals and objectives and following up on needs specific to SharePoint	Provide support for changes to be made to existing implementation to improve services for organization Encourage user adoption of changes by communication, awareness, and support for training Apply business focus and benefit to any initiative or need related to implementation
Meeting Facilitator	Those appointed by the Executive Sponsor to both oversee meetings and manage the committee as a whole for productive meetings	Organize and communicate with Committee Members Record and update decisions, initiatives, or concerns raised during meetings Schedule and maintain quarterly meetings
Business Unit Representation	Members of a business unit to represent the interest and impact of the SharePoint implementation	Have one or more members from each business unit to represent at all times Rotate members yearly Provide feedback and input to initiatives, needs, and decisions made regarding existing implementation
SharePoint Farm Administrator(s) or key technical representatives	SharePoint-related technical experts	

SharePoint Operations Team

The operations roles for SharePoint are focused on the detailed management of the SharePoint Service and are composed of several key sets of responsibilities. Each role is described by its specific areas of control as well as related operations groups, necessary rights, and responsible oversight members, as defined in Table 9.5.

TABLE 9.5   Structure of a SharePoint Operations Team

Role	Responsibilities and Tasks	Group	Permissions	Trustee
Active Directory Manager	–Active Directory Management –Exchange Management	Infrastructure	–Will not have access to portal or site configuration settings and will not be able to make any changes to the application	SharePoint System Architect
Network Engineer(s)	–WAN, LAN Monitoring –WAN, LAN Optimization –Load Balancing	Infrastructure	–Will not have access to portal or site configuration settings and will not be able to make any changes to the application	SharePoint System Architect
SharePoint Engineer(s)	–First level of support for complex day-to-day issues to support the organization's SharePoint users –Responsible for SharePoint services, policies, procedures, and governance/best practice enforcement –Serves as SharePoint champion(s) for almost all SharePoint areas	Enterprise Application Team	–Will not have system administrative or SQL administration rights –Local Full Control has full control given at the site collection level	SharePoint Farm Administrator
System Administrator(s)	–Responsible for maintenance of SharePoint servers from the hardware through the operating system (OS) –Responsible for SharePoint farm server infrastructure change requests –Responsible for day-to-day maintenance of SharePoint farm OS operations and uptime –Apply OS service packs, hot fixes, and updates	Infrastructure	–Will not have access to portal or site configuration settings and will not be able to make any changes to the application	SharePoint System Architect

Role	Responsibilities and Tasks	Group	Permissions	Trustee
Database Administrator(s)	–SQL Server database backup and recovery, SQL configuration, SQL upgrades and monitoring	Database Team	–Will not have access to portal or site configuration settings and will not be able to make any changes to the application –SQL Administrative rights	SharePoint System Architect

Administrative/Power User Roles

Administrative and power user roles are assigned to team members who are extremely knowledge about the technical aspects of SharePoint and familiar with its user interface. Members of these roles will provide administrative support to the organization's SharePoint user base. These include Site Collection Administrators, Site Owners, and Site Designers, as detailed in Table 9.6.

TABLE 9.6   Overview of the Roles and Responsibilities of Site Collection Administrators, Site Owners, and Site Designers

Roles	Responsibilities and Tasks	Training	Permissions	Trustees
Site Collection Administrator	–Manage features and solutions for the site collection on the production system –Perform SharePoint site provisioning within the site collection –Manage security –Manage site content –Perform subsite management –Act as liaison between SharePoint Operations Team and the business unit represented by the site collection –Create workflows –Be able to demonstrate functional knowledge of tools to others	Instructor led with good understanding of site administration, security, and content creation	–Access defined at the Site Collection level –No access at the system level –No access to Central Administration	SharePoint Farm Administrator

6

Roles	Responsibilities and Tasks	Training	Permissions	Trustees
Site Owner	–Create Site Owner content –Manage content –Manage permissions	Instructor led with good understanding of site administration, security, and content creation	–Access defined at the site level –No access at the system level –No access to Central Administration	Site Collection Administrator
Site Designer	–Manage the site layout and structure –Participate in design tasks for a SharePoint site as needed –Create out-of-box noncoded workflows	Instructor led with good understanding of site administration and content creation	–Access defined at the site level –No access at the system level –No access to Central Administration	Site Owner

Site Collection Administrators

Site Collection Administrators have full control over the entire site collection and also have access to additional areas, such as the Site Collection Recycle Bin and Content and Structure administration. There will be only a primary and secondary Site Collection Administrator. Additional responsibilities of Site Collection Administrators include these:

▶ Reporting, reviewing, and acting on any audit finding that indicates unauthorized access

▶ Supplying reports and related site usage information as requested

▶ Maintaining the audit log and related information

Site Owners

Site Owners have full control over an entire site and subsites, unless inheritance has been broken. The Site Owner is allowed to manage site permissions as well as create, modify, and delete SharePoint-related containers such as lists, apps, and libraries. There will be only a primary and secondary Site Owner per site. Additional responsibilities of Site Owners include the following:

▶ Ensuring that existing content is updated and relevant

▶ Ensuring that content is removed from the site if it is out-of-date, expired, or otherwise no longer relevant while adhering to the organization's records management and/or retention policy

▶ Remaining aware of content in other areas to ensure consistency and to ensure that duplicate content does not exist elsewhere

▶ Ensuring that published content adheres to branding, compliance, or other related policies

▶ Providing oversight to ensure that high-risk (confidential/inappropriate) material is not within the SharePoint environment

▶ Responsible for timely approval of user requests or assistance

▶ Ensuring that content types (that is, metadata) have been properly entered into lists and libraries

▶ Ensuring that content is posted to the correct location

Site Designers

Site Designers have Site Designer permission over a specific site and its subsites. Site Designers are allowed to perform the same functions as members of a site, as well as create, modify, and delete SharePoint-related containers such as lists, apps, and libraries. Site Designers are appointed as desired by the relevant Site Owner.

Other User Roles

The additional user roles of Member, Approver, and Visitor, shown in Table 9.7, are roles that are managed by the Site Owner. Your organization may tailor these roles to meet specific requirements of the organization. Users may belong to more than one group and may also be removed from lower-level roles when higher-level role permissions may encompass the permissions of the lower-level role.

TABLE 9.7   Overview of the Member, Approver, and Visitor Roles

Roles	Responsibilities and Tasks	Training	Permissions	Trustees
Member	–Create content (documents, list items) –Contribute to collaboration sites (blog, wiki) –Initiate workflows	Computer-based training (CBT) with good understanding of document libraries and lists	–Access defined at the SharePoint site level –No access at the system level	Site Owner
Approver	–Approve content (documents, list items) –Initiate workflows	CBT with good understanding of content approval and workflows	–Access defined at the SharePoint site level –No access at the system level	Site Owner
Visitor	–View content	N/A	–N/A	Site Owner

6

Developer Roles

Developer roles, as detailed in Table 9.8, allow for the modification of SharePoint sites, lists, apps, and other areas of SharePoint, either through code-based solutions and changes or via more superficial updates through web-based design tools for simple editing. Developer roles can widely differ based on the experience of the actual developer and her familiarity with Visual Studio 2012/2013, as well as how to properly package and deploy a solution or an app.

TABLE 9.8   Overview of the Developer Roles

Roles	Responsibilities and Tasks	Training	Permissions	Trustees
Developer	–Create custom workflows –Create custom web parts, apps, solutions, and features –Be responsible for building the framework and features of the portal –Modify SharePoint templates as needed –Write ASP.Net code –Participate in design tasks as needed –Participate in development and testing as needed –Create custom forms	Instructor-led training for Visual Studio, ASP.Net, and SharePoint Designer. Training can also include branding and responsive web design-related topics, as well as Team Foundation Server (TFS) for proper code and solution storage.	–Access is defined at the SharePoint application level. No access at the system level. –Access does not exist in the production environment.	SharePoint Application Architect

An individual Developer Role can vary based on the person's real-world experience and knowledge to complete tasks such as these:

▶ Implementing development standards within the organization for:

  ▶ Code and code-related security

  ▶ Builds, packaging, and release

▶ Implementing processes for:

  ▶ Solution life cycle

  ▶ Code reviews

  ▶ Security reviews

  ▶ Change management

▶ Providing overall custom development operational management for:

  ▶ Deployed solutions

  ▶ Updated business and functional requirements from the business

SharePoint Architecture Governance

The hierarchy of SharePoint and its underlying information architecture, as discussed in detail in Chapter 5, "Implementing a Best Practices SharePoint 2013/Office 365 Information Architecture," consists of web applications, site collections, subsites, lists, and libraries.

Web applications provide the main URL path and form the top-level taxonomy structure in the hierarchy, whereas site collections reside within the web application and provide separate security and features within SharePoint and/or Office 365's SharePoint Online. SharePoint sites and subsites are subsets of site collections and subsites have the capability to inherit security or features from the site collection but can provide unique security boundaries as well. The following section provides governance recommendations and an approach you can utilize for your organization's specific architecture and configuration.

Web Applications and Site Collection Governance Considerations

It is key to create policies to ensure that no new web applications are created without permission or awareness of a member of the SharePoint Steering Committee. It is equally important to ensure that site collections are being created that only utilize site templates that the organization has created that contain the appropriate lists, libraries, apps, web parts, and approved branding standards.

> **TIP**
>
> SharePoint site templates can be created without a great deal of time and effort and they have incredible ROI. Site templates can also ensure that SharePoint site provisioning is done in a governed manner. Perform the steps detailed at the following URL to create site templates for your organization: http://msdn.microsoft.com/en-us/library/jj938033.aspx

Criteria to Create a Site Collection

The following details a granular overview of the justification of governance policies your organization can implement regarding site collections:

▶ For security management benefits

Every Site Collection creates a security boundary between one collection of sites and another collection of sites. Each Site Collection has its own collection of SharePoint groups and Permissions.

▶ For privacy or management benefits and different site collection administrators

Each Site Collection has a role of "Site Collection Administrator" and one or more people assigned to that role. The "Site Collection Administrator" has Full Control access to all content contained within the sites of that collection. There are times when either for privacy or confidentiality reasons, you must have different people assigned to manage that collection of sites.

▶ For search separation

It is possible to assign a different Search Center for each Site Collection, thus allowing for a different scope of results to be queried by the users in that collection.

▶ For workflow separation

Custom workflows are enabled per Site Collection and may need to be separated due to security or functional requirements.

▶ To impose specific storage quotas

SharePoint site collections allow you to define different storage quotas and email warnings to notify users when they are approaching a defined threshold on their Site Collection storage. Different business units may have different requirements for the volume of data they must maintain.

▶ To impose specific site solution quotas

With a SharePoint Site Collection, you can define the maximum number of points sandbox solutions can use per day. Additionally, you can also configure an email warning when storage exceeds a certain number of points.

▶ To ensure governed site collection proliferation

Site collections within the organization should not duplicate the purpose of other available site collections and should be created in a methodical manner to lower resource allocation as well as the required related maintenance.

SharePoint 2013 has many features that can be enabled at the site collection level. You may not want the same features active on specific site collections because this can provide functionality that should not be available to some business units or users.

Sites and Subsites

A site is a single SharePoint subsite within a site collection and is also a hierarchical set of subsites that can be managed together. Subsites within a site have common features, such as shared permissions, galleries for apps, templates, content types, and web parts, and can share a common navigation.

A subsite can inherit permissions and navigation structure from its parent site or alternatively can be specified and managed independently. A site and subsites governance strategy should be implemented to specify which site template should be used when it is created.

TIP

Your organization must have a policy that is communicated to all users that specifies the steps users must take to request a new site. This policy should also include the required information users must submit in order to justify a new site's creation, along with the responsibilities they must adhere to if their site request is approved.

Site Governance Recommendation

The following are recommendations for your organization to consider when developing governance strategies and policies for SharePoint 2013 and/or Office 365's SharePoint Online sites, as well as the components and contents within these sites:

▶ Document libraries and lists should contain at least two organizationally approved core content types (that is, metadata fields) to ensure content management best practices, as well as related search results.

▶ All sites should be audited every four to six weeks to ensure that security and permission strategies are properly configured.

▶ All site content should be periodically monitored for sensitive or classified content.

▶ All pictures and media stored within a site should be periodically reviewed for content.

▶ Site quotas must be set within each site.

TIP

SharePoint 2013's software boundaries and limits regarding uploads and other features can be found at the following link: http://technet.microsoft.com/en-us/library/cc262787.aspx

Office 365's SharePoint Online software boundaries and limits regarding uploads and other features can be found at the following link: http://office.microsoft.com/en-us/office365-sharepoint-online-enterprise-help/sharepoint-online-software-boundaries-and-limits-HA102694293.aspx

▶ Navigation should be vetted and agreed on by stakeholders to ensure standardization and usability throughout SharePoint.

▶ RSS feeds should be limited to content related to the organization.

▶ Discussion boards and wikis must not contain defamatory content about the company or employees within the organization.

▶ Users must sign and/or agree to a "user agreement" before accessing the SharePoint environment that details governance strategies as well as compliance standards and acceptable usage.

▶ Any SharePoint Designer access and related edits must be tightly monitored and controlled. The organization may also consider disabling SharePoint Designer access entirely.

▶ A file-type exclusion list should be implemented within sites to avoid nonorganizational or possibly harmful files from entering the environment.

▶ Version control should be turned on within document libraries, along with the appropriate version settings to match the organization's requirements.

▶ The organization should implement a policy that mandates that in almost all cases SharePoint Site Owners should avoid breaking inheritance whenever possible from all subsites, libraries, and lists.

General Site Collection Management

SharePoint usage must comply with existing organization policies and standards, including any records retention and usage policies. The organization should impose a quota limitation based on content and related storage requirements. The following examples detail a scenario of quotas that an organization can enforce:

▶ Each user's My Site is allotted 200MB of storage.

▶ The maximum allocation for any site collection is 100GB of storage.

▶ There are three quota levels: Level 1 = 25GB, Level 2 = 35GB, Level 3 = 50GB.

▶ The default quota for site collections is 25GB.

▶ Site Collection Administrators receive alerts when storage is at 85% of the currently assigned quota.

▶ SharePoint Farm Administrators can increase quotas to the next level for site collections without additional approval based on business unit need.

▶ At 50GB, if business justification is provided, the site collection will be moved into a separate database and assigned the maximum quota capacity of 100GB with no exceptions.

▶ SharePoint best practice dictates that no single database will be larger than 200GB, and therefore there will be no more than two such site collections in this database.

When Site Collection Administrators are notified that their collection is approaching the quota limit, they will contact the Farm Administrator, who will work with them to review the current site and make adjustments to the existing content such as deleting, moving, or archiving. If no adjustments can be made, the site collection will be elevated to the next level quota.

If it is determined that the collection will continue to require additional storage space beyond the defined quota, downtime will be scheduled and the collection will be migrated to a dedicated database.

NOTE

As a best practice, it is recommended that Site Collection Administrators and site owners not be allowed to upload solutions into the site Solutions Gallery and functionality will be disabled.

Upload Limits and Restricted File Types

The following are examples of recommendations for upload limitations, as well as restricted file types for SharePoint sites. The recommended maximum size for a single document that is allowed to be stored within SharePoint is 2GB. The maximum size for a single upload operation should be initially set at 150MB.

The file types shown in Table 9.9 are recommended to be excluded from being uploaded and stored within SharePoint.

TABLE 9.9   Recommended File Types to Exclude from Uploading to SharePoint

Ade	adp	asa	ashx	asmx
Asp	bas	bat	cdx	cer
Chm	class	cmd	cnt	com
Config	cpl	crt	csh	der
Dll	exe	fxp	gadget	grp
Hlp	hpj	hta	htr	htw
Ida	idc	idq	ins	isp
Its	jse	json	ksh	lnk
Mad	maf	mag	mam	maq
Mar	mas	mat	mau	mav
Maw	mcf	mda	mdb	mde
Mdt	mdw	mdz	msc	msh
msh1	msh1xml	msh2	msh2xml	mshxml
Msi	ms-one-stub	msp	mst	ops
Pcd	pif	pl	prf	prg
printer	ps1	ps1xml	ps2	ps2xml
psc1	psc2	pst	reg	rem
Scf	scr	sct	shb	shs
shtm	shtml	soap	stm	svc
url	vb	vbe	vbs	vsix
ws	wsc	wsf	wsh	xamlx

Site Provisioning

One of the most important processes that an organization can put in place is a standardized site provisioning (that is, new site request) policy to ensure that content sprawl related to the existence of sites with the same or very similar content or purses be created and utilized.

The following is an example of a site provisioning policy that your organization can utilize and tailor to fit your specific requirements:

Employees, team members, and contractors with existing Active Directory accounts may request a SharePoint site via the following URL (that is, *siterequest*.epcgroup-example.com) where a formal request ticket must be submitted. Submitted requests must be approved by the Site Collection Administrator.

Table 9.10 details some of the criteria that your organization should consider utilizing as required fields or approval criteria in your formal site provision process.

TABLE 9.10   Fields and Criteria to Consider for Your Organization's Formal Site Provisioning Process

Requirements	Required Fields
–Requester has an existing Active Directory account.	–Requester name
–Site Owner has completed training. (*Note:* The level of training will be provided by the training team based on the recommendation provided.)	–Site Owner name
	–Preferred name of site
	–Requested site template from approved list
–Requested name for the site is unique and does not duplicate the name of a site already in use.	–Business justification for the creation of this new site
–Approval of the Site Collection Administrator is needed.	

In some cases, a new site request may be submitted that requires custom development. These site requests should go through the standard request process, as well as be approved by the SharePoint Executive Board. Table 9.11 details some of the criteria that your organization should consider regarding the approval and provisioning of customized sites and new functionality outside of the existing approved site templates.

TABLE 9.11   Criteria to Utilize for Custom Site Requests

Requirements	Required Fields
–SharePoint Executive Board approval is needed.	–Requester name
	–Site Owner name
–Requester has an existing Active Directory account.	–Preferred name of site
	–Requested site template from approved list
–Requester has completed training.	–Business justification for the request of this new site
–Requested name for the site is unique and is not already in use.	–Detailed list of customizations requested
	–Review existing sites and their apps\features to ensure no site duplication
	–Review the development costs of customizations
	–Request budget and resource allocation approval

By default, all new sites inherit the permissions of the parent site they are created under. A site is created with unique permissions only if ownership is assigned to an organization's employee with the approval of the appropriate Site Collection Administrator.

If an employee will no longer be handling Site Owner responsibilities, it is the responsibility of that Site Collection Administrator, in coordination with the business, to determine who will take over the Site Owner role.

Site Auditing

Auditing features are available for documents as well as list items that are not part of a document, such as items in task lists, issues lists, discussion groups, or calendars. Auditing features both address and log information for SharePoint features as well as events, such as those listed next.

The following audit settings should be enabled:

▶ Documents and Items

  ▶ Opening or downloading documents, viewing items in lists, or viewing item properties

  ▶ Moving or copying items to another location in the site

  ▶ Deleting or restoring items

▶ Apps, Lists, Libraries, and Sites

  ▶ Editing content types and columns

  ▶ Editing users and permissions

The following audit settings should be enabled by default but based around organizationally specific scenarios:

▶ Documents and Items

  ▶ Editing items

  ▶ Checking out or checking in items

▶ Apps, Lists, Libraries, and Sites

  ▶ Searching site content

Site Deletion Process

Site deletion is a significant impact process and should be controlled by Farm Administrators, or a similar organizational role, in conjunction with your organizations records management and/or records retention policies. Site Owners should submit a formal request for site deletion to the Farm Administrator, and no site should be deleted without an approved request being followed.

The deletion request should include the URL of the site to be deleted and the contact information of the Site Owner. Sites should not be deleted if any of the following criteria are met:

▶ The site contains active subsites.

▶ The site owner cannot be contacted to verify approval of the request.

▶ The site contains data that must be retained. If it is determined that the site contains data that must be retained, the site will be deleted only if the data that must be retained can be moved to another location or appropriately archived.

Security Governance for SharePoint 2013 and Office 365's SharePoint Online

Security has never been a hotter topic in IT. In most cases, however, even though it is being discussed by members of the organization and it dominates a good deal of technology news coverage, it is still often an afterthought for many SharePoint deployments.

In many SharePoint deployments, the organization's Active Directory (AD) deployment may have a good deal of duplication, custom groups, or old and expired information that has been created and stored over many years. Implementing a best practices SharePoint security strategy requires in-depth planning and knowledge of the overall information architecture (IA) design, as well as an understanding and awareness of the capabilities available.

The members of your organization's project team may be security experts but not necessarily SharePoint security experts, so there must be knowledge transfer, demos, and conversations around its capabilities to ensure that all team members are on the same page. It is important to understand not only what SharePoint's security can do but also what it may not be able to do out-of-the-box to meet specific or custom requests.

Protecting the content and intellectual property that is stored within SharePoint and/or Office 365 should be the number-one goal of the project. Your organization's intellectual property is what drives your business, as well as what gives you a competitive advantage.

Depending on the type of organization and business sector you are in, there are various regulations and compliance laws that you may be subject to, so implementing a SharePoint security model that will ensure a reduced- or zero-liability footprint is key. Understanding the granular details of the compliance framework and granular requirements faced by your business, as detailed in Figure 9.2, is key to designing your SharePoint security roadmap.

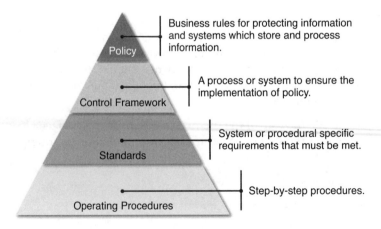

FIGURE 9.2   An overview of a compliance management framework.

For example, if your organization is in the healthcare sector, you know that you are subject to HIPAA, PHI, and PII regulations, but what about the newly enacted laws on HIPAA HITECH?

> **NOTE**
>
> For more information on the Health Information Technology for Economic and Clinical Health (HITECH) Act, refer to the following link: http://www.hhs.gov/ocr/privacy/hipaa/administrative/enforcementrule/hitechenforcementifr.html

There is a wide range of laws, compliance regulations, and related security considerations that you must be aware of to avoid compliance violations, fines, sanctions, and any possible reputation impacts that your company could incur in facing these issues.

The following are high-level examples of security considerations and corresponding scenario implications:

- Intellectual Property
    - New product release information, loss of competitive advantage, loss of marketing message or related efforts
- Public Health
    - Health records, insurance fraud, and so on
- Public Safety or Deployment Success
    - Protection of classified or sensitive information and mission plans

Permissions Management

When you are implementing your permission management strategy, there are some core standards you can begin with, such as these:

- The accounts running services should be Active Directory domain accounts.
- They should not be personal administration accounts.
- A central email account should be configured for all managed accounts.

In most cases, the organization's employees and contractors with existing Active Directory accounts will be granted access to the appropriate SharePoint Site collection, sites, lists, and libraries, as shown in Figure 9.3, using the employees' AD account and password.

User permissions and related permission policies should be implemented as follows:

- User Permissions
    - Permissions available within permission levels at the site collection level.

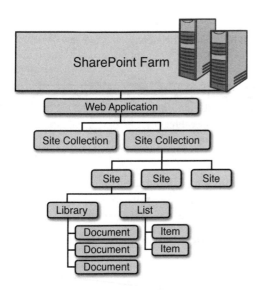

FIGURE 9.3   An overview of SharePoint's hierarchical architecture.

▶ Permission Policies

    ▶ Define groups of permissions (similar to permission levels).

    ▶ Only place with a "Deny" capability (that is, the default: deny write, deny all).

▶ User Policies

    ▶ Assign permission policies to users and groups for the entire web app (that is, deny the group the permission to delete items within an entire web app—applicable to a public-facing web app).

▶ User access will be also be managed through the use of SharePoint groups.

▶ Permissions will not be directly assigned to either Active Directory groups or individual user accounts.

▶ A combination of Active Directory groups and individual user accounts will be utilized as appropriate for individual and specific situations and added to the SharePoint group to control permissions.

Requests to access specific site collections should be made through the Site Collection Administrators through a built-in access request function. Access to specific Sites is controlled by the Primary Site Owner as determined via the Site Access Request setting and is handled through the built-in Access Request function. This practice is designed to provide the greatest flexibility and ease of management for security, content targeting, and communication.

Office 365 Compliance and Standards

In planning your organization's Office 365 security roadmap, it is key to take into consideration its published compliance and related standards, as detailed in Table 9.12.

TABLE 9.12   Overview of Office 365's Compliance and Standards

Category	Certification	Audience
International Standards and Controls	ISO 27001	All Customers
	Data Processing Agreement	
	SSAE 16 (Statement on Standards for Attestation Engagement)	
	SOC 1 (Type I and Type II) Compliance	
Industry Specific Compliance and Standards	FISMA	U.S. Government
	HIPAA/BAA	Healthcare Customers
	FERPA	Education-related Customers
Geography-Specific Standards	EU Safe Harbor	EU Customers
	EU Model Clauses	

Content Management Governance

Content within SharePoint includes not only documents but also workflows, libraries, lists, and calendars, as well as a wide variety of other content elements. Management of that content includes how it is maintained, classified, stored, deleted, recovered, and moved. Content should follow the organization's defined security policy and standards for information technology assets.

Web Content management applies to web pages, page layouts, and other web-based features of SharePoint sites and defines how the related content is created, edited, approved, and published for user consumption.

The following sections discuss content management governance and related best practices strategies.

Document, Content, and Records Management Governance

In SharePoint, the terms Document Management, Enterprise Content Management (ECM), and Records Management (RM) can sometimes be intertwined and used to describe very similar initiatives. Those topics are covered in granular detail in Chapter 10, "Enterprise Content Management (ECM), Records Management (RM), and eDiscovery Best Practices."

The following sections, as mentioned previously, cover governance strategies for content management and how best your organization can architect SharePoint to successfully manage these following proven strategies.

Document management, for example, can describe the policies that control the creation, editing, approval, publishing, retention, and disposal of content used through the SharePoint environment. Content may be created inside or outside of SharePoint and stored and managed within SharePoint. Content stored and managed within SharePoint is governed by policies to keep content relevant, minimize storage, and manage automation. SharePoint content must adhere to the organization's records retention policy at all times, and involving the legal department in your SharePoint initiative is key to ensuring that this is achieved.

Information that is created and/or transmitted in SharePoint may be subject to discovery in court litigation requests. It is incumbent upon SharePoint users to effectively maintain records in accordance with the organization's records retention policy.

Two terms commonly used when discussing records management and individual records are "retention" and "destruction." Retention of superfluous, nonrelevant information and correspondence beyond its disposition timeframe will result in decreased efficiency and effectiveness while mitigating legal risks.

Your organization's records retention schedule values should be added to SharePoint's core content type strategies and properties to allow for record declaration, data integrity, and disposition processing of SharePoint content in a manner that is compliant with the organization's records management policy, as depicted in Table 9.13. Records and record types are typically defined by the organization's legal department.

> **NOTE**
>
> Table 9.13 is a straightforward example to describe content that may be stored in SharePoint and how an organization's legal retention policy and related expiration policy may be enforced. This example and its legal retention policy should not be applied to your organization but rather used as an outline for how your specific content type strategy can be outlined and architected.

TABLE 9.13   Examples of Content Types and Related Legal Retention Policies

Content Type	Legal Retention Policy	Expiration Policy
Presentation	Active until superseded	EBD + 1 year
Press Release	Active + 1 year	EBD + 1 year
Procedure	Active + 6 years	EBD + 6 years
Project File	Active + 2 years	EBD + 2 years
Project Plan	Active + 2 years	EBD + 2 years
Report	Active + 1 year	EBD + 1 year
Voice Mail	Active + 30 days	EBD + 30 years

EBD is a standard term utilized for Expiration Basis Date.

Digital Asset Management

Digital asset management describes the life cycle of digital assets such as images, audio, and video files. Each asset type may require metadata or other controls based on type, as outlined in Table 9.14.

TABLE 9.14   Overview of Digital Asset Management File Types and Related Metadata

Asset Type	File Types	Metadata
Images	.jpg, .jpeg, .gif, .png, .bmp, .ico, .tiff	Resolution, Photographer, Image Size
Audio	.mp3, .wma, .wav	Duration, Composer, Artist, Genre
Video	.avi, .wmv, .mp4	Category, Genre, Release Date, Rendition

Metadata Management

A default set of content properties and keywords (metadata) will be utilized for documents and items created in the environment. These properties and keywords provide additional information about the content in the SharePoint environment and are technically referred to as content types. This not only provides a way for content to be categorized but also provides for more accurate search results in SharePoint 2013's search.

Defining Your Organization's Metadata Model

A metadata model, as shown in Figure 9.4, provides for a typical three-tier attribute architecture that provides flexibility to categorize your organization's content, as well as related processes, functions, and locational needs.

A metadata model should do the following:

▶ Deliver the core attributes (that is, content types) to support the SharePoint environment and related records management and retention policies

▶ Recommend opportunities to standardize labels and definitions for extended attributes that will enable the business to review and mandate for continued improvement and understanding of the organization's data

▶ Implement the architecture to support extended and local attributes (that is, content types)

During the development of your organization's content type strategy, it is key to take into consideration the different levels and locations of attributes to ensure that your plan is comprehensive and complete.

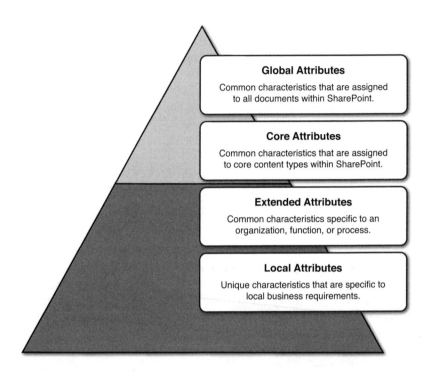

FIGURE 9.4   An overview of a SharePoint Metadata Model.

Recycle Bin

Content restoration can be controlled by the business user via the SharePoint Recycle Bin. The Recycle Bin captures item, file, list, library, app, and subsite deletions, which can be restored through the Recycle Bin. Subsites are stored in the Site Collection Recycle Bin (what is considered the second stage Recycle Bin) and can be restored only by Site Collection Administrators. Site collections are captured in the Site Collection Recycle Bin but cannot be restored through the user interface. PowerShell commands or scripts are required to retrieve site collections that have been deleted.

The Recycle Bin has two stages:

▶ The first stage Recycle Bin stores items for up to 90 days from the time the content was deleted, and then permanently removes the content. These items can be restored only by the business user who deleted the item.

▶ Items in the first stage Recycle Bin that have been deleted by a user other than the user requesting its retrieval can be restored by the Site Collection Administrator if the 90-day period has not expired.

▶ The second stage Recycle Bin stores content deleted from the first stage Recycle Bin before the 90-day deletion period, and for the remainder of the 90-day period it can be restored only by the Site Collection Administrator.

▶ Content held in the first stage Recycle Bin is included in any applicable Site Collection quota.

▶ The second stage Recycle Bin stores an additional 50% data volume of the assigned Site Collection quota.

▶ Only Site Collection Administrators may access the second stage Recycle Bin.

NOTE

Items that are no longer within the Recycle Bin will not be restored.

Workflow Governance Considerations

Out-of-the-box workflows may be configured only by users with appropriate permissions, which may fall within the role(s) of Site Designers, Site Owners, or Site Collection Administrators. Site Members may initiate or participate in existing workflows associated with a SharePoint list, library, app, or content type. SharePoint contains out-of-the-box workflows and also provides a platform for more complex workflow authoring and development, as shown in Figure 9.5.

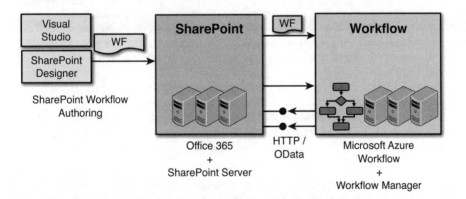

FIGURE 9.5   An overview of SharePoint 2013's workflows and authoring process.

9

The following considerations should be addressed when you are developing, deploying, and managing workflows within your organization:

▶ Which team members within your organization will define the business rules and related configuration of workflows?

    ▶ Will this be done on a site collection basis or a site-by-site basis?

    ▶ Does the organization have business analysts with technical understanding to properly convey business requirements and convert them into functional requirements?

▶ Will workflows be implemented that will work both on-premises and in a cloud architecture such as Office 365, Microsoft Azure, or Amazon Web Services and require hybrid cloud-related configurations?

▶ What task or process management tools are currently utilized or in place within the organization, and how will SharePoint's workflow capabilities impact those tools?

    ▶ Has an inventory of business processes been performed? If so, are there any that are in need of improvement that may be an opportunity for a "quick win" with the implementation of a new SharePoint workflow?

▶ What reporting tools are currently implemented within the organization?

▶ Are there any enterprise integration concerns with possible existing workflows or automated business processes (outdated technology, old code, incompatibility with the .NET framework, and so on)?

> **NOTE**
>
> SharePoint workflows can be implemented across various platforms, but it is key to understand the current workflow or business process automation playing field within your organization.

▶ What stakeholders or team members will be responsible for the management and proper operation of the organization's workflows and new process automation initiatives?

SharePoint 2013's workflow architecture for an on-premises environment, as depicted in Figure 9.6, does differ from that of a cloud-based Office 365 or Microsoft Azure SharePoint, as shown in Figure 9.7.

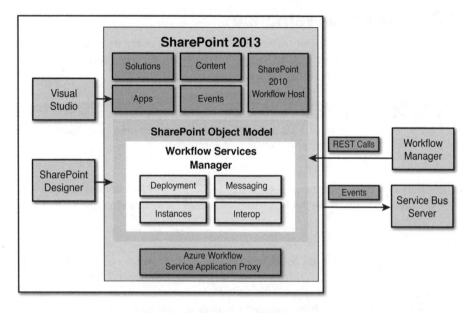

FIGURE 9.6   An overview of SharePoint 2013's on-premises workflow architecture.

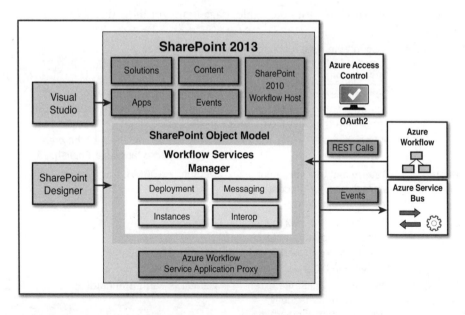

FIGURE 9.7   An overview of a cloud-based Office 365 or Microsoft Azure SharePoint 2013 architecture.

Social Computing Governance

Social Computing policies help control information sharing and usage through the common social functions that are a part of SharePoint and may require additional supporting policies such as the organization's Acceptable Usage Policy.

NOTE

Social Computing and SharePoint 2013's related functionality are covered in granular detail in Chapter 16, "Social Networking and My Site Strategies."

The guidelines provided here describe general usage scenarios and should be considered separately in the areas that allow for such features to be activated individually.

My Sites

My Sites represent the use of personal collaboration site collections for individual business users and can be activated and allowed for specific sets of users as needed. The organization's usage policy may or may not restrict the use of sites for individuals. However, all sites used for personal reasons will have reduced controls related to the standard site and site collection usage policies.

Table 9.15 describes the main areas for acceptable usage limits for individual My Sites.

TABLE 9.15   Areas for Acceptable Usage Limits for Individual My Sites

Usage	Description	Limit
Language Option	Determines whether My Sites can be created in languages other than the SharePoint farm core language	Default is unavailable without additional Multilingual User Interface (MUI) packs installed. Policy is that My Sites will be created using the core language English.
Storage Quota	Determines the maximum storage size for all content in the Site Collection	Default is 100MB.
User Solution	Determines the maximum number of solution points scored before solutions automatically disable	Disabled.
Blocked File Types	Determines which file extensions are automatically prevented from upload into a My Site Library	Default is Farm Standard.
Site Collection Administrator	Determines which users have Site Collection Administration rights to the site collection	Default is provisioned user.

Usage	Description	Limit
SharePoint Designer 2013	Determines whether SharePoint Designer 2013 is allowed to be used and which features of SharePoint Designer are allowed	Default is allowed. Standard is disabled.
Privacy Controls	Determines whether other users are allowed to see information in an individual profile as well as the default state of visibility	Default shows all directory-based properties to everyone and cannot be changed, but SharePoint-specific properties are manageable by the user. Standard is set to default.
Blog or Other Subsite	Determines whether the Blog subsite or other subsites may be created by a specific user	Default allows any subsite, including the Blog option, to be created. Standard is set to default.
OneDrive for Business	Determines whether the user may have personal content in OneDrive for Business and is synchronized with a personal site	Default allows OneDrive for Business to synchronize. Standard is set to disallow.

Additional policies applied to the shared My Site location are defined as outlined here:

▶ **Newsfeeds:** The Newsfeed provides a system of showing updates to individual users who have subscribed to automatic updates on other users, content, or sites. The organization's policy must consider whether to allow the usage of Newsfeeds.

> **NOTE**
>
> Your organization has the option to replace SharePoint 2013, Office 365's SharePoint Online My Site Newsfeeds with Yammer, but this is not something I would recommend upon your initial project phase.

▶ **Communities:** Communities are Site Templates that provide a forum experience within SharePoint. Communities enable you to categorize and cultivate discussions among a broad group of people across the organization.

▶ **Following and Microblogging:** Following is a user-initiated action that enables individuals to be updated on changes in a document, site, tag, or person, and provides the update on the individual's newsfeed. Related to Following, Microblogging offers users a simple system of providing status updates on their own profile that other users can follow.

> **NOTE**
>
> Microblogging is not restricted by default but cannot be seen by others unless that user is followed. Your organization must define its approach and policy around the features of Following and Microblogging.

▶ **Tagging and Notes:** Tags, including hashtagging, enable an individual user to mark pages, list items, and sites with single or multiple words that can be used as a bookmarking system as well as update system for an individual based on personal interest in any of those types of content.

These tags are displayed in the Tag Cloud web part in the My Site for that user for later reference. The organization's policy should typically be to allow the usage of Tagging and Notes.

▶ **Ratings:** Ratings provide a method for users to score the relevance and value of content in pages, lists, and libraries, which improves their discoverability in Enterprise Search queries. The default for Ratings is deactivated on most lists and libraries. Site Owners and Site Designers can enable ratings for lists and libraries within their sites at their own discretion without further approval.

Operational and Technical Policies and Standards

SharePoint and Office 365's SharePoint Online are designed to be available for customer use 24 hours per day, seven days per week, 365 days per year (24x7x365), excluding scheduled maintenance and upgrade times.

The SharePoint Steering Committee should detail the procedures for the announcement to employees regarding any scheduled interruptions and maintenance windows through the corporate communications venues. This includes, but is not limited to, email distributions and local announcements.

Enterprise Search Service

The Enterprise Search service involves the crawling, indexing, and querying of content discovered both internally and externally to the SharePoint farm. Table 9.16 outlines how the Enterprise Search service maintains expected usage for crawling and querying content.

TABLE 9.16   Overview of the Enterprise Search Service's Expected Usage for Crawling and Querying Content

Function	Purpose	Guidelines
Managed Properties	Defines which properties may be queried against as well as other refining or relevance	No policies have been defined. Discussions with various business units need to occur to develop a proper information architecture plan.
Crawl Schedule	Defines index freshness for updated search results	Standard policy is 15-minute incremental crawls for freshness on collaboration, daily incremental crawls for archival sources. Full crawls are scheduled on a weekly basis.

Function	Purpose	Guidelines
Content Sources	Defines what information sources are acceptable for search queries	All standard content sources (file shares, web sites, Exchange public folders, line-of-business data) are considered acceptable sources; other Search sources may be federated.
File Type Inclusion	Defines which file types will be queried against	Standard policy supports only out-of-box extensions; all other extensions that require a custom index filter must go through customization procedures.
Server Mappings	Defines how content URLs display in search results	Standard policy applies only to internal resources exposed on public sites, not enabled by default.
URL Removal	Removes URLs and associated index content from result sets and prevents such content from being crawled again	Standard policy is to use only when exposed content should be managed; limited to only Farm Administrator or Search Administrator.
Crawl Rules	Determines how certain paths or URLs are crawled, including inclusion, exclusion, or alternate login	Standard policy is no defined rules; managed only by Farm Administrator or Search Administrator as required; rules may be defined by approved request.

In addition, the following configurations are managed locally at the site collection level by Site Collection Administrators as needed:

▶ Query rules/scopes/result sources

▶ Keywords/promoted results

Managed Metadata Service

The Managed Metadata Service provides enterprise metadata availability for taxonomies and folksonomies, as well as publishable content types. The Managed Metadata Service is defined as a single Term Store that stores and manages all used Terms centrally and for the enterprise.

There is no provisioned Managed Metadata Service by default. The Farm Administrator is responsible for managing the security and availability of the Term Store, but designated business roles manage the Terms separately.

Table 9.17 provides the general guidelines for the Managed Metadata Service connections management. All use of the Term Store is shared for all web applications.

NOTE

The Managed Metadata Service is covered in granular detail in Chapter 10.

TABLE 9.17   General Guidelines for the Managed Metadata Service Connections Management

Function	Purpose	Guidelines
Default Keyword Location	Defines Term Store default location of all enterprise keywords created for all web applications connected to a Managed Metadata Service	Default is set to no central Term Store, but allows only one Term Store in the enterprise. Standard is to use designated Term Store for all Term Sets.
Default Term Set Location	Defines Term Store default location of Term Sets created for all web applications connected to a Managed Metadata Service	Default is set to no central Term Store. Standard is a single Term Store for all Term Sets.
Use Content Types	Configures a Content Type Hub to centralize the updating and management of Content Types to all web applications connected to a Managed Metadata Service	No Content Type Hub defined by default. Standard is to define Content Type Hub and designate management of Content Types centrally.
Push-down Content Type Publishing updates from the Content Type Gallery	Supports the updating of Content Types from the designated Content Type Hub to all web applications and their content connected to a Managed Metadata Service	Dependent on the Use Content Types function. Standard is to push-down if the Content Type Hub is in use.

User Profile Service

The User Profile Service manages user profile information connected to individual users within a SharePoint farm that may also be leveraged by other services for locating information about other users. The profile data is obtained from an external system such as Active Directory but stored and managed within the SharePoint farm. The User Profile Service also supports the use of all Social Computing functions and is required to take advantage of most of those services. Table 9.18 outlines the management of the User Profile Service.

TABLE 9.18   Overview of the Management of the User Profile Service

Configuration	Purpose	Guidelines
Synchronization Connection	Defines which external source is used as the primary source for profile properties	Default is not configured, but can be set to use Active Directory minimally. Standard is to use Active Directory as the sole external source.

Configuration	Purpose	Guidelines
Exclusion Filters	Defines whether specific types of users or synchronizing groups are required when profile properties are imported	Default is to not filter users and to synchronize groups. Standard is set to default.
Property Mappings	Defines which properties from an external source are mapped to existing profile properties	Default has 63 properties already mapped to Active Directory properties. Standard is set to default.
Synchronization Schedule	Defines how often the Timer Job updates content, as well as how much it updates	Default is to not schedule for any synchronization. Standard is to perform full synchronizations weekly and incremental synchronizations nightly.

Uptime and Performance Standards

SharePoint 2013 overall platform management should correspond with service level agreements (SLAs) to define the standard targets for supporting SharePoint and the related expectations of its user base.

Table 9.19 provides an outline of a high-level SharePoint SLA and the related responsiveness that the business can expect based on the priority, impact, or level of a specific issue.

TABLE 9.19   Example of a High-Level SharePoint Service Level Agreement

Priority	Response and Service Levels	
Critical:	Business Outage or significant customer impact that threatens future productivity.	
	Service Desk Acknowledge and Assessment Time:	0–15 minutes
	IT Acknowledge Time:	0–15 minutes
	Resolution Time:	0–2 hours
High:	High Impact problem where production is proceeding but in an impaired fashion. There is a time-sensitive issue important to long-term productivity that is not causing an immediate work stoppage.	
	Service Desk Acknowledge and Assessment Time:	0–15 minutes
	IT Acknowledge Time:	0–1 hour
	Resolution Time:	0–8 hours

9

Priority	Response and Service Levels	
Moderate:	Important Issue that does not have significant current productivity impact.	
	Service Desk Acknowledge and Assessment Time:	0–15 minutes
	IT Acknowledge Time:	0–8 hours
	Resolution Time:	0–3 days (elapse days)
Low:	Issue that has a low productivity impact. Service Desk continues to monitor.	
	Service Desk Acknowledge and Assessment Time:	0–15 minutes
	IT Acknowledge Time:	0–3 days
	Resolution Time:	0–3 weeks (elapse weeks)
Scheduled:	Scheduled tasks for the future.	
	Service Desk Acknowledge and Assessment Time:	Depends on the nature of the request.
	IT Acknowledge Time:	Depends on the nature of the request.
	Resolution Time:	Depends on the nature of the request.

Scheduled Outages and Availability

Required SharePoint system outages should follow normal change control processes. The organization's IT resources will provide advance notice of any planned system outages. Table 9.20 provides an example of an organization's scheduled outages and availability metric that would be typically published within SharePoint's service level agreement(s).

TABLE 9.20   Example of an Organization's Scheduled Outages and Availability Metric

Critical Hours	Monday to Friday: 7:00–18:00
	Saturday: 7:00–15:00
Non-Critical Hours	Monday to Friday: 18:01–6:59
	Saturday: 15:01–23:59
	Sunday: 00:00–23:59
Maintenance Window	Saturday: 22:00–8:00
Availability	99.900%

NOTE

Specific downtimes must be reported via change control.

Data Recovery Guidelines

SharePoint's components can be restored at different times and in different manners depending on their application. The data recovery guidelines chart, detailed in Table 9.21, outlines the options available for recovering deleted items, sites, and subsites, and for total disaster recovery, as well as specifying which responsible role should be contacted.

TABLE 9.21   Data Recovery Guideline Chart

Type	Level	Option	Support Roles	Time Allocated	Availability
Items	SharePoint Site	Versioning	Site Member, Site Owner	Immediate	Set at library level
Items, Lists	SharePoint Site	Recycle Bin	Site Owner, Site Collection Administrator	Immediate	90 days
Items, Lists	SharePoint Site	Site Collection Recycle Bin	Site Collection Administrator	Immediate	90 days or 50% of available site collection quota
Site	Server	Site Collection Recycle Bin	Site Collection Administrator, SharePoint Farm Administrators	Immediate	90 days or 50% of available site collection quota
Site Collection	Server	Site Collection restoration from previous backup	SharePoint Farm Administrators	2–5 days	90 days
Disaster Recovery/ Complete Outage	Server	Restoration from previous backup Required components: –Content databases –Customizations –Configurations –Binary files (SharePoint and operating system)	SharePoint Farm Administrators	24 hours	90 days

SharePoint's containment hierarchy, as shown in Figure 9.8, details how each level is broken down in relation to the chart in Table 9.21.

6

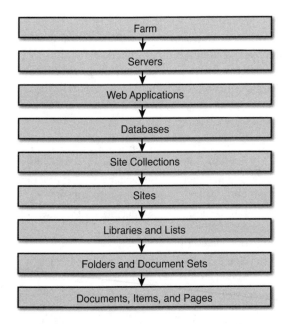

FIGURE 9.8   SharePoint's containment hierarchy.

Outage Planning Procedures

Changes or additions to production farm servers must comply with the organization change management procedure and must be approved by the SharePoint Operations Team.

Intended Downtime Procedure

Scheduled maintenance for the SharePoint environment is essential in order to install patches and upgrades and to maintain security.

Scheduled maintenance windows are determined by the SharePoint Operations Team in coordination with the organization's infrastructure team members, and maintenance should be coordinated through the SharePoint Operations Team.

Unintended Downtime Procedure

Unintended downtime is defined as a failure of some type that is both unscheduled and unexpected. Notification of unintended service interruption should be announced as soon as possible via standard communication channels.

Support Requirements and Schedules

All farms should perform backups of the SharePoint farm and SQL Server databases as indicated here:

▶ At least an incremental backup on a nightly basis

▶ A full backup on a weekly basis

NOTE

Backups should be retained for 90 days or as set forth by the organization's legal retention schedule.

In the case of a catastrophic event, corrupt data, or the need for the farm to be rebuilt, nightly backups are used to restore the location's SharePoint farm. Each location, if there are multiple locations, is required to have a Disaster Recovery build document and plan for the SharePoint environment.

The SharePoint environment is a business-critical application and must be considered as such in the Disaster Recovery Plan. A full disaster-recovery scenario should be executed once a year for the SharePoint farm.

This is done in accordance with the farm's disaster recovery policies. The scenario assumes a total loss of the SharePoint farm and restoration to the last known backup to full functionality in the recovery environment.

Mission-critical sites need to be restored based on SLAs for mission-critical sites defined by the organization's policies and standards.

SharePoint farm recovery must provide a full recovery from the last backup.

In the case of a true disaster in which the system is totally down and unavailable, the system should be restored up to the previous day's full backup within eight hours if possible.

Public and Hybrid Cloud Governance

In Chapter 7, "Implementing a SharePoint 2013 System Architecture with Future Hybrid Scalability in Mind," we discussed the architecture of the hybrid cloud and how the expansion of organization's having resources both on-premises and in the cloud is a becoming more and more common.

A lot of organizations and IT professionals are wondering how the cloud will impact their business and whether a hybrid SharePoint/Office 365 or Microsoft Azure environment makes sense for their IT strategy and related technology roadmap. I have been involved in several recent hybrid SharePoint implementations using SharePoint Server 2013 on-premises, as well as Office 365, Microsoft Azure, or SharePoint 2013 deployed within Amazon Web Services (AWS).

Specific hybrid governance considerations must be taken into account, such as how disaster recovery and backup procedures may change, as well as security and federation configurations, to ensure a seamless user experience. There are also business intelligence considerations with organizations wanting to provide on-premises data reporting in conjunction with data stored within the cloud. These considerations include common questions such as the following:

▶ How will moving to a hybrid cloud architecture impact my SharePoint planning and my ability to manage and integrate SharePoint across the enterprise, as depicted in Figure 9.9?

▶ How should my organization prepare for the possibility of rapid provisioning of new sites and related workloads in Office 365 while maintaining existing on-premises sites and workloads, and how can I implement a cohesive governance and management strategy?

▶ Should I attempt to supplement our small or initial cloud environment with additional features or customizations that are currently possible only on-premises?

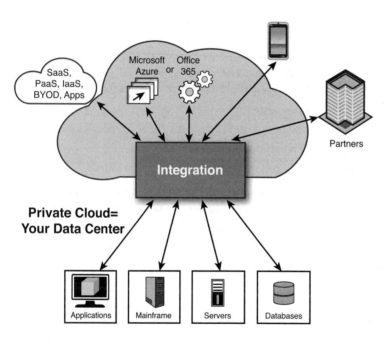

FIGURE 9.9   An overview of a hybrid cloud architecture and integration with the on-premises "private cloud."

A large number of organizations have concerns with the hybrid cloud regarding the "unknowns" they feel may impact them in regard to compliance and specific requirements that may stipulate that certain types of data be hosted in a particular location (that is, on-premises rather than in the cloud). These concerns also bring up questions such as the following:

▶ How can I calculate or fully understand the growing requirements of identity management?

▶ Can I implement a governance strategy to support growing service catalogs in a hybrid cloud architecture?

One major key to the success of a hybrid cloud architecture is ensuring that you have the ability to manage permissions across both SharePoint on-premises and Office 365's SharePoint Online or Microsoft Azure content, with the added ability to make mass updates across both environments (updating/adding content types to a large number of document libraries and so forth).

Customization Governance

SharePoint customizations and the development of custom solutions such as apps, web parts and workflows enable you to tailor your environment to meet unique requirements that are specific to your organization and business model. Customization requests tend to be initiated by user requests that are meant to meet a specific business challenge or streamline an existing process.

> **NOTE**
>
> Chapter 13, "Development Strategies and Custom Applications in SharePoint 2013 Office 365, and SharePoint Online," covers SharePoint 2013 related custom development best practices and strategies in granular detail.

It is important to communicate to your user base that they must adhere to the SharePoint Change Management policies and procedures when requesting any custom feature outside of the site templates and governed functionally provided to them within the existing SharePoint Service.

Users should initiate any customization request via the Change Management Approval Process, which is then communicated to SharePoint's Farm Administrator(s) or the designated individuals within the organization who handle change management requests.

The process diagram shown in Figure 9.10 illustrates a high-level overview of a SharePoint customization review process.

9

FIGURE 9.10   An illustration of a SharePoint customization review process.

Sandboxed Solutions

Sandboxed Solutions, also referred to as User Solutions, involve the deployment of site collection–limited code for the purpose of enhancing the functionality of a site through additional user interface changes such as JavaScript, custom lists and libraries, web parts, apps, templates, or other customizations that can be limited to a site collection.

Sandbox Solutions may be deployed only by the Farm Administrator, SharePoint Developer, or SharePoint Architect after complete testing. Sandbox Solutions may not be deployed by Site Owners or Site Collection Administrators.

Maintenance, Patching, and Updates

System software patches are updates created by manufacturers of core software components (OS/Windows Server 2012, IIS, Exchange Server, Lync Server, SQL Server, and Microsoft SharePoint Server). Normal system patches and maintenance should be deployed according to the organization's available maintenance or patching policy and windows in conjunction with the infrastructure team and the SharePoint Operations Team.

Customization Request Process

If a user's request for a custom solution is approved through the organization's SharePoint Change Management policies, there should be a defined process for the overall business and functional requirements handoff to IT and the development team. A SharePoint customization development and deployment process, as shown in Figure 9.11, provides an example of how this process should be defined within your organization.

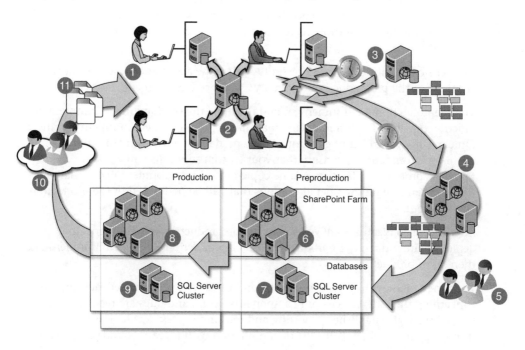

FIGURE 9.11   An overview of a SharePoint customization deployment process.

The following steps provide the outline for your organization's SharePoint customization development and deployment process:

1. The custom requirements are received from the organization's business analyst or team member who has been working with the "requester" to collect and outline the business and functional requirements for this custom development effort, and they are submitted to IT. IT members then converted these requirements into a formal project request with a related project plan and granular tasks and/or milestones.

2. Developers then begin development on the custom requirements utilizing Visual Studio 2012/2013 for development. Should the development team have any questions or clarifications during development, they will reach back out to the business

analyst or team member working with the requester for clarification. The develop team utilizes Team Foundation Server to track the development progress and store the custom source code. The development continues until it is complete and ready to be tested.

3. With the source code stored in a centralized location, the development team can create automated builds for integration and unit testing purposes. You can also automate testing activities to increase the overall quality of the customizations.

4. In large initiatives, there may also be an additional user acceptance testing (UAT) farm that is utilized by QA personnel to test and verify the builds in an environment that more closely resembles the production environment. Typically, a build verification farm has multiple servers to ensure that custom solutions are deployed properly.

5. After custom solutions have successfully undergone acceptance testing, you can continue to the preproduction or quality assurance environment.

6, 7. The preproduction environment should resemble the production environment as much as possible. This often means that the preproduction environment has the same patch level and configurations as the production environment. The objective of this environment is to ensure that your custom solutions will work in production. The production database can be copied to this environment occasionally so that you can imitate the upgrade actions that will be performed in the production environment.

8, 9. After the customizations are verified in the preproduction environment, they are deployed either directly to production or to a production staging environment and then on to production.

10. The production environment is used by end users who provide feedback and ideas concerning the different custom components. Issues and bugs are reported and tracked through established reporting and tracking processes, which is typically done through a custom SharePoint list in conjunction with a Team Foundation Server.

11. Feedback, bugs, and other issues in the production environment are turned into requirements, which are prioritized and turned into developer tasks. Multiple developer teams can work with and process bug reports and change requests received from end users of the production environment, and development can coordinate their solution packages. The framework and the functionality development teams may follow separate versioning models that need to be coordinated as they track bugs and changes.

Using SharePoint Designer

SharePoint Designer is a client-based tool for designing custom functionality, such as workflows for SharePoint Sites. It is separate from SharePoint Server but is supported and may be controlled for use in the SharePoint farm. SharePoint Designer is not designed for farmwide customization.

SharePoint provides four control settings that govern the use of SharePoint Designer. These control settings are configured at the Web Application or Site Collection level. Disabling a setting at the Web Application level prevents that setting from being enabled at the Site Collection level.

The settings shown in Table 9.22 are made available for your organization to govern SharePoint Designer.

TABLE 9.22   Settings Available to Assist in Governing SharePoint Designer

Setting	Description
Enable SharePoint Designer	Specify whether to allow Site Owners and Designers to edit the sites in this site collection using SharePoint Designer. Site Collection Administrators will always be able to edit sites.
Enable Detaching Pages from the Site Definition	Specify whether to allow Site Owners and Designers to detach pages from the original site definition using SharePoint Designer. Site Collection Administrators will always be able to perform this operation.
Enable Customizing Master Pages and Page Layouts	Specify whether to allow Site Owners and Designers to customize master pages and page layouts using SharePoint Designer. Site Collection Administrators will always be able to perform this operation.
Enable Managing of the Website URL Structure	Specify whether to allow Site Owners and Designers to view and manage the hidden URL structure of their website using SharePoint Designer. Site Collection Administrators will always be able to perform this operation.

In addition, each Web Application may allow for external workflow designers to create user-defined workflows, which applies to SharePoint Designer as well. Workflows may be created only by Site Designers, Site Owners, and Site Collection Administrators who have submitted a change request with prior approval.

User Interface Governance and Related Policies

User Interface Standards are meant to create and enforce a common look and feel for the organization's SharePoint and/or Office 365's SharePoint Online environment. These design elements are typically created by an organization's developer with assistance from a designer and applied to all SharePoint Sites within the environment in a governed manner.

Your organization must follow a defined process, as shown in Figure 9.12, when developing a SharePoint and/or Office 365 custom branding initiative to implement User Interface Standards.

9

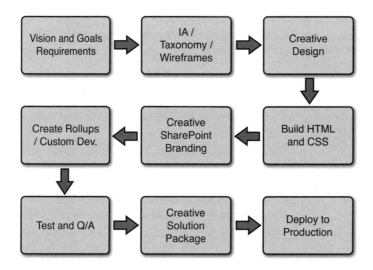

FIGURE 9.12   An overview of a recommended process for a custom SharePoint and/or Office 365 branding initiative.

The organization should have an approved "master page" as well as approved site themes, as shown in Figure 9.13, that slightly differ in color or layout from the approved branding standards. This allows for a governed user interface but also provides for departments or individual sites to maintain some unique feel or slight color scheme differences. This should appease most users and also steer away from a great deal of future custom branding requests that don't fall within the governed corporate branding standards. It is key to ensure that your organization's SharePoint or Office 365 user interface has all the main navigational elements in a common layout so that users can easily navigate and find the content they are looking for, no matter what site or subsite they may find themselves in, to avoid confusion.

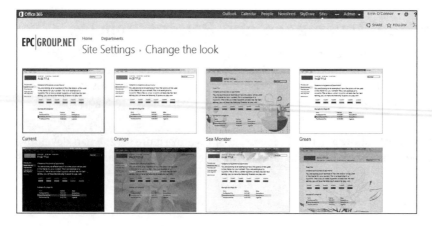

FIGURE 9.13   An example of available site themes in SharePoint 2013 and/or Office 365.

> **TIP**
>
> The themes available out-of-the-box in SharePoint 2013 are detailed at the following link: http://msdn.microsoft.com/en-us/library/jj927174.aspx

Chapter 14, "Search, Web Content Management, Branding, and Navigational Strategies," covers custom branding and user interface best practices in granular detail, as well as the policies you should enforce within your organization to ensure best practices branding and UI governance.

> **TIP**
>
> SharePoint 2013 supports a wide range of browsers, including Internet Explorer, Google Chrome, Mozilla Firefox, and Apple Safari. To learn more about SharePoint 2013's supported browsers and related updates, you can access the following URL: http://technet.microsoft.com/en-us/library/cc263526.aspx

Language Support

Language Support enables users to utilize different languages from within sites. Many organizations support a multilingual user interface with a core language standard of English but with available language packs that support Dutch, Czech, French, Slovak, Chinese Simplified, Chinese Traditional, Japanese, Malay, Thai, and Vietnamese.

> **TIP**
>
> For additional information on the SharePoint 2013 language packs, refer to the following link: http://technet.microsoft.com/en-us/library/ff463597.aspx

Acceptable Usage Policy to Enforce in Your Governance Strategy

The purpose of this policy is to establish acceptable and unacceptable use of electronic devices and network resources for the organization in conjunction with its established culture of ethical and lawful behavior, openness, trust, and integrity.

The organization provides computer devices, networks, and other electronic information systems to meet missions, goals, and initiatives, and it must manage them responsibly to maintain the confidentiality, integrity, and availability of its information assets. This policy requires the users of information assets to comply with company policies and protects the company against damaging legal issues.

Scope

All employees, contractors, consultants, temporary workers, and other workers, including all personnel affiliated with third parties, must adhere to this policy. This policy applies to information assets owned or leased by the organization or to devices that connect to the network or reside at a company site or location.

Policy Statements

The following are baseline policy standards for your organization's Acceptable Usage Policy:

▶ You are responsible for exercising good judgment regarding appropriate use of the company's resources in accordance with the policies, standards, and guidelines. Company resources may not be used for any unlawful or prohibited purpose.

▶ For security, compliance, and maintenance purposes, authorized personnel may monitor and audit equipment, systems, and network traffic per the organization's audit policies. Devices that interfere with other devices or users on the organization's network may be disconnected. Information Security standards prohibit actively blocking authorized audit scans. Firewalls and other blocking technologies must permit access to the scan sources.

System Accounts

▶ You are responsible for the security of data, accounts, and systems under your control. Keep passwords secure and do not share account or password information with anyone, including other personnel, family, or friends. Providing access to another individual, either deliberately or through failure to secure its access, is a violation of this policy.

▶ You must maintain any system-level and user-level passwords in accordance with the organization's password policy.

▶ You must ensure through legal or technical means that proprietary information remains within the control of the organization at all times. Conducting company business that results in the storage of proprietary information on personal or non-company-controlled environments, unless permitted via the organization's BYOD policy and agreement, including devices maintained by a third party with whom our organization does not have a contractual agreement, is prohibited. This specifically prohibits the use of an email account that is not provided by the organization or its customer and partners, for company business.

Computing Assets

▶ You are responsible for ensuring the protection of assigned company assets that includes the use of company-provided computer cable locks and other security devices. Laptops left at company locations overnight must be properly secured or placed in a locked drawer or cabinet. Promptly report any theft of company assets to IT or a designated manager.

▶ All PCs, tablets, laptops, smartphones, and workstations must be secured at all times, and you must lock the screen or log off when the device is unattended.

▶ Devices that connect to the company's network must comply with the minimum access policy.

▶ Do not interfere with corporate device management or security system software, including, but not limited to, antivirus software, malware software, information rights policies configured on the device, or mobile device management software.

Network Use

You are responsible for the security and appropriate use of the organization's network resources under your control. Using company resources for the following is strictly prohibited:

▶ Causing a security breach to the organization's network resources, including, but not limited to, accessing data, servers, or accounts to which you are not authorized; circumventing user authentication on any device; or sniffing network traffic.

▶ Causing a disruption of service to the organization's other network resources, including, but not limited to, ICMP floods, packet spoofing, denial of service, heap or buffer overflows, and forged routing information for malicious purposes.

▶ Violating copyright law, including, but not limited to, illegally duplicating or transmitting copyrighted pictures, music, video, and software.

▶ Exporting or importing software, technical information, encryption software, or technology in violation of international or regional export control laws strictly prohibited.

▶ Using the Internet or the organization's network in a manner that violates the organization's policies, or federal and local laws.

▶ Intentionally introducing malicious code, including, but not limited to, viruses, worms, Trojan horses, email bombs, spyware, adware, and keyloggers.

▶ Port scanning or security scanning on a production network unless authorized in advance by Information Security.

Electronics Communications

The following are strictly prohibited:

▶ Inappropriate use of communication vehicles and equipment, including, but not limited to, supporting illegal activities, and procuring or transmitting material that violates company policies against harassment or the safeguarding of confidential or proprietary information.

▶ Sending spam via email, text messages, pages, instant messages, voice mail, or other forms of electronic communication.

▶ Forging, misrepresenting, obscuring, suppressing, or replacing a user identity on any electronic communication to mislead the recipient about the sender.

▶ Posting the same or similar non-business-related messages to large numbers of newsgroups (that is, newsgroup spam).

▶ Use of a company email or IP address to engage in conduct that violates company policies or guidelines.

▶ Posting to a public newsgroup, bulletin board, torrent, or listserv with a company email or IP address.

You must exercise good judgment to avoid misrepresenting or exceeding your authority in representing the opinion of the company.

Enforcement

An employee found to have violated this policy may be subject to disciplinary action, up to and including termination of employment. A violation of this policy by a temporary worker, contractor, or vendor may result in the termination of their contract or assignment with the organization.

Summary

This chapter provided a detailed roadmap and strategy that you can utilize to build a tailored governance strategy for your SharePoint 2013, Office 365, and/or SharePoint Online implementation.

Additional Office 365-specific governance tasks such as Lync and additional considerations around OneDrive for Business that fall under administration activities will be covered in Chapter 15, "Administration and Maintenance Strategies."

Governance is sometimes a project within itself, and it does not always come with a great deal of recognition for those who take on this difficult task. However, it is one of the most important aspects, if not *the* most important aspect, in ensuring the long-term success of your implementation.

In Chapter 10, we will cover enterprise content management capabilities and strategies, as well as SharePoint 2013's search, which are, in contrast to governance, some of the most high-profile aspects of the overall initiative.

CHAPTER 10

Enterprise Content Management (ECM), Records Management (RM), and eDiscovery Best Practices

Microsoft's SharePoint 2013, along with its enterprise content management (ECM) and/or records management (RM) capabilities, as they are both referenced in many cases, continues to be recognized as an enterprise platform leader and as being in the "magic quadrant" that many organizations look for when measuring a platform's capabilities.

ECM and RM efforts also have one of the biggest pushes for SharePoint 2013 initiatives as organizations are understanding more than ever that they need to get a true handle on their data. This is true not only from a regulatory and compliance standpoint but also from an intellectual property and security perspective because lost knowledge is one of the most costly impacts an organization can experience in relation to their bottom line over time.

To personally gauge the interest of organizations' commitment to undertake these efforts, of the first 50 SharePoint 2013 implementations for our clients at EPC Group, after SharePoint 2013's official release in October 2012, 33 of those initiatives were SharePoint 2013 ECM- or RM-related projects.

This chapter covers ECM, RM, eDiscovery, and other SharePoint-related content management best practices and strategies your organization can follow to ensure that these extremely high-profile efforts are done right the very first time.

Proven ECM and RM Strategies for SharePoint 2013 and/or SharePoint Online

Microsoft will continue to update SharePoint's offerings over time with new features, service packs, and/or plans around SharePoint Server 2013 on-premises, as well as Office 365's SharePoint Online or implementing a separate SharePoint Online initiative on its own apart from Office 365's additional capabilities. It is key to understand the features and functionality that your organization will utilize during your records management and/or enterprise content management initiative.

> **TIP**
>
> When planning a SharePoint Server 2013 and/or SharePoint Online ECM or RM initiative, you must ensure that your organization's licensing and selected plan have the features you require. For more information regarding licensing and capabilities, refer to the following link: http://office.microsoft.com/en-us/sharepoint/collaboration-tools-compare-sharepoint-plans-FX103789400.aspx
>
> When you are utilizing SharePoint Online with Office 365's capabilities, there are integration considerations that can differ from a SharePoint Server 2013 on-premises deployment such as Microsoft Exchange Online and Lync. Also, many organizations are implementing hybrid SharePoint 2013 deployments with SharePoint Server 2013 on-premises with Microsoft Exchange Online. I believe that the hybrid model is one that will continue to grow throughout many organizations. For more information regarding SharePoint Server 2013's hybrid considerations, refer to the following link: http://technet.microsoft.com/en-us/library/dn197168.aspx

> **TIP**
>
> When reviewing your content management and related information management strategy, it is key to review the features that have been discontinued or modified in SharePoint 2013. A detailed overview of these discontinued or modified features can be reviewed at the following link: http://office.microsoft.com/en-us/sharepoint-help/discontinued-features-and-modified-functionality-in-microsoft-sharepoint-2013-HA102892827.aspx

I have been deeply involved in a large number of the ECM and RM initiatives at EPC Group over the past 15 years and have had the privilege of working with organizations and institutes of just about every shape and size or vertical in both the private and public sectors. Every project we have engaged in, to no surprise, is unique. Many organizations differ as to what they consider to be a "record," as well as the existing processes and systems that are in place and have been previously implemented.

You should not feel that implementing this type of initiative is impossible within your organization based on any perceived "current technology state" or hurdles, because there has never been a time in the past decade I can ever remember when organizations' leadership understands the importance of finally getting a handle on the organization's content and records. There is also a growing focus on being proactive regarding possible eDiscovery issues for many companies. You are most definitely not alone if you have been tasked with implementing this type of effort for your organization.

There are still many enterprise organizations throughout the globe that do not have an approved records retention schedule or may even have multiple versions or flavors of a retention schedule that are still in the process of being vetted and approved by their legal counsel.

I have had the privilege of being involved in projects with the world's largest airline in implementing one of their first records management systems, the world's second-largest oil and gas company's global ECM platform, and efforts related to the Department of Defense, as well as in meetings at the National Archives (NARA) discussing strategies and whiteboarding records retention architecture designs with some of their leading records archivists.

One of the most memorable discussions and working sessions I can recall was centered on nonclassified related documents and content regarding the Space Shuttle. The premise of this conversation was that these records were stored in various secured systems and the goal was to design an approach for the migration of these records from older versions of Microsoft SharePoint and other technologies while maintaining their "content databases" and version history integrity. The main requirement of this discussion was how this could all be accomplished in a seamless manner to meet the requirements of future Freedom of Information Act requests.

As I recall quite well, a few months ago I was working with a few team members at EPC Group on an ECM initiative for a client of ours in the manufacturing sector on the East Coast of the U.S. that had approximately 1,200 employees and five regional offices. I can tell you that the ECM/RM-related NARA-sized effort mentioned previously and ECM initiative for this manufacturing organization still had to follow all the same core strategies and processes and was complex in its own manner; so don't be underwhelmed or overwhelmed as each initiative is different and the granular requirements must be addressed.

When you hear someone on the project team, right before the effort is set to start, pose the question of "where do we even begin?" just know you're not alone. The sections that follow will assist you in approaching these efforts in a methodical manner to ensure your success.

Differences Between Enterprise Content Management and Records Management

One of the items you should ensure you have a clear understanding of is the organization's stance on what the differences are between a standard document and an official record and what the official legal criteria are that drive these definitions.

Documents of all types are stored throughout the organization in both SharePoint document libraries and areas such as file shares, laptops, and devices, in both structured and unstructured manners. Records tend to be considered evidence of the official activities of the organization and its governing policies. Are you confused yet? This can be a very gray area at times. I technically define records management as the practice of identifying, classifying, archiving, preserving, and destroying records according to a set of predefined standards.

Records usually have strict compliance requirements and related retention, access, and destruction policies. This can vary, though, based on the type of organization and the local or federal compliance policies that specifically relate to the business.

In the litigious world we live in today, it is best to err on the side of caution because courts can enforce strict penalties on organizations that are considered to not have a records management program, not have a consistently deployed records management program, or not have a vehicle to perform an audit of their records management program and related eDiscovery plan.

Your organization may have implemented or considered various techniques for converting an existing or "active" documents to a record, such as these:

▶ Creating a workflow that sends a document to a Records Center or centralized records management related site

▶ Manually declaring a document to be a record

The Association of Records Managers and Administrators, better known as ARMA, has a wealth of free information and resources you can access to determine specific records retention policies and related governing laws for your organization and can be found at the following link: http://www.arma.org/

There has also been another standard for which records management systems are judged, which is the U.S. Department of Defense's (DoD) 5015.2 standard or equivalent, which can be reviewed at the following link: http://jitc.fhu.disa.mil/cgi/rma/standards.aspx

This standard is set for the management of records that will be eventually transferred to the U.S. National Archives and Records Administration (NARA) and will include government personnel records, standards, directives, manuals, and documents that are scheduled for declassification or redacted items.

In countries in the EU, there is a similar standard named MoReq, which is applied across the EU. More information regarding MoReq can be found at the following link: http://ec.europa.eu/archival-policy/moreq/index_en.htm

> **NOTE**
>
> For more information on ways to plan the conversion of active documents to records in SharePoint Server 2013, refer to the following link: http://technet.microsoft.com/en-us/library/cc263464.aspx

Common Terminology Used Within ECM and RM Initiatives

Various common terms are used throughout ECM and RM initiatives, including the following:

▶ **Metadata:** In practical usage as it's most commonly described, it means data about data. For SharePoint, it is data that describes or classifies other content or documents in lists, apps, and libraries. It is also used to categorize people, discussions, and communities, or to describe conversations.

▶ **Enterprise Metadata Management:**

  ▶ Metadata as an enabler for different functionalities such as navigation, term, and search-driven pages.

  ▶ Used for key capabilities for term store managers to enhance term usage models.

  ▶ Drives multilingual capabilities.

  ▶ Enables taxonomy APIs exposed via CSOM (Client Side Object Model) and REST (Representational State Transfer) for extensibility purposes.

▶ **Taxonomy:** Formal hierarchy of terms and tags that are usually centrally administered and defined.

▶ **Folksonomy:** Informal list of ad hoc tags or terms that are built up over time through user-defined keywords.

▶ **Ontology:** Formal representation of knowledge as a set of concepts within a domain with relationships between those sets of concepts.

▶ **Term Store:** Database that houses taxonomies.

▶ **Term Set:** Secondary level of a taxonomy.

▶ **Term:** Element of the defined taxonomy.

SharePoint and Office 365's SharePoint Online ECM and RM Terminology

There are various common terms that are specific to SharePoint 2013 and Office 365's SharePoint Online that are used throughout ECM and RM initiatives, including the following:

▶ **Content Type:** A reusable collection of settings and rules applied to a certain category of content in SharePoint.

▶ **Content Type Hub:** A site collection that operates as a central source to share content types across the enterprise.

▶ **Content Type Syndication:** Publishing of content types across multiple sites, site collections, web applications, and/or farms.

Throughout this chapter, I provide references and links for you to access to get the most up-to-date information on SharePoint 2013 and Office 365's SharePoint Online.

10

NOTE

Microsoft's offerings for SharePoint Server 2013 on-premises in marketing materials and official press releases are always very clear. SharePoint Online and/or Office 365, though, are being referred to more and more as the same or very similar technology. I want to make this clear so that when you are in technical conversations with your team or reviewing certain materials, you understand how the technologies may be referenced, and it's key that you determine the specifics of the licensing or offering being deployed. When I use the reference or refer to Office 365's SharePoint Online, it is because most SharePoint Online initiatives are being done under the umbrella of Office 365, but you can procure licenses of SharePoint Online (that is, in the cloud) without Office 365.

Records Management Best Practices

Records management initiatives can be successfully accomplished by following a framework of defined guidelines and principles driven by compliance, collaboration, associated cost, and business continuity. It is key that the initiative has executive buy-in to both promote and enforce the overall records management initiative. You also must assign specific responsibility to a records management–related team with a recognized and central discipline within the enterprise.

Although this chapter focuses on more granular best practices and "in the consulting trenches" strategies, it can also help you to review right from the start how to create a record center using an enterprise site template. The following link regarding how to store and manage records in SharePoint 2013 covers a lot of the basics you may want to cover if you are new to Microsoft SharePoint's technology: http://office.microsoft.com/en-us/office365-sharepoint-online-enterprise-help/choose-how-to-store-and-manage-records-HA102771908.aspx?CTT=5&origin=HA102893868

It is key that you understand your organization's content life cycle, as shown in Figure 10.1, in terms of when a document is created through when it is archived and even possibly destroyed. This is where including your organization's legal or records team(s) in the very beginning of this effort is extremely important so that you are not developing a SharePoint ECM or RM platform without having the legal specifics set in stone.

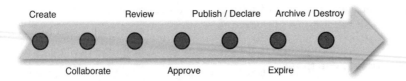

FIGURE 10.1   An overview of a document or record's content life cycle.

Initial Records Management Strategies in Building Your Core Team

The following elements should be a key part of your approach to building your core team and framework in implementing a successful records management initiative:

- ▶ Create classification schemes and apply standard indexing terms across the organization via metadata.

- ▶ Keep it as simple as possible at the beginning to not overwhelm the project team.

- ▶ Ensure that the project team members are properly trained and there are milestone items to develop a defined change management procedure.

- ▶ Ensure that there is a clear set of descriptions for the technology and a "glossary of approved terms" to avoid misunderstandings, as well as to ensure that new members are on the same page with the rest of the project team.

The Strategic Approach for Implementing Your Records Management Initiative

The following should be part of the core elements of your strategic approach for the overall records management initiative:

- ▶ Ensure that the ECM/RM team works closely with IT at all times for both capacity and overall infrastructure planning.

- ▶ Always focus your approach around scalability because the system will grow and this must be a core part of your overall SharePoint roadmap.

- ▶ Determine the clear path and approach for in-place versus the record center.

- ▶ Identify the organization's current retention schedule or any related development of a new or updated retention schedule.

- ▶ Ensure that the team thinks in terms of how best to possibly utilize the retention schedule's attributes and their possible mapping in SharePoint.

- ▶ Clearly define the organization's compliance requirements and obtain sign-off by executive leadership to ensure that all requirements have been identified.

- ▶ Work closely with the organization's IT security (that is, InfoSec) teams as well as key SharePoint team members to define the overall approach to Active Directory (AD) and SharePoint security groups and related policies.

- ▶ Define the organization's monitoring, auditing, and reporting requirements in relation to the organization's records management initiative.

- ▶ Plan for and deploy centralized "core" content types that follow with a file plan for your organization's strategy, as shown in Figure 10.2.

10

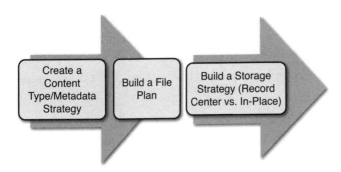

FIGURE 10.2   Define a centralized "core" content type strategy that follows with a file plan.

It is key to identify records management roles within your organization, such as the following:

▶ Records managers and compliance officers to categorize the records in the organization and to run the records management process

▶ IT personnel to implement the systems that efficiently support records management

▶ Content managers to find where organizational information is kept and to make sure that their teams follow records management practices

▶ Power users who work with content daily but also have ownership or responsibilities to ensure that policies are followed within a given site or sites

A major goal is to implement a process to ensure that records managers and content managers can survey document usage in the organization to determine which documents should become records and to be able to answer questions such as these:

▶ Where are records stored?

▶ How best can the defined retention periods be applied to records?

▶ How best can they continually communicate with the individuals responsible for updating and maintaining the content within various types of records?

Records Management Challenges

Many organizations throughout the globe have not implemented successful records management initiatives because of the inherent difficulty in applying retention policies to content. Another main issue IT has faced is the difficulty in providing a balanced centralized platform that is easy for users to adopt that will store both official records and standard documents and other content. Other major issues have been these:

▶ The high costs of complying with new laws and regulations and the ability to ensure that the system can adopt to updated requirements

- Aligning the organization's existing Active Directory (AD) and security architecture to provide access to controlled records

- The overall poor user adoption of records management solutions due to the lack of training and transparency to users regarding the importance of compliance

There are risks and other possible issues your organization may face by not having a records management or enterprise content management strategy in place, such as incurring added audit or related court fines or higher out-of-court settlements.

It is key for the entire project team to understand Microsoft SharePoint's permissions and how they are applied. The following links are useful references for you and the team to review to ensure you understand the granular aspects of the underlying platform:

- For more information regarding user permissions and permission levels in SharePoint 2013, refer to the following link:

  http://technet.microsoft.com/en-us/library/cc721640.aspx

- For more information regarding the use of fine-grained permissions in SharePoint Server 2013, refer to the following link:

  http://technet.microsoft.com/en-us/library/gg128955.aspx

Determine Your Organization's File Plan

Many organizations differ on terminology for records management strategies or what the overall file plan will look like when deployed. A SharePoint file plan consists of information such as this:

- Determine the organization's record coding schema

- Analyze record types

- Designate record owner(s)

- Review possible events that can occur for the record

- Formulate the retention period

- Determine the version management policy

- Decide on the archival or disposition

NOTE

For more information and resources regarding the creation of a file plan for SharePoint Server 2013, refer to the following link: http://technet.microsoft.com/en-us/library/cc261708.aspx

---

10

Planning SharePoint's Infrastructure for Records Management and/or Enterprise Content Management

It is key to continue to balance your business and functional requirements with the continued planning of the underlying infrastructure requirements of SharePoint during your records management or enterprise content management initiative. The following infrastructure elements should be continually reviewed as the organization's strategy is developed:

▶ Capacity planning

  ▶ Current inventory (size, total number of documents, and so on)

  ▶ Estimate growth: For more information regarding capacity planning in SharePoint Server 2013, refer to the following link:

  http://technet.microsoft.com/en-us/library/ff758645.aspx

▶ Scalability aspects

  ▶ RBS (Remote BLOB Storage): For more information regarding RBS in SharePoint 2013, refer to the following link:

  http://technet.microsoft.com/en-us/library/ee748649.aspx

  ▶ Single site versus distributed sites

▶ Overall server farm and underlying infrastructure design: For sample architectural design models for SharePoint 2013, refer to the following link:

  http://technet.microsoft.com/en-US/sharepoint/fp123594

▶ SharePoint 2013's new features and functionality considerations

  ▶ Minimal Download Strategy (MDS): For more information regarding the new MDS in SharePoint 2013, refer to the following link:

  http://msdn.microsoft.com/en-us/library/office/dn456544.aspx

  ▶ Query and index improvements

  ▶ Distributed Cache service: For more information regarding the management of the Distributed Cache service in SharePoint Server 2013, refer to the following link:

  http://technet.microsoft.com/en-us/library/jj219613.aspx

  ▶ Scalable search

  ▶ Request management: For more information regarding the new Request Management functionality in SharePoint 2013, refer to the following link:

  http://technet.microsoft.com/en-us/library/jj712708.aspx

> ▶ Shredded storage: For more information regarding Shredded Storage in SharePoint 2013, refer to the following link:
>
>   http://www.microsoft.com/en-us/download/details.aspx?id=39719

Key RM and ECM Features for SharePoint Server 2013 and SharePoint Online

The following sections detail the capabilities available within SharePoint Server 2013 as well as SharePoint Online. As mentioned at the beginning of this chapter, please ensure you have a deep understanding of the licensing model and capabilities available to you and your organization so that you are not planning for core features that may not be available with your current licensing model or offering.

Managed Metadata Service (MMS) in SharePoint Server 2013

Managed metadata is a collection of managed terms your organization can centrally store and then utilize as key attributes throughout SharePoint Server 2013. SharePoint Server 2013 has a native Term Store Management Tool that is utilized to create and manage term sets. Some of SharePoint Server 2013's managed metadata's granular features are as given here:

- ▶ Publish and subscribe model for distributed content types and related site policies

- ▶ Central management of social #hashtags

- ▶ Site-based retention policy

TIP

For more information and examples of managed metadata in SharePoint Server 2013, refer to the following link: http://technet.microsoft.com/en-us/library/ee424402.aspx

---

SharePoint Server 2013's managed metadata service application, a shared services application as shown in Figure 10.3, is what makes it possible to use managed metadata. The MMS enables you to share content types across site collections and web applications.

The managed metadata service enables you to publish a term store for your organization as well as an optional configuration for content types to use a managed metadata connection.

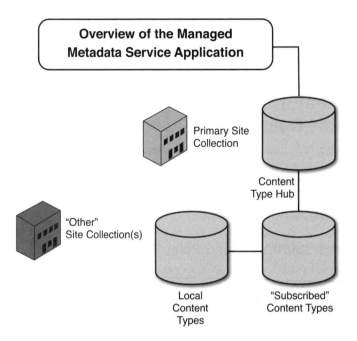

FIGURE 10.3   An overview of the managed metadata service application.

An extremely useful capability of the managed metadata service is that it can allow
records managers within your organization to administer and update metadata over time
without the need to provide them with SharePoint farm administration permissions. This
enables you to implement a much more secure overall SharePoint security model by
providing records managers with only the capabilities they need to perform their day-to-day
activities and not open up other areas of SharePoint to possible security holes.

You can utilize the managed metadata service to centrally define "product tags" to be
shared across multiple sites and related document libraries.

The managed metadata service also allows your organization to do the following:

▶ Define a term store for all common elements and synonyms

▶ Define managed metadata in record centers for specific files based on the value of a
specific attribute

▶ Consume from views, navigation, catalogs, and search

▶ Use MMS-enhanced navigation and search queries to create information "storefronts" and catalogs

▶ Select from list or type-ahead

▶ Utilize the Tags & Notes button on the Ribbon

TIP

For more information on the managed metadata service applications in SharePoint Server 2013, refer to the following link:
http://technet.microsoft.com/en-us/library/ee424403.aspx

TIP

A core element of the MMS is the available SharePoint Server 2013's managed metadata connections. It is also key to understand the appropriate permissions required for the service account for SharePoint managed metadata to avoid running into errors and troubleshooting issues that may be related to insufficient permission settings. For more information on managed metadata connections as well as the appropriate service account permissions, refer to the following link: http://technet.microsoft.com/en-us/library/ee519603.aspx

---

Term Store and Managed Metadata

As mentioned in the preceding section, the MMS enables you to define a term store, as shown in Figure 10.4, with related term sets and terms. The Term Store Management Tool, as shown in Figure 10.5, enables you to perform the actions to build the appropriate configuration for your organization.

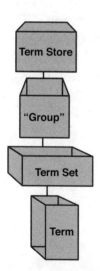

FIGURE 10.4   The MMS term store and related components.

TIP

For more information on the terms and term sets in SharePoint Server 2013, refer to the following link: http://technet.microsoft.com/en-us/library/ee519604.aspx

---

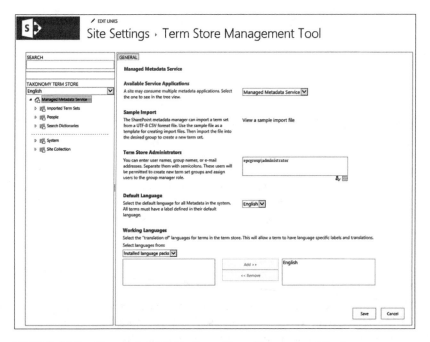

FIGURE 10.5   SharePoint 2013's Term Store Management Tool.

SharePoint Server 2013 allows for one term store per shared service application and you can then create many groups per term store. The managed metadata service creates a separate database or databases apart from the organization's SharePoint content databases.

The service is shared and consumed using the service application infrastructure. Within SharePoint's Central Administration, users with appropriate permissions can perform the actions to create metadata service applications (that is, term stores) and configure metadata service connections.

Term sets provide and/or provide for the following capabilities:

▶ Create and manage different hierarchies that share terms

▶ Allow the same term to have different parents in different term sets

▶ Configure each term set to have a unique sort order

▶ Allow or disallow end-user updates

Term management within your organization allows you to do the following:

▶ Copy terms

▶ Reuse terms

▶ Provide term description

▶ Merge terms

▶ Import terms

▶ Deprecate terms

▶ Delete terms

You can import term sets, as shown in Figure 10.6, and specify unique term set names for department or divisions, as shown in Figure 10.7.

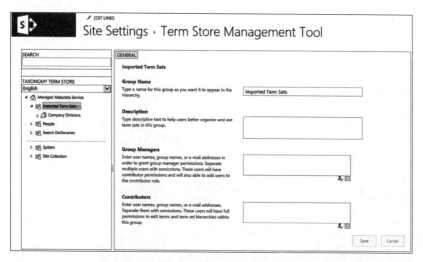

FIGURE 10.6   Importing term sets using the Term Store Management Tool.

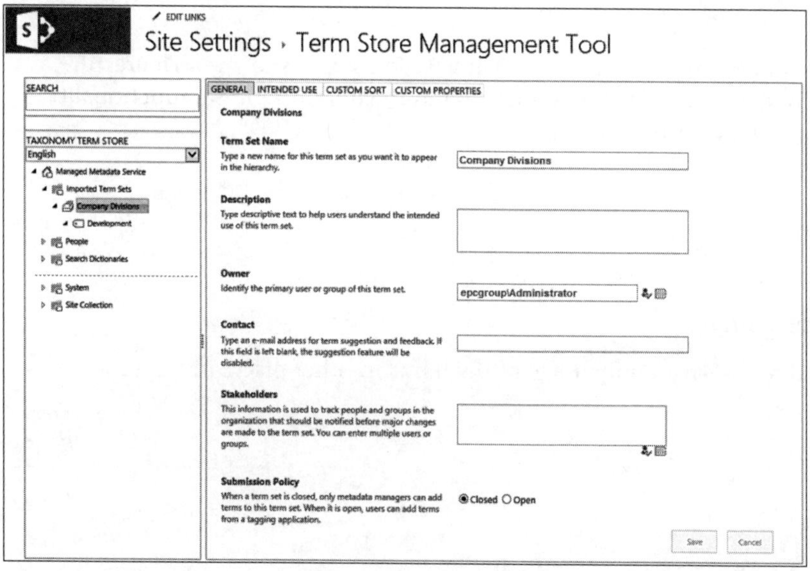

FIGURE 10.7   Importing terms sets for specific departments or divisions within your organization.

Within a specific organization or division, you can create term sets. In the example in Figure 10.8, a new term is being created for EPC Group's Application Development division.

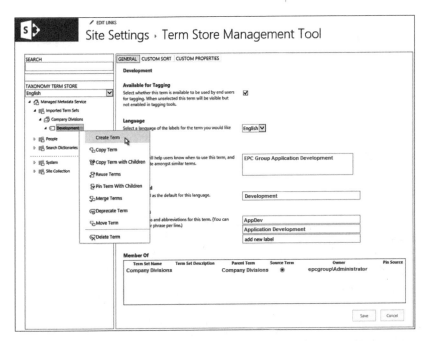

FIGURE 10.8   An example of a new term being created for a specific division within an organization.

You also have the option of importing a predefined term set, as shown in Figure 10.9, using a simple CSV file. There are limitations around the import term set functionality because it does not support the following:

▶ Synonyms

▶ Translations

▶ Custom properties

▶ Reused terms/pinning

   ▶ Pinned terms—read-only usage of the terms in other places in term hierarchy

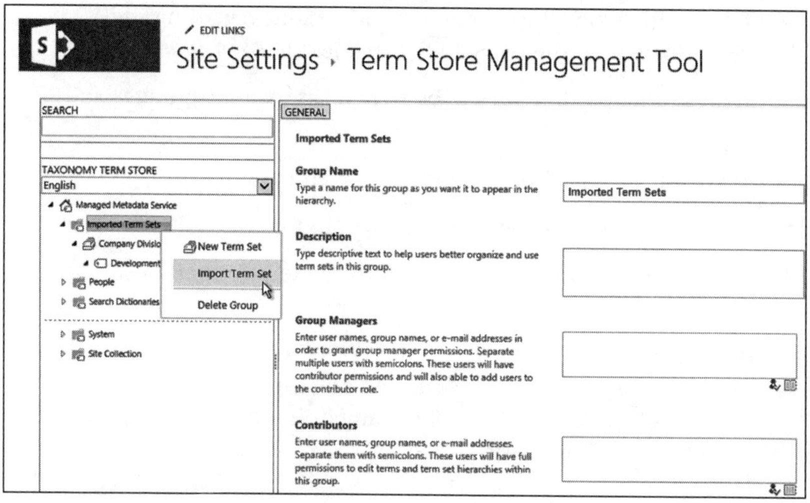

FIGURE 10.9   Importing a predefined term set.

TIP

There are several key tips and takeaways to remember when planning and implementing term sets. The following are some quick points for consideration:

▶ Adding a term set as a navigation source for a site is also referred to as a catalog. When a term set is added as a navigation source for a site, you are also able to define custom pages or pass selected tags to filtered view controls.

▶ Term sets can be copied, relocated, and reused from existing terms.

▶ Terms can be copied, reused, merged, deprecated, and so on.

▶ Keywords (that is, folksonomy) can be moved into a managed term set or deleted.

▶ Folksonomy is referred to as managed keywords that are usually "open" and allow users to add new terms interactively.

▶ Managed term stores are usually closed and require administrators to add new terms.

▶ Security is limited to the term set level.

▶ All child terms inherit this visibility setting.

▶ When dynamic external tags are being utilized, there are one-way data import limits and the BCS provides alternative tag techniques. The BCS data source can also be maintained externally or by publishing the source as an external list.

▶ Programming and customization are allowed (that is, C# and PowerShell) and native web parts can be utilized to display tags. You can also easily build web parts to add statistics on tag usage.

▶ Constraints and limitations exist, such as no granular security on tag definitions or tags as applied. Also, if you add price or color to a product tag, these will not be reflected in SharePoint search results.

When approaching information architecture design considerations regarding the MMS, you should consider the following "in the consulting trenches" lessons:

▶ Use MMS to centrally define product tags to be shared across multiple sites and libraries.

▶ Create centralized document repositories (Document Center and so on).

▶ Define a term store for all common elements and synonyms.

▶ Use MMS-enhanced navigation and search queries to create information storefronts and catalogs.

▶ Folksonomy consists of informal lists of ad hoc tags or terms that are built up over a period of time through user-defined keywords and are centrally stored in the MMS application. They can easily be enabled for all document libraries and can also be applied to content outside of SharePoint.

Content Types in SharePoint Server 2013

As mentioned in the preceding section, a content type is a reusable collection of settings and rules applied to a certain category of content in SharePoint. Content types define more granular attributes for documents, content, and library or list items. They enable you to associate information management policies to your SharePoint sites and site collections and play a key role in enforcing SharePoint governance.

Metadata in SharePoint is applied to content via an associated content type with a list or library. Content types can be extremely confusing when first described to your project team because they can be applied to so many different aspects of your SharePoint configuration and overall strategy. Workflows, site templates, lists, apps, library templates, and policies all have content types associated within them.

Your organization's information management and related ECM or RM efforts should entail defining core custom content types in a top-level site's content type gallery so that they can be not only applied to that site but inherited from all the sites below that site.

Custom content types can be housed in a content type hub that is defined in the managed metadata service instance and then made available to other site collections that are part of web applications associated with that managed metadata service instance.

For project team members who may not be familiar with content types, I would recommend sharing the following article with them regarding the planning of content types: http://technet.microsoft.com/en-us/library/cc262735.aspx

Out of all of the technical terminology used in a SharePoint Server 2013 or Office 365 SharePoint Online initiative, content type is the single most misunderstood or misused term.

Content Type Hub

A content type hub, as depicted in Figure 10.10, is associated with a site collection's content type gallery. In conjunction with SharePoint's managed metadata service instance, it can be made available to other site collections that are part of web applications associated with that managed metadata service instance.

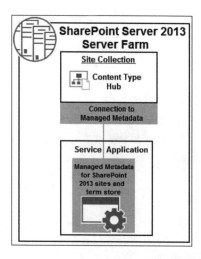

FIGURE 10.10   An overview of the content type hub within a SharePoint server farm.

NOTE

When you have shared content types from the content type galleries of multiple site collections, you must add a managed metadata service for each required content type hub. If your organization requires more than one managed metadata service, these must be documented in your information architecture governance strategy along with the granular details of what each service's term store will be utilized for within SharePoint.

Content Organizer

You can utilize SharePoint 2013's content organizer to route documents and automatically manage important library rules, maintenance activities, and other related tasks. To activate the content organizer feature on a site, a user with the appropriate permissions can select the Site Settings options from the "gear" icon and then, on the Site Settings Page under Site Actions, select the Manage Site Features option, as shown in Figure 10.11.

```
Site Actions
Manage site features
Save site as template
Enable search configuration export
Reset to site definition
Delete this site
```

FIGURE 10.11   SharePoint's Site Settings page.

When viewing the features within the site or site collection, the user should click on
Activate next to the Content Organizer feature, which will then activate this feature, as
shown in Figure 10.12.

FIGURE 10.12   Activating the Content Organizer feature.

The content organizer can automate tasks such as these:

▶ Manage a governed quote for the number of items in folders.

▶ Automatically create a new folder when a specific number of items is reached within
a folder.

▶ Create and then utilize custom rules within Site Administration, as shown in Figure
10.13, to determine and enforce where documents are routed or moved (to a specific
library or folder). These rules can be based on a specific combination of content
types and metadata that meets the needs of your organization, as shown in Figure
10.14.

```
Site Administration
Regional settings
Language settings
Site libraries and lists
User alerts
RSS
Sites and workspaces
Workflow settings
Content Organizer Settings
Content Organizer Rules
Site Closure and Deletion
Term store management
Popularity Trends
```

FIGURE 10.13   Available options within Site Administration to manage the Content Organizer's
rules and settings.

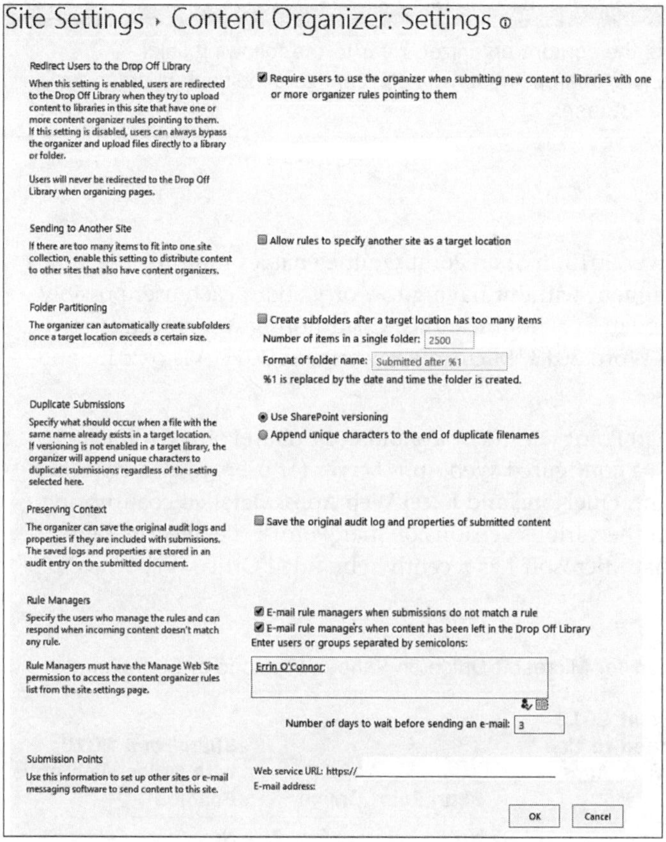

FIGURE 10.14   Configuring settings within SharePoint 2013's Content Organizer.

Note that in SharePoint Server 2013, this feature allows for content to be routed even if the underlying content is located in a different site collection.

▶ Place all uploaded documents in a Drop Off Library where an organization's users can ensure that metadata is applied or a custom process should be started and/or completed.

▶ Store audit logs regarding documents and continue to track the documents after they have been routed.

▶ Enforce SharePoint's version configurations by forcing a user uploading a document with a similar name to change the name or even automatically add new characters to ensure that both versions are stored and content that is not supposed to be updated is not overwritten.

10

TIP

For more information regarding the content organizer, refer to the following link: http://office.microsoft.com/en-us/sharepoint-server-help/configure-the-content-organizer-to-route-documents-HA102772938.aspx

Coauthoring

Coauthoring in SharePoint Server 2013 or SharePoint Online enables multiple users to collaborate and work on a document without having to worry about each user possibly interfering with each other's updates or modifications. Coauthoring works seamlessly with Office 2013 for Microsoft Word 2013, Microsoft PowerPoint 2013, Visio 2013, and Microsoft OneNote 2013.

When utilizing Office 365's SharePoint Online or a standalone SharePoint Online instance, you are able to utilize a configured Web Apps Server for users to also coauthor documents in Word, PowerPoint, OneNote, and Excel Web Apps. Detailed coauthoring support for Microsoft Office on the various versions of SharePoint is detailed in Table 10.1. It is important to note that Microsoft has recently rebranded Office Web Apps to Office Online.

TABLE 10.1   Coauthoring Support for Microsoft Office on Various Versions of SharePoint

Microsoft Office Version	SharePoint 2013 Configured to Use Office Web Apps Server	SharePoint Online	SharePoint 2010 with Office Web Apps Enabled
Excel 2013	No	No	No
Excel Web App	Yes	Yes	Yes
Excel 2010	No	No	No
OneNote 2013*	Yes	Yes	Yes
OneNote Web App	Yes	Yes	Yes
OneNote 2010*	Yes	Yes	Yes
PowerPoint 2013*	Yes	Yes	Yes
PowerPoint Web App	Yes	Yes	Yes
PowerPoint 2010*	Yes	Yes	Yes
Word 2013*	Yes	Yes	Yes
Word Web App	Yes	Yes	Yes
Word 2010*	Yes	Yes	Yes
Visio 2013*	Yes	Yes	Yes
Visio Web App	No	No	No
Visio 2010	No	No	No
Office 2007 client applications	No	No	No

Coauthoring's functionality enables two or more users to work on different sections or parts of a composite document without interfering with each other's work.

I have found this functionality to be extremely helpful in developing large PowerPoint presentations; several EPC Group team members can work on a composite slide show and add slides to the PowerPoint presentation deck in real time without one individual having to merge several decks together for review and final editing.

TIP

Excel 2013's client application does not support coauthoring workbooks in SharePoint 2013 or SharePoint Online. The Excel client application uses the Shared Workbook feature to support non-real-time coauthoring workbooks that are stored locally or on network paths. The coauthoring of Excel workbooks in SharePoint is currently supported only by using the Excel Web App, which is included with Office Online (Office Web Apps).

TIP

To get detailed information for both you and the project team to review on SharePoint 2013's coauthoring and its administration, refer to the following link: http://technet.microsoft.com/en-us/library/ff718235.aspx

This link is helpful to share because there are also some native videos available from Microsoft to help ease some of the possible concerns legal and compliance may have about this powerful feature.

In Table 10.1, versions that are denoted by * support coauthoring functionality, even when Office Web Apps are not configured or enabled in your organization's SharePoint environment.

Library and List Settings in SharePoint 2013

Libraries and lists are the most widely used features within SharePoint sites because they store the actual content, records, and files you will work on every day. Document libraries are commonly used to store content and records, and most of SharePoint 2013's document management features are delivered through these document libraries.

For example, SharePoint 2013's library and list features and their related settings provide you the options to manage content types, specify whether to require content approval for submitted items, and specify how SharePoint should handle the versioning on content. These lists and library settings also provide for the configuration of features such as approval workflows, provide the requirements of whether users must first check out a document when opening or editing, and provide the security settings and strategies to protect your organization's content.

To modify a library, a user with the appropriate permissions can select Library Settings in the Ribbon, as shown in Figure 10.15. When you are within the Library Settings page, as shown in Figure 10.16, you have a variety of options you can tailor to meet your organization's needs. Some library and list options vary; you may not see the exact same options in every library or list because some features, security settings, or other elements may limit what is available.

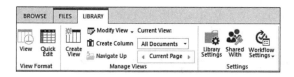

FIGURE 10.15   The Library Settings option within the Ribbon.

List Information		
Name:	SharePoint 2013 Field Guide Chapter Submissions	
Web Address:	https://	
Description:		

General Settings	Permissions and Management	Communications
▪ List name, description and navigation	▪ Delete this document library	▪ RSS settings
▪ Versioning settings	▪ Save document library as template	
▪ Advanced settings	▪ Permissions for this document library	
▪ Validation settings	▪ Manage files which have no checked in version	
▪ Column default value settings	▪ Workflow Settings	
▪ Audience targeting settings	▪ Generate file plan report	
▪ Rating settings	▪ Enterprise Metadata and Keywords Settings	
▪ Form settings	▪ Information management policy settings	

Columns

A column stores information about each document in the document library. The following columns are currently available in this document library:

Column (click to edit)	Type	Required
Created	Date and Time	
Modified	Date and Time	
Title	Single line of text	
Created By	Person or Group	
Modified By	Person or Group	
Checked Out To	Person or Group	

▪ Create column

FIGURE 10.16   The options shown when you select Library Settings from the Ribbon for a document library.

As mentioned at the beginning of this chapter, it is key to ensure that you are aware of the latest updates regarding the specific SharePoint Server 2013 or Office 365's SharePoint Online plan your organization has selected because Microsoft's updates and release cycles have changed from previous versions.

The following link provides information on planning document libraries in SharePoint 2013 that I would recommend you share with your organization's project team to ensure that everyone is on the same page and is using the correct technology terms in relation to lists and libraries: http://technet.microsoft.com/en-us/library/cc262215.aspx

> **TIP**
>
> I would not recommend selecting the option to include content when saving a library or list as a template. There may be sensitive data or simply irrelevant data that you would then have to delete each time after a new library or lists are created using the specified template. Also, errors can occur if the content in the library or list is too large based on the default size quota settings configured within SharePoint's template galleries.

▶ **Permissions for This Document Library** (or the name of the specific type of library or list)

For more information on how to edit permissions for a list, a library, or an individual item, refer to the following link:

http://office.microsoft.com/en-us/sharepoint-help/edit-permissions-for-a-list-library-or-individual-item-HA102833689.aspx

▶ **Manage Files Which Have No Checked In Version**

▶ **Workflow Settings**

For more information on workflows in SharePoint 2013, refer to the following link:

http://msdn.microsoft.com/en-us/library/office/jj163986.aspx

▶ **Generate File Plan Report**

This option allows you to specify the location where the file plan report should be saved after it is generated.

▶ **Enterprise Metadata and Keywords Settings**

For more information on how to add an enterprise keywords column to a list or library, refer to the following link:

http://office.microsoft.com/en-us/sharepoint-help/add-an-enterprise-keywords-column-to-a-list-or-library-HA102832526.aspx

▶ **Information Management Policy Settings**

For more information on how to create and apply information management policies, refer to the following link:

http://office.microsoft.com/en-us/sharepoint-server-help/create-and-apply-information-management-policies-HA101631505.aspx

Communications

▶ **RSS Settings**

For more information regarding how to manage RSS feeds as well as the related configuration for lists and libraries, refer to the following link:

http://office.microsoft.com/en-us/office365-sharepoint-online-enterprise-help/manage-rss-feeds-HA102771948.aspx

10

Columns

▶ **Create Column**

For more information on how to create, change, or delete a column in a list or library, refer to the following link:

http://office.microsoft.com/en-us/sharepoint-server-help/create-change-or-delete-a-column-in-a-list-or-library-HA102771913.aspx

▶ **Add from Existing Site Columns**

▶ **Column Ordering**

▶ **Indexed Columns**

Views

▶ **All Documents** (editing the out-of-the-box default view)

▶ **Create View**

For more information on how to create, change, or delete a view of a list or library, refer to the following link:

http://office.microsoft.com/en-us/sharepoint-server-help/create-change-or-delete-a-view-of-a-list-or-library-HA102774516.aspx

Every organization has unique requirements that you must plan for when designing SharePoint's information management and configuring the underlying lists and libraries. From determining your organization's granular companywide policy needs to the actual creation of site collections and their governed configuration, the project team must continually be kept up-to-date because communication is extremely important in achieving this task.

There will be extreme technical conversations between IT project team members and other business-related conversations with key department stakeholders who will relay their needs and what they actually do on a day-to-day basis, and those business requirements must be captured and transferred into a user-friendly and functional SharePoint platform.

The following link provides information about planning information management policies in SharePoint 2013 that I would recommend you share with your organization's project team to ensure that everyone is on the same page and is using the correct technical terminology: http://technet.microsoft.com/en-us/library/cc262490.aspx

Versioning in SharePoint 2013

Versioning is the method in SharePoint 2013 for which iterations of a document are numbered and saved. Versioning also provides for content approval functionality, which is the method by which SharePoint site users with appropriate permissions can control the publication of content and documents.

There are also check-in and check-out features in SharePoint 2013 that enable users to control when a new version of a document is created, and provide added capabilities for comments on changes that are made to documents when they are checked back in to the library.

Plan Versioning in SharePoint 2013

Various levels of versioning can be implemented, as shown in Figure 10.17, based on your organization's needs. The following versioning can be applied:

▶ No versioning enabled

▶ Create major versions

▶ Create major and minor versions (drafts)

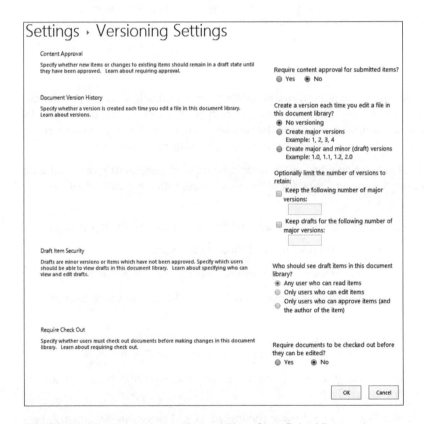

FIGURE 10.17   Versioning settings within a SharePoint Library.

Document IDs

SharePoint 2013's Document IDs capabilities enable you to manage and track items regardless of where they are stored. You can track important content such as a legal contract, and even if it is moved from one document library to another for appropriate reasons, that legal contract will retain its underlying Document ID.

Document ID capabilities enable you to easily track content from its creation through archival and also enable important documents that have been archived to be located for retrieval. Document IDs are a site collection level feature that can be easily activated, and when a document is generated, a unique ID is applied and automatically searchable.

> **NOTE**
>
> To activate and configure Document IDs in a site collection, refer to the following link: http://office.microsoft.com/en-us/sharepoint-server-help/activate-and-configure-document-ids-in-a-site-collection-HA102773259.aspx

Document Sets

Document Sets is a feature in SharePoint that enables your organization's users to incorporate multiple documents or files into a unique "set" or type of folder so that there is a relational set of attributes and unique elements that enable them to be managed as a single deliverable. Document Sets can provide your organization with the following:

▶ Organizations that want to manage "multidocument sets" consistently can configure a new Document Set content type for each work product they typically create and utilize.

▶ Policies, tagging, and templates can be applied to any document set that is created.

▶ Content types let you wrap up documents in formal metadata.

▶ This feature helps when you are working on multiple documents at the same time.

▶ By default, Document Sets inherit permissions from the library in which they are located.

▶ You can opt to specify unique permissions for a Document Set if you need to restrict or change who has access to the documents in an individual Document Set.

▶ Users interact with Document Sets in much the same way that they interact with regular SharePoint folders.

▶ All documents in a Document Set share the metadata and the entire set can also be versioned.

▶ Any kind of document that your SharePoint farm is configured to support can be included in a Document Set.

▶ You can enable users to group multiple documents that support a single project or task together into a single entity.

▶ You can organize unmanaged documents and enable collaboration on these documents.

▶ Ease workflow deployment on multiple items with SharePoint Designer 2013.

▶ Metadata has to be updated in only one place for it to be applied to all the documents contained within the Document Set.

▶ You can capture a version of all documents within a container.

▶ The site collection feature can be enabled or disabled.

> **NOTE**
>
> In Office 365, the Document Sets feature is currently available only with the Enterprise or "E" plans.

Document Sets and Folders present a similar interface to users; however, the functionality in Document Sets is specifically targeted to support business processes and the management of content as a single unit.

Document Sets are very straightforward to configure, and Microsoft is continuing to roll out added capabilities around this feature. For more information on Document Sets, refer to the following link: http://technet.microsoft.com/en-us/library/ff603637.aspx

Record Center Overview

In SharePoint Server 2013, it is key to understand the concept of in-place records management versus the utilization of the record center. You are able to manage records in the same document repository as other active documents or manage them in an archive (that is, record center). The in-place approach means the document stays where it is while information policies (retention policies) are applied to it and it is then declared as a record. This in-place approach fits into the existing site structure where the content creator(s) may be able to access their own content depending on the specifics of the information policies applied.

The record center approach entails the record being moved to the record center where it inherits retention rules. The record center approach allows for a more centralized management approach and tighter governance, which I strongly recommend. Not only does the record center, as shown in Figure 10.18, provide stronger governance, but it also allows for better scalability and the application of security and permission strategies with dedicated roles.

10

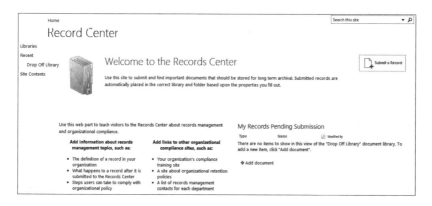

FIGURE 10.18   The record center in SharePoint 2013.

In some cases, though, you may utilize both the in-place and the record center approaches in a hybrid RM approach. A record may be kept in-place with other active documents, for example, on an existing project and then after the project has been completed the record would then be moved to the record center (records archive) along with other possible documents that may have been declared records during that project.

To help guide you in determining the correct approach, there are some factors that you can review and questions you can answer that will steer you in the best direction to meet the needs of your organization. The factors and related questions are as shown here:

▶ Does your organization have specific industry requirements or regulatory rules that determine whether a record must be stored within a record center?

▶ If you were to utilize the in-place approach, does your organization's governance model cover the policies, security, and oversight that will be needed to ensure compliance of the site for which the in-place record is managed?

▶ Does your organization's legal or compliance department or counsel have specific input due to their in-depth knowledge of your business?

▶ Does your disaster recovery (that is, backup and restore) strategy meet the requirements to back up the location where the record is stored?

▶ What is your organization's archival strategy for sites that may not be actively utilized, and would the in-place record be stored within a site that may be stagnant for a period of time where archival may be a factor?

I would recommend the utilization of the records center to not only err on the side of caution but ensure that your SharePoint roadmap and scalability strategy is able to meet the growing needs of the business over a several-year period.

As mentioned earlier in this chapter, it is key that the project team understand the core concepts of records management and be on the same page during project meetings regarding implementing this for your organization.

I also recommend reviewing and sharing the following links with your organization's project team members so that they can review many of the core concepts from a more high-level approach, as well as to ensure that any updates or new feature releases to SharePoint Server 2013 on-premises, future service packs, or in the cloud via Office 365's SharePoint Online are addressed:

▶ For information on how to create and configure a records center site, refer to the following link:

http://office.microsoft.com/en-us/office365-sharepoint-online-enterprise-help/implement-records-management-HA102893868.aspx

▶ For more information on planning ways to convert active documents to records in SharePoint Server 2013, refer to the following link:

http://technet.microsoft.com/en-us/library/cc263464.aspx

▶ For more information on how to use SharePoint Server 2013 records archive or manage records in place, refer to the following link:

http://technet.microsoft.com/en-us/library/ee424394.aspx

▶ For information regarding how to manage a connection to a document center or a records center in SharePoint 2013, refer to the following link:

http://technet.microsoft.com/en-us/library/ee424395.aspx

eDiscovery Strategies in SharePoint Server 2013

Not only do records stored on users' devices and in SharePoint become relevant in legal and compliance-related cases and incidents, but emails as well as even Lync conversations also fall into eDiscovery requests more and more every day. The new eDiscovery features and functionality in SharePoint Server 2013 provide improved methods to help protect your organization as well as its team members. Some of the new and added capabilities related to eDiscovery in SharePoint Server 2013 include the following:

▶ Improved support for searching and exporting content from file shares

▶ The capability to have a dedicated site collection for which you can perform eDiscovery queries across multiple SharePoint instances, farms, and Exchange servers that will store and preserve the items that are discovered

▶ Features that enable you to export discovered content from Exchange Server 2013 and SharePoint Server 2013 to ensure that you are able to meet timely requests or related court orders

▶ The capability for in-place preservation of Exchange mailboxes and SharePoint sites that also include SharePoint list items and SharePoint pages

10

▶ The capability to create Site Mailboxes to store email in a comprehensive manner
related to a specific project or effort

For more information on how to configure Site Mailboxes in SharePoint Server 2013,
refer to the following link:

http://technet.microsoft.com/en-us/library/jj552524.aspx

SharePoint Server 2013's capability for managing discovery cases and holds comes in the
form of a new eDiscovery Center site template, as shown in Figure 10.19, which creates
a portal through which you can access discovery cases to conduct the required searches.
When you have conducted the relevant searches, you are able to place content on hold as
well as export the content to meet the needs or your organization and its legal counsel.

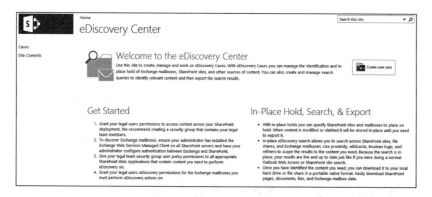

FIGURE 10.19   SharePoint Server 2013's eDiscovery Center site template.

It is important to remember that for each individual case, you must create a new site that
uses SharePoint Server 2013's eDiscovery Case site template. Every case correlates to a
collaboration site that includes a document library for you and your organization's legal
team members to use to store documents related to the management of the case while
demonstrating to the court or matter's governing body your company's preparedness and
due diligence in having a process in place for such matters. This not only benefits your
organization but also can give your organization the upper hand by ensuring that you
have all relevant information available for your counsel, because time is always of the
essence in these types of matters.

You are also able to associate the following items with each case:

▶ The source the information was derived from, such as SharePoint, Exchange, or File
Shares.

▶ The specific search criteria your organization ran to prove your due diligence and
extraordinary efforts to meet the court's or opposing counsel's request.

▶ The actual eDiscovery sets that may include all the sources and a complete list of
queries and filters, as well as the actual exports that were produced in relation to
the case.

An added plus to this process is that if additional requests are made by the court or requesting party, you can build on or add new queries to further refine searches and the related retrieved content.

When content in SharePoint Server 2013 is put on hold and is preserved, the state of the content at the time of that preservation is recorded, but that does not mean work on a project by team members must cease.

SharePoint still allows content to be updated or changed, but the content that was put on hold and preserved will not change; those "copies" or "records" are being preserved and the content the users are working on is simply new content and records that can also be preserved if needed at any time by implementation of a new hold on these updated records. This allows a project and your business to continue being productive as this matter is being resolved, which in many cases may take several years.

TIP

It is important to note that records managers or compliance officers who have permissions to use the eDiscovery features of SharePoint Server 2013 can access the original, preserved versions of content at any time.

TIP

When a SharePoint eDiscovery export is being performed, the locations where the content resides may cause the export type to differ.

For example, you may have documents that are exported from file shares where no version history is available, but documents from a SharePoint document library will have their version history intact when exported from SharePoint Server 2013.

If an item in a SharePoint list was included in the eDiscovery query results, the complete list is exported as a comma-separated values (.csv) file. SharePoint pages such as wiki pages or blogs are exported as MIME HTML (.mht) files.

Microsoft Exchange items or objects in an Exchange Server 2013 mailbox, such as tasks, calendar entries, email messages, contacts, and attachments, are exported as a .pst file.

To ensure compliance, a complete XML manifest that complies with the Electronic Discovery Reference Model (EDRM) specification is made available that provides an overview of all the exported information.

NOTE

To set up an eDiscovery Center in SharePoint Online, refer to the following link: http://office.microsoft.com/en-us/sharepoint-server-help/set-up-an-ediscovery-center-in-sharepoint-online-HA104042284.aspx

The following is a detailed list of capabilities of the SharePoint Server 2013 eDiscovery Center:

▶ SharePoint 2013 in-place holds

▶ Exchange 2013 in-place holds

▶ Query-based preservation

▶ Bulk metadata update

▶ Content drag and drop

▶ Exchange Site Mailboxes

▶ Improved video handling

▶ Search enhancements

▶ CMIS update to CMIS 1.0

Microsoft Exchange and SharePoint 2013 Integration Capabilities

The overall integration of Microsoft Exchange and SharePoint 2013 consists of the following:

▶ Site mailboxes have their own unique email address.

▶ Emails are stored in Microsoft Exchange.

▶ Documents and emails are stored in both SharePoint and Outlook.

▶ Your organization can manage emails as records that include Site Retention.

▶ You are able to drag emails from Outlook into SharePoint 2013.

▶ Mobile access is native to meet the needs of the ever-changing mobile IT world and BYOD demands.

Site Mailbox Feature in SharePoint Server 2013

SharePoint Server 2013's Site Mailbox feature, as shown in Figure 10.20, provides for the following capabilities:

▶ Creation of an Exchange Mailbox per site for which information management policies can be applied and governed

▶ The capability to drag emails in to SharePoint document library for which retention and information management policies are then available to be applied based on your organization's specific requirements or configuration

▶ The capability to apply an expiration policy for both SharePoint and Site Mailboxes

A high-level flow of SharePoint 2013's Site Mailbox functionality is depicted in Figure 10.20.

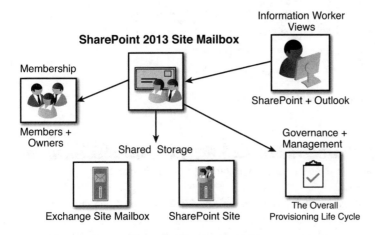

FIGURE 10.20   The high-level flow of SharePoint 2013's Site Mailbox functionality.

Site Mailboxes and Life Cycle Management

An overview of the provisioning of SharePoint Server 2013 Site Mailboxes follows:

▶ They are available to be provisioned OOTB from a SharePoint site, provided that Exchange 2013 integration is in place.

▶ They provide for customized self-service provisioning from Outlook.

▶ The Site Mailbox is deleted together with SharePoint site.

▶ Site deletion can be manual or policy driven in relation to any Site Mailbox considerations.

▶ Site Mailboxes are only marked for deletion in Exchange.

The overall life cycle of a Site Mailbox must be defined within your organization's information management policies. An example of SharePoint Server 2013's Site Mailbox overall life cycle is shown in Figure 10.21.

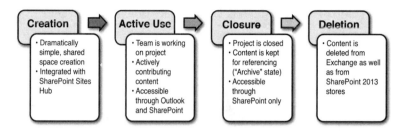

FIGURE 10.21   The life cycle of a Site Mailbox.

TIP

The following should be kept in mind at all times regarding SharePoint's Site Mailbox feature:

▶ The site connection must be restored when the SharePoint site's URL is changed or modified.

▶ Site Mailboxes can be accessed by any users with at least read/write access to the site.

▶ For information security precautions, it is important to use naming standards with the email address prefix as specified in your organization's provisioning policy.

Summary

In this chapter, we discussed the many options an organization must consider when implementing an ECM or RM initiative. There are both internal and external factors that must be considered, and security and compliance should be a driving factor in all configuration and policy decisions.

There is a wide variety of data, and your organization must, at some time in the near future, take on the task of implementing an information management policy and related records retention strategy to ensure compliance and mitigate risk.

In Chapter 11, "Upgrade and Migration Best Practices," we will cover strategies for upgrading as well as migrating content in a best practices manner from previous versions of SharePoint to a new SharePoint Server 2013 on-premises, Office 365 SharePoint Online, or combination hybrid SharePoint platform.

CHAPTER 11

Upgrade and Migration Best Practices

When approaching a SharePoint 2013 upgrade or migration initiative, you first must perform due diligence on what is currently implemented.

Due diligence in a SharePoint 2013 upgrade or migration initiatives means asking the right and sometimes tough questions while also putting in place strategies for the possible "unknowns" and surprises that may be in store for you in this journey to a successful "go-live" in SharePoint 2013.

In the first 10 chapters of this book, the core features of SharePoint 2013 were addressed, as well as "from the consulting trenches" lessons learned about how best to approach SharePoint's information architecture (IA) design. We also covered SharePoint 2013ECM/RM initiatives as well as considerations around the underlying SharePoint system architecture with a focus on scalability and governance to address the ever-changing hybrid IT world we live in today.

At the time of writing this chapter, I have been personally involved in more than 60 SharePoint 2013 upgrade and/or migration initiatives with my teams at EPC Group. Every organization's initiative requires a tailored strategy that best fits the underlying business and functional requirements, as well as one that has minimal impact on your users and fits into your available budget.

Just as I am sure I drove a few IT "purists" a little crazy in the preceding chapter, when referring to taking on an ECM and/or RM initiative, the same thing can be said here in this chapter. SharePoint 2013 upgrade initiatives almost always require content to be migrated over from the existing SharePoint platform(s) to the new SharePoint 2013 environment.

It's key to first scope out your organization's effort to determine, at a very granular level, exactly what you and the project team are being tasked with successfully completing.

Are you wanting to take on this initiative in a "forklift"-type approach in which everything that currently exists will be upgraded or migrated to SharePoint 2013 and then any updates or rearchitecture (that is, information architecture redesign, site consolidation, content cleanup, and so on) would then be performed in a later phase 2 initiative down the road?

Does your organization have both SharePoint 2007 and SharePoint 2010 implemented, and is the overall goal to consolidate everything into a centralized SharePoint 2013 platform?

In many SharePoint 2013 upgrade or migration initiatives, there are also non-SharePoint-based systems and content also in-scope to be migrated into SharePoint 2013. These efforts provide for SharePoint 2013 to "intake" the non-SharePoint system or platform so that it can then be decommissioned and additional ROI can be achieved now that "other platform" licenses or any "premier support" contracts will never again need to be renewed.

If your company is a mid-market to enterprise-size organization, you may even want to consider the possibility of renaming this effort or at least publicly referring to your new SharePoint 2013 upgrade or migration initiative as a "SharePoint 2013 upgrade and consolidation" project.

The following sections dig deep into these questions as well as ask a number of additional questions so that you can steer your SharePoint 2013 architecture design and tailor the project's business message, goals, internal perception, and technical execution in a manner that will ensure its success. The first few sections in this chapter reiterate the importance of ensuring that your organization's information architecture and system architecture designs have been put in place in a scalable manner, as well as digging into what your organization currently has implemented in terms of SharePoint and non-SharePoint systems and the goals and milestones you are wanting to achieve.

TIP

With my deep involvement with SharePoint since its original version 1 release back in 2001, it has been extremely beneficial to be able to witness and learn firsthand how this technology has evolved now into its fifth version release with SharePoint 2013. SharePoint and its "non-identical twin brother" in a public or hybrid cloud-based Office 365 and SharePoint Online are now the undisputed underlying flagship technology in Microsoft's enterprise solution stack.

I have seen firsthand the pitfalls and "gotchas" that can derail these types of initiatives and have the bumps and bruises from having fallen into them on more than a few occasions over the past decade. With the lessons learned "from the consulting trenches" in these experiences, this chapter provides the guidance needed to help you achieve a successful upgrade or migration to SharePoint 2013.

Focus on developing a path for our organization that will always attempt to limit the business impact on your SharePoint user base during this initiative. This includes having prepared materials such as questionnaires for possible interviews or specific questions defined that you may need to pose to stakeholders or power users about their existing site(s) and content.

Limiting business impact is also going to entail executing a small but very professional and ongoing internal public relations (PR) campaign and communication strategy tied directly to reasonable train-the-trainer expectations for existing SharePoint champions or power users.

Ensuring That Your System and Information Architecture Strategy Aligns with Your SharePoint Roadmap

In Chapter 5, "Implementing a Best Practices SharePoint 2013/Office 365 Information Architecture," SharePoint 2013 information architecture (IA) design strategies and recommendations were discussed and in Chapter 7, "Implementing a SharePoint 2013 System Architecture with Future Hybrid Scalability in Mind," SharePoint 2013's underlying system architecture was also covered in great detail. When you are at the point of actually kicking off and performing the upgrade or migration initiative to SharePoint 2013, it is key to ensure that those core elements have been designed and put in place to meet not only the current needs of the organization over the next 12 months but also the needs for at least the next 24 to 36 months via a SharePoint roadmap.

Scalability in SharePoint 2013's design and planning for the future will save your organization an incredible amount of budget as well as the intangible price that comes with achieving user buy-in and an overall satisfied user base that utilizes the tools and features being provided to them.

What does your organization currently have implemented? And if you could, "in a perfect world," descibe the exact scenario and path of how your SharePoint 2013 initiative should go, what would you say?

For example, on the previous 60-plus SharePoint 2013 upgrade or migration initiatives I have been a part of, I have outlined the overall requirements of five actual projects that organizations were able to achieve with SharePoint 2013 and/or Office 365's SharePoint Online.

> **NOTE**
>
> In reviewing these scenarios, put togethor your own high-level summary of what you are wanting to acheive in your organization's effort.

These five organizations with existing SharePoint as well as non-SharePoint platforms had the following technology landscapes implemented and overall project requirements for their new initiative:

▶ Our organization has SharePoint 2007 (MOSS) implemented with a fair number of customizations that were done via SharePoint Designer, and we are wanting to upgrade directly to SharePoint Server 2013. We have approximately 800 users and two data centers and would like to achieve a "big bang" migration by moving everything over all at once. We have about 250GB of content in our content databases and our site structure is really more departmental following our company's org chart.

▶ Our organization has SharePoint Server 2010 implemented with about 4,000 users, and we are utilizing several of SharePoint's ECM tools along with the record center. We have a lot of sites that are not being used because we did not have a defined site provisioning strategy when we first launched, so we would like to clean up or archive those sites so that they are not carried over to SharePoint 2013.

▶ Our organization has been utilizing SharePoint since the 2003 version. We upgraded to SharePoint 2007 using a migration tool several years ago, but we wanted to wait until SharePoint Server 2013 came out to move away from SharePoint 2007. There are a few departments that did stand up their own SharePoint 2010 environments, and we are not 100% sure of the content or how they are utilizing it; however, we will want to ensure that they are also in scope for this migration effort. We want this project to not only focus on getting us into SharePoint 2013 and off the older version but also focus on this as an opportunity to implement governance and new permission strategies and also implement some custom branding that aligns with our corporate brand. We are also very interested in taking advantage of the new built-in FAST technology in SharePoint 2013's search.

▶ Our organization has SharePoint Server 2010 implemented, as well as Project Server 2007, and our PMO department also has heavily utilized the SharePoint project sites that came along with Project Server. These project sites, built in Windows SharePoint Services 3.0 (WSS 3.0) are also part of the overall migration and upgrade effort because we do not want to continue to support the environment that these older SharePoint project sites reside on. We also have a compliance and security concern about all the "project documents" that reside in Project Server 2007's WSS 3.0 environment because they do not have an approved security model. We also want to make sure that all new projects, because we also want to upgrade soon to Project Server 2013, have their project sites in SharePoint 2013. In summary, this effort will be for upgrading our main intranet and collaboration environment, on SharePoint Server 2010, as well as migrating the WSS 3.0 project sites over to a new SharePoint 2013 environment.

▶ Our organization is in the healthcare arena. We have the free version of SharePoint 2010, SharePoint Foundation 2010, and it is being widely used across the entire organization. We also have offices and partners all over the world who need to be able to securely access a SharePoint 2013 environment. We are interested in utilizing

Office 365 for our external partners and then implementing a SharePoint Server 2013 on-premises environment due to our compliance requirements around HIPAA and PHI and our organization's president's overall concern about cloud security and the recent NSA leaks and press that are in the news. Our leadership does not feel comfortable storing our intellectual property or our highly sensitive HIPAA and PHI data in the cloud, but we do want to take advantage of the cloud and are looking at a hybrid SharePoint scenario. Also, we have tested Visual Studio 2013 and Visual Studio online and would be interested in implementing a development environment in Microsoft Azure for some of our new developers who will be learning SharePoint development.

These are just a few real-world examples of how each and every organization is unique in what they are trying to accomplish, as well as the hurdles and compliance concerns they are facing. All five of these projects were completed, and I am stating that because it is absolutely possible to migrate from SharePoint 2007 to SharePoint 2013 by following defined processes. It is also completely possible to migrate Windows SharePoint Services 3.0 and a SharePoint Server 2007 platform in addition to a highly utilized SharePoint Server 2010 environment with ECM and records retention requirements that all reside within one company.

Questions that I would pose to organizations with similar or a completely different and unique set of requirements are these:

▶ What is your experience with your organization's users regarding a "big bang" migration (that is, all at once) versus a granular migration that may take place over several weekends?

▶ What types of customizations have been implemented, and what tool or method was used to develop these customizations?

▶ Does your organization have an existing governance strategy that defines service level agreements (SLAs) or expectations of SharePoint's availability?

▶ Do the organization and executive management consider SharePoint to be a mission-critical application?

▶ How much data and what types of data exist within your environment(s)?

▶ Do you have any records retention or ECM/RM requirements that will be required to be implemented with the new SharePoint 2013 or Office 365's SharePoint Online environment?

▶ What has worked well in the past for training your organization's user base on new technologies, and do you have a defined trainer? Do you prefer a train-the-trainer type of strategy to possibly help lower the costs of ongoing training?

▶ Where are your data centers and offices located? Do you have offices or data centers in both North America and the EU? If so, what EU compliance policies must be followed when working with those users and their data?

▶ What is your organization's executive leadership's feeling regarding the cloud, and have there been any conversations regarding the implementation of a hybrid cloud strategy (that is, a completely federated SharePoint Server 2013 on-premises + Office 365's SharePoint Online + Exchange Online + Lync Online)?

▶ What does your current environment's underlying system architecture entail, and how is your organization utilizing virtualization?

▶ Do you have any existing Microsoft Azure or Amazon Web Services (AWS) environments that may run non-SharePoint-based or other custom applications that will also need to seamlessly integrate (that is, via Identify Management) with your overall new SharePoint 2013 platform?

▶ How is your organization's Active Directory (AD) environment configured, and are there any configuration concerns or possible updates that may need to be made to AD to ensure that a best practices security model is implemented?

▶ Does your IT department have dedicated developers who will be developing custom SharePoint 2013 or Office 365 apps in the future? Are you utilizing Visual Studio as well as Team Foundation Server for code management? Can you provide more insight regarding your organization's development and buy versus build policies?

▶ Are you looking at possible future business intelligence (BI) or reporting initiatives or looking to pull in external data sources from "other" line-of-business systems such as SAP? If so, there are some areas of consideration and planning that should be discussed and added into your organization's SharePoint roadmap so that SharePoint 2013 can "intake" those future requirements. This enables you to build and deliver new services such as BI or ECM to your organization's users without having to perform any major rearchitecture (information and system architecture scalability and roadmap planning).

These are just a few initial questions to help get you thinking more granularly about what you currently have implemented and how you may want to tailor your overall project implementation strategy to meet not only your user's current needs but also future "big ticket" types of initiatives in the future.

ITERATIVE MIGRATION VERSUS "BIG BANG" MIGRATIONS

Because a migration can be time-consuming due to the volume and nature of content to be migrated, the process can impact daily working operations because it will prevent access to necessary or useful content during the migration process. To mitigate this delay in access, it may be determined that your organization will continue to access and use content from the source environment (that is, existing SharePoint 2010 or SharePoint 2007 platform) during and after the main migration phase.

This is a key consideration for your project, but very large environments tend to benefit from an iterative migration over "a few separate weekends" rather than a big bang that could add unnecessary risks for the end users.

There are strategies that can be put in place for both iterative and "big bang" migrations that will limit the impact to any possible content changes or the need for any remigration into the destination environment. Your communication strategy should tie directly into your migration approach so that users are notified and kept up-to-date regarding the project's progress as well as when they can expect their sites to be affected.

Understanding and Reviewing Your Current Technology Landscape

Every organization has a unique set of business and functional requirements related to a SharePoint 2013 upgrade and/or migration effort. These requirements will be created and will continue to be built on based on various questions and related variables that the organization will need to answer and document to ensure that the environment is upgraded or migrated properly.

The following sections cover the various topical areas that you must address and document to ensure that the SharePoint 2013 upgrade or migration strategy is aligned with your organization's 24- to 36-month IT roadmap and that no key items or areas are overlooked.

What Software and Infrastructure Elements Are Currently Deployed Within Your Organization?

It is important to first get a high-level overview of what is currently deployed and being utilized by the organization. The following initial core questions must be answered and documented to ensure that your initiative is properly scoped:

- ▶ What SharePoint technologies and related versions are currently deployed within your organization?
  - ▶ Do you have instances of SharePoint Server 2010 installed?
    - ▶ If so, do you have the Enterprise or Standard Version?
    - ▶ Do you have FAST Search installed within the SharePoint 2010 environment?
    - ▶ Did you deploy My Sites, and if so, what is the current state of the My Site usage?
  - ▶ Do you have instances of SharePoint Foundation 2010 installed?
  - ▶ Do you have instances of Microsoft Office SharePoint Server 2007 (MOSS) installed?
    - ▶ If so, do you have the Enterprise or Standard Version?
    - ▶ Did you deploy My Sites, and if so, what is the current state of the My Site usage?

> ▶ Do you have instances of Windows SharePoint Service 3.0 installed?

> ▶ Do you have old remaining instances of SharePoint 2003 installed?

▶ How does the organization currently utilize Microsoft SharePoint?

> ▶ Does the organization utilize SharePoint as its centralized intranet platform?

>> ▶ Is Corporate Communication or Marketing involved in the management of the intranet content?

>> ▶ Is there any tailored branding applied, and who owns the overall "look and feel" of the organization's intranet?

> ▶ Is SharePoint being utilized for any enterprise content management or records management initiatives?

>> ▶ Does SharePoint integrate with any other ECM or RM systems your organization may also have deployed, such as Documentum?

>> ▶ Has your organization implemented any records retention or utilized any of the managed metadata, content type hub, or related features?

> ▶ Is SharePoint being utilized by teams and departments for collaboration (departmental team sites and so forth)?

> ▶ Is SharePoint being utilized or perceived by the organization as a "glorified file share" or file share "dumping ground?"

> ▶ Is SharePoint used for any business intelligence or reporting initiatives?

>> ▶ Is Microsoft PerformancePoint being utilized?

>> ▶ Has SharePoint been configured to work with SQL Server Reporting Services (SSRS)?

>> ▶ Are there any KPIs or dashboards within SharePoint?

>> ▶ Is Excel Services being utilized?

> ▶ Is SharePoint used for any workflow or business process automation initiatives?

>> ▶ Are the workflows being utilized out-of-the-box or have any custom workflows been created via SharePoint Designer or more complex ones via Visual Studio?

>> ▶ Do any of the workflow activities interact with "other" line-of-business systems or any third-party solutions?

> ▶ Is SharePoint being utilized as an extranet?

>> ▶ Who is the audience for the extranet? Is this for partners, customers, or clients with any custom security models or permissions applied?

▶ Is SharePoint being utilized as any Internet-facing websites?

    ▶ Have you utilized Web Content Management features such as any publishing or multilanguage sites?

▶ Is SharePoint being utilized to host or be a centralized platform for any custom .NET or other custom applications?

▶ Is SharePoint being utilized as a learning management system (LMS) or training platform for your organization?

▶ Is SharePoint being utilized for any knowledge management (KM) or advanced "social" or "professional" networking-related efforts?

    ▶ Have My Sites been widely adopted, and are there any tailored or custom features that have been applied to them?

    ▶ Have you implemented or integrated any third-party social application platforms such as Microsoft's Yammer, Sitrion (previously NewsGator), or Jive?

▶ Do you have any scanning (OCR) or paperless initiatives implemented that integrate with SharePoint?

    ▶ Have you implemented or integrated any third-party scanning solutions or applications?

▶ Does your organization have Microsoft Project Sever deployed within your organization?

    ▶ What version of Microsoft Project Server do you have deployed?

    ▶ Does the Microsoft Project Server deployment reside on any of the servers being utilized in your organization's Microsoft SharePoint implementations?

▶ Does your organization have any Microsoft Dynamics solutions implementation deployed within the organization?

    ▶ What Microsoft Dynamics solutions are deployed and what versions (releases and so on) are they?

▶ Does your organization have any other line-of-business (LOB) or major platforms that utilize or integrate with Microsoft SharePoint such as the following?

    ▶ SAP

    ▶ Oracle

    ▶ Documentum/eRoom

    ▶ LiveLink

▶ Does your organization have any third-party SharePoint-specific or SharePoint-related tools or solutions implemented due to SharePoint 2007's or SharePoint 2010's versions not having the out-of-the-box capabilities you may have required at that time? Do any third-party ISV solutions exist within your organization, such as the following?

   ▶ Metalogix

   ▶ Colligo

   ▶ HiSoftware

   ▶ AvePoint

   ▶ Bamboo Solutions

Deprecated Features in SharePoint 2013 That Previously Existed in SharePoint 2010

With SharePoint 2013's release, there have been a great number of improvements related to specific features, as well as the replacement of existing features by either new SharePoint 2013 features and functionality or deprecation due to technology updates and improved security. The following features that existed in SharePoint 2010 have been deprecated and are no longer directly available in SharePoint 2013:

▶ Document and Meeting Workspaces

▶ Bar codes

▶ Legacy Web Analytics feature

▶ Chart Web Part

▶ Internet Explorer 7 support

▶ PowerPoint Broadcasting

▶ Project Web Access

▶ Slide Libraries

▶ Visual Upgrade

▶ Microsoft.SharePoint.StsAdmin namespace

   For more information regarding the Microsoft.SharePoint.StsAdmin namespace and SharePoint 2013, refer to the following link:

   http://msdn.microsoft.com/en-us/library/microsoft.sharepoint.stsadmin.aspx

For a full list of deprecated and discontinued features in SharePoint 2013, refer to the following link: http://office.microsoft.com/en-us/sharepoint-help/discontinued-features-and-modified-functionality-in-microsoft-sharepoint-2013-HA102892827.aspx

Performing a Content and Configuration Assessment on Your Existing Environments

After you have a good understanding of the technology platforms and related components that currently exist, as well as what the organization wants to achieve regarding SharePoint's underlying system and information architecture (IA), an assessment of the actual content and related configurations should be performed.

The following checklist details the areas within your organization's existing SharePoint and related in-scope supporting environment(s) that must be thoroughly reviewed in a content and configuration assessment:

- ▶ Review and Document All the Current SharePoint Services Configured

    - ▶ Review the overall farm(s) topology

    - ▶ Document all database names in addition to the content databases listed previously

    - ▶ Document all service applications that have been configured and are being utilized

    - ▶ Document all service settings

    - ▶ Review and document all customizations and features and obtain the code or install package(s)

    - ▶ Review Web Applications

    - ▶ Review Alternate Access Mappings (AAMs)

    - ▶ Document authentication methods and providers

    - ▶ Document and review managed paths

    - ▶ Review and document any web.config modifications

- ▶ Content Database Analysis

    - ▶ How large are the databases, how many are there, and how long does it currently take them to back up or restore?

    - ▶ Do you have any extremely large content databases that must be taken into consideration?

    - ▶ Have you utilized Alternate Access Mappings that must be taken into consideration?

    - ▶ Have you implemented any redirects?

    - ▶ Do you have any host header named site collections?

    - ▶ Do you have the existing platform's underlying database information and configuration documented?

    - ▶ What customizations have been performed and how were they performed?

▶ Custom Application Assessment-Related Issues and Challenges

▶ What types of customizations have been deployed (WSP, Javascript, managed, and/or unmanaged)?

▶ What documentation do you have on current customizations?

▶ What issues will we have regarding upgradability and how best can we begin to test this?

▶ What third-party components will no longer be required due to the functionality being out-of-the-box in SharePoint 2013?

▶ Do you have a governed release process?

▶ What are the policies regarding available maintenance windows?

▶ Do we really want to bring over all or specific customizations, or would retraining the users to use the new out-of-the-box SharePoint 2013 features provide for better ROI?

▶ How many separate elements need to be tested?

▶ What branding and user interface changes have been made?

▶ Are there any custom workflows that exist, and if so, what tool were they developed in?

▶ Are any existing reporting features, such as SSRS or other BI (KPI, Dashboards, and so on), implemented? If so, are they business critical and who owns these reports?

PowerShell Procedures (Cmdlets) Available to Review and Analyze an Existing SharePoint 2010 Environment

Windows PowerShell cmdlets enable you to perform administrative tasks as well as key preparation and migration tasks that will be required to successfully upgrade and migrate your existing SharePoint environment to SharePoint 2013. It is important to remember too that you must first add the SharePoint Snap-In to PowerShell to be able to load SharePoint cmdlets and perform these procedures.

For more information regarding Windows PowerShell, refer to the following link: http://technet.microsoft.com/en-us/library/ee662539.aspx

The following PowerShell cmdlets procedures will enable you to gain critical insight into your existing SharePoint 2010 environment and begin to resolve items that may cause issues during the actual upgrade and migration process to SharePoint 2013. (Note that I have also listed a few procedures that utilize the stsadm to resolve any possible data issues.)

▶ Remove stale SPSites and SPWebs

  ▶ `Remove-SPSite`

  ▶ `Remove-SPWeb`

▶ Fix/resolve data issues within SharePoint

  ▶ `stsadm -o DatabaseRepair [-deletecorruption]`

  ▶ `stsadm -o ForceDeleteList`

  ▶ `stsadm -o VariationsFixupTool`

▶ Database alignment

  ▶ `Move-SPSite`

I would recommend the process of review and testing for "blocking" issues within your existing environment's databases as well as any deployed solutions and non-claims-based authentication sites to ensure that you document and address these issues before and during the actual migration.

▶ Run/re-run `Test-SPContentDatabase` on each database.

▶ Review any missing dependencies.

▶ Review known customizations using `Get-SPSolution` and its `SaveAs()` method.

▶ Ensure that you copy and deploy solution packages and/or feature folders to the new SharePoint 2013 environment.

▶ Identify large or "wide" lists and delete excess lookup, choice, or managed metadata columns.

▶ Consider upgrading any SharePoint 2010 non-claims-based assets to claims-based authentication:

  In SharePoint 2010, use `$wa.UseClaimsAuthentication = $true; $wa.Update()`.

Review and Analyze Your Current User Base

Your organization's users are going to be the most important assets to your upgrade or migration initiative, as well as possibly your biggest critics should things not go exactly as planned. It is important to review and analyze your user base and ask questions such as these:

▶ Who are the site collection owners and site owners?

▶ Who are our power users or super users?

▶ What has worked well for training on the current environment?

▶ What are the biggest complaints we receive from our users?

▶ What are the most popular or most used features?

▶ Are we currently allowing mobile devices or tablets (that is, BYOD)?

▶ What browsers are our users using, and do we have external users who we may not be able to control or recommend specific browser usage to?

▶ What version of Windows as well as what version of Microsoft Office is installed?

▶ What is our current MAC user base and how may that change?

▶ Are they currently using a messaging platform, and has Microsoft Lync or Skype been utilized or possibly piloted?

Training Strategy and Related Considerations

With any new technology implementation or related upgrade, training is critical to its long-term success. Training is covered in granular detail in Chapter 17, "SharePoint 2013, Office 365 and SharePoint Online: Training and End-User Adoption Strategies," but the following should be established during this effort:

▶ Begin working on establishing SharePoint 2013 training near the very beginning of your effort because the audiences for training must be identified and the development of a train-the-trainer strategy must be put in place. Time must be scheduled for the actual training of the internal "train-the-trainer(s)," who must be prepared and up to speed when training is set to be delivered.

▶ Ensure that your project's communication strategy and messages to your users about the overall project include information on training and what they should expect and when this may take place.

▶ Provide your development team with updated training specific to SharePoint 2013. I would recommend having them create a "trial" account for Microsoft Azure as well as utilize Visual Studio Online to start to get familiar with Microsoft's new developer toolsets.

▶ Set up a SharePoint training site within your existing SharePoint environment, and populate it with the available free training materials and videos that Microsoft provides.

Considerations with the New System Architecture and Preparations Required Within the Existing SharePoint Environment

The new SharePoint 2013 farm must be built and configured on different and separate Windows Server 2012 servers, which can be VMs, because your organization will require a database attach upgrade scenario to move into SharePoint 2013. It is also very important to ensure that the organization has properly planned for capacity (storage) because SharePoint Server 2013 will require more storage than previous versions of SharePoint. For more information regarding capacity planning for SharePoint Server 2013, refer to the following link: http://technet.microsoft.com/en-us/library/ff758645.aspx

The following recommendations should also be considered and implemented in your initiative:

▶ Ensure that you implement your SharePoint 2013 environment in conjunction with SQL Server 2012/2014 rather than SQL Server 2008.

▶ Ensure that you implement both high-availability and disaster recovery strategies.

▶ Perform the installation and preparation on the new SharePoint 2013 in parallel while the existing SharePoint environment is up and running. This will enable you to perform testing around functionality for the eventual upgrade.

▶ Review the current SharePoint environment's information architecture and plan for its rearchitecture or any new updates to its structure, such as new departments or teams.

▶ Perform a trial upgrade on a test farm first to ensure that possible issues are identified long before the actual migration is scheduled to take place.

▶ Ensure that the appropriate service packs and update(s) are applied to your existing SharePoint environment, including those that take RBS into consideration.

▶ Clean up templates, features, and existing web parts.

▶ Optimize your underlying environment before the upgrade to include considerations relating to Windows, Active Directory, and network optimization.

Planning for Risks and Underlying Time Constraints

The following necessary actions should be taken into consideration because there are inherent risks as well as time constraints in certain aspects of a SharePoint 2013 upgrade or migration effort:

▶ Realize that there will be time and duration constraints related to database sizes and related bandwidth and network latency.

▶ Plan to rebuild SharePoint 2013's search index following the upgrade.

▶ Perform one or more trial upgrades beforehand.

▶ Outline and prioritize the service application's upgrades as well as the web application's upgrades.

▶ Consider whether the organization needs to allow individual site collection upgrades to be performed by specific delegated users.

▶ Ensure that the environment is fully functioning before you begin to upgrade.

▶ Ensure that email alerts and/or the email server configurations in SharePoint are disconnected during the upgrade because you do not want the user base receiving a massive number of email alerts due to any tasks performed.

▶ Establish specific users who can assist you with validation testing so that this does not become a constraint or related delay if items are performed "off hours."

▶ Ensure that full backups of all related databases and SharePoint servers are performed before the migration.

▶ Consider how the URLs will be handled and whether your organization wants to keep the existing main SharePoint URLs. Be sure to take into consideration that changes in URLs will affect users with shortcuts and bookmarks, as well as documents that have embedded links in them from the existing SharePoint environment.

▶ Ensure that you script as many of the procedures as possible, such as the SQL Backup, File Copy, and SQL Restore:

  ▶ `Test-SPContentDatabase`

  ▶ `Mount-SPContent Database`

TIP

Continue to keep an eye out for items such as these:

▶ Content Editor web parts with embedded content that may need to be manually addressed

▶ Web part connections

▶ JavaScript and jQuery code that references the HTML DOM

▶ Broken web parts in source

▶ Alerts

▶ Fab 40 sites

  For more information on the "Fab 40," refer to the following link:

  http://technet.microsoft.com/en-us/sharepoint/bb407286.aspx

▶ "#" in quick launch, which may cause issues

Recommended Communication Strategy for IT

Within your initiatives communication strategy, it's critical that you keep your user base "in the loop" regarding the overall status of the project, any major impacting events, and project success or milestones. The following communications should be provided to the organization's end users as well as project team members to ensure complete transparency and help build use buy-in:

▶ Information on what will happen during the transition into the new version of SharePoint.

▶ Detailed information regarding when the actual upgrade will occur, as well as when it will be completed.

▶ Updates regarding what IT support will be available to them, as well as what the organization is providing regarding training.

▶ Specific emails to end users who may have existing custom solutions and what the new process or replacement features will look like and how it will perform in SharePoint 2013. (Note that the users with customizations should be able to train in a development or test environment so that they are comfortable with the new solution in SharePoint 2013 before the actual switch-over and go-live.)

▶ Information on any "chargebacks" or how the business and IT will be managing the cost for the migration.

▶ What new services IT will be providing that they can leverage using SharePoint 2013.

▶ Updates and extended training to site owners and power users regarding content publishing and content ownership.

▶ SLA information and what they can expect from IT in terms of support and uptime.

▶ Updates and assurances from IT regarding backup and recovery and the overall high-level disaster recovery strategy.

▶ Information on new site or new feature requests and the process that users must use to make these types of requests.

▶ Communication regarding OneDrive (previously SkyDrive) and the organization's usage policies.

▶ Information regarding the organization's SharePoint governance policies and possible end-user sign-off agreeing to abide by this governance.

▶ Information and updates regarding permission strategies or what users should do if they require access to a site they currently cannot access.

You may also want to provide your organization's end users, as well as project team members, with very high-level reports or updates during various phases of the initiative but try to avoid any communication that may cause the rehashing of any contentious issues that have already been covered. An example of a simple outline of the project that you may want to also incorporate into your organization's communication strategy is listed here:

1. Planning Phase

   A. Inventory settings.

   B. Test for blocking issues.

   C. Plan for customizations and user interface updates.

   D. Determine upgrade parameters.

   E. Create a project plan.

   F. Develop the change management and communications strategies.

   2. Preparation Phase

   A. Install new SharePoint 2013 environment(s).

   B. Mitigate any issues such as customizations discovered during the review of your current environment(s).

   C. Prepare the development teams for any required customization upgrades.

   3. Execution Phase

   A. Back up the existing environment and all related servers.

   B. Upgrade the existing service applications.

   C. Implement and configure the upgrade parameters.

   D. Upgrade the existing web applications.

   4. Verification Phase

   Verify that all items listed are in place, perform any cleanup, and then communicate the various messages at the defined communication strategy.

   5. Review Phase

   After the upgrade has been completed, review the upgrade Status page and logs, and begin testing the migrated sites.

Account Requirements to Perform a SharePoint 2013 Upgrade or Migration

There are specific accounts that will be required to successfully perform the upgrade and migration tasks that touch not only the database layer but also the web, search, and application servers involved. These accounts should be created to follow a naming convention that makes sense for your organization, and they also need to be created and ready at least a week before being required.

There are initiatives that are delayed due to last-minute account creation issues, so ensuring that these are put in place, tested, and ready to go for your team is critical.

To ensure that you have the appropriate SharePoint 2013 administrative and service account prepared for this initiative, refer to the following link: http://technet.microsoft.com/en-us/library/cc263445.aspx

---

NOTE

If other non-SharePoint-based systems are also involved in this effort, accounts and required permissions must also be ready for those assets.

Database Upgrades
▶ Active SQL Server login on the server that runs SQL Server

▶ Login must be a member of the DB_Owner database security role on the database being upgraded

▶ Login must be a member of the WSS_Admin_WPG database security role on the farm configuration database

▶ Member of the Farm Admin group

Site Collection Upgrades

▶ Member of the site collection administrator group

▶ Both primary and secondary site collection owners have this automatically

▶ Can also be a member of a full-control web application policy

Farm Upgrades

▶ Member of the Administrators local group on each server on which the upgrade will be run

Logical Architecture Site Planning for Your SharePoint 2013 Upgrade or Migration Initiative

Table 11.1 gives an example of the logical architecture of the SharePoint site migration planning, similar to what you will need to document for your organization. The documentation should detail the current locations of your organization's SharePoint sites as well as the proposed destination in the new SharePoint Server 2013 environment.

TABLE 11.1   Sample Overview of a SharePoint 2010 Logical Architecture's Current Site URL Locations and New Proposed Site URL Locations

Current Location	Proposed Location
IT.exampleOrganization.com	SP2013.exampleOrganization/IT
Manufacturing.exampleOrganization.com	SP2013.exampleOrganization/Manufacturing
Legal.exampleOrganization.com	SP2013.exampleOrganization/Legal
Finance.exampleOrganization.com	SP2013.exampleOrganization/Finance
Business.exampleOrganization.com	SP2013.exampleOrganization/Business
SupplyChain.exampleOrganization.com	SP2013.exampleOrganization/Supplychain
Development.exampleOrganization.com	SP2013.exampleOrganization/Dev
Quality.exampleOrganization.com	SP2013.exampleOrganization/Quality
HR.exampleOrganization.com	SP2013.exampleOrganization/HR
Research.exampleOrganization.com	SP2013.exampleOrganization/Research
Research2.exampleOrganization.com	Not migrated
HRTestSite.exampleOrganization.com	Not migrated

Regarding the example detailed in Table 11.1, the URLs were changed but this is something that must be strongly considered because URL changes can have a large end-user impact and should be minimized and avoided whenever possible. Any URL updates should be reviewed and approved by the SharePoint 2013 project sponsors. Host-named site collections enable you to assign a unique DNS name to the site collections and are the recommended method for the deployment of sites in SharePoint 2013. One major factor in this is that Office 365 utilizes host-named site collection and, with scalability and the future hybrid cloud environment that most organizations will be implementing, is the best practices approach to your architecture.

For more information on SharePoint 2013's host-named site collection architecture and deployment considerations, refer to the following link: http://technet.microsoft.com/en-us/library/cc424952.aspx

SharePoint 2013 Upgrade and Migration Strategy Overview

Based on the overall requirements and existing SharePoint environment(s) your organization has implemented, there are several available paths you may take to perform the actual upgrade to SharePoint 2013 as well as ensure that the content of the existing SharePoint 2007 or SharePoint 2010 environment is also successfully migrated.

Using a coexistence strategy is recommended when migrating to SharePoint 2013, which will entail temporarily maintaining both the previous SharePoint environment(s) and the new SharePoint 2013 environment(s) simultaneously. It is also key to understand the risks of this strategy:

▶ Changes may be made to content after the main or subsequent migrations.

▶ Client shortcuts that exist in the existing SharePoint environment will continue to exist.

▶ Hyperlinks to the existing SharePoint environment within documents will continue to exist.

▶ The previous SharePoint environment will continue to occupy resources until decommissioned.

▶ Undocumented customizations may fail to work in the new SharePoint 2013 environment.

If your organization has implemented FAST Search in your existing SharePoint 2010 environment, you will need to review and document its current configuration. For more information on SharePoint 2010 environments with FAST Search implemented, refer to the following link: http://technet.microsoft.com/en-us/library/dn130132(v=office.15)

Before you perform the actual migration processes, it is important to verify that the new SharePoint 2013 environment's installation and configuration has been completed as described in Chapter 12, "Installation and Configuration."

You can also find granular details regarding how to install SharePoint 2013 by referring to the following link: http://technet.microsoft.com/en-us/library/cc303424.aspx

Upgrading or Migrating SharePoint 2007 to SharePoint 2013

If your organization has an existing SharePoint 2007 environment, you can upgrade either SharePoint Server 2007 or Windows SharePoint Server 3.0 to SharePoint Server 2013 by following a database attach upgrade method. You are not able to directly upgrade SharePoint 2007 to SharePoint 2013 due to the major differences in the underlying architecture, but by performing a series of database attach upgrades of your existing SharePoint 2007 content into a temporary SharePoint 2010 environment, you can migrate them over to SharePoint 2013.

This temporary SharePoint 2010 environment utilized in SharePoint 2007 to SharePoint 2013 upgrade and/or migration initiative is sometimes referred to as the "staging" environment. It is critical that you prepare the temporary SharePoint 2010 environment correctly; you can do this by following the tasks detailed in the following link: http://technet.microsoft.com/library/cc263026(v=office.14)

TIP

To run the pre-upgrade checker on your existing SharePoint 2007 environment, you must have at least Service Pack 2 installed. This tool enables you to identify your SharePoint 2007 features and default templates, as well as other granular details required to successfully perform the database attach upgrade to a temporary SharePoint Server 2010 environment. For more information on the pre-upgrade checker for SharePoint 2007, refer to the following link:
http://technet.microsoft.com/en-us/library/dd793609(v=office.12).aspx

To ensure that you have the appropriate accounts and related permissions for the SharePoint 2010 environment, refer to the following link: http://technet.microsoft.com/library/cc288210(v=office.14).aspx

---

TIP

You can download a trial version of SharePoint Foundation 2010 or SharePoint Server 2010 for your temporary environment if you do not have a license agreement for the full product. Trial versions for Microsoft SharePoint can be found at the following link:
http://technet.microsoft.com/en-us/evalcenter/hh973397.aspx

Performing a Database Attach Upgrade from SharePoint 2007 to SharePoint 2010

You will first want to perform a database attach upgrade from SharePoint 2007 to SharePoint 2010. To do this, you will need to first back up a copy of your SharePoint 2007 content database and restore it to the new created temporary SharePoint 2010 farm. You can utilize SQL Server's Management Console, as shown in Figure 11.1, to back up and restore a copy of the content database. To do so, select the Restore Database option within the Management Console, and then specify the source location of the existing SharePoint 2007 environment and the destination of your temporary SharePoint 2010 environment. When performing this action, ensure that the option Overwrite the Existing Database, as shown in Figure 11.2, has been selected. After the Restore Database option procedure has been completed, you should receive a confirmation message, as shown in Figure 11.3, indicating that the database has been successfully restored.

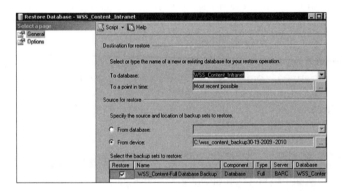

FIGURE 11.1   Backing up and restoring an existing SharePoint 2007 database.

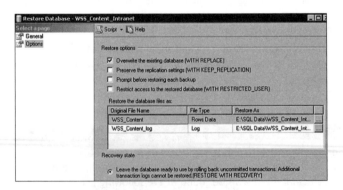

FIGURE 11.2   Ensuring that the Overwrite option is selected during the backup and restore procedure.

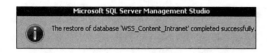

FIGURE 11.3   Notification of a successful restore of an existing SharePoint 2007 database into the SharePoint 2010 staging environment.

The next step is to perform test and validate the content database(s) that have been moved over into the temporary SharePoint 2010 staging environment. This is best accomplished via Windows PowerShell using the `Test-SPContentDatabase` PowerShell cmdlet. This PowerShell cmdlet tests and verifies that any custom components that are required for this content database have been installed and configured in the SharePoint 2010 environment. This also provides an opportunity for you to resolve any issues with customizations that should not be part of this migration effort or reside in these databases.

The PowerShell action listed here performs the testing and validation:

```
Test-SPContentDatabase -Name database name -WebApplication URL
```

In the example used, you would conduct this validation by first launching the SharePoint 2010 Management Shell and typing the preceding command, ensuring that you have entered your organization's database name and URL. This example uses the WSS_Content_Intranet content database referenced in Figure 11.1 and a sample URL of http://intranet.site.com:

```
Test-SPContentDatabase -Name WSS_Content_Intranet -WebApplication http://intranet.site.com
```

The `Test-SPContentDatabase` tool will provide a list of any missing setup files, web parts, and related errors, as well as information regarding how to resolve these issues if any arise. This tool will specify whether the missing features identified would block the upgrade from succeeding. Based on your organization's available project timeline as well as the importance of the feature identified, you can resolve the issues and features before or after the upgrade.

Add SharePoint 2007's Content Databases to the SharePoint 2010 Web Application

The next key step in this process is to add the content database(s) to the SharePoint 2010 Web Application. Before performing this action, you must ensure that there are no databases connected to the web application you will be attaching to in this SharePoint 2010 staging environment. You can verify this via SharePoint's Central Administration under the Application Management section by selecting Manage Content Databases, bringing up the screen shown in Figure 11.4.

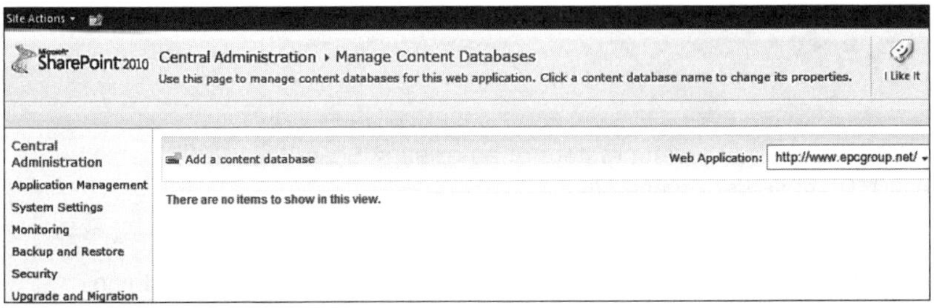

FIGURE 11.4   SharePoint 2010's Central Administration Manage Content Databases showing no current content databases.

> **NOTE**
>
> If an existing database is attached, you can easily remove it by clicking on the database name you would like removed and selecting the Remove Content Database option check box. Before performing any Remove Content Database action, you must validate that this database is not being utilized by the business and is simply a database that was created during the new temporary SharePoint 2010 configuration.

After you have verified that there are no databases attached to the SharePoint 2010 staging environment, you can then perform the action of adding the content database(s) to the SharePoint 2010 Web Application by utilizing the `stsadm.exe` feature via the `addcontendb` command-line parameter listed here:

```
stsadm -o addcontentdb -url URL -databasename database name
```

This example uses the WSS_Content_Intranet Content Database referenced in Figure 11.1 and a sample URL of http://intranet.epcgroup-testing.com as detailed here:

```
stsadm -o addcontentdb -url http://intranet.epcgroup-testing.com -databasename WSS_
Content_Intranet
```

This action initiates the upgrade process as detailed in Figure 11.5.

FIGURE 11.5   Adding a content database to a SharePoint web application.

After the procedure of adding a content database to a SharePoint 2010 web application is completed, SharePoint will provide you with detailed information, as shown in Figure 11.6, regarding whether the upgrade was completed, as well as any errors that may have been experienced during this process. If you receive any errors when adding a content database to a SharePoint 2010 web application, you should immediately review the upgrade log file to determine the underlying cause. In many cases, errors are experienced due to missing features that were not installed or activated in SharePoint 2010.

```
C:\Program Files\Common Files\microsoft shared\Web Server Extensions\14\BIN>stsa
dm -o addcontentdb -url http://intranet.epcgroup-testing.com -databasename WSS_C
ontent_Intranet

100.00%
Upgrade completed with errors. Review the upgrade log file located in C:\Progra
m Files\Common Files\Microsoft Shared\Web Server Extensions\14\LOGS\Upgrade-2009
0914-095657-657.log. The number of errors and warnings is listed at the end of
the upgrade log file.
```

FIGURE 11.6   Feedback regarding an error that has occurred during the attachment of a content database to a SharePoint 2010 web application.

After the content database is successfully attached into the temporary SharePoint 2010 environment's web application and your command prompt screen reflects 100% completed, you should also validate this via SharePoint's Central Administration under the Application Management section by selecting Manage Content Databases. The screen, as shown in Figure 11.7, should now reflect the upgraded database within the designated web application you specified during the upgrade.

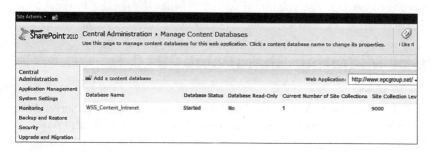

FIGURE 11.7   SharePoint 2010's Central Administration Manage Content Databases reflecting the new upgraded database.

NOTE

You also can view any upgrade status actions that have been performed via SharePoint's Central Administration under the Upgrade and Migration section by selecting Check Upgrade Status, as shown in Figure 11.8. This lists all previous upgrade attempts as well as summarizing the overall number of errors and warnings that you have encountered during this or previous upgrade efforts. The most common error that organizations experience relate to missing features that have not been properly installed in the new SharePoint 2010 farm that were relevant and utilized in SharePoint 2007.

TIP

All of SharePoint's upgrade logs are located in the following location by default: `c:\ Program Files\Common Files\Microsoft Shared\Web Server Extensions\14\LOGS`.

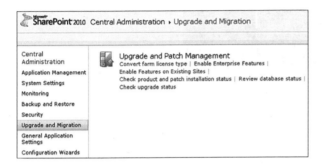

FIGURE 11.8   The Upgrade and Migration options within SharePoint 2010's Central Administration.

Now that your SharePoint 2007 environment is in a SharePoint 2010 environment, you can perform the required upgrade and migration tasks to finalize the process to move into SharePoint 2013. This process is covered in granular detail in the following section.

Upgrading or Migrating SharePoint 2010 to SharePoint 2013

If your organization has an existing SharePoint 2010 environment (SharePoint Server 2010 or SharePoint Foundation 2010) or you have a SharePoint 2007 environment and have followed the steps in the preceding section and are now in a new SharePoint 2010 temporary "staging" environment, you will be able to successfully upgrade to SharePoint Server 2013 by following the strategy and processes found in the following sections.

Your organization must have a fully functioning SharePoint 2013 environment implemented before performing a SharePoint 2010 to SharePoint 2013 upgrade or migration initiative. The SharePoint 2013 components on all Web Front End (WFE), application, and database servers that support the SharePoint 2013 environment must be fully functioning and available to begin to "intake" the upgrade of SharePoint 2013.

The actual installation and configuration of SharePoint 2013 is covered in great detail in Chapter 12; please reference its related configuration recommendation whenever a technical element is discussed in this chapter that you are not yet familiar with configuring. The following sections' procedures and upgrade tasks are detailed in a manner which assumes that the SharePoint 2013 environment is fully available.

Perform the Database Backups for the SharePoint 2010 Environment

To begin the upgrade and migration process from the SharePoint 2010 environment to the new SharePoint 2013 environment, you first need to perform a full backup of the SharePoint 2010 databases that are able (that is, compatible) to be migrated to SharePoint 2013. The following SharePoint 2010 databases, starting with the content databases, will now be backed up and then migrated over to the new SharePoint 2013 environment in the recommended order listed here:

1. Content databases.

2. Search Admin database.

3. Profile database.

4. Social database.

5. Managed Metadata database.

6. Secure Store database. (Passphrase is required.)

7. Access databases. (Do not migrate if this feature was not utilized in SharePoint 2010.)

8. Project Server databases. (Do not migrate if this feature was not utilized in SharePoint 2010.)

The service application databases, excluding the Access databases and Project Server databases, are detailed in Table 11.2.

TABLE 11.2   SharePoint 2010's Service Application Databases Compatible in a SharePoint 2013 Upgrade and Migration Initiative

Service Application	Default Database Name
Business Data Connectivity	BDC_Service_DB_*ID*
Managed Metadata	Managed Metadata Service_*ID*
PerformancePoint	PerformancePoint Service Application_*ID*
Search Administration	Search_Service_Application_DB_*ID*
Secure Store	Secure_Store_Service_DB_*ID*
User Profile: Profile, Social, and Sync databases	User Profile Service Application_ProfileDB_*ID*
	User Profile Service Application_SocialDB_*ID*
	User Profile Service Application_SyncDB_*ID*

To perform the database backups for the SharePoint 2010 environment, execute the following procedure:

1. In the existing SharePoint 2010 environment, utilize the SQL Server Management Studio and find the database you would like to back up to be migrated. Right-click on the individual database and then click on the Tasks option and select Back Up, as shown in Figure 11.9.

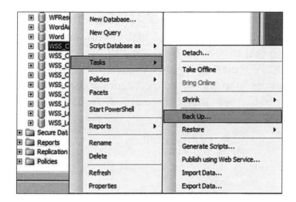

FIGURE 11.9   Performing a backup on one of the databases that will be migrated into the new SharePoint 2013 environment.

2. Select to the Full option in the Backup Type drop-down list, as shown in Figure 11.10, and then choose the Back Up to Disk option because these backups will be required to be backed up to disk.

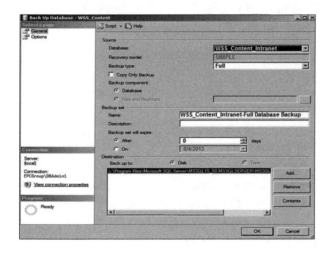

FIGURE 11.10   Specify the backup destination.

3. Specify the desired disk path for the backup by selecting the Add option, which will then open prompt you with additional options to specify where these backup files will be created. When you have completed specifying the desired locations for the backup, as shown in Figure 11.11, click OK in the main Backup form to start the database backup. You can monitor the progress in the Progress windows, and you will receive an additional prompt notifying you when the backup base been completed.

4. After each SharePoint 2010 database backup is completed, verify the file's existence and size as the location you specified when you were initially prompted to specify a desired disk path for the upgrade in step 3.

5. Repeat steps 1 through 4 to back up all the remaining SharePoint 2010 databases that will be required to successfully complete the upgrade and migration initiative and related tasks.

> **NOTE**
>
> You should start with backing up the content databases and then continue to back up other databases, including the Search Admin database, Profile database, Social database, Managed Metadata database, Secure Store database, Access databases, and Project Server databases. You might not have utilized Project Server or Access Databases in the previous SharePoint environment, and those may be able to be skipped over if your organization's technology landscape did not encompass those features.

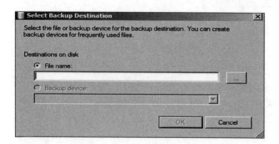

FIGURE 11.11   Select the appropriate backup destination for the back procedure.

Restore the SharePoint 2010 Databases into the New SharePoint 2013 Environment

1. To restore the databases that were previously backed up from the SharePoint 2010 environment into the new SharePoint 2013 environment, open the SQL Server Management Studio and select the Database and Restore Database option.

2. Under the Destination for Restore section, enter the name of the new database in the To Database selection box and then select From Device under the Source for Restore section, as shown in Figure 11.12.

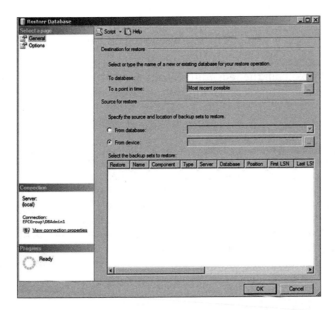

FIGURE 11.12   Populate the required restore fields with the information specific to this restore procedure.

3. Click on the file browser button that is to the right of the From Device option that you previously selected. A Specify Backup screen will appear, as shown in Figure 11.13; click the Add button.

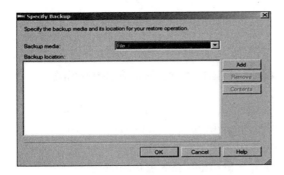

FIGURE 11.13   Select the location of the backup files to be restored.

4. After the Add option is selected, you will be able to browse to or specify the location and name of the Backup file that is currently being restored. Click OK after the file section process is completed, and this will update the Restore Database screen, as shown in Figure 11.14, with the restore options that have been specified for this restore option.

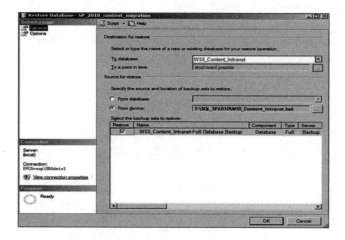

FIGURE 11.14   The granular information required regarding the source, destination, and available variables for the restore procure.

5. Click on the Options tab, and under the Select a Page section, on the left side of the Restore Database window and within the available Options that appear, choose the following settings:

   ▶ Select the Overwrite the Existing Database check box.

   ▶ Ensure that the radio button under the Recovery State has been selected for Read and Write Mode.

6. Click OK to start the restore process for the selected backup file.

7. Repeat steps 1 through 7 to perform restores for all the backups from the SharePoint 2010 databases. This is required to successfully complete the tasks and procedures remaining to successfully complete the overall SharePoint 2013 implementation.

Windows PowerShell Related SharePoint 2013 Upgrade and Migration Tasks

In the previous sections, the backup and restore procedures for providing the new SharePoint 2013 environment with access to the organization's existing content and service application databases was defined. It is now time to bring that content into the new SharePoint 2013 farm. There are very specific technical procedures that must be followed to ensure that these databases and their related content and items are successfully upgraded into the SharePoint 2013 environment.

The following list of tasks and procedures must be completed in order for this content to be made available to your organization's new SharePoint 2013 platform:

1. Upgrade content databases.

2. Upgrade service application databases and perform the related service application configurations.

3. Perform site collection health checks.

4. Upgrade site collections.

5. Review authentication impacts.

6. Recap useful PowerShell commands for upgrading to SharePoint 2013.

These six high-level task items entail several more granular layers of information and required attention from the project team; these elements are addressed in the following sections.

Upgrade Content Databases

You can test a content database for the SharePoint 2013 upgrade utilizing PowerShell and the `Test-SPContentDatabase` cmdlet, as shown in Figure 11.15. This will address issues within the content database before the actual migration, reducing risk as well as any end-user impact that unforeseen issues could have on any planned outages. The following shows an example of performing this PowerShell cmdlet:

```
Test-SPContentDatabase -ServerInstance SQLSERVERNAME
-Name DBNAME -WebApplication http://yourwebapptargetname
```

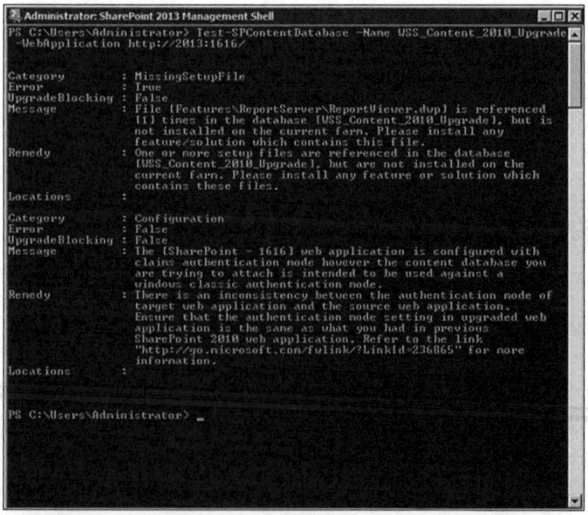

FIGURE 11.15   Using PowerShell to test a content database for the SharePoint 2013 upgrade using `Test-SPContentDatabase`.

In the example in Figure 11.15, a few issues were discovered in the content database that need to be resolved. After you perform the action to resolve those issues, you will use `Mount-SPContentDatabase` to mount the database in the new SharePoint 2013, as shown in Figure 11.16. There will be a percentage indicator that progresses and provides you with a way to gauge how long the procedure will take.

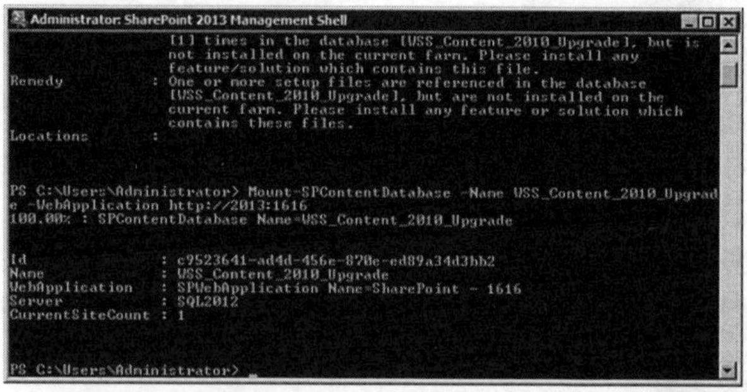

FIGURE 11.16   Using PowerShell to mount a content database to the new SharePoint 2013 environment.

You then need to perform the PowerShell command `Get-SPSite -ContentDatabase`, as shown in Figure 11.17, along with your organization's specific details, to continue the upgrade process. The following shows an example of performing this PowerShell cmdlet:

```
Get-SPSite -ContentDatabase CONTENTDBNAME -Limit All |
Upgrade-SPSite -VersionUpgrade
```

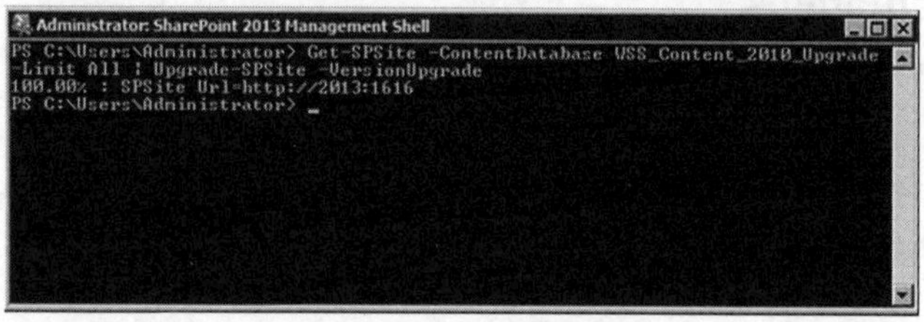

FIGURE 11.17   Performing a `PowerShell` action to continue the SharePoint 2013 upgrade process.

You will be able to gauge the overall time of the upgrade by documenting the time each of these content database upgrades takes and correlating the size of the database as well as any related complexities.

To check the status of the content database upgrade that is being performed, you can use `Get-SPSiteUpgradeSessionInfo`, as shown in Figure 11.18. The following shows an example of performing this PowerShell cmdlet:

```
Get-SPSiteUpgradeSessionInfo -ContentDatabase CONTENTDBNAME
-ShowInProgress -ShowCompleted -ShowFailed
```

FIGURE 11.18   Checking the status of a content database that is in the process of being upgraded.

Upgrading Service Application Databases and Performing the Related Service Application Configurations

As mentioned in a previous section, you can upgrade some of the SharePoint 2010 service application databases that are deemed compatible for the upgrade process. The following sections detail how to perform the actual upgrades of these service application databases.

Upgrading the Managed Metadata Service

To upgrade the managed metadata service, you are first required to create the new service application pool on the SharePoint 2013 environment that will house the previous SharePoint 2010's database. You accomplish this task by utilizing the New-SPServiceApplicationPool cmdlet, as detailed in Figure 11.19.

FIGURE 11.19   Creating the new service application pool on the SharePoint 2013 environment.

You then need to reference the restored database for the upgrade by using the `New-SPMetadataServiceApplication` cmdlet, as shown in Figure 11.20, to create the connection between the service application and the database.

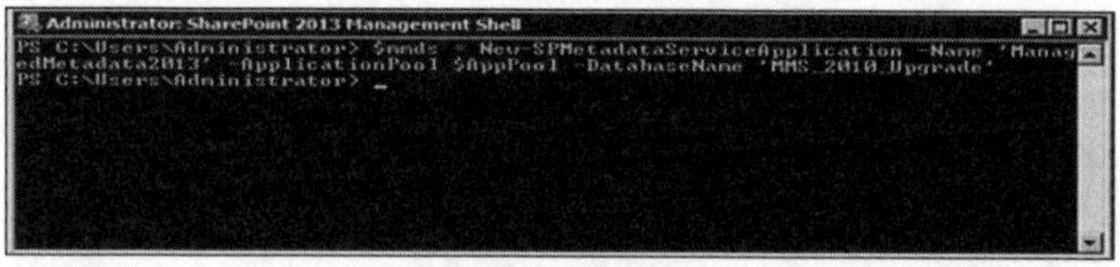

FIGURE 11.20   Referencing the restored database for the upgrade.

After you have created the new service application pool in the new SharePoint 2013 environment and properly referenced the database for this upgrade, you will now need to create the Service Application Proxy using a PowerShell cmdlet, as shown in Figure 11.21. This can be accomplished with the following PowerShell cmdlet:

```
New-SPMetadataServiceApplicationProxy
```

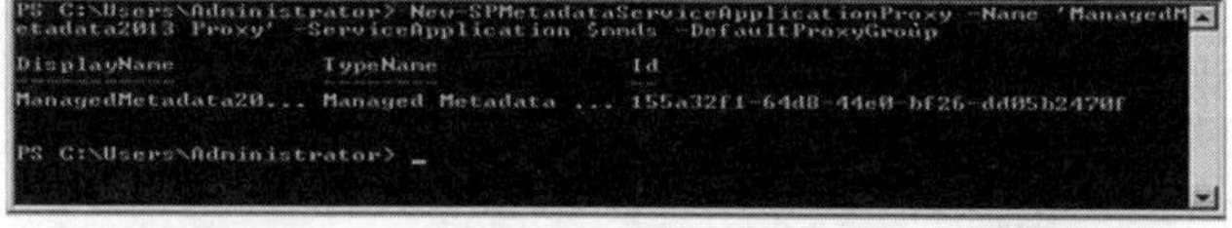

FIGURE 11.21   Creating the new service application pool in SharePoint 2013.

After this procedure is completed, the new Managed Metadata Service Application as well as the Term Store should be available and shown in SharePoint 2013's Central Administration. The last remaining task to perform is to update the content type hub URL by using the following PowerShell cmdlet:

```
Set-SPMetadataServiceApplication -Identity "ManagedMetadata2013"
-HubUri http://sitename
```

Upgrading the User Profile Sync

To successfully perform this upgrade, you must use the MIISkmu Encryption Key Management Tool `miiskmu` command to export the existing UPA key. Perform the actions listed via the MIISKMU tool. The Microsoft Identity Integration Server Encryption Key Management Wizard is the most effective method to use to export the key sets, and you should use the account credentials that run the current SharePoint 2010 UPA.

It is important that you have the GUID (that is, encryption key) available to complete the appropriate actions necessary. You can export the existing SharePoint 2010 environment's GUID by performing the following tasks:

1. In the server where User profile Service is currently running, open the command prompt CMD and go to `%Program Files%\Microsoft Office Servers\14.0\ Synchronization Service\Bin\`.

2. Enter `miiskmu.exe` and select the export key and click Next.

3. Enter your farm admin account details and domain and click Next.

4. Set the path where the key should be exported, and click Export.

For more information regarding this tool, refer to the following link: http://technet.microsoft.com/en-us/library/jj590361(v=ws.10).aspx

After you have obtained the key sets, you need to create a new service application pool to support the UPA by using the following PowerShell syntax:

```
$ups = New-SPProfileServiceApplication -Name "User Profile"
-ApplicationPool "Name of an Application Pool"
-ProfileDBServer "DB_SERVERNAME" -ProfileDBName "ProfilesDB"
-SocialDBServer "DB_SERVERNAME" -SocialDBName "SocialDB"
-ProfileSyncDBServer "DB_SERVERNAME" -ProfileSyncDBName "SyncDB"
-MySiteHostLocation "URL_to_MySite_Host"
```

The next step is creating a new Service Application Proxy to support the UPA by using the following sample PowerShell syntax:

```
New-SPProfileServiceApplicationProxy -Name UserProfile2013Upgrade
-ServiceApplication 12345678-90ab-cdef-1234-567890bcdefgh -DefaultProxyGroup
```

NOTE

The `ServiceApplication` specifies the GUID, in the form `12345678-90ab-cdef-1234-567890bcdefgh`; a valid name of a subscription User Profile Service application (for example, `ProfileSvcApp1`); or an instance of a valid `SPServiceApplication` object.

For more information regarding `New-SPProfileServiceApplicationProxy`, refer to the following link: http://technet.microsoft.com/en-us/library/ff607737.aspx

After these procedures are completed, the User Profile Service Application will be visible within SharePoint 2013's Central Administration.

NOTE

After this action is completed, be sure to copy the GUID/encryption key to the `bin` folder, as well as document it, because it will be required to complete this process. You can utilize the `/?` to find the GUID of the key.

The default location to run the `miiskmu.exe` file is `C:\Program Files\Microsoft Office Servers\15.0\Synchronization Service\Bin`.

You will then open a command prompt and inject the key via the MIISkmu tool, as shown in Figure 11.22, using the appropriate GUID you have documented via the following syntax:

```
miiskmu.exe /i Path {12345678-90ab-cdef-1234-567890bcdefgh}
```

FIGURE 11.22   Injecting the GUID via the MIISkmu tool.

Perform Site Collection Health Checks

Performing site collection health checks is key because they enable you to resolve issues that may exist and limit the risk or potential downtime that may be associated with resolving these issues during the available downtime period or maintenance window communicated to the user base for the migration.

The following is a summary of the health-check capabilities, as well as how you can perform the SharePoint Site Collection health checks:

▶ The health check looks for common and known issues such as these:

  ▶ Blocking upgrade issues

  ▶ Missing SharePoint 2013 templates

  ▶ Post-upgrade issues

  ▶ "Unghosted" files

▶ It is a site collection–level scoped tool.

▶ You can perform rule-based health checks.

▶ A user interface exists for site collection administrators.

▶ You can perform this via PowerShell cmdlet for Farm administrators:

  ▶ `Test-SPSite`

    ▶ Runs site collection health checks

    ▶ All rules by default or specify specific rule

▶ `Repair-SPSite`

   ▶ Automatically repairs all issues

▶ Examples of these PowerShell cmdlets:

   ▶ `Test-SPSite -Identity http://server/sitecollection`

   ▶ `Repair-SPSite -Identity http://server/sitecollection`

▶ This tool will execute automatically before site collection version-to-version-based upgrades and

   ▶ Will prevent upgrade if blocking issues are detected.

   ▶ Won't execute before any build-to-build-based upgrades.

▶ It reviews elements of any SharePoint 2010 Web Analytics:

   ▶ Existing features must be removed.

   ▶ New web analytics features are supported only in SharePoint 2013 mode.

▶ SharePoint 2010 Office Web Applications will be replaced with SharePoint 2013 Office Web Applications (now Office Online) for both SharePoint 2013 and SharePoint 2013 "modes":

   ▶ This ensures that you are aware of any PowerPoint Broadcast sites that must be removed.

To perform site collection health checks within SharePoint 2013, carry out the following steps:

1. On the Site Settings page for the site collection, in the Site Collection Administration section, as shown in Figure 11.23, click on Site Collection Health Checks.

2. On the Run Site Collection Health Checks page, click Start Checks, as shown in Figure 11.24, which then provides a complete list of all issues that were reviewed, as well as a list of issues that you need to resolve.

3. After you resolve the issues that were listed, go back to step 1 and perform the health check again until all issues are resolved.

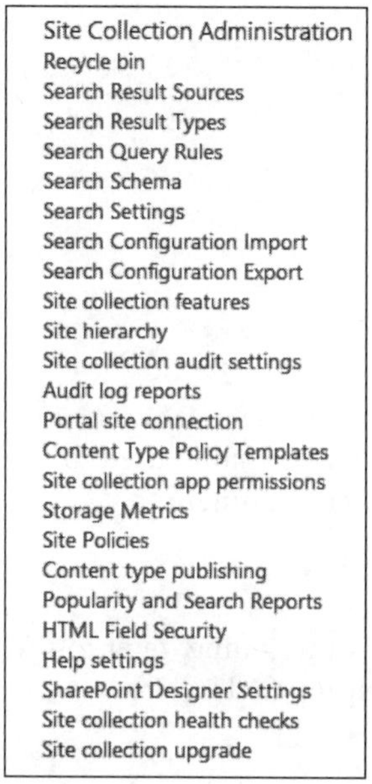

Site Collection Administration
Recycle bin
Search Result Sources
Search Result Types
Search Query Rules
Search Schema
Search Settings
Search Configuration Import
Search Configuration Export
Site collection features
Site hierarchy
Site collection audit settings
Audit log reports
Portal site connection
Content Type Policy Templates
Site collection app permissions
Storage Metrics
Site Policies
Content type publishing
Popularity and Search Reports
HTML Field Security
Help settings
SharePoint Designer Settings
Site collection health checks
Site collection upgrade

FIGURE 11.23   SharePoint's Site Collection Administration options.

Site Settings ▸ Site Collection Health Checks

Run site collection health checks

The Site Collection Heath Checks have never run for this version of the site collection. Click Start checks to run the heath checks now.

Start checks

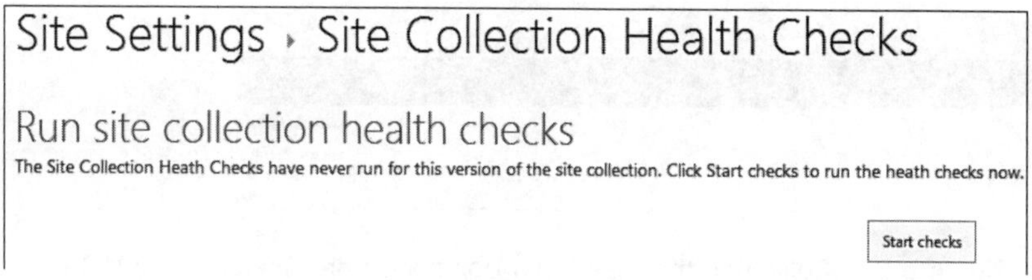

FIGURE 11.24   The Site Collections Health Check Site in SharePoint 2013.

Upgrade Site Collections

After you have performed site collection health checks, you can perform the actual upgrade of these site collections in SharePoint 2013 by utilizing SharePoint 2013's interface or via performing PowerShell cmdlets. To utilize SharePoint 2013's interface, click on the Site Collection Upgrade option shown in Figure 11.23 under the Site Collection Administration options, which opens the Site Collection Upgrade site. You can then click on Review Site Collection Upgrade Status, as shown in Figure 11.25.

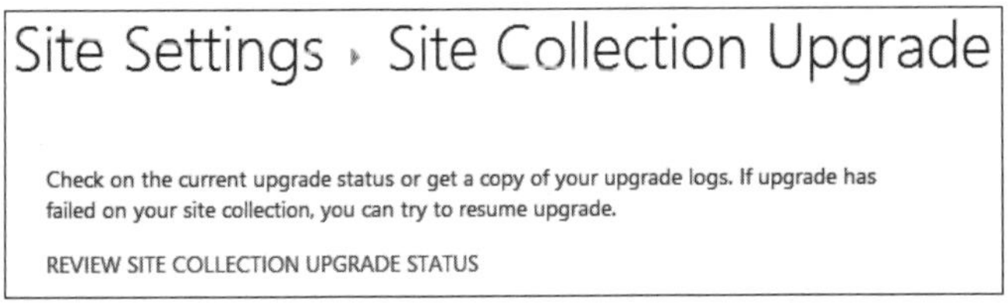

Site Settings ▸ Site Collection Upgrade

Check on the current upgrade status or get a copy of your upgrade logs. If upgrade has
failed on your site collection, you can try to resume upgrade.

REVIEW SITE COLLECTION UPGRADE STATUS

FIGURE 11.25   The Site Collection Upgrade site in SharePoint 2013.

To utilize PowerShell cmdlets to perform a site collection upgrade, you can use the
Upgrade-SPSite cmdlet. The following is an example of the PowerShell cmdlet used to
upgrade your SharePoint 2010 sites into the new SharePoint 2013 environment:

```
Upgrade-SPSite http://server/sitecollection -VersionUpgrade
```

For more information on how to upgrade site collection to SharePoint Online, refer to the
following article: http://office.microsoft.com/en-us/sharepoint-help/upgrade-a-site-
collection-to-sharepoint-online-2013-HA102865473.aspx

When a site collection has been upgraded to SharePoint 2013, your organization has the
option to maintain the existing SharePoint 2010 layout, as shown in Figure 11.26, or
choose to go right to SharePoint 2013's new upgraded interface.

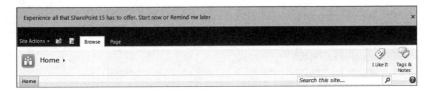

FIGURE 11.26   A Site in a Site Collection that has been Upgraded from SharePoint 2010 to
SharePoint 2013 without the UI changes applied.

The main drivers behind organizations opting to keep the existing SharePoint 2010 interface relate to SharePoint 2013 upgrade and migrations that are happening in a phased
manner over a period of time rather than in a "big bang" type of manner.

You want to minimize the user impact whenever possible, and based on your organization's training strategy, as well as for those organization migration timelines that may be
spread out over a period of weeks, this option may be extremely helpful.

In 80% of the migration that EPC Group performs, our clients opt to go right into
SharePoint 2013's interface. SharePoint's branding and overall user interface are covered
in more granular detail in Chapter 14, "Search, Web Content Management, Branding, and
Navigational Strategies."

Review Authentication Impacts

The underlying authentication architecture of SharePoint 2013 has been updated and enhanced not only to allow for more seamless integration with other Microsoft technologies such as Exchange Server 2013 and Lync Server 2013, but also to ensure support of the Open Authorization 2.0 (OAuth 2.0) web authorization protocol. The OAuth 2.0 protocol is widely used across platforms such as Google APIs, Facebook, and LinkedIn. SharePoint 2013 also allows for server-to-server authentication and app authentication utilizing OAuth 2.0, which includes granting permissions to apps in the SharePoint Store and App Catalog.

Previous versions of SharePoint allowed for classic-mode web applications, and those should be converted to claims-based authentication. For information on how to migrate from classic-mode to claims-based authentication in SharePoint 2013, refer to the following link: http://technet.microsoft.com/en-us/library/gg251985.aspx

---

TIP

After a web application has been converted to claims-based authentication, it is not possible to revert it to classic-mode authentication.

SharePoint 2013's authentication is covered in more granular detail in Chapters 12 and 15.

Recap of Useful PowerShell Commands for Upgrading to SharePoint 2013

There are many extremely useful PowerShell commands that can be utilized during your organization's SharePoint 2013 upgrade or migration initiative. For more information regarding Windows PowerShell options for SharePoint 2013, refer to the following link: http://technet.microsoft.com/en-us/library/ee890108.aspx

The following subsections provide examples of some of these specific commands.

Content Database

▶ `Mount-SPContentDatabase`

For more information, refer to the following link:

http://technet.microsoft.com/en-us/library/ff607581.aspx

   ▶ Initiates content database upgrade

   ▶ Runs internal consistency/orphans check

   ▶ Runs web application compatibility checks

   ▶ Customization references

      ▶ Web parts

      ▶ Features

▶ Site definitions

▶ Event handlers

▶ Authentication/security migration references

▶ Installed to reference authentication provider mismatch

▶ Test-SPContentDatabase

For more information, refer to the following link:

http://technet.microsoft.com/en-us/library/ff607941.aspx

▶ This performs tests on a content database:

▶ Will test a database that is not yet connected to the farm

▶ Enables you to test a database that is already connected to the farm

▶ List issues including orphans

▶ Missing referenced server-side customizations:

▶ Missing features

▶ Missing templates and site definitions

▶ Missing web parts

▶ Use the -ShowRowCounts option to find database row sizing metrics

▶ Site collections in content database but not in the configuration database site map and vice versa

▶ Upgrade-SPContentDatabase

For more information, refer to the following link:

http://technet.microsoft.com/en-us/library/ff607813.aspx

Site

▶ Test-SPSite

For more information, refer to the following link:

http://technet.microsoft.com/en-us/library/fp161259.aspx

▶ Upgrade-SPSite

For more information, refer to the following link:

http://technet.microsoft.com/en-us/library/fp161257.aspx

▶ Request-SPUpgradeEvaluationSiteCollection

▶ Repair-SPSite

For more information, refer to the following link:

http://technet.microsoft.com/en-us/library/fp161269.aspx

Farm

▶ Upgrade-SPFarm

For more information, refer to the following link:

http://technet.microsoft.com/en-us/library/fp161260.aspx

Services

▶ Restore-SPEnterpriseSearchServiceApplication Upgrade-SPEnterpriseSearch ServiceApplication

For more information, refer to the following link:

http://technet.microsoft.com/en-us/library/ff608082.aspx

▶ New-SPBusinessDataCatalogServiceApplication

For more information, refer to the following link:

http://technet.microsoft.com/en-us/library/ff607899.aspx

▶ Upgrade-SPEnterpriseSearchServiceApplicationSiteSettings

For more information, refer to the following link:

http://technet.microsoft.com/en-us/library/jj219545.aspx

▶ New-SPProfileServiceApplication

For more information, refer to the following link:

http://technet.microsoft.com/en-us/library/ff608036.aspx

▶ New-SPMetadataServiceApplication

For more information, refer to the following link:

http://technet.microsoft.com/en-us/library/ff607557.aspx

▶ New-SPSubscriptionSettingsServiceApplication

For more information, refer to the following link:

http://technet.microsoft.com/en-us/library/ff607823.aspx

▶ New-SPPerformancePointServiceApplication

For more information, refer to the following link:

http://technet.microsoft.com/en-us/library/ff608122.aspx

▶ New-SPProjectServiceApplication

For more information, refer to the following link:

http://technet.microsoft.com/en-us/library/ff607529.aspx

▶ New-New-SPSecureStoreApplication

For more information, refer to the following link:

http://technet.microsoft.com/en-us/library/ff607967.aspx

Testing, Validation, and Content Verification

There should be a defined period for selected users to test and validate that the content of their sites or site collections have been successfully moved to the new SharePoint 2013 farm. During this testing phase, your organization does have the option to allow users to continue to use the current SharePoint farm for their day-to-day tasks.

Upon successful completion of the testing and validation phase, a second migration pass will be executed. This time, only the new and modified content will be copied over and will take much less time than the original migration process.

The content verification process involves the user base, usually per department and work-group, to access and verify the integrity of their content, including the following:

▶ Availability

▶ Access

▶ Status

A defined process or use-case scenarios should be available for each group accessing their content to ensure that transparent usage of content may continue without interruption.

Custom Design Verification

The custom design verification process involves both the administration and the user bases to access and verify the proper functionality and operation of any customized components that existed in the previous SharePoint environment, including, but not limited to, the following:

▶ Web parts

▶ Master pages

▶ Page layouts

▶ Content types

- ▶ Navigation
- ▶ Menus
- ▶ Features

All customization options that have been approved and tested for migration should be identified and verified. Use-case scenarios should be created for your organization to ensure proper operation of customizations.

Cutover Process

The Cutover Process describes how the removal of the source environment will be handled after all content reaches the new SharePoint 2013 "destination" environment. The Cutover Process includes the following:

- ▶ Cutover Deadline schedule
- ▶ Disconnecting from source environment
- ▶ Decommissioning source environment

Cutover Deadline

The Cutover Deadline is a scheduled date to indicate when the source environment will no longer be in use or accessible. It is assumed that all testing and verification will have been completed by this date, because additional destructive activities will be implemented to repurpose resources or remove them from use.

The Cutover Deadline should be communicated well in advance of the final phase of Cutover, Decommissioning the Source Environment, so that all users are aware of the removal of this environment. It is not recommended that the source environment remain in the organization for any significant period, usually over two weeks, to prevent content from being changed in the nonproduction environment.

Upgrading\Migration Troubleshooting Steps

If you experience issues, it is key to first determine the cause of the failure. This can best be done by:

- ▶ Reviewing status page and upgrade logs:
    - ▶ Upgrade error log now
    - ▶ Full upgrade log
    - ▶ ULS log
- ▶ Finding issue instances using commands:
    - ▶ `Test-SPContentDatabase`
    - ▶ `stsadm -o EnumAllWebs`

When you identify an issue, you should first try to resolve it by doing the following:

▶ Installing any missing or updated customizations

▶ Activating missing services settings

▶ Activating missing farm settings

▶ Activating missing web application settings

After you have identified an issue and implemented the resolution, you can resume the process. If any errors or warning messages appear, you must continue to troubleshoot the issue via the upgrade logs or preferred methods. If you encounter an issue that you are not able to resolve, it is key to discuss its impact with the project team and determine whether any workarounds are available. It is also important that you document any update errors that you encounter and make them available to the team in case a similar issue should be encountered again by another team member.

Performance Testing

After the new SharePoint 2013 environment has been established within the new infrastructure, preliminary performance and capacity testing should be performed to verify the capability of sustaining expected workloads as defined by the organization's service level agreements and within the SharePoint Governance strategy. Performance testing is covered in greater detail in Chapter 15, "Administration and Maintenance Strategies."

Summary

This chapter covers the full spectrum of how to migrate an existing SharePoint 2007 or SharePoint 2010 environment into SharePoint 2013. We discussed how to implement a strategy to review your organization's existing platform as well as the considerations related to existing content and customizations that may exist and how these elements should be handled.

In Chapter 12, we will cover the actual installation and configuration of SharePoint 2013 and how to build a best practices scalable environment to meet the needs of your organization.

CHAPTER 12

Installation and Configuration

The actual act of performing the installation and initial configuration of SharePoint can be very straightforward but only after you have done the due diligence of architecting and designing your new SharePoint 2013 environment's information architecture (IA), as well as the underlying system architecture. It is also key to consider the governance strategies covered in Chapter 9, "Governance Strategies for SharePoint 2013, Office 365, and SharePoint Online," to ensure not only that the proper approach is being followed but also that the appropriate team members identified as owners of the specific tasks, areas, and milestones are included and/or updated during the actual installation and configuration process.

Key considerations during the installation and configuration of SharePoint 2013's IA that were discussed earlier in Chapter 5, "Implementing a Best Practices SharePoint 2013/Office 365 Information Architecture," are as listed here:

▶ Planning SharePoint 2013's taxonomy, navigational hierarchy, and overall topology.

▶ Ensuring that your organization's business and functional requirements are translated into the actual build and configuration of SharePoint 2013.

Additional key considerations, discussed earlier in Chapter 7, "Implementing a SharePoint 2013 System Architecture with Future Hybrid Scalability in Mind," that you should keep in mind during the actual installation and configuration of SharePoint are as given here:

▶ Ensuring that your organization has a clear understanding of the public, private, and hybrid cloud and related implementation considerations with an emphasis on preparing for the likelihood of a future Hybrid SharePoint Platform.

▶ SharePoint 2013's system architecture components and the key considerations related to future scalability and your organization's 24- to 36-month SharePoint roadmap.

▶ SharePoint 2013's search and scalability recommendations.

▶ SharePoint 2013's SQL Server 2012 scalability recommendations.

With these major considerations in mind, this chapter discusses the procedures and approach to actually installing SharePoint so that you can begin configuring it in the manner you have planned for based on the previous chapters in this book.

Detailing the Installation, Deployment, and Configuration Requirements

The purpose of this section is to detail and itemize the requirements for and process of building the organization's SharePoint 2013 farm in a highly functioning and continuously updated environment to meet expected workloads and performance for key projects and initiatives that will be accessed through SharePoint.

The following discussion contains a sample deployment by EPC Group. I have provided details regarding the architectural recommendations for this scenario of a 5,000-user enterprise SharePoint 2007 environment to SharePoint 2013 upgrade initiative, as well as descriptions of the implementation and configuration best practices that should be followed.

This following sections cover these topics:

▶ Implementation plan overview

▶ Requirements and recommendations

▶ Installation process

▶ Overview of the configuration process

▶ Upgrade and migration process for the scenario provided in this chapter, related to an organization upgrading their existing SharePoint 2007 environment to SharePoint 2013

Recommended Links to Periodically Review for Updates from Microsoft

The following links are extremely helpful references that the Microsoft SharePoint and SQL Server teams continuously update with the latest technology releases. I would recommend reviewing them periodically for updates and for additional reference purposes to ensure that your organization's technology deployment and related versions follow the published Microsoft recommendations:

▶ Microsoft's Deployment Guide for SharePoint 2013 eBook:

http://www.microsoft.com/en-us/download/details.aspx?id=30384

▶ Hardware and software requirements for SharePoint 2013:

http://technet.microsoft.com/en-us/library/cc262485.aspx

▶ Windows Server 2012 R2 main reference page and trial:

http://www.microsoft.com/en-us/server-cloud/products/windows-server-2012-r2/default.aspx#fbid=ar6seGOg6kQ

▶ Microsoft SQL Server 2012 64-bit trial:

http://www.microsoft.com/en-us/download/details.aspx?id=29066

▶ Microsoft SQL Server 2012 Service Pack 1 (SP1):

http://www.microsoft.com/en-us/download/details.aspx?id=35575

▶ SharePoint Server 2013 (180-day trial):

http://technet.microsoft.com/en-us/evalcenter/hh973397.aspx

▶ Initial deployment administrative and service accounts in SharePoint 2013:

http://technet.microsoft.com/en-us/library/ee662513.aspx

▶ Account permissions and security settings in SharePoint 2013:

http://technet.microsoft.com/en-us/library/cc678863.aspx

▶ Installation overview for SQL Server 2012:

http://technet.microsoft.com/en-us/library/bb500469.aspx

▶ Guidelines on choosing service accounts for SQL Server Services:

http://support.microsoft.com/kb/2160720

▶ Configure Windows service accounts and permissions:

http://technet.microsoft.com/en-us/library/ms143504.aspx

▶ Configure the Windows firewall to allow SQL Server access:

http://msdn.microsoft.com/en-us/library/cc646023.aspx

▶ Security considerations for a SQL Server installation:

http://technet.microsoft.com/en-us/library/ms144228.aspx

12

Implementation Plan Overview—"In the Trenches" Scenario

The goal of this scenario project is to migrate an enterprise manufacturing organization with 5,000 users from its current SharePoint 2007 farm to a new SharePoint 2013 deployment with a complete information architecture redesign. This scenario for the "XYZ" company's current SharePoint 2007 deployment has deviated from prescribed best practices and control procedures. The new implementation not only will bring into play the numerous additional features and functionality now available with SharePoint 2013, but also will allow this sample organization to bring the environment back into alignment of known best practices and governance.

Table 12.1 describes the key stages for this company scenario implementation plan, as well as the processes involved where appropriate.

TABLE 12.1   Key Stages for This Implementation Plan

Stage	Purpose	Details
Hardware/Software Requirements	Describes the minimum and expected requirements for building and deploying the infrastructure to support the solution.	Information regarding hardware and software gathering and preparation, and general structure definition regarding SharePoint given in this section
Installation	Describes the stages and processes involved in deploying each element and the order of installation to properly deploy the SharePoint infrastructure.	The main phases of implementation include: –Base server deployment –Database Tier –Application Tier –Web Front End Tier
Configuration	Describes the post-installation processes for configuring the SharePoint environment, because the content already exists and must be placed into this environment to support it.	The main phases of configuration include: –SQL configuration –SharePoint configuration
Migration	Describes the process for migrating existing content into the new SharePoint farm.	The main phases of migration include: –Recording configurations –Protecting content –Testing and remediation –Execution

> **NOTE**
>
> Each of these stages is described in detail in the following sections.

Hardware and Software Requirements

The requirements stage of the sample implementation plan details the basic and extended requirements for installing and configuring a fully operational SharePoint 2013 farm that will support the organization's content and required services. These requirements have increased from the existing SharePoint environment due to new functions and features available within SharePoint 2013.

SharePoint 2013 has increased hardware recommendations over previous versions of the product. Depending on the utilization of individual services, it is possible that additional hardware, either via an increase in RAM or processors or via the addition of a new server, could be required as usage demand increases.

The SharePoint farm of the sample organization XYZ is designed to support an anticipated user load of 5,000 to 6,000 concurrent users. The design makes use of a standard three-tier topology that takes into account the growth potential of the SharePoint platform as a solution provider. This design allows for scaling in either an upward or an outward direction because additional servers can be easily added to the initial farm configuration to support increased demand for services or user workload.

Table 12.2 provides granular details for the initial farm design, including topology and resource allocations.

TABLE 12.2   Initial Farm Design, Including Topology and Resource Allocations

Server Type	Purpose	Requirements
Database Server (2 nodes clustered) (Physical)	Key storage of content for the farm.	Servers: 2 node active/passive cluster, SAN storage CPU: 16 core RAM: 64GB Disk: TBD (current storage is 3.2TB) 320GB OS/paging @ TBD GB TempDB (10% of largest DB) TBD content @ TBD transaction logs @ TBD DB files

Server Type	Purpose	Requirements
Application Server (1): Central Administration, Excel Services, Managed Metadata, User Profile Service (Virtualized)	Provides dedicated and separated functionality for administration and service applications. Will run additional services as required by the farm.	Servers: 1 CPU: 16 core RAM: 32GB Disk: 760GB 160GB OS/paging 300GB office directories and logs 300GB for search failover
Application Server (1): Search Service—Admin, Crawler, Analytics Processing, Content Processing (Virtualized)	Provides dedicated Crawl and Analytics functionality for building the content index used by SharePoint searches.	Servers: 1 CPU: 16 core RAM: 32GB Disk: 760GB 160GB OS/paging 300GB office directories and logs 300GB search analytics processing
Web Front End (2 nodes network load balanced): Query Service, Index Service (Virtualized)	Main client communication point and content rendering layer; query processing handled on these systems.	Servers: 2 nodes network load balanced (network device) CPU: 8 core RAM: 24GB Disk: 920GB 120GB OS/paging 300GB office directories and logs 500GB search index component and BLOB cache

Software Requirements and Recommendations

The software requirements that are necessary for the organization XYZ's SharePoint farm entails the basic software expectations that will be required to set up and maintain the SharePoint farm. Additionally, prerequisites are expected per server type (such as SharePoint Server), and recommended levels of cumulative updates and service packs are also documented.

Table 12.3 describes the minimum software required to create the SharePoint farm.

TABLE 12.3   Minimum Software Required to Implement the SharePoint Farm for the Sample Implementation Scenario

Server Software	Purpose	Requirements
Windows Server 2012 R2	Base OS for supporting all SharePoint-related server functions; all servers in the farm will have this OS installed.	Windows Server 2012 R2, 64-bit
SQL Server 2012	Database layer requires SQL Server to store all SharePoint-related content; this software is necessary only for the SQL cluster nodes.	SQL Server 2012, 64-bit, Enterprise
SharePoint Server 2013	SharePoint Server 2013 is required for a farm of this size and that incorporates key services such Excel Calculation and Managed Metadata, and will be used for all Application and WFE roles.	SharePoint Server 2013, 64-bit, Enterprise

Note: SQL Server 2014 is also now available for SharePoint 2013 on-premises deployments.

Each of the servers involved in this requirement may also have associated cumulative updates or service packs that should be verified against the existing infrastructure or possibly applied for security and performance reasons.

Table 12.4 details the servers as well as any applicable updates to be implemented to meet the implementation requirements of the sample scenario provided in this chapter.

TABLE 12.4   Servers and Applicable Updates to be Implemented to Meet the Implementation Requirements of the Sample Scenario

Server Software	Applicable Updates	Notes
Windows Server 2012 R2	–Current: Service Pack 1	
SQL Server 2012	–Current: Service Pack 1	
	–Recommended: Service Pack 1	
	–KB 2765317	
	–Microsoft .NET Framework version 4.5	

Server Software	Applicable Updates	Notes
SharePoint Server 2013	–Current: April CU –The following are installed by using the SharePoint Products Preparation Tool: Web Server (IIS) Role Application Server Role Microsoft .NET Framework version 4.5 SQL Server 2012 R2 SP1 Native Client Microsoft WCF Data Services 5.0 Microsoft Information Protection and Control Client (MSIPC) Microsoft Sync Framework Runtime v1.0 SP1 (x64) Windows Management Framework 3.0, which includes Windows PowerShell 3.0 Windows Identity Foundation (WIF) 1.0 and Microsoft Identity Extensions (previously named WIF 1.1) Windows Server AppFabric Cumulative Update Package 1 for Microsoft AppFabric 1.1 for Windows Server (KB 2671763)	To use the SharePoint Products Preparation Tool to download and install additional software, an Internet connection is required during the installation process.

NOTE

Appropriate security updates and hotfixes should be applied as needed to the base OS.

A Proven Installation Process to Follow

After software, licensing, and other prerequisite software have been acquired and prepared, installation of the SharePoint farm can be executed in the following order:

1. Base OS and updates

2. SQL Server and updates

3. SharePoint servers and updates

Due to the desire for the new SharePoint 2013's farm architecture to be virtualized, virtual machines must be prepared, including the resource allocations (CPU, RAM, NIC) to host the Server Software. SQL Server will be hosted on physical hardware, but additional considerations for the SQL Cluster storage (via SAN technology) should also be prepared for the SQL Server installation.

All WFE, DB, and App Server Baseline OS Requirements

The base OS phase of the installation process entails the following:

- ▶ Installing the operating system
- ▶ Separating disk space
- ▶ Applying OS updates

> **NOTE**
>
> Additional configurations to the OS are handled in the configuration process.

Database Tier Installation Overview

After the base OS has been installed, the first set of servers to be installed for the SharePoint farm should most always be the Database Tier, because this must be in place before SharePoint may be installed. The process entails the following:

- ▶ Installing the first node of the SQL Server cluster into appropriate disk separations
- ▶ Applying updates to the first node
- ▶ Installing the second node of the SQL Server cluster into appropriate disk separations
- ▶ Applying updates to the second node

> **NOTE**
>
> Additional configurations for optimization and maintenance are handled in the configuration process.

Application Tier Installation Overview

The Application Tier introduces the two parts of the SharePoint farm that are handled in the backend that do not have direct communication with users. These servers handle the following roles:

- ▶ Central Administration/Application Services
- ▶ SharePoint Search components

The two-part installation process is as follows:

1. Install SharePoint Server on all designated SharePoint servers.

2. Apply SharePoint updates.

Because the role of the individual servers will be determined via Central Administration after running through the SharePoint configuration process, no further configuration is needed at this time.

Web Front End Tier Installation Overview

The Web Front End (WFE) Tier is primarily a designation for all servers in the SharePoint farm performing web-based functions such as client communication and content rendering. The installation process is similar to that for the Application Tier in that the WFE Servers are installed as SharePoint Servers but specific configurations are handled during the configuration process. The installation process is as follows:

1. Install SharePoint Server on all designated SharePoint servers.

2. Apply SharePoint updates.

> **NOTE**
>
> Defining the various server roles within your organization's SharePoint farm is handled during the configuration process.

Overview of the Configuration Process and Related Granular Tasks

The configuration phase will help define roles and services provided by the SharePoint farm, as well as allow for the support and customization required to care for functionality in the SharePoint content.

The configuration process handles these main areas:

▶ Base OS configuration

▶ SQL Server configuration

▶ SharePoint configuration

The Database Tier where SQL Server supports the SharePoint farm can be configured separately from the SharePoint Application/WFE Tiers, but it should be configured before the SharePoint servers are configured.

Base OS Configuration

Several configurations for the base OS can help with performance and maintenance of the base server system. The following describes the configurations to be applied:

1. Configure PageFile to organizational standards.

2. Stop unneeded services.

> **NOTE**
>
> Before application binaries are installed, standard tests will be conducted to ensure the viability of the hardware systems to follow Microsoft and EPC Group best practices.

SQL Server Configuration Process

The SQL Server Configuration phase focuses on the configuration of how SQL will be used in connection with SharePoint. Although many of the configurations to be applied are also best practices for using SQL Server database servers, they also apply well to SharePoint farms.

The following describes the configurations to be applied:

1. Configure the maximum RAM usage.

2. Set SQL Server collation to the SharePoint-specific format.

3. Configure the Lock Pages in Memory right.

4. Configure the use of Temp DBs.

5. Set the model DB settings.

6. Place data files and log files on separate spindles and separate from the OS.

Begin SharePoint Configuration

The SharePoint configuration phase focuses on building the SharePoint farm, providing customizations through farm solutions, and deploying necessary farm services that content and users will take advantage of in the new SharePoint farm.

The following describes the configurations to be applied:

▶ Configure the SharePoint farm.

▶ Add servers by roles.

▶ Deploy farm solutions.

▶ Configure SharePoint logging locations and frequencies.

▶ Configure service applications.

▶ Create and configure web applications.

▶ Create Site Quotas.

▶ Configure publishing user accounts.

Performing SharePoint's Software Installation

After the SharePoint binaries are installed on a base server configuration, to create a new farm you must run the SharePoint Products and Configuration Wizard. The first server that the SharePoint Products and Configuration Wizard is executed on will become the host for the Central Administration website. Although Central Administration can be moved to a different server later, you should start your build with this system. Central Administration is required for all other configuration procedures of the SharePoint farm.

The following describes the configurations for creating a farm:

1. Launch the SharePoint Products and Configuration Wizard.

2. Elect to Create a New Server Farm, as shown in Figure 12.1.

3. Specify the appropriate SQL Server configuration settings, as shown in Figure 12.2.

4. Assign a random port for the Central Administration website.

FIGURE 12.1   Select the Create a New Server Farm option.

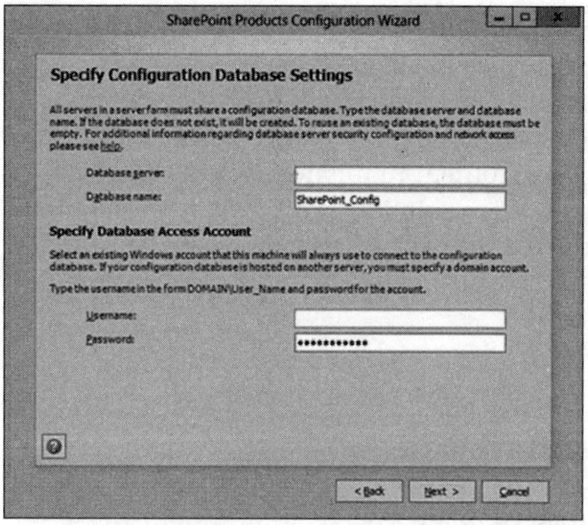

FIGURE 12.2   Specify the appropriate configuration database settings.

Add Servers by Role to Support Your Architecture

To add a new server to an existing farm, you run the SharePoint Products and Configuration Wizard on the server you want to add. After the server is part of the farm, you can assign it specific roles by starting or stopping the relevant SharePoint Services via Central Administration.

Application Roles within SharePoint 2013

The following describes the configurations for Application Servers:

1. Launch the SharePoint Products and Configuration Wizard.

2. Add the server to an existing farm.

3. Start the relevant services appropriate for the role.

Web Front End Roles within SharePoint 2013

The following describes the configurations for Web Front Ends:

1. Launch the SharePoint Products and Configuration Wizard.

2. Add the server to an existing farm.

3. Update the `web.config` file as needed.

4. Configure the BLOBCache location and settings.

5. Install any required SSL certificates to support HTTPS.

Deploy Farm Solutions for a Sample "Real World" Scenario

Existing features that may be enabled in the existing SharePoint farm will require solutions to be deployed into the new farm before they will function. Ensure that any third-party or custom solutions that are required by existing sites or data are updated for compatibility and deployed before migrating any content to the new system. This may include working with the client to review the existing solution and providing a demo of SharePoint 2013's new feature set that will replace the existing system's features.

The following subsections detail the additional features enabled to meet the needs of this sample scenario.

Configuring SharePoint Logging

By default, SharePoint 2013 writes diagnostic logs to the same drive and partition on which it was installed. Because diagnostic logging can use a large amount of drive space and compromise drive performance, you should configure SharePoint 2013 to write to another drive on which SharePoint 2013 is not installed.

You should also consider the connection speed to the drive on which SharePoint 2013 writes the logs. If verbose-level logging is configured, the server records a large amount of data. Therefore, a slow connection might result in poor log performance.

By default, the amount of disk space that diagnostic logging can use is unlimited. Therefore, restrict the disk space that logging uses, especially if you configure logging to write verbose-level events. When the disk reaches the restriction, SharePoint 2013 removes the oldest logs before it records new logging data.

You can configure diagnostic logging to record verbose-level events. This means that SharePoint 2013 records every action it takes. Verbose-level logging can quickly use drive space and affect drive and server performance. You should use verbose-level logging to record more detail only when you are making critical changes or troubleshooting a specific problem. Ensure that you then reconfigure logging to record only higher-level events after you make the change or fix the issue.

Configuring Service Applications in SharePoint 2013

SharePoint 2013 uses an Application Service model to provide functionality to the SharePoint farm. Application Services include such features as Search, Business Connectivity Services, and Excel Calculation Services. In this sample scenario, it has been determined that the organization will implement at least the following services:

- ▶ Excel Calculation Services
- ▶ Business Connectivity Services
- ▶ Managed Metadata Services
- ▶ User Profile Services

> **NOTE**
>
> Additional services may be deemed useful but will need to be analyzed as to their distribution and impact on the configurations already planned.

Creating and Configuring Web Applications in SharePoint 2013

Web applications provide the host URL for access to all content stored within SharePoint. Each web application consumes additional RAM and processing power on the host server. It is recommended that no server host more than 10 application pools for performance reasons. The organization's current SharePoint farm, as used in this sample scenario of an organization upgrading from SharePoint 2007 to SharePoint 2013, supports 15 different web applications. It is the goal of this project to consolidate those into a single web application under one URL.

Creating Site Quotas to Help Enforce SharePoint Governance

SharePoint stores all content within SQL databases. Best practice dictates that the size of these databases not exceed 200GB, for both performance and recovery purposes. Site collections cannot span multiple databases; therefore, to ensure that the content databases associated with your SharePoint deployment do not grow beyond these recommended limits, you should implement Site Quotas to control how large site collections can become. After a site collection has reached its quota limit, no new content can be added to that collection until some existing content is removed.

Configuring Object Cache User Accounts

The object cache stores properties about items in SharePoint Server 2013. Items in this cache are used by the publishing feature when it renders web pages. The goals of the object cache are to reduce the load on the computer on which SQL Server is running, and to improve request latency and throughput. The object cache makes its queries as one of two out-of-box user accounts: the Portal Super User and the Portal Super Reader. These user accounts must be properly configured to ensure that the object cache works correctly. The Portal Super User account must be an account that has Full Control access to the web application. The Portal Super Reader account must be an account that has Full Read access to the web application.

Steps for configuring these accounts include the following:

1. From within Central Administration, select the web application that contains publishing sites.

2. Create a user policy granting the Super User Full Control.

3. Create a user policy granting the Super Reader Full Read.

Virtual Machine Topology (for the Sample Scenario)

Because the organization's SharePoint farm will be primarily virtual, with the SQL servers being physical, the recommendation for allocating virtual servers to physical servers should follow a formula to allow for both load balancing and fault tolerance. The basic configuration could be in the following allocation:

- ▶ Virtual Server Machine #1
  - ▶ One WFE Server
  - ▶ Application Server with Central Administration
- ▶ Virtual Server Machine #2
  - ▶ One WFE Server
  - ▶ Application Server with Search components

Overview of the Migration Process

The Migration phase details the general order in which the migration will occur, based on importance and need. Because there are multiple web applications associated with the current organization's SharePoint environment, the new SharePoint farm will consolidate these different web applications into a single structure.

Performing the Database Attach Method

This will be a multiple-phase process, and the content for each web application will be migrated individually. The basic migration process is as follows:

1. Clean up and remove data no longer needed from the current SharePoint 2007 farm.
2. Set SharePoint 2007 to Read-Only.
3. Back up all existing content databases.
4. Restore databases and attach to a temporary SharePoint 2010 farm.
5. Backup the newly upgraded databases.
6. Restore and attach this data to the SharePoint 2013 farm.
7. Back up data from additional web applications and restore to a new URL in the consolidated web application.
8. Test content integrity and functionality.

This process is twofold, meaning that there will be a test phase and a final phase, both of which will follow the same process. Refer to Chapter 11, "Upgrade and Migration Best Practices," for the development of the migration plan for more detailed best practices for migration processes.

Content Cleanup and Taxonomy/IA Re-architecture

This effort would also require initiatives for the restructuring of content in conjunction with the migration process. The procedural outline for content cleanup is as follows:

1. Clean up and remove data no longer needed from the current SharePoint 2007 farm.

2. Create the basic site structure for the new taxonomy within the SharePoint 2013 farm.

3. Copy content from SharePoint 2007 to its new location within the SharePoint 2013 taxonomy.

4. Test content integrity and functionality.

5. Rerun migration tasks to copy any newly created or changed data from 2007 to 2013.

Testing and Performance

After the SharePoint 2013 environment has been established in the destination infrastructure, user acceptance testing (UAT) should begin to ensure that the content is accurate and accessible. Any corrective measures necessary to bring the farm to full operational status should be made at this time.

The following tasks are handled in this effort:

▶ User acceptance testing

▶ Corrective actions as needed

In this sample scenario, the organization's SharePoint 2013 farm will be placed on new hardware, with a new farm configuration, and use existing content from the original SharePoint 2007 farm. After the content has been put in place, proper usage testing and performance analysis should be completed, and eventually followed with more regular samplings to track trends and forecast usage.

After the environment is stabilized, a thorough restructuring of the content can take place to bring the system into alignment with best practice and governance policies.

Reviewing the Bits Installation and Configuration

The SharePoint application bits were installed on the servers using the installation account SP2013Install. The complete installation option was chosen as per SharePoint best practices. The file location was changed from the default `c:\` location and instead pointed at `D:\Microsoft Office Servers`. The Active Directory group, SPFarmAdmins, was added to the Local Administrators group on all SharePoint Servers.

A SQL Server alias was configured for all the SharePoint Servers using the `CliConfg.exe` utility. TCP/IP was enabled and the alias SP2013SQL was created and mapped to the server.

Reviewing the Farm Configuration

In this sample scenario, on the application server, SP2013App, the SharePoint Products and Configuration Wizard was started, still logged onto the system as the SharePoint install account SP2013Install. The option to create a new farm was chosen.

For the database connection, the database server used was the newly created alias, SP2013SQL. The database name used was EPCGroup_SharePoint_Config. This is the SharePoint configuration database, and it contains all the central information regarding the structure and components of the newly created farm.

The account assigned as the Central Administration application account was also SP2013Install. At the conclusion of the wizard, the option to run the Farm Configuration Wizard was not chosen, because all elements and services will be configured manually. Table 12.5 summarizes the database configuration selected during this implementation scenario.

TABLE 12.5   Database Configuration Selected During This Implementation Scenario

Option	Configuration
Install Choice	Create New Farm
Database Server	SP2013SQL
Database Name	EPCGroup_SharePoint_Config
Central Administration Account	SP2013Install
Passphrase	************(Use Your Company Standards)
Central Administration Port	(Per Your Preference)
Authentication	NTLM

The outgoing email was set to use EPCGroup.internal as the email server. The organization should change the From and Reply to addresses to a functional and monitored email address of their choice within the organization.

The SharePoint Products and Configuration Wizard was then run on both SP2013Web1 and SP2013Web2, with the option to join an existing farm, thereby making these servers part of the newly created SharePoint farm. The Active Directory group, SPFarmAdmins, was then added to the Farm Administrators group in Central Administration and the BUILTIN\Administrators group was removed. All of the service accounts that you previously created were then registered with SharePoint as Managed Accounts via Central Administration so that they could then be used by services and applications.

The Farm Configuration Wizard was run in order to install the State Service, with all other options being deselected. The option to create a site collection at the conclusion was skipped.

Web Applications Configuration Review (Examples)

The three web applications and their settings shown in Tables 12.6, 12.7, and 12.8, created to meet the functional requirements of this sample project scenario, are detailed next.

TABLE 12.6   Web Application and Related Configuration for the EPCGroup_Content Database for This Implementation Scenario Example

Option	Configuration
Web Application	EPCGroupNET
Host Name	EPCGroup.epc.internal
Database Name	EPCGroup_Content
Application Pool	Create New
App Pool Name	EPCGroupInternalWebs AppPool
Managed Account	(Domain)\spInternalWebApps
Authentication	NTLM

The root site collection was created using the Publishing Portal template. "User A" was assigned as the Primary Site Collection Administrator and "User B" as the Secondary Site Collection Administrator. This should be changed to reflect proper ownership of this site according to company policy.

TABLE 12.7   Web Application and Related Configuration for the EPCGroup_Chub_Content Database for this Implementation Scenario Example

Option	Configuration
Web Application	EPCGroup Chub
Host Name	EPCGroupChub.internal
Database Name	EPCGroup_Chub_Content
Application Pool	Use Existing
App Pool Name	EPCGroupInternalWebs AppPool
Authentication	NTLM

The root site collection was created using the Publishing Portal template, with "User A" assigned as the Primary Site Collection Administrator and "User B" as the Secondary Site Collection Administrator. This should be changed to reflect proper ownership of this site according to the organization's policy.

TABLE 12.8   Web Application and Related Configuration for the EPCGroup_CThub_Content Database for This Implementation Scenario Example

Option	Configuration
Web Application	EPCGroup My Sites
Host Name	Mysites.epc.internal
Database Name	EPCGroup_CThub_Content
Application Pool	Create New
App Pool Name	EPCGroupMySites AppPool

Option	Configuration
Managed Account	(Domain)\spInternalWebApps
Authentication	NTLM

The root site collection was created using the My Site host site template, with "User A" assigned as the Primary Site Collection Administrator and "User B" as the Secondary Site Collection Administrator. This should be changed to reflect proper ownership of this site according to company policy.

A Web Application User Policy was added to both the EPCGroupNet and the MySites web applications granting spSuperReader Full Read access and spSuperUser Full Control access as required for the publishing object cache to function properly.

Service Applications (Examples)

The five service applications created to meet the functional requirements of this sample project scenario are detailed in Tables 12.9, 12.10, 12.11, 12.12, and 12.13.

TABLE 12.9   The Service Application for the Business Connectivity Service and the Related Settings for This Implementation Scenario Example

Option	Configuration
Service Application	Business Connectivity Service
Application Pool	Create New
App Pool Name	EPCGroupServiceApps AppPool
Managed Account	(Domain)\spAppServices

TABLE 12.10   The Service Application for the Search Service and the Related Settings for This Implementation Scenario Example

Option	Configuration
Service Application	Search Service
Search Account	EPCGroup\spCrawl
Admin Application Pool	Create New
App Pool Name	EPCGroupSearchAdmin AppPool
Managed Account	(Domain)\spAppServices
Query Application Pool	Create New
App Pool Name	EPCGroupSearchQuery AppPool
Managed Account	EPCGroup\spAppServices

Two crawl schedules were created for the Search Service Application. A full crawl is scheduled to run weekly every Monday at 3:00 a.m. An incremental crawl is scheduled to run daily at 1:00 a.m. The organization should adjust these schedules to suit their needs and availability. A full crawl was triggered to populate search results.

TABLE 12.11   The Service Application for the Secure Store Service and the Related Settings for This Implementation Scenario Example

Option	Configuration
Service Application	Secure Store
Application Pool	Use existing
App Pool Name	EPCGroupServiceApps AppPool
Key	No key generated

TABLE 12.12   The Service Application for the User Profile Service and the Related Settings for This Implementation Scenario Example

Option	Configuration
Service Application	EPCGroup User Profile Service
Application Pool	Use existing
App Pool Name	EPCGroupServiceApps AppPool
Profile Database	EPCGroup_Profile_DB
Sync Database	EPCGroup_Sync_DB
Social Database	EPCGroup_Social_DB
Sync Instance	EPCGroup-SP2013App1
MySite URL	http://mysites.epcgroup.internal
Managed Path	/personal
Naming Format	Username

TABLE 12.13   The Service Application for the Managed Metadata Service and the Related Settings for This Implementation Scenario Example

Option	Configuration
Service Application	EPCGroup Managed Metadata
Application Pool	Use existing
App Pool Name	EPCGroupServiceApps AppPool
Database	EPCGroup_Managed_Metadata_Service_DB
Hub URL	http://chub.epcgroup.internal

12

Summary

The actual installation and configuration of SharePoint 2013 requires many business requirements gathering and technical roadmap decisions to be put in place by the organization before the actual installation so that SharePoint is implemented and architected right the very first time.

This chapter followed a sample scenario of an enterprise 5,000-user manufacturing company with an existing SharePoint 2007 environment and the upgrade and migration of its content into a new SharePoint 2013 environment.

It is key to refer to Chapters 5 and 7 to ensure that your organization's information architecture design, as well as system architecture design, is properly planned and vetted by the business so that the installation and configuration will go smoothly and also scale to future IT and SharePoint roadmap requirements.

CHAPTER 13

Development Strategies and Custom Applications in SharePoint 2013, Office 365, and SharePoint Online

Overview of SharePoint 2013, Office 365, and Microsoft Azure Development Strategies

This chapter covers the latest tools and technologies for performing custom development on SharePoint Server 2013, Office 365, SharePoint Online, and Microsoft Azure environments. I will also discuss development strategies for organizations that plan to have these technology assets deployed both on-premises and in the cloud and require applications that are compatible as well as secure in a hybrid cloud environment.

The new SharePoint app model, as depicted in Figure 13.1, has been designed in a distributed nature to support applications regardless of where they are hosted, as depicted in Figure 13.2, to ensure that SharePoint will be able adapt and evolve over time and scale with your business.

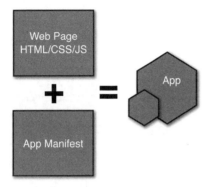

FIGURE 13.1   A high-level overview of the SharePoint app model.

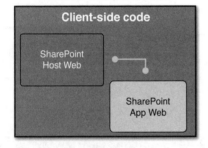

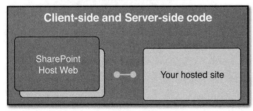

FIGURE 13.2   An overview of the hosting architecture for apps.

The new SharePoint app model provides an array of customization options for your organization's business and/or technical requirements to support areas such as the following:

▶ Compatibility around a full-screen interface

▶ Entails the customization of the ribbon or menu actions

▶ Needs to be an app part

▶ Requires workflows and/or remote event receivers

▶ Needs to pull in data from other systems

▶ Requires custom lists, fields, or views

Microsoft has recently released the new Office 365 API Tools, which opens up the possibilities of integrating data, as well as the capability to continue to streamline the security models and lower some of the fears and possibly realistic perceived risk regarding the storage of sensitive (PHI, PII, HIPAA, and so on) data within the cloud. This will continue to press the hybrid cloud development model as these APIs come out of "preview" and the first production Office 365 API Tools are officially released.

The overall options to a developer have widened and the use of HTML has become prevalent in achieving development requests of end users and the business. We will discuss the new SharePoint app and related APIs in the following sections, including security and identity management elements such as OData (Open Data Protocol) and OAuth (Open Authorization) that provides for secure access to data and resources.

The core developer skill sets for SharePoint 2013, Office 365, and/or SharePoint Online requires a strong understanding of the .NET Framework 4.5.1, which is released with Visual Studio 2013 as well as being included in Windows 8.1. You also need to have good working knowledge of JavaScript and be very comfortable with HTML and CSS. In addition, you need to have knowledge of SharePoint 2013's APIs as well as Microsoft Azure's SDK and offerings and the updated underlying foundational changes around SharePoint 2013's workflows and Windows Workflow Foundation 4.

Windows Workflow Foundation 4 is hosted in the new Workflow Manager Client, as shown in the diagram in Figure 13.3, and is built on the messaging functionality of Windows Communication Foundation (WCF).

> **NOTE**
>
> Microsoft has rebranded Windows Azure to Microsoft Azure.

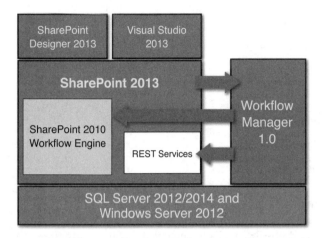

FIGURE 13.3   A high-level overview of SharePoint 2013 Workflow and the Workflow Manager.

TIP

For you to be able to perform development activities in SharePoint 2013, Office 365, SharePoint Online, and Microsoft Azure, there are core technologies and tools you must have available, as detailed here:

► **SharePoint 2013 development environment:**

You will need a SharePoint 2013 development environment prepared with the proper configurations and variables in mind to meet the needs of your development requirements. This includes the installation media for SharePoint 2013, Windows Server 2012, SQL Server 2012/2014, and so forth.

► **Visual Studio 2013 and tools**

For more information on Visual Studio 2013, refer to the following link:

http://www.visualstudio.com/en-us/downloads

► **Microsoft Office 2013 Professional**

► **An Office 365 Developer Site**

To sign up for an Office 365 Developer Site, refer to the following link:

http://msdn.microsoft.com/en-us/library/office/fp179924(v=office.15).aspx

► **Microsoft Azure SDK and tools**

For more information on the Microsoft Azure SDK, as well as the tools and downloads available, refer to the following link:

http://azure.microsoft.com/en-us/downloads/

► **Microsoft Azure Trial Subscription**

To obtain a trial subscription of Microsoft Azure, refer to the following link:

http://azure.microsoft.com/en-us/pricing/free-trial/

TIP

Workflow activities, which are implementations of activity classes and are implemented declaratively by using XAML (Extensible Application Markup Language), represent the underlying managed objects that drive the overall workflow behavior. Workflow actions, which are defined by the author of the workflow, are wrappers that encapsulate the underlying activities and are easily reviewable in SharePoint Designer 2013.

For more information regarding XAML and the .NET 4.5 Framework, refer to the following link: http://msdn.microsoft.com/en-us/library/ms752059(v=vs.110).aspx

---

Even if your organization's current initiative or identified business requirements are focusing on just on-premises or a cloud-based infrastructure, you must be prepared for future hybrid cloud initiatives and the related development that goes along with them. The "hybrid cloud development mind-set" will be the new focus and leading strategy for most organizations' development efforts over the next decade.

Recommending that you test and familiarize yourself with tools that may not be required for your project's scope, such as signing up for an Office 365 Developers site or testing Microsoft Azure and its SDK, is not going to create a situation in which you are wasting your time or simply "playing around with the latest fun development toys" available on the market as it would have been in previous releases of SharePoint. In the past releases of SharePoint and in my previous two books on SharePoint 2007 and SharePoint 2010, I never recommended going out and performing this type of familiarization with tools that may never be in scope. However, a complete shift in the IT landscape has taken place in the past few years and even past few months, and it's an absolute necessity to prepare for scalability and the possibility of a hybrid cloud scenario.

With the new unified architecture mind-set of SharePoint 2013, Microsoft's recent release of Office 365 API Tools, and the corresponding unified project system in Visual Studio, you will actually be improving on your organization's overall application development life-cycle strategy and the ROI you can provide to your team. Developing with the thought process of "erring on the side of caution" and ensuring that any custom apps, features, workflows, or solutions you are developing are also compatible with the cloud may actually take some extra time in terms of development hours.

The flip side of the coin here is that if you do not develop with "cloud compatibility" in mind, you may end up in a situation down the road where your organization wants to try out Office 365 or Microsoft Azure for one department, business unit, or external vendor. This could force you to then nearly completely redesign a custom app to make it compatible for a new business case in which it may take 70 hours of time to accomplish when you could have instead spent 5 or 6 additional hours in the first place to ensure that the app was scalable and compatible.

There are also the related internal business processes that most organizations require to initiate a new custom development project or initiative. You do not want to put yourself in a situation in which you are forced into a "phase 2" development effort when a type of "change order" could have been discussed with the project team about the importance of this compatibility and additional level of effort it may take in the initial "phase 1" effort.

Even if you know that this additional effort is going to be denied, it is important to follow this best practice and provide the best advice to the business, even if they do not want to listen. This may help you on the off chance a discussion comes up internally and you are asked, "Why didn't we just develop this to be compatible with both an on-premises and a cloud-based environment?"

.NET Framework 4.5/4.5.1 and SharePoint 2013

With all the new features released in the new version of SharePoint 2013, the underlying .NET Framework is at the very core of the managed execution environment and the required services to its running applications.

There are two main components of the .NET Framework:

▶ **The common language runtime (CLR):** This is the execution engine that handles running applications.

▶ **The .NET Framework Class Library:** This library consists of reusable code that developers call within the custom applications they are developing, as shown in Figure 13.4.

FIGURE 13.4   An overview of the components that make up .NET.

The following is a list of the services provided via the .NET Framework for running applications:

▶ Memory management allocating and releasing memory

▶ Multitargeting via the targeting of the portable class library, which provides compatibility for multiple platforms

▶ Development frameworks and technologies that include ASP.NET, ADO.NET, and Windows Communication Foundation

▶ An extensive class library of types and their members from the .NET Framework Class Library

▶ Language interoperability via compilers targeting the .NET Framework and emission of an intermediate code, which is then compiled at run time to enable programmers to develop applications in their preferred language

▶ Version compatibility between .NET Frameworks

▶ Side-by-side execution via allowing multiple versions of the common language runtime to exist on the same computer, thus allowing multiple versions to coexist

Capability to Select from Any Programming Language Supported by the .NET Framework
The .NET Framework enables you to select from any of the supported programming languages to achieve your development goals. There is underlying interoperability that enables the language that you prefer and select to interact with all the other .NET Framework applications regardless of the languages for which they were developed. Within SharePoint 2013, Office 365, SharePoint Online, and Microsoft Azure, the development languages that are typically utilized via Visual Studio are C#, ASP.NET, and JavaScript.

For more information on how best to get started on this framework, refer to the following link:

http://msdn.microsoft.com/en-us/library/hh425099.aspx.

To download the latest .NET Framework (4.5/4.5.1), refer to the following link: http://msdn.microsoft.com/en-us/library/5a4x27ek.aspx

Updated .NET Framework Features Commonly Discussed Within SharePoint 2013 Initiatives
There are a large number of new features and tools as well as key improvements to the .NET 4.5 Framework, but there are a few that are core to new high-profile updates and features in SharePoint 2013 that are commonly discussed by SharePoint project team members and SharePoint administrative with the development team.

The following is a small subset of new features and updates to the .NET Framework 4.5 that are commonly discussed within a new SharePoint 2013, Office 365, SharePoint Online, or Microsoft Azure initiative:

- New .NET Framework tool called the Resource File Generator (`Resgen.exe`) that enables you to create a `.resw` file for use in Windows Store apps from a `.resources` file embedded in a .NET Framework assembly
- New .NET for Windows Store apps, which can be built in C#
- Updates to Windows Workflow Foundation that include changes and improvements in the following areas:
    - The addition of state machine workflows with the capability to set breakpoints on states as well as the capability to copy and paste transitions in the Workflow Designer
    - New activities for creating state machine workflows that include StateMachine, State, and Transition
    - An Enhanced Workflow Designer feature related to search capabilities in Visual Studio, as well as new panning support that enables the visible portion of a workflow to be changed without use of the scrollbars
- Updates to the Windows Presentation Foundation (WPF) that include changes and improvements in the following areas:
    - The new Ribbon control, which enables you to implement a ribbon user interface that hosts a Quick Access Toolbar, Application Menu, and tabs

▶ Improved performance when displaying large sets of grouped data, and when accessing collections on non-UI threads

▶ Capability to set the amount of time that should elapse between property changes and data source updates

▶ New features for Windows Communication Foundation applications that include changes and improvements in the following areas:

▶ Capability to configure ASP.NET compatibility mode more easily

▶ Validation of WCF configuration files by Visual Studio as part of the build process so that you can detect configuration errors before you run your application

▶ New HTTPS protocol mapping to make it easier to expose an endpoint over HTTPS with Internet Information Services (IIS)

Licensing Apps for Office and SharePoint

With the continued growth in popularity of the Office Store and the apps for Office and SharePoint, many organizations are wanting to add their own custom application to the store to meet a need of the Microsoft business community. The process for adding apps in the seller dashboard is surprisingly very streamlined, and the "go to market" time has been very reasonable based on the personal experiences I have had, as well as those of my clients.

Summary of the Submission Process from Start to Finish

In this section, I outline the overall submission process, as shown in Figure 13.5, as well as links that you must visit to download the appropriate information regarding your submission. To begin the process of submitting your app to the Office Store, perform the following:

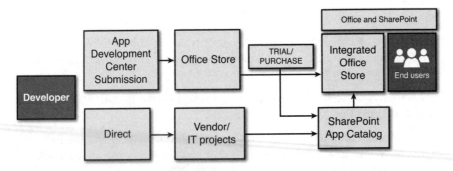

FIGURE 13.5   Getting your application published on the Office Store.

1. Review and download the checklist provided by Microsoft that helps answer some initial questions regarding your app and its architecture at the following link:

   http://msdn.microsoft.com/en-us/library/office/dn356576(v=office.15).aspx

2. The first document you should review is "Validation Checklist for Apps for Office and SharePoint," at the following link:

   http://msdn.microsoft.com/en-us/library/office/jj938162(v=office.15).aspx

   There are some key validation items that you should consider from a business and overall profitability standpoint because there are costs associated with not only having developed the app but also continuing to maintain it. Some organizations like to have an app from their organization on the store from more of a marketing and PR perspective than from a revenue perspective.

3. After you have completed the validation checklist items, you should create a seller account on the Office Store, as well as provide Microsoft with the required business or personal documentation they require and your payout detail information.

   Microsoft provides both a "company account," for corporations, LLCs, and other registered state and local entities, and an "individual account" for independent developers.

   To sign up for a company account or an individual account, refer to the following link:

   http://go.microsoft.com/fwlink/?LinkId=248605

4. After you have signed up for an account, you should immediately submit the verification documents, as well as required tax documents and payment information, because the verification process must, in most cases, be completed and required paperwork received before you can upload and submit an app for review and validation. The list of payout and tax information can be found at the following link:

   http://msdn.microsoft.com/en-us/library/office/dn336975(v=office.15).aspx#BKMK_PayoutTax

   Microsoft provides additional information via the "Microsoft Seller Dashboard FAQ" page that can be found at the following link:

   http://msdn.microsoft.com/en-us/library/office/dn336975(v=office.15).aspx#BKMK_ReceivePayout

5. You can continue to check the status of your account by logging in to your seller account, selecting the Account tab, and then, under Manage, selecting Status for the most recent updates on approval.

6. You should have your app ready to be updated and 100% complete so that you can upload it after your account is approved. This includes performing antivirus scans and final verifications listed on the "Publish Apps for Office and SharePoint to the Office Store" page, which can be found at the following link:

   http://msdn.microsoft.com/en-us/library/office/jj220037(v=office.15).aspx

7. After your account is approved, you can submit your app for verification and approval by using your seller account's interface or by the new Visual Studio publishing process, which allows you to publish within the related Microsoft Visual Studio development environment. For more information on how to publish an app for SharePoint by using Visual Studio, refer to the following link:

http://msdn.microsoft.com/en-us/library/office/jj220044(v=office.15).aspx

8. You have probably already decided on a final price for your app or a range that you are thinking would fit well into the overall gallery of existing apps, but I would recommend reviewing Microsoft's "Decide on a Pricing Model for Your App for Office or SharePoint" page at the following link:

http://msdn.microsoft.com/en-us/library/office/dn456317(v=office.15).aspx

9. You should also review the "Licensing Your Apps for SharePoint" page for additional insights into the best price or licensing model that would best fit your needs, which can be accessed at the following link:

http://blogs.msdn.com/b/officeapps/archive/2012/11/09/licensing-your-apps-for-sharepoint.aspx

10. After your app is live and users are purchasing it, you can utilize Microsoft's seller interface to verify that you are being paid your licensing fees (e.g., for your "paid" apps). An overview of the metrics and available options to verify this can be found at the following page:

http://blogs.msdn.com/b/officeapps/archive/2012/11/01/creating-and-verifying-licensing-in-a-paid-app-for-office.aspx

11. After your app has been live in the Office Store, you may find that you need to conduct maintenance or want to provide updates. Microsoft has a page that provides recommendations and options called "How to: Update, Un-publish, and Track Your App Metrics," which can be found at the following page:

http://msdn.microsoft.com/en-us/library/office/dn270534(v=office.15).aspx

Preparing a SharePoint 2013 Development Environment

It is important to combine the various factors for the type of development that you will be performing, your knowledge of the underlying business requirements of the organization, and the underlying system and information architecture the organization has deployed to properly prepare your own SharePoint 2013 development environment.

As mentioned previously, regardless of whether your organization's implementation is strictly hosted on-premises or is in the cloud, it is still important that you dive into the various development areas and capabilities of both hosting models and obtain a firm grasp on what a hybrid cloud SharePoint 2013 or Office 365 environment might contain. This will assist you in deploying scalable solutions and understanding the range of tools at your disposal.

Based on the variables listed previously regarding the type of development environment that would best fit your needs, I recommend that you follow the steps contained in the MSDN references listed next on how best to prepare and build an environment tailored to your needs. I recommend this not only because they are tremendously helpful, but also because they contain technology updates from Microsoft. New capabilities are frequently being released for both SharePoint 2013 and Office 365 and integration tools via Microsoft Azure, and it is key you factor in any of these changes.

> **NOTE**
>
> Whenever possible, your local development environment should be implemented on a virtual environment.

13

▶ To set up an on-premises development environment for apps for SharePoint 2013, refer to the following link:

http://msdn.microsoft.com/en-us/library/office/fp179923(v=office.15).aspx

▶ To set up an environment for developing apps for SharePoint on Office 365, refer to the following link:

http://msdn.microsoft.com/en-us/library/office/fp161179(v=office.15).aspx

▶ To set up an environment for creating a basic app for SharePoint by using "Napa" Office 365 Development Tools (the Office 365 API Tools), refer to the following link:

http://msdn.microsoft.com/en-us/library/office/jj220041(v=office.15).aspx

▶ To sign up for an Office 365 Developer Site, refer to the following link:

http://msdn.microsoft.com/en-us/library/office/fp179924(v=office.15).aspx

> **TIP**
>
> During your development activities in SharePoint 2013, Office 365, or SharePoint Online, you may hear a reference to ASP.NET MVC. MVC stands for "model–view–controller."
>
> ASP.NET MVC is an open-source web application framework that implements this model–view–controller pattern, and you can utilize it for an app in SharePoint 2013.
>
> For more information regarding ASP.NET MVC, as well as to access the free framework download, refer to the following link: http://www.asp.net/mvc/mvc4

There are core requirements (for example, installation steps and prerequisites) that you must have prepared when building your actual development environment. Development environments are not as resource intensive as your QA or Prod environments, but at the same time you do not want to "skimp" on the resources you procure. For detailed information on installation and configuration of SharePoint 2013's components, refer to Chapter 12, "Installation and Configuration."

TIP

You also can utilize Microsoft Azure virtual machines for your development environment. Microsoft has released an Azure developer image that contains SharePoint 2013 and Visual Studio 2013 Ultimate RC preinstalled. The Azure developer image also contains scripts to provision and configure SharePoint 2013 with or without an Active directory running on a different machine.

If you implement an Azure developer image for your development needs, you can access your organization's on-premises source control from Visual Studio on the virtual machine by using an Azure point-to-site connection.

For more information about Azure point-to-site connections, refer to the following link:

http://msdn.microsoft.com/en-us/library/windowsazure/dn133792.aspx.

For more information regarding Microsoft Azure virtual machines, refer to the following link: https://azure.microsoft.com/en-us/solutions/infrastructure/

Requirements Gathering for the Development of a New Solution

There are a number of questions that you should ask yourself regarding the app you are wanting to develop to ensure you are documenting the most granular requirements from both a development and user perspective. A short example of these questions is as follows:

▶ How will the users be using the solution?

▶ How will the solution be deployed into production and managed?

▶ What are the quality attribute requirements for the solution?

▶ What are the underlying security and compliance requirements?

▶ What types of SLAs are required around uptime and business continuity (e.g., Backup, Restore, and Disaster Recovery)?

▶ What are the performance requirements, and are there factors that you are aware of regarding the user base, concurrency, localization, or configuration?

▶ How can the solution be designed to be flexible and maintainable over time?

Reviewing the SharePoint App Model and the Composition of an App for SharePoint

The new SharePoint app model introduces new technologies for you to master and requires an overall change in your thinking and development approach so that you are developing custom applications that can be extensible, if needed, beyond "your data center."

SharePoint 2013's development's extensibility means that no matter what "data center" is being discussed or selected, the custom applications that you develop must be able to live and thrive in all these environments.

As in the previous 12 chapters, I will provide links to some of the latest and greatest resources available as Microsoft's continues to update their architecture around SharePoint applications that run on both on-premises and the Office 365 platform.

SharePoint 2013's service upgrades include new APIs and other changes that could affect your application, so it has never been more important to stay on top of the latest news and release cycles so that you are developing in a best practices and "intelligent" manner and are in the know so that any applications you develop do not have problems due to any issues in tenancy updates.

When you are reviewing the new SharePoint app model, it is important to first have a clear understanding of what exactly an "App for SharePoint" is.

An app's configuration with SharePoint is derived from an underlying app manifest, which is an XML file that declares the app's basic properties. The app manifest file can utilize various authentication schemes (app principals), as well as declare the permissions the app requires. The app manifest can also include tokens that are replaced at build/run time that enable you to reference your app and pass context so that you can properly provide details regarding the SharePoint language as well as where the app resides or has been installed.

As was mentioned at the beginning of this chapter, SharePoint app model works in a distributed nature, and based on this you can select where the app's code will run by selecting and specifying hosting options. There are three main providers:

▶ **Provider-hosted apps**

Provider-hosted apps, as depicted in Figure 13.6, require that they must be hosted either on a dedicated server or via a third-party hosting service. This provides you with the option to run the apps either in your organization's on-premises environment's dedicated server or within the cloud.

Provider-hosted apps support WebForms as well as MVC.

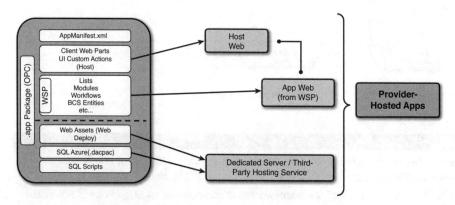

FIGURE 13.6   High-level overview of a provider hosted app.

▶ **Autohosted apps**

Autohosted apps, as depicted in Figure 13.7, are cloud specific and are automatically deployed by SharePoint into Microsoft Azure Web Sites and SQL Azure.

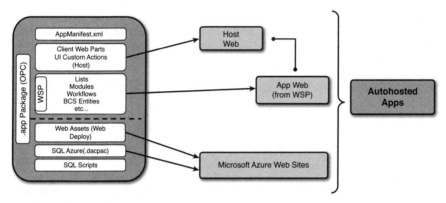

FIGURE 13.7   High-level overview of an autohosted app.

▶ **SharePoint-hosted apps**

SharePoint-hosted apps, as depicted in Figure 13.8, are hosted by SharePoint itself and are comprised of HTML and JavaScript.

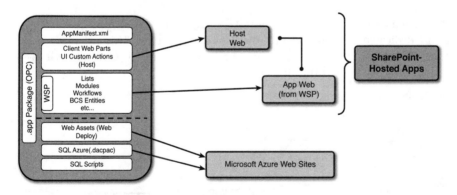

FIGURE 13.8   High-level overview of a SharePoint hosted app.

TIP

There is also the configuration option for hybrid apps in which SharePoint components run in SharePoint while components hosted in the cloud run in the cloud.

To get a better understanding of the framework and components of SharePoint client-side code, refer to Figure 13.9.

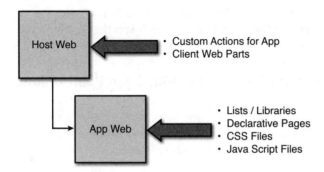

FIGURE 13.9   An overview of the framework and components of SharePoint Client-side Code.

13

The Cloud App Model

SharePoint 2013 includes a new cloud app model, as shown in Figure 13.10, which enables your organization to create apps for SharePoint that are self-contained pieces of functionality meant to extend SharePoint's capabilities and be "cloud ready" for both on-premises (e.g., private cloud) as well as in the cloud (e.g., public cloud) or work with resources in both environments in a hybrid cloud architecture.

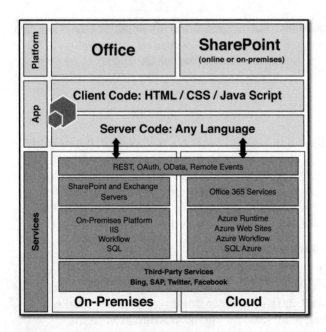

FIGURE 13.10   An overview of the new Cloud App Model.

The new cloud app model embraces web standards for technologies such as HTML, JavaScript, REST, OData, and OAuth and enables you to build a web app that is connected to Office and SharePoint APIs and services.

Configuring an App in SharePoint 2013, Office 365, SharePoint Online, and Windows Azure

To successfully configure and deploy an app within a SharePoint 2013 on-premises environment or within the Office 365 cloud, it is key to understand the granular underlying configuration requirements to ensure security and proper authentication.

> **NOTE**
>
> For the latest information from Microsoft on how to plan for app authentication in SharePoint 2013, which also includes the recent 2014 updates, refer to the following link:
>
> http://technet.microsoft.com/en-us/library/jj219806(v=office.15)

Key Considerations in Configuring SharePoint Apps

It is important to keep the following consideration in mind to ensure that you are configuring your environment in a secured manner:

> **NOTE**
>
> For more information on how to configure an environment for apps for SharePoint 2013, refer to the following link: http://technet.microsoft.com/en-us/library/fp161236(v=office.15)

▶ Apps do not support Kerberos.

Each app runs in its own isolated domain, and to enable the configuration required for Kerberos, you would have to configure the service principal name (SPN). In this configuration, we would be have to configure SPNs for every app, which would cause major underlying issues as well as unnecessary resource utilization on the servers. If Kerberos is enabled for your web applications, SharePoint apps can fall back onto NTLM (Windows NT Challenge/Response authentication protocol).

▶ SharePoint-hosted apps do not support SAML authentication.

By default, SharePoint-hosted apps (on-premises) will not properly be redirected when configured using SAML authentication; however, Microsoft Azure Active Directory does support the SAML 2.0 web browser single sign-on (SSO) profile. For more information regarding SAML 2.0 and Microsoft Azure, refer to the following link:

http://msdn.microsoft.com/en-us/library/windowsazure/dn195589.aspx

> **NOTE**
>
> Microsoft enables you to configure an app domain for each web application zone and use alternate access mapping (AAM) and host-header web application configuration. For more information about configuring apps in AAM or host-header environments, refer to the following link: http://technet.microsoft.com/en-us/library/dn144963.aspx

Configuring Apps Authentication

In SharePoint 2013, OAuth is used to establish a trust that enables users to grant a third-party site access to information that is stored with another service provider without sharing usernames and passwords and without sharing all the data that they have in SharePoint.

The following is a high-level overview of the process a user signing in to their SharePoint 2013 on-premises environment would take to attempt to establish a trust with OAuth, as shown in Figure 13.11:

1. A user signs in to SharePoint 2013 and is authenticated.

2. The user then opens a provider-hosted app (for example, Azure).

3. The app was granted permission at install time by a user to access a SharePoint list.

4. The app is rendered as an embedded IFrame or loaded full frame by POSTing the necessary context information.

5. That app then calls back to SharePoint to access the SharePoint resources on behalf of the user.

6. When it calls back, it includes a token for both the current user and the app.

7. SharePoint validates that both have rights to access the content.

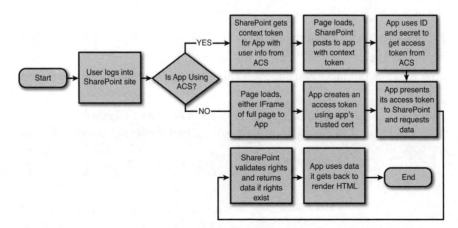

FIGURE 13.11   The process of a SharePoint 2013 on-premises user attempting to establish an OAuth trust.

The following is a high-level overview of the configuration steps required for deploying SharePoint Apps, as shown in Figure 13.12, and performing the required OData trust level configurations:

Before you begin

Buy a domain for apps from a domain provider   **ContosoApps.com**

On your DNS Server

(1) Create a forward lookup zone for apps   **ContosoApps.com**

(2) Create a CName alias from the app domain to the SharePoint domain   ***.ContosoApps.com -> SharePoint.Contoso.com**

For SSL (https://URLs)

(3) Create a wildcard SSL certificate for the new app domain   **http://*.ContosoApps.com**

On your SharePoint Servers

(4) Configure the Subscription Settings service Application by using Windows PowerShell.

(5) Configure the App Management service application (Central Administration or Windows PowerShell).

(6) Configure the App URLs in Central Administration   **Domain: ContosoApps.com**
Prefix: Apps

FIGURE 13.12   Overview of the process for deploying SharePoint Apps.

▶ Configuring the underlying SharePoint 2013 app deployment prerequisites requires the following:

  ▶ The initial step that is required is to ensure that an app domain name has been determined for the configuration.

  ▶ After the domain name is acquired, it should be configured in your organization's DNS.

  ▶ After the domain name and DNS have been obtained and specified, as shown in Figure 13.13, you must then create a new wildcard SSL certificate for the app.

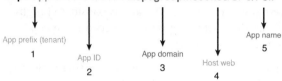

FIGURE 13.13   An app URL with the proper constructs submitted for an OData trust.

▶ Configuring the SharePoint farm requires you to complete the following tasks:

  ▶ Create a SharePoint service application and enable services.

  ▶ Configure the app settings in SharePoint.

▶ Authentication configuration for the app requires the following steps:

  ▶ Configure SharePoint for low-trust apps.

  ▶ Configure SharePoint for high-trust apps.

TIP

For tips and FAQ on OAuth and remote apps for SharePoint, refer to the following link:
http://msdn.microsoft.com/en-us/library/fp179932.aspx

Configuring SharePoint for Low-Trust Apps

Low-trust apps are those that Microsoft Azure Access Control Services (ACS) acts as the authentication provider and common authentication broker \ trust broker between SharePoint and the app.

ACS is where SharePoint requests a context token that it can send to the location hosting the app. The app then uses the context token to request an access token from ACS. When received, this is used by the app to talk back to SharePoint.

For additional information regarding low-trust applications and app permissions, refer to the section regarding low-trust application at the following link: http://msdn.microsoft. com/en-us/library/office/dn268593(v=office.15).aspx

Configuring SharePoint for High-Trust Apps

High-trust apps are those for which you are not using ACS as the trust broker; they require a certificate to establish trust and must generate their own access token by using the server-to-server security token service that is part of SharePoint 2013.

This type of trust is known as a server-to-server (S2S) trust relationship and is between the SharePoint farm and the app; this ensures that you must perform the trust for each individual app for each high-trust app that uses different certificates, and in SharePoint there is no context token.

There can be some confusion about whether high trust actually means full trust. It does not, but a high-trust app must still request app permissions. The app is considered high-trust because it is trusted to use any user identity that the app needs, because the app is responsible for creating the user portion of the access token.

When an app is not SharePoint-hosted and requires some server-side processing logic, this is the approach on-premises apps should take in most situations.

For additional information regarding the proper guidelines for using the high-trust authorization system in apps for SharePoint 2013, refer to the following link: http://msdn.microsoft.com/en-us/library/jj945118(v=office.15).aspx

For information as well as a PowerShell example on how to create high-trust apps for SharePoint 2013, refer to the following link: http://msdn.microsoft.com/en-us/library/office/fp179901.aspx

---

TIP

To help you understand the differences in configuring SharePoint for low-trust apps versus high-trust apps, I will summarize the main differences and reasons for their terming this *low* and *high*.

A SharePoint 2013 on-premises is a high-trust, provider-hosted application that uses the server-to-server protocol. The application is considered "high-trust" because it is trusted to use any user identity that the application needs and then create the user portion of the access token. A high-trust application is not intended to run within Office 365; the S2S protocol is typically configured behind an organization's firewall. A high-trust application uses a certificate instead of a context token to establish trust. In SharePoint 2013, the SPTrustedSecurityTokenIssuer provides access tokens for server-to-server authentication.

Low-trust applications are those that utilize a trust broker like Microsoft Azure Access Control Services to act as a token issuer between SharePoint and the application. In low-trust apps, SharePoint requests a context token from ACS and then routes it to the location hosting the application. The application then uses the context token to extract the refresh token and uses the refresh token to request an access token from ACS. After the access token is received, it is used by the application to talk back to SharePoint.

SharePoint low-trust (cloud-based) applications rely on the OAuth 2.0 authorization code flow (grant type) to delegate limited rights to applications to act as users.

The SharePoint environment must establish a trust and communicate with a token issuer as SharePoint relies on Microsoft Azure Active Directory (AD). Microsoft Azure AD, in exchange, must be aware of SharePoint and the client application in order to grant them the necessary tokens to work together.

Low-trust applications can't interact with content outside of the app web, which is the SharePoint subweb that contains your app by default. To do this, you need to specify permissions to the host web. The host web is the SharePoint web that hosts the app web for the app. These requested permissions are then approved or denied by the installer of the app during installation. If denied (not trusted), the permissions automatically prevent the app from installing and then cancel the operation.

13

TIP

For more information on how to plan for server-to-server authentication in SharePoint 2013, refer to the following link: http://technet.microsoft.com/en-us/library/jj219546(v=office.15).aspx

SharePoint 2013's APIs, Office 365 API Tools, and the Development Options for Accessing Data and Resources

SharePoint 2013's APIs enable apps, as well as other elements, to connect and integrate with SharePoint's core features. The APIs, as depicted in Figure 13.14, provide apps the capability to view content or integrate with a workflow or even perform searches. For example, if you were developing an app for a business intelligence initiative, SharePoint 2013's APIs would enable your app to connect to SharePoint's BCS and other elements in a secure manner to access specific data.

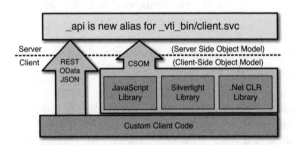

FIGURE 13.14   An overview of the SharePoint 2013 Remote API framework.

SharePoint 2013 APIs can really initially be put into three major "buckets" to help better understand their overall capabilities:

▶ Server-side object model

▶ Client-side object model

▶ REST APIs

TIP

For more information on how to choose the right API set for your specific business and functional goals in SharePoint 2013, refer to the following link: http://msdn.microsoft.com/en-us/library/office/jj164060(v=office.15).aspx

Server Object Model in SharePoint 2013

The server object model in SharePoint 2013 is the largest API set, and it covers all features and functionality both from an administrative perspective and for an end user. The server object model's core assembly is `Microsoft.SharePoint.dll`, which is installed in the Global Assembly Cache (GAC). Table 13.1 details the server object model's most utilized classes.

TABLE 13.1   The Server Object Model's Most Utilized Classes

Server Object Model	SharePoint Object
SPSite	Site Collection
SPFarm	Farm
SPList	List
SPListItem	List Item
SPWeb	Web

The server object model in SharePoint 2013, for example, can be utilized to create server-side utility application or can even be used to create Timer Job services to run in the background. It is extremely useful in modifying list items, performing searches, modifying and/or manipulating permissions, or assisting with business continuity elements with backup and restore.

I recommend reviewing a very detailed "business case" example available on MSDN on how the server object model can be utilized from an administrative perspective because this may help to identify similar tasks within your organization's environment. This example, which relates to the administrative task for working with user profiles and organization profiles by using the server object model, can be viewed at the following link: http://msdn.microsoft.com/en-us/library/office/jj163142(v=office.15).aspx

Client-Side Object Model (CSOM)

The client-side object model (CSOM) updates, retrieves, and manages data in SharePoint 2013, and it is available in several different forms to support many of SharePoint 2013's core capabilities, as depicted in Figure 13.15. The CSOM provides for:

▶ **.NET Framework redistributable assemblies**

  ▶ For more information regarding the .NET client APIs for SharePoint 2013, refer to the following link:

    http://msdn.microsoft.com/en-us/library/office/jj193041(v=office.15).aspx

  ▶ For more information regarding the .NET server API reference for SharePoint 2013, refer to the following link:

    http://msdn.microsoft.com/en-us/library/office/jj193058(v=office.15).aspx

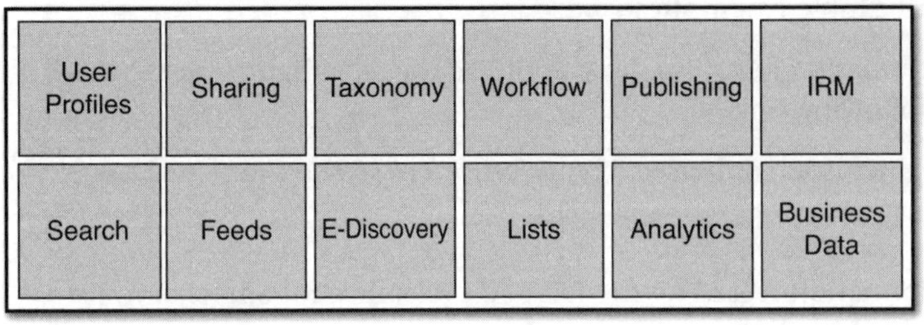

User Profiles	Sharing	Taxonomy	Workflow	Publishing	IRM
Search	Feeds	E-Discovery	Lists	Analytics	Business Data

FIGURE 13.15   An overview of the core SharePoint 2013 features that the CSOM API supports.

▶ **Office 365 API Tools**

   ▶ For more information regarding the new Office 365 API Tools, refer to the following link:

   http://msdn.microsoft.com/en-us/library/office/dn605893(v=office.15).aspx

   ▶ To download the new Office 365 API Tools, refer to the following link:

   http://visualstudiogallery.msdn.microsoft.com/7e947621-ef93-4de7-93d3-d796c43ba34f

▶ **JavaScript library**

   ▶ For more information regarding the JavaScript API and how it interacts with SharePoint 2013, as depicted in Figure 13.16, refer to the following link:

   http://msdn.microsoft.com/en-us/library/office/jj193034(v=office.15).aspx

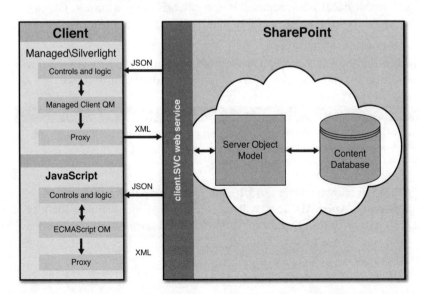

FIGURE 13.16   An overview of underlying interactions in CSOM within SharePoint 2013.

▶ **Silverlight redistributable assemblies**

  ▶ For more information regarding how to utilize the Silverlight Object Model, refer to the following link:

    http://msdn.microsoft.com/en-us/library/office/ee538971(v=office.15).aspx

▶ **REST APIs**

  ▶ For more information regarding the REST API reference for SharePoint 2013, refer to the following link:

    http://msdn.microsoft.com/en-us/library/office/dn593591.aspx

▶ **Windows Phone assemblies**

  ▶ For an overview of Windows Phone SharePoint 2013 application templates in Visual Studio, refer to the following link:

    http://msdn.microsoft.com/en-us/library/office/jj163786(v=office.15).aspx

With CSOM providing such a wide array of available APIs, I recommend referring to the following API index look-up page on MSDN that lists the most frequently used types and related objects: http://msdn.microsoft.com/en-us/library/office/dn268594(v=office.15).aspx

Office 365 API Tools

Microsoft has recently introduced the next step in the evolution of the Office 365 platform by releasing the Office 365 API Tools, as shown in Figure 13.17. This continues to extend the platform and opens up more possibilities around the hybrid cloud with the capability to access SharePoint 2013 on-premises. It also extends the platform in Office 2013 by adding the capability for both sites and native applications to consume Office 365 data.

Native applications running on Windows 8, iOS, Android, and other device platforms, will be able to consume Office 365 data by using REST APIs and standard OAuth flows.

NOTE

This first preview release of Office 365 API Tools supports a limited number of SharePoint, Exchange, and Microsoft Azure Active Directory data sources.

The Office 365 API Tools, as shown in Figure 13.18, are part of a platform that is built on an entirely new Microsoft Azure AD. They will provide for the more seamless identity management that is so critical to bringing more compliance and governance to these environments.

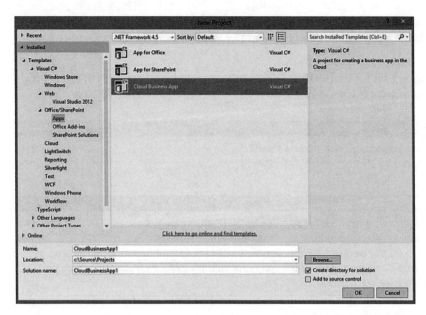

FIGURE 13.17   Creating a Cloud Business App via the new Office 365 API Tools.

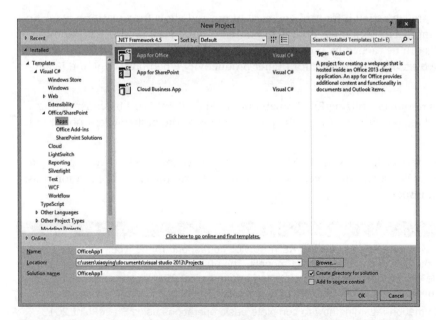

FIGURE 13.18   Creating a new App for Office via the new Office 365 API Tools.

There has also been an updated set of tools in Visual Studio developed in parallel so that the overall application life-cycle management (ALM), as well as future Release Management components such as Team Foundation Server, will be able to serve all data sources and tenants.

The Office development tools and templates in Visual Studio can be downloaded at the following link: http://visualstudiogallery.msdn.microsoft.com/7e947621-ef93-4de7-93d3-d796c43ba34f

I recommend signing up for a free Office 365 Developer Site by referring to the following link: http://msdn.microsoft.com/en-us/library/office/fp179924(v=office.15).aspx

> **NOTE**
>
> These tools were previously code named "NAPA."

> **TIP**
>
> Microsoft has released a new SharePoint Server 2013 Client Components SDK that can be utilized to enable remote and local development with SharePoint Server 2013. For more information on the new SharePoint Server 2013 Client Components SDK, as well as to access this free download, refer to the following link: http://www.microsoft.com/en-us/download/details.aspx?id=35585

REST APIs

The REST APIs are very straightforward and easy to use and allow for a platform-agnostic development approach. Each query that is submitted is done via a unique URL, and the returned results can be cached by proxy servers. The REST APIs are easier to utilize than a SOAP-based web service and provide for higher productivity when JavaScript and jQuery are used.

You can access resources utilizing REST capabilities in SharePoint 2013 by constructing a RESTful HTTP request, using OData, which corresponds to the desired client object model API.

The client.svc service handles the HTTP request and serves the appropriate response in either Atom or JSON (JavaScript Object Notation) format, and the client application must then parse that response.

> **TIP**
>
> The endpoints in the SharePoint 2013 REST service correspond to the types and members in the SharePoint client object models. The utilization of these HTTP requests allows for the use of these REST endpoints to perform typical CRUD (create, read, update, and delete) operations against SharePoint entities like SharePoint sites or lists.
>
> For more information regarding how to complete basic operations using SharePoint 2013 REST endpoints, refer to the following link: http://msdn.microsoft.com/en-us/library/office/jj164022(v=office.15).aspx

The URI (uniform resource identifier) for these REST endpoints closely mimics the API signature of the resource in the SharePoint client object model, as the main entry points for the REST service represent the site collection and site of the specified context that is submitted. To provide an overview of this, a specific site collection can be accessed by using the following:

http://*server*/*site*/_api/*site*

If you are wanting to access a specific site, you would do so by using the following:

http://*server*/*site*/_api/*web*

The *server* always represents the name of the server and the *site* represents the name of the site or the path to the specific site. By using this as a baseline, you can then construct more specific REST URIs by utilizing the object model names of the APIs from the client object model separated by a forward slash (/).

TIP

The differences between a URI, a URN, and a URL can be confusing due to the similarities of the concepts of all three of these terms.

▶ A URI is a uniform resource identifier, which is a string of characters used to identify a name or a resource on the Internet. A URI identifies a resource by location, by name, or both. A URI has two specializations known as URL and URN.

▶ A URL is a uniform resource locator, which is a subset of the URI. The URL specifies where an identified resource is available, as well as the mechanism for retrieving it, and defines how the resource can be obtained.

▶ A URN is a uniform resource name is actually a URI that uses the URN scheme but does not imply availability of the identified resource.

This means that both URNs (names) and URLs (locators) are URIs, and a specific URI may be both a name and a locator at the same time.

To clarify this in an example, EPC Group is the consulting firm that I work for and the name "EPC Group" can be used as an "identification." There are also a few firms overseas named EPC Group but they are in manufacturing and in other business verticals; so just telling you the company name "EPC Group" does not provide you any specifics on just the face value of the "identification" provided.

Think of the differences, in terms of performing a Bing or Google search, between the terms "EPC Group" and "EPC Group SharePoint 2013 Office 365 Houston." The second search term provides additional metadata, which then will provide more specifics to identify the correct company and its location.

A URN is very similar to a name and a URL is similar to a street address; the URN defines the actual identity whereas the URL provides a location. So in summary, a URL is a URI that identifies a specific resource and also provides the means by which you can locate the resource by describing the way to access it.

Note that some new browser updates, such as in Google Chrome, are now dropping the protocol from the display within the browser, which visually turns URLs into URIs.

For a complete REST API reference list as well as related samples, refer to the following link: http://msdn.microsoft.com/en-us/library/office/jj860569(v=office.15).aspx

The REST APIs and OData in SharePoint 2013

REST APIs in SharePoint 2013 are now compatible with OData, the industry standard for creating and consuming data APIs. The official reference for OData, as well as to track updates regarding this industry standard, can be found at the following link: http://www.odata.org

OData's official description, in essence, states that OData builds on core protocols like HTTP and commonly accepted methodologies like REST, resulting in a uniform way to expose full-featured data APIs.

In terms of SharePoint 2013, OData is a protocol for interacting with RESTful web services. It was released under Microsoft's open specification promise; it works on top of standard HTTP using HTTP GET, POST, PUT, and DELETE verbs and returns standard ATOM or JSON formatted results.

For more information regarding Microsoft's open specifications promise, refer to the following link: http://www.microsoft.com/openspecifications/en/us/programs/osp/default.aspx

RESTful web services are basically those services or applications that conform to REST constraints, and any service that does not conform to the required constraints should not be considered RESTful. There is a very strong focus on resources within RESTful web services and they should be simple for a developer to utilize. These services should follow these four principles:

- ▶ Utilize HTTP methods appropriately

- ▶ Expose data in a directory structure

- ▶ Be stateless

- ▶ Transfer either XML or JSON formatted results, as shown in Figure 13.19

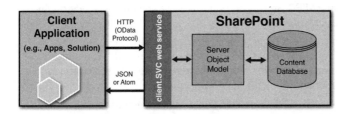

FIGURE 13.19   An overview of a RESTful HTTP request using OData.

For more information regarding additional technical specifications that may affect your specific organization's deployment, refer to Microsoft's Open Data Protocol Q&A at the following link: http://msdn.microsoft.com/en-us/data/ee844254.aspx

Microsoft has also recently released a 300-plus page OData/open specifications whitepaper for protocols, file formats, languages, and standards, as well as overviews of the interaction among each of these technologies, which can be accessed at the following link: http://msdn.microsoft.com/en-us/library/dd541188.aspx

REST and Search in SharePoint 2013

The new Search capabilities in SharePoint 2013 include a Search REST service that you can utilize to add search features and functionality to your organization's client applications as well as your mobile applications that support REST web requests.

This capability enables you to use the Search REST service to submit Keyword Query Language (KQL) or FAST Query Language (FQL) queries in apps for SharePoint, mobile apps, and remote client apps. In addition, the new Search REST service also supports both HTTP POST and HTTP GET requests.

For GET requests, you would construct the URI for query GET requests to utilize the Search REST service by using the following:

```
/_api/search/query
```

The GET request specifies the query parameters in the URL and can utilize two options for constructing GET requests as detailed here:

```
http://server/_api/search/query?query_parameter=value&query_parameter=value
```

or

```
http://server/_api/search/query(query_parameter=value&query_parameter=<value>)
```

For POST requests, you would construct the URI for query POST requests to utilize the Search REST service by using the following:

```
/_api/search/postquery
```

The POST requests are passed via the query parameters in the request in JSON format, and the HTTP POST version of the Search REST service supports all the parameters supported by the HTTP GET version.

You should utilize POST requests whenever the following is true:

▶ You have concerns about the length of your URL due to URL length restrictions that may be experienced with a GET request.

▶ You cannot specify the query parameters via a simple URL such as those in pass parameter values that contain a complex type array because there is added flexibility around the construction of POST requests.

You must ensure that whenever a call is made to the Search REST service, the specific query parameters are included with the request because these query parameters are used to construct the underlying SharePoint search query. These query parameters are specified in different manners between GET and POST requests:

▶ GET requests specify the query parameters in the URL.

▶ POST requests pass the query parameters in the body in JavaScript JSON format.

For more information regarding the SharePoint Search REST API, refer to the following link: http://msdn.microsoft.com/en-us/library/office/jj163876(v=office.15).aspx

For more information regarding the keyword query language syntax, refer to the following link: http://msdn.microsoft.com/en-us/library/office/ee558911(v=office.15).aspx

For more information regarding the FAST query language syntax, refer to the following link: http://msdn.microsoft.com/en-us/library/office/ff394606(v=office.15).aspx

Security and Identity Management Considerations for Application Development

There are various security, identity management, and authentication considerations when developing custom applications and related features in SharePoint 2013, Office 365, SharePoint Online, and Microsoft Azure. You should always keep in mind SharePoint 2013's "claims first" authentication architecture during your development, as well as in discussions with the business about their custom requirements.

With SharePoint 2013's user authentication based on claims, user authentication results in creation of a claims token, which tracks name-value pairs related to the token subject. These claims tokens are stored in memory using the FEDAUTH token format.

Overview of App Authentication

SharePoint 2013's app authentication is supported in CSOM as well as in REST API endpoints but is not supported for custom web services. Three types of app authentication are utilized by SharePoint 2013:

▶ Internal authentication

▶ External authentication using server-to-server trusts

▶ External authentication using OAuth

Internal Authentication

Internal authentication is utilized when an incoming call targets a CSOM or REST API endpoint or when an incoming call carries a claims token with an established user identity. Internal authentication is also utilized when an incoming call targets the URL of an existing SharePoint 2013 app web. This authentication does not support app-only authentication to elevate privilege(s).

There is no programming effort required in terms of access tokens; internal authentication is automatically utilized with client-side calls from pages in the app web, and it can also be utilized from remote web pages that are using the cross-domain library.

For more information regarding how to access SharePoint 2013 data from apps using the cross-domain library, refer to the following link: http://msdn.microsoft.com/library/office/fp179927

External Authentication

External authentication, which users both S2S and OAuth, is utilized for server-side code in the "remote web" and issues CSOM or REST API calls against the SharePoint host. The incoming calls can target host web and other sites within your organization's tenancy.

External authentication does require custom app code to be developed to create and manage access tokens which carry the app's identity as well as user identity because the app is required to transmit an access token in the request header when making a call to SharePoint 2013.

Apps Granted Permissions

In SharePoint 2013, how an app is granted permissions is not identical to how a user is granted permissions. App permissions have only two options, which are that they are or are not granted permissions, because it is really a simple "yes or no" type of scenario.

App permissions have no permissions hierarchy, unlike the user permissions strategy and available security hierarchy within a given site collection.

Apps with Default Permissions

An app that has been provided with default permissions has full control over the app web, as well as access to incoming query string parameters, but does not have default access to the host web. An app with default permissions must include a permission request within its application manifest because the installer actually grants or denies permissions during the installation of the app and will automatically cancel any app install if permissions are denied.

For more information regarding authorization and authentication for apps in SharePoint 2013, refer to the following link: http://msdn.microsoft.com/en-us/library/office/fp142384(v=office.15).aspx

Adding a Permission Request

As mentioned previously, an app must have a permissions request added to its application manifest. You can achieve this by opening the `AppManifest.xml` file in the manifest designer in Visual Studio and adding a permission request for each permission to SharePoint that the web application requires.

For more information as well as code examples on how to add permissions to an application manifest, as well as using the manifest designer, refer to the following link: http://msdn.microsoft.com/en-us/library/office/fp179886(v=office.15).aspx

For more information as well as code examples regarding exploring the app manifest and the package of an app for SharePoint 2013, refer to the following link: http://msdn.microsoft.com/en-us/library/office/fp179918(v=office.15).aspx

The Visual Studio 2013 SDK provides for project templates, tools, tests, and reference assemblies that are required to build extensions for Visual Studio 2013. This can be downloaded at the following link: http://www.microsoft.com/en-us/download/details. aspx?id=40758

Server-to-Server Trust Architecture

The new S2S authentication architecture, as shown in Figure 13.20, enables your organization's infrastructure to share resources between various servers in your SharePoint farm. The S2S Trust also provides for access services to other servers such as those that support your Exchange Server 2013 or Lync Server 2013 platforms.

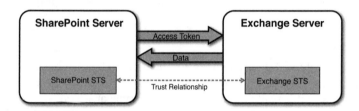

FIGURE 13.20   An overview of the server-to-server authentication architecture.

The S2S authentication protocol does not just support those servers that run your organization's other major "Microsoft application stack" technologies; SharePoint 2013 supports resource sharing and accesses any server within your organization that is compliant with the S2S protocol.

An S2S Trust consists of the following:

▶ Trusted connection between app and SharePoint

▶ OAuth and Access Control Services for on-premises farms

▶ Trust between servers configured using SSL certificates

▶ App code that contains the required access to a private key of an SSL certificate

▶ Creation of a security token service on SharePoint servers

NOTE

For more information on how to plan for server-to-server authentication in SharePoint 2013, refer to the following: http://technet.microsoft.com/en-us/library/ jj219546(v=office.15).aspx

> **TIP**
>
> Azure Access Control Service, which is also referred to as Access Control Service, or ACS, is a Microsoft Azure service that provides an easy way for you to authenticate users to access your web applications and services without having to add complex authentication logic to your code.
>
> The following features are available in ACS:
>
> ▶ Integration with Windows Identity Foundation (WIF)
>
> ▶ Support for Active Directory Federation Services (ADFS) 2.0
>
> ▶ An OData-based management service that provides programmatic access to ACS settings
>
> ▶ Support for popular web identity providers (IPs) including Microsoft accounts (formerly known as Windows Live ID), Google, Yahoo, and Facebook
>
> ▶ A Management Portal that allows administrative access to the ACS settings
>
> For more information about Azure Access Control Service, refer to the following link: http://azure.microsoft.com/en-us/documentation/articles/active-directory-dotnet-how-to-use-access-control/

There are nine overall key steps you must take in the configuration of an S2S trust:

1. Create an x509 certificate.

2. Make the certificate's public key accessible to SharePoint.

3. Utilize Windows PowerShell to create a trusted security token issuer based on public key.

4. Develop a provider-hosted app that has access to the private key file.

5. Create S2S access tokens with the help of the `TokenHelper` class.

6. Pass access token by calling into SharePoint using the CSOM or REST API.

7. Select one of the two available methods to make a certificate available.

8. Pass the file path of the certificate to SharePoint.

9. Expose the certificate from the app as a metadata endpoint.

   For more information on how to configure server-to-server authentication in SharePoint 2013, refer to the following:

   http://technet.microsoft.com/en-us/library/jj219532(v=office.15).aspx

The underlying architecture of an S2S trust contains the following elements and configurations:

▶ To utilize this type of service, you need to generate the set of public and private keys and an X.509 certificate that contains the public/private key pair.

  ▶ The private key is used to sign certain aspects in the access token.

▶ A public key is registered with the SharePoint farm.

   ▶ The public key creates a trusted security token issuer.

▶ The app creates an access token to call into SharePoint, as shown in Figure 13.21.

   ▶ The app creates an access token with a specific client ID and signs it with a private key.

   ▶ A trusted security token issuer validates the signature.

▶ SharePoint establishes the app identity.

   ▶ The app identity maps to a specific client ID.

   ▶ Multiple client IDs can be associated with a single x.509 certificate.

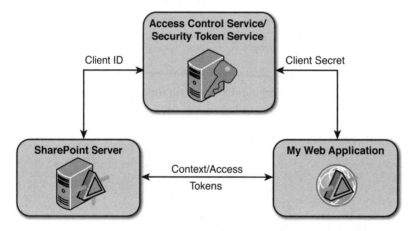

FIGURE 13.21   An overview of a RESTful HTTP request using OData.

TIP

For more on how to create high-trust apps for SharePoint 2013, refer to the following link:
http://msdn.microsoft.com/en-us/library/fp179901.aspx

Development Tools and Related Strategies for Public, Private, and Hybrid Environments

There have been many improvements as well as options added to Visual Studio 2013 to address the new technology releases of SharePoint 2013, Office 365, SharePoint Online, and Microsoft Azure.

As I mentioned in the beginning of this chapter, I highly recommend that your organization's developers have both on-premises and cloud development environment tools available so that they can become familiar with them, and also ensure that compatibility of a future architecture, as shown in Figure 13.22, is taken into consideration.

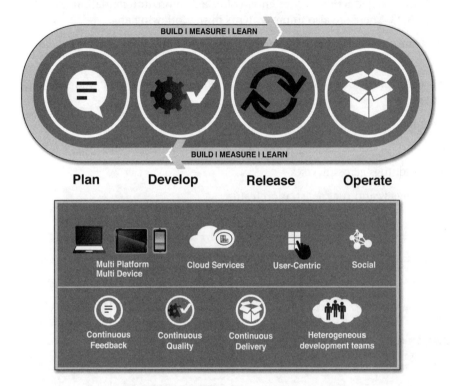

FIGURE 13.22   An overview of a hybrid cloud architecture, as well as a supporting hybrid cloud application development life-cycle strategy.

Visual Studio 2013 and Related Tools and SDK

Visual Studio 2013 is the enterprise development tool that should be used on almost any development initiative because the application life-cycle management as well as code repository integration and new SharePoint 2013 integration features make it the only tool available on the market with its capabilities.

Visual Studio 2013 has four available additions:

- ► Visual Studio Ultimate
- ► Visual Studio Premium
- ► Test Professional
- ► Visual Studio Professional

Visual Studio 2013 Advanced Development Environment
Visual Studio 2013 comes with several user interface improvements, with a more friendly "look and feel," and updated icons with brighter colors and more differentiation, as shown in Figure 13.23. There are also improvements in the following areas:

▸ Improved team explorer home page and pop-out panels for pending changes and builds

▸ CodeLens (also called code information indicators) for greater project awareness and team integration

▸ Scrollbar enhancements with code preview

▸ Peek definition for in-code reference preview

▸ Synchronize settings across devices

▸ Automatic preview and trial registration features

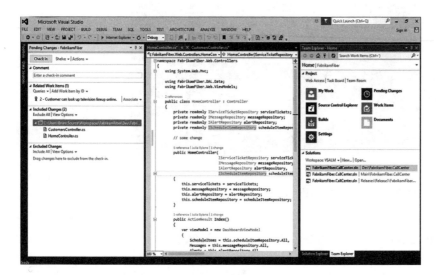

FIGURE 13.23   An overview of Visual Studio 2013's new user interface.

What's New in Visual Studio 2013 and .NET 4.5.1
The new Visual Studio 2013 has focused on three main areas of improved functionality to match that of the new .NET 4.5.1 framework, which are developer productivity, app performance, and continuous innovation, which provide for the following new features and capabilities:

▸ **Developer Productivity**

  ▸ Sixty-four-bit edit and continue

  ▸ Method return value inspection

- ▶ Async debugging enhancements, as shown in Figure 13.24

- ▶ Windows store development improvements

- ▶ ADO.NET connection resiliency

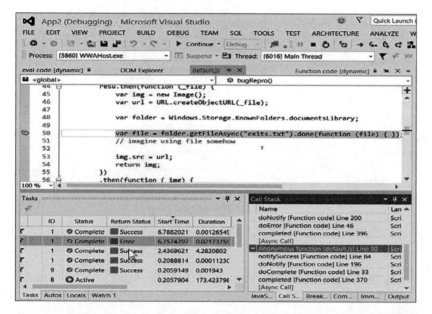

FIGURE 13.24   Visual Studio 2013 performing an Async debugging procedure.

- ▶ **App Performance**

  - ▶ ASP.NET application suspension

  - ▶ Multicore JIT improvements

  - ▶ On-demand large-object heap compaction

  - ▶ Consistent performance before and after servicing the .NET Framework

- ▶ **Continuous Innovation**

  - ▶ Curated .NET Framework NuGet packages

  - ▶ New and enhanced .NET libraries

Application Life-Cycle Management and Visual Studio 2013

The new features in the Visual Studio 2013 release had a strong focus on providing organizations with a way to manage the entire life cycle of the project while being able to
improve team efficiencies with teams and manage backlogs.

The new agile portfolio management capabilities within Team Foundation Server (TFS) are
meant to not only address any backlogs but also shorten the cycle times of new or existing
initiatives. This is meant to lead to reduced risk as well as the associated costs of having to

redesign or rework solutions, as shown in Figure 13.25, because the transparency is much greater from initial requirements gathering all the way through design, development, and UAT.

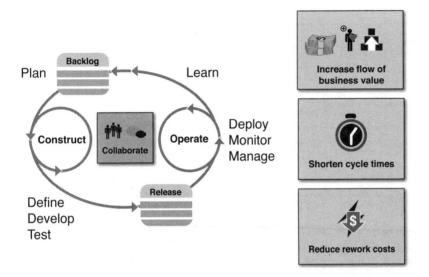

FIGURE 13.25   An overview of the new ALM capabilities and the related goals they are meant to address.

CodeLens

CodeLens is probably one of the best features ever released in Visual Studio. It is almost like having a bit of "artificial intelligence" built in because it can let you know ahead of time whether one small change or update you are about to make will break large amounts of code.

The CodeLens feature can provide you with details about the code that you would never be able to come up with, and it does it on the fly.

This feature, though, has taken a lot of heat regarding its licensing strategy. It is currently available only in Visual Studio Ultimate, which most organizations do not have or really need to purchase. It's a bit of a hidden gem that you may not ever be able to work with, but I am interested to see what the upcoming licensing models will provide for this feature.

You want to make a change to some code, but you're uncertain what else will be affected if you do or whether you'll end up chasing the ripples of your change throughout your entire code base. It's important to know the answer because it affects the size of the work in front of you.

CodeLens, as shown in Figure 13.26, provides a heads-up display with code indicators layered over the code editor for both classes and methods. Another great feature is the history and information that it can provide you about the code, which includes changing sets and authors and automatically providing unit tests for you behind the scenes. It is compatible with C#, Visual Basic, and C++. Keep your eyes open regarding the upcoming licensing changes because I am hopeful that Microsoft will unlock this feature to the masses.

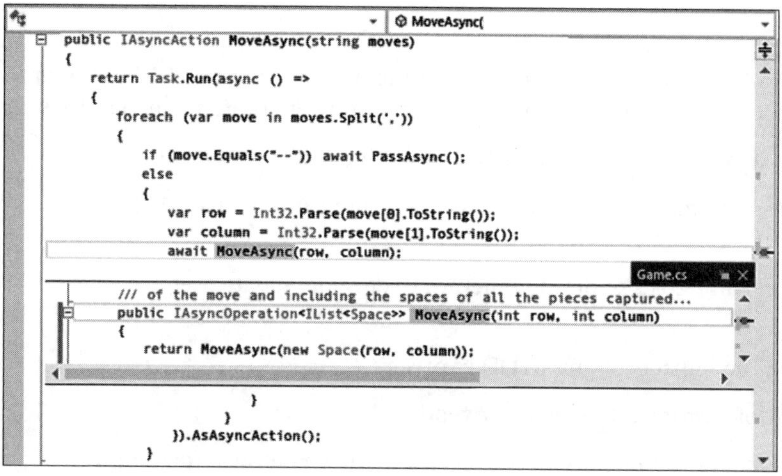

FIGURE 13.26   CodeLens in Visual Studio 2013.

Scrollbar in Visual Studio 2013

There is a new customizable scrollbar feature in Visual Studio 2013, as shown in Figure 13.27, that enables you to click on the vertical scrollbar and then select Scroll Bar Options. At that point, you will see several new areas that can be modified, including an option to turn on annotations.

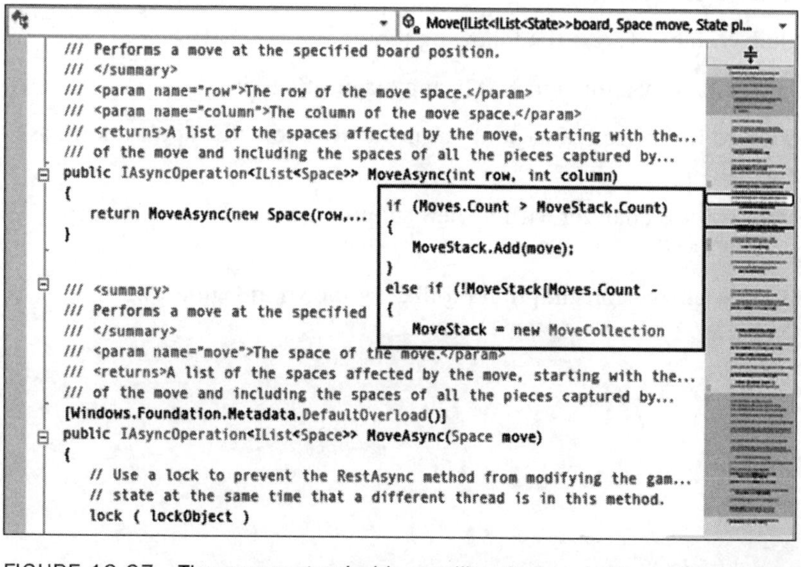

FIGURE 13.27   The new customizable scrollbar feature in Visual Studio 2013.

By turning on annotations, you will be shown special items throughout, as well as break-points and where bookmarks are located. This feature enables you to reveal any syntax errors the editor has identified, which may save you time by enabling you to catch some-thing big or even very small before you compile your code.

Performance and Diagnostics Hub

The Performance and Diagnostic Hub is a new of feature in Visual Studio 2013 that you and your organization could immediately put to work to provide for items such as these:

▶ Baseline understanding of SharePoint 2013/Office 365 usage

▶ Baseline server performance based on any custom applications that utilize the BCS or other APIs to access external data

▶ Gathering SharePoint 2013/Office 365 metrics to develop updated service level agreements

▶ Understanding the impacts of any BYOD efforts

▶ Extranet traffic of customers, partners, or vendors

▶ Performing an audit on your current SharePoint platform before a migration initiative

▶ Understanding the impacts of any cloud initiatives

▶ Gathering data to help the organization make IT roadmaps as well as SharePoint roadmap updates

The new Performance and Diagnostic Hub feature allows for nearly all of Visual Studio's diagnostic tools to be run from one interface and for much easier analysis of various reports due to their being centralized.

Within one single hub, you can access the following tools:

▶ Windows 8.1, HTML, JavaScript, and XAML app diagnostic tools

▶ The various tools to run performance and diagnostic tests for .NET applications, as shown in Figure 13.28

▶ XAML UI responsiveness analyzer with its new support for Windows Store apps implemented with XAML

▶ The HUB app's new energy consumption profiler, as shown in Figure 13.29

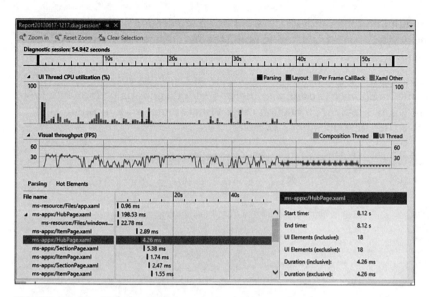

FIGURE 13.28   The new Performance and Diagnostic Hub viewing a recently run diagnostic report.

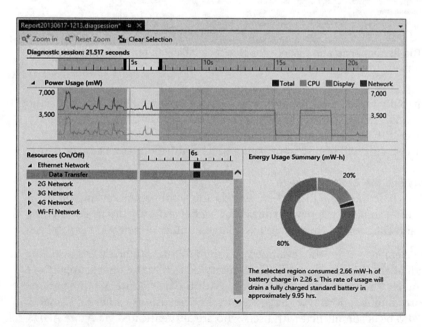

FIGURE 13.29   The energy consumption profiler within the new centralized Performance and Diagnostics Hub.

The energy consumption profiler provides analysis on an application's impact on the battery life of the device, as well as providing estimates on the amount of overall power that will be consumed.

Other new tools provided are the Memory Dump Analysis capability for managed .NET applications and the IntelliTrace performance indicators for diagnosing performance problems, as shown in Figure 13.30, in production using Visual Studio 2013 in conjunction with System Center 2012 R2's Operations Manager.

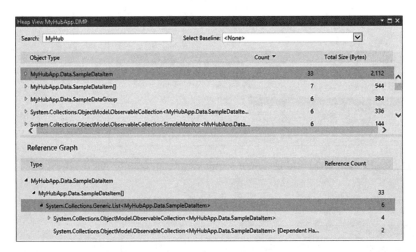

FIGURE 13.30   The Performance and Diagnostics Hub's capability to provide a centralized location to analyze many types of reports at once.

Providing the capability for an administrator and a developer to work together in diagnosing an issue will lead to that issue being resolved in a much faster manner because both the hardware side and the software side can work together and troubleshoot from two different perspectives. This will lead to items being quickly ruled out as a cause or issue.

Revamped Security and the Browser Link
Visual Studio 2013's base has gone through an underlying architectural revamp on its security model to offer some of the new features that we have already discussed, such as the Performance and Diagnostics Hub, as well as a large number of new ALM capabilities.

The most notable element within the revamped security is Visual Studio 2013's available support of individual and Windows authenticated users, as well as the direct support of Microsoft Azure Active Directory enhanced tooling. With the new Azure AD integration, the features, reports, and diagnostics we have seen in the screenshots earlier on Visual Studio 2013 can also be accomplished with users who are authenticated via Azure AHD.

The capabilities for a more open and capable security model also provide enhancements for the Browser Link, which can test applications, sites, and site design performance degradation due to items such as a navigational issue, database or search processing, and user connectivity and throughput.

Developers can set their sights on app design while actually editing HTML or CSS in Visual Studio without any manual refresh or multiple browsers or browser connections. An interesting metric that can be captured by Browser Link in Visual Studio 2013 is the actual optimization for browsers, as well as any variables to feature response time.

For more information on Visual Studio 2013, refer to the following link: http://www.visualstudio.com/en-us/downloads

TIP

To download a trial of Visual Studio 2013, as well as add-ons and related software such as the Microsoft .NET Framework 4.5.1, refer to the following link: http://www.visualstudio.com/en-us/downloads

TIP

The Developer Dashboard in SharePoint 2013 has been improved to provide more information in a more accurate way to track and debug issues with page rendering time. Features include the following:

▶ Running in a separate window to avoid affecting rendering of the actual page

▶ Detailed request information per page with chant view

▶ Dedicated tab for ULS log entries, as shown in Figure 13.31, for a particular request

▶ Additional detailed information included for request analyzing

▶ Turned Off by default but can be enabled (On) or disabled (Off) by using the PowerShell listed next

To enable the Developer Dashboard, use the following Windows PowerShell snippet code:

```
$content = ([Microsoft.SharePoint.Administration.SPWebService]:
:ContentService)
$appsetting =$content.DeveloperDashboardSettings
$appsetting.DisplayLevel =
[Microsoft.SharePoint.Administration.SPDeveloperDashboardLevel]:
:On
$appsetting.Update()
```

13

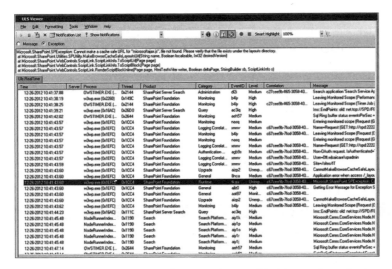

FIGURE 13.31   Reviewing ULS log entries provided for each particular request of the Developer Dashboard in SharePoint 2013.

TIP

To turn on and off reporting services events in the Reporting Services Category, perform the following tasks:

1. From SharePoint Central Administration, click Monitoring.

2. Click Configure Diagnostic Logging in the Reporting group.

3. Find SQL Server Reporting Services in the category list.

4. Click the plus symbol (+) to expand the subcategories under SQL Server Reporting Services.

5. Select the subcategories to be added to the trace log.

6. At the bottom of the categories list, select an event level for the least critical event to report to the trace log. Select None to disable tracing.

TIP

You can use data from the Unified Logging Service (ULS) logs in SharePoint 2013 to troubleshoot issues within the farm. The ULS logs can collect data at varying levels depending on the logging settings. You can use Windows PowerShell to filter the data, display it in various ways, and output the data to a data grid with which you can filter, sort, group, and export data to Excel 2013. For more information regarding the ULS logs, as well the details options and PowerShell cmdlets required, refer to the following link:
http://technet.microsoft.com/en-us/library/ee748656(v=office.15).aspx

Visual Studio Online

To utilize Microsoft's description, "Visual Studio Online, formerly Team Foundation Service is the home for your project data in the cloud. Get up and running in minutes on our cloud infrastructure without having to install or configure a single server. Set up an environment that includes everything from hosted Git repos and project tracking tools, to continuous integration and an IDE, all packaged up in a monthly per-user plan. Connect to your project in the cloud using your favorite development tool, such as Visual Studio, Eclipse, or Xcode."

This service was released for general availability in April of 2014 and the first official pricing was released in May of 2014. I personally think that Microsoft may position Visual Studio Online as a cloud leader in application life-cycle management solutions for organizations that may want to implement a new ALM initiative and that do not feel comfortable taking on that initiative internally and on-premises.

The Visual Studio Online versus Visual Studio 2013 on-premises issue is similar in some ways to the Office 365 and SharePoint Online versus SharePoint 2013 on-premises but without the overtones of compliance and regulatory concerns. I have had several conversations with EPC Group's clients regarding the IT roadmaps and the different options available, and there have been intellectual property concerns regarding placing source code in the cloud.

For some organizations in certain business verticals, their "code" and that IP is everything to them and the core of their business, whereas others have nonsensitive code that is for non-mission-critical business systems.

I would encourage you to sign up for a free trial to test the service even if your organization is traditionally an on-premises–only organization.

Currently, Visual Studio Online, as shown in Figure 13.32, has the following plans available:

▶ **Visual Studio Online Basic**

   For more information on Visual Studio Online Basic, refer to the following link:

   http://www.visualstudio.com/en-us/products/visual-studio-online-basic-vs

▶ **Visual Studio Online Professional**

   For more information on Visual Studio Online Professional, refer to the following link:

   http://www.visualstudio.com/en-us/products/visual-studio-online-professional-vs

▶ **Visual Studio Online Advanced**

   For more information on Visual Studio Online Advanced, refer to the following link:

   http://www.visualstudio.com/en-us/products/visual-studio-online-advanced-vs

	Visual Studio Online			
PRODUCTS EXPLORE DOWNLOADS GET STARTED NEWS SUPPORT				
User Plans Compare Shared Resources				
Compare				
Categories and capabilities	Visual Studio Online Advanced	Visual Studio Online Professional	Visual Studio Online Basic	Visual Studio Premium with MSDN
Maximum number of users with this plan on an account	Unlimited	10 users	Unlimited	Unlimited
Unlimited team projects and private, hosted code repos using TFVC or Git	■	■	■	■
Project planning and bug tracking tools, including Kanban boards and team velocity forecasts	■	■	■	■
Integration with popular development tools, including Visual Studio, Eclipse, and Xcode	■	■	■	■
Work in one IDE to create solutions for the web, desktop, cloud, server, and phone		■		■
Support for Office 365 business apps		■		■
Track complex projects with hierarchical portfolio backlogs	■			■
Visualize project data with work item chart authoring	■			■
Discuss projects with teammates and monitor project events in Team Rooms	■			■
Send feedback requests to users and stakeholders	■			■

FIGURE 13.32   An overview of the current available plans on Visual Studio Online, as well as their related offerings and capabilities.

SharePoint Designer 2013 Introduction

SharePoint Designer 2013 is a free download from Microsoft. In previous versions it had been a tool that was tightly integrated with SharePoint (SharePoint 2010 and SharePoint 2007) for updating the user interface, as well as creating "light to mid-level" development and customization requests and quickly turning them around into a workable and tailored SharePoint 2010 or SharePoint 2007 solution.

SharePoint Designer 2013's main role in SharePoint 2013 revolves around the creation of custom workflows and the related automating of business processes. SharePoint Designer 2013 is not compatible with OAuth. With the OAuth protocol becoming so key and integrated into SharePoint 2013, Office 365, SharePoint Online, and Microsoft Azure, SharePoint Designer 2013 has been taken "out of the game" and should now be mainly used for workflow development and related BPM (business process automation).

TIP

SharePoint Designer 2013 is a free download that can be accessed at the following link: http://www.microsoft.com/en-us/download/details.aspx?id=35491

It is also important to note that the Design View that existed in SharePoint Designer 2010 has been removed in this latest release.

Visual Studio is the tool you should use as your organization's governed and standardized core development platform due to the architecture changes that have been introduced in the on-premises and cloud technologies of SharePoint 2013, Office 365, SharePoint Online, and Microsoft Azure. This is underlined even more with the release of the Office 365 API Tools because SharePoint Designer 2013 can no longer provide the capabilities or even access the areas it could in past version releases.

Microsoft Azure Development and SDK

Microsoft Azure currently has four main groupings related to their features and services:

▶ Infrastructure Services

▶ Develop Modern Applications

▶ Insights from Data

▶ Identity and Access Management

NOTE

Microsoft Azure has a documentation library available, as shown in Figure 13.33, to help answer questions, as well as to review the frequent updates published on its structure and underlying security model along with cloud compliance and regulatory concerns.

FIGURE 13.33   An overview of the documentation center available on Microsoft Azure.

These four main groupings related to their features and services are then broken down further, as shown in Figure 13.34, to provide an overview of the additional offerings:

- ▶ Infrastructure Services
    - ▶ Virtual Machines
    - ▶ Storage, Backup, and Recovery
    - ▶ Big Compute
- ▶ Develop Modern Applications
    - ▶ Web
    - ▶ Mobile
    - ▶ Media
    - ▶ Integration
    - ▶ Dev-Test
- ▶ Insights from Data
    - ▶ SQL Databases
    - ▶ HDInsight
- ▶ Identity and Access Management
    - ▶ Active Directory
    - ▶ Multifactor Authentication

To obtain a free trial subscription of Microsoft Azure, refer to the following link: http://azure.microsoft.com/en-us/pricing/free-trial

To download the Microsoft Azure SDK and available command-line tools, as shown in Figure 13.35, refer to the following link: http://azure.microsoft.com/en-us/downloads/

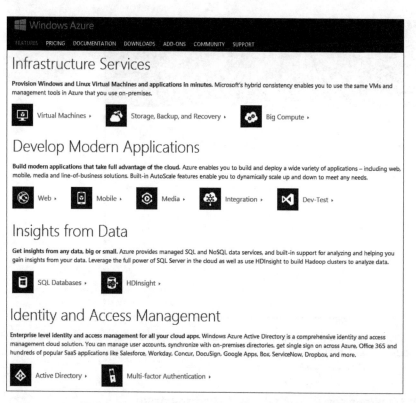

FIGURE 13.34   An overview of the available Offerings and Features of Microsoft Azure.

When you are reviewing your organization's development requirements and the resources you may currently have on-premises, as well as those that you may be reviewing in the cloud, it is key to have a clear understanding of what the disaster recovery architecture model would entail along with the published SLAs from the provider. A high-level overview of Microsoft Azure's DR architecture is shown in Figure 13.36.

13

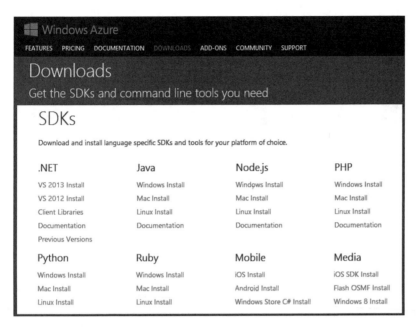

FIGURE 13.35   Microsoft Azure's available downloads to obtain the latest SDK, as well as any available command-line tools that you may require.

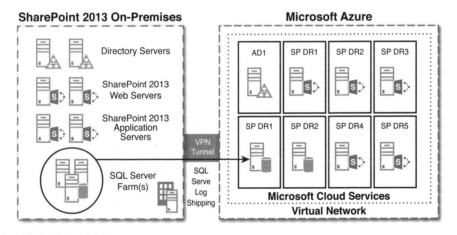

FIGURE 13.36   Microsoft Azure's disaster recovery architecture.

In Microsoft Azure, there is a 99.95% service level agreement (SLA) for extranet connectivity, which is really the industry standard across the board. Microsoft Azure's latest SLA can be found at the following link: http://azure.microsoft.com/en-us/support/legal/sla/

This SLA covers the actual hardware along with the datacenter, network, and any power grid failure, as well as hardware upgrades and related software maintenance in their datacenter(s). The two elements that are not covered are VM container crashes and guest OS updates.

When you review your organization's overall approach to development, as well as the actual hosting and provider selection, it is key to start from the disaster recovery metrics and SLAs and then work your way back through your specific requirements. This is a completely different way of thinking than that of the past, but this is the new approach in discussions of cloud and hybrid cloud initiatives.

Team Foundation Server and Code Management

The following sections review the latest updates in Visual Studio 2013's Team Foundation Server. This service provides the capability to build, test, and manage your repositories and processes during and after a development initiative.

The latest information on this new release of TFS in Visual Studio 2013 can be found at the following link: http://www.visualstudio.com/en-us/products/tfs-overview-vs.aspx

Release Management Process

TFS's release management process, as shown in Figure 13.37, in the latest release is made up of a comprehensive deployment solution for .NET teams. Just as with the Visual Studio 2013 development tools covered in earlier sections, TFS has taken advantage of the new release analytics and reporting capabilities of the updated underlying framework and security model.

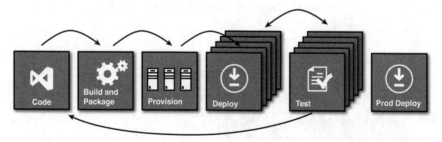

FIGURE 13.37   An overview of TFS's release management process and its focus on consistency.

TFS's Release Management Client for Visual Studio 2013 is available in the three following licensing models:

▶ Visual Studio Test Professional

▶ Visual Studio Premium

▶ Visual Studio Ultimate

At a high level, the Release Management feature provides for and performs three core things:

▶ Automates deployments directly from TFS to all the environments, including production. Part of the deployment procedure may include things like taking backups, generating test data, provisioning Servers on Azure, or executing your auto-mated tests. Basically everything you need in order to start working on a given stage.

▶ Ensures that all deployments are done the same way from the same binaries so that by the time you deploy your application to production, your deployment proce-dure has been tested over and over, removing a lot of those release-related risks and headaches.

▶ Automates the approval workflow through all the environments, reducing delays and coordination issues to a minimum. Testers receive a notification when a new version is ready for them, so they can either confirm that the application meets the stage requirements or stop the release of that specific version. Along the way, Release Management provides tracking of each attempted release.

The Release Management Server automates all the manual tasks involved in releasing applications and puts them into its process editor for deployment. There are optional configurations for your specific needs, but the centralized approved deployment process, end-to-end, which is repeatable and traceable, as depicted in Figure 13.38, is at its core.

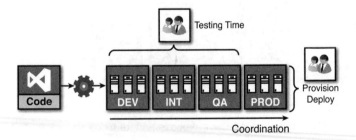

FIGURE 13.38   Implementing the Release Management Server to provide an approved, repeatable, and traceable process.

Microsoft InfoPath 2013

Microsoft has announced that Microsoft InfoPath 2013 will be the last release of InfoPath and that they will be releasing a new forms solution sometime around mid-to-late 2014 or early 2015.

TIP

The press release regarding InfoPath 2013 being the last version of InfoPath to be released states, "In an effort to streamline our investments and deliver a more integrated Office forms user experience, we're retiring InfoPath and investing in new forms technology across SharePoint, Access, and Word. This means that InfoPath 2013 is the last release of the desktop client, and InfoPath Forms Services in SharePoint Server 2013 is the last release of InfoPath Forms Services. The InfoPath Forms Services technology within Office 365 will be maintained and it will function until further notice.

If you're an InfoPath customer, we want to reassure you that we're working on migration guidance in parallel as we're building our next generation of forms technology. Until we have more detailed technology roadmap and guidance to share with you, we encourage you to continue using InfoPath tools. We also want to remind you that the InfoPath 2013 desktop client and InfoPath Forms Services for SharePoint Server 2013 will continue to be supported through 2023 as part of our Lifecycle support policy."

The official press release from Microsoft can be found at the following link: http://blogs.office.com/2014/01/31/update-on-infopath-and-sharepoint-forms/

Windows PowerShell

Windows PowerShell is covered in great detail in Chapter 15, "Administration and Maintenance Strategies." PowerShell is an administrative tool that provides great value in maintaining and administrating a SharePoint 2013 implementation but does not provide for custom development.

There are several references to Windows PowerShell throughout this chapter's content and related references, but in each case it is to perform an administrative-type task such as starting an underlying SharePoint 2013 service so that other services can then consume that service or related data set.

Developing Workflows in SharePoint 2013, Office 365, and SharePoint Online

There has been a complete update to SharePoint 2013's workflow capabilities and overall workflow architecture, as shown in Figure 13.39, with new features as well as the underlying workflow engine itself receiving a major overhaul. The workflows in SharePoint 2013 run within Workflow Manager by services, processes, and logic received from SharePoint 2013. This means these processes that have been moved to Workflow Manager no longer have to run in the SharePoint 2013 content farm and can utilize separate server resources and is decoupled (i.e., now runs independently) from SharePoint 2013 to also support other platforms.

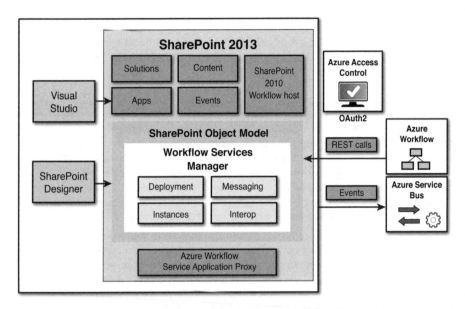

FIGURE 13.39   An overview of the new SharePoint 2013 workflow architecture with the added workflow execution now used in the Microsoft Azure Workflow (WAW).

Some of the driving factors of these changes had to do with being able to provide a workflow solution to SharePoint 2013 users that would be able to function in an independent manner and bypass any possible performance or scalability limits of SharePoint with on-premises, cloud, and hybrid cloud in mind.

Workflow Manager has a new infrastructure, built on Windows Workflow Foundation 4.5 (WF 4.5), and is a fully declarative authoring environment that gives your organization's information workers the ability to use tools such as SharePoint Designer 2013 and Visio 2013 to ensure the creation of workflows in a very visual and "swim lane" diagram-type manner, as shown in Figure 13.40. There is a new set of Visual Studio 2013 workflow project templates for developers to craft very complex workflows with custom actions and capabilities to provide enterprise-level workflows to the masses.

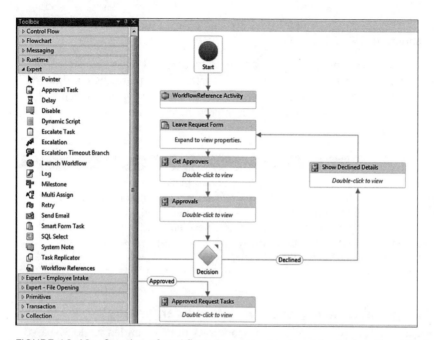

FIGURE 13.40   Creation of workflows in a very visual and "swim lane" architected type manner.

TIP

Workflow Manager is a separate download and must be configured to communicate with the SharePoint Server 2013 farm. To download Workflow Manager, refer to the following page and the different options it provides: http://technet.microsoft.com/en-us/library/jj193525.aspx

---

NOTE

InfoPath also supports elements of SharePoint 2013 workflow, but with Microsoft phasing InfoPath, I would not recommend using InfoPath for this or any other custom development requirement in SharePoint.

To ensure a seamless experience across both on-premises and cloud-based environments, Workflow Manager integrates with the new SharePoint 2013 app model, which enables workflows to reside in SharePoint 2013, Office 365, SharePoint Online, and Microsoft Azure.

The integration with the SharePoint 2013 app model enables organizations to use the APIs, web services, and design templates covered earlier in this chapter. This has enabled developers to create "workflow-specific apps" for the automation of very common manual processes within the organization, which I have seen provide an instant boost to overall SharePoint user adoption.

Microsoft put a great deal of time into creating an extremely useful free video series regarding a wide array of key workflow topics, such as architecture planning configuration, installation, custom development, and information worker training, which can be found at the following link: http://technet.microsoft.com/en-us/library/dn201724(v=office.15).aspx

> **TIP**
>
> If your organization has legacy SharePoint 2010 workflows that need to be utilized within the SharePoint 2013, you should refer to the SharePoint workflow Interop. This feature is a "bridge" between the two platforms that may meet your needs and save you from having to redesign a workflow that may be able to rely on this new feature. For more information on the SharePoint workflow Interop, refer to the following link: http://msdn.microsoft.com/en-us/library/office/jj670125(v=office.15).aspx

Workflow Manager and New Workflow-Related Terminology

Workflow Manager, built on WF 4.5, allows for workflows to be extended via REST-based web services and is multitenant capable, which is key to the capability to service not only SharePoint 2013 but also Office 365, SharePoint Online, and Microsoft Azure. The Microsoft Azure service bus, as shown in Figure 13.41, provides for the hosted and widely available infrastructure to allow for the massive communication elements, as shown in Figure 13.42, required for workflows that have large-scale event distribution and service publishing. The service bus provides for the available connectivity options for Windows Communication Foundation and other service endpoints.

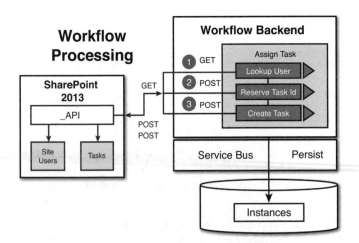

FIGURE 13.41   A high-level overview of a workflow that is processing and connecting to external locations.

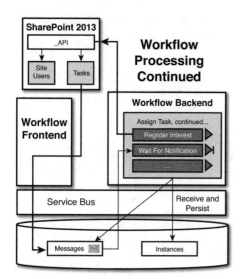

FIGURE 13.42   An overview of the massive communication elements and large-scale event capabilities of SharePoint 2013 workflows.

A lot of specific technical terms are used with the new Workflow Manager and the new overall architecture of SharePoint 2013 workflows that you will need to understand. These terms will come up in technical conversations with IT and with the business, and they can become a bit confusing and sometimes seem to overlap each other.

The following lists the key business and technical features in Workflow Manager provides for the following workflows capabilities:

▶ Fully declarative workflows

▶ High density and multitenancy capable workflows

▶ Workflow artifact management

▶ Tracking and monitoring of workflows and their related events

▶ Provides for instance management

▶ Provides for expressive workflows

▶ Visual designer capable workflows that can be structured in Visio 2013 and/or SharePoint Designer 2013

Understanding Custom Actions and Activities in Workflows
Custom workflow actions are reusable workflow steps that run within Workflow Manager via the SharePoint REST API and are compatible with Visual Studio 2013 as well as SharePoint Designer 2013. They are used at different levels within a "copy," department, or functional unit for interacting with the Workflow Manager. These "wrapper objects" encase the underlying activities in a format that can be modified via SharePoint Designer.

Custom workflow activities are "objects" of custom code that handle the method calls to the underlying APIs and web services that drive workflow behaviors and allow for the inclusion of business logic in code.

For more information on custom actions and activities references in SharePoint 2013, refer to the following link: http://msdn.microsoft.com/en-us/library/office/jj163867(v=office.15).aspx

Configuring Workflow Manager

When you approach the installation and configuration of Workflow Manager, you will first want to ensure that your environment has the underlying prerequisites installed:

▶ .NET Framework 4.5

▶ Service Bus 1.0

▶ Workflow Client 1.0

▶ PowerShell 3.0

Workflow Manager must be installed on a support platform configuration that contains the following:

▶ Windows Server 2012 x64 or Windows Server 2008 R2 SP1 x64

▶ SQL Server 2012/2014 or SQL Server 2008 R2 SP1

TIP

SQL Server can be installed on the same physical server with Workflow 1.0 and Service Bus as well as on a separate server. The Service Bus databases can reside on multiple machines and do not require a single database to be created.

When you download the installation files and then start the install, there is a web platform installer that automatically checks for these prerequisites and installs them so that you do not need to install them separately. You can begin the installation by obtaining the required files, which includes the web platform installer, at the following link: http://technet.microsoft.com/en-us/library/jj193448.aspx

NOTE

Before you execute the installation, you must ensure that you have the proper system requirements, available accounts, and related appropriate permissions in place, as well as the underlying network ports/connection open on the firewall. To ensure that you have these system configurations in place before executing the installation, refer to the following link to verify the underlying system architecture's readiness: http://technet.microsoft.com/en-us/library/jj193451.aspx

TIP

You also can perform an offline installation of Workflow Manager if the machine does not have Internet access or you may be building a VM instance that can be performed by following the steps listed at this link: http://technet.microsoft.com/en-us/library/jj906604.aspx

After you have the system requirements in place, as mentioned previously, you can perform the installation and configuration of Workflow Manager.

After the web platform installer has finished installing Workflow Manager, the Workflow Manager Configuration Wizard automatically loads to enable you to specify the granular elements of your environment.

NOTE

You also have the option to configure Workflow Manager using Windows PowerShell. For more information on using PowerShell for the configuration, refer to the following link: http://technet.microsoft.com/en-us/library/jj193506.aspx

Configuring SharePoint 2013 with the New Workflow Manager Configuration

After you have installed and configured Workflow Manager, you can configure your SharePoint environment to this underlying workflow component. You must use the fully qualified domain name (FQDN) site URL of the workflow farm along with the specified port number while configuring SharePoint.

The following contains the overview of the steps:

1. Create a new site collection before starting the configuration.

2. If you installed Workflow Manager on another server or server clusters, as shown in Figure 13.43, you must also install and configure the Workflow Client on the actual SharePoint server, because this is required to register the workflow service successfully. For more information on installing the Workflow Client, refer to the following link:

   http://technet.microsoft.com/en-us/library/jj658562.aspx

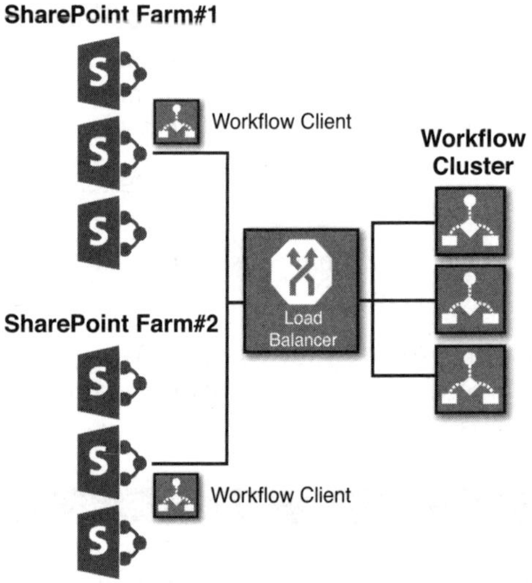

SharePoint Farm#1

FIGURE 13.43   An overview of the Workflow Manager being installed within a separate server farm.

NOTE

You will also need to install the Workflow Manager Tools 1.0 for Visual Studio. You can find more information on this by referring to the following link: http://technet.microsoft.com/en-us/library/jj658562.aspx#WFToolsInstallation

---

3. You will then need to "pair" the installations of Workflow Manager with SharePoint 2013 by using a PowerShell cmdlet as follows:

    `Register-SPWorkflowService`

    For more information on the `Register-SPWorkflowService` "pairing" via PowerShell, refer to the following link:

    http://msdn.microsoft.com/en-us/library/office/dn411563(v=office.15).aspx

4. It is also key to ensure that you have properly configured outgoing email for your SharePoint 2013 farm so that you can use the Send Email action in workflow. For more information regarding how to configure outgoing email for a SharePoint 2013 farm, refer to the following link:

    http://technet.microsoft.com/en-us/library/cc263462.aspx

TIP

You can monitor your organization's workflow farm after Workflow Manager is installed and users have started the processing workflows within the SharePoint 2013 environment by using System Center Operations Manager Workflow Management Pack. This is a fantastic tool to monitor and ensure that your workflow configuration is stable and supporting your user base. More information on the System Center Operations Manager Workflow Management Pack can be found at the following link: http://www.microsoft.com/en-us/download/details.aspx?id=35384

Available Authoring Tools for Workflows in SharePoint 2013

The redesigned architecture of SharePoint 2013's workflows also coincides with a new set of related authoring tools to design, create, and develop workflows for your organization. The three main tools for authoring SharePoint 2013 workflows are SharePoint Designer 2013, Visio 2013, and Visual Studio 2013.

The following section provides an overview of each of these tools as well as the related recommended usage of them within your organization to ensure that your workflows are "enterprise ready" regardless of whether your organization is 50 or 50,000 users. The workflow capabilities of SharePoint 2013 are one of the most high-profile and "advertised" features of this new release, so it is important that you develop, build, and deploy your workflows in a manner which ensures that they are properly tested before "going live" to your user base.

SharePoint Designer 2013's Workflow Capabilities

SharePoint Designer 2013 is not a tool whose mission and capabilities are centered on the design of SharePoint's UI or geared to perform "low to medium" customizations for lists and libraries, but instead it has reemerged as a powerful workflow tool with integrated capabilities for the new workflow architecture.

SharePoint Designer 2013 now has a visual experience that uses a Visio 2013 add-in to allow for a "swim line" diagram type of workflow development and a new action that enables no-code web service calls from within a workflow in which RESTful web services are supported, as shown in Figure 13.44.

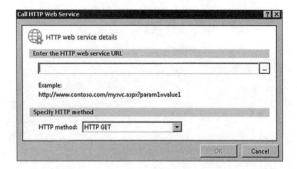

FIGURE 13.44   SharePoint Designer 2013 allows for no-code web service calls.

Some other new features of SharePoint Designer 2013 are listed here:

▶ Support of authoring 2010 and 2013 workflows that provide you with the option to select the platform on which you want to build a workflow, as shown in Figure 13.45

▶ New actions for creating a task and starting a task process

▶ State Machine for workflows for states and conditions

▶ Nested conditions that enable the representation of a complex business processes to be performed more easily

▶ Looping feature that enables you to loop a specific number of times between stages or actions, as shown in Figure 13.46

▶ Impersonation feature to enable an action to execute with higher-level access

▶ A new Dictionary data type used for storing name-value pairs

▶ New workflow building blocks such as Stage, Loop, and App Step, which enable a workflow author to group a number of individual actions and conditions as a single unit

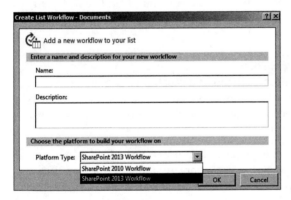

FIGURE 13.45   SharePoint Designer 2013 provides the option to select the platform on which you want to build a workflow.

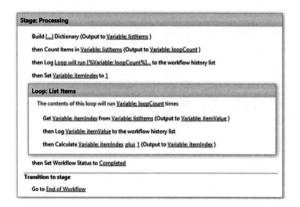

FIGURE 13.46   SharePoint Designer 2013's looping feature that enables you to loop a specific number of times between stages or actions.

TIP

For a quick reference to workflow actions in the SharePoint 2013 Workflow platform that can be utilized by SharePoint Designer 2013, refer to the following link: http://technet. microsoft.com/en-us/library/jj164026(v=office.15).aspx

---

TIP

For more information on workflow development in SharePoint Designer 2013, as well as design example and scenarios, refer to the following link: http://technet.microsoft.com/ en-us/library/jj163272(v=office.15).aspx

---

Visio 2013's Workflow Capabilities

You can utilize Visio 2013 to create workflows in a manner that allows for a clear visual view into the workflow that you are creating by utilizing its shapes. Visio 2013 is really an "initial design point" for information workers who do not have programming backgrounds to design a visual workflow, via these Visio 2013 shapes, and then export it to SharePoint Designer 2013, which then converts shapes to activities before publishing the workflow to a site.

Visio 2013 comes with a SharePoint 2013 Workflow template, as shown in Figure 13.47, that you can utilize to design SharePoint 2013 workflows. This template contains a SharePoint 2013 Workflow Actions stencil, and SharePoint 2013 Workflow Conditions and SharePoint Workflow Terminators stencils.

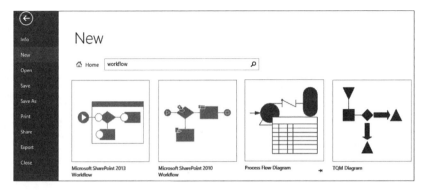

FIGURE 13.47   Visio 2013's SharePoint 2013 Workflow template.

These three stencils contain shapes that correspond to specific actions and conditions you can use to build a new SharePoint 2013 workflow in a "drag and drop" manner onto Visio's drawing canvas, as shown in Figure 13.48.

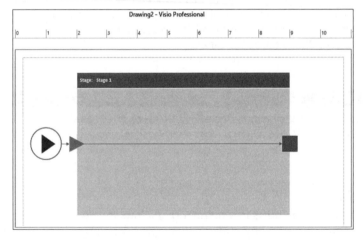

FIGURE 13.48   A newly created SharePoint 2013 Visio Workflow template and its initial blank canvas.

TIP

For more information on workflow development in Visio 2013, as well as design example and scenarios, refer to the following link: http://technet.microsoft.com/en-us/library/jj163272(v=office.15).aspx

For more information on the shapes in the SharePoint Server 2013 workflow template in Visio 2013, refer to the following link: http://technet.microsoft.com/en-us/library/jj164055(v=office.15).aspx

Visual Studio 2013 and Custom Workflow Development

Visual Studio 2013 can be utilized for the creation of complex and enterprise workflow solutions that use web services, custom actions, and all the capabilities provided by the SharePoint 2013 workflow object model. The SharePoint 2013 workflow object model is built on the .NET Framework 4.5 object model for Windows Workflow Foundation 4 and provides four major workflow services:

▶ Instance management service, which manages workflow instances and their execution

▶ Deployment service, which manages the deployment of workflow definitions

▶ Interop service, which manages the Interop bridge for supporting legacy workflows (e.g., SharePoint 2010 workflows)

▶ Messaging service, which manages message queuing and transport

The workflow object model provides an ideal approach for requirements such as the development of the following:

▶ Alternate workflow user interface requirements

▶ Mobile workflow experiences for cross-browser and cross-device (device-agnostic) compatibility

▶ Management of workflow to align with apps

▶ Requirements of additional custom tools or third-party add-ons or related features

The SharePoint workflow object model contains the following namespaces containing both SharePoint namespaces as well as Microsoft Office namespaces:

▶ Microsoft.SharePoint namespaces

    ▶ Microsoft.SharePoint.Workflow

    ▶ Microsoft.SharePoint.Workflow.Application

    ▶ Microsoft.SharePoint.WorkflowActions

    ▶ Microsoft.SharePoint.WorkflowActions.WithKey

    ▶ Microsoft.SharePoint.WorkflowServices

    ▶ Microsoft.SharePoint.WorkflowServices.Activities

▶ Microsoft.Office namespaces

    ▶ Microsoft.Office.Workflow

    ▶ Microsoft.Office.Workflow.Actions

    ▶ Microsoft.Office.Workflow.Feature

13

▶ Microsoft.Office.Workflow.Routing

▶ Microsoft.Office.Workflow.Utility

Visual Studio 2013 contains templates for building workflow-specific apps, as shown in Figure 13.49, and then provides options within Visual Studio's Solution Explorer to add new SharePoint components such as lists or libraries.

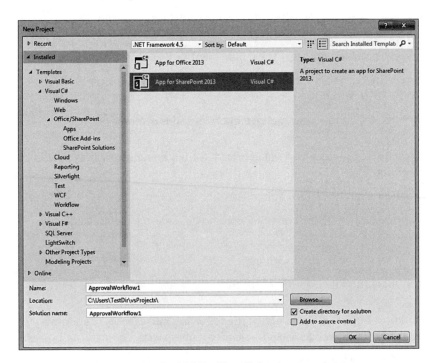

FIGURE 13.49   Visual Studio 2013's SharePoint App template.

For example, if you were to select the option to Add and then select New Items and choose List, the SharePoint Customization Wizard would load, as shown in Figure 13.50. Here, you can provide additional granular details regarding a list or library to which the new custom app's workflow would be applied.

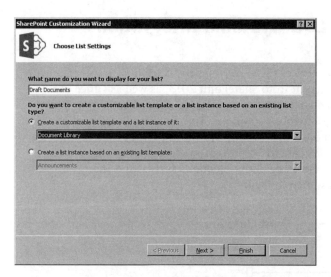

FIGURE 13.50   SharePoint Customization Wizard within Visual Studio 2013.

For more information on how to create a SharePoint workflow app using Visual Studio 2012/2013, refer to the following link: http://msdn.microsoft.com/en-us/library/office/dn456545(v=office.15).aspx

> **TIP**
>
> For more information on working with web services in SharePoint 2013 Workflows using Visual Studio 2012/2013, refer to the following link: http://msdn.microsoft.com/en-us/library/office/dn532193(v=office.15).aspx

Visual Studio 2013 also has an updated visual workflow designer surface that lets you create custom workflows, forms, templates, and custom workflow activities, all within the enhanced designer environment. SharePoint workflows developed in Visual Studio 2013 are packaged and deployed as SharePoint features and are no longer compiled and deployed as .NET Framework assemblies.

With Microsoft's press release regarding InfoPath 2013 being the last version of InfoPath it will release, Visual Studio 2013 no longer uses InfoPath forms and now relies on ASP.NET forms for users, which will ensure scalability, as well as cross-platform and cross-tenant compatibility.

> **TIP**
>
> For more information on working with tasks in SharePoint 2013 workflows using Visual Studio 2012/2013, refer to the following link: http://msdn.microsoft.com/en-us/library/office/dn551366(v=office.15).aspx

BCS, External, and LOB Systems Integration Strategies

SharePoint Business Connectivity Services (BCS) provides the capability to integrate with data that is stored outside of SharePoint in to SharePoint 2013, as well as Office 365 and Microsoft solutions. The BCS enables data to be integrated into SharePoint, Office 365, SharePoint Online, and other Microsoft solutions. This database been integrated in reports, lists, as well as in other areas of your organization's BI initiatives. SharePoint 2013's search can integrate with BCS data in order to provide your users with search results from data across the enterprise using native elements such as the SharePoint 2013 search's connector framework, as shown in Figure 13.51.

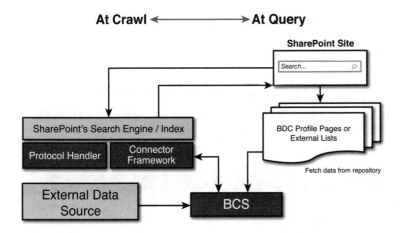

FIGURE 13.51   An overview of SharePoint 2013 search's connector framework and its integration with the BCS.

The BCS's updated capabilities allow for data to be viewed as well as updated from external report systems in a "push/pull" scenario.

The capability to provide for a centralized infrastructure for managing connections to external sources is key to not only ensuring security but also managing performance, resource, and scalability elements.

> **NOTE**
>
> For more information on the BCS client object model reference for SharePoint 2013, refer to the following:
> http://msdn.microsoft.com/en-us/library/office/jj164116(v=office.15).aspx

With SharePoint 2013's UI being the common interface for accessing all remote or LOB data sources, you can apply branding as well as governance with SharePoint for the "one-stop shop" scenario. Your organization may have data in SAP or Oracle, but you more than likely want to use SharePoint 2013's interface as the centralized UI to provide key reports from these systems as well as from SharePoint. A large number of organizations have implemented the SQL Server Reporting Services (SSRS) framework, as shown in Figure 13.52, in the past to pull in data from their SQL Server environments to integrate with SharePoint, but the available data source does not have to stop at being only SQL Server.

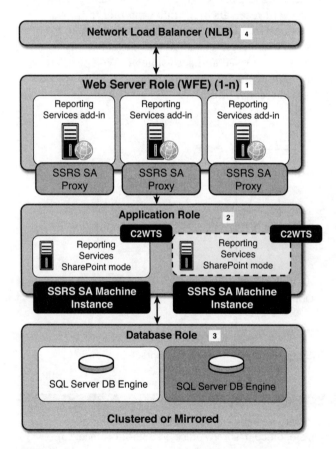

FIGURE 13.52   SQL Server Reporting Services architecture overview.

The BCS provides for the management of authentication to external systems and can also index data in external systems for searching through SharePoint 2013 while being able to still "security trim" search results to only users with access to "their specific data."

There has also been a major update in the BCS being compatible with the cloud and hybrid cloud to be able to provide support for the notification of events in external systems, as well as the inclusion of BCS support in apps.

Office 365 supports both WCF and OData-based BCS entities, which are the most scalable approach and architecture for systems that are on separate environments and accessed via HTTP or HTTPS. Office 365 also supports the secure store service, and the BCS and secure store are managed at a tenant level that will meet your scalability as well as hybrid cloud federated security requirements for any future initiatives.

BCS and External Events

SharePoint 2013 adds a model for subscribing to events triggered in external systems; you can develop custom code for these event receivers in a similar manner to how a SharePoint event receiver would be developed. With the capability to subscribe to events triggered in external systems with custom event receivers, as well as the capability to access applications and data sources that are exposed and accessible via WCF services as well as OData endpoints, as shown in Figure 13.53, you now have the ability to take almost any BI, reporting, or enterprise-wide search initiative.

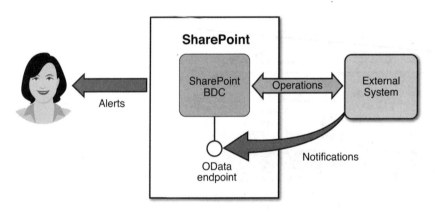

FIGURE 13.53   An overview of the BCS connecting with external events.

NOTE

For more information on how to use OData sources with the BCS in SharePoint 2013, refer to the following: http://msdn.microsoft.com/library/office/jj163802(v=office.15)

SharePoint 2013 apps can include external content type definitions and the accompanying BCS models within them, although they are limited to one per app, and you should keep in mind that the OData connector is the only connector allowed for this type of connection.

> **NOTE**
>
> For more information on the BCS REST API reference for SharePoint 2013, refer to the following link: http://msdn.microsoft.com/en-us/library/office/jj163227(v=office.15).aspx

The BCS and OData

There are several factors to keep in mind when planning the use of OData with the BCS:

- ▶ OData is an available source in Visual Studio but is not available in SharePoint Designer 2013.

- ▶ OData provides the capability for a lighter payload of data, which benefits underlying network latency, as well as the public cloud, hybrid cloud, and mobile initiatives.

- ▶ An OData feed can be created via a WCF data service as well as via a WebAPI.

Summary

This chapter covered the full spectrum of SharePoint 2013, Office 365, and SharePoint Online and Azure development. We reviewed strategies for how best to prepare for development in on-premises, cloud, and hybrid cloud scenarios, and we also reviewed SharePoint 2013's new app model and the APIs, including the new Office 365 API Tools, that you have at your disposal within the overall development framework.

We discussed the security and identity management considerations your organization should keep in mind now for current initiatives but also for future scalability and to support multiple tenants.

We also discussed the different tools available for you to perform custom development, and provided a deep dive into workflow development best practices and business process automation. We then finished the chapter by discussing the BCS and gaining secure and seamless access to external data sources.

In the next chapter, we will discuss SharePoint 2013's search best practices, web content management (WCM), branding, and related navigational strategies for your organization.

CHAPTER 14

Search, Web Content Management, Branding, and Navigational Strategies

In this chapter, we will focus on some of the more "sexy" features of SharePoint 2013, Office 365, and SharePoint Online to include industry-leading search capabilities, as well as how to leverage web content management (WCM) and branding features to increase user adoption and "wow" your end users.

In Chapter 10, "Enterprise Content Management (ECM), Records Management (RM), and eDiscovery Best Practices," we covered the terms related to metadata, content types, and the term store, as well as other core underlying content management capabilities.

This chapter will help you to continue to bring all the major elements together while "popping the hood" on new and more granular configurations to help you maximize your SharePoint 2013, Office 365, and/or SharePoint Online investment and ensure its long-term success while opening users' eyes to new possibilities for these additional capabilities. Search in SharePoint 2013 now brings together the core search capabilities that were available previously in SharePoint 2010's Search as well as FAST Search for SharePoint 2010 into a single engine architecture, as referenced in Figure 14.1, called SharePoint 2013 Search.

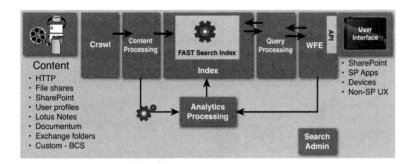

FIGURE 14.1   SharePoint 2013's Search architecture.

It is important to note that there are different limitations that can be set regarding SharePoint Server 2013 on-premises versus an Office 365 or SharePoint Online deployment. This topic is covered in later sections of this chapter, but for information regarding limits to SharePoint Online search, refer to the following link: http://office.microsoft.com/en-us/sharepoint-help/search-limits-for-sharepoint-online-HA104141011.aspx?CTT=1

Overview of Search in SharePoint 2013, Office 365, and SharePoint Online

There are key service applications and services that power SharePoint's search to enable your organization's data to easily be found on-demand as well to enable the accuracy of your search results.

SharePoint 2013's Search applications and related services are as listed here:

▶ SharePoint Server Search service

   This service is responsible for crawling content, as shown in Figure 14.2, on your organization's search index and is automatically started on all servers that run search topology components. This service is unique because it cannot be stopped or started from the Services on Server page. For more information regarding the PowerShell cmdlets in relation to the SharePoint Server Search service, refer to "Start-SPEnterpriseSearchServiceInstance," which can be found at the following link:

   http://technet.microsoft.com/en-us/library/ff607852(v=office.15).aspx

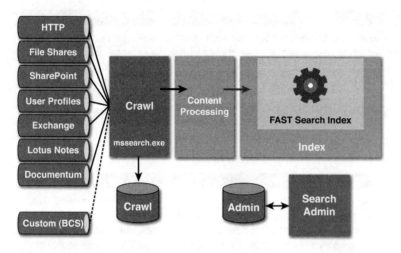

FIGURE 14.2   An overview of SharePoint 2013's Crawl component.

▶ Search Query and Site Settings service

This service load balances queries within the search topology and runs on the servers that run the Query Processing components. This service detects farm-level changes to the search service and stores them in the Search Admin database. This service automatically starts on all servers that are running the Query Processing component.

▶ Search Host Controller service

This service manages the overall search topology components and is automatically started on all services that are running topology components.

TIP

The terms "Federated Search" and "Scopes" are now referred to as "Result Sources" in SharePoint 2013.

TIP

SharePoint 2013's Search uses a componentized model that is based on a Shared Services architecture. A Search service application and proxy is provisioned and the Search Admin page is then accessed via Central Administration in SharePoint Server 2013 or for SharePoint Online via the Office 365 Admin Center under the SharePoint tab in the SharePoint admin center. For a complete overview of SharePoint Online search administration, refer to the following link: http://office.microsoft.com/en-us/office365-sharepoint-online-enterprise-help/sharepoint-online-search-administration-overview-HA103728204.aspx

> **TIP**
>
> For search to properly work, the SharePoint 2013 Search service must configure a default crawl account, which is also referred to as the default content access account. This account must be an active, Active Directory Domain Services domain account. This account should not be set up as an individual or a specific person in IT because I have personally seen SharePoint search issues caused by this account being deactivated and an entire organization's SharePoint search cease to work until the account issue was resolved.

> **TIP**
>
> As you become more experienced with SharePoint 2013 Search, I would recommend reviewing and learning more about how to construct Keyword Query Language (KQL) queries for Search; there is an entire syntax reference library you can utilize that may come in handy down the road as you become an expert in SharePoint 2013's Search. For more information on Keyword Query Language queries, refer to the following link: http://msdn.microsoft.com/en-us/library/office/ee558911.aspx#kql_operators

Underlying Search Components

The underlying architecture of SharePoint Search 2013 consists of six main components:

▶ Crawl component

▶ Content Processing component

▶ Analytics Processing component

▶ Admin component

▶ Index component

▶ Query Processing component

> **TIP**
>
> For an overview of the search schema in SharePoint Server 2013, refer to the following link: http://technet.microsoft.com/en-us/library/jj219669.aspx

When you are looking at SharePoint 2013's Search capabilities and how it actually crawls content, it is important to understand that this is a two-part process and two related components drive this activity. The Crawl component and the Content Processing component work together as the Crawl component fetches the actual data and then those crawled items are sent over to the Content Processing component to extract links, meta-data, and other rich information.

There is a continuous crawl option in SharePoint 2013 that frequently reviews sites to ensure that the search results are up-to-date, and these can be configured based on your organization's needs and any performance restrictions, as well as the overall amount of content that is being crawled. For more information on how to manage continuous crawls in SharePoint Server 2013, refer to the following link: http://technet.microsoft.com/en-us/library/jj219802(v=office.15).aspx

To set a crawl, you must first have a content source you would like this service to review and return results to you and your organization's users. By default, when a Search service application is created, a content source named "Local SharePoint sites" is automatically created and starts crawling all SharePoint sites within the local SharePoint server farm. Users will only be able to see search results that their permissions allow them to see due to SharePoint's search being security trimmed, but this default content source, "Local SharePoint sites," does automatically put all of your SharePoint sites in-scope for search when a SharePoint service application is originally configured.

For more information regarding how to start, pause, resume, or stop a crawl in SharePoint Server 2013, refer to the following link: http://technet.microsoft.com/en-us/library/jj219814(v=office.15).aspx

14

TIP

Microsoft is planning to release a new product by the name of Oslo whose goals is to tie together search silos in one centralized manner. This product is set to be released later in 2014, but for more information regarding Oslo, refer to the following link: http://blogs.office.com/2014/03/11/introducing-codename-oslo-and-the-office-graph/

Crawl Component of SharePoint 2013's Search

SharePoint 2013's Search contains a Crawl component that is executed via `MSSearch.exe`, and crawled items are sent over to the Content Processing component for further processing before being finally routed over to the Index component.

SharePoint 2013's Crawl components consist of the following:

▶ Out-of-the-Box connectors

The following connectors are available out-of-the-box in SharePoint 2013:

   ▶ SharePoint

   ▶ HTTP

   ▶ File Share

   ▶ BDC—which also includes these other connectors that are built on the BDC framework:

      ▶ Exchange public folders

      ▶ Lotus Notes

      ▶ Documentum connector

      ▶ Taxonomy connector

> ▶ Requires the term store to be provisioned for crawling

> ▶ People Profile Connector

>   Note that this requires the profile store to be deployed and configured.

▶ Features that are extensible through BCS

▶ Local disk cache

▶ Crawled items tracked in crawl database

The crawl database is used by the Crawl component to store information about crawled items and to track crawl history. The crawl database also holds information such as the last crawl time, the last crawl ID, and the type of update during the last crawl.

▶ Configurations stored in Admin database

The Admin database contains information about the crawl servers via their synchronized registry and corresponding information regarding content sources and schedules.

▶ Crawl modes

> ▶ Full crawl

> ▶ Incremental crawl

> ▶ Continuous crawl

These crawls "crawl" the various content sources and return both the crawled items in terms of their actual content and their associated metadata, which is then routed to the Content Processing component.

For more information regarding how to plan crawling and federation in SharePoint 2013, refer to the following link: http://technet.microsoft.com/en-us/library/jj219577(v=office.15).aspx

---

TIP

When you are measuring the performance of SharePoint 2013's Crawl components, it is important to review how your environment reacts in terms of high CPU utilization because the CPU load will rise in conjunction with the number of documents crawled per second. You should also monitor the corresponding network and disk load for any possible bottlenecks that may cause performance degradation during a crawl as the network load is generated as the content is downloaded by the crawler from the hosts.

Disk load, on the other hand, is generated when items are temporarily stored during the crawl for these crawled items for processing by the Content Processing component.

For more information regarding how to manage crawling in SharePoint Server 2013, refer to the following link:
http://technet.microsoft.com/en-us/library/ee792876(v=office.15).aspx

For more information on best practices for crawling in SharePoint Server 2013, refer to the following link: http://technet.microsoft.com/en-us/library/dn535606(v=office.15).aspx

Content Processing Component of SharePoint 2013's Search

SharePoint 2013 Search's Content Processing component, as shown in Figure 14.3, receives the crawled content from the Crawl component and performs document parsing, link extraction, metadata, and property mappings. After items are processed, they are sent over to SharePoint Search's Index component to be indexed.

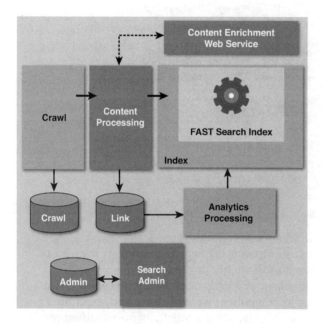

FIGURE 14.3   SharePoint 2013's Content Processing components.

SharePoint 2013's Content Processing component consists of the following:

▶ Analyses of content for indexing

▶ Overview processing flow

▶ Available dictionaries

    For more information regarding the creation of custom entity extraction dictionaries, refer to the following link:

    http://technet.microsoft.com/en-us/library/jj219480(v=office.15).aspx

▶ Stateless node for SharePoint

▶ Schema mapping components

▶ Capability to stores links and anchors in the Link database for analytics

▶ Additional extensible capabilities, as shown in Figure 14.4, through web service call-outs

▶ The configurations stored in admin database

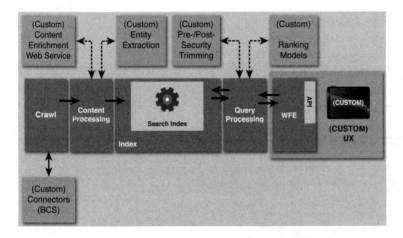

FIGURE 14.4   SharePoint 2013's additional extensibility capabilities.

The Content Processing component transforms crawled items into artifacts that can be included in the search index by parsing document and property mappings. The Content Processing component also performs linguistic processing or language detection at the time of indexing. In SharePoint 2013, this component writes information about links and URLs directly to the Link database, as well as generating phonetic name variations for SharePoint 2013's people search.

There are also capabilities to enable a content web service call-out to enrich data before an item is added to the index via the extensibility capability, which includes working with managed properties that can be provided to and from a web service.

TIP

You can create additional content sources in SharePoint 2013's Central Administration as well as edit or delete any existing content source at any time. For more information on how add, edit, or delete a content source in SharePoint Server 2013, refer to the following link: http://technet.microsoft.com/en-us/library/jj219808(v=office.15).aspx

You can also delete items from the search index or from search results in SharePoint Server 2013. For more information regarding how to delete these items, refer to the following link: http://technet.microsoft.com/en-us/library/jj219587(v=office.15).aspx

In Office 365/SharePoint Online search administration, as shown in Figure 14.5, you can perform actions such as creating a new result source or managing an existing resource source, as well as performing a number of other administrative search functions.

For more information on how to manage result sources in SharePoint Online, refer to the following link: http://office.microsoft.com/en-us/office365-sharepoint-online-enterprise-help/manage-result-sources-HA103639370.aspx#_Toc342634787

FIGURE 14.5   Office 365/SharePoint Online search administration.

TIP

In SharePoint 2013's Search, a Crawl component will automatically communicate with all crawl databases within the corresponding farm, and there is no need to map a Crawl component to specific crawl database as was required in previous versions of SharePoint.

Analytics Processing Component of SharePoint 2013's Search

In SharePoint 2013's Search, the analytics are now performed by the Analytics Processing component during a crawl within the Search service application. The new Analytics Processing component utilizes both the links database and the analytic reporting database, which improves overall speed and accuracy.

The Analytics Processing components, as shown in Figure 14.6, contain core features such as these:

▶ Search analytics

▶ The map-reduce feature

▶ Capability to learn by usage

The search analytics component analyzes not only the crawled items but how users actually interact over time with the search results.

▶ Overall usage analytics to include previous views stored in the event store

▶ Enriching the index by updating index items

▶ Usage reports in the Analytics Reporting database, as shown in Figure 14.7

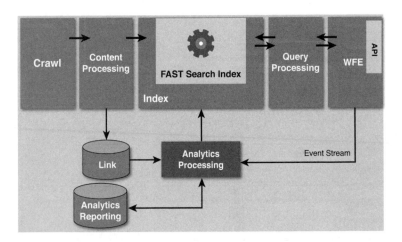

FIGURE 14.6   The Analytics Processing component in SharePoint 2013.

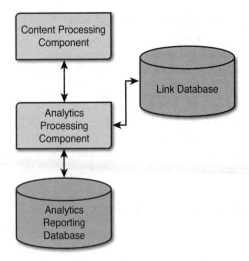

FIGURE 14.7   The Analytics Reporting database in SharePoint 2013.

This feature has the capability to analyze the action a user performs (for example, viewing a page) and then collect the data regarding the event in the relevant usage files and publish them into the event store, where they are stored and processed, to enable the system to familiarize itself with "learned behavior."

The Analytics Processing component routes the results to the Content Processing component for it to be included in the search index. You also can utilize its additional extensibility capabilities to develop code to handle custom events, as well as scale the component to meet the underlying requirements and usage of your organization. You are able to do the following:

▶ Add additional Analytics Processing roles for faster analysis

▶ Add additional Link databases to increase capacity for links as well as user search clicks

▶ Add additional reporting databases to scale to meet your reporting needs, as well as to improve SQL throughput in retrieving reports

The Most Popular Items feature within SharePoint 2013's Ribbon, as shown in Figure 14.8, is driven by the Analytics Processing component of SharePoint 2013's new search architecture.

FIGURE 14.8   The Most Popular Items feature in SharePoint 2013.

The Analytics Process component within SharePoint 2013's Search capabilities also provide for the following:

▶ View counts

▶ Sort by popularity

▶ Recommendations

▶ Relevancy based on usage

▶ Search reports

▶ Suggested sites for you to follow and the reminder of sites you are looking at that you have previously viewed

Search Admin Component of SharePoint 2013's Search

SharePoint 2013 Search's Admin component is responsible for all search provisioning as well as any topology changes. This component manages the life cycle and monitor state for these components:

▶ Crawl component

▶ Content Processing component

▶ Analytics Processing component

▶ Index component

▶ Query Processing component

Within SharePoint 2013's architecture, you can deploy multiple Search Admin components for high availability and fault tolerance, including the Search Admin database, which stores search configuration data such as these:

▶ Query rules

▶ Topology

▶ Managed property mappings

▶ Content sources

▶ Crawl rules

  For more information on how to manage crawl rules in SharePoint Server 2013, refer to the following link:

  http://technet.microsoft.com/en-us/library/jj219686(v=office.15).aspx

▶ Crawl schedules

▶ Underlying analytics settings and configurations

▶ Ranking model configuration

  Via PowerShell cmdlets, the SharePoint search service administrator can perform the following operations on SharePoint 2013 rank models:

  ▶ List ranking models

  ▶ Specify a default ranking model

  ▶ Change an existing custom ranking model

  ▶ Delete an existing custom ranking model

  ▶ Create a new ranking model

  ▶ Import and export a ranking model to XML

TIP

Microsoft has provided connectors for SharePoint Server 2013's Search to allow for seamless interaction with other major technologies such as Microsoft Exchange, Lotus Notes, and Documentum.

To learn more about how to configure and use the Exchange connector for SharePoint 2013, refer to the following link: http://technet.microsoft.com/en-us/library/jj591608(v=office.15).aspx

To learn more about how to configure and use the Lotus Notes connector for SharePoint Server 2013, refer to the following link: http://technet.microsoft.com/en-us/library/jj591606(v=office.15).aspx

To learn more about how to configure and use the Documentum connector in SharePoint Server 2013, refer to the following link: http://technet.microsoft.com/en-us/library/ff721975(v=office.15).aspx

14

SharePoint 2013 enables you to export and import customized search configuration settings between site collections and sites. The settings that you export and import also include these:

▶ All customized query rules

▶ Result sources

▶ Result types

▶ Ranking models

    ▶ Ranking models describe which criteria are included in sorting, as well as how much they contribute to the rank score and how they relate to one another.

    ▶ Custom ranking models are managed through Windows PowerShell as well as via the user interface (UI).

    ▶ You can select a ranking model for a specific query at query time by setting the `RankingModelId` of the query.

▶ Site search settings

▶ Exportation of customized search configuration settings from a Search service application and importation of those settings to site collections and sites

NOTE

It is not possible to import customized search configuration settings into a Search service application or export the related default search configuration settings. For more information regarding the export and import of customized search configuration settings in SharePoint Server 2013, refer to the following link: http://technet.microsoft.com/en-us/library/jj871675(v=office.15).aspx

Search Index Component of SharePoint 2013's Search

SharePoint 2013 Search's Index component provides for the overall feed and query, which consists of receiving processed items from the Content Processing component and then persisting those items to index the appropriate files. This also entails receiving queries from the Query Processing component and then providing result sets in return.

The Index component also provides for features and underlying capabilities such as these:

▸ Provides replication of index content between replicas (for example, Index components) within the same index partition because this index partition is a logical portion of the entire search index

  ▸ Each and every partition is served by one or more Index components, and the primary replica is set by default to maintain a persisted journal of new and updated items, which is then copied to the other replicas within the partition.

  ▸ Every replica exists for added fault tolerance as well as increased query throughput, and the underlying index can scale in multiple manners.

▸ Provides flexibility required during topology changes to apply index partition changes when a topology change occurs

---

NOTE

For more information on how to reset the search index in SharePoint Server 2013, refer to the following link: http://technet.microsoft.com/en-us/library/jj219652(v=office.15).aspx

---

Search Query Component of SharePoint 2013's Search

SharePoint 2013 Search's Query Component performs the actual linguistic processing at the time of a query, which includes word breaking, stemming, query spell-checking, and the native thesaurus capabilities.

The Query Component receives the queries and then analyzes and processes them in order to optimize precision and relevancy. After the query is processed, it is submitted to the Index component while also providing guidance as to which query rules should apply and are applicable. The Query Component also provides guidance as to which index the query should be sent to, as well as whether there are any pre- or post-processing procedures that should be conducted on the query. When this is done, the index returns a result set to the Query Processing component, which then processes it and returns it to the appropriate point in the process.

TIP

SharePoint 2013 utilizes a new ranking model to calculate the relevance rank of search results. This ranking model also can influence the order of search results by using SharePoint Search's query rules, the search schema, and ranking models.

This enables the most relevant, searched, and selected terms to be ranked via a calculated method to help ensure that the most accurate search results are displayed in an order influenced by relevance as well as usage within the organization. For more information on search result ranking in SharePoint Server 2013, refer to the following link: http://technet.microsoft.com/en-us/library/dn169065(v=office.15).aspx#Ranking_Models

Search Diagnostics and Health Monitoring

SharePoint 2013 provides for a number of native query health reports to assist you in monitoring the health and performance of SharePoint's search and also to ensure that your users are retrieving the content they are attempting to query.

SharePoint 2013's native query health reports are as listed here:

▶ Trend

▶ Overall

▶ Main Flow

▶ Federation

▶ SharePoint Search Provider

▶ People Search Provider

▶ Index Engine

There are several reports we have found to be very useful for our clients at EPC Group that I would recommend you deploy, such as these:

▶ Usage Reports

    ▶ Number of Queries

▶ Search Reports

    ▶ Top Queries for (for example, Day and Month)

    ▶ Abandoned Queries (for example, Day and Month)

    ▶ No Result Queries (for example, Day and Month)

    ▶ Query Rule Usage (for example, Day and Month)

For more information on how to view search diagnostics in SharePoint Server 2013, refer to the following link: http://technet.microsoft.com/en-us/library/jj219611(v=office.15).aspx

Hybrid Search: SharePoint Server 2013 and Office 365 Integration

One of the most common configurations that is starting to emerge into today's IT landscape is that of a hybrid cloud architecture. SharePoint Server 2013 can integrate with cloud-based solutions such as Office 365 or SharePoint Online in a secure and federated manner that will enable a user with proper search permissions to return results from on-premises in SharePoint Server 2013 as well as in Office 365 in the cloud, as shown in Figure 14.9.

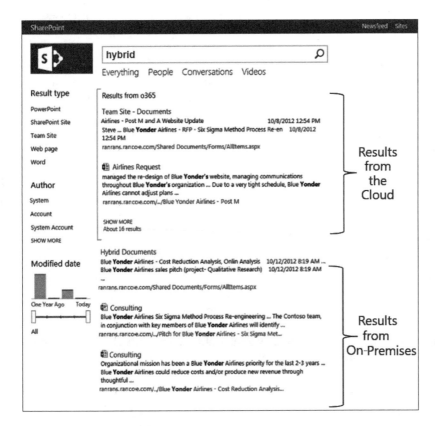

FIGURE 14.9   The results of a hybrid cloud search from a user searching both SharePoint Server 2013 and Office 365.

The following is a summary of a hybrid SharePoint Server 2013 and Office 365 search integration and the related components:

▶ The remote SharePoint Index allows for the search to be federated between the on-premises SharePoint Server 2013 environment and the cloud-based Office 365 environment for a hybrid cloud environment architecture.

▶ This sample configuration provides query capability, and additional configurations can be implemented to support crawl.

▶ The hybrid cloud architecture requires the following:

   ▶ Configuration of an OAuth trust between your on-premises SharePoint 2013 farm and your Office 365 tenancy

▶ The creation of a result source for the remote farm

▶ An externally addressable endpoint for the on-premises farm (for example, reverse proxy) that can be reached via the Office 365 sites

▶ This sample configuration allows you to query the result source directly or create a query rule to also allow for user queries to the cloud-based Office 365 or remote farm when needed.

▶ A token is created for the user and security trimmed results are returned, which requires two-way AD synchronization between the SharePoint Server 2013 on-premises environment and Office 365.

▶ By using a query rule, you can integrate the results from both farms into a single display for users and tailor the UI as desired.

Search Web Parts in SharePoint 2013, Office 365, and SharePoint Online

There are several new web parts for Search in this latest release of SharePoint that provide users an entirely new experience when conducting search. The following is a list of the core search-related web parts in SharePoint 2013, Office 365, and/or SharePoint Online:

▶ Content Search Web Part (CSWP)

The Content Search Web Part utilizes various capabilities to display dynamic content within SharePoint pages. Each Content Search Web Part within a page is directly associated to a search query and displays the results for that search query while providing options to easily tailor the way the results reflect within the web part.

  ▶ Exposes results as JSON (JavaScript Object Notation) on the page.

  ▶ Customize search results rending.

  ▶ Client-side solution using returned results as JSON.

For more information on JSON, refer to the following link:

https://developer.mozilla.org/en-US/docs/JSON

  ▶ Server side via custom Display Templates.

  ▶ Content is editable only at the source.

For more information regarding the Content Search Web Part in SharePoint 2013, refer to the following link:

http://msdn.microsoft.com/en-us/library/jj163789.aspx

▶ Refinement Web Part

The Refinement Web Part enables users to filter the search results from a Search Results Web Part into additional categories to allow for more intelligent decision making on the result set. For more information regarding how to configure properties in the Refinement Web Part, refer to the following link:

http://technet.microsoft.com/en-us/library/gg549985(v=office.15).aspx

▶ Search Box Web Part

The Search Box Web Part is typically utilized on the home page of the Search Center (e.g., `default.aspx`). Numerous configuration options are available and to find out more about these, refer to the following link:

http://technet.microsoft.com/en-us/library/gg576963(v=office.15).aspx

▶ Search Navigation Web Part

The Search Navigation Web Part displays links to the different major search verticals such as Everything, People, Conversations, and Videos. For more information regarding how to configure properties in the Search Navigation Web Part, refer to the following link:

http://technet.microsoft.com/en-us/library/gg576964(v=office.15).aspx

▶ Search Results Web Part

The Search Results Web Part displays the results of a search query entered in a Search Box Web Part. The Search Results Web Part, OOTB (e.g., native), is used on all search vertical pages and displays the actual search results returned. The web part also relays search results to the Refinement Web Part.

For more information regarding how to configure properties in the Search Results Web Part, refer to the following link:

http://technet.microsoft.com/en-us/library/gg549987(v=office.15).aspx

You can add refiners to a page to narrow the items that are shown in a Content Search Web Part, and help users quickly browse to specific content. Refiners are based on managed properties from the search index. To display refiners on a page, you must first enable the managed property that you want to use as a refiner, and then add a Refinement Web Part to the page where you want the refiners to appear.

▶ Refinement Web Part

In SharePoint 2013, you can add refiners to a page to help you continue to narrow the scope of a search to find very specific content. These refiners, for which you first must enable the managed property you are wanting to use as a refiner, enable you to then add a Refinement Web Part to the page where you are wanting these specific refiners to appear. For more information regarding how to configure the Refinement Web Part, refer to the following link:

http://technet.microsoft.com/en-us/library/jj679900(v=office.15).aspx#BKMK_ConfigureRPWP

NOTE

You must have the relevant publishing features enabled to include the cross-site publishing feature in order to utilize web parts such as the Refinement Web Part. For more information regarding the cross-site publishing feature, refer to the following link: http://technet.microsoft.com/en-us/library/jj635883(v=office.15).aspx

---

TIP

For information regarding all of SharePoint 2013's Search web parts, as well as their related configuration, refer to the following link: http://technet.microsoft.com/en-us/library/jj679900.aspx

---

Tailoring the Search UI of SharePoint 2013 and Office 365

When the user interface of SharePoint 2013, Office 365, or SharePoint Online is being updated, the update should be performed in a governed manner that follows the branding and UI standards of the organization. A later section of this chapter goes into great detail regarding how to engage in a custom branding effort for your SharePoint 2013, Office 365, and/or SharePoint Online initiative, and this also covers the pages and sites associated with SharePoint's search.

The search UI itself has specific characteristics you can tailor or configure as a "one off" branding initiative or to simply offer a set of specific and tailored search result–type pages to meet a department's or a specific user's needs.

SharePoint's search UI configuration elements mainly consist of the following:

► Result types

► Display templates

► Query suggestions

► Thumbnail preview features

These new search UI–related features can now be administered by site and site collection administrators but must follow the organization's overall governance strategy in relation to permissions and specific user capabilities.

Result Types

Result types in SharePoint 2013 are similar in nature to query rules in that they enable you to define rules, as shown in Figure 14.10, for when a specific search result can trigger a specified display template. A display template contains the list of managed properties that can be utilized in the results and also can control how the results themselves should be rendered.

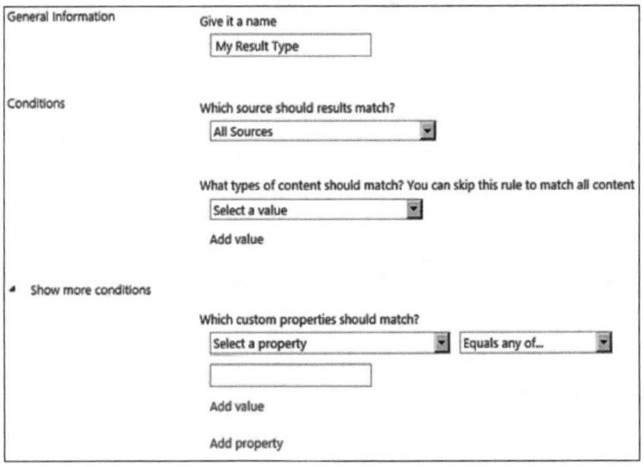

FIGURE 14.10   Providing custom metrics for a result type.

There are a wide range of options that can be utilized around defining the specific rules for when a result type should perform a specific action.

The underlying framework enables you to create custom comparisons based on equality, greater than or less than, and logical operators, for example, "Equality (= or !=), comparison (< or >), or logical (AND or OR or NOT)." Multiple rules can also be combined for a specific condition while also giving you the option to use managed properties in a rule.

Display Templates

Display templates provide the actual rendering of an individual search result and provide for a dynamic array of options to create very visual and interactive search results.

With the new focus on allowing HTML, you are not limited to a specific HTML editor. Based on your organization's governance strategy, you may be able to utilize not only SharePoint Designer 2013 but also Visual Studio, Notepad, Dreamweaver, and other tools you are comfortable editing in.

You are able to create custom HTML display templates and drive search results that work in conjunction with underlying placeholder tags that specify the output of a managed property (result title, author, and so on). For example, Figure 14.11 details a SharePoint 2013 search that was run using a sample custom result type and corresponding display template for a .TXT file stored in SharePoint Server 2013.

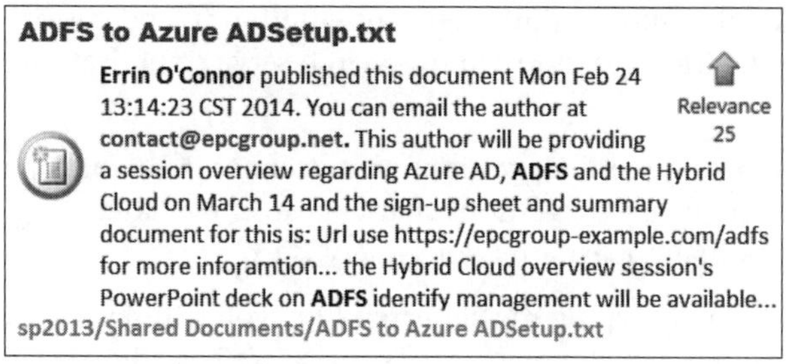

ADFS to Azure ADSetup.txt

Errin O'Connor published this document Mon Feb 24 13:14:23 CST 2014. You can email the author at contact@epcgroup.net. This author will be providing a session overview regarding Azure AD, **ADFS** and the Hybrid Cloud on March 14 and the sign-up sheet and summary document for this is: Url use https://epcgroup-example.com/adfs for more inforamtion... the Hybrid Cloud overview session's PowerPoint deck on **ADFS** identify management will be available...

Relevance 25

sp2013/Shared Documents/ADFS to Azure ADSetup.txt

FIGURE 14.11   An example of a custom result type and corresponding display template for a .TXT file stored in SharePoint Server 2013.

SharePoint 2013 natively contains a number of display templates you can review and copy to a new filename. This way, you can begin modifying and quickly start to learn and test to perfect this new capability. Display templates contain the following characteristics:

▶ They define the visual layout of a Result Type.

▶ A template is really just HTML.

▶ You can edit a template with any HTML designer including Dreamweaver, SharePoint Designer, Visual Studio, Notepad, and so on.

▶ You add placeholders to your HTML file where managed properties should be emitted.

▶ It gives you a real WYSIWYG experience when you're designing templates.

▶ A set of display templates is included OOTB; you can find them in the Master Pages/Display Templates/Search folder.

▶ Site collection admins can upload new display templates.

After you have spent some time developing and testing this feature to "get your feet wet," you can upload the display template to a site, to a site collection, or at a farm level from which it can then be added to a Search service application.

Query Suggestions

Query suggestions enable you to take advantage of the suggestions that SharePoint 2013 provides via a personal query log of all the queries you execute. This personal query log is utilized to provide query suggestions from SharePoint 2013 by remembering the search queries that you have executed before, as well as search results that you've selected and clicked on in the past.

SharePoint 2013's search also pulls in frequent queries from all users within the organization to include relevant results to your query that others also found to be useful and accurate. This builds on a foundation of SharePoint's search learning with you and your organization to provide query suggestions as another option to find relevant content, in addition to the standard browse and "findability" experience that you would get with just a standard raw search. SharePoint 2013 also allows additional configuration to add custom inclusions and exclusions for query suggestions to users via the Search service application administration pages.

SharePoint 2013 provides for two variants of query suggestions that occur at different times during the search process. There are query suggestions that appear as you are typing in the search box, as well as suggestions that appear after your query is executed.

In the first query suggestion variant, as you're typing in the search box, you will see a list of queries you have previously executed, which you can click on, as well as a list of other queries from users across the farm whose queries have led to two or more successful searches, as shown in Figure 14.12.

FIGURE 14.12   The query suggestion feature in SharePoint 2013's Search showing previous successful searches.

In the second query suggestion variant, after your search is executed, SharePoint will provide a list of additional choices based on search results that you personally clicked on when you executed the same query at a previous time within the platform. This feature enables you to quickly execute a search for content that you may routinely search for via the utilization of the same query to find specific documents or list or library items. To summarize, this feature allows for the following:

▶ Your personal SharePoint activity factors into the query suggestions.

▶ It includes weighting based on sites that you have previously visited.

▶ It uses the most frequent queries across all users that "match" the search terms.

▶ The behavior of the query suggestions turns into more of a "browse and find" kind of experience.

▶ You can also add inclusion and exclusion lists for suggestions via the Search service application admin pages.

Thumbnail Preview

SharePoint 2013 utilizes Office Online (Office Web Apps) to provide the capability to view a thumbnail preview, as shown in Figure 14.13, of a document or piece of content without actually having to open the specified content.

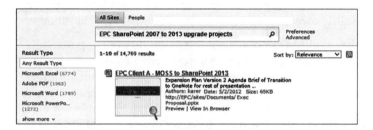

FIGURE 14.13   SharePoint 2013's thumbnail preview example.

Similar to YouTube or Bing videos, hovering your pointer over presentations enables you to view short animations as well as zoom in and out to ensure that the selection is the correct content you are trying to retrieve. There is no delay if the content that you hovered over to view the thumbnail preview is not the content you need; you can simply view the other search results and click on the other items to also preview them before making your ultimate selection.

This feature has been a resounding hit for our clients at EPC Group. It saves time by ensuring that the document they are previewing is correct by enabling them to quickly look for things such as formatting, logos, color schemes, and other easily identifiable markings.

TIP

SharePoint 2013's default authentication is claims-based authentication, and most organizations that have upgraded or migrated from a previous version of SharePoint 2010 have converted any classic-mode web applications to claims-based authentication or opted to create a new claims-based web application in SharePoint 2013.

It is important to be aware that if your organization still has any classic-mode web applications, the thumbnail preview feature will have issues and will not properly function, which can cause confusion for your user base.

For more information on how to migrate from classic-mode to claims-based authentication in SharePoint 2013, refer to the following link: http://technet.microsoft.com/en-us/library/gg251985(v=office.15).aspx

Web Content Management Feature Deep-Dive

SharePoint 2013 does come with a number of new WCM features, as well as major improvements in features that were available in SharePoint 2010's release. The following sections covering WCM closely tie in to the final section of this chapter, "Implementing Custom Branding for SharePoint 2013, Office 365, and SharePoint Online," because there are many considerations regarding configurations that work in tandem with one another.

The improvements in cross-site publishing as well as the capability to present powerful video to users while introducing new content embedding capabilities have been met with great feedback by end users and content owners. New features for content authoring, the use of digital assets (as shown in Figure 14.14), image renditions, clean URLs, and more powerful metadata navigation capabilities enable SharePoint administrators to meet the needs of the business while being able to lean on the out-of-the-box capabilities of SharePoint 2013.

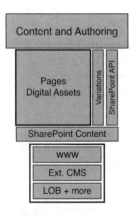

FIGURE 14.14   An overview of content authoring in SharePoint 2013.

The following list includes the core features of SharePoint 2013's WCM capabilities:

▶ Custom error/404 pages

▶ Search Engine Optimization (SEO) tools and the Analysis Engine, as shown in Figure 14.15

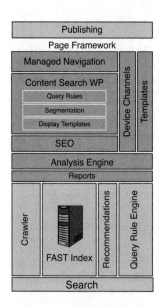

FIGURE 14.15   An architecture overview of Search Engine Optimization, the Analysis Engine, and the related page framework functionality.

▶ Image Renditions and Video Improvements, as shown in Figure 14.16

▶ Cross-Site Publishing

▶ Product Catalog

▶ Managed Navigation

▶ Friendly URLs

FIGURE 14.16   An overview of the improved user experience with new image and video capabilities.

Custom 404/Error Pages

The capability to create a custom error or 404/Not Found page is a "nice-to-have capability" that a lot of organizations really do not take advantage of in their implementations. I do think this is something that should be implemented because it takes only a small amount of time to tailor a standard error page, as shown in Figure 14.17, and it provides users with more direction regarding next steps and how to possibly provide themselves with self-help support. It is not, however, taken advantage of in many deployment efforts.

FIGURE 14.17   A standard error or 404/Not Found page.

You can create a custom 404/Not Found page via SharePoint's interface or using Windows PowerShell.

NOTE

To create a Publishing Site, you can create a new site collection and then select the Publishing tab and then the Publishing Portal option, as shown in Figure 14.18.

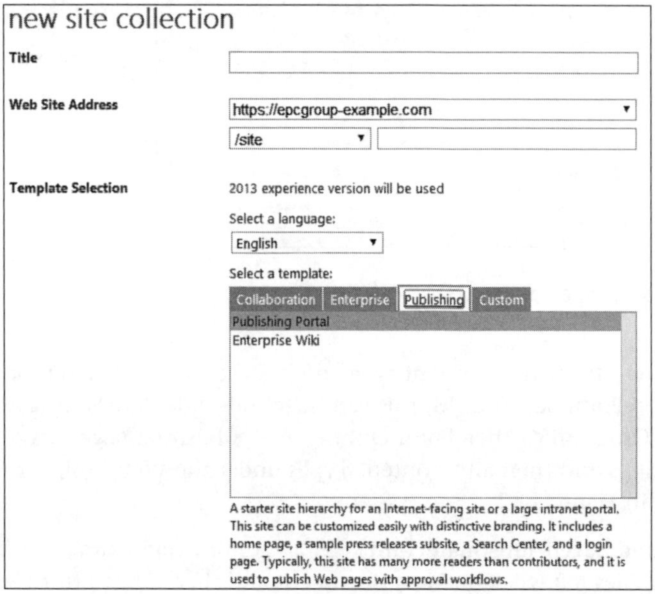

FIGURE 14.18   Creating a new Publishing Site in Office 365's SharePoint Online.

All the Publishing Sites contain a 404/Not Found page named PageNotFoundError.aspx, which resides in the Pages library (as shown in Figure 14.19), which you can find by clicking on Site Contents. You can then open PageNotFoundError.aspx and edit it to meet your organization's specific needs.

FIGURE 14.19   The Pages library in Office 365's SharePoint Online.

SharePoint 2013 and Office 365's SharePoint Online also contain a new Error Page content type, which can be located in the Site Content Types gallery, as shown in Figure 14.20.

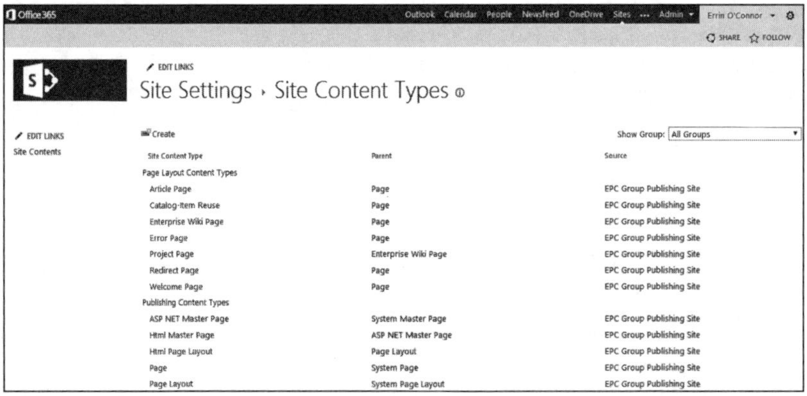

FIGURE 14.20   The Site Content Types gallery.

This content type inherits from the "Page" content type and has the standard layout of 404/Not Found pages. In SharePoint Server 2013, this can be found under Site Settings and then Content Types. In Office 365's SharePoint Online, in a publishing page this can be found under Site Settings and then Site Content Types under the Web Designer Galleries category, as shown in Figure 14.21.

To create a new 404/Not Found page using SharePoint's UI, an administrator can go to the Pages Library and, under the Files tab, click on New Document and then select Error Page, as shown in Figure 14.22.

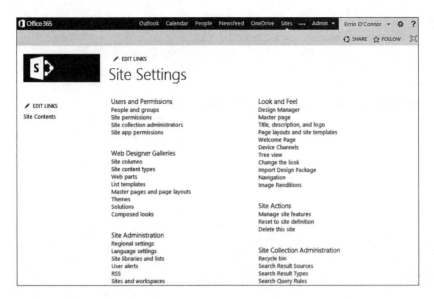

FIGURE 14.21   Showing Web Designer Galleries within the Site Settings page of a publishing page in Office 365's SharePoint Online.

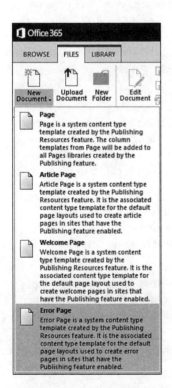

FIGURE 14.22   Creating a new error page using SharePoint's user interface.

The Create Page screen, as shown in Figure 14.23, then loads, and then you can specify the details and modify the configurations required for this new error page for your organization. After you have completed the custom configurations, you must check in and publish the page to make it available.

FIGURE 14.23   The Create Page for specifying the details for the new custom error page for your organization.

Search Engine Optimization Tools and the Analysis Engine

SharePoint 2013 provides for search engine optimization enhancements for organizations that are utilizing SharePoint as their Internet-facing site. These SEO enhancements provide organizations with improved search results for external and anonymous Internet users performing a search via a search engine such as Google or Bing. By improving search results via these SEO enhancements, your organization will have a competitive edge and have a much better chance of being recognized and increasing your organization's overall bottom line.

SharePoint 2013 includes features such as XML sitemaps, friendly URLs, home page redirects, and custom SEO properties. These features enable you to define meta tag descriptions and browser titles for sites, as well as variation capabilities to drive any multi-language requirements of your organization.

SharePoint Server 2013 on-premises implementations enable you to tailor your sitemaps as well as specify the search engines you would like your site to ping. SharePoint Online capabilities in Office 365 generate an updated XML sitemap for your organization within 24 hours of site and related topology or navigational changes.

An overall high-level list of new SEO improvements follows:

▶ Clean URLs

▶ Home page redirects

- Country code top-level domains (ccTLDs)

- XML sitemaps

- SEO properties including meta tag descriptions

- Webmaster tools integration

Image Renditions and Video Improvements

SharePoint 2013 provides for new and added capabilities for managing and presenting images and videos within sites and related pages. SharePoint 2013's image renditions capability enables you to dynamically modify the image to best fit the overall "site presentation" and experience you are wanting to display to your users. These renditions are actual thumbnails that are created automatically and cached to enable you to have consistently sized images to display within your site.

> **TIP**
>
> For more information regarding image renditions in SharePoint 2013, as well as in Office 365's SharePoint Online, refer to the following link: http://office.microsoft.com/en-us/ office365-sharepoint-online-small-business-help/add-and-customize-images-on-your-website-HA102825650.aspx

This feature enables you to optimize your sites and pages payload to help ensure that you won't have images that are causing major bandwidth and page load issues. It also enables you to crop an image to target a specific area within a picture, similar to how you would perform cropping when uploading a picture to a LinkedIn or My Site profile.

SharePoint 2013's video improvements and new capabilities include the capability to meet specific business requirements like creating an enterprise podcast series. The additional video capability improvements in SharePoint 2013, Office 365, and/or SharePoint Online include the following:

- Embedding videos in any content page

- Automatically generating a new video thumbnail

- Renditions for videos just like those of image renditions

- New capabilities to support external videos

- Multiple encodings for single video

- A new native HTML 5 video player

- Fallback capability to Silverlight as needed

- A new video content type

- Allowing content authors to select a specific frame from a video and then utilize the selected frame as the thumbnail preview image

For more information on the enhanced video experience and capabilities in SharePoint 2013, refer to the following link: http://blogs.office.com/2013/03/08/enhanced-video-experience-in-sharepoint-2013/

> **NOTE**
>
> To be able to utilize the automated thumbnail creation feature, the Desktop Experience feature must be installed and configured on the front-end web server(s) of SharePoint Server 2013.

Content authors have the ability to insert an IFrame element into an HTML field on a site that utilizes embedded dynamic content that already exists from other sites and pages such as videos, maps, or other relevant content.

SharePoint automatically trusts some external domains that are already approved for use in IFrames, and SharePoint administrators and site collection owners can customize and implement governance around the field security settings that allow whether external domains are trusted for use within the environment.

> **NOTE**
>
> To modify and update the field security settings for a site collection, click HTML Field Security on a site's Site Settings page.

> **TIP**
>
> To utilize image renditions within your organization in SharePoint Server 2013, you must first ensure that you have enabled the BLOB cache. For more information regarding how to enable this feature, as well as additional information on the configuration of cache settings, refer to the following link: http://technet.microsoft.com/en-us/library/cc770229.aspx

Cross-Site Publishing

The Cross-Site Collection Publishing feature in SharePoint Server 2013 enables you to utilize one or more authoring site collections to author and store documents and content, as well as one or more Publishing Site collections to control the overall design of the site and its content display. An authoring site collection contains catalogs which are lists, libraries, and pages with content that is tagged with specific metadata and terms (e.g., content types), as shown in Figure 14.24. These catalogs are then indexed by SharePoint's search and are available to the Publishing Site collection.

Queries for data are issued by the indexed Publishing Site collection and are shown on pages by using web parts (e.g., SharePoint 2013 Search Web Parts), as shown in Figure 14.25. In essence, you then brand the content on the Publishing Site via custom master pages, page layouts, and display templates, which are covered in a later section, "Implementing Custom Branding and a Tailored 'Look and Feel' for SharePoint 2013, Office 365, and SharePoint Online."

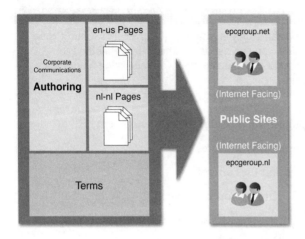

FIGURE 14.24   An overview of cross-site publishing and the related components.

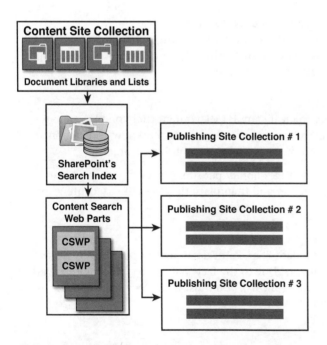

FIGURE 14.25   An overview of cross-site publishing and interaction with SharePoint's Content Search Web Parts.

This capability of using "catalog-enabled" sites works extremely well for organizations that want to heavily utilize features such as a content repositories or knowledge base/knowledge management, or for a product catalog.

TIP

The cross-site publishing is currently available only in SharePoint Server 2013, but if your organization is utilizing SharePoint Online, you can use the author-in-place method to publish content. It is also important to note that the search-driven publishing features are available only for private site collections.

In SharePoint Server 2013, cross-site publishing provides the following benefits:

▶ Provides a broad range of possible site architectures

▶ Allows for a mix of authored pages and list content

▶ Separates content authoring from branding and rendering

▶ Allows content to be shared anonymously with users on the Publishing Site

▶ Can be used across site collections, web applications, and farms

▶ Allows for a mix of authored pages and list content

Available Types of Content to Be Utilized for Cross-Site Publishing

There are multiple types of content that can be utilized for cross-site publishing in the libraries and lists of the authoring site collection(s). The following list describes the types of content you can use in an authoring site collection:

▶ Pages library

You can utilize a Pages library to create any HTML content that you plan to reuse across site collections and take advantage of the approval workflow and content scheduling features that are part of the SharePoint publishing feature set.

Note that you can have only one Pages library per site. However, you can have multiple sites within a site collection and then place the Pages library content into separate catalogs.

▶ Document library

You can utilize one or more standard SharePoint document libraries to store files such as Word and Excel documents. Due to the fact that these types of files are also considered binary large object files (BLOBs), you must treat Document libraries in the same manner in which you treat Asset libraries.

▶ List

You can utilize one or more lists to store any type of data that is better stored in a list than in Pages library content.

▶ Asset library

You can utilize one or more Asset libraries to store binary large object files such as pictures, audio, or video files, as long as those files contain the primary content that you are wanting to show on the Publishing Site.

Asset libraries that are used to contain BLOBs that are referenced by pages or lists, such as PDFs or product images, represent a different type of content and are handled differently for utilization in cross-site publishing.

Term Set Tagging in Cross-Site Publishing

Term sets are used to tag content in authoring sites, and when content is tagged with one or more terms, the terms become part of the metadata (e.g., content types) that is associated with the content.

When the search system adds content to the index, it also adds the associated metadata, and that metadata is later used in the Publishing Site collections when content is shown on pages and when it is utilized for managed navigation.

Catalog Configuration in Cross-Site Publishing

After you share lists and libraries for use as catalogs, you can then start to reuse this content across Publishing Site collections. When these lists or libraries are shared as a catalog, you must specify that you want to share them with other sites and site collections or optionally choose to enable anonymous access to the content in the catalog.

Each catalog allows you to select up to five fields that are used to uniquely identify items in the catalog, and you also specify a single managed metadata field that is used as a navigation term set in the Publishing Site collections.

After a library or list is shared as a catalog and the content has been crawled and indexed, you can then connect to it from a Publishing Site collection. There must be at least one piece of content added to a list or library before it is shared as a catalog, and you must also tag it with a term from the tagging term set. When the managed metadata site column that is associated with the tagging term set is created, it is required to be a single value field.

Catalog Connections in SharePoint 2013

For content to be shared from an authoring site collection, a catalog of connections must be configured in the Publishing Site collection that will consume those catalogs.

When you configure catalog connections, you specify which catalogs the Publishing Site collection will use to show this content and specify granular details for information such as whether to integrate catalog content into the site or where the categories to use for navigation should reside. You also specify the term set that was used for tagging, as well as how category item URLs should be constructed.

Category Pages and Catalog Item Pages in SharePoint 2013

Category pages and catalog item pages are page layouts that you can use to show structured catalog content consistently across a site. By default, SharePoint Server 2013 can automatically create one category page layout and one catalog item page layout per catalog connection. Pages based on these layouts are created in the Pages library of a Publishing Site when you connect the site to a catalog. These pages have the following consideration:

▶ When you edit the HTML page layouts, they are automatically synced back to the corresponding ASPX pages, but if you prefer to edit the ASPX pages directly, you should first delete the HTML version of the page.

For more information regarding cross-site publishing in SharePoint 2013, refer to the following link: http://msdn.microsoft.com/en-us/library/office/jj163225(v=office.15).aspx#SP15_CrossSitePublising_CrossSitePublishingAPIs

Product Catalog in SharePoint 2013

The Product Catalog feature in SharePoint 2013 is based on the SharePoint Product Catalog site template and is a site that allows a content owner or content manager to create content that will be utilized and published within a site or even within SharePoint's search.

You can optionally activate the Cross-Site Collection Publishing feature on a specific site rather than creating this site template if you want to use SharePoint lists and libraries as catalogs. It is important to note that there are additional configuration options that must be enabled if you choose to activate the cross-site collection publishing feature rather than creating a SharePoint Product Catalog site from the template.

NOTE

The Product Catalog is available only for On-Premises Enterprise SharePoint.

For more information on the SharePoint Product Catalog, refer to the following link: http://technet.microsoft.com/en-us/library/jj656774(v=office.15).aspx

---

Managed Navigation in SharePoint 2013

Managed navigation enables you to define and maintain the navigation on a site by using term sets, as shown in Figure 14.26, because this navigation enables you to add to or supplement SharePoint's OOTB SharePoint navigation that is, by default, based on your implementation's overall site structure. The managed navigation structure is created by adding terms to term sets via the Term Store Management tool, as shown in Figure 14.27, which also enables you to copy the navigation term set and translate it into the languages that are used for variations labels within your organization.

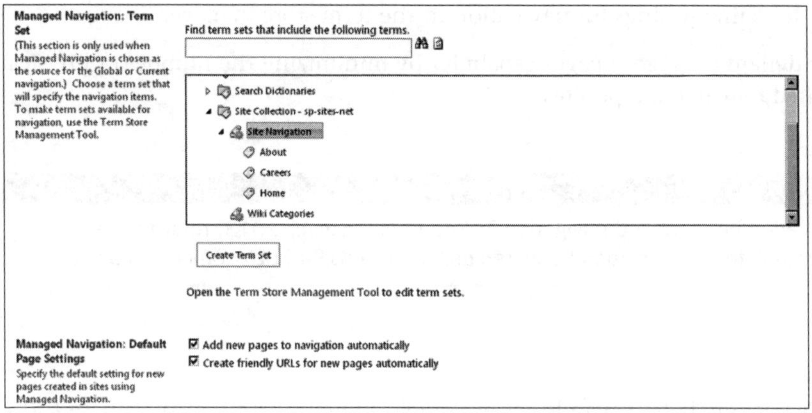

FIGURE 14.26   SharePoint 2013's managed navigation: Term Set configuration page.

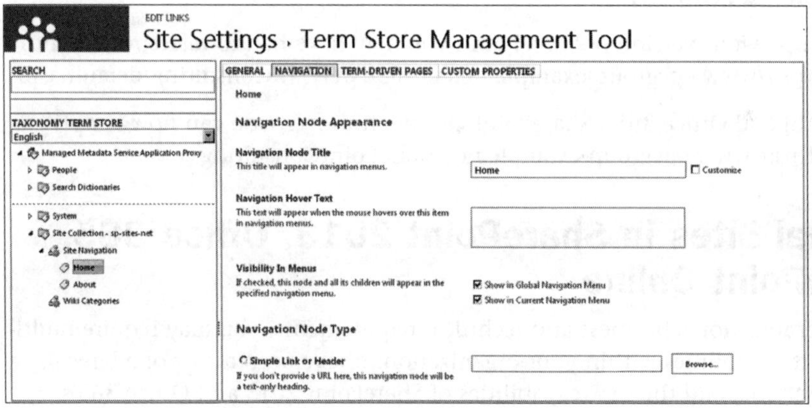

FIGURE 14.27   SharePoint 2013's Term Store Management tool.

You can combine some elements of term sets from different site collections in order to create an overall navigational structure of a site.

In summary, SharePoint 2013's managed navigation's key elements:

▶ Enable you to drive your navigation and URLs based on term store hierarchies

▶ Provide for clean URLs for actual end users

    ▶ www.epcgroup-example.net/careers

    ▶ www.epcgroup-example.net/about-us

▶ Enable you to define settings for navigation in the term store manager

▶ Provide for dynamic category pages capability by minimizing the number of physical pages required for catalog type sites

---

TIP

For more information on managed navigation in SharePoint Server 2013, refer to the following link: http://technet.microsoft.com/en-us/library/dn194311(v=office.15).aspx

---

Friendly URLs

SharePoint 2013's Friendly URLs capability is extremely straightforward in that these URLs are links that correspond directly to a term within your organization or on a particular site or page, as well as correspond to your organization's navigation term set. The `.aspx` is no longer required after the site or page name, and the `default.aspx` page can be dropped from the URLs reference entirely.

For example, in a previous version of SharePoint, you may have had to reference an entire URL like this: https://www.epcgroup-example.net/sites/SharePointConsulting/default.aspx

In SharePoint 2013 and Office 365's SharePoint Online, however, you can now simply reference this: https://www.epcgroup-example.net/SharePointConsulting

Multilingual Sites in SharePoint 2013, Office 365, and SharePoint Online

Based on your organization's business and technical requirements, you may require multilingual SharePoint capabilities within your organization. I have been a part of a large number of these efforts, and the new capabilities of SharePoint 2013 and Office 365's SharePoint Online have made this task much easier on the project team and the level of measurable success within your reach.

A lot of organizations, for example, state that they support "English only" within their SharePoint environments, but there seems to be custom site collections pop-up at times with language packs or custom deployments in other languages to support specific locations. There is the new Multiple Language Interface (MLI), which, in essence, tells a specific site's interface to be available and utilize a specific language pack. It is also important to note that this feature changes elements such as titles, navigations elements, and menus, but any embedded "custom text" or content does not automatically change to the specified language. You can think of this content as being in "a container of its own" and outside of the feature set, so it is important to keep this in mind in your planning.

The Variations feature makes multilingual sites possible. It is available for Publishing Sites and creates a duplicate copy of the site and updates it into the specified variation language when it is published and translated.

You will need to install at least a few core language packs for the languages your organization wants to support. There are more than 40 available language packs for SharePoint 2013, as listed in Table 14.1. Although you may not think you will initially or possibly ever utilize other language packs, there may be documents that are emailed or uploaded to SharePoint from partners, clients, or team members that have other languages embedded in them or were possibly created from a template set in another language, causing search to not properly return search results for this content. With that in mind, I would recommend at least installing the following language packs within your implementation:

- ▶ Chinese (Traditional)
- ▶ English
- ▶ French
- ▶ German
- ▶ Portuguese (Brazil)
- ▶ Spanish

14

TABLE 14.1   Language Packs for SharePoint Foundation 2013, SharePoint Server 2013, and SharePoint Online

Language	SharePoint Server 2013	SharePoint Online
Arabic	Yes	Yes
Basque (Basque)	Yes	Yes
Bulgarian	Yes	Yes
Catalan	Yes	Yes
Chinese (Simplified)	Yes	Yes
Chinese (Traditional)	Yes	Yes
Croatian	Yes	Yes
Czech	Yes	Yes
Danish	Yes	Yes
Dutch	Yes	Yes
English	Yes	Yes
Estonian	Yes	Yes
Finnish	Yes	Yes
French	Yes	Yes
Galician	Yes	Yes
German	Yes	Yes
Greek	Yes	Yes
Hebrew	Yes	Yes
Hindi	Yes	Yes

Language	SharePoint Server 2013	SharePoint Online
Hungarian	Yes	Yes
Indonesian	Yes	No
Italian	Yes	Yes
Japanese	Yes	Yes
Kazakh	Yes	Yes
Korean	Yes	Yes
Latvian	Yes	Yes
Lithuanian	Yes	Yes
Malay (Malaysia)	Yes	No
Norwegian (Bokmål)	Yes	Yes
Polish	Yes	Yes
Portuguese (Brazil)	Yes	Yes
Portuguese (Portugal)	Yes	Yes
Romanian	Yes	Yes
Russian	Yes	Yes
Serbian (Cyrillic)	Yes	No
Serbian (Latin)	Yes	Yes
Slovak	Yes	Yes
Slovenian	Yes	Yes
Spanish	Yes	Yes
Swedish	Yes	Yes
Thai	Yes	Yes
Turkish	Yes	Yes
Ukrainian	Yes	Yes
Vietnamese	Yes	No

TIP

Language packs for SharePoint Server 2013 can be downloaded via the Microsoft Download Center at the following link: http://www.microsoft.com/en-us/download/details.aspx?id=37140

When you install language packs, you are required to install them on each and every SharePoint Server (e.g., web front-end and application servers) within your organization's farm.

Internet Explorer as well as other popular browsers managed the regional settings used by the browser within the browser itself.

TIP

For information on how to change your Internet Explorer language settings, refer to the following links: http://windows.microsoft.com/en-us/windows-vista/change-your-internet-explorer-language-settings

---

For more information on language packs in SharePoint Server 2013, refer to the following link: http://technet.microsoft.com/en-us/library/ff463597(v=office.15).aspx

Translation Services with SharePoint 2013

SharePoint 2013 has a new Machine Translation Service service application that enables you to update your site or page's content to be translated by a cloud service depending on the security and proxy settings on your organization and related governance policies.

I have worked on several initiatives that have language packs with a few different variations, so having a content owner of the translated or variation site is key so that the content owner can review it for any errors or proper "word usage" for that region before publishing. For example, EPC Group recently completed a SharePoint Server 2013 and Office 365 hybrid cloud deployment with an organization based in the U.S. but with several offices in South America in which Portuguese was the standard language of these other offices. The Translation Service as well as variations, via SharePoint 2013's variations capabilities, did not 100% properly translate the Portuguese of these offices due to regional dialect, and it was key to establish a content owner for these sites that worked closely with the U.S. office to ensure that all content was accurate.

For more information on the Machine Translation Service in SharePoint 2013, refer to the following link: http://msdn.microsoft.com/en-us/library/office/jj163145(v=office.15).aspx

Variations in SharePoint 2013

Variations in SharePoint Server 2013, as depicted in Figure 14.28 as well as Figure 14.29, drive the core multilingual capabilities that make this powerful feature possible. Users within your organization who visit a site are automatically redirected to the appropriate variation site based on the language setting of their web browser.

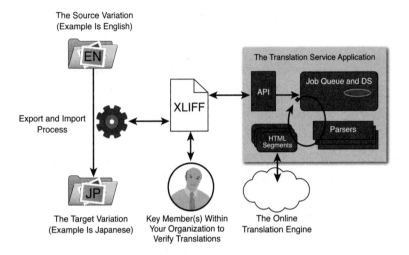

FIGURE 14.28   SharePoint 2013's Variations.

Variations provide for:

▶ The use of industry-standard XLIFF file format, which can include an entire list or library or simply one page or navigation element

▶ Improved throughput for creating new language sites

Content authors can nominate lists on source variation sites to be propagated to target variation sites, and list items such as documents and images propagate independently from pages. The Variations feature can provide significant performance improvements as well as enabling bulk export of pages. There is also added logging functionality around variations to help administrators monitor as well as improve the usefulness of the feature by reviewing error messages and logs and resolving any underlying issues.

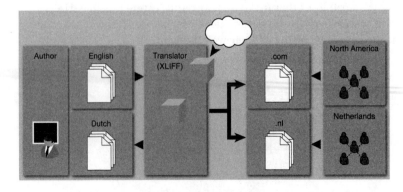

FIGURE 14.29   An example of SharePoint 2013's Variations in action.

Implementing Custom Branding for SharePoint 2013, Office 365, and SharePoint Online

It is key to approach any branding or custom "look and feel" initiative with as much of a browser- and device-agnostic approach as possible and to utilize Responsive Web Design (RWD) methodologies to drive and set expectations for both your underlying business requirements and your functional and technical requirements.

RWD is a design approach aimed at tailoring sites and pages to provide the most powerful viewing experience available while assuming that most browsers and mobile devices will at some point view the tailored site and its content, while also taking into consideration the additional and available native features of SharePoint.

For example, when navigation-related development considerations in responsive web design are being approached, the following items must be taken into consideration:

▶ Floating elements

▶ Drop-down menu

▶ Collapsible menu or features

▶ Any elements or content that may be "off canvas"

▶ Focus on navigational design and not around any device

SharePoint branding initiatives can add a great deal of value by enhancing the companies' user experience to increase the overall usability as well as likability of SharePoint. In many project engagements, EPC Group and our clients work to implement SharePoint without calling it SharePoint. Providing a tailored brand to your new 2013 implementation can increase usage by up to 30%, and that can correlate to true ROI.

Many organizations do not see the need to brand SharePoint and/or Office 365's SharePoint Online, and that can be understood because in a lot of cases the company's previous custom branding culture tends to bleed over into their overall approach to SharePoint 2013, Office 365, and SharePoint Online branding. For those organizations that do want to brand their implementation, I will cover some best practices and experiences from some of EPC Group's recent branding, mobility, and responsive web design initiatives.

SharePoint 2013, Office 365, and SharePoint Online Branding Considerations

Your organization's design should be extremely user-friendly while serving a variety of users' viewpoints from their device to their location. There should be a core set of expectations on which browsers need to be supported, at a core, for your SharePoint responsive web design initiative. Along with this, there should also be a related set of device expectations that the team will utilize which must be added to your organization's overall governance strategy. Assuming that your deployment is an internal secure platform and not an Internet-facing site, you should be able to get a baseline on the device and browser question.

There are considerations related to SharePoint 2013 and Office 365's SharePoint Online ribbon elements and how they will merge or change with any design that is secure and requires authentication versus an anonymous Internet-facing site that does not require authentication that may have limited ribbon elements. Your organization must consider the images, videos, and media content in scope because there may be sizing issues or diminished quality on specific devices if the images are not clear or are not developed or stored in a recommended format. All initial images should be reviewed and "mocked up" in wireframes during the initial design and requirements-gathering sessions.

Branding for the Future with Mobile First in Mind

EPC Group's Mobility and Branding team follows certain design and development paths, as shown in Figure 14.30, for any responsive web design initiative. These core foundations are key to ensuring an initiative's overall short- and long-term success. EPC Group's short list of responsive web design best practices is to always identify base breakpoints based on the design while utilizing a temporary background image for columns and possibly an overall background image to ensure that all areas blend and there are no glaring "white spaces" regardless of any device. In many cases, you want to start with a specific pixel block.

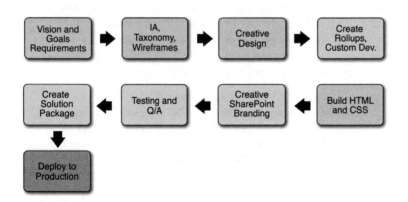

FIGURE 14.30   EPC Group's SharePoint 2013, Office 365, and SharePoint Online branding methodology approach.

Your organization should consider device channels in your custom branding initiative, which will enable you to tailor specific pages to specific devices to even include device- and page-specific interfaces as well as changing the order of content based on the specific device.

Optimize Experience for Mobile and Device Channels

SharePoint Server 2013 supports targeting different devices, as shown in Figure 14.31, such as smartphones and tablets, and designers can create channels that allow a single Publishing Site to be rendered in multiple ways by using different designs that target different devices.

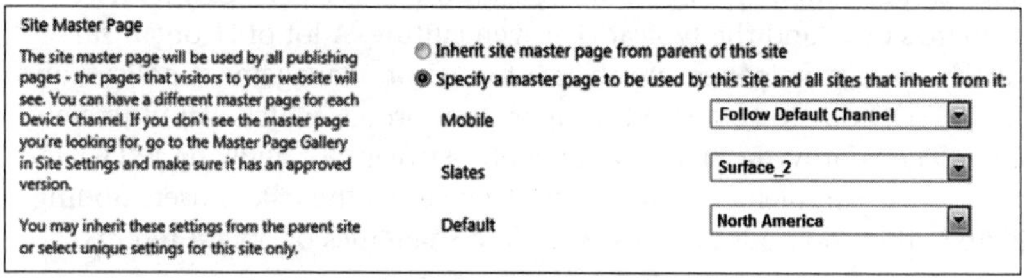

FIGURE 14.31   Native support of specific devices.

Device Channels

You can create device channels for your organization by using tools such as Design Manager, and then you map these channels to mobile devices or browsers by using substrings of each incoming device's user agent string. A specific device can belong to multiple channels, which allows for device channels to be ranked. After you define different device channels, you can then map a master page to each of the channels. A master page can reference a different CSS file than the master page for the default channel, and all page layouts that you create will work with all the channels that are developed. To differentiate page layout designs between channels, you must use the Device Channel Panel control. SharePoint 2013 Publishing Sites are automatically optimized for mobile development, which enables you to use the device channels feature of a Publishing Site to define channels for one or more devices and learn from how this functions to give yourself and your team a reference point to quickly learn from.

You are also provided with the option to assign an alternative master page to each device channel, as well as provide it with unique chrome while still being able to include or exclude portions of any page layout in a channel.

The following provides a high-level overview of SharePoint 2013 capabilities for device-based rendering via device channels:

▶ Different channels are defined at the site collection level.

▶ You can define "channels" for single devices or groups of devices based on rights and the underlying user agent of the device.

▶ You can assign alternate master pages per channel.

▶ This feature provides the capability to selectively include and exclude portions of page layouts per channel by using specific controls.

▶ If required, you can provide cookie-level override for end users.

The Device Channel Panel enables you to control a page layout and decide what content is rendered within a channel. The Device Channel Panel is a container that is mapped to one or more channels, and if one or more of those channels are active when the page is rendered, all the contents of the Device Channel Panel are automatically rendered.

SharePoint 2013 BYOD and Mobile Device Management (MDM) Best Practices

Remote workers and workers empowered with bring-your-own-device (BYOD) policies can touch the boundaries of IT and the typical IT-driven culture. A lot of IT organizations are playing catch-up in governance and their information management policies and have pushed back on BYOD due to the added complexity it brings, which can ultimately force specific polices to be approved. There is a trade-off between not allowing BYOD and the work required to actually implement a BYOD strategy versus the risk of users finding shortcuts and utilizing other methods or access points to share files or obtain reports.

BYOD is also bring a 24/7 "working window" into the picture that some organizations may see as encroaching on the work/life balance but also what may define the actual workplace or given workday. One of the major issues with BYOD has related to the security risks that may open, but in the case of SharePoint 2013 and Office 365's SharePoint Online, there are solutions in Microsoft's System Center in Windows Intune that can assist in resolving all of those challenges.

There must be a balance of privacy in conjunction with other obligations such as legal risks that may come with:

▶ Protecting your organization's team members' personal information (for example, PII, PHI, and HIPAA data).

▶ Enforcing a policy that requires the user who is requesting BYOD to become aware of any possible challenges or privacy-related data and ensure that the user consents or "signs off" on a usage or related company policy.

SharePoint Comparing Approaches and Level of Effort for SharePoint 2013, Office 365, and SharePoint Online Branding

There are different levels of branding that organizations can undertake when implementing a custom "look and feel" for their overall platform. The following list details some examples of the core elements of a full, medium, and low level of effort branding and "look and feel" initiative:

▶ A full branding effort entails the following:

    ▶ Developing custom master pages

    ▶ Implementing tailored page layouts

    ▶ Developing tailored display templates

    ▶ Implementing a responsive web design initiative that corresponds to the testing of pages via mobile and tablet browsers via emulators or simulators

    ▶ Working and developing in Visual Studio 2013/2012, Design Manager, or other development-related applications

> ▶ A medium branding effort entails the following:
>
>> ▶ Utilizing the Design Manager for Publishing Sites
>>
>> ▶ Implementing custom CSS and background images
>>
>> ▶ Working and developing in Visual Studio 2013/2012, or other development-related applications
>
> ▶ A low-level branding effort entails the following:
>
>> ▶ Working with page editing and themes as well as Composed Looks
>>
>> ▶ In SharePoint 2013, making additional modifications within a Composed Looks gallery for small color changes and for specific URLs

HTML-Based Master Pages and Page Layouts

In SharePoint 2013 and Office 365's SharePoint Online, both master pages and page layouts can now be edited in HTML. The Design Manager can create a new minimal master page or page layout and can also convert existing HTML designs to functioning master pages. In both of these cases, there is an associated HTML file for editing that can be modified in the desired HTML editor of your choice.

TIP

It is important to note that the Designer Manager is available only in Publishing Sites.

Also, every time you save SharePoint updates to branding elements, the system automatically regenerates the corresponding master page or page layout.

Cascading Style Sheets (CSS) in SharePoint 2013

CSS is used to override default SharePoint 2013 branding, and it allows for the following custom CSS options:

▶ CSS can be applied to a page with Script Editor Web Part or Content Editor Web Part.

▶ CSS can be applied to a custom Master Page, but this does require some knowledge of master pages and their underlying configuration best practices.

▶ The alternate CSS feature in Publishing Sites is an option, but you must first activate the Publishing features or create a Publishing Site.

▶ You can utilize features such as Internet Explorer's F12 Developer Tools or Firebug for Firefox to view and highlight elements in the browser to see what style is being applied to the HTML element and how CSS classes are overriding each other.

UI Customization with Familiar Design Tools and Native Capabilities

SharePoint 2013 and Office 365's SharePoint Online can be customized via Visual Studio 2013/2012 as well as SharePoint's native Design Manager, but these efforts can also be performed using tools such as Dreamweaver, Expression Blend, or other tools you may be comfortable using.

These customizations and tailored designs are performed using industry standards such as HTML5, CSS, and JavaScript, as well as the utilization of the underlying .NET Framework 4.5, C#, and ASP.NET.

Chapter 13, "Development Strategies and Custom Applications in SharePoint 2013, Office 365, and SharePoint Online," covers core and advanced development strategies for SharePoint 2013 and Office 365's SharePoint Online that provide greater insight regarding additional development options you can utilize in your custom branding and "look and feel" initiative.

Visual Studio 2013/2012 Design Support

For enterprise and mid-size organizations, Visual Studio is the go-to tool for development for custom branding and "look and feel" initiatives because it provides for not only the required set of development tools but related testing and troubleshooting feature sets. Visual Studio is covered in much greater detail in Chapter 13.

If you are developing a highly visible app or customization for an organization with a user base of 500-plus users, I would always recommend using Visual Studio, which is an enterprise tool for development. There are exceptions, though, such as if you are modifying only a small component or customizations where there is not a major impact or if you are tailoring an existing customization already in-place. In such cases, you can opt to use a much less complex and even a free tool. More information on Visual Studio can be found at the following link: http://msdn.microsoft.com/en-us/library/dd831853.aspx

SharePoint 2013's Design Manager

SharePoint 2013's new Design Manager is a native tool that is available for organizations that are performing design-related tasks. It becomes available when the SharePoint publishing feature is enabled.

SharePoint 2013's Design Manager provides the following capabilities:

- ▶ Provides guidance to modify master pages and page layouts
    - ▶ Helps in converting HTML designs to be used in SharePoint as master pages
- ▶ Allows editors to continually update HTML pages
    - ▶ Converts required changes for master pages and page layouts
    - ▶ Offers snippets for helping build designs
- ▶ Provides export and import capabilities
- ▶ Empowers web designers and developers by
    - ▶ Offering completely revamped CSS classes
    - ▶ Allowing web part rendering with <DIV> tags

- ▶ Minimizing ramp-up time
- ▶ Providing assistance and capabilities for uploading templates and allowing them to be modified on the fly
▶ Features the Design Manager in the Site Actions drop-down after the publishing feature is enabled

SharePoint 2013's Design Manager provides the capabilities to create as well as import design packages. The following is an overview of the features supported in these areas:

▶ Design Manager has the capability to automate the creation of design packages and this includes:

- ▶ Master pages
- ▶ Page layouts
- ▶ CSS
- ▶ Images

▶ It can be easily imported into another site even on a different farm.

▶ Design Manager allows for the creation of a simple sandbox solution.

▶ When your site design is ready, you can simply upload your custom HTML, created via the editor of your choice, and supporting files and then use Design Manager to convert the HTML file into an ASP.NET master page (.master file) and apply the master page to a SharePoint site.

▶ The Design Manager can create a new page layout as the HTML version is automatically associated with the corresponding ASP.NET page (.aspx file) that SharePoint interprets.

▶ After HTML files are converted, you can continue to use an HTML editor to update and tailor your design as well as preview and save files.

TIP

Whenever you save HTML versions of a master page or page layout files, SharePoint 2013 automatically updates the associated SharePoint master page and page layouts to reflect your changes.

SharePoint's 2013 Themes/Composed Looks (OOTB)

SharePoint 2013 comes with various OOTB themes/composed looks, as shown in Figure 14.32, that your organization can first view to find any elements that you may like or want to reuse in your overall custom branding design. These themes also enable you to apply this simple "branding" on sites that the organization was not previously planning to brand.

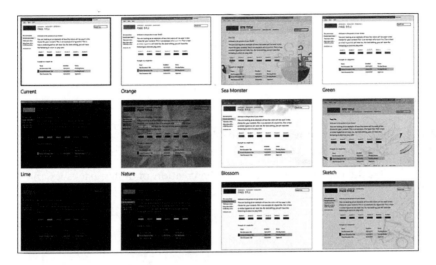

FIGURE 14.32   SharePoint 2013 out-of-the-box themes.

No matter what themes or customizations you may be implementing for your organization's custom branding or "look and feel" initiative, you must always remember to keep in mind the responsive web design and browser and device-agnostic needs facing your users and organizations. Remember that there is a wide variety of devices that your organization's implementation may one day be required to support.

SharePoint's 2013 Snippet Gallery

The Snippet Gallery in SharePoint 2013 can display options on the ribbon for assisting in editing a master page or page layout. The available options displayed on the ribbon in conjunction with the Snippet Gallery are based on the type of design action you are performing. Microsoft provides a set of common snippets that you can copy and paste into your HTML master page or page layout. These include the most common SharePoint functional areas such as the following:

- ▶ Navigation
- ▶ Breadcrumbs
- ▶ Search box
- ▶ Title/logo
- ▶ Sign in
- ▶ Web parts

TIP

For more information regarding the Snippet Galley, refer to the following link:
http://msdn.microsoft.com/en-us/library/office/jj822367(v=office.15).aspx

Summary

This chapter covered the core underlying structure of SharePoint 2013, Office 365, and SharePoint Online search, as well as the configurable components your organization can take advantage of to provide not only ROI from the new platform but also increased user adoption.

We also discussed the available Web Content Management feature available to ensure that you "wow" your users with your organization's sites and pages with new capabilities related to images and videos as well as new embedding features.

The core elements of providing multilingual sites for your organization were also covered, as well as the strategies and related tools you can utilize to provide your organization with a custom branding or tailored "look and feel" for your implementation.

In Chapter 15, "Administration and Maintenance Strategies," we will cover core administration and maintenance strategies, including deep-dives into not only SharePoint Server 2013 but also Office 365 and SharePoint Online to include related administration of Microsoft Lync and other integrated technologies.

14

CHAPTER 15

Administration and Maintenance Strategies

SharePoint 2013, Office 365, and SharePoint Online Administration Overview

As you start to dive into this chapter, it is key to take a quick look back at the items we have covered so far, as well as your organization's SharePoint governance strategy that ultimately drives the overall administration and maintenance of SharePoint 2013, Office 365, and SharePoint Online. We have covered a great deal of the administrative and maintenance-related tasks for the features and functionalities available by approaching the actual design and configuration with administration in mind.

In Chapter 9, "Governance Strategies for SharePoint 2013, Office 365, and SharePoint Online," the different roles and related responsibilities were identified regarding administration-related tasks and how the organization should plan and execute SharePoint's support to meet the identified service level agreements (SLAs).

In Chapter 18, "Disaster Recovery (DR) and Business Continuity Management (BCM) Considerations," the granular tasks for DR such as backup and restore, are covered in greater detail, but they are also outlined at a high level in this chapter to assist with your project planning efforts.

In this chapter, we will discuss the various elements within the overall platform that must be administered and maintained to ensure a highly available and secure environment.

The administration and maintenance tasks and responsibilities will be affected by the overall design and architecture that has been implemented, as well as the services that the organization is providing within the overall platform.

The administration and maintenance of SharePoint 2013, Office 365, and SharePoint Online include interaction with the individual(s) responsible for your organization's Active Directory, SQL Server, Exchange and network configurations, and system architecture.

> **NOTE**
>
> I would recommend reviewing and providing your infrastructure team with a recent publication from Microsoft regarding best practices for SQL Server in a SharePoint Server farm, which Microsoft has continued to keep up-to-date with the latest features and changes, that can be accessed at the following link: http://technet.microsoft.com/en-us/library/hh292622(v=office.15).aspx

Platform Monitoring and Auditing for On-Premises, Cloud, and Hybrid Cloud Implementations

Whether your organization is implementing a SharePoint 2013 on-premises environment (private cloud) or an Office 365 and/or SharePoint Online (public cloud) or a combination of the two in a hybrid cloud scenario, you can utilize various tools to monitor and audit almost any aspect of an environment's servers, databases, applications, system performance, and content growth, as well as other key metrics.

There should be a preventive and proactive mind-set regarding monitoring and maintaining the environment to identify potential issues and address them before they cause negative impacts and affect the underlying user base.

The following provides an overview of the recommended monitoring and auditing tools that cover the different aspects of the underlying platforms:

▶ **SharePoint Health Analyzer Overview**

   ▶ This tool is available for SharePoint 2013 on-premises deployments. You can access it from the central administration home page by clicking on the Monitoring option, as shown in Figure 15.1, and then selecting Health Analyzer. This tool can be utilized to analyze and resolve problems in the following areas:

   ▶ Performance

   ▶ Security

   ▶ Configuration

   ▶ Platform availability

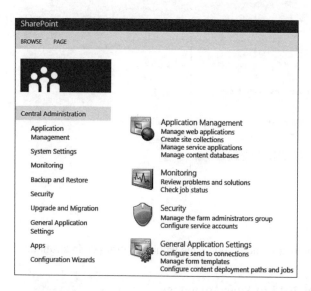

FIGURE 15.1   SharePoint 2013's on-premises deployment's Central Administration page.

▶ You can create predefined runes for the Health Analyzer to run at scheduled intervals, which will trigger a rule if an error is detected, which will then provide you recommendations and ways in which the error or issue can be resolved.

▶ **Timer Jobs**

   ▶ This tool is available for SharePoint 2013 on-premises deployments. You can access it from the central administration home page by clicking on Monitoring and then Timer Jobs, as shown in Figure 15.2. SharePoint 2013 uses configurable timer jobs to collect health data and then writes the data to the logging folder and to the logging database. This data is then used in reports to display the health status of the farm servers. You can reschedule a timer job as well as enable or disable it, and run it on demand.

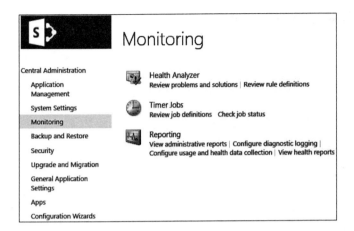

FIGURE 15.2   SharePoint 2013's on-premises monitoring page within Central Administration.

▶ **Using Reporting in SharePoint 2013 to Your Advantage**

   ▶ This tool is available for SharePoint 2013 on-premises deployments. You can access it from the central administration home page by clicking on Monitoring and then Reporting, as shown in Figure 15.2. This feature lets you configure diagnostic logging and data collection, and view administrative and health reports.

▶ **System Center 2012's Operations Manager (SCOM) with System Center Management Pack for SharePoint Server 2013**

   ▶ System Center 2012's Operations Manager is a powerful monitoring platform that lets you monitor services, devices, and operations across your entire organization. The System Center Management Pack for SharePoint Server 2013 monitors events and collects SharePoint component-specific performance counters in one central location and provides alerts for any errors or issues, which you then can immediately act on to resolve.

      ▶ To download the System Center Monitoring Pack for SharePoint Server 2013, refer to the following link:

         http://www.microsoft.com/en-us/download/details.aspx?id=35590

      ▶ To download the System Center Monitoring Pack for SharePoint Foundation 2013, refer to the following link:

         http://www.microsoft.com/en-us/download/details.aspx?id=35591

▶ **Windows PowerShell and Its Administration Capabilities**

    ▶ Windows PowerShell is a powerful tool for monitoring SharePoint 2013 that is available for both on-premises and SharePoint Online. It utilizes PowerShell cmdlets to obtain the granular logs for specific information that you want to monitor or obtain. Additional information and granular options related to Windows PowerShell are covered later in this chapter.

    For more information on how to view diagnostic logs using PowerShell, refer to the following link:

    http://technet.microsoft.com/en-us/library/ff463595(v=office.15).aspx

---

NOTE

Windows PowerShell cannot be utilized to manage Office 365 Small Business or Office 365 Small Business Premium.

▶ **Event Viewer Overview**

    ▶ Event Viewer is a Microsoft Management Console (MMC) snap-in that provides for the ability to easily browse and manage event logs.

    For more information on the Event Viewer, refer to the following link:

    http://technet.microsoft.com/library/cc766042

▶ **Developer Dashboard in SharePoint 2013**

    ▶ The Developer Dashboard in SharePoint 2013 has been improved to provide more information in a more accurate way to track and debug issues with page-rendering time. It provides for the following capabilities:

        ▶ Detailed request information per page with chant view

        ▶ A dedicated tab for ULS log entries for particular request

▶ **Office 365 Admin Center: Office 365's Central Hub**

    ▶ The Office 365 Admin Center, as shown in Figure 15.3, is the central page for Office 365 administrators to view the overall platform's health and up-to-date usage. This centralized location provides a place for administrators to manage Office 365 services, as shown in Figure 15.4, in SharePoint Online, Exchange Online, and Lync Online.

15

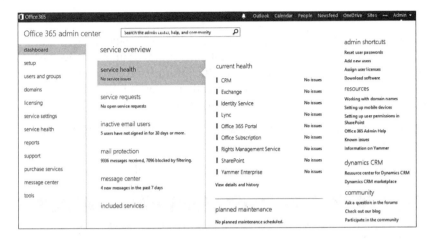

FIGURE 15.3   The Office 365 Admin Center.

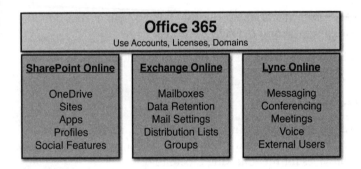

FIGURE 15.4   An overview of Office 365's core technologies.

The Office 365 Admin Center provides for the following capabilities:

▶ A central location to perform tasks related to users and groups such as these:

   ▶ Adding, editing, or removing users

   ▶ Resetting passwords

   ▶ Assigning licenses

   ▶ Managing security permissions, security groups, and delegated administrators

   ▶ Configuring single sign-on and directory synchronization

> ▶ A central location to manage your Office 365 domains

> ▶ Access to a knowledge base for troubleshooting issues, as well as links to view solutions to common issues and access troubleshooting tools

> ▶ Creation of a new service request online or reviewing of existing service requests

> ▶ Option to purchase subscriptions and Office 365 services as well as manage licenses

> ▶ Ability for admins to view the service status for all Office 365 services, as well as view upcoming planned maintenance

It is key that you utilize these tools to perform daily and weekly reviews of the underlying platform and related system's health, test and ensure that the backup jobs are being successfully performed, and continually review key metrics around usage, search, and storage.

The monitoring and related maintenance you perform and the related processes you follow must be documented and kept up-to-date within your organization's SharePoint 2013 and/or Office 365 governance strategy; this will ensure that your platform can perform at the levels expected by your end users.

15

TIP

The Microsoft Office Configuration Analyzer Tool (OffCAT) provides a detailed report of your installed Office programs, and these reports include several parameters about your organization's Office program configuration. The OffCAT highlights known problems that are found when it performs a scan of your organization's computer. For any problems listed in the report, you are provided a link to a Microsoft (public-facing) article regarding each problem or issues so that you can read about possible fixes. For more information regarding the Office Configuration Analyzer Tool, refer to the following link: http://www.microsoft.com/en-us/download/details.aspx?id=36852

SharePoint 2013 Administration Considerations

SharePoint 2013 administration encompasses a wide range of tasks and topics, from ensuring security-related best practices and maintenance to ensure your sites are secure, to reviewing the underlying performance and reviewing the backup and DR jobs to ensure that the processes are functioning as expected.

Microsoft has provided a great high-level layout of the administration tasks, as shown in Figure 15.5, which include the following:

> ▶ Application Management

>> ▶ Manage web applications

>> ▶ Create site collections

- ▶ Manage service applications

- ▶ Manage content databases

▶ Monitoring

- ▶ Review problems and solutions

- ▶ Check job status

▶ Security

- ▶ Manage the farm administrators group

- ▶ Configure service accounts

▶ General Application Settings

- ▶ Configure send to connections

▶ Configuration Wizards

- ▶ Farm configuration wizard

▶ System Settings

- ▶ Manage servers in this farm

- ▶ Manage services on server

- ▶ Manage farm features

- ▶ Configure alternate accessing mappings

▶ Backup and Restore

- ▶ Perform a backup

- ▶ Restore from a backup

- ▶ Perform a site collection backup

▶ Upgrade and Migration

- ▶ Convert farm license type

  - ▶ For more information on configuring licensing in SharePoint Server 2013, refer to the following link: http://technet.microsoft.com/en-us/library/jj219627(v=office.15).aspx

- ▶ Check product and patch installation status

- ▶ Check upgrade status

▶ Apps

- ▶ Manage App Catalog

- ▶ Manage App Licenses

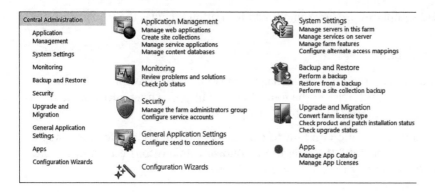

FIGURE 15.5   An overview of SharePoint 2013's Central Administration, which provides a nice layout for expected administrative tasks and duties.

TIP

To ensure that your organization takes into consideration browser compatibility and support in SharePoint 2013, refer to the following link: http://technet.microsoft.com/en-us/library/cc263526(v=office.15).aspx

For information regarding mobile device browser support in SharePoint 2013, refer to the following link: http://technet.microsoft.com/en-us/library/fp161353(v=office.15).aspx

Application Management

SharePoint 2013's Application Management, as shown in Figure 15.6, provides the core capabilities of providing sites and features to the organization.

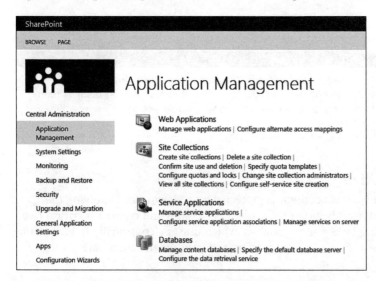

FIGURE 15.6   An overview of Application Management in SharePoint 2013.

SharePoint 2013's Application Management administration includes the management of the following:

▶ Web Applications

   ▶ For information on how to manage permissions for a web application in SharePoint 2013, refer to the following link: http://technet.microsoft.com/en-us/library/ff607719(v=office.15).aspx

   ▶ For more information on how to manage permission policies for a web application in SharePoint 2013, refer to the following link: http://technet.microsoft.com/en-us/library/ff608071(v=office.15).aspx

▶ Site Collections

   ▶ For more information on how to manage site collections in SharePoint 2013, refer to the following link: http://technet.microsoft.com/en-us/library/ff607925(v=office.15).aspx

   ▶ For more information on how to administer sites and site collections in SharePoint 2013, refer to the following link: http://technet.microsoft.com/en-us/library/cc789335(v=office.15).aspx

▶ Service Applications

   ▶ For more about service applications and services in SharePoint 2013, refer to the following link: http://technet.microsoft.com/en-us/library/ee704554(v=office.15).aspx

   ▶ For a complete list of service applications in SharePoint 2013, refer to the following link: http://social.technet.microsoft.com/wiki/contents/articles/12512.sharepoint-2013-service-applications-list.aspx

▶ Databases

NOTE

This information has been covered in Chapter 5, "Implementing a Best Practices SharePoint 2013/Office 365 Information Architecture," but it is also a good point of reference within these administration sections for readers who would like to review specific information on these direct topics.

Security Administration

Ensuring that your organization's content is protected by reviewing and applying the correct roles, groups, and organization's security model to sites and content is critical (see Figure 15.7). The following tasks and procedures, which must be continually followed and repeated, will ensure a best practices strategy to protect your organization data:

▶ Reviewing sites that have broken the default inheritance to meet a specific business need, which includes:

    ▶ Assigned explicit permissions

    ▶ Permissions that are inherited by child objects

▶ Managing the membership of the site collection administrators group

▶ Configuring managed accounts and service accounts

▶ Specifying authentication providers

▶ Managing trust as well as reviewing S2S configurations, etc.

▶ Reviewing the content that is allowed within SharePoint such as the approved file types

▶ Perform SharePoint 2013's security administration tasks that include:

    ▶ Reviewing SharePoint's user role assignments and how their inheritance structure is applied (e.g., parent/child relationship) by performing reviews on:

        ▶ Sites

        ▶ Subsites

        ▶ Lists

        ▶ Libraries

        ▶ Folders

        ▶ Items

        ▶ Documents

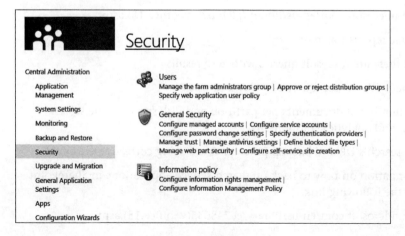

FIGURE 15.7   An overview of security administration within SharePoint 2013's Central Administration.

Search Administration

SharePoint 2013's search is one of the most high-profile features of SharePoint. It must be maintained and monitored to ensure that your users are getting the results expected and that search is up-to-date and relevant, as well as fully functional.

For more information on how to administrate search in SharePoint 2013, refer to the following link: http://technet.microsoft.com/en-us/library/ee792877(v=office.15).aspx

SharePoint 2013's search administration includes the following tasks:

▶ Reviewing, daily and weekly, SharePoint's search topology UI and ensuring that all components are in a "green" status, as shown in Figure 15.8.

  For more information on how to manage the search topology in SharePoint Server 2013, refer to the following link:

  http://technet.microsoft.com/en-us/library/jj219705(v=office.15).aspx

Search Application Topology						
Server Name	Admin	Crawler	Content Processing	Analytics Processing	Query Processing	Index Partition 0
IndexServer1	✓	✓	✓	✓		✓
IndexServer2		✓				⚠
WebFrontEnd1					✓	

FIGURE 15.8   Reviewing SharePoint 2013's search application topology.

▶ Monitoring performance reports, crawler health, and query health

  For more information on how to scale search for performance and availability in SharePoint Server 2013, refer to the following link:

  http://technet.microsoft.com/en-us/library/jj219628(v=office.15).aspx

▶ Reviewing usage reports for trends

▶ Ensuring that there are no result queries with zero results

▶ Getting familiar with the top queries by day and week

▶ Verifying the number of documents per partition and disk space on the search index, crawler, and analytics components

▶ Ensuring that search's DR and backup procedures are being correctly performed

  For more information on how to back up search service applications in SharePoint 2013, refer to the following link:

  http://technet.microsoft.com/en-us/library/ee748635(v=office.15).aspx

▶ Implementing query rules and best bests over time to improve the user's search experience

▶ Ensuring the that required services on the server have been enabled, as shown in Figure 15.9, to provide the content and capabilities for search to perform as expected

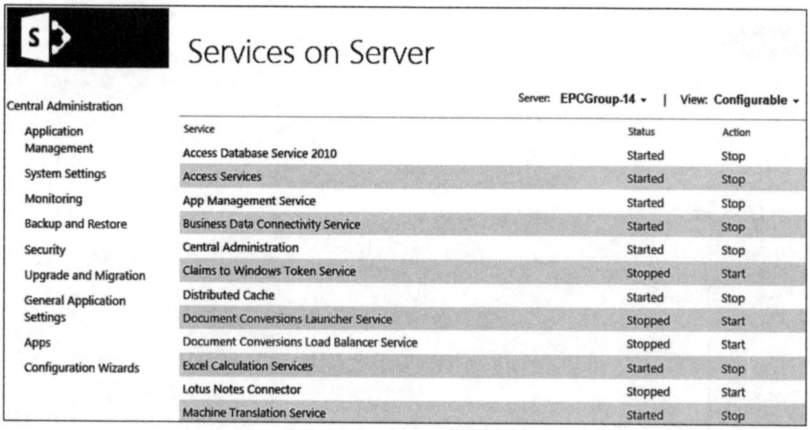

Services on Server

Central Administration

Server: EPCGroup-14 ▾ | View: Configurable ▾

Service	Status	Action
Access Database Service 2010	Started	Stop
Access Services	Started	Stop
App Management Service	Started	Stop
Business Data Connectivity Service	Started	Stop
Central Administration	Started	Stop
Claims to Windows Token Service	Stopped	Start
Distributed Cache	Started	Stop
Document Conversions Launcher Service	Stopped	Start
Document Conversions Load Balancer Service	Stopped	Start
Excel Calculation Services	Started	Stop
Lotus Notes Connector	Stopped	Start
Machine Translation Service	Started	Stop

Central Administration sidebar:
Application Management
System Settings
Monitoring
Backup and Restore
Security
Upgrade and Migration
General Application Settings
Apps
Configuration Wizards

FIGURE 15.9   Reviewing the services on the server that have been enabled.

TIP

The distributed cache in SharePoint 2013 uses 10% default RAM in the pool, and the size of the cache affects the speed and size of recent SharePoint newsfeeds. It is key to review health analyzer reports to ensure that the distributed cache is functioning correctly within your organization's farm.

TIP

To ensure that you are aware of the latest software updates, including update rollups, service packs, feature packs, critical updates, security updates, or hotfix updates available from Microsoft for SharePoint 2013, refer to the following link: http://technet.microsoft.com/en-us/sharepoint/jj891062.aspx

For information on how to deploy these updates based on your specific environment's configuration and the related update provided by Microsoft, refer to the following link: http://technet.microsoft.com/en-us/library/cc263467(v=office.15).aspx

For more information regarding SharePoint 2013's SP1 as well as Office 365's SP1, refer to the following link: http://blogs.technet.com/b/office_sustained_engineering/archive/2014/02/25/announcing-the-release-of-service-pack-1-for-office-2013-and-sharepoint-2013.aspx

SharePoint Admin Center in Office 365

SharePoint Online administration provides for the wide range of administration tasks and topics to ensure that your environment is configured to meet your organization's expectations. The SharePoint Online Admin Center, as shown in Figure 15.10, provides for the following main administrative areas:

FIGURE 15.10   SharePoint Online Admin Center.

- ▶ Site Collections
    - ▶ Create new site collections, either private site collections or public websites
    - ▶ Site collection properties
    - ▶ Site collection storage quotas
    - ▶ Update links
    - ▶ Manage site collection ownership
    - ▶ Buy additional storage for the tenant
    - ▶ Sharing settings for the site collection
    - ▶ Update site collection server resource quotas
    - ▶ Add domain

- ▶ OneDrive for Business
  - ▶ Change the OneDrive for Business storage limit for individual users
- ▶ InfoPath
  - ▶ Specify user browser-enabled form template settings
  - ▶ Specify exempt user agents
- ▶ User Profiles, as shown in Figure 15.11
  - ▶ People management
  - ▶ Organizations management
  - ▶ My Site settings management

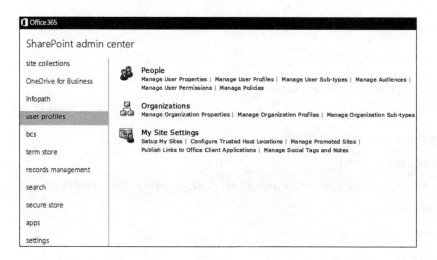

FIGURE 15.11   SharePoint Online User Profiles page.

- ▶ BCS, as shown in Figure 15.12
  - ▶ Manage BDC models and external content types
  - ▶ Manage connections to online services
  - ▶ Manage connection to on-premises services

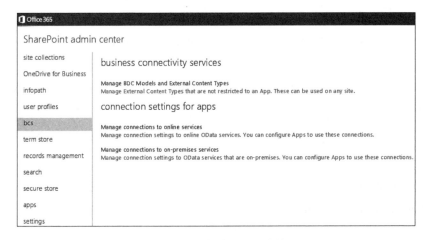

FIGURE 15.12   SharePoint Online BCS page.

▶ Term Store

    ▶ Specify whether terms are available for tagging

    ▶ Specify the language of the labels for the terms

    ▶ Provide a description for terms

    ▶ Specify default labels

    ▶ Browser taxonomy terms store and search dictionaries and the system settings

▶ Records Management

    ▶ Specify sent to connections

    ▶ Specify connection settings

    ▶ Add and remove a connection

▶ Search

    ▶ Manage search schema

    ▶ Manage search dictionaries

    ▶ Manage authoritative pages

    ▶ Modify query suggestion settings

    ▶ Manage results sources

    ▶ Manage query rules

    ▶ Remove search results

    ▶ View usage reports

- ▶ Modify search center settings

- ▶ Export search configurations

- ▶ Import search configurations

- ▶ Modify crawl log permissions

▶ Secure Store

- ▶ Create a new secure store target application

- ▶ Delete a secure store target application

- ▶ Edit a secure store target application

- ▶ Set and modify secure store application credentials

▶ Apps

- ▶ Manage app catalog settings

- ▶ Purchase apps

- ▶ Manage app licenses

- ▶ Configure app store acquisition settings

- ▶ Monitor apps and track usage

- ▶ Manage app permissions

▶ Settings

- ▶ Specify enterprise social collaboration (for example, SharePoint newsfeed or Yammer.com service)

- ▶ Specify external sharing

- ▶ Specify global experience version settings

- ▶ Specify information rights management (IRM) capabilities

- ▶ Specify team site default locations, as well as site classification and URL requirements

- ▶ Specify whether to enable or disable Office on demand

- ▶ Specify whether to enable or disable preview features

Exchange Admin Center in Office 365

The Exchange Admin Center, as shown in Figure 15.13, provides for the wide range of administration tasks and topics to ensure your Exchange environment is configured to meet your organization's expectations.

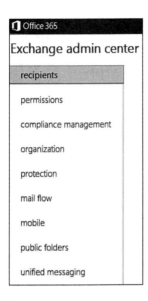

FIGURE 15.13   Office 365's Exchange Admin Center menu.

The Exchange Admin Center allows for the following settings to be managed from the Office 365 portal:

▶ Recipients

    ▶ Mailboxes

    ▶ Groups

    ▶ Resources

    ▶ Contacts

    ▶ Shared

    ▶ Migration

▶ Permissions

    ▶ Admin roles

    ▶ User roles

    ▶ Outlook web app policies

▶ Compliance Management, as shown in Figure 15.14

    ▶ In-place eDiscovery and hold

    ▶ Auditing

    ▶ Data loss prevention

▶ Retention policies

▶ Retention tags

▶ Journal rules

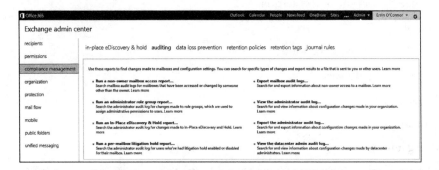

FIGURE 15.14   Exchange Admin Center Compliance Management options.

▶ Organization

   ▶ Calendar sharing policies

   ▶ Apps to add functionality to your Outlook web app experience

▶ Protection

   ▶ Malware filters

   ▶ Connection filters

   ▶ Content filters

   ▶ Outbound spam

   ▶ Quarantine

▶ Mail Flow

   ▶ Rules

   ▶ Delivery reports

   ▶ Message trace

   ▶ Accepted domains

   ▶ Connectors

- ▶ Mobile
  - ▶ Mobile device access management
  - ▶ Mobile device mailbox policies
  - ▶ Exchange ActiveSync access settings
- ▶ Public Folders
  - ▶ Add, edit, or delete public folders
  - ▶ Public folder mailboxes
- ▶ Unified Messaging
  - ▶ UM dial plans
  - ▶ UM IP gateways

The Exchange Admin Center allows for commonly used Exchange Online service settings such as these:

- ▶ Management of users' email accounts
- ▶ Management of groups, contacts, and distribution lists
- ▶ Access to Outlook Web Access
- ▶ Spam and malware filtering, as well as related rules
- ▶ Compliance management, as well as eDiscovery, auditing, retention tags, and journal rules
- ▶ Management of rules, delivery reports, accepted domains, and message trace
- ▶ Email on phones using Exchange ActiveSync
- ▶ Facebook and LinkedIn contact sync
- ▶ Calendar settings
- ▶ External contacts
- ▶ Shared mailboxes
- ▶ Distribution groups
- ▶ Password expiration policy
- ▶ How to grant and revoke access to mailboxes
- ▶ Connected accounts
- ▶ Inbox rules and automatic reply

TIP

The Office 365 Best Practices Analyzer for Exchange Server 2013 is an automated tool that evaluates the health and readiness of your on-premises Exchange Server 2013 environment. It can also be utilized for organizations that want to establish a hybrid Exchange Server 2013 configuration or want to leverage Exchange Online exclusively.

You will be required to have an Office 365 or Azure Active Directory user ID to download this tool, and after you have downloaded the Office 365 Best Practices Analyzer for Exchange Server 2013, you will not be required to sign in to the Office 365 Admin Center to rerun the checks.

For more information regarding this tool, refer to the following link: http://community. office365.com/en-us/wikis/deploy/office-365-best-practices-analyzer-for-exchange-server-2013.aspx

Lync Admin Center in Office 365

The Lync Admin Center, as shown in Figure 15.15, provides for the wide range of administration tasks and topics to ensure that your Lync environment is configured to meet your organization's expectations.

FIGURE 15.15   Office 365's Lync Admin Center menu.

The Lync Admin Center enables the following settings to be managed from the Office 365 portal:

▶ Users

▶ Organization, as shown in Figure 15.16

  ▶ General for configuring presence privacy and mobile phone notifications

  ▶ External Communications for specifying allowed or blocked domains, as well as for selecting whether to allow for public IM connectivity with Skype users and other public IM service providers

▶ Dial-in Conferencing

    ▶ Provider

    ▶ Dial-in users

▶ Meeting Invitation

FIGURE 15.16   The Office's Lync Admin Center options on the organization's external communications page.

The following Lync Online settings can be managed from the Office 365 portal:

▶ Edit user settings

▶ Domain federation

▶ Instant messaging notifications on mobile devices

▶ Dial-in conferencing

▶ Online presence

▶ External communications

▶ Recording

▶ Instant messaging notifications on mobile devices

▶ Enable or disable PIC

SQL Server 2012/2014 Best Practice Administration for SharePoint 2013

There are various key strategies and administration best practices to follow to ensure that your organization's SharePoint 2013 environment is providing optimal performance and that the growth of the underlying content databases is governed in SQL Server 2012/2014 to ensure a fully recoverable environment in a disaster recovery scenario.

> **NOTE**
>
> For more information regarding storage and SQL Server capacity planning and configuration for SharePoint Server 2013, refer to the following link: http://technet.microsoft.com/en-us/library/cc298801(v=office.15).aspx

These are the key SharePoint 2013 and SQL Server integration and configuration points:

▶ SharePoint 2013's farm configuration information is stored in the configuration database in SQL Server.

▶ The majority of SharePoint content is stored in SQL Server.

▶ SharePoint 2013's central administration content is stored within its own content database.

▶ Most SharePoint 2013 service applications have at least one content database.

▶ All SharePoint 2013 web apps have at least one content database.

SharePoint 2013's content databases have key considerations of their own:

▶ SharePoint 2013 site collections reside in only one content database.

▶ SharePoint 2013 content databases can contain multiple site collections; you can utilize quota templates to specify the maximum number of site collections allowed.

▶ You can control the size of databases from within SharePoint 2013.

The following are key SharePoint 2013 and SQL Server 2012/2014 administration and related configuration best practices:

▶ Ensure that any one SharePoint 2013 content database remains under 200GB to ensure recoverability in a reasonable amount of time to meet your organization's DR SLAs.

▶ Use database autogrowth as sparingly as possible unless your underlying requirements require such a configuration approach.

    ▶ Reduces fragmentation

    ▶ Improves overall performance

▶ Create multiple TempDB files on multiple disks.

▶ Provide for dedicated server/instance with SQL Server alias.

▶ Do not allow spousal installations.

▶ Ensure that you modify the model database settings.

▶ Spread data files and transaction log files across multiple physical drives or locations on RAID 5/10.

▶ Avoid shrinking database files.

▶ Ensure that you have a comprehensive and repeatable database maintenance plan for the overall SharePoint SQL Server database farm(s).

▶ Ensure that your organization is utilizing the appropriate number of processors in your parallel plan execution via the configuration of the maximum degree of parallelism (MDOP). For more information on server configuration, see http://technet.microsoft.com/en-us/library/ms189094.aspx.

▶ Monitor disk seconds per read/write to ensure <20ms.

▶ Defragment drives containing content database files.

▶ Ensure that your organization's backup and restore (DR strategy) performs regular backups of database and transaction logs.

▶ Be prepared and proactive to account for SharePoint's content database content growth as this happens in 95% of all implementations.

▶ Ensure that you presize your tempdb to approximately 20% of the size of the single-largest SharePoint 2013 content database.

▶ Document all instances and related versions of SharePoint and SQL Server, as well as related updates, service packs, and patches.

It is key to understand SQL Server system databases and their underlying hierarchy as follows:

▶ **Master:** Configuration database of SQL Server

▶ **Msdb:** SQL Server automation

▶ **Tempdb:** Temporary storage work area

▶ **Model:** Template for all new databases

SQL Server Maintenance Strategies for SharePoint 2013

The following are key SharePoint 2013 and SQL Server 2012/2014 maintenance best practices that your organization should consider implementing and that must be documented in your SQL Server maintenance plans:

▶ Log sizing configurations are set to full logged, which is the default, which generates extremely large transactions logs.

▶ Backups:

  ▶ Local disk are easy but are very storage intensive.

  ▶ Agents are remote but require extra software.

▶ RBS maintenance must ensure that you are aware of BLOB orphans.

  ▶ For more information on how to plan for RBS in SharePoint 2013 as well as references regarding BLOG orphans, refer to the following link: http://technet. microsoft.com/en-us/library/ff628583(v=office.15).aspx

SharePoint 2013 Backup and Recovery

The backup and recovery options, as well as the development of a disaster recovery (DR) and business continuity management strategy (BCM) strategy for your organization's SharePoint 2013, Office 365, and/or SharePoint online implementation, are covered in Chapter 18.

For a SharePoint 2013 on-premises (private cloud) implementation, you can utilize the Backup and Restore page within SharePoint's Central Administration, as shown in Figure 15.17. You also can utilize Windows PowerShell for backup and restore. For more information on PowerShell backup and recovery cmdlets in SharePoint 2013, refer to the following link: http://technet.microsoft.com/en-us/library/ee890109(v=office.15).aspx

FIGURE 15.17   SharePoint 2013's Backup and Restore page within Central Administration for a private cloud implementation.

For an Office 365 and SharePoint Online cloud (public cloud) implementation, the backup and business continuity is managed by Microsoft via the Office 365 SLAs and overall availability metrics that can be viewed at the following link: http://blogs.office. com/2013/08/08/cloud-services-you-can-trust-office-365-availability/

The Office 365 backup, restore, and business continuity SLAs include those for Exchange Online, Lync Online, SharePoint Online, Yammer, and Microsoft Dynamics CRM Online; you can also restore these by contacting Microsoft by creating a new server request, as shown in Figure 15.18, or by contacting technical support at 1-800-865-9408.

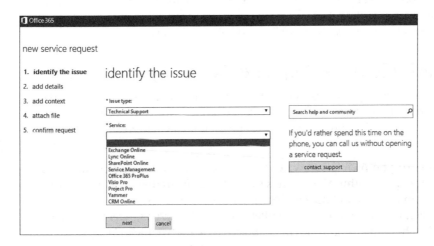

FIGURE 15.18   Creating a new service request by using the Office 365 Support and Service Request option from within Office 365.

TIP

The SharePoint Online SLAs provide for the following backups and related restore options:

▶ Site collection backups are taken every 12 hours and retained for 14 days.

▶ For a site collection to be restored, you must contact Microsoft technical support by creating a new service request (support ticket) or by calling technical support at 1-800-865-9408.

▶ The only currently supported restore option is a full site collection restore.

▶ The site collection restore uses the same URL when it is restored, so you will lose any data that is currently hosted within the SharePoint Online site collection at that URL. You should create a separate and/or temporary site or site collection and move any current or new data that has been created since the site collection backup you are asking to be restored.

Windows PowerShell Administration Overview

Windows PowerShell is a very powerful tool for performing administrative and main-tenance-related tasks for your organization's SharePoint 2013 environment, as well as SharePoint Online, Exchange Online, and Lync Online. Microsoft provides a great deal of information to assist you in learning PowerShell. One of those tools is the Windows PowerShell for SharePoint Command Builder, as shown in Figure 15.19, which you can access at the following link: http://www.microsoft.com/resources/TechNet/en-us/Office/media/WindowsPowerShell/WindowsPowerShellCommandBuilder.html

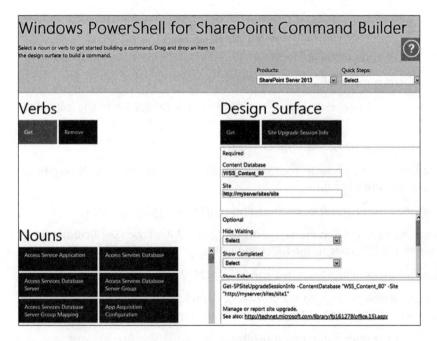

FIGURE 15.19   The Windows PowerShell for SharePoint Command Builder.

NOTE

To download the Windows PowerShell Command Builder user's guide for SharePoint 2013, Office 365, SharePoint Online, and SharePoint 2010, refer to the following link: http://download.microsoft.com/download/5/5/C/55CBF854-D7FD-43D9-B6F0-813AB33AC360/Windows-PowerShell-command-builder-guide.docx

---

PowerShell is available both for SharePoint 2013 on-premises and for SharePoint Online via the SharePoint Online Management Shell, which enables you to manage users, sites, and various other areas within SharePoint Online. This enables you to perform these types of administrative tasks without having to rely on the SharePoint Online Administration Center. For an introduction to the SharePoint Online management shell, refer to the following link: http://technet.microsoft.com/en-us/library/fp161388(v=office.15).aspx

Windows PowerShell Resources and References

Microsoft offers many resources that detail examples of Windows PowerShell cmdlets and scenarios to ensure that you can successfully utilize Windows PowerShell to perform various administrative, maintenance, support, upgrade, and development tasks. The following provides an overview of the additional online resources available:

▶ **SharePoint 2013 on-premises: Windows PowerShell**

   ▶ For an overview of Windows PowerShell for SharePoint 2013, refer to the following link:

   http://technet.microsoft.com/en-us/library/ee662539(v=office.15).aspx

   ▶ For an overview on how to use Windows PowerShell to administer SharePoint 2013, refer to the following link:

   http://technet.microsoft.com/en-us/library/ee806878(v=office.15).aspx

   ▶ For an index of PowerShell cmdlets for SharePoint 2013, refer to the following link:

   http://technet.microsoft.com/library/ff678226(office.15).aspx

   ▶ For an overview on how to configure licensing by using Windows PowerShell, refer to the following link:

   http://technet.microsoft.com/en-us/library/jj219627(office.15).aspx

   ▶ For an overview on App management using Windows PowerShell cmdlets in SharePoint 2013, refer to the following link:

   http://technet.microsoft.com/en-us/library/jj219772(v=office.15).aspx

   ▶ For an overview on how to manage service applications and the related cmdlets in SharePoint 2013, refer to the following link:

   http://technet.microsoft.com/en-us/library/ee906561(v=office.15).aspx

   ▶ For an overview on PowerShell cmdlets regarding SQL Server 2012 Reporting Services (Reporting Services SharePoint Mode), refer to the following link:

   http://msdn.microsoft.com/en-us/library/gg492249.aspx

▶ **SharePoint Online: Windows PowerShell**

   ▶ For an index of Windows PowerShell cmdlets for SharePoint Online, refer to the following link:

   http://technet.microsoft.com/en-us/library/fp161364(v=office.15).aspx

   ▶ To set up the SharePoint Online Management Shell Windows PowerShell environment, refer to the following link:

   http://technet.microsoft.com/en-us/library/fp161372(v=office.15).aspx

> ▶ For an overview of the available detailed references for Windows PowerShell for SharePoint Online, refer to the following link:
>
> http://technet.microsoft.com/en-us/library/fp161397(v=office.15).aspx

▶ **Exchange Online: Windows PowerShell**

> ▶ For an overview of Exchange Online Windows PowerShell cmdlets, refer to the following link:
>
> http://technet.microsoft.com/en-us/library/jj200780(EXCHG.150).aspx
>
> ▶ For information on how to connect to Exchange Online Using remote PowerShell, refer to the following link:
>
> http://technet.microsoft.com/en-us/library/jj984289(v=exchg.150).aspx
>
> ▶ For information on how to manage remote PowerShell access in Exchange Online, refer to the following link:
>
> http://technet.microsoft.com/en-us/library/jj984292(v=exchg.150).aspx

▶ **Lync Online: Windows PowerShell**

> ▶ For information on how to use Windows PowerShell to Manage Lync Online, refer to the following link:
>
> http://technet.microsoft.com/library/dn362831.aspx

▶ **Microsoft Azure AD: Windows PowerShell**

> ▶ For an overview on how to manage Microsoft Azure AD using Windows PowerShell, refer to the following link:
>
> http://technet.microsoft.com/en-us/library/jj151815.aspx

System Center 2012 Overview

Microsoft's System Center 2012 provides a comprehensive way for you to manage your organization's environmental infrastructure, as well as the devices and services to which it is connected. System Center 2012, as depicted in Figure 15.20, provides for infrastructure provisioning and monitoring, application performance monitoring, automation, and IT service management.

15

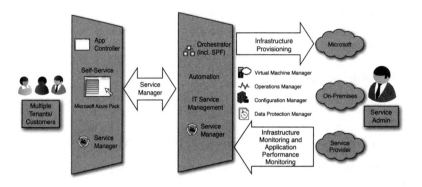

FIGURE 15.20   A high-level overview of System Center 2012.

The following list provides a high-level overview of System Center 2012 and some of its key capabilities:

▶ Comprehensive management of your organization's Windows Server, SharePoint, Exchange, SQL Server, and Azure resources

▶ Capabilities to ensure the optimization of apps and workloads by providing analytics and reports to ensure that you can predictably meet your application SLAs

▶ Infrastructure provisioning for key business and technical requirements such as workload scaling to meet specific performance metrics and related needs

▶ Infrastructure monitoring for resources that are physical, virtual, or architected in a hybrid cloud model

▶ Comprehensive IT service management to provide the necessary service management processes such as managing custom service request offerings, as well as linking them to an underlying organizational chargeback model

For more information on System Center 2012, refer to the following link:
http://www.microsoft.com/en-us/server-cloud/products/system-center-2012-r2/default.aspx

Administration of Mobile Devices

Microsoft's latest version of Windows Intune enables organizations to manage mobile devices as well as desktop and laptop devices in a unified manner. With Windows Intune, you can upload and publish software packages as well as deploy and configure management and security policies from a central location in a "one stop shop" manner.

Windows Intune also provides the capability to disable lost or stolen devices and wipe them to ensure that your organization's intellectual property is safe and you are able to minimize the risks that happen during these types of events. This allows for BYOD initiatives to take hold due to the ability to lower the risk and provide IT as well as the business with real answers to compliance and regulatory concerns regarding these types of efforts.

Windows Intune enables you to ensure that devices that are allowed to access company data follow any password governance as well as device encryption and can also disable mobile devices that have too many failed login attempts.

For more information on Windows Intune, refer to the following link: http://www.microsoft.com/en-us/server-cloud/products/windows-intune

Summary

This chapter covered SharePoint 2013, Office 365, and SharePoint Online administration and maintenance recommendations for your organization to develop a comprehensive strategy that aligns with your underlying SharePoint governance strategy.

We discussed the various native capabilities of the platforms for you to perform these tasks, as well as how you can utilize Windows PowerShell to automate and perform maintenance in a repeatable fashion.

In the next chapter, we will discuss the social capabilities of SharePoint 2013, Office 365, and SharePoint Online to allow for increased sharing and collaboration within your organization.

15

Social Networking and My Site Strategies

Overview of Social Capabilities in SharePoint 2013, Office 365, and SharePoint Online

Over the past two releases of SharePoint and into this latest release of SharePoint 2013 and its new cloud-based version of SharePoint Online and Office 365, Microsoft has continued to add and improve on the platform's social capabilities.

In this new release of SharePoint 2013, Microsoft has successfully brought together all the various "social moving pieces" to provide organizations with the industry's leading social and "professional networking" platform to increase sharing, knowledge transfer, and collaboration in a secure and seamless manner.

SharePoint 2013's new social features include the following:

▶ Community

▶ Social tagging

▶ Capability to easily share content and activities

▶ Capability to follow documents, people, sites, news-feeds, tags, and activities

▶ Improved activity streams

▶ Improved My Sites

▶ Improved Yammer integration

▶ Microblogging and improved newsfeed capabilities

▶ Tailoring of your personal scope of interest to personal, site, and company feeds

▶ Capability to now include "likes," "@mentions," and "#tags"

The following sections cover the new social features and capabilities of SharePoint 2013, Office 365, and SharePoint Online, as well as sample scenarios for which your organization can utilize those features to provide these capabilities in a governed and secure manner.

For an overview of social computing terminology and concepts in SharePoint Server 2013, refer to the following link:http://technet.microsoft.com/en-us/library/jj219804.aspx

SharePoint Communities: Best Practices and Proven Strategies

The new community site, as shown in Figure 16.1, is created from a template similar to that of a team site, but is tailored with specific "social" features that also add a more competitive feel in terms of providing incentives for users to participate. This new community site has the capability to award users "badges" as well as "likes" to their posts, as well as providing "#tags" to follow trending topics that provide a corporate Facebook and Twitter combination with these components.

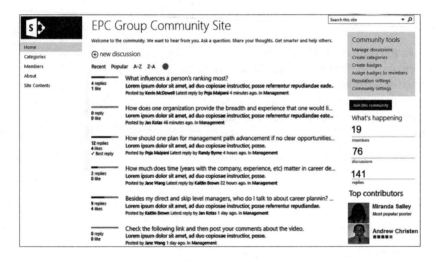

FIGURE 16.1   The new SharePoint 2013 community site.

Community sites are composed of the following features and underlying capabilities:

▶ A template that is available similar to a new team site template in SharePoint 2013

▶ Sites that contain features that are tailored to long-standing groups to facilitate discussion in a specific domain or profession

▶ A template that can be easily customized for the topic and goals of the community that consists of the following:

  ▶ Four basic pages: Home, Categories, Members, and About

  ▶ Membership and joining workflow

  ▶ The Activity Dashboard, Top Contributors, My Membership, Discussion List, and Owner Tools web parts

▶ A site that requires routine attention and facilitation by dedicated moderators

▶ A template that is well integrated into the overall social fabric of SharePoint 2013, Office 365, and SharePoint Online

▶ Integration for a community into SharePoint 2013's additional social components

▶ A community portal template for showcasing and promoting the various communities to users within your organization

▶ Lync integration for instant communication with other members of your community

▶ Community- and discussion-specific search features

Community sites provide for the following roles, features, and related capabilities:

▶ Community users and members roles for discovering, joining, and participating in a community

▶ Community owner roles for adding users and members, as well as configuring settings and permission

▶ Community moderator roles for monitoring, facilitating, managing, and promoting content

One of the most common areas of concern that organizations have regarding not having implemented the social capabilities of SharePoint in the previous two versions (SharePoint 2010 and SharePoint 2007) was the lack of native administration tools, as well as a way to enforce the organization's social governance policies, defined in the overall SharePoint governance strategy. A great new feature that you can easily configure is the Enable Reporting of Offensive Content option within a community's settings, as shown in Figure 16.2. I feel that this feature is mislabeled and should have been more generic in being named "Enable Reporting of Inappropriate, Sensitive, or Offensive Content," but it does have the same underlying effect.

16

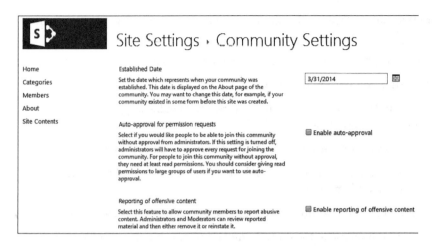

FIGURE 16.2   The Community Settings page that contains the option to enable reporting of offensive content.

NOTE

The Enable Reporting of Offensive Content feature is not enabled by default.

For example, without the Enable Reporting of Offensive Content feature enabled, a user who feels that a discussion post violates the community rules would not have the "Report to Moderator" feature, as shown in Figure 16.3, available to easily report the item. This features is also extremely useful if a user finds personal or even regulatory content or information (for example, PII, PHI, HIPAA) was accidentally listed and would like to immediately bring this to the moderator's attention.

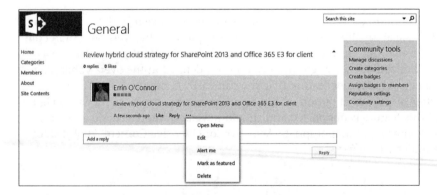

FIGURE 16.3   The drop-down options available when a user clicks on a discussion post when the Enable Reporting of Offensive Content option has not been activated.

The Enable Reporting of Offensive Content setting should be enabled in all communities within your organization. After it is activated, a user will then be provided an additional option in a post's drop-down list, Report to Moderator, as shown in Figure 16.4, which is key to helping community members be proactive about governing their specific community.

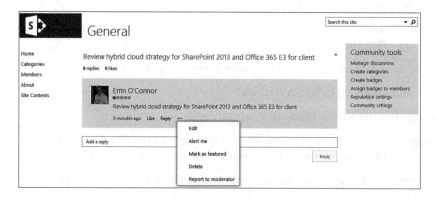

FIGURE 16.4   The Report to Moderator option is available in the drop-down option of a discussion post when the Enable Reporting of Offensive Content option is activated.

SharePoint 2013 provides for four main community categories:

▶ Communities of practice

Community for a group of people who share a unique skill, role, or profession to share experiences, best practices, and advice

▶ Communities of purpose

Community that exists to accomplish a specific goal, need, or mission

▶ Communities of interest

Community consisting of a group of people who share a common interest in or passion for a topic or domain

▶ Communities for social interaction

Community consisting of a group of people who primarily interact for the sake of interaction and socializing to build new relationships based on a common characteristic, culture, or geography commonality

Within the four main community categories, there are also four main types of communities:

▶ Private community

This type is available to only specified members.

▶ Permissions allow for the site to be shared only with specific users or groups.

▶ No approval settings are available.

▶ Closed community

Everyone can view the content of the site, but only members who have approved requests for membership can contribute.

  ▶ Permissions allow you to grant visitor permissions to everyone within the organization so that they can view the site and request to join.

  ▶ The approval settings allow you to enable access requests on the site.

▶ Open community with explicit join settings

Everyone can view the site and can automatically join to contribute to the site.

  ▶ Permissions allow you to grant visitor permissions to everyone within the organization so that they can view the site and automatically join as a member.

  ▶ The approval settings are set to auto-approval to allow users to automatically join the site.

▶ Open community without explicit join

Everyone can contribute to the community.

  ▶ Permissions allow you to share the site with everyone in the organization and grant member permissions so that the new users can all contribute.

  ▶ The approval settings do not provide for a join button to be visible and the auto-following for new members is not enabled.

For more information on communities in SharePoint Server 2013, refer to the following link: http://technet.microsoft.com/en-us/library/jj219805(v=office.15)

There is a centralized community portal template that can be created as a central hub for showcasing the various communities within your organization to your user base. The community portal performs the following:

▶ Aggregates all communities across an enterprise

  ▶ Sorts communities by popularity (membership, recent activity, age, and so on)

▶ Uses search to populate the list of the communities

  ▶ Provides the capability to be scoped to exclude communities created as subsites

  ▶ Does not list the community sites created via feature activation and does not aggregate to the portal

  ▶ Enabled search results to be security trimmed

  ▶ Shows only communities to which the visitor/user has access

A community is created via the community site template, as shown in Figure 16.5; it can be created as a site and subsite, but it is recommended that it be created as the root of a site collection. Also, any existing SharePoint site is provided the capability to activate the community site feature, as shown in Figure 16.6, to have this common functionality, although it is recommended that it be created at the root of a site collection.

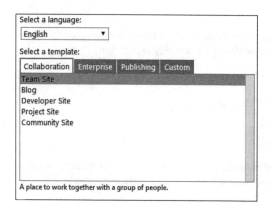

FIGURE 16.5   The community site template is available when you are creating a new site.

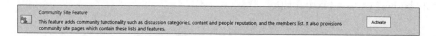

FIGURE 16.6   The community site feature can be activated within an existing SharePoint site.

For more information on how to plan for communities in SharePoint Server 2013, refer to the following link: http://technet.microsoft.com/en-us/library/jj219489(v=office.15)

For more information on how to create and configure communities in SharePoint Server 2013, refer to the following link: http://technet.microsoft.com/en-us/library/jj219543(v=office.15)

Community Features That Promote User Interaction

There is a competitive nature in communities that enables users who participate in discussions and act as "subject matter experts" (SMEs) to build a reputation, unique to each community, by other members' "likes" or star ratings. A community member's discussion or reply can also be tagged with the "best answer" tag, which also builds on the reputation of that user within a specific community. A community tracks each member's activity to build reputation and gathers metrics such as these:

- ▶ "Likes" or star ratings provided by other community members

- ▶ "Best answers" tags provided for an answer provided by a community member

- ▶ The number of posts, replies, and likes

Ratings can reflect as likes, as shown in Figure 16.7, or stars, as shown in Figure 16.8. If you choose to switch between the two options, you will not lose the underlying data.

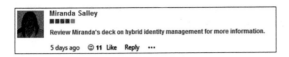

FIGURE 16.7   A community member's discussion receives "likes" from other community users based on its content, which builds on a user's SharePoint community reputation.

FIGURE 16.8   A community member's discussion receives stars from other community users based on a post's content, which builds on a user's SharePoint community reputation.

Community owners can also set achievement level settings, as shown in Figure 16.9, by configuring custom achievement levels, and community members gain points based on their participation to attain a level of achievement. These community levels are displayed as an image or a "badge" or as a textual title.

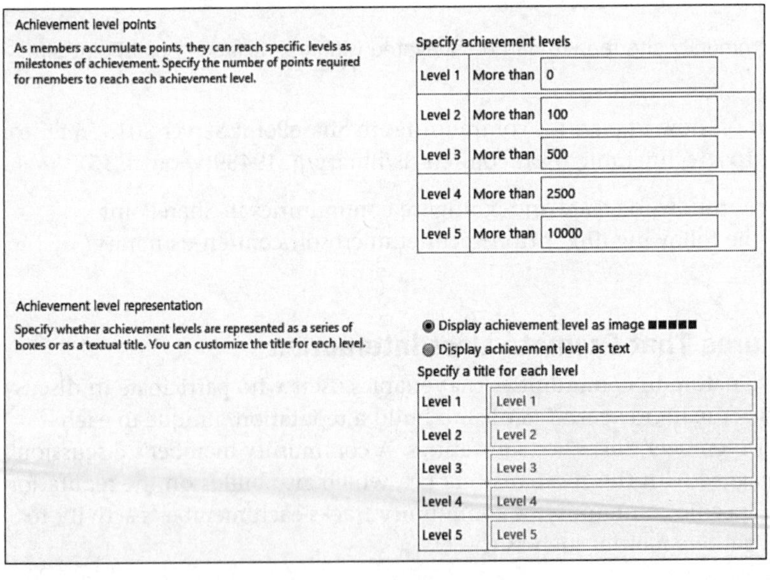

Achievement level points

As members accumulate points, they can reach specific levels as milestones of achievement. Specify the number of points required for members to reach each achievement level.

Specify achievement levels

Level 1	More than	0
Level 2	More than	100
Level 3	More than	500
Level 4	More than	2500
Level 5	More than	10000

Achievement level representation

Specify whether achievement levels are represented as a series of boxes or as a textual title. You can customize the title for each level.

◉ Display achievement level as image ■ ■ ■ ■ ■
◉ Display achievement level as text

Specify a title for each level

Level 1	Level 1
Level 2	Level 2
Level 3	Level 3
Level 4	Level 4
Level 5	Level 5

FIGURE 16.9   A community's underlying ability for its owner(s) to reach specific achievement levels within the community.

NOTE

A community's ratings settings can be enabled or disabled by the community's owner.

TIP

Discussions are always placed within a category format created by the community. SharePoint 2013 provides for an improved discussion experience that allows for rich media, rich text, and copy and paste, and is UX streamlined for reviewing.

The following elements provide insight into posts and related communications within a community:

► A discussion can be marked as a "Question."

► Replies can be made to the root post or to a reply.

► Members can mark any reply to their discussion as the "best reply."

► "Liking" the root post or individual replies adds to thread's reputation.

► Posts or replies can be reported to the moderator by any member.

The metrics tracked within a community then apply custom reputation levels and badges with a related icon such as "MVP" of a community or "Moderator." The community's moderator actually can provide custom attributes and even apply a "featured discussion" tag to popular posts.

Understanding Community Membership and Roles

The following list provides an overview of community membership:

► A community's membership is maintained in a SharePoint list.

► This membership list does not explicitly define site permissions for a member.

► When a site is shared by a member, the sharing activity itself does not automatically add the users who received the invitation to a community's members list.

► A user who joins a community automatically "follows" it.

► Leaving a community hides a member from the list but retains the points the member has earned in his participation in case he rejoins the community.

Community Owners

Community owners are assigned specific activities and responsibilities:

► Creating the community site via the community site template

► Maintaining community settings:

    ► Basic settings such as established date, as well as the monitoring reports and any reporting of post-related abuse

    ► Reputation settings and badges

▶ Customizing the community:

  ▶ Handling site icon, description, and theming

  ▶ Editing the home and about pages

  ▶ Establishing the categories for which the discussions and posts will be organized

  ▶ Adding apps, lists, libraries, calendars, pages, and other content

▶ Maintaining the community's permissions for users to ensure that they are up-to-date and relevant

▶ Sharing and promoting the community

▶ Managing the auto-approval feature to ensure that it is applicable and fits into the overall community model

Community Visitors and Members

Community visitors and members are assigned and/or can perform the following activities:

▶ Visiting and consuming content

▶ Following, joining, and maintaining membership in a community

▶ Participating with relevant posts that are beneficial to the community

▶ Monitoring any inappropriate or sensitive content that they feel should not have been shared

NOTE

Any reported content is stored in a hidden list, and the author of the reported content is not notified of the action.

Community Moderators

Community moderators have specific activities and responsibilities that they are assigned:

▶ Monitoring, facilitating, and managing the overall community, which includes these tasks:

  ▶ Ensuring that posts get replies and questions get answered

  ▶ Monitoring and utilizing the answered/unanswered filter

  ▶ Reviewing best replies for completeness

  ▶ Recategorizing discussions into their proper categories

  ▶ Maintaining high-quality and appropriate content

- ▶ Addressing reported content

- ▶ Editing or deleting incorrect or inappropriate content

- ▶ Arbitrating arguments and keeping the community positive and productive

▶ Maintaining a healthy and vibrant community (a critical responsibility)

▶ Promoting content and people:

- ▶ Featuring content

- ▶ Marking replies as "best reply"

- ▶ Helping specific discussions stand out

- ▶ Marking question as "answered"

- ▶ Boosting the reputation of the members who write the best replies

- ▶ Assigning "badges"

My Sites in SharePoint 2013, Office 365, and SharePoint Online

The My Site social architecture in SharePoint 2013, as shown in Figure 16.10, has undergone several major updates, and the "personal site" (My Site), as it is now being technically referenced, drives a great deal of the overall social technologies and experience in this new release.

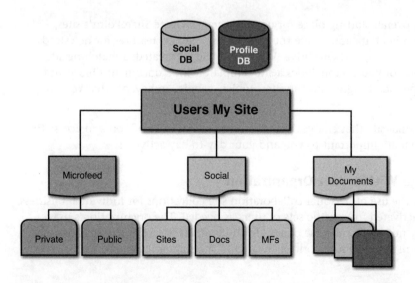

FIGURE 16.10   A high-level overview of SharePoint 2013's social architecture.

The My Site, as shown in Figure 16.11, drives the aggregation of the way users perform their everyday tasks within three difference major hubs. The personal site (My Site) drives sites, newsfeed, and OneDrive for Business. The My Site is the new "central platform location" that ties together the underlying technology which surfaces user profile data, search results, activity feeds, and tagging capabilities for all users within your organization.

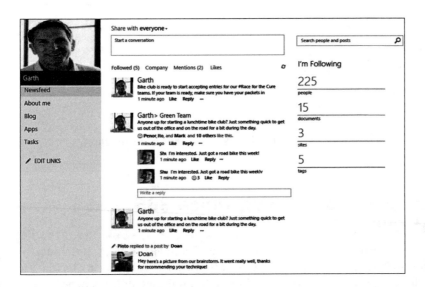

FIGURE 16.11   A SharePoint 2013 or Office 365 SharePoint Online My Site.

The My Site is the overall starting place for users to then navigate SharePoint's sites, lists, content, and other data and where they can access the new features for newsfeeds, hashtags, community sites, and OneDrive. When a My Site is created, a matching site collection is created for you that includes a site template with a document library and several apps that provide insight into the sites, topics, people, and events that you are interested in.

A My Site is a personal site that enables you to store personal information and access the events and data that are important to you and your day-to-day activities.

My Sites Usage Within Your Organization

My Sites represent the use of personal collaboration site collections for individual business users and can be activated for specific sets of users as needed. The organization's usage policy may or may not restrict the use of sites for individuals. However, all sites used for personal reasons will have reduced controls related to the standard site and site collection usage policies.

Table 16.1 describes the main areas for acceptable usage limits for individual My Sites.

TABLE 16.1   Areas for Acceptable Usage Limits for Individual My Sites

Usage	Description	Limit
Language Option	Determines whether My Sites can be created in languages other than the SharePoint Farm core language.	Default is unavailable without additional Multilingual User Interface (MUI) packs installed. Policy is that My Sites will be created using the core language English.
Storage Quota	Determines maximum storage size for all content in the site collection.	Default is 100MB.
User Solution	Determines maximum number of solution points scored before solutions automatically disable.	Disabled.
Blocked File Types	Determines which file extensions are automatically prevented from upload into a My Site Library.	Default is Farm Standard.
Site Collection Administrator	Determines which users have Site Collection Administration rights to the Site Collection.	Default is provisioned user.
SharePoint Designer	Determines whether SharePoint Designer is allowed to be used and which features of SharePoint Designer are allowed.	Default is Allowed. Standard is Disabled.
Privacy Controls	Determines whether other users are allowed to see information in an individual profile as well as the default state of visibility.	Default shows all directory-based properties to everyone and cannot be changed, but SharePoint-specific properties are manageable by user. Standard is set to default.
Blog or Other Subsite	Determines whether the Blog subsite or other subsites may be created by a specific user.	Default allows any subsite, including the Blog option, to be created. Standard is set to default.
OneDrive	Determines whether a user's OneDrive contains appropriate business content.	Default allows OneDrive to synchronize. Standard is set to disallow.

Additional policies applied to the shared My Site location are defined as outlined here:

▶ **Newsfeeds:** The newsfeed provides a system of showing updates to individual users who have subscribed to automatic updates on other users, content, or sites. The organization's policy must consider whether to allow the usage of newsfeeds.

▶ **Communities:** Communities are site templates that provide a forum experience within SharePoint. Communities enable you to categorize and cultivate discussions among a broad group of people across the organization.

▶ **Following and Microblogging:** Following is a user-initiated action that enables individuals to be updated on changes in a document, site, tag, or person, and provides the update on the individual's newsfeed. Related to following, microblogging gives a user a simple system of providing status updates on their own profile that other users can follow.

> **NOTE**
>
> Microblogging is not restricted by default but cannot be seen by others unless that user is followed. Your organization must define its approach and policy regarding the features of following and microblogging.

▶ **Tagging and Notes:** Tags, including hashtagging, enables an individual user to mark pages, list items, and sites with single or multiple words that can be used as a bookmarking system as well as update system for an individual based on personal interest in any of those types of content.

These tags are displayed in the Tag Cloud web part in the My Site for that user for later reference. The organization's policy should typically be to allow the usage of tagging and notes.

▶ **Ratings:** Ratings provide a method for users to score the relevance and value of content in pages, lists, and libraries, which improves their discoverability in Enterprise Search queries. The default for ratings is deactivated on most lists and libraries. Site owners and site designers can enable ratings for lists and libraries within their sites at their own discretion without further approval.

Understanding the Underlying System Architecture Behind My Sites

When an organization deploys My Sites for their users, the underlying SharePoint 2013 system architecture creates a web application, a My Site host site collection, an individual site collection, and several SharePoint service applications and features. The individual site collection is created after a user provisions a My Site, but the other moving pieces described are configured during the initial My Site deployment and shared among all the users who are part of the My Sites deployment.

My Sites consist of the following main functional areas:

▶ Newsfeed

  ▶ Provides you with updates on social activities for items and people you are following, including:

    ▶ People posts

    ▶ People profile changes

- ▶ Changes on followed documents

- ▶ Items tagged with followed tags

- ▶ Mentions and likes

- ▶ All of your activities

- ▶ Site feed activities

- ▶ Company feeds

  - ▶ I'm Following

    - ▶ Suggestions based on people "following" people, documents, and sites

  - ▶ Trending Tags

- ▶ About Me

  - ▶ Your personal profile page that includes information about you, as well as specifics on your role, job title, manager, and department. The more information you fill in, such as your expertise, the more likely that SharePoint search will be able to recommend you to others in the organization who may be looking for assistance with your subject-matter expertise.

- ▶ OneDrive for Business

  - ▶ For more information on how to plan for OneDrive for Business in SharePoint Server 2013, refer to the following link:

    http://technet.microsoft.com/en-us/library/dn232145(v=office.15).aspx

- ▶ Blog

- ▶ Apps

- ▶ Tasks

  - ▶ The task feature provides the ability to have a single, aggregated view of all user tasks across SharePoint sites, Project sites, and Microsoft Exchange.

  - ▶ Aggregation occurs through a new SSA named "Work Management" (WM).

    - ▶ WM uses a hidden list in a user personal site to cache all the aggregated data.

    - ▶ Users can also create new personal tasks that get stored in that list.

  - ▶ WM also provides the ability to write back tasks updated on the original location.

    - ▶ The Work Management Service is not federated and must run in the personal site content farm.

    - ▶ WM is integrated with the newsfeed and provides for the ability to follow up conversations through the My Tasks list.

Distributed Cache Service

SharePoint 2013 social architecture and related features rely heavily on My Sites data as well as the Distributed Cache service, which provides for the following:

▶ Two lists, the Microfeed list and the Social list

For an overview of microblog features, feeds, and the Distributed Cache service in SharePoint Server 2013, refer to the following link:

http://technet.microsoft.com/en-us/library/jj219700(v=office.15).aspx

▶ Personal site document libraries

▶ Profile database

The Distributed Cache service, which is built on top of the Windows Server AppFabric Cache, provides caching functionality to features and services in SharePoint Server 2013. The Distributed Cache service provides caching for the following:

▶ Authentication (e.g., FedAuth cookie for claims-based authentication)

▶ Newsfeeds

For information on how to plan for feeds and the Distributed Cache service in SharePoint Server 2013, refer to the following link:

http://technet.microsoft.com/library/jj219572(office.15).aspx

▶ OneDrive client access

▶ Security trimming

▶ Page load performance

For more information on how to manage the Distributed Cache service in SharePoint Server 2013, refer to the following link: http://technet.microsoft.com/en-us/library/jj219613(v=office.15).aspx

User Profile Service Application

A prerequisite for provisioning My Sites is the configuration of the User Profile service application, as shown in Figure 16.12, which stores information about your organization's users in a central location for access by SharePoint 2013's social computing features.

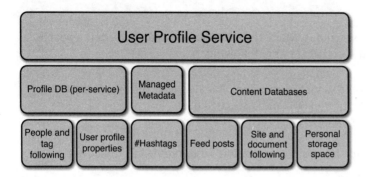

FIGURE 16.12   A high-level overview of the User Profile service.

For an overview of the User Profile service application in SharePoint Server 2013, refer to the following link: http://technet.microsoft.com/en-us/library/ee662538(v=office.15).aspx

The User Profile service application provides a central location where service administrators configure and administer the following features:

▶ User profiles

These profiles contain detailed information about people in an organization and display all the available properties related to each user in a single location with social tags, documents, and other items related to that user.

▶ Profile synchronization

This provides a reliable way to synchronize groups and user profile information that is stored in the SharePoint Server 2013 profile database together with information that is stored in directory services across the enterprise.

▶ Audiences

Audiences provide a way to target content to users based on their job or task, as defined by their membership in a SharePoint Server group or distribution list, by the organizational reporting structure, or by the public properties in their user profiles.

▶ My Site

As detailed previously, My Sites are personal sites that give users in your organization a central location to manage and store documents, links, and information about colleagues. They also provide a way for users to access the information and content they have specified they are interested in following.

▶ Social tags and notes

This feature enables users to add social tags to documents, content, and other SharePoint items. This feature enables users to leave notes on profile pages of a My Site or any SharePoint page.

16

▶ Newsfeed

This provides a user's social hub where the users can see updates from the people, documents, sites, and tags that they are following.

When you create a User Profile service application, SharePoint Server creates three databases for storing user profile information and associated data:

▶ Profile database

This database is used to store your organization's user profile information.

▶ Synchronization database

This database is used to store configuration and staging information for synchronizing profile data from external sources such as the Active Directory Domain Services (AD DS).

▶ Social tagging database

This database is used to store social tags and notes created by users. Each social tag and note is associated with a profile ID.

For information on how to create, edit, or delete User Profile service applications in SharePoint Server 2013, refer to the following link: http://technet.microsoft.com/en-us/library/ee721052(v=office.15).aspx

Yammer Overview

The Yammer platform provides a way to connect users across disparate business applications by providing a common conversation layer. Within Yammer's newsfeed, you can view icons indicating private messages, as well as read the content posted within the groups of which you are a member.

You can create groups for specific projects or teams, as well as share posts from within a team with a specific individual or another group that may be able to provide additional information on the topic being discussed.

Yammer has several similarities to SharePoint 2013's newsfeeds. You can actually configure a Yammer newsfeed to replace a SharePoint newsfeed, and it does provide a very easy way to post new messages to a targeted group with additional hashtag capabilities.

Yammer also allows for external networks and for non-organizational team members to join in on specific conversations that may be relevant, for example, if they are a vendor or supplier to your organization. Yammer provides a people directory that is a searchable database of all your organization's team members that lists not only contact information but also skill sets and interests to provide additional metadata in helping you narrow your search.

The most powerful feature of Yammer, in my opinion, is its capability to integrate with other applications such as SharePoint or even Salesforce as it provides Yammer APIs for use with .NET and REST endpoints.

For more information on Yammer APIs, refer to the Yammer developer center at the following link: https://developer.yammer.com/

For additional information on how Yammer and SharePoint 2013 integrate, you can review and download a whitepaper from Microsoft detailing the various integration points and best practices at the following link: http://technet.microsoft.com/en-us/library/dn270535(v=office.15).aspx

For information on how to synchronize and authenticate users from your on-premises Active Directory to Yammer and Office 365, refer to the following link: http://technet.microsoft.com/en-us/library/dn457819(v=office.15).aspx

Summary

This chapter covered SharePoint 2013, Office 365, and SharePoint Online social capabilities for communities and My Sites. We discussed the usage of communities within your organization, as well as the different roles and related responsibilities that manage them.

We also discussed My Sites and the updated underlying architecture that drives these new centralized "personal sites" and the moving pieces that are required for them to be provisioned. We closed the chapter by touching on Yammer and some of its high-level capabilities.

In the next chapter, we will discuss training and end-user adoption strategies for SharePoint 2013, Office 365, and SharePoint Online.

16

SharePoint 2013, Office 365, and SharePoint Online: Training and End-User Adoption Strategies

When developing a new training strategy for your organization, it should be approached in a context that matches where your organization is currently at within your overall implementation. If you are developing a training strategy in conjunction with a new implementation effort or upgrade/migration initiative, it is important to tie your training project into your overall implementation and communication strategy. If you already have your SharePoint 2013, Office 365, or SharePoint Online implementation complete or have been "live" for some time and are looking to improve on or implement a new training initiative, then you can approach this in terms of a more separate or "siloed" initiative.

The landscape of SharePoint 2013, Office 365, and SharePoint Online training is vastly different than that of previous releases such as SharePoint 2007 or SharePoint 2010. SharePoint training used to be big business for "training-specific" companies that could convince organizations to have 10 to 20 of their users attend a four- or five-day training class for a specific type of user, such as "end-user training," "administrator training," or "developer" training.

I am not saying that this type of offering is not still available or does not offer value, because there are many "training-specific" companies still offering these types of courses, but the feedback I have received over the years from current and previous clients, as well as from those at SharePoint conferences or "user groups" who have taken this type of training, has been mixed at best.

One of the major issues with this type of "canned" training is the mixed user "student" audience that makes up a given class and the vast differences in the level of knowledge they may or may not already have about the technology.

The focus of your organization's training initiatives should be on your tailored environment (showing your branding, navigation, and so on) and what you are actually trying to accomplish, as well as the underlying requirements of your users. This must be done in a manner that ensures the right balancing act of governance and user empowerment, as shown in Figure 17.1, by training and related user activities.

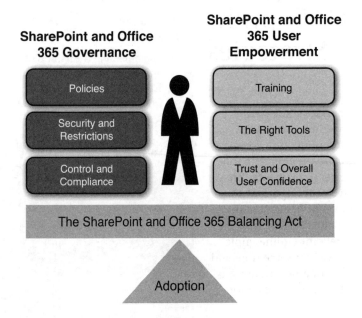

FIGURE 17.1   Ensuring the right balancing act of governance and user empowerment by training and related user activities.

Key Considerations and Strategies to Ensure Long-Term Training Success

As with any initiative, you must involve key business stakeholders while also not only identifying the business need for this training but providing a strategy to ensure that it has long-term ROI for the organization. This is going to be a high-profile initiative that affects the day-to-day activities of just about everyone in your organization who utilizes SharePoint, so it must be done right.

Are there previous technology initiatives that have implemented successful training that you can review to see how they worked with your organization's user base? I ask this question because every single organization is different, and the culture and users themselves vary in terms of how they "feel" they should be trained. This does not mean you have to follow the same strategy of a previous training initiative, because users do not always know what is best for them in terms of learning a new technology and may have preconceived notions about it.

Also, when thinking about preconceived notions that users may have, they may have a feeling about SharePoint based on previous experiences in SharePoint 2010, 2007, or even 2003 at a prior job or even a previous rollout. In that case, they may feel that

▶ SharePoint is just a glorified file share.

▶ SharePoint is too complex for what I need in order to do my job.

▶ It is not secure enough to store my documents.

▶ It is ugly and has a terrible interface and is not easy or enjoyable to use.

▶ It is not strong enough in terms of searching and finding my content.

What Type of Training Should You Offer?

There are many types of training you can offer your organization's users, but whichever path you choose to follow, it must be tailored to your organization. SharePoint training can be offered or performed via the following:

▶ Instructor, as depicted in Figure 17.2, in a classroom-type setting

▶ Dedicated training site with videos, "one-pagers," FAQs, and such

▶ One-on-one mentoring

▶ Internal user groups

▶ Power-user workshops

▶ Web-based training by an instructor via WebEx or Lync, as depicted in Figure 17.3

17

FIGURE 17.2   Instructor-led training in a classroom setting for your organization's SharePoint 2013, Office 365, and/or SharePoint Online initiative.

FIGURE 17.3   Providing web-based training by an instructor via WebEx or Lync.

It is important to understand the end-state result of what you want to achieve from training and apply metrics to it that will enable you to determine its success. Set some initial benchmarks for the method or methods of training you are offering, and see which one is providing the best results.

Training must focus on the business goals and what SharePoint 2013, Office 365, or SharePoint Online is being used for, such as the following:

▶ Collaboration platform

▶ Enterprise content management (ECM)/records management (RM) solution

▶ Enterprise search solution

▶ Organizational intranet

▶ Extranet platform for external access for vendors, suppliers, and so forth

▶ Business process automation platform (workflows and so on)

▶ Business intelligence (BI) solution (KPIs, dashboards, reporting, and so on)

Training must also focus on the culture and specific details of your organization and its user base, and you must develop your training around knowing the answer to questions such as these:

▶ Where are my users located?

▶ What are the organization's demographics?

▶ Does the organization strive to be innovative or "leading edge" or to be more structured and "safe" around new technologies?

No matter what methods you choose to develop your training around, you must ensure that it is engaging or users will quickly lose interest and also communicate their opinions to other users. You must showcase the platform's overall solutions and not just specific features. Try to provide use cases or "success stories" about how the platform has helped a specific set of users or department achieve certain criteria.

Internal Power User or Monthly SharePoint User Group for Your Organization

There are public SharePoint and Office 365 user groups all over the country, but you should consider setting up one internal to your organization. I have seen this get great traction and really provide the opportunity for users to share stories about what has worked for them, as well as what hasn't, and how they have gone about achieving success.

This helps empower a cross-functional user group of end users as well as power users and site owners.

These "internal user groups" help to promote governance as well, and users come together in a "homeowners association" type of manner in which they all feel they are on the same team and want to improve the overall community.

Focus on a Tailored Curriculum for Your Organization

In most all cases, canned training does not work for SharePoint 2013, Office 365, or SharePoint Online initiatives unless its goal is to ensure that all users are "level set" and have a baseline set of knowledge that you can then build your training on.

When you develop tailored training and a corresponding tailored curriculum, you must do so in a manner that focuses on your organization's business drivers and map out specific training roles and tasks. After you have determined your training delivery methods, you can start to build the components of your overall training effort that includes the following:

▶ Standardized PowerPoint training decks

▶ Custom videos

▶ One-pagers that focus on a specific function

▶ Classroom standards on how many students each class should be limited to, as well as elements like time limits

▶ Breakout workshops around governance or search

▶ Leveraging of your organization's users who feel strongly about the benefits of the platform

Training Requirements and Required Knowledge of Your Users

In Chapter 9, "Governance Strategies for SharePoint 2013, Office 365, and SharePoint Online," the types of users that are required to support as well as ensure your implementation's long-term success are covered in detail. When you're reviewing the makeup of your organization's user base, the following is a sample layout of your organization's user types and the related information and topics that they will need to understand in granular detail:

▶ **Administrators**

  ▶ Overall installation, configuration, and maintenance

  ▶ Installation prerequisites

  ▶ Deep understanding of Active Directory, SharePoint security groups, and SSL, as well as service accounts

  ▶ Overview of SQL Server 2012/2014 and installation requirements and related permissions

  ▶ SharePoint's overall farm topology and its logical architecture

  ▶ Complete understanding of the organization's SharePoint 2013, Office 365, and/or SharePoint Online roadmap, scalability, and capacity planning

  ▶ Deep understanding of web applications, site collections, user profiles, and content databases

  ▶ Deep understanding of the configuration and administration of the user profile service

  ▶ Configuration of managed paths

  ▶ Understanding of all of SharePoint 2013's Service Applications, such as the managed metadata service and the Distributed Cache service

  ▶ Deep understanding of metadata, as well as managed terms, taxonomies, document sets, and so on

▶ Deep understanding of SharePoint 2013's search and related search service and available configurations

▶ Site Feature utilization and any corresponding site templates

▶ Deep understanding of the organization's BYOD and/or mobility strategies and the concept of responsive web design

▶ Creation of lists and libraries, as well as how to create list and library templates

▶ Understanding of RBS, Shredded Storage, and large files, as well as allowed and governed file types

▶ Understanding of SharePoint 2013 and Office 365 Tenancies and hybrid cloud concepts

▶ Implementation of My Sites and their unique site collections

▶ Deep understanding of navigation and the available features and configurations

▶ Understanding of licensing and what the organization has procured

▶ Understanding of the terminology of SharePoint Server 2013, as well as Office 365 and SharePoint Online

▶ Deep understanding of how Microsoft Exchange and Microsoft Lync integrate with the platform

▶ Deep understanding of Office Web Apps Server and App Store

▶ Understanding of Windows Server 2012 and how SharePoint works with its core components such as IIS

▶ Deep understanding of how to configure OneDrive for Business and how to implement governance and quotas per the organization's standards

▶ Windows PowerShell cmdlets and their capabilities

▶ Timer jobs, Business Connectivity Services, email configurations, and alerts

▶ Understanding of how SharePoint 2013, Office 365, and SharePoint Online correspond to business requirements of the organization

▶ Understanding of SharePoint branding and how master page customizations and UI changes can affect the environment

▶ Deep understanding of virtualization (Hyper-V, VMware, and so on)

▶ Disaster recovery, backups, and restores

▶ Monitoring and viewing of available log files

▶ Performance SLAs and related troubleshooting

▶ Understanding of the organization's compliance and regulatory requirements

17

▶ **Developers**

  ▶ Deep understanding of the .NET Framework 4.5, C#, ASP.NET, and so on

  ▶ Deep understanding of server-side SharePoint development, server-side APIs, and server-side data access

  ▶ Deep understanding of HTML, CSS, JavaScript, CAML, LINQ for SharePoint, and AJAX

  ▶ Deep understanding of remote Event Receivers

  ▶ Understanding of how customizations affect the overall topology and architecture

  ▶ The organization's governance policies regarding deployment practices and techniques

  ▶ Packaging extensibility and development artifacts, as well as Team Foundation Server (TFS) and code management

  ▶ Deep understanding of the SharePoint 2013 APIs, Office 365 API Tools, and Microsoft Azure APIs

  ▶ Understanding of the hybrid cloud and the available identity management, security, and federation options

  ▶ Visual Studio 2013/Visual Studio 2012 and Visual Studio Online, as well as the licensing available to the organization

  ▶ Core debugging and logging options, as well as the developer dashboard and unified logging service

  ▶ JavaScript and its utilization in SharePoint

  ▶ Using Windows PowerShell cmdlets and a deep understanding of their capabilities

  ▶ Deep understanding of farm and sandbox solutions

  ▶ Complete understanding of the SharePoint App Model

  ▶ The SharePoint Object Model

  ▶ SharePoint 2013, Office 365, and SharePoint Online custom branding, UI development, master pages, and so on

  ▶ Build solutions that run on the server and use the SharePoint server-side API

  ▶ Understanding of strategies on how to leverage client object models (CSOM)

  ▶ Best practice approach to authentication including the claims-based authentication approach and Office 365's security model for developing all customizations with cloud compatibility in mind (e.g., the new Office 365 API Tools)

  ▶ Understanding of SharePoint 2013's Windows Workflow Foundation 4

- ▶ Understanding of the concepts to consume and interact with external data sources

- ▶ Development requirements of SharePoint 2013's enterprise content management (ECM) capabilities, including managed metadata, term store, custom terms, catalogs, and so on

- ▶ Microsoft Azure auto-hosted apps and their framework and interaction within a hybrid cloud environment

- ▶ Understanding of chrome control and ribbon extensibility options and best practices

- ▶ Understanding of how SharePoint 2013, Office 365, and SharePoint Online correspond to business requirements of the organization

- ▶ Deep understanding of OAuth 2.0

- ▶ Deep understanding of SharePoint Designer 2013's workflow capabilities

- ▶ Understanding of the platform's eDiscovery capabilities, as well as site mailboxes and interaction and integration with Microsoft Exchange

- ▶ Understanding of the organization's compliance and regulatory requirements

- ▶ **Power Users/"Super Users"**

  - ▶ Understanding of Active Directory and SharePoint security groups

  - ▶ Understanding of the organization's SharePoint 2013, Office 365, and/or SharePoint Online roadmap and governance strategy

  - ▶ Understanding of site collections and content database growth considerations regarding sizing limitations and performance

  - ▶ Understanding of metadata, taxonomies, and document sets

  - ▶ Understanding of SharePoint 2013's search and available features

  - ▶ Site Features and how they can be utilized

  - ▶ Understanding of the organization's BYOD and/or mobility strategies

  - ▶ Creation of lists and libraries, as well as how to utilize list and library templates

  - ▶ Understanding of SharePoint 2013 and Office 365 terminologies and the overall hybrid cloud concept

  - ▶ Understanding of My Sites and governance

  - ▶ Understanding of available navigation features

  - ▶ Understanding of Office Online (for example, previously named Office Web Apps) and what is available to users in terms of apps and the app store

  - ▶ Understanding of OneDrive for Business and the organization's utilization and policies

17

▶ Understanding of the organization's SLAs regarding disaster recovery, backups, and restores

▶ Understanding of how SharePoint 2013, Office 365, and SharePoint Online correspond to business requirements of the organization

▶ Understanding of how to use all basic SharePoint features and capabilities such as lists and libraries, etc.

▶ Understanding of basic end-user support and change management principles

▶ Deep understanding of site creation requirements and policies on how to request a new site

▶ Understanding of the organization's site customization request policies and availability

▶ Ability to explain to the organization's end users features such as navigation, filtering and sorting, and alerts

▶ Core concepts of metadata, content types, and the importance of "tagging" content

▶ Available workflows provided by the organization

▶ List and library management, as well as site maintenance requirements

▶ Understanding of the organization's compliance and regulatory requirements

▶ **Site Owners/Content Managers**

▶ Ability to add and manage users

▶ Understanding of templates and their available features

▶ Understanding of how SharePoint 2013, Office 365, and SharePoint Online correspond to business requirements of the organization

▶ Understanding of My Sites and the organization's related governance strategy

▶ Overall roles and responsibilities provided to site owners and the overall user and group hierarchy of the platform

▶ Ability to manage the content on a site as well as to keep it up-to-date and relevant

▶ Deep understanding of permissions, as well as site and document sharing

▶ Understanding of the organization's SLAs on disaster recovery, backups, and restores

▶ Understanding of OneDrive for Business and the organization's utilization and policies

▶ Ability to manage discussions within blogs or lists

▶ Ability to create new lists such as calendars or other common and "non-admin" tasks

▶ Ability to explain to the organization's end users features such as navigation, filtering and sorting, and alerts

▶ Understanding of the structure of the organization's "help desk" or support available and who their key contacts are for assistance

▶ Available workflows provided by the organization

▶ Understanding of the organization's compliance and regulatory requirements

▶ **End Users/Typical Business Users**

▶ Ability to add and edit content as well as understanding of how to utilize the web parts and apps within their site

▶ Understanding of My Sites and overall site governance

▶ Understanding of the context of where SharePoint fits in their organization, as well as to their day-to-day activities

▶ Ability to perform standard tasks and actions such as search, uploading of content, editing of content, check-in and check-out, and so on

▶ Understanding of the structure of the organization's "help desk" or support available and who their key contacts are for assistance

▶ Understanding of the organization's compliance and regulatory requirements

Change Management's Integration with Your Training Strategy

As your organization's SharePoint 2013, Office 365, and/or SharePoint Online implementation evolves, there will undoubtedly be updates and changes that must align to those of the underlying business. With these changes, your organization must also continue to update not only your roadmap and governance strategy but also your training strategy.

In Chapter 9, we discussed the development and implementation of a change management strategy, and this strategy must align with your overall training strategy. The training strategy's major change management elements will include updates to the following:

▶ Underlying technology roadmap and strategy changes

▶ Support strategies and available resources

▶ The underlying culture of the organization relating to collaboration and professional networking

▶ Governance updates to include compliance, security, and regulatory, as well as BYOD and mobility

▶ Business structure changes (reorganization, additional or new business units, hierarchy changes, acquisitions, and so on)

17

▶ Business intelligence (BI) and reporting capability requirements and related offerings

▶ Training budget and new training initiatives based on the success of these initial efforts

There is a "care and feeding" aspect to training to ensure that your organization makes training an ongoing event for users, and not just a yearly or sporadic-type event around major release changes.

Measuring the ROI and Effectiveness of Your Organization's Training Initiatives

Training is something that is judged by every participant, and those involved will always have good and bad elements to any feedback that is given. You should implement a way to compare the overall effectiveness of users both before and after training to not only justify these continued efforts but show users why they need to be onboard with this effort and be willing participants and champion this process.

Your training will be able to be more easily measured in terms of ROI if you have set goals and identified underlying "quick wins" that users can take with them after the training is completed and immediately put into practice. These training efforts should also decrease the overall support required by IT for simple and very common issues, which is a metric that is easily captured and measured. You may also see a jump in requests for new features or sites, which is a good thing and means that users are interested. It is key, for this very reason, that you discuss the new site request or custom feature request your organization has implemented during training. This way, attendees will know how to properly make these types of requests.

Using Training to Drive User Adoption

A major part of your training should include regular activities that are centered on increasing user adoption. These can also be training workshops or "lunch and learns" that can take place in a physical room together with a set class or virtually via a web-based solution like Lync or WebEx.

Your marketing or corporate communications department should also be included in this, and if any existing corporate newsletters exist, I would recommending adding a "department showcase" or "user showcase" around a success story with the platform, as well as items such as a "tip of the week" or "did you know" type of element.

When you showcase a specific department or users' real-world success stories, the overall user audience will be able to better map a business need they may have in mind to a SharePoint solution, which will quickly further adoption.

You can quickly ensure user adoption by implementing common and core company processes on SharePoint 2013, Office 365, and/or SharePoint Online, such as employee onboarding or human resources–related activities. Identifying "quick wins" such as easy access to common forms or reports can ensure adoption while also providing traction for

SharePoint to eventually replace other existing systems, because users want an easy-to-use centralized solution or "one-stop shop" to perform all of their activities.

Your organization's training should also continually enforce the importance of keeping information current while also removing outdated content or duplicate content stored in other systems so that you can refer to content in SharePoint as the "one version of the truth" for the organization.

SharePoint's new search capabilities are one of the most powerful and easily recognized ways to drive user adoption for the solution, because users not only can quickly find their content and information but also can perform actions such as previewing content in the hover panel by simply resting the pointer on a specific search result.

The people search capabilities are also extremely popular with users and are a core way to bring together the organization in allowing users to find the right resources with the skill sets and experience they seeking. For more information on implementing people search in SharePoint Server 2013, refer to the following link: http://technet.microsoft.com/en-us/library/hh582311(v=office.15).aspx

Keys to Driving SharePoint 2013, Office 365, and/or SharePoint Online Adoption

There are defined and proven ways in which you can increase overall user adoption, and these are "in the consulting trenches" strategies that we have used at EPC Group to help clients quickly realize ROI on the new platform.

The following are key elements and strategies to ensure that your organization will drive user adoption to the new platform:

▶ Ensure that you have executive sponsorship or a core business leader who will assist you in projecting your messages to the organization's overall user base.

This does not mean that the organization's CEO or CIO must be the executive sponsor or core business leader. Although that would be optimal, you need to find an individual or individuals who can provide you with their time and actively communicate the value and benefit of SharePoint.

▶ Ensure that your organization's project team and related support personnel are available and passionate about helping users; this will go a very long way and will be communicated by those users to others in the organization. You may have the most well-architected and planned-out implementation around, but if you are not there for your users, they will quickly lose faith in the system, as well as overall interest.

▶ Implement at least light branding to your user interface that includes your organization's logos or core color scheme.

▶ Ensure that all users have the same Microsoft Office version installed so that all users have the same capabilities and experience.

▶ If available to your organization, try to champion the integration of Microsoft Lync with the new platform. Lync is a great way to show how seamless content, information, and access to people can be under one platform's umbrella.

▶ Implement both train-the-trainer and power-user training programs.

▶ Implement a centralized training site with training videos, as depicted in Figure 17.4, as well as FAQs and one-pagers so that users can access training information and content 24/7 without the need to ask for assistance. This site should also link to free Microsoft training materials, as well as other free training sites such as those on YouTube and other available media.

▶ Promote "quick wins" and achievements by the users of the platform in emails or the organization's newsletter.

**Training Videos Recorded and
Available on Demand 24/7**

FIGURE 17.4   Providing a training site with training videos for your users to access 24/7.

Do You Require a Business Case for Training?

Your organization may not be one that always values training initiatives, and you may need to build a case study or provide a detailed request or summary regarding why this effort is important. It is key to show that the proposed training is in line with your overall underlying business strategy and that there are specific ways you can improve the organization's ROI for the platform.

When you are developing your overall training initiative and related strategy, you must ensure that you do so in such a manner that the goals you are setting are achievable. The business and those who will need to approve the budget for this effort will ask questions such as these:

▶ What are the costs associated with implementation of this training, and what are our options?

▶ Is this training something we will own and be able to reuse after the training is completed?

▶ How will we reach users in other locations and how does this training strategy address this?

▶ Isn't the platform supposed to be easy enough for anyone to learn?

▶ Can users just go purchase books to learn about this new technology?

▶ Would we save money by outsourcing this training or by developing our own internal training material?

You must ensure that your training strategy business case or any justification you may need to submit for this effort includes key areas that your training will address and where ROI can be ensured, such as these:

▶ This training will ensure that users utilize the system in a compliant and governed manner that protects our organization's intellectual property.

▶ This training will ensure that users are aware of the legal and responsible usage policies they must follow as developed by the organization.

▶ This training will lower the organization's overall support costs by ensuring that they are not only trained on core features but made aware of the self-support and training materials provide by the organization.

Implementing a SharePoint and/or Office 365 Training Site for Your Organization

The implementation of a training site for self-service support to your organization's user base is a guaranteed win and will provide instant ROI. This site should include areas such as these:

▶ A document library containing one-pagers on how to perform common tasks or basic how-to actions.

▶ Support and training videos that are topic driven and approximately three to five minutes in length on average.

Whenever possible, these videos should relate to your specific environment and show your organization's branding, layout, and navigation structure.

▶ Links to the official "forms" or documents to request a new SharePoint site or custom feature.

▶ A glossary for "official" terminology.

▶ A suggestion area to request new videos or training material.

▶ Links to the organization's official governance document or strategy.

▶ Online evaluations and suggestion box.

▶ Blog and discussion capabilities for peer-to-peer support.

Free Training Material and Courses Available from Microsoft

An abundance of free training materials and videos are available from Microsoft that your organization can take advantage of and reuse to save time as well as budget for your training initiative.

For example, there are SharePoint 2013 training videos from Microsoft that can be easily found by performing the following:

1. Within your browser, go to Bing Videos: http://www.bing.com/videos/.

2. Search for the term "SharePoint 2013."

3. Under Source, select "MSN Video," as shown in Figure 17.5.

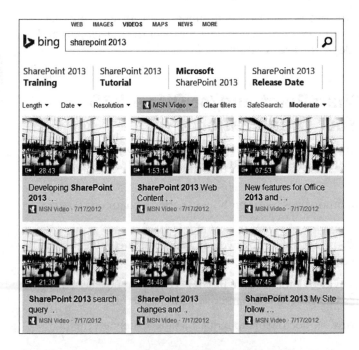

FIGURE 17.5   Performing a Bing search for SharePoint 2013 videos.

You will get hours of free videos from Microsoft that are great for end users or power users that you can download and reference or link to within your organization's SharePoint 2013/Office 365 training site.

The following are links to additional free Microsoft SharePoint 2013, Office 365, SharePoint Online, and other integrated Microsoft solutions for your reference:

▶ Microsoft Virtual Academy (Home): http://www.microsoftvirtualacademy.com/#?fbid=hcVrAZ5GmgD

▶ Microsoft Virtual Academy SharePoint 2013:

http://www.microsoftvirtualacademy.com/product-training/sharepoint#?fbid=hcVrAZ5GmgD

▶ Microsoft Learning SharePoint 2013:

http://www.microsoft.com/learning/en-us/sharepoint-training.aspx

▶ SharePoint 2013 training courses on Microsoft.com:

http://office.microsoft.com/en-us/sharepoint-help/training-courses-for-sharepoint-2013-HA104030990.aspx

▶ SharePoint 2013 training for IT pros on TechNet via Microsoft.com:

http://technet.microsoft.com/en-US/sharepoint/fp123606

▶ SharePoint 2013: Presentation: IT pro training:

http://www.microsoft.com/en-us/download/details.aspx?id=30361

▶ Microsoft Virtual Academy Office 365:

http://www.microsoftvirtualacademy.com/product-training/office-365#?fbid=hcVrAZ5GmgD

▶ Microsoft Learning Office 365:

http://www.microsoft.com/learning/en-us/office365-training.aspx

▶ Training courses for Office 365 for business:

http://office.microsoft.com/en-us/office365-suite-help/training-courses-for-office-365-for-business-HA104031723.aspx

▶ Microsoft Virtual Academy Lync:

http://www.microsoftvirtualacademy.com/product-training/lync#?fbid=hcVrAZ5GmgD

▶ Microsoft Learning Lync Server:

http://www.microsoft.com/learning/en-us/lync-server-training.aspx

17

▶ Microsoft Virtual Academy Microsoft Azure:

http://www.microsoftvirtualacademy.com/product-training/windows-azure#?fbid=hcVrAZ5GmgD

▶ Microsoft Virtual Academy Microsoft Exchange 2013:

http://www.microsoftvirtualacademy.com/product-training/exchange#?fbid=hcVrAZ5GmgD

▶ Microsoft Virtual Academy System Center:

http://www.microsoftvirtualacademy.com/product-training/system-center#?fbid=hcVrAZ5GmgD

▶ Microsoft Ignite:

http://ignite.office.com/Resource-Library

▶ MSDN SharePoint 2013 Developer Training Courses: SharePoint 2013:

http://msdn.microsoft.com/en-US/office/dn448488

Summary

In this chapter, we discussed the some of the key considerations around developing a training strategy for your organization's SharePoint 2013, Office 365, and/or SharePoint Online implementation. We covered the elements that should be included in this training effort, as well as how best to ensure that it is adopted and how it can provide instant ROI to your organization.

We also discussed areas in which you may get push-back from the organization regarding developing a training initiative and how best to address the issues. In the next chapter, we will discuss disaster recovery strategies and business continuity management to ensure that your environment is backed up and can adjust to major or minor events so that your organization's priceless data will be safe and your environment will be able to be quickly restored.

CHAPTER 18

Disaster Recovery (DR) and Business Continuity Management (BCM) Considerations

Developing a Best Practices Approach to Disaster Recovery and Business Continuity for SharePoint 2013

When you are developing a disaster recovery (DR) and business continuity management (BCM) strategy for your organization's SharePoint 2013 platform, there are many factors that must be taken into consideration, as well as existing DR strategies your organization may already have in place.

These factors can differ based on the business vertical your organization is in, which can add external factors related to legal and regulatory compliance, as well as how IT and the business view the criticality of the SharePoint platform and whether or not it is mission critical. In most cases, SharePoint is viewed as one of the most business-critical platforms in the organization, and the DR and business continuity management service level agreements (SLAs) are or should be very strict in regard to response time of an incident.

Other elements to consider include the damage to SharePoint's reputation within the organization as a trusted system that users can depend on in storing content and records and their view of its future reliability. This is critical because you do not want users going against governance policies and storing content in other locations because they have lost faith in the platform due to lengthy downtime or lost data.

There must be clear direction and an accurate inventory regarding SharePoint's farm-level restoration, which should also encompass the possibility of a catastrophic loss of the SharePoint Server 2013 environment, as well as loss of any hybrid connectivity in case of a cloud-based outage.

Your organization must develop clear documentation and processes that include the full scope of the records of all files, databases, and configurations necessary to return content and services to business-critical operation.

As mentioned in previous chapters, Microsoft will continue to offer updates to both SharePoint 2013 on-premises and Office 365's SharePoint Online plans in their new release cycle strategy. To ensure that your organization has the more updated information on the offerings and versions your organization has procured, refer to the following article regarding how to prepare to back up and restore farms in SharePoint 2013: http://technet. microsoft.com/en-us/library/ff806332.aspx

Preparation for SharePoint 2013 DR/BCM

Preparation describes the key areas and components of a SharePoint Server farm and outlines the critical items the responsible parties within your organization must protect through proper inventory and backup procedures to provide as complete a restoration as possible. Failure to itemize and back up any of these components or configurations may result in an inability to return expected levels of service and data availability.

Because a SharePoint 2013 platform consists of servers, services, and content, each component represents a critical aspect of the ability to provide a fully functioning SharePoint farm. Even if your organization has deployed a relatively small SharePoint environment, the following sections and related components are just as vital to those of a large enterprise environment to ensure proper functionality and restoration of the organization's SharePoint platform. These components include the following:

▶ SharePoint databases, including all content databases and Shared Services Provider (SSP) databases

▶ Customizations, including web parts, apps, site and list definitions, master pages, style sheets, and features

  For more information on how to back up customizations in SharePoint 2013, refer to the following link:

  http://technet.microsoft.com/en-us/library/ee748642.aspx

▶ SharePoint configurations, including farm configuration databases, alternate access mappings, email settings, and service accounts

▶ SharePoint binaries, including software, service packs, and cumulative updates and hotfixes

▶ Internet Information Services (IIS) configurations, including IIS metabase and Inetpub directories

▶ Operating system binaries, including OS, hardware drivers, software updates, and server components

SharePoint Content

The SharePoint-specific content that needs to be addressed is usually the bulk of the backup and restore operations. SharePoint content includes all content found in the content databases, such as the site collection and all included sites, documents and list items, and even security, configurations, and associations.

The content database is by far the most important element of a SharePoint disaster recovery scenario but certainly not the only item that is required for some disaster recovery scenarios. For the latest updates from Microsoft regarding how to back up content databases in SharePoint 2013, refer to the following link: http://technet.microsoft.com/en-us/library/ee428327.aspx

In particular, the content databases will help restore the following:

▶ Entire site collections

▶ Any subsite in any site collection

▶ Any document library or list in any site in a site collection

▶ Web parts and apps in web pages

▶ Site- and list-level configurations

▶ Security and user information

For scenarios requiring the restoration of any of these items, the content database is required. However, be aware that some items, such as security or web parts, require entire site or in some cases entire site collection restores to gain access to this information.

Web Infrastructure DR Considerations

Elements related to how SharePoint provides and controls access to any contained content are handled through the web infrastructure portion of the logical architecture of a SharePoint farm. Web applications, authentication providers, application policies, and other web-related items are required to properly restore a web infrastructure that interfaces with SharePoint.

A SharePoint content database is attached directly to a web application and is therefore accessed through the web application itself. Failure to have an accessible web application, or having a web application with an incorrect configuration, may result in SharePoint content being inaccessible.

18

In addition, since web applications are websites in Internet Information Services, physical files and file locations are also necessary to record and maintain.

Web infrastructure elements include the following:

- ▶ Web applications
- ▶ Web application settings
    - ▶ General settings
    - ▶ Activated features
    - ▶ Associated content databases
    - ▶ Alternate access mappings
- ▶ Authentication providers
- ▶ Web application policies

IIS-related elements include these:

- ▶ Host headers and/or port numbers
- ▶ SSL or anonymous access configuration
- ▶ Application pool and associated application pool ID/Inetpub folder
- ▶ SSL Certificates
- ▶ Web.config customizations

Shared Services DR Considerations

Aside from content, SharePoint also utilizes a number of services that are managed within or through SharePoint and are connected and shared to all web infrastructure components of SharePoint, in particular, web applications. Also, if you have SharePoint 2013 as well as a previous version of SharePoint installed, such as SharePoint 2010, this may be managed through a Shared Service Provider or a service application.

> **NOTE**
>
> For more information regarding how to back up service applications in SharePoint 2013, refer to the following link: http://technet.microsoft.com/en-us/library/ee428318.aspx

A Shared Service Provider has associated web applications, service accounts, administration host sites, and service and content databases. All of these items need to be recorded and preserved to provide the unique information provided by the Shared Service to return the environment to a functioning, usable system.

Components of a Shared Service Provider include these:

▶ Application host

▶ Associated web applications

▶ Service and content databases

▶ Service accounts

Each Shared Service may have its own set of configurations and may need to be recorded to maintain functioning service for your organization's SharePoint platform. However, protecting or recording the entirety of a Shared Service Provider can provide enough information to re-create one if it fails for any reason.

A service application is a later architecture supported by SharePoint that has similarities and differences to a Shared Service Provider. Similar to Shared Service Providers, a service application provides a specific service component for consumption by the entire farm, and some types of services can be shared with other farms.

Unlike Shared Services, the service application architecture is not monolithic. It defines separate services rather than groups of services, and thus multiple associations may be made to one service application, multiple service applications of the same type may be defined, and multiple cross-associations, including those of other farms, can be configured.

Components for service applications are identical to those or a Shared Service Provider, except that they are used for only specific service applications rather than groups of service applications.

Support Systems and Configurations

As you know, SharePoint requires the Windows Server operating system (OS) in order to function, because it is not a standalone system. As mentioned previously, IIS is leveraged from Windows Server to support the system function. Access accounts, also referred to as service accounts, are provided through Active Directory (AD) and are used for many cross-farm services and functions.

NOTE

For information regarding installing IIS 8.0 in Windows Server 2012, refer to the following link: http://www.iis.net/learn/get-started/whats-new-in-iis-8/installing-iis-8-on-windows-server-2012

However, within all of this, SharePoint still requires its own binary installation files, which may also include hotfixes, cumulative updates, or service packs. Each of these layers of the support systems is required to return a failed installation or an entire SharePoint farm if necessary. Furthermore, additional third-party applications that extend and enhance SharePoint functionality should also be considered and recorded.

Support systems include the following:

▶ Windows OS version and all applied patches and updates

▶ SharePoint Farm Build Version for patches and updates

▶ SharePoint installation media and license keys

▶ Active Directory Service accounts and passwords

> ▶ Setup/Admin accounts
>
> ▶ Database Access account (i.e., Farm account)
>
> ▶ Application Pool accounts (i.e., Content, Central Admin, SSPs)
>
> ▶ Farm Search Service account(s)
>
> ▶ Default Content Access account
>
> Note that this may be the same as the Farm Search Service account. For more information on how to back up the Search Service applications in SharePoint 2013, refer to the following link:
>
> http://technet.microsoft.com/en-us/library/ee748635.aspx

▶ Third-party applications

▶ Custom or third-party solution (.wsp) files

> For more information on how to back up solutions in SharePoint 2013, refer to the following link:
>
> http://technet.microsoft.com/en-us/library/ee428315.aspx

Inventory of SharePoint 2013 and Related Components

The inventory of SharePoint 2013 provides a checklist of all important files, configurations, and other details necessary to back up, record, and have available to document both the required backup items and the necessary restoration items.

The following indicates all the important SharePoint-specific components and files that should be backed up regularly:

▶ Farm configuration

> For the latest information regarding how to back up farm configuration, refer to the following link:
>
> http://technet.microsoft.com/en-us/library/ee428320.aspx

▶ Shared Service Provider

▶ Single sign-on database and encryption keys

▶ InfoPath form templates

- ▶ Web applications and content databases
- ▶ Site collections and subsites
- ▶ SharePoint Root (the 15 hive)

Farm configurations that should be documented include:

- ▶ Alternate access mapping settings
- ▶ Farm-level search settings
- ▶ External service connection settings
- ▶ Workflow management settings
- ▶ Email settings
- ▶ A/V settings
- ▶ Usage analysis processing settings
- ▶ Diagnostic logging settings
- ▶ Content deployment settings
- ▶ Timer job settings
- ▶ HTML viewer settings
- ▶ Recycle Bin settings and other web application general settings
- ▶ Administrator-deployed form templates
- ▶ Default quota templates
- ▶ Database names and locations
- ▶ Crawler impact rules
- ▶ Activated features
- ▶ Blocked file types

Additionally, supporting files for SharePoint functionality over the network include the following:

- ▶ `Web.config` customizations
- ▶ Inetpub custom content
- ▶ C:\Inetpub\wwwroot\wss\VirtualDirectories
- ▶ Custom solutions (`.wsp`) files
- ▶ App for SharePoint content and packages
- ▶ App Management Service

18

▶ Secure Store Service application database

For more information regarding the backup of the Secure Store Service in SharePoint 2013, refer to the following link:

http://technet.microsoft.com/en-us/library/ee748648.aspx

▶ Third-party or custom assembly files (C:\Windows\Assembly)

▶ Connection information (SQL Alias)

Furthermore, specific configurations may be configured to return services to normal functioning levels, including these:

▶ User Profile Services and Audiences settings

For more information regarding how to back up the User Profile service applications in SharePoint Server 2013, refer to the following:

http://technet.microsoft.com/en-us/library/gg576965.aspx

▶ Search settings

▶ Usage analysis settings

▶ Excel Services settings

▶ Business Data Catalog entities, permissions, and objects

▶ Document conversion settings

▶ InfoPath settings

Table 18.1 provides a workspace to document vital or unique files for your organization. It is important to note that there may be additional items that are unique to your organization that you must be aware of and include in this list.

TABLE 18.1   Example of the Vital and Unique Files an Organization's DR and BCM Strategy Must Include

Inventory Component	Purpose	Location
SharePoint_Config	Farm Configuration Database	SQL Server
MySites_Content	My Sites Content Database	SQL Server
SharePoint_AdminContent_[GUID]	Central Administration Content Database	SQL Server
WSS_Content	Main Content Database	SQL Server
ManagedMetadata_Content	Managed Metadata Services Database	SQL Server
UPS_ProfileContent	User Profile Services Database	SQL Server
UPS_SocialContent	Social Tagging Database	SQL Server

Inventory Component	Purpose	Location
UPS_SyncContent	User Profile Synchronization Database	SQL Server
SearchService_Content	Search Administration Database	SQL Server
SearchService_AnalyticsReporting_DB	Search Analytics Database	SQL Server
SearchService_CrawlStore_DB	Search Crawl Database	SQL Server
BCS_Content	Business Connectivity Services Database	SQL Server
SharePoint Root	SharePoint templates and files	`Program Files/Common Files/Microsoft Shared/ web server extensions/15`
IIS Support Files	IIS web application configuration files	`Inetpub/wwwroot/wss/ virtualdirectories/*`
SQL Alias	SQL Alias connection configuration	`C:\windows\system32\ cliconfig.exe` to read configuration
IIS Metabase	IIS configuration	IIS configuration
Windows Registry	SharePoint registry keys	`Regedit.exe`
Custom Assembly Files	Custom code functionality	`C:\windows\assembly`
Custom Solutions	Farm-deployed solutions	`SQL\SharePoint_Config`
SSL Certificates	Security for web applications	Personal Certificate Store of local machine

Backup of SharePoint 2013 and Related Content and Components

This section focuses on the specific content to be backed up and the process for performing these actions. In some cases, there is not a specific backup order, and in some cases the entire farm can be backed up, which will eliminate unnecessary steps because they will be included in that backup. However, it may be beneficial to keep portions of a complete backup to restore only that element and make the return of that component occur in a shorter timeframe to meet any specific business needs. It is important that backups occur regularly and are scheduled appropriately in accordance with your organization's SLAs. For more information regarding backup solutions in SharePoint 2013, refer to the following link: http://technet.microsoft.com/en-us/library/ee428315.aspx

For example, if only a site in a site collection needs to be restored, a single Site Collection backup could be configured and scheduled to handle this.

18

This section covers the following:

- ▶ Full farm backup

- ▶ Content-only backup

- ▶ Shared Services Provider backup

- ▶ SharePoint Root backup

- ▶ IIS-based backup

- ▶ System State backup

Full Farm Backup

A full farm backup is performed for a complete catastrophic failure recovery; this backs up all aspects of SharePoint to provide a complete SharePoint-specific environment restoration. This restoration will include the farm configuration, the SSP, the Index Partition, and all content databases and components.

It is important to note that this type of backup does not take into account any web infrastructure considerations outside of web applications, custom code or assemblies, web.config, customizations, or SharePoint file system files.

Central Administration Backup

The following steps provide the process for performing a full farm backup. This backup will be performed through Central Administration.

Performing a Farm Backup Through Central Administration

To perform a farm backup through Central Administration, take the following steps:

1. Verify that the user account that is performing this procedure is a member of the Farm Administrators SharePoint group.

2. In Central Administration, on the home page, in the Backup and Restore section, click Perform a Backup, as shown in Figure 18.1.

FIGURE 18.1   SharePoint 2013's Central Administration Backup and Restore.

3. On the Perform a Backup – Step 1 of 2: Select Component to Backup page, select the farm from the list of components, and then click Next.

4. On the Start Backup – Step 2 of 2: Select Backup Options page, in the Backup Type section, select either Full or Differential.

5. In the Back Up Only Configuration Settings section, click Back Up Content and Configuration Settings.

6. In the Backup File Location section, as shown in Figure 18.2, type the UNC path of the backup folder, and then click Start Backup.

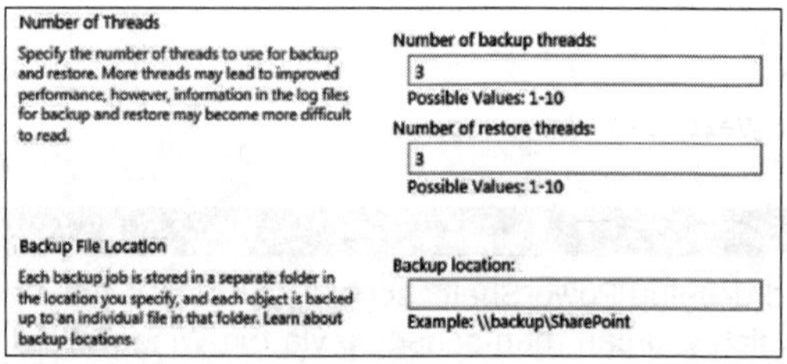

FIGURE 18.2   Specifying the backup file location for a SharePoint 2013 Central Administration backup.

You can view the backup job status on the Backup Status page by clicking Refresh, and the page also refreshes every 30 seconds automatically. Backup and recovery are Timer service jobs, so it may take a few seconds for the backup to start.

If you receive any errors, you can find more information by looking in the `spbackup.log` at the UNC path that you specified in step 3.

NOTE

This backup cannot be automated through Central Administration.

PowerShell Backup

Because Central Administration cannot automate a backup, it is a good practice to use the Windows PowerShell cmdlets that help you complete as well as schedule backup and recovery operation in SharePoint 2013.

Using PowerShell to Back Up a Farm

To utilize PowerShell to back up a farm, carry out these steps:

1. On the Start menu, click All Programs, click Microsoft SharePoint Products, and then click SharePoint 2013 Management Shell.

   OR

   On the Start screen, click SharePoint Management Shell.

   OR

   Right-click Computer, click All apps, and then click SharePoint Management Shell.

2. Type the following command, and then press Enter:

   ```
   Backup-SPFarm -Directory BackupFolder
   -BackupMethod {Full | Differential} [-Verbose]
   ```

> **NOTE**
>
> To automate SharePoint's backup, you should develop PowerShell "scripts" for both a full SharePoint backup and deferential backup, which you can then schedule via the Windows Task Scheduler. For more information regarding the available Windows PowerShell cmdlets, refer to the following link: http://technet.microsoft.com/en-us/library/ee890109(v=office.15).aspx

Schedule a Backup Using PowerShell

To schedule a backup using PowerShell, perform the following steps:

1. In the Windows Server 2012 Task Scheduler, select the option to Create Basic Task.

2. Provide a unique name for the PowerShell backup task, and then click Next.

3. Select how often you want this task performed (for example, weekly), and then click Next.

> **NOTE**
>
> To automatically perform this backup periodically, select an interval such as Weekly or Monthly. To perform this backup one time, or to delay a single backup, select One Time Only.

4. Choose a time and start date for your backup.

5. Select the Start a Program action, and then click Next. When the Start a Program dialog box opens, type in the command to run PowerShell and specify the file location of the PowerShell script. Then click Next.

6. Click Finish. You will need to repeat these steps to specify any new and/or different types of desired PowerShell backups.

Additional Supporting Backups

It is also necessary to back up other areas related to SharePoint to return full functionality to the farm. These are the additional backups that may be required:

▶ SharePoint Root backup

▶ IIS Inetpub backup

▶ System State backup

Content-Only Backup

A Content-Only Backup uses SQL Server backup tools to back up and protect content related to a SharePoint farm. This is performed directly against the SQL Server and the required content and configuration databases used by SharePoint. Although this section describes SQL Server backup, it does not describe scheduling an SQL Server Backup.

The following outlines the steps involved in using SQL Server to perform a backup on most of the SharePoint content. Note that this backup method does not back up the Index Partition used for Search and a full crawl must be run after a database recovery using this method.

Back Up SharePoint Content Through SQL Server

To back up SharePoint content through SQL Server, carry out the following actions:

1. Start SQL Server Management Studio and connect to the database server.

2. In Object Explorer, expand Databases.

3. Right-click the configuration database (usually named SharePoint_Config), point to Tasks, and then click Back Up.

4. In the Back Up Database dialog box, select the type of backup you want to perform from the Backup Type list.

5. Under Backup Component, select the Database option.

6. In the Name text box, type a name or use the default.

7. In the Description text box, type a description of the backup.

18

8. Under Backup Set Will Expire, specify how long the backup should be kept, or use the default. When the backup set expires, the backup set can be overwritten by any subsequent backups with the same name. The backup set is set to never expire (0 days) by default.

9. In the Destination section, specify a location to store the backup set, or use the default.

10. Click OK to back up the database.

11. Repeat steps 3 through 10 for the following databases:

  ▶ Content databases

  ▶ Databases for SSPs

  ▶ Search databases for the SSPs

  ▶ Search databases

NOTE

You can back up databases to snapshots in SharePoint Server 2013 Enterprise Edition only by using SQL Server tools. For more information regarding how to back up databases to snapshots in SharePoint Server 2013, refer to the following: http://technet.microsoft.com/en-us/library/ee748594.aspx

Other Content to Back Up

This same methodology can be used to back up any individual content database. However, Microsoft does not support a configuration database restore, and SharePoint does not tolerate a configuration database restored in a different environment and may prevent a successful restoration even if the backup was sound.

In this case, an alternative Recovery farm may be used with a different configuration database but the same content databases.

NOTE

It is also possible to use Central Administration to back up a web application.

Back Up a Web Application with Central Administration

To back up a web application with Central Administration, perform the following steps:

1. Verify that the user account that is performing this procedure is a member of the Farm Administrators group.

2. In Central Administration, on the home page, in the Backup and Restore section, click Perform a Backup.

3. On the Perform a Backup – Step 1 of 2: Select Component to Back Up page, select the web application from the list of components, and then click Next.

4. On the Start Backup – Step 2 of 2: Select Backup Options page, in the Backup Type section, select either Full or Differential.

5. In the Back Up Only Configuration Settings section, click Back Up Content and Configuration Settings.

6. In the Backup File Location section, type the Universal Naming Convention (UNC) path of the backup folder, and then click Start Backup.

You can view the backup job status on the Backup Status page by clicking Refresh. The page also refreshes every 30 seconds automatically. Backup and recovery is a Timer service job, which may take a few seconds for the backup to start.

If you receive any errors, you can find more information by looking in `spbackup.log` at the UNC path you specified earlier.

Back Up a Web Application with PowerShell

To back up a web application with PowerShell, do the following:

1. Start the SharePoint 2013 Management Shell.

2. At the Windows PowerShell command prompt, type the following command:

```
Backup-SPFarm -Directory <BackupFolder>
-BackupMethod {Full | Differential} -Item <WebApplicationName> [-Verbose]
```

NOTE

Refer to the earlier section, "Schedule a Backup Using PowerShell," to schedule reoccurring backups and related tasks.

Shared Services Provider Backup

A Shared Services Provider backup protects the content and configuration databases associated with a Shared Service Provider. Although it is not necessary to back this up separately if a full farm backup is employed, there can be a benefit in restoring only content related to the SSP in a manner similar to restoring content databases.

Content included with backing up an SSP/SA includes the following:

▶ SSP/SA web application

▶ SSP/SA database

▶ One or more SSP/SA content databases

▶ User profile data

▶ Session state data

▶ Search data, including the search database and index

18

When an SSP is being backed up, any associated My Sites will be backed up as well. However, a separate backup for My Sites can be performed as with any other content database. Because it is generally recommended to keep My Sites on a web application separate from both the SSP and other web applications, My Sites backups can usually be performed separately as needed if this is the configuration used.

For backing up an SA, the My Sites web application must be backed up separately. This operation is exactly like backing up a standard content web application.

Back Up a Shared Service Provider with Central Administration

To back up a Shared Service Provider with Central Administration, carry out these actions:

1. Verify that the user account that is performing this procedure is a member of the Farm Administrators SharePoint group.

2. In Central Administration, on the home page, in the Backup and Restore section, click Perform a backup.

3. On the Perform a Backup – Step 1 of 2: Select Component to Backup page, select the service application from the list of components, and then click Next. To back up all the service applications, select the Shared Service Applications node.

4. On the Start Backup – Step 2 of 2: Select Backup Options page, in the Backup Type section, select either Full or Differential.

5. In the Backup File Location section, in the Backup Location box, type the path of the backup folder, and then click Start Backup.

You can view the backup job status on the status page by clicking Refresh. The page also refreshes every 30 seconds automatically. Backup and recovery uses the Windows SharePoint Services Timer Service to schedule jobs, so it may take a few seconds for the backup to start.

If you receive any errors, you can find more information by viewing the `spbackup.log` at the UNC path you specified previously.

Back Up a Service Application with PowerShell

To back up a service application with PowerShell, do the following:

1. Start the SharePoint 2013 Management Shell.

2. At the Windows PowerShell command prompt, type the following command:

```
Backup-SPFarm -Directory <BackupFolder>
-BackupMethod {Full | Differential} -Item
<ServiceApplicationName> [-Verbose]
```

NOTE

Refer to the earlier section, "Schedule a Backup Using PowerShell," to schedule reoccurring backups and related tasks.

SharePoint Root Backup

A SharePoint Root Backup is a backup performed against a SharePoint Server, in particular the location that is commonly known as the 15 hive. Specifically, this location is by default set at the following location: `%COMMONPROGRAMFILES%\Microsoft shared\Web server extensions\15`

This location is common across all SharePoint Servers and normally stores the same content across all servers as well. Normally, the machine running Central Administration becomes the main target for a backup.

This backup can be performed by any common file system backup, such as Windows Backup, or other third-party backup tools. Additionally, a copy of this location and all its subfolders may be made and placed in a safe location.

IIS-Based Backup

Because SharePoint is dependent on IIS, it is important to back up IIS or relevant portions of it. Depending on how much customization has been made to IIS, a full IIS metabase backup may be necessary. However, the key area for SharePoint is the Inetpub location.

The IIS Inetpub location stores the custom content and custom `web.config` file used by the web application to properly handle SharePoint communication through IIS.

It may be that this location has not been customized, but often the `web.config` file may store third-party information. The web.config also tends to store other customizations that may not be present anywhere else and may result in issues regarding web pages from SharePoint loading if the web.config is not returned to its properly configured state.

The IIS Inetpub location related to SharePoint is located by default in the following location:

`C:\Inetpub\wwwroot\wss\VirtualDirectories`

This backup can be performed by any common file system backup such as Windows Backup or other third-party backup tools. Additionally, a copy of this location and all its subfolders may be made and placed in a safe location.

The IIS metabase can be backed up through a System State backup.

System State Backup

A System State backup is a common backup that protects the OS from failure or other compromises so that a newly installed OS can be returned to functioning capacity after the System State backup is applied. Files from the OS included in the backup from a server that is not a Domain Controller or a Certificate Server include the following:

▶ The boot file

▶ The COM+ class registration database

▶ The registry

There are many registry entries for SharePoint functionality, but most can be either
replaced or updated along with a full farm backup.

Backup Considerations

There are several decision points for managing a backup schedule, and all of them impact
the success, degree of granularity, and speed of the recovery required for your organization. Although the recovery scenarios are covered in the following section, a few items
should be evaluated and decided on before the schedule is implemented.

Table 18.2 details the backup options as well as considerations you should review based
on your organization's specific requirements.

TABLE 18.2   Backup Options and Considerations

Backup Option	Consideration
Full or Differential	–Full backups must always be taken before any Differentials are allowed.
	–The more Differentials taken before the next Full backup, the longer the overall backup time will take.
	–The more Differentials taken, the longer the restore process will take, but it will require fewer overall backup files.
Schedule or Manual	–Scheduling provides automation but requires scripts.
	–Scripts should be backed up.
	–Test that Schedules are actually being kept.
SharePoint or Other Method	–SharePoint will not back up local OS or application files.
	–SharePoint can include the Index Partition.
	–SQL Server will not back up SharePoint files or other OS or application files.

Additional Backup Considerations for Your Organization

Table 18.3 details additional backup considerations that may factor into your organization's overall DR and BCM requirements.

TABLE 18.3   Additional Backup Considerations for Your Organization

Backup Option	Consideration	Notes
System State	Backs up registry, IIS metabase	Handled with Server backup
SQL Server backups	Protecting data in SQL Server but not Index Partition	SQL backups
File System	Back up SharePoint root, Inetpub, or other local files	Handled with Server backups

Additional Documentation Considerations for Your Organization

Table 18.4 details additional documentation considerations that your organization may require to be added to your overall DR and BCM requirements.

TABLE 18.4   Additional Documentation Considerations for Your Organization

Configuration Option	Purpose	Location
Host Headers	Access to SharePoint web applications	IIS and DNS entries
Email Configurations	Provides email service to or from SharePoint	Central Administration
Managed Paths	Provides URL placeholders for site collections	Central Administration, web applications
Alternate Access Mappings	Provides URL-based mapping inside SharePoint for SharePoint content only	Central Administration, web applications
Farm Version	Indicates levels of service packs, cumulative updates, and hotfixes applied	Central Administration, servers in farm
Application Pools	Identifies service accounts and w3wp threads in use	IIS
Service Accounts	Defines which Active Directory account provides network or service functions	Active Directory

18

Service Account Considerations for Your Organization

Table 18.5 details additional considerations for service accounts for your organization.

TABLE 18.5   Service Account Considerations for Your Organization

Service Account	Purpose	Configuration
SharePoint Local Admin	Manages all aspects of the SharePoint Server, including command-line and local server management, and may also install/patch SharePoint	Local Administrators
Farm Administrator	Manages SharePoint through Central Administration but does not run functions locally	Products Configuration Wizard, IIS Application Pools, Farm Administrators SharePoint Group
Search Service	Runs the Local Search Services and acts as the Default Content Access Account	Office SharePoint Search, Shared Service Provider
Shared Service Provider Administrator	Manages the Shared Service Provider functions	IIS Application Pools, Shared Service Provider personalization permissions

Web Application Documentation Considerations

Table 18.6 details web application documentation considerations for your organization.

TABLE 18.6   Web Application Documentation Considerations

Configuration	Notes
Host Header/Port Number	IIS configuration
Email Configurations	Outgoing or incoming
Application Pool and Application Pool ID	IIS configuration
Authentication Provider	SSL requires certificate, Kerberos requires SPN
Managed Paths	Web application
Content Database Settings	Content databases
Alternate Access Mappings	Alternate Access Mappings
SSL Certificate	IIS configuration

Restoration of the Environment

The restoration procedures cover restoring elements of the SharePoint farm as defined by your organization's business continuity management guidelines and/or service level agreements. It is essential that all necessary content and configuration details have been backed up and/or documented to replace or reconfigure any necessary details or content for the content within the executed restoration process.

Business continuity management in this restoration section focuses on returning SharePoint to an operational state with minimal or no data loss. However, operational states and minimal data loss can vary and are entirely dependent on availability of software or hardware, integrity of content, and documented configurations.

As mentioned, this section focuses on the procedures for returning a SharePoint farm to an operative, minimal-data-loss state, and should accompany the organization's backup procedures outlined in the preceding section. Other procedures, such as restoring services or content, may also be described for less catastrophic data loss and business continuity interruption. For more information on the latest updates from Microsoft regarding restoration in SharePoint 2013, refer to the following link: http://technet.microsoft.com/en-us/library/ee428303.aspx

Farm Restoration

The following information outlines the process for restoring the main elements of a SharePoint farm.

Complete Catastrophic Restore

This restoration process assumes that the SharePoint Server is no longer viable and must be replaced. It is assumed that there is a functioning SQL Server as well, although additional information regarding restoring an SQL Server may be documented here but is outside the scope of this document. Content databases may need to be restored at this time. The required steps required to complete a catastrophic restore are as follows:

1. Install the original OS version of Windows for the server, which should match the current SharePoint Server OS version.

2. Add the setup/admin service account to the local Administrators group and provide the Sysadmin server role to SQL Server.

3. Remove the previous SharePoint Server computer account from Active Directory and join the new server to Active Directory.

4. Add IIS to the OS and install the same level of the .NET Framework that was previously being used by the original SharePoint Server farm.

5. Install SharePoint 2013 on the new server using the setup/admin account mentioned previously, using the Advanced Installation and Complete Role options in the Setup Wizard, but do not run the Products Configuration Wizard when the installation completes.

6. Apply all updates to the SharePoint binaries or service packs.

7. After all updates have been properly applied, run the Products Configuration Wizard.

8. In the Products Configuration Wizard, create a new farm, specify the SQL Server and/or Server instance, and provide the name of the SharePoint Configuration Database. Also, provide the Farm Service account information.

18

9. For Central Administration, choose an existing port number or use a random one, and then choose the proper authentication type (NTLM is the default).

10. After the farm is created, start the appropriate services within Central Administration and provide any information requests for service accounts.

11. Start all other services necessary that were previously utilized.

12. Create each web application necessary, applying the same configurations used previously in the SharePoint Server:

   ▶ SSP

   ▶ My Sites

   ▶ Content

   ▶ Extensions

13. Create or extend web applications and new web applications and provide the following information:

   ▶ Port and host header

   ▶ SSL if applicable

   ▶ Application Pool and Application Pool ID credentials

   ▶ SQL Server name/instance and name of associated content database (root first if there is more than one)

   ▶ Extend any web applications if necessary

14. Associate additional content databases with web applications, as well as add content databases and enter the required name of the database.

15. Restore the SSP through Central Administration. Next, choose the web application created previously:

   ▶ My Sites—clear the check box

   ▶ Select the My Sites web application

   ▶ Provide the SSP Service credentials

   ▶ Provide the name of the SSP database

   ▶ Provide the name of the SSP search database

   ▶ Provide the index file location

16. Reset IIS after SSP is restored.

17. Reinstall third-party applications or SharePoint Solutions.

18. Apply additional configuration changes such as the following:

- ▶ AAMs

- ▶ `vxweb.config`

- ▶ Assembly cache code

- ▶ IIS settings (SSL Certificate)

- ▶ Customizations in SharePoint Root

- ▶ Web application policies

- ▶ Outgoing/incoming email settings

19. Run a full crawl to fully update the search database through the SSP.

20. Check and test access and functionality.

Farm Restoration Only

If a full farm backup has been taken and is intact, it can be possible to recover the farm as a whole if a misconfiguration or data loss occurs. It is important to note that the farm will be restored to the original location, which means it will overwrite existing databases. A farm can be restored through Central Administration, depending on what is available.

Restore Through Central Administration

To execute a restore through Central Administration, carry out these steps:

1. Verify that the user account that is performing this procedure is a member of the Farm Administrators SharePoint group.

2. In Central Administration, on the home page, in the Backup and Restore section, click Restore from a Backup.

3. On the Restore from Backup – Step 1 of 3: Select Backup to Restore page, from the list of backups, select the backup job that contains the farm backup, and then click Next. You can view more details about each backup by clicking the + next to the backup.

4. On the Restore from Backup – Step 2 of 3: Select Component to Restore page, select the check box that is next to the farm, and then click Next.

5. On the Restore from Backup – Step 3 of 3: Select Restore Options page, in the Restore Component section, make sure that farm appears in the Restore the Following Component list:

- ▶ In the Restore Only Configuration Settings section, make sure that the Restore Content and Configuration Settings option is selected.

18

▶ In the Restore Options section, under Type of Restore, select the Same
Configuration option. A dialog box will appear that asks you to confirm the
operation. Click OK.

▶ Click Start Restore.

6. You can view the general status of all recovery jobs at the top of the Backup and
Restore Job Status page in the Readiness section. You can view the status for the
current recovery job in the lower part of the page in the Restore section. The status
page updates every 30 seconds automatically. You can manually update the status
details by clicking Refresh. Backup and recovery are Timer service jobs. Therefore, it
may take several seconds for the recovery to start.

If you receive any errors, you can review them in the Failure Message column of the
Backup and Restore Job Status page. You can also find more details in the `Sprestore.log`
file at the UNC path that you specified in step 3.

1. When the restore process has completed, you may need to restart one or more
service applications. In Central Administration, on the home page, in the
Application Management section, click Manage Services on Server.

2. On the Services on Server page, start any services related to service applications
that you want to run by clicking Start in the Actions column next to the service
application.

Restore Through PowerShell
To execute a restore through PowerShell, this is the process to follow:

1. Click Microsoft SharePoint 2013 Products.

2. Click SharePoint 2013 Management Shell.

3. At the Windows PowerShell command prompt, type the command

```
Restore-SPFarm -Directory <BackupFolder>
-RestoreMethod Overwrite [-BackupId <GUID>]
<Type the appropriate cmdlet, including parameters and
values, and enclose the values for the parameters in
"placeholder" tags >
```

where `<BackupFolder>` is the name and path for the backup folder where the service
application was backed up.

4. To restart a service application, at the Windows PowerShell command prompt, type
the following command:

```
Start-SPServiceInstance -Identity <ServiceApplicationID>
```

Content-Only Restoration

If the SharePoint farm is intact, which means that the Configuration Database is at an operational state but content is lost, then content-only recovery is possible. In this case, the content database must have a valid backup and the SharePoint Server must also be intact. Any portion from the web application down into the site content may have issues and can be restored, depending on what has been backed up.

Restore with Central Administration

To execute a restore with Central Administration, perform the following:

1. In Central Administration, on the home page, in the Backup and Restore section, click Restore from a Backup.

2. On the Restore from Backup – Step 1 of 3: Select Backup to Restore page, from the list of backups, select the backup job that contains the content database backup, and then click Next.

3. On the Restore from Backup – Step 2 of 3: Select Component to Restore page, select the check box that is next to the content database, and then click Next.

4. On the Restore from Backup – Step 3 of 3: Select Restore Options page, in the Restore Options section, under Type of Restore, click the Same Configuration option. A dialog box appears that asks you to confirm the operation. Click OK.

5. Click Start Restore.

Restore with PowerShell

To execute a restore with PowerShell, follow these instructions:

1. Start the SharePoint 2013 Management Shell.

2. At the Windows PowerShell command prompt, type the command

```
Restore-SPFarm -Directory <BackupFolder>
-RestoreMethod Overwrite -Item <ContentDatabase>
[-BackupId <GUID>] [-Verbose]
```

where `<BackupFolder>` is the name and path for the backup folder where the service application was backed up and `<ContentDatabase>` is the name of the content database.

Additional Considerations

Additional considerations for restoration should also be undertaken for purposes of speed and granularity, as detailed in Table 18.7.

TABLE 18.7   Additional Considerations for Restoration to Increase Speed and Granularity

Consideration	Description
Change Log	Documentation providing date, time, and party making any configuration change to the SharePoint farm.
Recovery Farm	An independent farm already configured and set to provide speed for recovering almost any element of the farm.
Trial Restoration	Procedural practice in restoring any level of content up to catastrophic recovery.
Farm Solutions	Solutions deployed to the farm via `.wsp` files are easier to maintain and update.
Smaller Content Database	Smaller content databases allow for faster recovery times.
Naming Conventions	For databases, web applications, or anything restored in tandem to keep their relationships clear and easily understood.
Patch Backups	Backing up before and after applying patches brings database content closer to the latest patch and thus makes it faster to restore.

Summary

The goal of this chapter is to ensure that you and your organization are taking into consideration the multiple moving parts within a SharePoint farm and how best to develop a disaster recovery plan as well as business continuity management strategy.

Many organizations develop these plans and related strategies but do not perform quarterly or regular tests to ensure all parties within your organization are ready to take on their related responsibilities during these important events.

Also, it is important to have physical copies of DR and BCM strategies so that in the event of a catastrophic power failure, you have backup copies if the system is down and the electronic copies are not accessible.

Index

A

acceptable usage limits for My Sites, 596

acceptable usage policy, enforcing governance strategies, 319-322

Access Services, 13

accessing SharePoint 2013, 68

   device support, 68

account requirements for upgrades or migration, 378-379

ACS (Access Control Service), 461

ADFS (Active Directory Federation Services), 104

Admin Center, 557-559, 566-569

administration

   mobile devices, 582-583

   SQL Server 2012/2014 best practices, 575-577

   tasks, 559-561

      Application Management, 561-562

      search administration, 564-565

      security administration, 562

   Windows PowerShell, 579-583

administrative and training governance, 43

administrator training, 610-611

AES (Advanced Encryption Standard), 115

aligning system and information architectures with roadmap, 363-367

Analytics Processing component of search, 509-511

anti-spam, Office 365 security, 114

APIs

   CSOM, 450-452

   Office 365 API Tools, 452-454

   REST APIs, 454-458

   OData, 456-457

   search, 457-458

   server object model, 450

App Catalog, 109-111

   configuring for web applications, 111

App Management Service, 13

Application Management, 561-562

Application Tier installation, 415-416

apps, 58-60, 109-111

   APIs

      CSOM, 450-452

      Office 365 API Tools, 452-454

      REST APIs, 454-458

      server object model, 450

   audience, 59-60

   authentication, 458-462

      adding permission requests, 459-460

      default permissions, 459

      external authentication, 459

      granted permissions, 459

      internal authentication, 458-459

      S2S, 460-462

   authentication, configuring, 445-447

   autohosted apps, 442

   cloud app model, 443-444

   configuring, 444-449

   examples of, 60

   high-trust apps, configuring, 447-449

   licensing, 436-438

   low-trust apps, configuring, 447

   provider-hosted apps, 441

   SharePoint app model, 440-442

   SharePoint-hosted apps, 442

   submission process, 436-438

B

restores, performing

>   complete catastrophic restores, 643-645

>   with PowerShell, 646

>   service account considerations, 642

>   shared services provider backups, 637-638

>   SharePoint Root backups, 639

>   System State backups, 639-640

>   unintended downtime procedures, 310-311

>   web application documentation consider-
>   ations, 642

base OS configuration, 417

batch files, performing backups with, 634

BCM (business continuity management)

>   best practices, 623-624

>   preparing for

>   content considerations, 625

>   support systems, 627-628

>   web infrastructure considerations,
>   625-626

BCS (Business Connectivity Services), 29-30,
496-499

BDC (Business Data Connectivity), 29-30

best practices, 3-4

>   BCM, 623-624

>   BYOD, 233-234

>   defining for Communications Management
>   Plan, 34

>   DR, 623-624

>   governance, 269-284

>   mission statement, defining, 270

>   principles for SharePoint usage, 273

>   roles and responsibilities, 273-275

>   IA design, 119-121

>   analysis process, 130

>   questions to ask, 127-128

>   records management, 131

>   taxonomy, structuring, 130-131

IM

>   document libraries, 81

>   user base, identifying, 80-81

MDM, 546

migration, 361-363

My Site architectural configuration, 90-91

RM, 328-333

>   core team, building, 329

>   initiative, implementing, 329-330

scalability, 24

SQL Server 2012/2014 administration,
575-577

best replies, 90

BI (Business Intelligence), 13, 235-239

>   capabilities of SharePoint Server 2013,
>   25-26

>   database connections, 246-251

>   connection string method, 249-251

>   custom SQL commands, creating,
>   251-254

>   username and password method,
>   247-249

>   Excel Power View, 242-243

>   Excel Services, 241

>   external data sources, 245-247

>   IA initiatives, 126

>   Microsoft BI stack, 237

>   PerformancePoint, 243-244

>   Power BI, 266-267

>   PowerPivot, 241-242

>   REST service connections, 256-257

>   SOAP service connections, 254-255

>   SSBI, 239-240

>   Visio Services, 244

>   XML data connections, 257-259

"big bang" migration versus iterative migration,
366-367

BitLocker 256-bit AES encryption, 115

BLOBs, RBS, 63

E

H

preparing for, 216-218

selecting for deployment, 82-84

hybrid farm topology, 226-227

hybrid Office 365 initiative, 105-109

identity providers, 108

Lync 2013, 105-106

MSOL, 108

Office 365 Secure Store, 108-109

reverse proxy, 108

security, 106-108

hybrid search integration, 515-517

I

IA (information architecture), 119-122

aligning with roadmap, 363-367

analysis process, 130

BI initiatives, 126

Content IA, 123

Context IA, 122-123

designing, questions to ask, 127-128

document libraries, creating, 147-148

libraries

deleting, 154-155

General Settings, 151-154

RSS Settings, 157

settings, modifying, 150-151

Workflow Settings, 157

list templates, creating, 145-147

lists, 138-147

creating from built-in templates, 139-141

custom lists, creating, 141-145

deleting, 154-155

General Settings, 151-154

permissions, 155-156

RSS Settings, 157

settings, modifying, 150-151

Workflow Settings, 157

logical architecture

service applications, 134

site collections, 136-137

URLs, 137

web applications, 134-136

zones, 136

performing administrative tasks, 134-136

PHI, 129

PII, 128

records management, 131

SBU information, 128

sensitive PII, 128-129

site columns, defining, 148-149

taxonomy, structuring, 130-131

technical components, 131-132

Users IA, 124-125, 130

IaaS (infrastructure as a service), 207-208

Windows Azure, 209-211

identifying

core tasks for SharePoint initiative, 44-52

ECM/RM requirements, 18-20

power users, 8-9

stakeholders for Communications Management Plan, 33

user base, 80-81

identity management

capabilities of SharePoint Server 2013, 26

Office 365 integration scenarios, 106-108

identity providers, 108

iFrames, 24

IM (information management), best practices

document libraries, 81

user base, identifying, 80-81

implementation strategy

Communications Management Plan, 33-36

best practices, 34

communication matrix, 34-35

communication schedule, 35-36

J-K

Q

R

T

U

SharePoint 2013 Field Guide
Advice from the Consulting Trenches

EPC GROUP.NET

SAMS

Errin O'Connor
The EPC Group Team of Experts

Safari
Books Online

FREE
Online Edition

Your purchase of **SharePoint® 2013 Field Guide** includes access to a free online edition for 45 days through the **Safari Books Online** subscription service. Nearly every Sams book is available online through **Safari Books Online**, along with thousands of books and videos from publishers such as Addison-Wesley Professional, Cisco Press, Exam Cram, IBM Press, O'Reilly Media, Prentice Hall, Que, and VMware Press.

Safari Books Online is a digital library providing searchable, on-demand access to thousands of technology, digital media, and professional development books and videos from leading publishers. With one monthly or yearly subscription price, you get unlimited access to learning tools and information on topics including mobile app and software development, tips and tricks on using your favorite gadgets, networking, project management, graphic design, and much more.

Activate your FREE Online Edition at
informit.com/safarifree

STEP 1: Enter the coupon code: RKIIQVH.

STEP 2: New Safari users, complete the brief registration form.
Safari subscribers, just log in.

If you have difficulty registering on Safari or accessing the online edition,
please e-mail customer-service@safaribooksonline.com